Depositaries in European Investment Law

DEPOSITARIES IN EUROPEAN INVESTMENT LAW

TOWARDS HARMONIZATION IN EUROPE

DR. SEBASTIAAN NIELS HOOGHIEMSTRA, LL.M.

Published, sold and distributed by Eleven International Publishing
P.O. Box 85576
2508 CG The Hague
The Netherlands
Tel.: +31 70 33 070 33
Fax: +31 70 33 070 30
e-mail: sales@elevenpub.nl
www.elevenpub.com

Sold and distributed in USA and Canada
International Specialized Book Services
920 NE 58th Avenue, Suite 300
Portland, OR 97213-3786, USA
Tel.: 1-800-944-6190 (toll-free)
Fax: +1 503 280-8832
orders@isbs.com
www.isbs.com

Eleven International Publishing is an imprint of Boom uitgevers Den Haag.

ISBN 978-94-6236-850-7
ISBN 978-94-6274-877-4 (E-book)

© 2018 Sebastiaan Hooghiemstra | Eleven International Publishing

Printed in The Netherlands

For Laura, Hans, Kim and Enzo

TABLE OF CONTENTS

LIST OF ABBREVIATIONS

AFM	Autoriteit Financiële Markten (The Netherlands)
AIF	Alternative Investment Fund
AIFM	Alternative Investment Fund Manager
AIFMD	Alternative Investment Fund Managers Directive
AIFMD (Commission) Regulation	Commission Delegated Regulation (EU) No 231/2013
AIFMD (Commission) Regulation I	Commission Implementing Regulation (EU) No 447/2013
AIFMD (Commission) Regulation II	Commission Implementing Regulation (EU) No 448/2013
AIMA	Alternative Investment Management Association
ALFI	Association of the Luxembourg Fund Industry
AMF	Autorité des Marchés Financiers (France)
AuM	Assets under Management
BaFin	Bundesanstalt für Finanzdienstleistungsaufsicht (Germany)
BCBS	Basel Committee on Banking Supervision
BIS	Bank for International Settlements
CASS	Client Asset Sourcebook (UK)
CBI	Central Bank of Ireland
CCP	Central Counterparty
CEPS	Center for European Policy Studies
CESR	Committee of European Securities Regulators
CJEU	Court of Justice of the European Union
CP	Consultation Paper
CRD	Capital Requirements Directive
CRO	Chief Risk Officer
CRR	Capital Requirements Regulation
CSD	Central Securities Depository
CSSF	Commission de Surveillance du Secteur Financier (Luxembourg)
DB	Defined Benefit
DC	Defined Contribution
DNB	De Nederlandsche Bank (The Netherlands)
DP	Discussion Paper
EBA	European Banking Authority
EBF	European Banking Federation
EC	European Commission
ECB	European Central Bank
ECJ	European Court of Justice
ECOFIN	Council of European Finance Ministers
ECR	European Court Report
EEA	European Economic Area
EEC	European Economic Community
EFAMA	European Fund and Asset Management Association
EFTA	European Free Trade Area
EIOPA	European Insurance and Occupational Pensions Authority
ELTIF	European Long-Term Investment Fund
ELTIFR	European Long-Term Investment Fund Regulation

EMIR	European Market Infrastructure Regulation
ESA	European Supervisory Authority
ESC	European Securities Committee
ESFS	European System of Financial Supervision
ESMA	European Securities and Markets Authority
ESRB	European Systemic Risk Board
EU	European Union
EuSEF	European Social Entrepreneurship Funds
EuSEFR	EuSEF Regulation
EuVECA	European Venture Capital Fund
EuVECAR	EuVECA Regulation
FAIFs	Funds of Alternative Investment Funds
FATCA	Foreign Accounts Tax Compliance (US)
FATF	Financial Action Task Force on Money Laundering
FCA	Financial Conduct Authority
FCD	Financial Collateral Directive
HNWI	High-net Worth Individual
IAS	International Association of Insurance Supervisors
IDD	Insurance Distribution Directive
IIID	Initial Investor Information Document
SIF	Fonds d'investissement spécialisés, Spezialfonds
FR	Final Report
FSA	Financial Services Authority (UK)
FSAP	Financial Services Action Plan
FSMA	Financial Services and Markets Act 2000 (UK)
FUND	Investment Funds Sourcebook
GATS	General Agreement on Trade in Services
GATT	General Agreement on Tariffs and Trade
GDP	Gross Domestic Product
HNWI	High Net Worth Individual
IAIS	International Association of Insurance Supervisors
ICSD	International Central Securities Depository
IMA	Investment Management Association
IORP	Institutions for Occupational Retirement Provision
IORPD	Institutions for Occupational Retirement Provision Directive
IOSCO	International Organization of Securities Commissions
KAGB	Kapitalanlagegesetzbuch – Capital Investment Code (Germany)
KIID	Key Investor Information Document
L. Rev.	Law Review
Luxembourg AIFM Law	Loi du 12 juillet relative aux gestionnaires de fonds d'investisse-ment alternatifs et – portant transposition de la directive 2011/61/UE (…) in Luxemburg
MFN	Most favoured Nation
MiFID	Markets in Financial Instruments Directive
MiFIR	Markets in Financial Instruments Regulation
MMF	Money Market Fund
MMoU	Multilateral Memorandum of Understanding
NAV	Net Asset Value
NURS	Non-UCITS retail schemes
OECD	Organisation for Economic Cooperation and Development
OEIC	Open-ended Investment Company

OPC	Organisme de Placement Collectif
OPC-Law 2010	Loi du 17 décembre 2010 concernant les organismes de placement collectif in Luxemburg
OPC-Law 2002	Loi du 20 décembre 2002 concernant les organismes de placement collectif et modifiant la loi modifiée du 12 février in Luxemburg
OPCVM	Organisme de Placement Collectif en Valeurs Mobilières
OTC	Over-The-Counter
PE	Private Equity
PEPP	Pan-European-Pension-Product
PPP	Personal Pension Product
PRA	Prudential Regulation Authority
PS	Policy Statement
QIF	Qualifying Investor Funds
QIS	Qualified Investor Scheme
RTS	Regulatory Technical Standards
SFT	Securities Financing Transactions
SI	Statutory Instrument
SICAR	Investment Companies in Risk Capital Regimes (investment company in risk capital)
SICAV	Société d'Investissement à Capital Variable (investment company with variable capital)
SIF Law	Loi du 13 février 2007 relative aux fonds d'investissements spécialisés
SLD	Securities Law Directive
SPV	Special Purpose Vehicle
SRD	Shareholder Rights Directive
SSRN	Social Science Research Network
TC	Third Country
TFEU	Treaty on the Functioning of the European Union
TTCA	Title Transfer Collateral Arrangements
UCITS	Undertakings for Collective Investment in Transferable Securities
UCITSD	Undertakings for Collective Investment in Transferable Securities Directives
UCITSG	Gesetz über bestimmte Organismen für gemeinsame Anlagen in Wertpapieren in Liechtenstein – UCITS Act (Liechtenstein)
WTO	World Trade Organization

1   INTRODUCTION

1.1   BACKGROUND

A few decades after the four freedoms were introduced that allowed several types of financial intermediaries the freedom to provide services throughout all EEA Member States,[1] it appears that this right is still undermined for depositaries providing services under the European investment law directives.[2]

Interestingly enough, a *de facto* passport[3] in this field already exists.[4] CRD IV,[5] IORPD II[6] and MiFID II,[7] all regulate the safekeeping of securities and the provision of custody services.[8] MiFID II lists the provision of safekeeping services, including custodianship for financial instruments, as ancillary service, and allows this service to be 'passported',[9] in addition to the investment activities/services for which investment firms are authorized.[10] Similarly, CRD IV allows the safekeeping of securities and the provision of custody services to be passported, in addition to the deposit-taking activity of credit institutions.[11] Under IORPD II, the safekeeping of securities and the provision of custody services are subject to a mutual recognition approach.[12] IORPD II allows, in addition to

---

1   Financial intermediaries, such as credit institutions, IORPs and insurance intermediaries currently enjoy the freedom of an European passport that is, indirectly based upon Arts. 49 and 56 TFEU. *See* D.A. Zetzsche, *The AIFMD and the Joint Principles of European Asset Management Law* 865 (D.A. Zetzsche ed., Kluwer 2015).
2   MiFID II, the AIFMD, UCITSD V and IORPD II are being referred to in this book as the 'European investment laws'.
3   *See also* C.P. Buttigieg, *The Case for a European Depositary Passport*, http://studylib.net/doc/13128849/the–case–for–a–european-depository-passport.
4   *See* for a discussion during the UCITSD II proposal on the 'the facto' European passport for custodians: European Parliament, *Report of the Committee on Legal Affairs and Citizen's Rights on the 1993 UCITS Proposal*, A5-0268/1993, 1 October 1993, http://goo.gl/rRSdJO.
5   Directive 2013/36/EU of the European Parliament and of the Council of 26 June 2013 on access to the activity of credit institutions and the prudential supervision of credit institutions and investment firms, amending Directive 2002/87/EC and repealing Directives 2006/48/EC and 2006/49/EC Text with EEA relevance, L 176/338, 27 June 2013 ('CRD IV').
6   Directive (EU) 2016/2341 of the European Parliament and of the Council of 14 December 2016 on the activities and supervision of institutions for occupational retirement provision (IORPs) (recast), OJ L 354/37, 23 December 2016, 37 ('IORPD II').
7   Directive 2014/65/EU of the European Parliament and of the Council of 15 May 2014 on markets in financial instruments and amending Directive 2002/92/EC and Directive 2011/61/EU, OJ L 173, 12 June 2014, 349 ('MiFID II').
8   *See* Art. 21(8) AIFMD; Art. 22(5) UCITSD V; Annex I n. 12 CRD IV; Annex I s. A MiFID II.
9   *See* D.A. Zetzsche & T.F. Marte, *The AIFMD's Cross-Border Dimension, Third-Country Rules and the Equivalence Concept* 474 (D.A. Zetzsche ed., Kluwer, 2015).
10   S.N. Hooghiemstra, *Depositary Regulation* 485 (D.A. Zetzsche ed., Kluwer 2015).
11   *Ibid.*, 484.
12   Art. 33(3) IORPD II.

UCITS /AIF depositaries, investment firms and credit institutions harmonized under the CRD IV and MiFID II to be appointed as a depositary regardless of whether the depositary is established in the IORP home Member State.[13] Notwithstanding the fundamental principle of the freedom to provide services,[14] the AIFMD[15] and UCITSD V only allow UCITS ManCos and AIFMs to appoint a depositary that is established or has a branch office in the EEA Member State in which the respective UCITS or AIF is established.[16] Strictly speaking, credit institutions or investment firms, which, under CRD IV, MiFID II and IORPD II, are allowed to provide custody services on a cross-border basis, may not exercise 'passporting rights' under the UCITS V and AIFMD, because these European directives preclude depositaries from doing so.[17] It would therefore be worthwhile to investigate whether depositaries under the AIFMD and UCITSD V should be allowed to enjoy passporting rights and whether and to what extent this fits in under the current 'de facto passports' available under European investment law.[18] If so, a cross-sectoral depositary passport could be considered and modelled after the cross-sectoral passport for investment management[19] services.[20]

1.2   THE CASE FOR THE INTRODUCTION OF A CROSS-SECTORAL EUROPEAN PASSPORT FOR DEPOSITARIES

It is undisputed that the introduction of an AIF/UCITS or even a 'cross-sectoral' depositary passport would lead to economies of scale, increased competition, lower costs and

---

13 *See* for home and host Member States referred to as 'product' and 'distribution' states: D.A. Zetzsche, *Drittstaaten im Europäischen Bank- und Finanzmarktrecht* 62-63 (G. Bachmann & B. Breig eds., Mohr Siebeck, Tübingen 2014).

14 Arts. 49 and 56 TFEU.

15 Directive 2011/61/EU of the European Parliament and of the Council 8 June 2011 on Alternative Investment Fund Managers and amending Directives 2003/41/EC and 2009/65/EC and Regulations (EC) No 1060/2009 and (EU) No 1095/2010, OJ L 174, 1 July 2011, 1 ('AIFMD').

16 Art. 21(5) AIFMD; Art. 23(1) UCITSD V.

17 *See* European Parliament, *Report of the Committee on Legal Affairs and Citizen's Rights on the 1993 UCITS Proposal*, A5-0268/1993, 1 October 1993, http://goo.gl/rRSdJO.

18 AIMA, *AIMA Position Paper UCITS V*, September 2012, http://giegold.korova.co/wp-content/uploads/2012/10/UCITS-V-AIMA-Position-Paper.pdf.

19 Portfolio management and risk management are both considered to be 'investment management'. *See* Point 1(a) and (b) Annex I and Art. 4(1)(w) AIFMD and Annex II, Art. 6(2) UCITSD V. *See also* D.A. Zetzsche & D. Eckner, *Risk Management* 336 et seq. (D.A. Zetzsche ed., Kluwer 2015).

20 The AIFMD, IORPD II, UCITSD V allow AIFMs and UCITS ManCos that fulfill various additional criteria to manage IORPs and discretionary mandates as well. *See* Art. 6(3)(a) UCITSD V and Art. 6(4)(a) AIFMD; *Cf.* J.-P. Casey, *Shedding Light on the UCITS-MiFID Nexus and Potential Impact of MiFID on the Asset Management Sector*, ECMI Policy Brief n. 12, April 2008; C.M. Grundmann-van de Krol, *Verlenen van MiFID-diensten door beheerders van beleggingsinstellingen en icbe's: enkele knelpunten*, 38 Ondernemingsrecht 198 (2014); Under Art. 32 IORPD II, IORPs may appoint for the management of investment portfolios, investment managers in accordance with UCITSD V, IORPD II, the AIFMD, CRD IV and MiFID II, as well as IORPs under IORPD II.

more innovation.[21] The introduction of such a passport would allow 'global custodians' to offer depositary services throughout the EEA at low costs. Currently, the depositary markets in Liechtenstein and other small Member States are underdeveloped. The reason for this is that the AIFMD/UCITSD V depositary locational restrictions make it too expensive for 'global custodians' to offer their services in these markets as, at the minimum, an establishment of a branch is required in these Member States. Currently, Liechtenstein AIFs and UCITS are required to appoint a depositary in Liechtenstein. Liechtenstein is, however, a financial centre in which the fund industry is in the development stage and small compared to renowned fund jurisdictions, such as Ireland and Luxembourg. No international depositary players are, till now, active in Liechtenstein and its depositary structures rely heavily upon local banks. These banks, however, invest limitedly in their depositary services as costs can only be offset in the local market. Depositary services in the local market are more expensive than in, for example, Luxembourg, and provided with a lower degree of quality. Traditionally, delegation structures were used prior to the introduction of the UCITSD V/AIFMD as a countermeasure in which local banks delegated their tasks to global custodians in, for instance, Zürich. Contrary to what has been argued in the AIF/UCITS depositary passport discussion,[22] these delegation structures led in many cases to higher quality depositary services provided in small Member States at lower costs. The introduction of a depositary passport would allow players from small Member States to enter big markets allowing them to invest more in depositary services and offering more choice for clients in the markets in big Member States. In addition, the introduction of an AIF/UCITS or even a cross-sectoral depositary passport would allow AIFMs/UCITS ManCos to appoint one depositary for all AIF/UCITS managed in the EEA.[23] The introduction of a (cross-sectoral) depositary passport would, thus, enable depositaries to offer their services on the European level and to consolidate services on a cross-sectoral and cross-border basis.

Notwithstanding the benefits of introducing an AIF/UCITS depositary passport, a European passport for UCITS and AIF depositaries has so far been multiple times considered, but not introduced due to investor protection concerns.[24] MEP Perreau de Pinninck in 1993 after the introduction of the 'ancillary European passport' under the ISD[25] and Second Banking Directive[26] considered that a European depositary passport for

---

21 *See* Chapter 3, Section 3.1.1.1.2.
22 *See infra*, Section 1.2.3.
23 *See* the response of Axa Investment Managers to the UCITSD VI Consultation, http://ec.europa.eu/finance/consultations/2012/ucits/docs/contributions/registered-organisations/axa-investment-managers_en.pdf.
24 *See infra*, Section 1.2.3.2.
25 Council Directive 93/22/EEC of 10 May 1993 on investment services in the securities field, OJ L 141, 11 June 1993, 27 ('Investment Services Directive; ISD').
26 Second Council Directive 89/646/EEC of 15 December 1989 on the coordination of laws, regulations and administrative provisions relating to the taking up and pursuit of the business of credit institutions and amending Directive 77/780/EEC, OJ L 386, 30 December 1989, 1 ('Second Banking Directive').

UCITS should not be introduced for two reasons.[27] First, it was considered that the depositary function was going beyond merely performing the 'custodian' function under the ISD and Second Banking Directive. Second, depositaries in the UCITS domain had not been harmonized to effectively perform the controlling function.

Prior to introducing an AIF/UCITS or 'cross-sectoral' depositary passport, the question that would, thus, need to be answered is whether the differences between depositaries and custodians justify the locational restriction applicable to AIF/UCITS depositaries. Furthermore, it should be verified whether AIF, UCITS and IORP are sufficiently harmonized or what should be done to make the introduction of a cross-sectoral depositary passport acceptable.

1.2.1   Depositaries versus Custodians

Indeed, the depositary function goes beyond the function performed by 'custodians' under MiFID II/CRD IV and national regimes.[28] 'Custodians' merely perform a safekeeping function and 'depositaries' perform the safekeeping of assets and monitoring duties. 'Custodians' and depositaries perform the same tasks under the safekeeping function.[29] Nevertheless, the additional monitoring task assigned to depositaries reflects that the role of a depositary goes beyond that of a mere custodian. Depositaries are mandatorily required to be appointed in EEA sectoral laws regulating 'investment intermediaries'[30] that perform discretionary investment and risk management for investors/members of 'collective investment undertakings'[31] in which members/investors 'fully bear investment risks'. Due to the fiduciary and collective investment nature of these investment relationships, a depositary is required to monitor the 'investment intermediary' on behalf of the joint investors/members. The controlling/monitoring duty is, however, limited to merely checking the compliance of the discretionary investments made by 'investment intermediaries' with the common terms under the legal form employed, including the investment policy, that investors/members have contracted themselves into.[32] The marginal controlling/monitoring duty does not imply the full involvement of the depositary in the investment decisions that are made by 'investment intermediaries'. This would impair the discretionary nature of these collective investment relationships. Instead, the monitoring/controlling duty has a 'technical nature'.[33] If, for example, a fund agreement agreed upon

---

27 European Parliament, *Report of the Committee on Legal Affairs and Citizen's Rights on the 1993 UCITS Proposal*, A5-0268/1993, 1 October 1993, http://goo.gl/rRSdJO.

28 *See* for the 'custodian' function: Chapter 6.

29 *See* Chapter 7, Section 7.2.

30 AIFMs, UCITS ManCos, investment firms authorized as portfolio manager or investment advisor and IORP governing boards are considered as 'investment intermediaries'.

31 AIFs, UCITS and IORPs can be regarded as 'collective investment undertakings'. For that purpose, the AIFMD excludes IORPs from the scope of the AIFM.

32 *See*, in particular, for AIF/UCITS depositaries: Chapter 4, Section 4.6.3.4.

sets out that the investment portfolio of an AIF may not have more than 10% of its assets invested in the timber industry, the depositary upon exceeding this limit will remind the AIFM to decrease its exposure to this industry. Depositaries, however, do not interfere with the investment decision of how and to what extent the AIFM invests in the timber industry. The controlling duty is assigned to depositaries for these relationships as to overcoming collective action problems and as it is the cheapest solution under the 'cheapest cost avoider theory'.[34]

The monitoring/controlling duty and the different functions of depositaries is also reflected in the separate set of legislation depositaries under the AIFMD, UCITSD V and IORPD II are subjected to. Depositary provisions under these sectoral laws have 'lex specialis' provisions addressing the different role of depositaries in 'fiduciary governance'.[35] On the contrary, 'custodians' are under European investment law mainly appointed in the case of individual investment relationships, such as discretionary portfolio management and 'execution only' services. The main difference is that investors may give investment instructions and remain to have ultimate control over the (discretionary) investment decisions made. For the purpose of the European passport discussion, indeed, depositaries are fundamentally different from 'custodians'.

1.2.2 Overcoming the 'European Depositary Passport Paradox'

A 'de facto European depositary passport' is granted to IORP depositaries, whereas this is not available for AIF/UCITS depositaries. This is highly remarkable as depositaries perform the same functions with the same underlying investor protection objective. This inconsistency can be rightfully called an 'European depositary passport paradox' as the eligible entities and, in particular, the depositary function itself under the AIFMD and UCITSD V has been harmonized to a much larger extent than under IORPD II.[36]

The AIFMD 'transitional relief' regime[37] suggests that the duties, delegation and depositary's liability regime are sufficiently harmonized on the European level for the introduction of a European passport. Under this regime, credit institutions appointed as an AIF depositary were allowed to be appointed under a 'mutual recognition regime' provided that the AIF home Member State in which the AIF is established for which the depositary is appointed has implemented this option in its AIFMD implementation laws.[38] The 'trial phase' of this 'transitional relief regime' ended in early 2017. The

---

33 In Germany, they refer to this duty as 'technische verwaltung' ('technical management').
34 G. Calabresi, *The Costs of Accidents: A Legal and Economic Analysis* (Yale University Press 1970).
35 In this book, 'fiduciary governance' is being referred to as the tri-partite relationship between an 'investment intermediary', depositary/custodian and investors/members under the AIFMD, UCITSD V, IORPD II and MiFID II.
36 *See* for the AIFMD/UCITSD V depositary regime: Chapter 4; *See* for the IORPD II depositary regime: Chapter 5.
37 *See* Chapter 2, Section 2.1.2.2.2.

AIFMD 'transitional relief regime', thus, seems to suggest that a European depositary passport could be introduced provided that eligible entities would be limited to 'credit institutions'. This suggestion seems to be confirmed by Recital 36 AIFMD, which considers that:

> the Commission is invited to examine the possibilities of putting forward an appropriate horizontal legislative proposal that clarifies the responsibilities and liabilities of a depositary and governs the right of a depositary in one Member State to provide its services in another Member State.

Giving the similarities under the UCITSD V depositary regime, similar considerations could be made regarding the introduction of a UCITSD V depositary passport.

In the light of this, the absence of a European passport for AIFs and UCITS remains, however, to be even more remarkable considering the fact that 'eligible depositary entities' under IORPD II are not limited to credit institutions nor any other EEA regulated entities, such as investment firms.[39] The 'de facto' IORP depositary passport under IORPD II, thus, does not comply with the modern approach towards European passports in which maximum harmonization of both the financial intermediary and its operations is required. This seems to suggest that the introduction of a 'cross-sectoral depositary passport' would require full harmonization of the depositary as a financial intermediary and also the harmonization of the IORP depositary duties, delegation and liability standards would be necessary for a consistent approach.

1.2.3   The AIFMD/UCITSD V Depositary Passport 'Investor Protection Concerns'

Throughout the past few decades, the introduction of an AIF/UCITS depositary passport has been discussed numerous times. The concerns expressed are similar as for the 'management passport' that has been introduced under UCITSD V and was also adopted under the AIFMD. For this reason, first the concerns and solutions related to the introduction of this 'management passport' under UCITSD IV[40] are being discussed before an assessment will be made whether and to what extent this discussion might offer a solution for investor protection concerns raised for the introduction of an AIF/UCITS depositary passport.

---

38   *Ibid.*
39   Art. 33(3) IORPD II.
40   Directive 2009/65/EC of the European Parliament and of the Council of 13 July 2009 on the coordination of laws, regulations and administrative provisions relating to undertakings for collective investment in transferable securities (UCITS) (recast), OJ L 302, 17 November 2009, 32 ('UCITSD IV').

1.2.3.1   The Concerns Raised upon Introduction of the 'Management Passport' under UCITSD IV

Upon the introduction of a 'management company passport' under UCITSD IV, a similar discussion has taken place as is currently the case for the introduction of an AIF/UCITS depositary passport.[41] The main issue in both discussions was the 'splitting of financial supervision' between the Member State in which the UCITS and the depositary were established, at the one, and the Member State in which the UCITS ManCo is established, on the other hand.[42] The main argument for not introducing a UCITS 'management passport' until UCITSD IV was that fragmented regulation and supervision of the UCITS structure would have an impact on investor protection and the confidence of investors.[43]

The original UCITSD I text did not allow UCITS established as contractual funds and unit trusts to appoint a UCITS ManCo in another Member State.[44] The rationale behind this was that these legal forms did not enjoy legal personality and, therefore, the UCITS ManCo was required to be established in the same Member State. UCITSD I was based upon the most common method applied by Member States at that time of granting the legal title of the UCITS' assets to the (legal entity of the) UCITS ManCo.[45] UCITSD I required UCITS ManCos of these types of UCITS to represent units trusts and common funds in all legal affairs. The UCITSD I text did not require UCITS investment companies to be established in the same Member State as the UCITS ManCo appointed.[46] This was the case as UCITSD I was originally based upon the idea that UCITS investment companies would have own legal capacity and, thus, would be self-managed.[47] The costs and efficiency benefits of 'third party asset management' were, however, also noticed by UCITS investment companies and, therefore, they almost exclusively appointed third party UCITS ManCos. UCITSD I did not foresee this. During the implementation of UCITSD III[48] that took many obstacles away and paved the way to today's success, CESR, contrary to the UCITSD III text, clarified that

---

41 European Commission, *Report of the Expert Group on Investment Fund Market Efficiency*, July 2006, http://ec.europa.eu/internal_market/investment/docs/other_docs/reports/efficiency_en.pdf; European Commission, *White Paper of on enhancing the single market framework for investment funds*, 15 November 2006, (COM (2006) 686 final), http://ec.europa.eu/internal_market/securities/docs/ucits/whitepaper/whitepaper_en.pdf.

42 C.P. Buttigieg, *The Development of the EU Regulatory and Supervisory Framework applicable to UCITS: A Critical Examination of the Conditions and Limitations of Mutual Recognition*, March 2014, 189, http://sro.sussex.ac.uk/48285/1/Buttigieg%2C_Christopher_P..pdf.

43 C. Kremer & T. Seale, *Passport benefits may not be worth risk*, Financial Times (13 October 2008).

44 *See* Chapter 2, Section 2.1.2.1.

45 D.A. Zetzsche, *Prinzipien der kollektiven Vermögensanlage* § 19 (Mohr Siebeck 2015).

46 J.P.S. Worley, *UCITS III and the Freedom to Provide Fund Management Services*, www.avukati.org/common/fileprovider.ashx?id=633123978903617500.

47 *Ibid.*

48 *See* for 'UCITSD III': Directive 2001/107/EC of the Parliament and of the Council of 21 January 2002 amending Council Directive 85/611/EEC on the coordination of laws, regulations and administrative relat-

the legislator's intention does not seem to have been to impose to UCITS home Member State to recognize the possibility for a foreign management company to set up an investment company in their own constituency.[49]

UCITSD I-III, thus, required all UCITS, appointed UCITS ManCos and depositaries to be established in the same Member State to ease the UCITS home Member State supervision task.[50]

ISD/MiFID I investment firms authorized for portfolio management already enjoyed the benefits of an European passport since the mid-1990s. The increased harmonization of investment firms under MiFID I took away obstacles that impaired investment firms from exercising this passport, whereas UCITS ManCos could only exploit efficiency gains on the basis of delegation arrangements. Being aware of the potential efficiency gains resulting from a similar European passport for UCITS ManCos, the European Commission initiated discussions and consultations with stakeholders for the introduction of such a passport.[51]

A handful of Member States, including Ireland and Luxembourg, opposed the introduction of a depositary passport.[52] They held that the introduction of such a passport would lead to fragmentation of regulation and supervision of the UCITS structure.[53] CESR, upon a request of the European Commission, provided technical advice on under what conditions the principle of mutual recognition could be introduced for UCITS ManCos.[54] CESR found three possible problems in which a 'management company passport' could endanger investor protection: difficulties of the depositary in fulfilling its

---

ing to undertakings for collective investment in transferable securities (UCITS) with a view to regulating management companies and simplified prospectuses, OJ L 41, 13 February 2002, 20 ('UCITSD III (Manager Directive)'); Directive 2001/108/EC of the European Parliament and of the Council of 21 January 2002 amending Council Directive 85/611/EEC on the coordination of laws, regulations and administrative provisions relating to undertakings for collective investment in transferable securities (UCITS), with regard to investments of UCITS, OJ L 41, 13 February 2002, 35 ('UCITSD III (Product Directive)').

49 See question 6 'can an open-ended investment company designate a management company in another EU jurisdiction'. CESR, *Consultation Paper – CESR's Guidelines for Supervisors Regarding the Transitional Provisions of the Amending UCITS Directives (2001/107/EC and 2001/108/EC)*, CESR/04-434, October 2004.
50 See Chapter 2, Section 2.2.1.
51 European Commission, *Commission Proposes Improved EU Framework for Investment Funds*, IP/08/1161, 16 July 2008.
52 ALFI, *ALFI Contribution to the CESR Consultation Paper on UCITS Management Company Passport*, www.-alfi.lu/de/publications-statements/alfi-statements/alfi-response-cesr-consultation-paper-09-624; C. Niedner & A. Sawires, *Passport Flexibility*, 96 European Lawyer 45 (2010); N. Tait & S. Johnson, *Brussels Drops Pan-Europe Funds Plan*, Financial Times (24 May 2008).
53 C.P. Buttigieg, *The Development of the EU Regulatory and Supervisory Framework Applicable to UCITS: A Critical Examination of the Conditions and Limitations of Mutual Recognition*, March 2014, 189, http://sro.sussex.ac.uk/48285/1/Buttigieg%2C_Christopher_P.pdf.
54 CESR, *Covering letter: Advice to the Commission on the UCITS Management Company Passport*, CESR08-067, 31 October 2008.

duties, problems for investor in addressing his/her complaints and a possible 'letterbox entity' that would be left to the UCITS home Member State to supervise.[55] The first two arguments were, however, immediately challenged by CESR. Physical presence of the depositary in the country of the UCITS ManCo was not considered necessary for the performance of its obligations. In addition, due to the UCITS distribution channels a direct relationship between UCITS ManCos and investors was already often absent. A 'management company passport' would, thus, not lead to a worse situation for investor complaints. The third argument, however, needed careful consideration. In this regard, CESR considered that

> effective supervision could be jeopardized if the fund is just a virtual/legal construction emptied of any substance and devoid of any activity, leaving supervisors in a situation where they have difficulty in discharging their responsibilities.[56]

CESR provided the ultimate solution for this problem by setting out detailed requirements on the cooperation and exchange of information between relevant financial supervisors.[57] In addition, CESR countered the letterbox entity concerns by requiring that the depositary from an investor protection point of view would remain to be located in the UCITS home Member State.[58] On this point CESR considered that depositaries should be held liable in accordance with the rules of the UCITS home Member State due to the non-harmonization in this area. For this reason, investors that subscribe to a UCITS in a given Member State should be protected by the supervision rules, depositary regime and investor compensation rules.[59] CESR, thus, made an attempt to protect investors on the presumption that investors would not invest in UCITS of Member States that have low-quality depositary regulation.

These considerations together with the further harmonization of organizational and conduct of business requirements of UCITS ManCos provided the ultimate foundation of the introduction of an UCITS 'management company passport' in UCITSD IV.[60]

---

55 European Commission, *Exposure Draft – Initial orientations for Discussion on Possible Adjustments to the UCITS Directive: Management Company Passport*, 5, http://ec.europa.eu/internal_market/investment/docs/legal_texts/orientations/mcpexposure_en.pdf.
56 *Ibid.*
57 CESR, *Advice to the Commission: UCITS Management Company Passport*, CESR08-867, October 2008; CESR, *Guidelines for supervisors regarding the transitional provisions of the amending UCITS Directives (2001/107/EC and 2001/108/EC)*, CESR/04-434b (2005).
58 European Commission, *supra* note 55, 23.
59 *Ibid.*
60 CESR, October 2008, *supra* note 57.

1.2.3.2 The Investor Protection Concerns upon Introducing an AIF/UCITS Depositary Passport

Similarly as for the 'management company passport' discussion, custodians already upon the introduction of the ISD enjoyed an ('ancillary') European passport. As a compromise of introducing the European 'management passport' under UCITSD IV and the AIFMD, the depositary remained to be required to be established in the UCITS/AIF home Member State. The remarks of CESR upon introducing the UCITS 'management passport' suggest that the 'investor protection concerns' are, in particular, related, in particular, to the minimum harmonization of UCITSD I-IV and pre-AIFMD depositaries.[61] The 'transitional European AIF depositary passport' granted to credit institutions,[62] however, seems to suggest that the efforts undertaken to sufficiently harmonize depositaries in the AIFMD and UCITSD V domain is sufficient provided that eligible entities are restricted to heavily regulated credit institutions (and, possibly, investment firms).[63]

Indeed, the introduction of an AIF/UCITS depositary passport would add an additional layer of fragmented supervision in the UCITSD V and AIFMD domain.[64] Limiting such depositaries to credit institutions and investment firms under MiFID II would, however, ensure that any supervisory issues could be resolved with the involvement of the 'colleges of supervisors'.[65] Furthermore, the argument could be brought up by Member States that the introduction of an AIF/UCITS depositary passport leads to the 'UCITS' being a 'letterbox entity'.[66] UCITS, essentially, are liquid AIFs that are required to comply with 'UCITSD V product regulation'.[67] In this regard, 'product regulation' should be understood as consisting of regulated legal forms and limits related to the investment policy that complements 'manager regulation', i.e. the 'intermediary regulation' applicable to AIFMs and UCITS ManCos.[68] The regulation of legal forms is, under both the AIFMD and UCITSD V, left over to individual Member States. This is the case as legal forms under all AIFMD and UCITSD V Member State implementations merely establish a separate asset patrimony consisting of fund assets that ensures asset segregation and limited liability.[69] The fiduciary governance aspect of legal forms is, almost completely,

---

61 *See* European Commission, *supra* note 55, 23.
62 Under the AIFMD proposal, the AIFMD intended to pave the way for an AIF depositary passport by limiting eligible entities to credit institutions. *See* European Commission, *Proposal on a Directive of the European Parliament and the Council on Alternative Investment Fund Managers and amending Directives 2004/39/EC and 2009/.../EC*, Brussels, 30.4.2009, COM(2009) 207 final.
63 *See* Chapter 2, Section 2.1.2.2.2.
64 C.P. Buttigieg, *The Development of the EU Regulatory and Supervisory Framework applicable to UCITS: A Critical Examination of the Conditions and Limitations of Mutual Recognition*, March 2014, 200, http://sro.sussex.ac.uk/48285/1/Buttigieg%2C_Christopher_P..pdf.
65 *Ibid.*, 211.
66 European Commission, *supra* note 55, 5 and 23.
67 D.A. Zetzsche & C.D. Preiner, *Scope of the AIFMD* (D.A. Zetzsche ed., Kluwer 2015).
68 *See* for 'intermediary', 'product' and 'sales regulation': D.A. Zetzsche, *Introduction* (D.A. Zetzsche ed., Kluwer 2015).
69 *Ibid.*

provided for by the intermediary and sales regulation applicable to AIFMs/UCITS Man-cos and depositaries under the AIFMD and UCITSD V. The UCITS/AIF home Member State upon the introduction of an European AIF/UCITS depositary passport, thus, remains only to be responsible for the authorization of UCITS and AIFs, if required. The role primarily focusses on checking the AIF/UCITS' investment policy prior to distribution. The introduction of an AIF/UCITS depositary passport, thus, does not lead to a 'letterbox entity' in the AIF/UCITS home Member States as AIFs/UCITS are primarily governed/represented by their AIFM s/UCITS ManCos and depositaries as intermediaries. The fund itself, unless internally managed, does not carry out any material activities.

The 'de facto depositary passport' under IORPD II seems to confirm this view. IORPs and IORP asset managers are under IORPD II not required to be established in the IORP home Member State., UCITS and IORPs are, thus, merely 'bundles of contracts' that are governed/represented by their investment intermediaries and depositaries.

Not introducing an AIF/UCITS depositary passport in UCITSD V and the AIFMD seems, thus, to be largely driven by a national protectionist agenda of certain Member States that do not want foreign depositaries to compete with their national depositaries.

1.3   Research Questions

Depositaries may provide cross-border custody services under IORPD II and MiFID II, whereas AIF and UCITS depositaries are precluded from doing so. This contradiction creates a paradoxical tension for depositary obligations under European investment law.

In particular, it seeks to find out whether a 'cross-sectoral'[70] depositary passport should be introduced that allows depositaries to perform cross-border services not only for IORPs and clients under MiFID II, but also for AIFs and UCITS.

In this book the view is taken that not introducing an European passport for depositaries is a disregard of the fundamental freedom of services, which characterizes the creation of an internal market for international financial services in the European Economic Area that cannot be justified in terms of investor protection.

Consequently, this book explores the question whether depositaries in European investment law should be allowed to enjoy the right of a cross-sectoral European passport.

In supporting this thesis, this book seeks to answer this question by the following sub-questions:
-   what inconsistencies in attributing an European depositary passport are to be found in European investment law?

---

70 European law had the tendency to first harmonize various sectors, such as the insurance and banking sector. Currently, European law not only harmonizes legislation within a certain sector but also harmonizes the legislative standards throughout various sectors as to ensure consistency.

- to what extent do financial intermediaries have to be harmonized on the EEA level to obtain a European passport?
- do the differences between depositaries and custodians justify the difference in treatment?
- what preconditions need to be fulfilled to introduce a European AIF/UCITS depositary passport and/or a cross-sectoral European depositary passport?

These questions need to be considered before a full European AIF and UCITS depositary passport and, eventually, a cross-sectoral depositary passport can be introduced.

1.4   METHODOLOGY

Having already established the basis of the theoretical outlook of this research, which is also pertinent to the lens to which the evidence collected will be looked at, it is now necessary to reflect upon how evidence will be collected to support the arguments espoused in this book. In studying the application of the European passport concept on depositaries, the study assesses the arguments pro/contra the introduction of an AIF/UCITS depositary passport of the European Commission,[71] its mandates and interest groups,[72] a law and economics analysis on the European passport and a study of positive norms applying to depositaries/ custodians in European investment law.[73] The latter involves a study regarding positive law, academic literature and the application of the comparative method.

Positive law, as the primary resource of this book in studying depositaries/custodians aims to provide, is an essentially descriptive analysis of a large number of technical and coordinated legal rules to be found in European investment law. The aim of this method of research is to collate, organize and describe all legal rules concerning depositaries in European investment law.[74]

The European Commission, its mandates and various interest groups have issued consultations, reports, recommendations and proposal at the European level on the de-positary/custodians laws on the European level.[75] These will, in particular, be taken into

---

71 European Commission, *Communication from the Commission to the Council and to the European parliament – Regulation of UCITS depositaries in the Member States: review and possible developments*, 30 March 2004, COM(2004) 207 final; FEFSI, *Position Paper on Depositaries*, 4-5 (6 November 2002).

72 AIMA, *supra* note 18; FEFSI, *supra* note 71.

73 F.C. Von Savigny, *System des heutigen Römischen Rechts § 33, A: Auslegung der Gesetze* 213 (Berlin 1840).

74 R. Zippelius, *Juristische Methodenlehre* (C.H. Beck 2012).

75 European Commission, *supra* note 71; FEFSI, *supra* note 71; European Commission, *Commission Staff Working Document of 12 July 2005* (SEC(2005) 947) – *Annex to the Green Paper on the enhancement of the EU Framework for Investment Funds*, http://ec.europa.eu/finance/investment/docs/consultations/green-paper-background_en.pdf; European Commission, *Report of the Expert Group on Investment Fund Market Efficiency*, July 2006, http://ec.europa.eu/internal_market/investment/docs/other_docs/reports/efficiency_en.pdf; European Commission, *White Paper of on Enhancing the Single Market Framework for Investment Funds*, 15 November 2006 (COM (2006) 686 final), http://ec.europa.eu/internal_market/securities/docs/ucits/whitepaper/whitepaper_en.pdf.

account when analysing the inconsistencies of the European depositary passport and why the European legislator has so far not adopted the European passport for AIF/UCITS depositaries (Part I), setting out the research parameters of what it requires to apply the European passport to (AIF/UCITS) depositaries/custodians (Part II), what differences there are between depositaries and custodians that justify this difference in treatment (Part III) and providing recommendations and proposals that on the European level could be applied to introduce a cross-sectoral European depositary passport (Part IV).

The comparative method is of great importance in this study.[76] It serves two purposes. First, it clarifies aspects of depositary regulation on the European level that have so far not been in detail clarified. Second, the approach of the European investment law directives towards the regulation of depositaries varies in the degree of harmonization. The AIFMD and UCITSD V regulate depositaries in detail,[77] whereas IORPD II and MiFID II do not clarify in detail what entities are eligible to be appointed, what organizational structure and responsibilities depositaries should have.[78] At present, studies, in particular, do not highlight the similarities and differences of depositaries/custodians in the IORPD II and MiFID II domain, the comparative method seeks to identify basic regulatory principles for IORP depositaries and MiFID II custodians.

The comparative study is being treated as essentially being the interpretation of the various Member States of the depositary regulation in European investment law. The recommendations and proposals provided in Part IV of this research aim to be applied by all Member States. Although France, Germany, Ireland, Luxembourg, the Netherlands and the UK dominate in terms of asset under management, no specific Member States are systematically studied in this book.[79] The latter approach is taken because a possible European legislative act needs to be decided upon on the European level. Basing a proposal upon merely a few Member State laws representing 31 EEA Member States would likely undermine this proposal. For this purpose, the comparative study mainly brings examples of the dominating Member States regarding small interpretative issues on the European level. For issues in depositary/custodian regulation, which are completely regulated to a minimum extent on the European level, such as the 'PE-depositary',[80] the research is based upon mapping exercises of Member State laws. The outcomes of these mapping

---

76 M. Van Hoecke, *Methodology of Comparative Legal Research*, http://rem.tijdschriften.budh.nl/tijdschrift/lawandmethod/2015/12/RENM-D-14-00001#content_RENM-D-14-00001.5738700789; G. Samuel, *An Introduction to Comparative Law Theory and Method* 81-82 (Hart Publishing 2014); M. Siems, *Comparative Law* (Cambridge University Press, 2014); M. Van Hoecke, *Do "Legal Systems" Exist? The Concept of Law and Comparative Law* 43-57. (S. Donlan & L. Heckendorn Urscheler eds., Ashgate 2014); K. Zweigert & H. Kötz, *Introduction to Comparative Law* 35 (Clarendon Press 1998).

77 Hooghiemstra, *supra* note 10.

78 EIOPA, *EIOPA's Advice to the European Commission on the Review of the IORP Directive 2003/41/EC*, EIOPA-BOS-12/015, 15 February 2012; Annex I s. A MiFID II.

79 *See* D.A. Zetzsche, *Prinzipien der kollektiven Vermögensanlage* (Mohr Siebeck 2015).

80 D.A. Zetzsche, *Fondsregulierung im Umbruch – ein rechtsvergleichender Rundblick zur Umsetzung der AIFM-Richtlinie*, ZBB 22 (2014).

exercises, to the extent relevant, are categorized into different groups as to formulate general similarities and differences as how certain European investment law provisions are being implemented in the laws of Member States. The latter approach guarantees an efficient outcome, which is realistically to be implemented on the European level.

With black letter analysis, the focus is on primary sources, in this research mainly statute and to a lesser extent, academic commentary.[81] As such, it focuses on the law in books rather than the law 'in action', thereby overlooking the sociological and political implications. To this extent, the limited available literature[82] in European investment law will be used, especially, in considering the differences between depositaries and custodians in the European investment law domain as elaborated in Part III of this research.

This analysis made on the basis of this methodology offers the foundations for the commentary offered on the emergence and significance of the depositary in European investment law with the aim of identifying an underlying system that could provide the basis for the recommendations and proposals for a cross-sectoral European passport of depositaries.

1.5 LIMITATIONS

The emphasis of this research project is on the eventual introduction of a cross-sectoral European depositary passport. Depositaries will be solely studied from a regulatory law perspective. The study deals with regulatory law issues concerning the European passport and the depositary/custodian as a financial intermediary from a comparative perspective within the scope of MiFID II, the AIFMD, UCITSD V and IORPD II. This study includes the so-called AIFMD/UCITSD V 'product regulations', including the use of the depositary under EuVECAR[83]/EuSEFR,[84] MMFR[85] and ELTIFR.[86] Regulatory laws and legal fields touching upon depositaries, such as custody transfer law and (international) private law, will not be dealt with in this study.

It is obvious that, in view of the amount of issues related to the subject of research, a certain trade-off has to be made between comprehensive and thoroughness within the

---

81 J.B. Murphy, *The Philosophy of Positive Law: Foundations of Jurisprudence* (Yale University Press 2005); J. Raz, *The Concept of a Legal System* 141 (Clarendon Press 1980); J.B.M. Vranken, *Methodology of Legal Doctrinal Research*, https://pure.uvt.nl/ws/files/1296852/Vranken_Methodology_of_legal_doctrinal_research_110118_publishers_embargo1y.pdf.

82 *See infra* 1.6.1. on 'scientific relevance'.

83 Regulation (EU) No. 345/2013 of the European Parliament and of the Council of 17 April 2013 on European venture capital funds, OJ L 115, 25 April 2013, 1 ('EuVECAR').

84 Regulation (EU) No. 346/2013 of the European Parliament and of the Council of 17 April 2013 on European social entrepreneurship funds, OJ L 115, 25 April 2013, 18 ('EuSEFR').

85 Regulation (EU) 2017/1131 of the European Parliament and of the Council of 14 June 2017 on money market funds, OJ L169/8, 30 June 2017, 8 ('MMFR').

86 Regulation (EU) 2015/760 of the European Parliament and of the Council of 29 April 2015 on European long-term investment funds, OJ L 123, 19 May 2015, 98 ('ELTIFR').

limits of this study. In this study, the author favours comprehensiveness. The chosen approach implicates that not every single and possible detail of depository regulation will be addressed in this study. In this respect, this study aims to take a pragmatic approach and will not extend beyond the limits set out in this proposal.

1.6 Scientific and Societal Relevance

1.6.1 Scientific Relevance

Currently there is no research with respect to the introduction of a cross-sectoral European passport for depositaries under European investment law.

After UCITSD II, that contained a proposal for the mutual recognition of EEA depositaries failed, various initiatives and studies on UCITS depositaries have been directly or indirectly initiated by the European Commission and were conducted from 2004 to 2012.[87] The European Commission in all these studies concluded that a lack of harmonization regarding the eligibility, organizational requirements, functions and responsibilities, delegation and liability regime would have to be overcome first before a European passport for UCITS depositaries could be seriously considered. Although some convergence over the years had taken place into the domain of eligible entities and the safekeeping function performed, the divergences regarding the types of oversight duties and the interpretation of the oversight duties imposed by UCITSD I–IV remained an obstacle that was not yet adequately addressed.[88] The various studies conducted influenced the adopted AIFMD and UCITSD V, as well as, the IORPD II depositary/custodian regime.[89] In spite of these revised legislative acts, the European Commission only reviewed a possible introduction of a depositary passport under UCITSD VI.[90] None of the initiatives and studies on the European level has so far considered the introduction of a cross-sectoral European depositary passport.

Apart from this, such a study is also not yet assumed by academic articles and books.

---

87 European Commission, 2004, *supra* note 71; FEFSI, *supra* note 71; European Commission, 2005, *supra* note 75; European Commission, July 2006, *supra* note 75; European Commission, November 2006, *supra* note 75; *See also* European Commission, *Working Document of the Commission Services (DG Markt) – Consultation Paper on the UCITS Depositary Function*, July 2009, http://ec.europa.eu/internal_market/consultations/docs/2009/ucits/consultation_paper_en.pdf; European Commission, *Consultation Paper on the UCITS Depositary Function and on the UCITS Managers 'Remuneration*, 14 December 2010, MARKT/G4 D (2010) 950800, 16, 17, http://ec.europa.eu/finance/consultations/2010/ucits/docs/consultation_paper_en.pdf.

88 Hooghiemstra, *supra* note 10.

89 EIOPA-BOS-12/015, 15.

90 European Commission, *Consultation Document – Undertakings for Collective Investment in Transferable Securities (UCITS) Product Rules, Liquidity Management, Depositary, Money Market Funds, Long-term Investments*, July 2012, http://ec.europa.eu/finance/consultations/2012/ucits/docs/ucits_consultation_en.pdf.

In general, the depositary in European investment law seems to be an unexplored area of law. Some authors have written on depositary law in relation to UCITS and AIFs.[91] These studies, however, are highly descriptive in nature.[92]

This research is necessary since the current harmonization trends in European investment law indicate that there is an increasing need for the introduction of a depositary passport that serves the needs not only of AIFs and UCITS, but also of MiFID II clients and IORPs.

1.6.2   Societal Relevance: The Growing Importance of Depositaries

The rise of European AuM and possible cost reductions resulting from the introduction of a (cross-sectoral) European depositary passport show the growing importance of depositaries and their societal relevance.

1.6.2.1   The Rise of European AuM

Total asset under management (AuM) in Europe increased 11% in 2012 and close to 9% in 2013, to reach an estimated EUR 16.8 trillion at the end of 2013.[93] Europe ranks second, after the US, in managing 33% of the EUR 47 trillion global asset management industry.[94] The social relevance is given since all these assets are safekept by European depositaries.[95]

In Europe, discretionary mandates (MiFID II) represented 52% of the total AuM at the end of 2012. Discretionary mandates are dominated by two markets: the UK and France, which together managed approximately 66% of all total European discretionary mandates at the end of 2012.[96]

---

91 S.N. Hooghiemstra, *De AIFM-richtlijn en de aansprakelijkheid van de bewaarder*, 6 TvFR 178 (2013); Hooghiemstra, *supra* note 10; C.P. Buttigieg, *supra* note 3; C.P. Buttigieg, *The Alternative Investment Fund Managers Directive in Malta: Past, Present ... What Next?*, 15, https://ssrn.com/abstract=2602750; See C.P. Buttigieg, *The 2009 UCITS IV Directive: A Critical Examination of the Framework for the Creation of a Broader and More Efficient Internal Market for UCITS*, https://ssrn.com/abstract=2137202; T. Dolan, *UCITS V Brings Convergence of the Depositary Role with AIFMD*, 1 JIBFL 64B (2015).

92 *See, e.g.* I. Riassetto, *Le nouveau régime applicable aux dépositaires issu de la directive OPCVM V*, 3 Bulletin Joly Bourse 113 (2015).

93 EFAMA, *Asset Management in Europe*, Facts and Figures 7th Annual Review, June 2014, 10, www.efama.org/Publications/Statistics/Asset%20Management%20Report/Asset%20Management%20Report%202014.pdf.

94 The world's largest market is the US, which represents EUR 21.5 trillion in AuM and makes up approximately 46% of the global asset management industry. See EFAMA, *Asset Management in Europe*, Facts and Figures 7th Annual Review, June 2014, 12, www.efama.org/Publications/Statistics/Asset%20Management%20Report/Asset%20Management%20Report%202014.pdf.

95 *See* IOSCO, *Standards for the Custody of Collective Investment Schemes' Assets – Final Report*, FR 25/2015, November 2015, https://www.iosco.org/library/pubdocs/pdf/IOSCOPD512.pdf.

96 The UK managed 47% and France 19%. See EFAMA, *supra* note 94, 18.

The share of AIF and UCITS assets in total AuM stood at 48%. Of the latter 48%, over 75% were invested in UCITS, whereas approximately 25% were invested in AIFs.[97] In the UCITS domain, over 80% is invested by fund domiciled in four jurisdictions: Luxembourg (32.4%), France (20.6%), Ireland (14.4%) and the United Kingdom (11.5%).[98] The European AIF sector, apart from Germany, is also dominated by these four Member States.[99]

The potential total aggregated amount of IORPs amount to 110,127 representing approximate assets of 2.9 trillion for around 75 million beneficiaries in June 2014. Of these 110,127 IORPs, only 75 are currently active cross-border IORPS.[100] Currently, 29 IORPs are domiciled in the UK, 25 in Ireland and 11 in Belgium. Together these Member States domicile 88% of the active cross-border IORPs.[101]

Overall, the European depositary industry is, thus, today entrusted with the safekeeping of more than EUR 16.8 trillion of assets.

1.6.2.2   Possible Cost Reduction of a Depositary Passport
Not only the rise of AuM in the European investment management industry, but also a possible cost reduction of the introduction of a (cross-sectoral) European depositary passport shows the growing importance of depositaries and their societal relevance.

AIF/UCITS depositaries must be located in the Member State in which the AIF/UCITS for which they are appointed, is established,[102] Over 80% of all assets may, thus, only be safekept by depositaries in six EEA Member States, whereas in a fully competitive European market these assets could be held by depositaries established in all thirty-one EEA Member States.[103]

In spite of recent trends affecting the custody sector, including increased global competition, the disappearance of local custodians and the emergence of a handful of global players, the European depositary fees are still significantly higher compared to the US.[104] The cost of custody calculated as a percentage of the assets held in custody varies in Europe for UCITS and AIFs between 0.25bp and 1.25bp, whereas the costs of custody in the United States ranges from 0.2bp to a maximum of 0.5bp.[105] The costs of custody in

---

97 EFAMA, *supra* note 94, 5 and 6.
98 *See* European Commission, *Impact Assessment – Proposal for a Directive of the European Parliament and of the Council Amending Directive 2009/65/EC on the Coordination of Laws, Regulations and Administrative Provisions Relating to Undertakings for Collective Investment in Transferable Securities (UCITS) as Regards Depositary Functions, Remuneration Policies and Sanctions* (COM(2012) 350) (SWD(2012) 186), 10.
99 EFAMA, *Trends in the European Investment Fund Industry in the Third Quarter of 2014*, Quarterly Statistical Release November 2014, No. 59, 8, www.efama.org/Publications/Statistics/Quarterly/Quarterly%20Statistical%20Reports/141128_Quarterly%20Statistical%20Release%20Q3%202014.pdf.
100 EIOPA, *Report on Cross Border IORP Market Developments*, 2014, 4, https://eiopa.europa.eu/Publications/Reports/EIOPA-BoS-14-083-Market-Development-Report-2014-deff.pdf.
101 *Ibid.*
102 Art. 21(5) AIFMD; Art. 23(1) UCITSD V.
103 *See* European Commission, *supra* note 98.
104 *See* European Commission, *supra* note 75.

Europe are, thus, between 200% and 500% higher than in the US. Given the fact that the cost of custody is normally calculated as a percentage of the assets that are held in custody on an annual basis, full competition by means of a depositary passport could, thus, save the European investors billions of Euros on an annual basis. Not even to speak about the increase in quality of services by way of which the enhancement of the introduction of a cross-sectoral European depositary passport could affect millions of investors. Therefore, it is clear that this research topic has societal relevance.

1.7   Study Outline

The purpose of this book is to assess whether a common European passport for depositaries servicing not only IORPs and clients of investment firms, but also UCITS and AIFs, should be introduced. For that purpose, this research is divided into four parts, each answering one sub-question.

Part I gives an overview of the 'depositary passport paradox' in European investment law, i.e. the problem of the inconsistency of the European depositary passport under the European investment law directives, which is the key problem addressed in this book. In order to point out the inconsistencies, first the locational restrictions of depositaries/custodians under the European investment laws are being discussed. In addition, the policy discussion related to the introduction of a European depositary will be addressed that sets out the historical context and indicates the reasons why such a passport so far has not been introduced. Part I concludes that for the introduction of a 'cross-sectoral European depositary/passport', two points need to be clarified. First, under what conditions do EEA and TC financial intermediaries obtain a European passport under EEA regulatory law and second, what is a depositary and to what extent does a depositary differentiate from a custodian. Before a proposal for a cross-sectoral European passport in Part IV is being made, Part II addresses the first question and Part III the second question.

Part II addresses to what extent financial intermediaries have to be harmonized on the EEA level to obtain a European passport. It explores the political economy of a European passport for EEA financial intermediaries and the 'joint principles' under various legislative acts, including authorization, operational, notification and enforcement conditions that EEA financial intermediaries, generally, need to fulfil in order to obtain a European passport. In addition, Part II studies the 'external dimension' of the European passport, i.e. the European passport granted to third country financial intermediaries. To this end, it will be studied what additional conditions EEA financial intermediaries under various European legal acts need to fulfil in order to enter the internal market. The latter serves to determine under what conditions a (cross-sectoral) European passport for third country financial intermediaries could be introduced.

---

105 *See* European Commission, *supra* note 98, 12.

Part III aims to define what a depositary is and whether and to what extent depositaries and custodians differ. This serves two purposes. First, Part III clarifies out whether a difference in treatment of depositaries, on one hand, and custodians on the other, throughout European investment law is justified from an investor protection perspective. Second, Part III seeks to find out whether common regulatory principles for depositaries and custodians, similar to those for asset managers that conduct investment management under the European investment law directives, are to be found, which would possibly justify a cross-sectoral European depositary passport. To this end, the positive norms applying to depositaries and custodians in various sectoral EEA laws will be studied to define the similarities and differences.

Part IV seeks to develop a cross-sectoral European depositary passport under European investment law. For this purpose, Part IV assesses whether and to what extent depositaries and custodians fulfil the preconditions of the introduction of an European passport for EEA and TC financial intermediaries as set out under Part II.

The eventual conclusion will be that depositaries and custodians are both safekeeping assets and, thus, 'custodians'. Depositaries, on top of being a 'custodian', however, also monitor asset managers by conducting controlling duties. The remaining problems related to the introduction of a cross-sectoral depositary passport, such as the non-harmonization of eligible depositary/custodian entities, can, thus, be regulated under a cross-sectoral regulatory framework in MiFID II, whereas the specific 'depositary' tasks may be regulated on the sectoral level. By undertaking this regulatory response, the European regulatory solves the issues related to the introduction of a cross-sectoral European depositary passport within the existing legal framework of European investment law.

PART I
THE EUROPEAN DEPOSITARY
PASSPORT PARADOX

2   LOCATIONAL DEPOSITARY RESTRICTIONS UNDER THE EUROPEAN INVESTMENT LAWS

Notwithstanding the fundamental principle of freedom to provide services under consti-tutional EEA law,[1] the AIFMD and UCITSD V restrict the choice of depositaries. The AIFMD and UCITSD V require depositaries to be 'established' in the funds' domicile.[2] Credit institutions, investment firms and UCITS depositaries that are under the terms of CRD IV, MiFID II and IORPD I/II allowed to provide custody services on a cross-border basis, may not exercise 'passporting rights' under the UCITSD V and the AIFMD.

Strictly speaking, there is, thus, inconsistency in locational depositary restrictions, i.e. a European 'depositary passport paradox' in European investment law. The chapter pro-ceeds by discussing the locational restrictions of depositaries/custodians under the Euro-pean investment laws. In addition, the policy discussion related to the introduction of a European depositary will be discussed that sets out the historical context and indicates the reasons why such a passport so far has not been introduced.

2.1   THE EUROPEAN DEPOSITARY/CUSTODIAN PASSPORT UNDER EUROPEAN INVESTMENT LAWS

In practice, the same investment firms and credit institutions are acting as a custodian for discretionary mandates and 'execution-only'[3] services under MiFID II/CRD IV, a deposi-tary under the AIFMD/UCITSD V and a depositary/custodian under IORPD II. Never-theless, the European investment laws, i.e. MiFID II, CRD IV, the AIFMD, UCITSD V and IORPD II, are inconsistent in granting a depositary/custodian passport to these de-positaries/custodians. They are both inconsistent throughout the directives and on a cross-sectoral basis. These inconsistencies are highlighted through this section and are referred to as the 'European depositary passport paradox'.

2.1.1   The European Passport for 'Custodians' under MiFID II/CRD IV

An 'ancillary' European passport for 'custodians' was being introduced under the Second Banking Directive and the ISD. Under both the Second Banking Directive and ISD, the 'safekeeping and administration of securities' could be provided as a so-called 'ancillary

---

1   *See* Art. 49 and 56 TFEU.
2   Art. 21(5) AIFMD and Art. 23(1) UCITSD V.
3   *See* Annex I s. A. n. 1 and n. 2 MiFID II; Art. 25(4) MiFID II.

service'. Credit institutions that were authorized for 'core services', such as deposit-taking and lending,[4] could be, additionally, authorized for acting as a custodian alongside these 'core services'. The ISD built upon this framework by allowing investment firms to be authorized for the ancillary service 'safekeeping and administration of financial instruments for the account of clients' in connection with investment services and activities, such as, amongst others, portfolio management and investment advice.[5] Throughout the updates of the Second Banking Directive to CRD IV and the ISD to MiFID II, the safekeeping and administration of securities remained an 'ancillary service' for which no separate authorization procedure nor a 'stand-alone' European passport is in place.[6]

2.1.2   The Location of the Depositary under the AIFMD and UCITSD V

Both the AIFMD/UCITSD V impose locational restrictions for depositaries. Under Article 23(1) UCITSD V and Article 21(5) AIFMD a depositary shall either have its registered office or be established in the UCITS/EEA-AIF home Member State.

Originally, this restriction was introduced under the UCITSD I 'product regulation approach'. UCITSD I harmonized and allowed European 'mutual funds', i.e. liquid retail collective investment undertakings, to be marketed throughout the EEA. The EEA-wide marketing of these financial products was only allowed under the condition that these undertakings complied with an investment policy composing of financial instruments and other liquid financial assets. UCITSD I was focussing on the product and was introducing a marketing passport. UCITS ManCos were, thus, only allowed to sell but not to manage UCITS on a cross-border basis.[7] The 'product regulation approach' required only the product and not the intermediaries, i.e. UCITS ManCos and depositaries, to be fully harmonized. Instead, UCITS ManCos and depositaries only needed to comply with 'principle-based' minimum requirements.[8] Consequently, the minimum harmonization of the organizational and conduct of business requirements applying to UCITS ManCos and depositaries implied that no European passport could be attributed to these intermediaries to provide services to UCITS on a cross-border basis.[9] As a result of the 'product regulation approach', UCITS ManCos and depositaries were under UCITSD I required to

---

4   Annex List of Activities subject to Mutual Recognition, n. 12 'safekeeping and administration of securities' Second Banking Directive; Annex I s. C, n. 1 'safekeeping and administration in relation to one or more of the instruments listed in Section B' ISD.

5   Annex I s. A MiFID II.

6   *See* Chapter 6, Section 6.2.1.

7   The UCITS ManCo passport was introduced under UCITSD IV. *See* C.P. Buttigieg, *The 2009 UCITS IV Directive: A Critical Examination of the Framework for the Creation of a Broader and More Efficient Internal Market for UCITS*, https://ssrn.com/abstract=2137202.

8   C.P. Buttigieg, *The Development of the EU Regulatory and Supervisory Framework Applicable to UCITS: A Critical Examination of the Conditions and Limitations of Mutual Recognition*, March 2014, 66, http://sro.sussex.ac.uk/48285/1/Buttigieg%2C_Christopher_P.pdf.

9   *Ibid.*

be established in the same Member State as the UCITS home Member State. The ratio-nale behind this was that the UCITS home Member State would be equipped the best to verify compliance of the UCITS ManCo, depositary and UCITS with UCITSD I and enforce compliance, if necessary.[10] The introduction of UCITSD III and IV led to the harmonization of UCITS ManCos to such an extent that a 'management passport', i.e. the right to manage UCITS on a cross-border basis throughout the EEA, was introduced.

The AIFMD built upon the work done for UCITS and introduced both a marketing and management passport for AIFMs on the basis of an 'intermediary regulation ap-proach'. Unlike for UCITS, the AIFMD focussed on the harmonization of AIFMs and not on the harmonization of AIFs. Upon the introduction of the AIFMD and subsequent adoption of UCITSD V, also the depositary regulatory framework has been substantially harmonized. A depositary passport, i.e. the right of a depositary to act on a cross-border basis on the basis of the free provision of services, however, has so far not been intro-duced.[11] Instead, depositaries are required to be 'established' in the home Member State of the UCITS/EEA-AIF. Established under the AIFMD means that either the registered office or a branch office is required to be located in the UCITS/AIF home Member State for which a depositary is appointed. The AIFMD, however, takes an inconsistent ap-proach as it deviates from the locational restriction applying to EEA-AIFS for TC-AIFs. In the same vein, the AIFMD transitional relief granted individual Member States until 22 July 2017 an option for their AIFMs managing EEA-AIFs to appoint credit institu-tions established in other Member States as a depositary.[12] The AIFMD is not only in-consistent in the locational restrictions that apply to depositaries. The absence of a Eu-ropean passport allows the Competent Authorities of the individual Member States to determine under what conditions a branch office of a depositary is being established within their domicile.

This section continues to discuss the 'depositary passport paradox' for AIF and UCITS depositaries. It will first address the locational restrictions of UCITS depositaries in further detail. This section will then address the inconsistent locational restriction applying to depositaries that apply to EEA-AIFs and TC-AIFs, on the one hand, and between an EEA-AIFM and a TC-AIFM managing an AIF, on the other.

---

10 *See* European Commission, *White Paper of on Enhancing the Single Market Framework for Investment Funds*, 15 November 2006 (COM (2006) 686 final), http://ec.europa.eu/internal_market/securities/docs/ucits/whitepaper/whitepaper_en.pdf;

11 Under the AIFMD transitional relief, Competent Authorities of the home Member State of an AIFM could allow, until 22 July 2017, allow credit institutions that are established in another Member State to be ap-pointed as a depositary. *See* Art. 61(5) AIFMD.

12 *See* Art. 61(5) AIFMD.

2.1.2.1   The Location of the Depositary for UCITS

Under Article 23(1) UCITSD V, a depositary shall either have its registered office or be established in the UCITS home Member State.

Under UCITSD V it is not defined what 'established' for depositaries means. 'Established' for depositaries under Art. 4(1)(j)(iii) AIFMD means 'having its registered office or branch in'. This definition is consistent with the section 'cross-border activities' as defined in various European legal initiatives that grant a European passport to financial intermediaries.[13]

The UCITS depositary location restrictions has to be read in conjunction with the eligible entity provision under UCITSD V.[14]

The initial UCITSD V draft had as its objective to limit UCITSD V eligible depositary entities to credit institutions and investment firms authorized under CRD IV and MiFID II.[15] Under this proposal the cross-border activities under CRD IV and MiFID II could have been used to determine whether a depositary is 'established', i.e. has its registered office or branch in the UCITS home Member State. Ever since the First Banking Directive[16] and ISD have been adopted, CESR, the predecessor of ESMA, has sought to clarify the conditions under which investment firms and credit institutions would be entitled to make use of their passporting rights.[17] The ongoing clarification under these directives of the 'cross-border activities' would have been useful. The final version of UCITSD V, however, did not limit eligible depositary entities to credit institutions and investment firms.[18] Instead, Member States were allowed the discretion to choose whether a credit institution,[19] national central bank [20] or 'other eligible entities'[21] would be eligible to be appointed as a UCITS depositary within their domicile.[22] Member States have taken different approaches in implementing this option. Some Member States have not implemented this option at all,[23] whereas other Member States have taken different approaches

---

13 D.A. Zetzsche, *The AIFMD and the Joint Principles of European Asset Management Law* 865 (D.A. Zetzsche ed, Kluwer 2015).

14 *See* for these eligible entity provisions: Art. 23(2) UCITSD V.

15 Art. 23a(2) UCITSD V Draft proposal.

16 First Council Directive 77/780/EEC of 12 December 1977 on the coordination of laws, regulations and administrative provisions relating to the taking up and pursuit of the business of credit institutions, OJ L 322, 17 December 1977, 30 ('First Banking Directive').

17 *See* CESR/07-337b.

18 Art. 23(2) UCITSD V.

19 Art. 23(2)(b) UCITSD V.

20 Art. 23(2)(a) UCITSD V.

21 Art. 23(2)(c) UCITSD V.

22 Art. 23(1) UCITSD V.

23 The following Member States, for example, only allow credit institutions to be appointed as a UCITSD V depositary: Austria: § 41(1) Investmentfondsgesetz 2011 (InvFG 2011); Croatia: Art. 4(7) Act on Open-Ended Investment Funds with a Public Offering (Official Gazette 44/16); Denmark: Art. 2 (1) n. 11 Act n. 597 of 12 June 2013 on investment associations; Germany: § 68 (2) and (3) KAGB; Luxembourg: Art. 17(3) OPC law 2010.

by either allowing all legal entities fulfilling these criteria to be appointed[24] or to specify the types of legal entities, such as investment firms,[25] CSDs,[26] prime brokers[27] or eligible legal entities authorized under national law[28] fulfilling the additional UCITSD V criteria that are allowed to be appointed as a UCITS depositary.

The cross-border activity definitions of 'registered and branch office' under EEA legislation applying to EEA entities, including investment firms,[29] CSDs,[30] prime brokers[31] established as credit institution or investment firms qualifying as 'other legal entities' under national legislation, could have been used. Nevertheless, the problem is that various Member States, such as Ireland and Malta, allow eligible legal entities authorized under national law that fulfil additional UCITSD V criteria to be appointed as a UCITS depositary. For these eligible legal entities, criteria under the respective national laws define what 'be established in the UCITS home Member State' means.[32]

Ireland allows Irish companies to be eligible as 'other eligible institution' provided that the company is wholly owned by either an EEA/TC credit institution[33] or an equivalent EEA/TC institution[34] that guarantees the liabilities of the company and that has a paid-up share capital of at least EUR 5 million.[35] Similarly, Malta allows Maltese companies to be appointed as a depositary that are wholly owned by an EEA credit institution provided that the liabilities of the company are guaranteed by that credit institution.[36] Under the

---

24 Cyprus: Art. 88(I)(2) Open-Ended Undertakings for Collective Investment (UCI) Law of 2012 Consolidated with Law 88(I)/2015; Liechtenstein: Art. 32(2)(c) UCITSG; the Netherlands: Art. 4:62n(a) Wft.

25 Czech Republic: § 69(1)(c) 240/2013 Sb.ZÁKON ze dne 3. července 2013 o investičních společnostech a investičních fondech; France: Art. L214-10-1 I.(a) n. 5 CMF; Liechtenstein: Art. 32(2)(a) and (b) UCITSG; the Netherlands: Art. 4:62n(c); Malta: Art. 13(2)(e) Investment Services Act (custodians of collective investment schemes) Regulations 2016; UK: COLL 6.6A.8R(3)(b)(i).

26 Finland: Finnish Government Bill, draft legislation for Managers of Alternative Investment Funds, 05.09.2013, 218; See also §16, Chapter 2 of the Act amending the Clearing Operations Act; See also Chapter 14, Section 3 Finnish Law on Alternative Investment Funds; Poland: Art. 71(3) Act of 27 May 2004 on Investment Funds.

27 See CSSF, Circular14/587, as amended by Circular CSSF 15/608, Sub-Chapter 7.3. Organisational arrangements at the level of the depositary and the UCITS in case of the appointment of a prime broker.

28 Ireland: Art. 35(2)(c) (Undertakings for Collective Investment in Transferable Securities) Regulations 2011 (S.I. No. 352 of 2011); Malta: Art. 13(2)(e) Investment Services Act (custodians of collective investment schemes) Regulations 2016; UK: COLL 6.6A.8R(3)(b)(i).

29 See supra note 25.

30 See supra note 26.

31 See supra note 27.

32 Cf. R.K.Th.J. Smits, De AIFMD-bewaarder; praktische gevolgen voor Nederlandse beleggingsinstellingen, 11 V&O 200-204 (2012).

33 Art. 35(2)(c) (Undertakings for Collective Investment in Transferable Securities) Regulations 2011 (S.I. No. 352 of 2011).

34 This is assessed by the Irish Central Bank. See Art. 35(2)(c)(iii) (Undertakings for Collective Investment in Transferable Securities) Regulations 2011 (S.I. No. 352 of 2011).

35 Art. 35(2)(c) (Undertakings for Collective Investment in Transferable Securities) Regulations 2011 (S.I. No. 352 of 2011). See for similar depositaries under the AIFMD: Art. 22(3)(iii) AIFM Regulations.

36 Art. 13(2)(d) Investment Services Act (CAP 370) (Custodians of Collective Investment Schemes) Regulations, 2016.

Irish UCITSD V implementation, non-EEA credit institutions may, thus, through wholly owned subsidiaries with little substance (indirectly), offer depositary services to UCITS not only within Ireland, but also by means of a branch within other EEA Member States. The wholly owned subsidiary under Irish law is an 'EEA legal entity' and meets both the 'registered office' and, depending upon the assessment of Competent Authorities in question, the branch office requirement under the UCITSD V 'established in' definition. Non-EEA legal entities under the Irish UCITSD V implementation, thus, formally meet the requirement that they only may act as a UCITS depositary for Irish AIFs if they have their registered office in Ireland. In addition, they may act as a UCITS depositary in other EEA domiciles if they have a branch office within that EEA Member State. Non-EEA legal entities that do not have a subsidiary with an EEA registered office may not act as a depositary in any EEA Member State.[37] Even not if they have a branch office in the UCITS home Member State in which they want to act as UCITS depositary.[38]

The registered office may, however, be a 'letterbox'[39] as the substance of 'other legal entities' authorized under national law has not been further defined and the UCITSD V only sets out some basic principles regarding the organizational requirements of these entities that need to be applied by national Competent Authorities.[40] The main problem is that this 'letterbox entity' may be established in another Member State as a 'branch'. UCITSD V, however, does not further define the criteria that a depositary 'branch office' needs to fulfil in order to be considered as being 'established in' a UCITS home Member States. The substance of a branch office, de facto, depends upon the national legislation and practical application of the 'branch office' requirement by the Competent Authorities of individual EEA Member States. Individual Member States, thus, have discretion in determining what operational activities UCITS depositaries are required to perform in the Member State in which the branch office of the depositary is established and what activities are allowed to be performed in the Member State in which the registered or branch office established in another Member State of the depositary is established. The Netherlands, for example, has a 'representative office approach' towards branch offices of EEA depositaries.[41] Branch offices in the Netherlands are, de facto, representative offices representing the registered office of a depositary in another Member State that do not itself provide depositary services.[42] Typically, a branch office carries out activities such as sales and marketing and relationship management.[43] The Netherlands allows these branch offices of EEA depositaries to conduct their operational depositary services in

---

37 Art. 23(2)(b) UCITSD V.
38 *Ibid.*
39 C.P. Buttigieg, *The Alternative Investment Fund Managers Directive in Malta: Past, Present ... What Next?*, https://ssrn.com/abstract=2602750.
40 Art. 23(2)(c) UCITSD V.
41 R.K.Th.J. Smits, *supra* note 32.
42 *See* on representative offices under MiFID I: CESR/07-337b, 13.
43 R.K.Th.J. Smits, *supra* note 32.

the Member State in which the registered office of the depositary is established or a so-called 'center of excellence/operational hub' located elsewhere.[44]

The locational restriction of UCITS depositaries is, thus, in practice not only arbitrary for 'other legal entities' authorized under the national laws of individual Member States but also for depositaries established as EEA legal entities. From an investor protection point of view, this can be justified for EEA legal entities that are authorized under EEA legislation and allowed to offer services under these legal initiatives on a cross-border basis. This is not the case for 'other legal entities' authorized under national legislation.

Irrespective of the eligible entity, it seems to depend upon the legislator and the national Competent Authorities of the individual Member States whether depositaries under the UCITSD V have a de facto 'European passport' or whether the locational restrictions of the UCITSD V are effectively enforced. Only the introduction of a European passport for UCITS depositaries based upon harmonized substantial and supervisory criteria would lead to clarification from an investor protection point of view.

2.1.2.2   The Location of the Depositary for AIFs

In determining whether and to what extent the AIFMD is applicable to a depositary, it is of utmost importance to know whether the depositary is located within or outside the European Union. The AIFMD makes, on the one hand, a distinction between EEA-AIFs and TC-AIFs, and, on the other hand, between an EEA-AIFM and a TC-AIFM managing an AIF, as shown in the following table.

Location of the Depositary – Depending on the Location of the AIF

	EEA-AIF	TC-AIF
EEA-AIFM	Home Member State AIF	Third country where the AIF is established Home Member State of the AIFM managing the AIF
TC-AIFM	Home Member State AIF	Third country where the AIF is established Member State of reference of the AIFM managing the AIF

2.1.2.2.1   *Location of the Depositary for EEA-AIFs*

Article 21(5) AIFMD requires a depositary for EEA-AIFs to be established in the home Member State of the EEA-AIF.[45] Following Article 4(1)(j)(iii) AIFMD, established means

---

44   *Ibid.*

45   Art. 21(5)(a) AIFMD; A transition relief from this mandatory rule is provided by Art. 61(5) AIFMD. On the basis of this relief, the Competent Authorities of the home Member State of an AIF or, in case where the AIF is not regulated, the Competent Authorities of the home Member State of an AIFM could until 22 July 2017

that depositaries of EEA-AIFs should have their registered office or branch in the same country as the EEA-AIF. The location of the depositary for EEA-AIFs has been adopted from UCITSD I-V. Similarly as for UCITS, the AIF depositary locational restriction is influenced by the eligible entities under the AIFMD. The original idea of limiting UCITSD V entities to credit institutions and investment firms under the initial draft UCITSD V was inspired by the AIFMD that limits eligible entities for (liquid) EEA-AIFs to credit institutions, investment firms and prime brokers.[46] The UCITSD IV eligible entities under AIFMD were planned to be 'phased-out' under the ultimate limitation of entities proposed under the draft UCITSD V. Under the initial UCITSD V proposal,[47] eligible entities under both the AIFMD and UCITSD V would have been limited to credit institutions, EEA investment firms and prime brokers that are credit institutions or EEA investment firms.[48] The UCITSD IV entities have to be dynamically interpreted under the AIFMD. For this reason, the so-called 'other legal entities' subject to minimum principle-based requirements under UCITSD V remain eligible under the AIFMD Member State implementations. The implications of allowing these 'other legal entities' under the AIFMD/UCITSD V Member State implementations to be eligible to be a depositary are under both directives the same.

Article 21(3)(a) and (b) AIFMD only allows credit institutions and investment firms that have their registered office in the EEA to act as a depositary for EEA-AIFs.[49]

Non-EEA investment firms that are under the MiFID II[50] third country regime able to provide the ancillary service[51] of safekeeping and administration of financial instruments for the account of clients within the EEA are under the AIFMD, thus, precluded from acting as a depositary. This holds even true for non-EEA investment firms that have established a branch in the same Member State as an EEA-AIF.

The AIFMD is on this point inconsistent with the rationale behind the MiFID II third country regime.

First, similar to the AIFMD, third country service providers under MiFID II are subject to additional third country requirements. Only third country firms that are estab-

---

allow credit institutions that are established in another Member State to be appointed as a depositary; *See also* Buttigieg, *supra* note 39.

46 Art. 21(3) AIFMD.

47 European Commission, *Proposal for a Directive of the European Parliament and of the Council amending Directive 2009/65/EC on the coordination of laws, regulations and administrative provisions relating to undertakings for collective investment in transferable securities (UCITS) as regards depositary functions, remuneration policies and sanctions*, 03.07.2011, COM(2012) 350 final ('UCITSD V Proposal').

48 *See* S.N. Hooghiemstra, *Depositary Regulation* (D.A. Zetzsche ed, Kluwer 2015).

49 Art. 21(4)(a) AIFMD.

50 Arts. 39-43 MiFID II.

51 These investment firms also have to provide the service of safekeeping and administering financial instruments as ancillary service, in addition to, one or more investment services/activities under Annex 1 MiFID II.

lished in countries whose legal and supervisory framework are considered to be offering equivalent investor protection are allowed to operate on a cross-border basis. Non-EEA investment firms that are authorized by a Member State Competent Authority under the MiFID II third country regime to operate though an EEA branch in a Member State are allowed to act as a custodian for professional and, under certain conditions, retail clients residing within the EEA, whereas they are precluded from acting as a depositary for EEA-AIFs.

Second, the AIFMD allows non-EEA entities to act as a depositary for TC-AIFs that are marketed to investors within the EEA on the basis of being of 'the same nature' as EEA credit institutions and investment firms. Non-EEA entities subjected to the more stringent harmonized MiFID II third country regime are, to the contrary, precluded from acting as a depositary for EEA-AIFs that are marketed to the same investors within the EEA.

Third, the AIFMD allows other institutions eligible under UCITSD IV/V subject to minimum prudential standards to be appointed as a depositary for EEA-AIFs, whereas investment firms falling under the MiFID II third country regime that are subject to the same organizational, prudential and capital requirements as investment firms are precluded from doing so.

Allowing non-EEA investment firms that have established a branch within the EEA to act as an AIF depositary within that EEA Member State would, thus, be consistent with the MiFID II TC regime.

2.1.2.2.2   *Transitional Relief – AIFMs managing EEA-AIFs*

The Competent Authorities of the home Member State of an AIF or, in case where the AIF is not regulated, the Competent Authorities of the home Member State of an AIFM could until 22 July 2017 allow credit institutions[52] that are established in another Member State to be appointed as a depositary.[53] The European Commission clarified that 'where the AIF is not regulated' should be interpreted as EEA-AIFs that have not (yet) obtained either an authorization or registration within an EEA Member State.[54]

EEA Member States had, thus, the option to (temporary) diverge from the AIFMD's mandatory requirement that depositaries of EEA-AIFs shall be established in the home Member State of the AIF.[55] This option was both available to EEA-AIFMs, as well as, TC-AIFMs that are managing EEA-AIFs.[56] Apart from this locational restriction, depositaries appointed by AIFMs that were making use of this option were required to fully comply with all other provisions laid down by Article 21 AIFMD.

---

52   Art. 21(3)(a) AIFMD.
53   Art. 61(5) AIFMD.
54   *See* Dutch Act Financial Markets Amendment Act 2014 (Second Amendment, 3 September 2013), 21.
55   Art. 21(5)(a) AIFMD.
56   Art. 61(5) AIFMD refers to the location restriction as laid down in Art. 21(5)(a) AIFMD that applies to both EEA-AIFMs and TC-AIFMs that are managing EEA-AIFs.

In practice, this option was, however, of limited importance given the temporary nature and the limited amount of Member States that have implemented this option in their
legislation.[57]

2.1.2.2.3 Location of the Depositary for TC-AIFs

The depositary location requirements for TC-AIFs have a wider scope than for EEA-
AIFs. The location of a depositary for TC-AIFs depends upon whether the AIFM is
located within or outside the EEA.

For TC-AIFs with an EEA-AIFM, the depositary must be established:[58]

- in the third country where the AIF is established;[59] or
- in the home Member State of the AIFM[60] managing the AIF.[61]

Besides the option of appointing a depositary that is located in the third country where
the TC-AIF is established, an EEA-AIFM may also decide to appoint a depositary within
its home Member State.

For TC-AIFs, a TC-AIFM has either the choice of appointing a depositary:

- in the third country where the AIF is established;[62] or
- in the Member State of reference[63] of the AIFM managing the AIF.[64]

The latter becomes available to TC-AIFMs from a date to be specified by the European
Commission under AIFMD. TC-AIFMs will then be able to obtain a marketing passport

---

57 Czech Republic: Art. 657(2) Czech Act on investment Fund and Investment Companies; Finland: Chapter
   23, § 3, Part IX Transitional Provisions Finnish AIFM Act; Netherlands: Art. VII (7) Wet van 12 juni 2013
   tot wijziging van de Wet op het financieel toezicht, het Burgerlijk Wetboek, de Wet op de economische
   delicten en enige fiscale wetten ter implementatie van richtlijn n. 2011/61/EU van het Europees Parlement
   en de Raad van de Europese Unie van 8 juni 2011 inzake beheerders van alternatieve beleggingsinstellingen
   en tot wijziging van de Richtlijnen 2003/41/EG en 2009/65/EG en van de Verordeningen (EG) n. 1060/2009
   en (EU) n. 1095/2010 (PbEU 2011, L 174) (Stb. 2013, 228) amended by: Art. XVIIa Wet van 25 november
   2013 tot wijziging van de Wet op het financieel toezicht en enige andere wetten (Wijzigingswet financiële
   markten 2014) (Stb. 2013, 487); UK: Art. 77(1) The Alternative Investment Fund Managers Regulations,
   2013, S.I (2013) No.1773.
58 Art. 21(5) AIFMD.
59 Art. 21(5)(a) AIFMD.
60 According to Art. 4(1)(q) AIFMD, 'home Member State of the AIFM' means the Member State in which the
   AIFM has its Registered Office. The registered office is the basic criterion to determine the location of an
   AIFM. However, the 'real seat' and 'registered seat' are unlikely to differ when it comes to an AIFM. The
   letter-box entity approach requires portfolio management and risk management to be exercised at the location where the AIFM is registered and may not be delegated. So in practice, there might be less legal
   uncertainty in determining the location for the AIFM and the location depositary as compared to the AIF.
   See for a possible conflict of laws in this regard D.A. Zetzsche & T. Marte, *The AIFMD's Cross-Border
   Dimension, Third-Country Rules and the Equivalence Concept* (D.A. Zetzsche ed, Kluwer 2015).
61 Art. 21(5)(b) AIFMD.
62 Art. 21(5)(a) AIFMD.
63 *See* Zetzsche & Marte, *supra* note 60.
64 Art. 21(5)(c) AIFMD.

under the AIFMD, allowing them to market both EEA-AIFs and TC-AIFs to (professional) investors across the EEA.[65]

2.1.2.2.4   A Quasi-Depositary Passport Regime for TC-AIFs

The free choice for AIFMs to appoint either an EEA or non-EEA depositary for TC-AIFs is remarkable considering the fact that depositaries appointed for EEA-AIFs always need to be established in the same Member State as where the fund is located. The AIFMD seems to be inconsistent with the UCITS rationale of linking the depositary to the fund to ensure that the depositary comes under the same supervisory regime as the fund. AIFMs managing EEA-AIFs must appoint a depositary within the same Member State. EEA-AIFMs are not allowed to appoint a depositary in a different EEA Member State that underlies the harmonized AIFMD regime for EEA depositaries, whereas AIFMs managing TC-AIFs have the choice to appoint either an EEA or a non-EEA depositary.

The AIFMD only allows third country depositaries to be appointed that are subject to 'effectively enforced' prudential regulation (including minimum capital requirements) and supervision equivalent to EEA law.[66] However, this extraterritorial effect of the AIFMD on depositaries in third countries leads to minimum harmonization, whereas EEA depositaries that underlie the AIFMD, MiFID II and CRD IV are harmonized to a much larger extent. The AIFMD depositary location regime functions as a quasi-depositary passport regime for AIFMs managing TC-AIFs that can exploit economies of scale and may enter into regulatory arbitrage, whereas AIFMs managing EEA-AIFs are not able to do so.

2.1.2.3   Conclusion

A depositary passport, i.e. the right of a depositary to act on a cross-border basis by the cross-border free provision of services under the AIFMD/UCITSD V, has so far not been introduced.[67] Instead, depositaries are required to be 'established' in the home Member State of the UCITS/EEA-AIF. Established under the AIFMD means that either the registered office or a branch office is required to be located in the UCITS/AIF home Member State for which a depositary is appointed. The locational restriction under the AIFMD/UCITSD V has to be read in conjunction with the eligible entities under the AIFMD/UCITSD V. Originally, both the AIFMD and UCITSD V were planned to 'phase out' all eligible entities for (liquid) EEA-AIFs/UCITS other than EEA credit institutions and investment firms. The final UCITSD V, however, allows discretion to individual Member States to decide that 'other legal entities' under national law that fulfil minimum require-

---

65 Art. 37 AIFMD.
66 For details, *see* Chapter 4, Section 4.5.
67 Under the AIFMD transitional relief regime, Competent Authorities of the home Member State of an AIFM could until 22 July 2017 allow credit institutions that are established in another Member State to be appointed as a depositary. *See* Art. 61(5) AIFMD.

ments to be appointed as a UCITS depositary. A dynamic interpretation of UCITSD IV eligible entities under the AIFMD grants Member States the option to allow AIFMs to appoint these 'other legal entities' as an AIF depositary as well. 'Established' for depositaries under Art. 4(1)(j)(iii) AIFMD means 'having its registered office or branch in'. A restriction of eligible entities under the AIFMD/UCITSD V to credit institutions and investment firms would have 'transposed' the 'establishment definitions' under CRD IV and MiFID II to UCITSD V and the AIFMD. Leaving the discretion to Member States to allow 'other legal entities' to be appointed under their implementation laws results in uncertainty related to what 'established in' means. In addition, the absence of a European passport for depositaries under the AIFMD/UCITSD V allows the Competent Authorities of the individual Member States to determine under what conditions a branch office of a depositary is being established within their domicile. This varies from Member State to Member State. Some Member States, such as the Netherlands, see a 'representative office' as a branch, whereas other Member States apply stricter criteria. Furthermore, the AIFMD takes an inconsistent approach as it deviates from the locational restriction applying to EEA-AIFs for TC-AIFs. In the same vein, the AIFMD transitional relief allowed Competent Authorities of the home Member State of an AIFM until 22 July 2017 credit institutions that are established in another Member State to be appointed as a depositary.[68] The absence of European passport, thus, not only leads to diverging interpretations of what constitutes 'established in', but is also inconsistent in the locational restrictions that apply to depositaries appointed for EEA- and TC-AIFs. The absence of a European passport, thus, not only allows the Competent Authorities of the individual Member States to determine under what conditions a branch office of a depositary is being established within their domicile. Only the introduction of a European passport for UCITS depositaries based upon harmonized substantial and supervisory criteria under the AIFMD and UCITSD V would lead to clarification from an investor protection point of view.

2.1.3   The Depository Mutual Recognition Approach under IORPD II

Article 33(3) IORPD II requires Member States not to restrict IORPs from appointing, depositaries *established in another Member State* and duly authorized in accordance with CRD IV or MiFID II, or accepted as a depositary for the purpose of UCITSD IV/V or the AIFMD.[69] The idea of granting a European passport to financial intermediaries that are subject to 'harmonized European prudential standards' does not apply to IORP depositaries.[70] The locational freedom also applies to 'other legal entities' complying with the

---

68 *See* art. 61(5) AIFMD.
69 Art. 33(3) IORPD II.
70 *See* Chapter 5, Section 5.3.2.

UCITSD V minimum standards that are authorized as UCITS depositaries under the national laws of individual Member States.

2.1.3.1   'Established in another Member State'

IORPD II does not clarify what 'established in another Member State' means. The AIFMD provides guidance on this point. Article 21(5) AIFMD requires a depositary for EEA-AIFs to be established in the home Member State of the EEA-AIF. Following Article 4(1)(j)(iii) AIFMD, established means that depositaries of EEA-AIFs should have their registered office or branch in the same country as the EEA-AIF. This also includes non-EEA investment firms that are duly authorized for acting as a custodian under MiFID II and have established a branch within a Member State.[71] Similar as for EEA-AIF and UCITS depositaries, 'established in' may be interpreted in various ways by the Competent Authorities of individual Member States as the depositary/custodian eligible entities are not completely harmonized under European law. UCITSD V 'exports' this uncertainty, thus, not only to the AIFMD, but also to IORPD II. Apart from this, the 'mutual recognition' approach seems to have a wider scope under IORPD II than under IORPD I.

2.1.3.2   Mutual Recognition under IORPD II – Applying to Depositaries and or Custodians?

Under Article 19(2) IORPD I, Member States were required not to:

> restrict institutions from appointing, for the custody of their assets (emphasis added by author), custodians established in another Member State and duly authorised in accordance with Directive 93/22/EEC or Directive 2000/12/EC, or accepted as a depositary for the purposes of Directive 85/611/EEC.

Taken a grammatical approach, Member States could under IORPD I not prevent Member States to allow an IORP to appoint a depositary or custodian established in another Member State 'for the custody of their assets'. A grammatical interpretation implied that Member States were forced to accept custodians under CRD I and ISD, or depositaries accepted under the UCITSD I-IV, but only for the safekeeping of IORP assets. IORPs that either appointed or were compulsorily required by IORPD I Member State implementation laws to appoint a depositary for safekeeping and oversight duties could, on the basis of this, be prohibited by Member State laws.

Such a grammatical interpretation would be in line with UCITSD IV/V and the AIFMD that both require a depositary to be established, i.e. to have a registered office or a branch, in the same Member State as an UCITS /EEA-AIF. In practice, however, this

---

71   *See* Chapter 4, Section 4.3.1.2.

grammatical approach of Article 19(2) IORPD I was not applied by the majority of the Member States. Only some Member States, such as Hungary,[72] Poland,[73] Slovakia[74] and Spain[75] under their Article 19 IORPD I Member State implementation laws restricted the appointment of a IORP depositary/custodian to domestic credit institutions. Most Member States allowed both depositaries for the safekeeping of assets (custodians) and depositaries appointed for safekeeping of assets and oversight duties to be appointed that were established in other Member States. Liechtenstein[76] and Malta[77] even explicitly allowed non-EEA institutions to be appointed as an IORP depositary provided that additional conditions were fulfilled.

Under IORPD II, depositaries established in another Member State may be appointed and the clause 'for the custody of their assets' has been removed. Depositaries are under Article 33(1) and (2) IORPD II either a depositary for the safekeeping of assets or a depositary appointed for safekeeping of assets and oversight duties in accordance with the IORPD. 'For the custody of their assets' was replaced by 'for both safekeeping and safekeeping and oversight duties' under IORPD II. The current practice that Member States under IORPD I do not differentiate between the appointment of 'depositaries' and 'custodians' established in another Member State has, thus, been confirmed by IORPD II.

The latter, however, leads to a 'de facto' depositary passport,[78] i.e. the right for depositaries to provide services on a cross-border basis *and* the right to establish a branch in another Member State, for IORPD II depositaries that is not in place for EEA-AIFs and UCITS. This was received in the consultation phase by mixed responses in the industry. Some commentators emphasized the more efficient provision of depositary services, which is ultimately beneficial to the members and beneficiaries.[79] Others pointed out that if depositaries would be allowed to perform an oversight function, the depositaries should be established in the same country where the IORP is located as this function could not satisfactorily be performed on a cross-border basis.[80] The 'de facto European IORP depositary passport' creates a paradoxical tension between the AIFMD and UCITSD V, on the one hand, and IORPD II on the other. UCITSD IV/V depositaries,

---

72 § 50(1) CXVII 2007 Law on occupational pensions and institutions.
73 Art. 158 Act of 28 August 1997 Law on the Organisation and Operation of Pension Funds.
74 § 56 (1) Act on Supplementary Pension Savings.
75 Art. 82(1) Real Decreto 304/2004, de 20 de Febrero, Por el que se aprueba el Reglamento de Planes y Fondos de Pensiones.
76 Art. 12 Gesetz vom 24. November 2006 betreffend die Aufsicht über Einrichtungen der betrieblichen Altersversorgung (Pensionsfondsgesetz; PFG).
77 B.6 Custody of Retirement Fund's Assets, B.6.1 General Conditions, Directives for Occupational Retirement Schemes, Retirement Funds and Related Parties under the Special Funds (Regulation) Act, 2002.
78 EIOPA, *Summary of Comments on Consultation Paper: Response to the Call for Advice on the Review of the IORP Directive 2003/41/EC: Second Consultation – EIOPA-CP-11/006*, EIOPA-BoS-12/016, 15 February 2012, Comment 95 (State Street).
79 *Ibid.*
80 *Ibid.*, Comment 58 (ADEPO).

investment firms and credit institutions under IORPD II may act as a depositary on a cross-border basis, whereas this is prohibited for EEA-AIF and UCITS depositaries.[81] This paradoxical tension is even exacerbated by the fact that under IORPD I implementation various Member States, such as Liechtenstein and Luxembourg, had depositary regimes in place that are similar to the depositary function as was implemented in their UCITSD I-IV implementation laws.[82] In fact, their IORPD I depositary regimes provided less regulation than their UCITSD I-IV depositary regulation, but none of the Member States required the depositary to be 'established' in their Member States. Under the expectation that the IORPD II implementation laws will not diverge much compared to IORPD I on this point, AIFMD/UCITSD V depositaries that are subjected to a larger degree of EU harmonization are not granted a European passport, whereas IORPD I/II depositaries subject to minimum harmonization do benefit from a 'de facto' IORPD II depositary passport. This problem is being referred to in this book as the 'European depositary passport paradox'.

2.1.3.3   Cooperation between Supervisory Authorities

The 'de facto depositary passport' under IORPD II is supported by cooperation that is required amongst relevant supervisory authorities. Article 33(4) IORPD II requires that Member States shall take the necessary steps to enable their Competent Authorities to prohibit the free disposal of assets located within their territory at the request of the Competent Authorities in the IORP home Member State.

EIOPA stated that the effectiveness of the powers and procedures followed by the Competent Authorities suffer from a lack of experience among Member States.[83] EIOPA, however, concluded that there was not enough evidence to conclude that additional provisions regarding powers and procedures were needed to facilitate the de facto European IORPD II depositary passport and concluded that more details in implementing measures would need to be adopted when further analysis of this issue would show the need to do so.[84]

2.1.3.4   Conclusion

Article 33(3) IORPD II requires Member States not to restrict IORPs from appointing, depositaries *established in another Member State* and duly authorized in accordance with

---

81 Art. 19(2) sub-para. 2 IORPD I.
82 Liechtenstein: Art. 12 Gesetz vom 24. November 2006 betreffend die Aufsicht über Einrichtungen der betrieblichen Altersversorgung (Pensionsfondsgesetz; PFG); Luxembourg : Art. 18 (1) and Art. 42 (1) Loi du 13 juillet 2005 relative aux institutions de retraite professionnelle sous forme de société d'épargne-pension à capital variable (sepcav) et d'association d'épargne-pension (assep) et portant modification de l'article 167, alinéa 1 de la loi modifiée du 4 décembre 1967 concernant l'impôt sur le revenu.
83 EIOPA-BOS-12/015, 469.
84 *Ibid.*

CRD IV or MiFID II, or accepted as a depositary for the purpose of UCITSD IV/V or AIFMD.[85] The 'de facto European IORP depositary passport' creates a paradoxical tension between the AIFMD and UCITSD V, at the one, and IORPD II at the other hand. UCITSD IV/V depositaries, investment firms and credit institutions under IORPD II may act as a depositary on a cross-border basis, whereas this is prohibited for EEA-AIF and UCITS depositaries.[86] This paradoxical tension is even exacerbated by the fact that under IORPD I implementation various Member States, such as Liechtenstein and Luxembourg, had depositary regimes in place that are similar to the depositary function as was implemented in their UCITSD I-IV implementation laws.[87] This leads to a 'European depositary passport paradox'.

2.1.4   Conclusion

In practice, the same investment firms and credit institutions are acting as a custodian for clients under MiFID II/CRD IV, a depositary under the AIFMD/UCITSD V and a depositary/custodian under IORPD II. The European investment laws, i.e. MiFID II, CRD IV, the AIFMD, UCITSD V and IORPD II, are inconsistent in granting a depositary/custodian passport to these depositaries/custodians. They are both inconsistent throughout the directives and on a cross-sectoral basis. On a cross-sectoral basis, MiFID II and CRD IV have an 'ancillary' European passport for 'custodians' in place.[88] To the contrary, the AIFMD and UCITS require the depositary of UCITS and EEA-AIFs to be established in the UCITS/EEA-AIF home Member State,[89] whereas the same entities acting as a depositary/custodian under IORPD II do have a 'de facto' European passport.[90] Not only are the European investment laws inconsistent throughout the directives, also the directives themselves are inconsistent. The AIFMD, for example, differentiates between a strict locational requirement for EEA-AIFs, whereas there is a 'quasi-depositary passport regime' in place for depositaries appointed for TC-AIFs.[91] The inconsistency in granting a European passport for depositaries under the European investment laws leads to an 'European depositary passport paradox'.

---

85 Art. 33(3) IORPD II.
86 Art. 19(2) sub-para. 2 IORPD I.
87 *See supra* note 82
88 Annex I n. 12 CRD IV; Annex I s. A MiFID II.
89 Art. 21(5) AIFMD and Art. 23(1) UCITSD V.
90 Art. 33(3) IORPD II.
91 *See also* C.P. Buttigieg, *The Case for A European Depositary Passport*, http://studylib.net/doc/13128849/the–case–for–a–european-depositary-passport; Hooghiemstra, *supra* note 48.

2.2   THE EUROPEAN DEPOSITARY PASSPORT DEBATE

For a better understanding of all legal issues related to the European depositary passport, it is of importance to examine the debate regarding the European depositary passport in a historical context. For this purpose, the concerns raised upon introducing such a passport during the adoption of the various UCITS directives, the AIFMD, the ISD/MiFID I/II and IORPD I/II will be studied to get a better overview of the present situation.

2.2.1   *UCITSD I-VI*

Throughout UCITSD I-VI the UCITS depositary passport debate has developed itself.

2.2.1.1   **UCITSD I**

UCITSD I required the depositary to have its registered office in the same Member State as that of the UCITS ManCo or be established in that Member State if its registered office is in another Member State.[92] UCITSD I, thus, required to have the depositary's registered office within the EEA. Branches of non-EEA banks could not be appointed as a depositary.[93] Subsidiaries of non-EEA entities were allowed, as long as the entity was established in the same Member State as the UCITS for which it was being appointed and the UCITS ManCo Member State.[94] The latter was only possible if the respective entity fulfilled the national Member State criteria of being an eligible depositary under UCITSD I.[95] At the time of the adoption, the restriction was justified in light of two legal considerations[96]: the oversight function that was performed by the depositary required a close relationship with the UCITS ManCo (investment company), and the same Competent Authority at that time was responsible for the authorization of the UCITS concerned, and also, if applicable, for its UCITS ManCo and the choice of the depositary.[97] In order to give legal effect to these arrangements, it was considered necessary for the depositary to be established in the same Member State as the UCITS and the UCITS ManCo, the registered office of the entities being taken as the decisive criterion.

---

92 *See* Art. 8 and 15 UCITSD I.
93 Commission of the European Communities, *Toward a European Market for the Undertakings for Collective Investment in Transferable Securities – Commentary on the provisions of Council Directive 85/611/EEC of 20 December 1985* ('Van Damme Report'), 27, http://goo.gl/K0iUzv.
94 *Ibid.*
95 Council Directive 85/611/EEC of 20 December 1985 on the coordination of laws, regulations and administrative provisions relating to undertakings for collective investment in transferable securities (UCITS), OJ L 375, 31 December 1985, 3 ('UCITSD I').
96 European Commission, *Completing the Internal Market: White Paper from the European Commission to the European Council*, COM(85)310 Final, 14 June 1985, http://europa.eu/documents/comm/white_papers/pdf/com1985_0310_f_en.pdf.
97 Commission of the European Communities, *supra* note 93, 28.

The 'establishment criterion' was introduced under UCITSD I and has to be seen in the light of the First Banking Directive. Upon the adoption of UCITSD I, only UCITS as a product was harmonized. Both UCITS ManCos and depositaries were required to fulfil principle-based requirements.[98] It was, thus, logical that the UCITS Manco, depositary and UCITS were required to be established by the same Member State.[99] The Second Banking Directive and ISD that introduced a European passport on the basis of the mutual recognition principle backed by harmonization of substantial and supervisory standards was not in place yet. In 1977 the First Banking Directive, the outcome of almost 12 years of negotiations, was being adopted.[100] The main objective was to liberate the banking market by allowing banks to set up branches without obstacles throughout the EEA. However, it was recognized that this would be a process that would be completed through time.[101] The First Banking Directive was the first initiative that allowed a bank to establish a branch in another Member State. De facto, however, this 'criterion' still posed important obstacles to the 'freedom of establishment'. European banks that had their registered office in another Member State and wanted to establish a branch in a 'host Member State' were still required to be authorized in their host Member State.[102] In addition, credit institutions remained subjected to the supervisor of the host Member State and were restricted in the range of permitted activities.[103] Finally, branches were required to be provided with so-called 'endowment capital' as if they were newly established domestic credit institutions.[104] 'Establishment' under the First Banking Directive, thus, either constituted the establishment of a new legal entity as credit institution within a Member State (registered office) or a branch of another EEA Member State that was a de facto full authorization.

The entities allowed to be eligible as a depositary under UCITSD I were also not harmonized yet. This was due to the fact that only banks and insurance undertakings were to a limited extent harmonized under European law and all other developments still needed to take off. Depositaries were, however, for the largest part credit institutions.[105]

The 'establishment criterion' under UCITSD I, thus, meant that financial intermediaries (mainly credit institutions) that were required to be located in the UCITS home Member State either had their registered office in that Member State or had a branch

---

98 Art. 4(2) UCITSD I.
99 *Ibid.*
100 B. De Meester, *Liberalization of Trade in Banking Services – An International and European Perspective* 270 (Cambridge University Press 2014).
101 *Ibid.*
102 *See* Art. 3 First Banking Directive; *Cf.* A. Bande, *Banking Integration in the EU: A Process Marked by a Battle between Systems*, 9, https://www.utwente.nl/en/bms/pa/staff/donnelly/Thesis%20-%20A%20A%20Bande%202020%2008%2012.pdf.
103 *See* Art. 3 First Banking Directive; *Cf.* E.B. Kapstein, *Governing the Global Economy – International Finance and the State* 136 (Harvard University Press 1994).
104 Art. 3 First Banking Directive.
105 FEFSI, *Position Paper on Depositaries*, 4-5 (6 November 2002).

that was, de facto, fully authorized in that Member State. These obstacles provided little incentives for banks to establish branches in foreign Member States. The First Banking Directive, thus, was the cornerstone for the development of the European passport concept that was introduced under the Second Banking Directive and ISD. The 'establishment criterion' under UCITSD I based upon the First Banking Directive, however, was never amended after the introduction of the Second Banking Directive and the ISD. The 'established in' criterion, thus, throughout the years has gotten a different meaning compared to the time this restriction was being introduced under UCITSD I.

2.2.1.2   UCITSD II

Following the introduction of UCITSD I, the adoption of UCITS in Europe was slow. This was mostly due to the divergent legal implementations of the various Member States.[106] The original UCITSD I investment and marketing restrictions prevented the European fund industry to fully exploit the benefits of a single market.[107] To address the dissatisfaction with UCITSD I, the European Commission presented a UCITSD II proposal in 1993[108] that was revised in 1994.[109]

The initial and amended UCITSD II draft considered that Member States should not restrict the freedom of UCITS to choose a depositary established in another Member State entailing both the freedom of services, as well as, the freedom of establishment. Depositaries were required to have an establishment in the same Member State as that of the UCITS, unless a credit institution or investment firm would be appointed that obtained an authorization to provide the safekeeping and administration services under the Second Banking Directive or ISD. It was generally felt that the Second Banking Directive and ISD that introduced a European passport laid down the necessary conditions to allow UCITS to appoint a credit institution or investment firm authorized for providing safekeeping and administration services as a depositary in another Member State.[110] The harmonized authorization, business organizational requirements together with the harmonization of financial supervision created an adequate level of protection that seemed to take away the rationale for not allowing depositaries to operate on the basis of a European passport.[111]

---

106 N. Moloney, *EC Securities Regulation* 205 (3rd edn., Oxford University Press 2014).

107 D. Pope & L. Garzaniti, *Single Market-Making: EC Regulation of Securities Markets*, 14(3) Company Lawyer 44 (1993); D. Ciani, *European Investment Funds: The UCITS Directive of 1985 and the Objectives of the Proposal for a UCITS II Directive*, 4(2) Journal of Financial Regulation and Compliance 150-156 (1996).

108 European Commission, *Proposal for a Directive Amending Directive 85/611/EEC on the Coordination of Laws, Regulations and Administrative Provisions Relating to Undertakings for Collective Investment in Transferable Securities (UCITS)*, COM(93), 9 February 1993final – syn 453, http://aei.pitt.edu/9161/1/9161.pdf.

109 European Commission, *Amended Proposal for a Directive Amending Directive 85/611/EEC on the Coordination of Laws, Regulations and Administrative Provisions Relating to UCITS*, Com(94)329, http://goo.gl/cMcOCa.

110 *See* Recital 9 amended UCITSD II draft (1994).

111 Buttigieg, *supra* note 39.

The amended UCITSD II draft (1994) imposed additional requirements on top of those required by the original UCITSD II draft (1993) to make this politically acceptable. To exercise this freedom, credit institutions or investment firm were proposed to:[112]

- comply with the UCITSD I depositary provisions, including:
  - the depositary's duty of loyalty and conflicts of interest rules;
  - the conditions for the replacement of the UCITS ManCo and the depositary as laid down in the fund rules; and
  - liability;
- declare that it has full knowledge of the legislation applicable to it when providing cross-border depositary services;
- provide the Competent Authorities responsible for supervision of the unit trust with all information they may require;
- conform to the supervisory rules provided for within cooperation agreements concluded between authorities of the relevant Member States.

Competent Authorities of the UCITS home Member State were entrusted to request the Competent Authority responsible for supervising the depositary to cooperate to assess its organization.[113] The above-mentioned cooperation agreements obliged the Competent Authority supervising the depositary to take appropriate measures to resolve irregular situations that the UCITS home Member State Competent Authority was unable to resolve.

Apart from this, the initial and amended UCITSD II draft considered it desirable to make institutions and firms of third countries eligible as a UCITS depositary.[114] Member States were, under the UCITSD II draft proposals, permitted to allow branches of institutions or firms having their head office outside the EEA to be appointed as UCITS depositary provided that this resulted not in more favourable treatment for TC depositaries than EEA depositaries.[115]

Notwithstanding the benefits of introducing a depositary passport, UCITSD II was never adopted. The introduction of European depositary passport was one of the main issues and led to major disagreements in the European parliament.[116] These two issues were raised by MEP Perreau De Pinninck in his report on the UCITSD II proposal in which he recommended that a depositary should continue to be established in the same

---

112 European Commission, *Amended proposal for a Directive Amending Directive 85/611/EEC on the Coordination of Laws, Regulations and Administrative Provisions Relating to UCITS*, Com(94)329, http://goo.gl/cMcOCa.

113 *Ibid.*

114 Recital 10, Art. 8(5) and Art. 15(5) amended UCITSD II draft (1994).

115 *Ibid.*

116 Clifford Chance, *Single Market Update Services*, 9 Journal of Internal Banking and Financial Law 457 (1996).

Member State as the UCITS for which the depositary is appointed.[117] De Pinninck raised two main arguments.

First, that the safekeeping of assets and administrative services carried out by credit institutions and investment firms under the Second Banking Directive and ISD was not comparable to the role of the depositary under UCITSD I.[118] In particular, he remarked that the UCITS depositary does not restrict itself to the safekeeping of assets (collection of dividends or interest, presenting securities for redemption, acting in cases of capital increases or new issues, etc.) as investment firms and credit institutions under the Second Banking Directive and ISD do. Instead, depositaries also add high value in supervising the UCITS ManCo, such as compliance with the UCITS investment policies and calculating the cash value of the fund. The controlling duties of UCITS depositaries in his opinion go beyond the mere safekeeping and administration of securities under the ISD and Second Banking Directive.

Second, De Pinninck felt that allowing a depositary passport would lead to less coordination/cooperation between the UCITS ManCo and depositary and create legal complexities. A lack of harmonization of requirements that eligible entities must satisfy, the requirements related to the safekeeping and controlling duties to be performed and the liability of depositaries towards UCITS and their investors was not in place. The differences in Member State implementations did not provide sufficient guarantees in terms of investor protection that would facilitate a depositary passport. The UCITSD II proposal was not based upon enough harmonization of substantive depositary requirements to allow a European passport for depositaries to function properly.[119] The UCITSD II proposals proved to be controversial and were ultimately withdrawn.[120]

2.2.1.3   UCITSD III/IV

The depositary passport was one of the reasons of the UCITSD II failure and was not part of the UCITSD III and IV proposal. The European Economic and Social Committee, however, still stressed the point that the introduction of a depositary passport would be essential for the further rationalization of the internal market for UCITS.[121] Various reports and studies reflected that the absence of a depositary passport became an anomaly and that significant economies of scale could be obtained by introducing one.[122]

---

117 European Parliament, *Report of the Committee on Legal Affairs and Citizen's Rights on the 1993 UCITS Proposal*, A5-0268/1993, 1 October 1993, http://goo.gl/rRSdJO.
118 *Ibid.*
119 Buttigieg, *supra* note 39.
120 Moloney, *supra* note 106.
121 European Parliament 1993, *supra* note 117.
122 European Commission, *Commission Staff Working Document of 12 July 2005* (SEC(2005) 947) – *Annex to the Green Paper on the enhancement of the EU Framework for Investment Funds*, http://ec.europa.eu/finance/investment/docs/consultations/greenpaper-background_en.pdf; European Commission, *Report of*

2.2.1.3.1   Commission Communication 2004

The Council along proposals for the 2001 UCITS Product Directive and the 2001 UCITS Management Directive requested the Commission to report on UCITS depositary regulation in Europe.[123] The European Commission indicated in various research reports and consultations during the adoption of UCITSD III and IV the risk for investor protection that a depositary passport could entail.[124] The national UCITSD I-III depositary implementation laws showed large differences. The Commission Communication was based on an internet consultation in autumn 2002 concerning the different national rules impeding the development of the internal market in the case of UCITS depositaries.[125] The survey identified major disparities between national rules that explained the national depositary markets.[126] Four main areas of action were formulated: prevention of conflicts of interest, clarification of depositary's liability, convergence of national prudential rules, and moves to enhance investor transparency and information.

Apart from the Commission Communication in 2004, various other initiatives and studies, including the Green Paper in 2005, a report of the Expert Group on investment market efficiency and a subsequent White Paper addressing the single market framework for investment funds on the UCITS depositary, have been conducted between 2004 and 2008.

2.2.1.3.2   Green Paper 2005

The Green Paper issued by the European Commission in 2005 launched a discussion whether UCITS, UCITS ManCos and depositaries could benefit from further rationalization.[127] At that time, both the UCITS ManCo and depositary were required to be located in the UCITS home Member State. Upon the adoption of UCITSD I, integrated super-

---

the Expert Group on Investment Fund Market Efficiency, July 2006, http://ec.europa.eu/internal_market/investment/docs/other_docs/reports/efficiency_en.pdf.

123 European Commission, *Communication from the Commission to the Council and to the European Parliament – Regulation of UCITS Depositaries in the Member States: Review and Possible Developments*, 30 March 2004, COM(2004) 207 final.

124 FEFSI, supra note 105; European Commission 2005, supra note 122; European Commission 2006, supra note 122; European Commission 2006, supra note 10; See also European Commission, Working Document of the Commission Services (DG Markt), Consultation Paper on the UCITS Depositary Function, July 2009, http://ec.europa.eu/internal_market/consultations/docs/2009/ucits/consultation_paper_en.pdf; European Commission, Consultation Paper on the UCITS Depositary Function and on the UCITS Managers 'Remuneration, 14 December 2010, MARKT/G4 D (2010) 950800, 16, 17, http://ec.europa.eu/finance/consultations/2010/ucits/docs/consultation_paper_en.pdf.

125 Plan to harmonize national rules on UCITS depositaries; See http://eur-lex.europa.eu/legal-content/EN/TXT/HTML/?uri=LEGISSUM:l24036d&from=EN; European Commission 2004, *supra* note 123; FEFSI, *supra* note 105.

126 *Ibid.*

127 *Cf.* European Commission, *Impact Assessment – Proposal for a Directive of the European Parliament and of the Council amending Directive 2009/65/EC on the coordination of laws, regulations and administrative provisions relating to undertakings for collective investment in transferable securities (UCITS) as regards*

vision was considered to be essential to ensure effective performance of UCITS ManCo and depositary services.[128] Stakeholders indicated the desire for greater freedom in the choice of the depositary. However, they agreed that the harmonization of the status mission and responsibilities of UCITS ManCos and depositaries would be a prerequisite for granting a European passport to both UCITS ManCos and depositaries.[129] The European Commission, in addition, considered it to be of the essence that the investor protection implications of splitting the responsibility of financial supervision of UCITS, the depositary and UCITS ManCo amongst the Competent Authorities of different Member States would have to be studied in detail.[130]

Upon introducing a UCITS ManCo passport, the European Commission later considered that the depositary must not be located in the same Member State as the registered office of the UCITS ManCo, but located in the UCITS home Member State. The European Commission considered that this was necessary from an investor protection point of view as the investors that subscribe to a UCITS located in a certain Member State should be subject to the investor protection rules of that Member State, including supervision rules, depositary and investor compensation rules.[131]

2.2.1.3.3   Expert Group on Investment Market Efficiency

The Expert Group on investment market efficiency concluded in its report in July 2006 that the requirements of UCITS having a local depositary and UCITS ManCo artificially imposes a geographic organization of the UCITS value chain and leads to an unnecessary duplication of costs across fund domiciles.[132] The Expert Group, however, believed that preconditions had to be met prior to establishing a depositary passport.[133]

---

depositary functions, remuneration policies and sanctions (COM(2012) 350) (SWD(2012) 186), 52; European Commission 2005, *supra* note 122.
128 European Commission 2006, *supra* note 10.
129 European Commission, *Exposure Draft – Initial Orientations for Discussion on Possible Adjustments to the UCITS Directive: Management Company Passport*, 23.
130 *Ibid.*
131 European Commission, Appendices to the report on Investment Fund Market Efficiency, July 2006, 50, http://ec.europa.eu/internal_market/investment/docs/other_docs/reports/annex_efficiency_en.pdf; European Commission, Commission Staff Working Document of 16 July 2008 (SEC(2008) 2263) Accompanying the Proposal for a Directive of the European Parliament and of the Council on the Coordination of laws, Regulations and Administrative Provisions Relating to Undertakings for Collective Investment in Transferable Securities (UCITS): Impact Assessment of the Legislative Proposal Amending the UCITS Directive, 16 July 2008, (COM(2008) 458 final) (SEC(2008) 2264); Cf. the arguments of CESR related to a 'local point of contact' for common contractual funds: Ref: CESR/08-867; CESR, CESR's advice to the EC on the UCITS Management Company Passport, October 2008, CESR/08-867, 9-11. European Commission, supra note 129.
132 European Commission 2006, *supra* note 122.
133 *Cf.* European Commission 2012, *supra* note 127.

The preconditions for granting more freedoms for the depositary would include a clarification on the depositary's role and responsibilities.[134] In particular, further work was needed to determine which elements of the depositary would need to be harmonized and under which conditions this could be best achieved. To that extent the Group recommended a two-stage approach. In the short term, the Group recommended that branches of EEA banks should be allowed to act as a depositary for locally domiciled funds and that Member States should allow the depositary to delegate custodial functions to licensed custodians located elsewhere in the EEA. In the long term, the Group recommended that the European Commission should undertake a harmonization of the capital requirements for depositaries and investigate the legal barriers that should be removed.[135]

2.2.1.3.4 Impact Assessment – White Paper on 'Enhancing the Single Market Framework for Investment Funds'

In a subsequent White Paper addressing the single market framework for investment funds, again the depositary passport was being addressed. For this purpose, three different options were being considered.[136] The first option related to a 'full depositary passport'. The second option on merely introducing a passport for the 'custodial function', whereas the controlling function would still be required to be performed in the UCITS home Member State and the third option considered a non-legislative harmonization through 'Level 3 guidelines' for depositaries to organize themselves on a pan-European basis. The White Paper, however, concluded that the Green Paper failed to demonstrate the need for requiring action on the European level and that, therefore, no legislative measures were more efficient.[137]

The studies by interest groups and the European Commission itself that were made in preparation of UCITSD III/IV resulted in the European Commission having the objective to remove discrepancy in national rules governing depositaries in UCITSD V/VI and the AIFMD.[138]

2.2.1.4 UCITSD V/VI

After the Madoff case brought uncertainties related to the depositary function within the UCITSD I-IV framework, the European Commission undertook an effort to map the national divergences of the UCITSD I-IV depositary regime to develop a new UCITSD V depositary regime.[139] This mapping exercise revealed main differences in the eligible

---

134 European Commission 2006, *supra* note 129.
135 *Ibid.*
136 European Commission 2006, *supra* note 10.
137 *Ibid.*
138 European Commission 2004, *supra* note 123.
139 CESR, *Mapping of duties and liabilities of UCITS depositaries (2010)*, CESR/09-175.

entities, the safekeeping and controlling task, delegation and liability regimes of depositaries throughout the EEA.[140] In the need to clarify and harmonize the depositary functions, respondents to the 2009 UCITSD V consultation highlighted the need to clarify the UCITS depositary safekeeping and supervisory functions.[141] Three reasons for this were being identified[142]: first, the UCITS depositary regime had remained mostly unchanged since the introduction of UCITSD I. Second, differences and inconsistencies in the application of depositary rules in the Madoff fraud highlighted legal uncertainties in the industry. Finally, there was a need for a consistent approach between the UCITS depositary rules and other EU initiatives, such as MiFID I and CRD I.[143]

Respondents in both the 2009 and 2010 consultation viewed that the full harmonization of the status, role and liability regime of UCITS depositaries had to be a prerequisite for a UCITS depositary passport.[144] In particular in the 2010 consultation, the European Commission envisaged that the depositary passport issues would need to be reviewed after a new UCITS depositary framework had come into force.[145]

It was envisaged that a provision is introduced into the UCITS Directive creating a commitment to assess and re-examine the need to address depositary passport issues, to be undertaken a few years after the new UCITS depositary framework has come into force.

After implementing UCITSD IV, the European Commission launched a consultation related to UCITSD VI.[146] Again, the European Commission sought to put the European depositary passport on the agenda. The main point of the European Commission was that the AIFMD and UCITSD V harmonized the rules governing entities eligible to act as depositaries, the definition of safekeeping duties and oversight functions, the depositary's liability and the conditions for delegation of the custody function to such an extent that the introduction of a depositary passport could be considered.[147] Respondents, however, mainly highlighted during the consultation that the AIFMD and UCITSD V harmonized regimes would first need to be implemented in practice in order to resolve any issues that would need to be addressed prior to the introduction of such a passport.[148]

---

140 *Ibid.*
141 *Cf.* European Commission 2012, *supra* note 127; European Commission 2009, *supra* note 124.
142 European Commission, *Feedback on Public Consultation on UCITS V*, http://ec.europa.eu/finance/consultations/2010/ucits/docs/summary_of_responses_en.pdf; European Commission, *Feedback Statement – Summary of Responses to UCITS Depositary's Consultation Paper*, 9, http://ec.europa.eu/internal_market/consultations/docs/2009/ucits/feedback_statement_en.pdf.
143 *Ibid.*
144 European Commission 2009, *supra* note 124; European Commission 2010, *supra* note 124.
145 *Ibid.*
146 European Commission, *Consultation Document – Undertakings for Collective Investment in Transferable Securities (UCITS) Product Rules, Liquidity Management, Depositary, Money Market Funds, Long-term Investments*, July 2012, http://ec.europa.eu/finance/consultations/2012/ucits/docs/ucits_consultation_en.pdf.
147 *Ibid.*
148 *See* Reponses to the UCITSD VI Consultation: http://ec.europa.eu/internal_market/consultations/2012/ucits/registered-organisations/state-street-corporation_en.pdf; *See* Buttigieg, *supra* note 91.

2.2.2   The AIFMD

During the AIFMD negotiation process on the Level 1 text, the introduction of a depositary passport was one of the main issues. Small Member States, such as Malta, were clearly in favour of the introduction of such a passport as it was generally felt that the restriction on the free movement of depositaries would negatively affect their fund domiciles.[149] As a result, Article 17(3) draft AIFMD intended to introduce a European depositaries passport for credit institutions authorized in the EEA. This would have allowed depositaries to both establish branches and provide depositary services on a cross-border basis. During discussions in the Council, a number of (big) Member States, however, requested that the text should be amended and required that depositaries would have to be established in the EEA-AIF home Member State. It was generally felt that the prevention of the depositary passport was the preference of these Member States to retain control over their depositary business that service their domestic AIFs and distrust towards other Member States in terms of supervision over these depositaries.

A compromised solution was agreed upon in the final AIFMD draft by introducing a transitional provision for EEA credit institutions appointed as a depositary during a period of 4 years whereby Member States were given the discretion to allow domestic AIFs to appoint a depositary in other Member States.[150] In addition, Recital 36 AIFMD invited the European Commission to introduce a horizontal legislative proposal that clarifies the responsibilities and liabilities of depositaries and the introduction of a depositary passport. The latter allowed small Member States to develop their domestic depositary industry, whereas the European Commission was given extra time to review legislative conditions for the introduction of a European depositary passport.

2.2.3   ISD-MiFID I/II/Second Banking Directive- CRD IV

The ancillary service nature of 'safekeeping and administration of securities' originally introduced under the Second Banking Directive has not evolved and is still the same under CRD IV.[151] To the contrary, the 'ancillary service nature' under ISD has been regularly discussed over time. Prior to adopting MiFID I, it has been discussed whether 'custodianship' should be upgraded to a full-fledged investment service or not.[152] The European Commission considered that 'custodianship' should remain a 'non-core service'. The European Commission considered that the functions and related risks differ from the core

---

149 Buttigieg, *supra* note 39.
150 Art. 61(5) AIFMD.
151 Annex I n. 12 CRD IV; Annex I s. A MiFID II.
152 European Commission, *Preliminary Orientations for Revision of the Investment Services Directive (ISD)*, IP/
   01/1055, July 2011, Annex 1: Definition and Scope of Investment Services Directive, 6.

provisions of investment firms.[153] Internalized settlement arrangements held within the organization, however, was considered to be included in the 'custodianship' definition.

The European Commission further reasoned that an alternative could be to strictly limit custodianship to safekeeping assets/funds and account administration and to exclude settlement from the scope of an European 'custodian passport'.[154] The European Commission did not prefer this option as ICSDs and CSD provide settlement services for international clients. The introduction of the ECD, allowing for cross-border settlement, however, made this need obsolete.

In the light of the adoption of the CSDR[155] regulating the latter, the original MiFID II draft proposed to upgrade the safekeeping and administration of financial instruments for the account of clients to a full-fledged investment service.[156] Following this proposal, any firm providing the service of safekeeping and administration of financial instruments for the account of clients would have been on a stand-alone basis subject to a separate authorization procedure.[157] This would have implied that under MiFID II, compared to MiFID I, not every investment firm,[158] but merely those entities with an authorization for safekeeping, would have been eligible as a custodian. CSDs were to be excluded from the scope of MiFID II.

This proposal was, however, not adopted in the final version of MiFID II.[159] Under MiFID II, the safekeeping and administration of financial instruments for the account of clients, thus, remains an ancillary service. CSDs, also in the final MiFID II version, were excluded from the scope of MiFID II. Member States remained, however, free to specify the types of entities that can be authorized for purely providing safekeeping/custodian services within their domiciles.[160] The non-harmonization in this area will, thus, also in the future continue to raise a number of questions as to whether the European legal framework for custodians needs to be further harmonized and strengthened to ensure a level playing field in terms of investor protection measures across all Member States.[161]

---

153 *Ibid.*

154 *Ibid.*, 7.

155 Regulation (EU) No 909/2014 of the European Parliament and of the Council of 23 July 2014 on improving securities settlement in the European Union and on central securities depositories and amending Directives 98/26/EC and 2014/65/EU and Regulation (EU) No 236/2012, OJ L 257, 28 August 2014, 1 ('CSDR').

156 *See* Annex 1 s. A Proposal for a Directive of the European Parliament and of the Council on markets in financial instruments repealing Directive 2004/39/EC of the European Parliament and of the Council (Recast), 20.10.2011 COM(2011) 656 final ('MiFID II Proposal').

157 *Ibid.*

158 Generally speaking, the MiFID custody rules apply to all 'MiFID investment firms', such as brokers, dealers, asset managers and advisers. *See* D. Frase, *Custody* 276 (D. Frase ed., Sweet & Maxwell 2011).

159 *See* for criticism on the proposed MiFID II upgrade for custodianship: H. Motani, *The Proposed EU Legislation on Securities Holding*, 69 (H.P. Conac, U. Segna & L. Thévenoz eds., Cambridge 2013).

160 Legal Certainty Group, *Second Advice of the Legal Certainty Group – Solutions to Legal Barriers related to Post-Trading within the EU*, August 2008, 25, 32.

161 Question 3, Bank of New York Mellon Response to the MiFID/MiFIR II Questionnaire of MEP Markus Ferber – 12 January 2012.

2.2.4 IORPD I/II

Upon adopting IORPD I,[162] it was considered that "restrictions regarding the free choice of approved (...) custodians limit competition in the internal market and should therefore be eliminated."[163] Article 19(2) IORPD I required Member States not to restrict IORPs from appointing, for the *custody* of their assets, *custodians* established in another Member State and duly authorized in accordance with the ISD, CRD or accepted as a depositary for the purpose of UCITSD I-III.

Introducing a 'de facto European passport' on a mutual recognition basis for appointing custodians in another Member State for the 'custody of their assets' was, however, only partly consistent with the two points that Perreau De Pinninck raised during the European passport discussion of the UCITSD II proposal. Obviously, IORPD I only sought to liberalize the 'custodian' market for the 'custody of assets'. The 'custody of assets' could be interpreted as 'the safekeeping and administration of assets' provided by credit institutions and investment firms under the ISD and CRD I for which a European passport was already earlier introduced in the early 1990s. Nevertheless, the IORPD I implementation of several Member States, including Liechtenstein and Luxembourg, did not introduce a custodian for the safekeeping of assets, but a depositary that was required to carry out safekeeping and controlling/monitoring tasks. Liechtenstein, Luxembourg and most other Member States requiring an IORP depositary, however, still allowed entities to be established in another Member State to carry out the IORP 'depositary function'.[164] This was contrary to the reasoning under UCITSD I that the UCITS depositary function in carrying out safekeeping and controlling tasks was going beyond the mere safekeeping task of credit institutions and investment firms under the Second Banking Directive and ISD. Other Member States, such as Croatia,[165] France[166] and Malta,[167] indeed only allowed custodians in another Member State to be appointed for 'custody of their assets'. IORPD I, however, allowed authorized UCITS depositaries to be appointed, whereas the European Commission in various policy documents and MEP Perreau De Pinninck in his report clearly indicated that first the eligible entities and, consequently, the authorization and business organizational requirements of UCITS depositaries would need to be authorized prior to introducing a UCITS depositary passport. The IORPD I approach towards custodians/depositaries was, thus, inconsistent with the UCITSD I-IV approach.

---

162 Directive 2003/41/EC of the European Parliament and of the Council of 3 June 2003 on the activities and supervision of institutions for occupational retirement provision, OJ L 235, 23 September 2003, 10 ('IORPD I').
163 Recital 28 IORPD I.
164 *See supra* note 82.
165 Art. 79 (1) The Mandatory and Voluntary Pension Funds Law of 7 May 1999.
166 L.143-4 du Code des Assurances.
167 B.6 Custody of Retirement Fund's Assets, *supra* note 77.

Despite various commentaries in the IORPD II consultation process,[168] Article 33(3) IORPD II still abided by the mutual recognition principle introduced under IORPD I. The wording, however, changed. Instead of referring to 'custodians', Article 33(3) IORPD II refers to 'depositaries established in another Member State'. Depositaries within the meaning of IORPD II are being referred to as depositaries for 'safekeeping and safekeeping and oversight duties'. IORPD II, thus, recognized that Member States took different approaches in their IORPD I implementations by requiring a custodian, depositary or no custodian/depositary at all to be appointed under national legislation.[169] The eligible entities list allowed to be appointed in another Member State was expanded by entities accepted as a depositary under the AIFMD. 'Other legal entities' authorized under national law are allowed to be appointed under both UCITSD V and the AIFMD qualify as 'accepted depositaries' under IORPD II. In addition, the IORPD II safekeeping and controlling tasks of IORPD II depositaries continue to have a minimum harmonization nature. Although the Level 1 safekeeping and controlling task have been (partly) copied out of UCITSD V and the AIFMD, the corresponding AIFMD/UCITSD V Level 2 provisions have not been adopted in a Level 2 IORPD II instrument.

The inconsistency with the UCITSD II proposal reasoning for not introducing a UCITS depositary passport because the eligible entities and tasks for UCITS depositaries have been harmonized to a limit, thus, also continues to exist under IORPD II.

2.2.5   Conclusion

For a better understanding of all legal issues related to the European depositary passport, it is of importance to examine the debate regarding the European depositary passport in a historical context. For this purpose, the concerns raised upon introducing such a passport during the adoption of the various UCITS directives, the AIFMD, the ISD/MiFID I/II and IORPD I/II, have been studied to get a better overview of the present situation.

Notwithstanding the benefits of introducing a depositary/custodian passport, a European passport for UCITS and AIFMD depositaries has so far been considered multiple times, but not introduced. MEP Perreau de Pinninck, after the introduction of the 'ancillary European passport' under the ISD and Second Banking Directive, considered that a European depositary passport for UCITS should not be introduced for two reasons.[170] First, it was considered that the depositary function was going beyond mere performing the 'custodian' function under the ISD and Second Banking Directive. Second, the depositaries in the UCITS domain had not been harmonized to effectively perform the controlling function. This reasoning, however, does not explain why currently not a de-

---

168 EIOPA, *supra* note 78.
169 *See* CEIOPS-OP-03-08 final, 12-13, 56-58.
170 European Parliament 1993, *supra* note 117.

positary passport has been introduced under the substantially harmonized depositary function under the AIFMD and UCITSD V. Neither does this explain why depositaries and custodians under IORPD II in a minimum harmonized regime enjoy a 'de facto European passport', why the AIFMD grants transition relief for credit institutions and a quasi-depositary passport for TC-AIFs.

2.3   CONCLUSION

In practice, the same investment firms and credit institutions are acting as a custodian for discretionary mandates and 'execution only'[171] services under MiFID II/CRD IV, a depositary under the AIFMD/UCITSD V and a depositary/custodian under IORPD II. The European investment laws, i.e. MiFID II, CRD IV, the AIFMD, UCITSD V and IORPD II, are inconsistent in granting a depositary/custodian passport to these depositaries/custodians. They are both inconsistent throughout the directives and on a cross-sectoral basis. On a cross-sectoral basis, MiFID II and CRD IV have an 'ancillary' European passport for 'custodians' in place.[172] To the contrary, the AIFMD and UCITS require the depositary of UCITS and EEA-AIFs to be established in the UCITS/EEA-AIF home Member State,[173] whereas the same entities acting as a depositary/custodian under IORPD II do have a 'de facto' European passport.[174] Not only are the European investment laws inconsistent throughout the directives, also the directives themselves are inconsistent. The AIFMD, for example, differentiates between a strict locational requirement for EEA-AIFs, whereas there is a 'quasi-depositary passport regime' in place for depositaries appointed for TC-AIFs.[175] The inconsistency in granting a European passport for depositaries under the European investment laws led to a 'European depositary passport paradox'.

For a better understanding of all legal issues related to the European depositary passport, it is of importance to examine the debate regarding the European depositary passport in a historical context. For this purpose, the concerns raised upon introducing such a passport during the adoption of the various UCITS directives, the AIFMD, the ISD/MiFID I/II and IORPD I/II have been studied. The 'ancillary European passport' for investment firms and credit institutions under MiFID II and CRD IV has never been updated to a full-fledged investment service as concerns have been raised regarding the scope of 'safekeeping and administration' and, in practice, such a 'low margin service' is only being offered in connection with other investment services/activities. The non-harmonization in this area will, however, also in the future continue to raise a number of ques-

---

171 *See* Annex I s. A. n. 1 and n. 2 MiFID II; Art. 25(4) MiFID II.
172 Annex I n. 12 CRD IV; Annex I s. A MiFID II.
173 Art. 21(5) AIFMD and Art. 23(1) UCITSD V.
174 Art. 33(3) IORPD II.
175 *See also* Buttigieg, *supra* note 91; *See also* Hooghiemstra, *supra* note 48.

tions as to whether the European legal framework for custodians needs to be further harmonized and strengthened to ensure a level playing field in terms of investor protection measures across all Member States.[176] The adoption of the CSDR might help in clarifying the scope of such an initiative.

Notwithstanding the benefits of introducing a depositary/custodian passport, a European passport for UCITS and AIFMD depositaries has so far been multiple times considered, but not introduced. MEP Perreau de Pinninck after the introduction of the 'ancillary European passport' under the ISD and Second Banking Directive considered that a European depositary passport for UCITS should not be introduced for two reasons.[177] First, it was considered that the depositary function was going beyond mere performing the 'custodian' function under the ISD and Second Banking Directive. Second, the depositaries in the UCITS domain had not been harmonized to effectively perform the controlling function.

This reasoning, however, does not explain why currently not a depositary passport has been introduced under the substantially harmonized depositary function under the AIFMD and UCITSD V. Neither does this reasoning explain why depositaries and custodians under IORPD II enjoy a 'de facto European passport' under a minimum harmonized regime and why the AIFMD grants transition relief for credit institutions and a quasi-depositary passport for TC-AIFs. For this reason, Part II addresses the conditions under which a European/TC passport could be granted to (AIF/UCITS) depositaries, whereas Part III discusses the extent to which depositaries and custodians are different.

---

176 Question 3, *supra* note 161.
177 European Parliament 1993, *supra* note 117.

PART II
THE EEA'S APPROACH TOWARDS THE CROSS-BORDER PROVISION OF FINANCIAL SERVICES

3   EEA Cross-Border Regulation for Financial Intermediaries

Ever since the adoption of the Maastricht Treaty, market liberalization in the EEA has taken a huge leap forward based on the free movement of persons, capital, establishment and goods. The same holds true for financial products and services provided by financial intermediaries. Since the early 1990s, EEA legislation has developed an 'internal dimension' and an 'external dimension' related to the cross-border provision of financial services by financial intermediaries. The so-called 'internal dimension' is based upon the four freedoms and regulates the cross-border provisions of financial services by EEA financial intermediaries. The 'external dimension' regulates the cross-border provision of financial services in the internal market by TC financial intermediaries and is based upon international law commitments and EEA secondary law.

The concept of the 'European passport' is at the heart of the 'internal dimension' of the EEA internal market for financial services.[1] It is a general concept that lays down the conditions for the 'mutual recognition' principle. The general idea is that financial products or services that are 'produced' (and marketed) in a 'home Member State' may, under conditions set out in European legislative acts, be marketed throughout the internal market without incurring further conditions imposed by 'host Member States'.[2] The concept is based upon centralized rulemaking and supervision that prevents *a race to the bottom* and ensures a 'level playing field' for all EEA financial intermediaries in the EEA internal market.

Since the early 1990s the 'European passport' as a concept has rapidly spread throughout EEA financial legislation. Various types of European passports are currently applied in the EEA, including passports for market infrastructures (CCPs), disclosure/information requirements (PRIIPR[3]), financial intermediaries (CRD IV, MiFID II) and financial products (IORPD II, UCITSD V).[4] Although the European passport of all these types is based upon the same principles, the focus of this chapter is on the cross-border provision of financial services and, in particular, European passports for financial intermediaries.

---

1   *See* E. Ferran, *Building an EU Securities Market* (Cambridge University Press 2004).
2   Host Member State do have some competences: *See* Recital 2, 7, Art. 86 MiFID II, Recital 4 CRD IV, Recital 85 Solvency II and Art. 21 UCITSD V ('reporting requirement for UCITS ManCos').
3   Regulation (EU) No. 1286/2014 of the European Parliament and of the of 26 November 2014 on key information documents for packaged retail and insurance-based investment products, OJ L 352, 9 December 2014, 1 ('PRIIPR').
4   D.A. Zetzsche, *Drittstaaten im Europäischen Bank- und Finanzmarktrecht* 101 et seq. (G. Bachmann & B. Breig eds., Mohr Siebeck, Tübingen 2014).

Along the development of the European passport as primary regulatory concept for EEA financial intermediaries, the EEA developed its 'external dimension', i.e. the conditions under which TC financial intermediaries may provide financial services in the internal market. TC financial intermediaries are not subject to the same centralized rule-making and supervision as EEA financial intermediaries. Moreover, the harmonization of financial regulation at the international level varies from sector to sector. Banking and insurance legislation are harmonized to a large degree, whereas other sectors, such as asset management, are hardly harmonized. For this reason, the EEA determines in EEA secondary legislation whether and to what extent TC financial intermediaries may provide certain services within the EEA. The degree in which markets are opened to those intermediaries varies on a sectoral basis. UCITSD V, for example, only allows TC financial intermediaries to be active in the internal market through the establishment or acquisition of an EEA subsidiary authorized as UCITS ManCo or as a delegate of an EEA-based UCITS ManCo. MiFIR,[5] however, grants a full European TC passport to TC firms providing investment services/activities to, for example, eligible counterparties. Generally, TC relationships are characterized by requiring equivalency of TC regulatory and supervision regimes. In addition, 'legal representation' in the form of a branch, subsidiary or legal representative is required and cooperation agreements and information exchange between relevant Competent Authorities have to be in place.

This chapter studies the EEA's approach towards the cross-border provision of financial services in more detail. In particular, the conditions under which European and TC European passports are granted to EEA and TC financial intermediaries are studied as to determine under what conditions a (cross-sectoral) European/TC passport could be granted to 'depositaries' and 'custodians'.

3.1 THE INTERNAL DIMENSION OF THE CROSS-BORDER PROVISION OF FINANCIAL SERVICES

The internal dimension of the cross-border provision of financial services has as its advantage that it leads to market efficiency and economies of scale and scope. The cross-border provision of financial services within the EEA, however, leads to 'risk asymmetry' that results from financial intermediaries that are located in a different EEA Member State than the Member State in which the financial services are being provided. For this reason, regulation is in place that intends to ward off any externalities resulting from 'risk asymmetry'. In the past, this led to a large degree of legal fragmentation posing hurdles to the cross-border provision of financial intermediaries that could not be resolved by the 'four freedoms' due to the 'prudential carve-out' that justifies the infringements on the

---

5 Regulation (EU) No. 600/2014 of the European Parliament and of the Council of 15 May 2014 on markets in financial instruments and amending Regulation (EU) No 648/2012, OJ L 173, 12 June 2014, 84 ('MiFIR').

freedom of capital and establishment. This section explains that EEA secondary law, i.e. positive integration, is the only viable means in which an internal market for the cross-border provision of financial services can be established.

3.1.1   A Law and Economics Theory of the Internal Market for Financial Services

Since the Treaty of Rome, the establishment of a 'common market', 'single market' and 'internal market' have been policy objectives in, amongst others, achieving a free market for financial services without barriers in the EEA. This section explains the law and economics rationale behind the internal market for financial services. It discusses market efficiency and economies of scale and scope as primary advantages of the internal market for financial services. In addition, this section explains the externalities of an internal market for financial services by explaining the concept of 'risk asymmetry' resulting from the divergence between 'production' and 'distribution' Member States.[6] Finally, this section concludes by explaining how the harmonization of EEA substitutes for 'risk asymmetry' and, thus, achieves 'risk symmetry'.

3.1.1.1   Market Efficiency and Economies of Scale and Scope
An internal market for financial services without barriers is the primary objective of EEA financial legislation as it increases market efficiency and economies of scale and scope.

3.1.1.1.1   Market Efficiency
A successful integration of the European market for financial services in the EEA leads to operative, allocative and institutional (market) efficiency.[7]

The establishment of an internal market for financial services leads in the first place to operational efficiency.[8] This type of efficiency can be defined as the ratio between the input to operate a financial institution and the output gained from operating financial services.[9] In the financial services context, input factors to be considered would be transaction costs, including staff, application for authorizations to operate and other types of investments.[10] Output factors would be, amongst others, revenue, innovation, new clients and the time-to-market.

---

6   'Production Member States' could be seen as 'home Member States' under passporting arrangements, whereas 'distribution Member States' could be seen as 'host Member States'.

7   E. Davies, A. Dufour & B. Scott-Quin, *The MiFID: Competition in a new European equity market* 163-197 (G. Ferrarini & E. Wymeersch, Oxford 2006).

8   *See* D. Gros, *The Economics of Brexit: It's not about the Internal Market*, https://www.ceps.eu/publications/economics-brexit-it%E2%80%99s-not-about-internal-market.

9   R.E. Bailey, *The Economics of Financial Markets* 22 (Cambridge University Press 2005).

10   F.A.G. den Butter, *Managing Transaction Costs in the Era of Globalization* 58 (Edward Elgar Publishing 2012).

Considering the input factors, financial institutions offering their products and services are benefiting from lower transaction costs.[11] Authorization and notification requirements under European passport arrangements, for example, only need to be fulfilled in one Member State while having a large market to offer their financial products and services without worrying about multiple authorization application and the establishment of subsidiaries that would have led to a duplication of legal costs. Prices in an EEA internal market for financial services decline as fixed costs are shared amongst a larger client base.[12] Firms may organize themselves anywhere in the EEA, in small and big Member States and, as a result, have the potential to maximize their efficiency and become more competitive. In addition to reducing transaction costs, financial institutions from either smaller or bigger EEA Member States may market products and services to all of the European Union's 500 million citizens resulting in more revenue. Actors from smaller Member States are able to compete and more likely to invest and innovate as their client potential significantly increases. Finally, the time-to-market for firms aiming to market their products and services in multiple Member States is heavily reduced. Instead of applying for an authorization to conduct financial services activities to 31 regulators and comply with 31 different sets of legislations only a single authorization and notification process suffices under modern European passport arrangements.

An internal market for financial services also leads to allocative efficiency, firms only locate themselves where the marginal benefit is equal to its marginal costs.[13] The bigger European economic market leads to more supply and demand for financial services increasing the liquidity for the market of services. The more supply and demand, the more innovation and a larger plurality of financial services being offered. The location of a supplier will be determined under competitive pressure there where its marginal benefits is slightly higher than its marginal costs in order to generate those profits giving firms the incentive to innovate and offer new products and services.[14]

Financial services providers will decide to locate themselves only there where the market sees them as most desirable and where there is high demand for their services. Most likely considering legal and non-legal factors, such as economic and social factors, firms primarily establish themselves in financial centres in Europe.[15] Firms are likely to establish themselves following their clients' needs and specialized financial services.[16] Basic services are provided on a local basis, whereas specialized financial services are centred in order to justify the costs for specialization.[17] They provide the expertise and

---

11 D. Dietrich, *Transaction cost economics and beyond: towards a new economics of the firm* (Routledge 1994).
12 Zetzsche 2014, *supra* note 4, 56.
13 J. Sloman, A. Wride, D. Garratt, *Economics* 293 (Pearson 2012).
14 Zetzsche 2014, *supra* note 4, 55.
15 D.A. Zetzsche, *The AIFMD and the Joint Principles of European Asset Management Law* 869-870 (D.A. Zetzsche ed, Kluwer 2015).
16 D.A. Zetzsche, Competitiveness of Financial Centers in Light of Financial and Tax Law Equivalence Requirements (R.P. Buckley, E. Avgouleas & D.W. Arner eds., Cambridge University Press 2016).
17 *Ibid.*

infrastructure to offer these specialized services resulting in a service industry which co-ordinates their interests to further their business.

An efficient internal market for financial services enhances cross-border activity and leads to a transfer from capital and resources from multiple Member States to a few Member States in which a flourishing financial sector is established that offers the best conditions leading to a loss of tax revenues, political influence and employment.[18] Allocative efficiency should, thus, not be seen as Pareto efficiency,[19] but as Kaldor–Hicks efficiency. By shifting resources the gain of the EEA financial sector would be greater than the loss in benefit of the other EEA Member States.[20]

An internal market for financial services could, however, at the downside lead to market failures when firms fail to allocate their resources efficiently. This might occur because of concentrated market power of an oligopoly of Member States that are only attractive enough to be established in. Pre-condition for allocative and operational efficiency is institutional efficiency. European laws have either unified or harmonized business practices/conditions across the 31 EEA Members to make a well-functioning internal market. The legal framework backing this up caters for integrity and stability of the European markets for financial services as a whole.[21] The latter enables the free market access of supply and demand leading to more liquidity and diversity at better service quality and lower prices.[22] The internal market for financial services, thus, leads to operative, allocative and institutional (market) efficiency.

3.1.1.1.2   Economies of Scale and Scope
Scale of economies are the biggest advantage of an internal market for financial services. The European investment fund industry is the most successful example of this.

Following, the IOS scandal in the 1960s and 1970s,[23] big fund distribution markets, such as Germany, for example, introduced legislation to protect their domestic markets.[24] Legal costs borne by fund managers residing in small Member States to obtain market access in big distribution markets increased significantly. For this reason, investments by fund managers in the quality of their services were only done to a limited extent in these Member States.[25] Instead, fund managers preferred to establish themselves in the big distribution markets itself.

---

18 Zetzsche 2014, *supra* note 4, 55.
19 Bailey, *supra* note 9, 22.
20 J. Hicks, *The Foundations of Welfare Economics,* 49 The Economic Journal 696–712 (1939).
21 N. Vokuhl, *Kapitalmarktrechtlicher Anlegerschutz und Kapitalerhaltung in der Aktiengesellschaft* 180 (Nomos 2007).
22 S. Kress, *Effizienzorientierte Kapitalmarktregulierung – eine Analyse aus institutionenökonomischer Perspektive* 59 (Wiesbaden 1996).
23 D.A. Zetzsche, *Prinzipien der kollektiven Vermögensanlage* § 14.C.III. (Mohr Siebeck 2015).
24 G. Müller, *Die Rechtsstellung der Depotbank im Investmentgeschäft nach deutschem und schweizerischem Recht* (Benningen 1969).
25 D.A. Zetzsche & T.F. Marte, *The AIFMD's Cross-Border Dimension, Third-Country Rules and the Equivalence Concept* 61 (D.A. Zetzsche ed, Kluwer 2015).

The introduction of a European (marketing) passport under UCITSD I was a double-edged sword in this regard. It enabled fund managers residing in small Member States, such as Ireland, Liechtenstein and Luxembourg, with a limited client base to market their UCITS in Member States with a bigger client basis. Liechtenstein, for example, became an EEA Member in 1995. Liechtenstein itself only has 36.000 inhabitants providing a small client basis for a successful fund industry. Its EEA Membership in conjunction with its implementation of the UCITSD I enabled a growth of its fund industry from 5 million CHF in 1995 to more than 40 billion CHF in 2017.[26]

Without the existence of an internal market for financial services, it would have not been worthwhile for any financial intermediaries to obtain an authorization to market financial services/products in small Member States, such as Liechtenstein, as the costs would exceed the benefits.[27] From the perspective of the large Member States, the competition of intermediaries of small Member States in marketing financial products/services in their domestic market leads to more competition, more innovation and financial services/products of a higher quality for lower prices.[28]

An internal market for financial services, thus, benefits small and big Member States.

3.1.1.2 Risk Asymmetry and the Concept of 'Production' and 'Distribution' Member States

The internal market for financial services enhances market efficiency and leads to economies of scale and scope. Conversely, the market access that an internal market facilitates may create negative externalities,[29] such as the insolvency of financial intermediaries or fraud that is particularly fuelled by 'risk asymmetry'.[30]

'Risk asymmetry' in an internal market for financial services[31] results from home Member States that might be inclined by political and economic motivations to stimulate their financial services/products that are 'produced' in their Member State (production state) by subjecting their financial intermediaries and products to a minimum set of regulation and/or lax enforcement of the regulatory framework in place.[32] If those products and services are primarily marketed outside of that home Member State, the positive effects of lax regulation and supervision are being enjoyed by the home Member State

---

26 *See* https://www.lafv.li/DE/Fonds/Statistik/FondsvermogennachStichtag.

27 *See, for instance,* the broad discussion about the European passport of financial intermediaries in the UK after the Brexit: K. Lannoo, *EU Financial Market Access after Brexit,* CEPS Policy Brief, September 2016, https://www.ceps.eu/system/files/Brexit%20and%20the%20financial%20sector_0.pdf.

28 Dietrich, *supra* note 11; K. Lannoo, *EU Retail Financial market Integration: Mirage Or Reality?* ECRI Policy Brief No. 3 (June 2008).

29 R. Gilson & R. Kraakman, *Market Efficiency after the Financial Crisis: It's Still a Matter of Information Costs,* 100 Va. L. Rev. 313 (2014).

30 *See* Zetzsche 2016, *supra* note 16, 401-402.

31 This idea has been earlier published in: H. van Meerten & S.N. Hooghiemstra, *PEPP – Towards a Harmonized European Legislative Framework for Personal Pensions,* https://ssrn.com/abstract=2993991.

32 Zetzsche 2014, *supra* note 4, 62-63.

as 'production state', whereas the negative effects of that are to be borne by 'distribution states', i.e. the host Member States. This might lead to so-called 'risk asymmetry' that has been evidenced by the 'Icesave scandal'[33] in which Icelandic Supervisory Authorities with lax supervision allowed badly capitalized credit institutions to offer deposits to Dutch and British customers based upon the European passport to boost their domestic financial services industry.[34]

The degree of risk asymmetry in a specific field of financial services depends upon the degree in which home and host Member States of financial intermediaries have the same level of substantive laws and enforcement in protecting investors and preventing systematic risks.[35] The level of equivalency of the latter determines the risk of regulatory arbitrage, risk asymmetry and a possible *race to the bottom*.

To what extent risk asymmetry poses a threat to investor protection and systematic risks depends on the demand and supply of financial services within home and host Member States regarding a specific type of financial service.[36] Member States could either have a high supply and demand for a specific financial service, whereas financial intermediaries in other Member States primarily provide supply-side financial services ('production Member State') or demand-side services ('distribution Member States').[37] In those Member States where demand and supply for a given financial service is even, legislators and Competent Authorities are expected to have introduced high-quality financial regulation that is strictly enforced to cater for investor protection and prevent systematic risks. This would be in the best interests of both the intermediaries' and investors'/clients' interests.[38]

An imbalance of supply and demand within a particular Member State may either give legislators and Competent Authorities the incentive to overly protect financial institutions in 'production Member States' or investors in 'distribution Member States'.[39]

Financial intermediaries established in production Member States with a small domestic market are, by absence of a common European legislative framework, likely to be

33 I. Fridriksson, *The Banking Crisis in Iceland in 2008*, www.bis.org/review/r090226d.pdf; Stefansson & T. Saethorsson, *Cross-Border Issues in EU Deposit Guarantee Schemes: With a Focus on the Icelandic Case*, 63-82, http://pure.au.dk/portal-asb-student/files/12991/Thesis_without_Appendix.pdf.
34 E.G. Gunnarsson, *The Icelandic Regulatory Responses to the Financial Crisis*, 1 European Business Organization Law Review 139 (2011); S. Benediktsdottir, J. Danielsson & G. Zoega, *Lessons from a Collapse of a Financial System*, https://www.tcd.ie/Economics/assets/pdf/version-20-ben-dan-zoega-revised.pdf; Z. Li, *Securities Regulation in the International Environment*, 110-115, http://theses.gla.ac.uk/691/1/2009zhaoliphd.pdf; M. Guðmundsson, *The Fault Lines in Cross-Border Banking: Lessons From the Icelandic Case*, OECD Journal Financial Market Trends, Issue 2 (2011).
35 Zetzsche 2016, *supra* note 16, 401.
36 Zetzsche & T.F. Marte, *supra* note 25, 474-475; D. Llewellyn, *The Economic Rationale for Financial Regulation* (FSA 1999).
37 The terms 'production' and 'distribution' Member State were introduced by: Zetzsche 2014, *supra* note 4, 60 and 61.
38 *Ibid.*, 61.
39 Zetzsche 2016, *supra* note 16, 410-411.

subjected to less strict laws and enforcement than financial institutions established in 'distribution Member States' with a large domestic consumer base. For this purpose, a difference should be made between laws and enforcement between prudential require- ments preventing a financial institution from insolvency, at the one, and conduct of business rules preventing fraud, at the other hand. 'Production Member States' have a strong interest in enforcing laws that prevent the insolvency of a financial institution, whereas the foreign client base would likely provide for less incentives to enforce conduct of business rules. EEA law substitutes for 'risk asymmetry'.

3.1.1.3   EEA Law as a Substitute for Risk Asymmetry

EEA law in the financial services domain substitutes for risk asymmetry. By harmonizing regulation at the EEA level to which financial service intermediaries are subjected to a level playing field is being created in which both intermediaries established in 'produc- tion' and 'distribution' Member States operate on the same minimum standards.[40] The harmonization of substantive EEA laws ensures a minimum degree of investor and mar- ket protection.[41] This is complemented by 'home state control' [42] and the 'ESFS'.[43]

The rationale of 'regulatory competition' initially led to a tendency of 'minimum har- monization' by means of directives. The idea was that some degree of regulatory diversity would lead to more efficient financial law as Member States would tailor their laws ac- cording to the needs of financial intermediaries. Excessive 'goldplating',[44] i.e. additional national regulatory standards in (host) Member States, led, however, to a fragmented market. This problem was acerbated by the 'Big 5 Bias'. Five Member States, including France, Germany, Italy, Spain and the UK, have more than half of the EEA's population. Regardless of the efficiency of the laws in these Member States, financial intermediaries were complying with the 'goldplating' standards applicable in these Member States as they disproportionally represent a large consumer base. The inefficiencies of minimum harmonization led to a preference of financial intermediaries to establish themselves in

---

40 *See* for intermediary, product and sales regulation: D.A. Zetzsche, *The Anatomy of European Investment Fund Law*, https://ssrn.com/abstract=2951681.

41 *See infra* 3.2.4.1.

42 P.H Verdier, *Mutual Recognition in International Finance*, 52 Harvard International Law Journal 56 (2011).

43 T. Möllers, *Auf dem Weg zu einer neuen europäischen Finanzmarktaufsichtsstruktur – Ein systematischer Vergleich der Rating-VO (EG) Nr. 1060/2009 mit der geplanten ESMA-VO*, 8 Neue Zeitschrift für Ge- sellschaftsrecht 285 (2010).

44 Directorate General for Internal Policies, *'Gold-plating' in the EAFRD – To What Extent Do National Rules Unnecessarily add to Complexity and as a Result, Increase the Risk of Errors?*, IP/D/ALL/FWC/2009-056, 27 February 2014, www.europarl.europa.eu/RegData/etudes/etudes/join/2014/490684/IPOL-JOIN_ET% 282014%29490684_EN.pdf; W. Voermans, *Gold-Plating and Double Banking: An Overrated Problem?* 79- 88 (H. Snijders & S. Vogenauer eds., Sellier European Law Publishers 2009); J.H. Jans & L. Squintani, A. Aragão, R. Macrory & B.W. Wegener, *'Gold Plating' of European Environmental Measures*, 6.4. Journal of European Environmental and Planning Law 417-435 (2009).

large Member States to avoid regulatory costs and the choice not to offer financial services in small Member States.

This forced the EEA to move to a maximum harmonization strategy that enhanced the internal market for financial services. This is exemplified by the fund industry. Upon the adoption of UCITSD I, France was the biggest fund domicile. The gradual (maximum) harmonization of UCITS under UCITSD I-V, however, led to Luxembourg as the primary choice for UCITS.[45] EEA law in the financial services domain based upon maximum harmonization, thus, substitutes for risk asymmetry.

3.1.2   The Internal Dimension – The Four Freedoms

The Treaty of Rome, concluded in 1957, obliged the Member States to 'establish a common market and progressively approximate the economic policies of the Member States'.[46] The primary aim of the treaty was the establishment of a customs union that ultimately would result in the elimination of tariffs imposed in intra-Community trade and the establishment of a common external tariff.[47] The Customs Union was established by a schedule of regulatory measures that led to the harmonization of indirect taxes[48] and the creation of the European Monetary System.[49] The Treaty provided for the 'four freedoms', i.e. the free movement of goods, persons, services and capital that were designed to support the establishment of a customs union.

The 'four freedoms' introduced by the Treaty of Rome and also adopted in the EEA Treaty,[50] still to date determine the internal dimension of the EEA. Relevant for EEA financial services are, in particular, the freedom of capital, establishment and services.

3.1.2.1   The Freedom of Capital

The free movement of capital laid down in Article 63(1) TFEU prohibits any restrictions on the movement of capital between Member States and between Member States and third countries.[51]

---

45 Zetzsche 2015, *supra* note 23.
46 Art. 1 Treaty establishing the European Economic Community as amended by the Single European Act. Treaties establishing the European Communities, abridged (Luxembourg: Office of Official Publications of the European Communities, 1987); *See* E. Grabitz & M. Hilf, *Das Recht der Europäischen Union* (C.H. Beck 2009).
47 S.J. Key, *Financial Integration in the European Community*, Board of Governors of the Federal Reserve System – International Finance Discussion Papers No. 349 (April 1989), 5.
48 Commission of the European Communities, *Completing the Internal Market: White Paper from the Commission to the European Council*, 11-18 (Office of Official Publications of the European Communities 1985).
49 P. Ludlow, *The Making of the European Monetary System: A Case Study of the Politics of the European Community* (Butterworth Scientific 1982).
50 Arts. 78-88 EEA Agreement.
51 G. Baber, *The Free Movement of Capital and Financial Services: An Exposition? Hardcover – Unabridged* (Cambridge Scholars Publishing 2014).

The free movement of capital is the only 'freedom' under the TFEU that has been significantly modified since its adoption in the original Rome Treaty.[52] The requirement that this freedom was only applicable to residents of EU Member States under the Rome Treaty has been modified in the EC Treaty and the reference to third countries was added. This was maintained under the TFEU. Both EU and non-EU nationals may, thus, invoke the free movement of capital in the courts of EU Member States.[53]

Apart from the scope, also the substance of the provision on the free movement of capital has changed through the years. The current TFEU definition is the result of original provisions that were so unclear that individuals had problems in enforcing their rights before their national courts.[54] To date, the TFEU still does not contain a definition on the meaning of 'movement of capital'. In the absence of a definition, the CJEU has reiterated that the nomenclature annexed to the Council Directive 88/361/EEC should serve as an indicator.[55] Examples of 'movement of capital' mentioned in the nomenclature are, amongst others, direct investments, investments in real estate, operations in securities normally dealt in the capital market, operations in units of collective investment undertakings, operations in securities and other instruments.[56] Restrictions on the free movement of capital are allowed if EEA Member States have a legitimate national or public security concern.[57] Article 65(1) TFEU allows Member States to act to prevent infringements of national law and regulations in the area of prudential financial regulation.

3.1.2.2 The Freedom of Establishment

Following Article 49(1) TFEU, the freedom of establishment prohibits the restrictions on the freedom of establishment of nationals of a Member State in the territory of another Member State. The prohibition applies to primary[58] and secondary[59] establishments.

---

52 J.A. Usher, *The Evolution of the Free Movement of Capital*, 31 Fordham International Law Journal 1533 (2007).

53 CJEU (Judgment of 14 December 1995), Joined cases C-163/94, C-165/94, C-250/94, *Sanz de Lera*, ECLI: EU:C:1995:451.

54 Usher, *supra* note 52.

55 *Ibid.*

56 Annex I Council Directive of 24 June 1988 for the implementation of Article 67 of the Treaty (88/361/EEC).

57 *See* for the grandfathering provisions: Art. 64(1) TFEU, *See also*: the public policy or public security: Art. 65 (1b) TFEU and Art. 52(1) TFEU.

58 *See* on primary establishment the following cases: CJEU (Judgment of 21 June 1974), C-2/74, *Reyners*, ECLI: EU:C:1974:68, paras. 15-16; CJEU (Judgment of 5 November 2002), C-208/00, *Überseering*, ECLI:EU: C:2002:632, paras. 78–82; CJEU (Judgment of 10 July 1986), C-79/85 *Segers*, ECLI:EU:C:1986:308, para. 14; CJEU (Judgment of 9 March 1999), C-212/97, *Centros*, ECLI:EU:C:1999:126, paras. 26–27; CJEU (Judgment of 30 September 2003), C-167/01, *Inspire Art*, ECLI:EU:C:2003:512, paras. 96–98, 105.

59 CJEU (Judgment of 13 July 1993), Case C-330/91, *Commerzbank*, ECLI:EU:C:1993:303, para. 13; CJEU (Judgment of 10 July 1986), C-79/85 *Segers*, ECLI:EU:C:1986:308, para. 13;CJEU (Judgment of 28 January 1986), C-270/83, *Commission v. France*, ECLI:EU:C:1986:37, para. 18; CJEU (Judgment of 16 July 1998), Case C-264/96, *Imperial Chemical Industries*, ECLI:EU:C:1998:370, para. 20; *See* on the right of secondary

Examples include the restriction on the setting-up of agencies, branches or subsidiaries by nationals of any Member State established within the EEA.[60]

Article 49 TFEU, however, only applies to 'nationals of any Member State'. Natural and legal persons[61] from third countries may, thus, not rely upon the freedom of establishment, unless a third country has established a subsidiary 'in accordance with the law of a Member State and has their registered office, central administration or principle place of business within the Union'.[62] The freedom of establishment is, thus, limited to secondary establishments of third country nationals. The freedom may, thus, not invoke by branches of third country nationals as it does not have legal personality. To benefit from this freedom, third country nationals, thus, need to establish a subsidiary within the EU (legal person). Claims on the free movement of establishment are, thus, for third country nationals restricted on the basis of its personal scope, whereas EU Members States may be derogated from restrictions on this freedom for EU nationals.

Following Article 52 TFEU, the freedom of establishment may be derogated by Member States by law, regulation or administration sanctions on grounds of public policy, public security or public health. Prudential financial regulation is, thus, derogated on the basis of public policy.

3.1.2.3   The Freedom to Provide Services

Following Article 56(1) Member States are prohibited from restricting the freedom to provide services[63] in respect of nationals of Member States who are established in a Member State other than that of the person for whom the services are intended. The freedom of services applies to nationals that want to provide services in another Member State without establishing a branch or subsidiary in that Member State. Similarly to the free movement of establishment, the personal scope of this freedom is limited to EEA nationals, non-EU nationals cannot invoke this freedom.

---

establishments of credit institutions: CJEU (Judgment of 5 October 2004), Case C-442/02, *Caixabank France*, ECLI:EU:C:2004:586, paras. 13–14; In the latter case, the CJEU stated that CRD I does not entitle credit institutions that are authorized in one Member State to set up a subsidiary in another Member State. *See* CJEU (Judgment of 5 October 2004), Case C-442/02, *Caixabank France*, ECLI:EU:C:2004:586, para. 7.

60   *See* Art. 49(1) TFEU.
61   Art. 54 TFEU.
62   The 'real and continuous' link principle was required by the 1961 General Programme on the abolition of restrictions on the freedom of establishment. *See* General Programme for the abolition of restrictions on the freedom of establishment within the European Economic Community, OJ 1962 2/36 English special edition: Series II Vol. IX, p. 7 (Title I: Beneficiaries); Later the principle got adopted also in various European financial legislative acts: *See, for instance*, Art. 13(2)(a) CRD IV under which a credit institution must have their head and registered office in the same Member State.
63   *See* Art. 57 TFEU.

On the basis of Article 61 TFEU, Member States may apply restrictions, as long as they have not been abolished, without distinction on grounds of nationality or residence to all persons to whom services are provided. Again, prudential regulation qualifies under this derogation.

3.1.2.4 Overlapping Fundamental Freedoms

The laws of Member States may infringe more than one fundament freedom. Convergence of the justifications and restrictions that are accepted for the fundamental freedoms renders the precise qualification of the fundamental freedom infringed irrelevant for intra-EEA cases. The qualification of the precise fundamental freedom infringed, is, however, relevant for TC financial intermediaries. The only fundamental freedom that applies to third countries is the free movement of capital. The TFEU does not contain any priority or exclusion rules. Laws may infringe both the freedom of capital and establishment, or services and establishment.[64] Some cases even touch upon the four freedoms simultaneously.[65] Throughout CJEU case law there are three approaches being used by the CJEU to ensure that the four freedoms are not being abused by TC financial intermediaries:

- the CJEU is reluctant to apply the free movement of capital if there is an overlap with another freedom;[66]
- the free movement of capital applies but the restricted is 'grandfathered';[67]
- restrictions affecting TC financial intermediaries are easier justified on the basis of a 'prudential carve-out'.[68]

The four freedoms, apart from the free movement of capital, thus, do not apply to TC financial intermediaries. If TC financial intermediaries are affected by an infringement of this freedom, the CJEU usually uses one of these approaches to avoid that the free move-

---

64 For a long time the literature, however, assumed that more freedoms could apply to a single case. *See* W. Schön, *Der kapitalverkehr mit Drittstaaten und das international Steuerrecht* 489-501 (R. Gocke, D. Gosch & M. Lang eds., C.H. Beck 2005).

65 *See* the following case on Denmark's pension taxation rules : CJEU (Judgment of 30 January 2007), C-150/04, *Commission v. Denmark*, ECLI:EU:C:2007:69.

66 *See, in particular* A-G Opinion (16 March 2006), C-452/04, *Fidium Finanz AG v. Bundesanstalt fur Finanzdienstleistungsaufsicht*, ECLI:EU:C:2006:182, para. 41 et seq.

67 H. Rehm & J. Nagler, *Verbietet die Kapitalverkehrsfreiheit nach 1993 eingefuhrte Auslanderungleichbehandlung?*, 15 Internationales Steuerrecht 861(2006); CJEU (Judgment 13 March 2007), C-524/04, *Test Claimants in the Thin Cap Group Litigation v. Commissioners of Inland Revenue*, ECLI:EU:C:2007:161; CJEU (Judgment of 24 May 2007), C-157/05, *Winfried L. Holböck v. Finanzamt Salzburg-Land*, ECLI:EU:C:2007:297, paras. 40-41; D. Hohenwarter & P. Plansky, *Die Kapitalverkehrsfreiheit mit Drittstaaten im Lichte der Rechtssache Holböck*, SWI 346 (2007).

68 CJEU (Judgment of 12 March 1996), C-441-93), *Panagis Pafitis and others v Trapeza Kentrikis Ellados*, ECLI:EU:C:1996:92, para. 49; CJEU (Judgment 12 October 2004), C-222/02, *Peter Paul and others v Germany*, ECLI:EU:C:2004:606, para. 44; A-G Opinion (16 March 2006), C-452/04, *Fidium Finanz AG v. Bundesanstalt fur Finanzdienstleistungsaufsicht*, ECLI:EU:C:2006:182, para. 42; A-G Opinion (26 January 1995), *Alpine Investments BV v Minister van Financiën*, ECLI:EU:C:1995:15, para. 44.

ment of capital is being 'abused' by TC financial intermediaries. Again, prudential regulation qualifies under any circumstance as a valid derogation from the free movement of capital.

Mere negative integration on the basis of invoking the 'four freedoms' to establish an internal market was for both EEA and TC financial intermediaries, thus, was not possible. Instead, positive integration in the EEA granting a European passport based upon maximum harmonization and the ESFS was necessary to unleash the potential of the internal market for financial services.

3.2   THE JOINT PRINCIPLES OF THE EUROPEAN PASSPORT OF EEA FINANCIAL INTERMEDIARIES

The EEA internal market for financial intermediaries is based upon the principle of 'mutual recognition'. The concept of the European passport is now widespread and commonly used to enhance the development of the EEA internal market for financial intermediaries that are active in a wide range of sectors.[69] The European passport and the overarching principle of 'mutual recognition' are based upon two cornerstones: the 'single rulebook', i.e. a thick set of harmonized rules[70] and a coordinated institutional framework for financial supervision comprising of 'home state control' and the ESFS that allows host Member States to defer supervision to home Member States and ESAs.[71] The European passport as regulatory tool is unique and not to be found in any other multilateral, regional or bilateral forms of cooperation at the international level.[72] The reason for this is the degree of centralized rulemaking and supervision at the EEA level on which the regulatory tool is based.[73] This section proceeds as follows. First, the internal market for financial intermediaries, the general concept of the European passport, positive integration, legal instruments and the role of the Lamfalussy procedure are being discussed. This section concludes by discussing in detail the 'single rulebook' and coordinated institutional framework for financial supervision in detail.

3.2.1   An Internal Market for Financial Intermediaries

The European passport as a common concept for EEA financial intermediaries has been introduced in many EEA secondary legislation initiatives. The concept is now widespread

---

69   An earlier version of this section has been earlier published in: van Meerten & Hooghiemstra, *supra* note 31.
70   C.M. Grundmann-van de Krol & J.B.S., Hijink, *Who is Afraid of a Single Rulebook?* 3-16 (F.G.B. Graaf, R.H. Maatman & L.J. Silverentand eds., Kluwer 2012).
71   N. Moloney, *Brexit, the EU and its Investment Banker: Rethinking 'Equivalence' for the EU Capital Market*, LSE Legal Studies Working Paper No. 5/2017, 5, https://ssrn.com/abstract=2929229.
72   Verdier, *supra* note 42.
73   IOSCO, *IOSCO Task Force on Cross-Border Regulation – Final Report*, FR 23/2015, (2015), 31 et seq.

in European financial legislation as it is evidenced that it is effective in the development of an internal market for financial intermediaries. The most commonly used TFEU legal basis for a legal instrument is the common 'internal market'.[74] Referring to the wording 'European passport' implies that the concept is used to establish an internal market for financial intermediaries in a particular sector on the basis of 'positive integration'.[75] 'Positive integration' is used to establish an underlying legal framework for harmonization in the EEA as to overcome widely differing national rules for financial intermediaries in sectors that are not yet harmonized and for which no European passport exists. A recent example of a sector that is considered to be harmonized is the internal market for PEPPs and its providers.[76]

The European Commission and EIOPA seek to establish an internal market for PEPPs and its providers on the basis of 'positive integration'.[77] This approach is logical as national rules for existing PPPs differ widely. EIOPA believes this is due to the fact that – in order to safeguard the interests of personal retirement savers – individual countries have introduced national rules of general good.[78] These rules relate to, amongst others, investment restrictions and requirements with regard to capping cost and charges.[79] Although the national rules of general good touch upon the free movement of persons,[80] the free movement of establishment/services and the free movement of capital, negative integration by directly invoking the 'fundamental freedoms' by means of the CJEU is excluded as Member States in the financial services domain are able to justify obstacles related to establishing an 'internal market' for PPPs on the basis of consumer protection ('the general good').[81] Positive integration is, thus, the only means in which an internal market for not only personal pensions and their providers/distributors but also other financial intermediaries that are not harmonized at the EEA level and for which no European passport exists, can be achieved.

Before the legal instruments that are used to establish a European passport on the basis of 'positive integration' are discussed, the European passport as a concept will be addressed.

---

74 *Cf.* Arts. 53, 62 and 114 TFEU.
75 F.W. Scharpf, *Negative and Positive Integration in the Political Economy of European Welfare States* 15-39 (G. Marks ed, Sage Publisher 1996).
76 *See* van Meerten & Hooghiemstra, *supra* note 31.
77 Scharpf, *supra* note 75.
78 EIOPA-CP-15/006, 13.
79 EIOPA-16/457, 60.
80 *See, for instance,* for IORPD II: H. Van Meerten & P. Borsjé, *A European Pensions Union*, National Bank of Slovakia, Series 2014, May, 5, 22, https://ssrn.com/abstract=2425478.
81 Zetzsche 2014, *supra* note 4, 111-114.

3.2.2   The General Concept of the 'European Passport'

The so-called 'European passport' is at the heart of the EEA system for financial services. It is a general concept that lays down the conditions for the 'mutual recognition' principle. The general idea is that financial products or services that are 'produced' (and marketed) in a 'home Member State' may, under the conditions set out in European legislative acts, be marketed throughout the internal market without incurring further conditions imposed by 'host Member States'.[82] The 'passporting' regulatory tool in European financial legislation is unique and not replicated in any other multilateral, regional or bilateral initiatives.[83]

There are various types of European passports that are currently applied in the EEA, including passports for market infrastructures (CCPs), disclosure/information requirements (PRIIPR), financial intermediaries (CRD IV, MiFID II[84]) and financial products (IORPD II, UCITSD V).[85] Although the European passports of all these types are based upon the same principles, the focus of this chapter is on European passports for financial intermediaries.

The underlying concepts of the European passport are 'risk asymmetry' and 'economies of scope and scale'.[86] To facilitate the 'mutual recognition' approach and overcome 'risk asymmetry', the European passport has to be based upon a harmonization of substantive law and financial supervision.[87] These legal frameworks are based upon positive integration and EU legal instruments.

3.2.3   Positive Integration and EU Legal Instruments

For the purpose of positive integration in the EEA to establish a European passport for financial intermediaries, there are several legal instruments available to achieve an 'internal market' for financial intermediaries. Based upon Articles 53, 62 and 114(1) TFEU, the European Parliament and the Council may adopt measures for the approximation of the provisions laid down by law, regulation or administrative action in Member States that

---

82 Host Member State do have some competences: *See* Recital 2, 7, Art. 86 MiFID II, Recital 4 CRD IV, Recital 85 Solvency II and Art. 21 UCITSD V ('reporting requirement for UCITS ManCos').

83 Moloney, *supra* note 71, 5.

84 K.W.H. Broekhuizen & W.A.K. Rank, *Het Europees paspoort voor beleggingsondernemingen* 255-271 (D. Busch, D.R. Doorenbos, C.M. Grundmann-van de Krol, R.H. Maatman, M.P. Nieuwe Weme & W.A.K. Rank eds., Kluwer 2007).

85 Zetzsche 2014, *supra* note 4, 101 et seq.

86 *Ibid.*, 102-108, 110-111; M. Lehmann & D.A. Zetzsche, *Brexit and the Consequences for Commercial and Financial Relations between the EU and the UK*, https://ssrn.com/abstract=2841333; Zetzsche & Marte, *supra* note 25, 474.

87 K. Lannoo & M. Levin, *Securities Market Regulation in the EU – Everything You Always Wanted to Know about the Lamfalussy Procedure*, CEPS Research Report in Finance and Banking, No. 33, (May 2004), 4.

have as their object the establishment and functioning of the internal market. Typically, financial regulation at the EEA level is being based upon the so-called 'Lamfalussy procedure'. Before the Lamfalussy procedure will be addressed, first the choice of policy instruments and the principles of proportionality and subsidiarity at the EEA level will be discussed.

3.2.3.1   The Choice of EU Policy Instruments

The legal acts of the EU are listed in Article 288 TFEU. There are regulations, directives, decisions, recommendations and opinions. EU institutions may adopt any of these legal acts if they are empowered to do so by the Treaties.[88] The sources of law laid down in Article 288 TFEU are referred to as 'secondary legislation' as it is based upon the Treaties that are 'primary legislation'.

Articles 289, 290 and 291 TFEU establish a hierarchy of secondary legislation between legislative acts, delegated acts and implementing acts. Legislative acts are adopted through the ordinary or a special legislative procedures, whereas delegated acts are non-legislative acts of general application that supplement or amend certain non-essential elements of a legislative act.[89] Delegated acts may be delegated to the European Commission by the European Parliament and the Council.[90] The European Parliament and the Council set out the objectives, content, scope and duration of the delegation and the conditions to which the delegation is subject in the legislative act.[91] Implementing acts are adopted by the European Commission if uniform conditions for implementing legally binding acts are needed. In specific cases that are duly justified and in areas of common foreign and security policy, the Council may only adopt implementing acts.[92]

There are under Article 288 TFEU various types of EU secondary legislation. The legal acts in the financial services domain include regulations, directives, decisions, recommendations and opinions.

Regulations function as a 'European law', i.e. no implementation at the Member State level is necessary and they are directly enforceable in all Member States (self-executing). Regulations have the object of maximum harmonization and leave no discretion for

---

88 'Treaties' on the EU level include: the Treaty on European Union (TEU); the Treaty on the Functioning of the European Union (TFEU); the protocols related to these treaties; the Character of Fundamental Rights of the European Union; the Treaty Establishing the European Atomic Energy Community (Euratom); international agreements; the principles of proportionality and subsidiarity of Union law and EU secondary legislation.

89 European Commission, *Better Regulation "Toolbox"*, Tool #15: The choice of policy instruments, 87, http://ec.europa.eu/smart-regulation/guidelines/docs/br_toolbox_en.pdf.

90 *See* for an overview how the mechanisms work out under IORPD II: A. van den Brink & H. van Meerten, *EU Executive Rule-Making and the Second Directive on Institutions for Occupational Retirement Provision*, 12 UU Law Review 1 (2016).

91 European Commission, *supra* note 89.

92 Art. 291 TFEU.

'goldplating'[93] by Member States.[94] They are designed to ensure uniform application of EU law in all Member States and supersede national laws incompatible with their substantive provisions.[95]

Directives are a European legislative act that obliges Member States to achieve a result. This requires Member States to implement the act at the Member State level. How the directive is implemented depends upon whether the directive has maximum or minimum harmonization as its objective that is usually being taken from the recitals and other policy documents upon adopting the directive.[96] directive, however, leave to national authorities the choice of form and methods how to implement the act. Member States are given some discretion in implementing directive to take account of specific national circumstances. Member States are, however, obliged by Article 4(3) TFEU to guarantee the effectiveness of EU law in accordance with the principle of sincere cooperation. Directives that are not timely implemented or have led to a 'wrong' implementation may have 'direct effect', i.e. may be directly invoked as if it was a law in itself.[97]

Decisions are binding in its entirety to those to whom they are addressed. Individuals may invoke rights to Member States, natural or legal persons conferred by a decision.

Communications from the European Commission and advices/guidelines given by the ESAs[98] are not legally binding in itself and do not confer any rights or obligations on those to whom they are addressed by, in particular, provide guidance as how EU law has to be interpreted. In the financial services domain these include communications from the European Commission and advices/guidelines given by the ESAs.[99] A Commission Communication is legally not binding and always leads to minimum harmonization that allows discretion to Member States how to implement the Communication in their national law.[100] ESA Guidelines are legally not binding in itself, unless any other legislative act explicitly delegates competences to ESAs related to a specific matter to be clarified by an ESA guidelines.[101] ESA advice is to be asked by the European Commission prior to

---

93 Directorate General for Internal Policies, *supra* note 44; Voermans, *supra* note 44; Jans *et al, supra* note 44.
94 Art. 288 TFEU.
95 European Commission, *supra* note 89.
96 C. Gerner-Beuerle, *United in Diversity: Maximum versus Minimum Harmonization in EU Securities Regulation*, 3 Capital Markets Journal 317 (2012).
97 *See* Francovich case, joined cases C-6/90 and C-9/90); *See also* the Faccini Dori Case C-91/92, ECR, p. I-3325 et seq., point 25).
98 *See* Art. 288 TFEU.
99 *See* Art. 288 TFEU; European Commission, *supra* note 89.
100 The Financial Services Action Plan ('FSAP ') was an European Union's attempt to create a single market for financial services by harmonizing financial services within the EU to a larger degree. The FSAP was initiated in 1999 and its implementing measures were completed by 2004. *See, e.g.* the simplified prospectus under UCITSD III: Commission staff working document, *Impact Assessment – Brussels, accompanying the Proposal for a Directive of the European Parliament and of the Council on the coordination of laws, regulations and administrative provisions relating to undertakings for collective investment in transferable securities*, (UCITS) {COM(2008) 458}{SEC(2008) 2264} SEC(2008) 2263, 57-59.
101 *See* Art. 290, 291 TFEU.

adopting Level 1 and Level 2 instruments. The advice concerned Level 2 is only mandatory in the cases that are expressly indicated in Level 1 instruments. The European Commission, however, remains to be responsible and is not legally obliged to follow up the
ESA advice.

3.2.3.2   The Principles of Subsidiarity and Proportionality

All EU acts need to be in line with the fundamental principle of subsidiarity as laid down
in EU law. Following Article 5 TFEU, the EU:

> shall act only if and in so far as the objectives of the proposed action cannot be
> sufficiently achieved by the Member States, either at central level or at regional
> and local level, but can rather, by reason of the scale or effects of the proposed
> action, be better achieved at Union level.

The principle has been introduced by the Treaty of Maastricht and is important not only
from a legal but also from a political and economic perspective.[102] The principle shields
off undesirable EU acts, serves as a constitution principle and requires EU legislative acts
to justify any proposals.[103]

Even though the principle has been introduced a long time ago, the CJEU has till date
not rejected any EU legislation that had been challenged by Member States on the basis of
this principle. The CJEU generally applies a 'form over substance approach', i.e. the CJEU
sees the principle of subsidiarity as a political principle and checks primarily whether the
legislative institutions in the legislative process have considered the principle sufficiently.[104]

This principle has, however, gained importance upon the adoption of the TFEU by
introducing two procedures. First, national parliaments may under the TFEU review
legislative draft proposals on the basis of the principle of subsidiarity and a new Subsidiarity and Proportionality Protocol allows Member States to challenge EU legislation on
the basis of this principle. Second, national Member States are allowed to make claims on
substantial factors, including the scope of the cross-border effects, the (economic) benefits of EU legislation, the scale of the problem and the national benefits that are at
stake.[105] By introducing these two procedures under the TFEU, EU acts specify in more
detail the considerations from a subsidiarity and proportionality perspective.[106]

---

102 G. Gelauf, *Subsidiarity and Economic Reform in Europe* (Springer 2008).
103 H. van Meerten, A. van den Brink & S.A. de Vries, *Regulating Pensions: Why the European Union Matters*
   (Netspar Discussion Paper) 10, http://papers.ssrn.com/sol3/papers.cfm?abstract_id=1950765.
104 A. Von Bogdandy, *Founding Principles* (A. Von Bogdandy & J. Bast, eds., Hart Publishing 2010).
105 Van Meerten & Borsjé, *supra* note 80.
106 *Ibid.*

3.2.3.3   The Lamfalussy Process

In the post-FSAP era,[107] the so-called 'Lamfalussy procedure' is being used for EEA financial service initiative in fostering harmonization in pursuing the internal market and the recent 'capital markets union initiative'. Positive integration is sought be means of introducing a European passport for financial intermediaries on the basis of the 'internal market' that requires a qualified majority to adopt measures concerned with the EU.[108] The Lamfalussy framework is the legislative framework on which a European passport is being based. The Lamfalussy procedure was being developed to accelerate the speed of accomplishing an internal market for financial services.[109]

The framework is being structured in four levels. The so-called Level 1 legislative acts are being agreed upon between the Council of ministers and the involvement of the European Parliament. By means of a regulation or a directive, the general framework, including the general principles to be regulated, are being set out. Directives and regulations as 'binding-acts' under the Lamfalussy process, require democratic control and ensure that legislative competences are delegated to European institutions subject to this control.[110] At Level 2, the European Commission with the assistance of the ESAs elaborate the certain aspect as indicated in the Level 1 initiative in directives or regulations. At Level 3, a committee comprised of the ESAs advices on the regulation and implementation of the supervision. ESAs may publish guidelines deliberately or be asked by Level 1 or Level 2 instruments to do so. At Level 4, the European legislation is implemented by the Member States and the European Commission ensures that this is done correctly, if necessary by commencing an infringement procedure pursuant to Article 258 TFEU.

3.2.3.4   The Trend towards Maximum Harmonization

The primary legal instruments being used for harmonization of both at Level 1 are directives and regulations. Recently, the 'maximum harmonization approach' has led to an increasing use of the regulation as a legal instrument. This has, however, not always been the case.

The first generation of 'product passports', including IORPs and UCITS under IORPD I and UCITSD I, have been adopted as a directive rather than a regulation. Although both legal instruments take precedence over Member State laws, the nature of

---

107 *See* K. Lee, *Investor Protection in European Union: Post FSAP Directives and MiFID*, https://ssrn.com/abstract=1339305; European Commission, *Commission Staff Working Document of 11 April 2013: Consumer Protection in Third-Pillar Retirement Products*, 7, http://ec.europa.eu/dgs/health_food-safety/dgs_consultations/ca/docs/swd_consumer_protection_thirds_pillar_pensions_en.pdf. Directorate General for Internal Policies, *Consumer Protection Aspects of Financial Services*, IP/A/IMCO/ST/2013, 07 February 2014, www.europarl.europa.eu/RegData/etudes/etudes/join/2014/507463/IPOLIMCO_ET%282014%29507463_EN.pdf.
108 *See* Arts. 53, 62 and 114 TFEU.
109 Lannoo & Levin, *supra* note 87.
110 *Ibid.*

the instrument is entirely different. Regulations as 'European laws' have direct effect, whereas directives offer Member States the possibility to choose the means by which the objectives set out by the directive would be achieved. The directive as a legal instrument was chosen over regulations under the first generation of 'product passports' as directives by nature accommodate the principles of subsidiarity and proportionality between EU law and institutions and national law and institutions at the Member State level better. As a consequence of regulating by directives, Member States were responsible for transposing EU law into national law. The objective of (product) regulation in the IORPD I and UCITSD I were minimum harmonization. As a result of this characteristic, Member States had the possibility to set higher standards, provided that they do not discriminate, i.e. restrict access from financial products in Member States that satisfy the minimum standard set out by the directive.

Many Member States made use of their discretion under the IORPD I and UCITSD I to set higher standards or abiding to different interpretations of similar terms resulting in the hindrance of an internal market of IORPs and UCITS. A decade after the implementation of IORPD I, this is exemplified by IORPs of which currently not even 100 are operating on a cross-border basis, whereas UCITS did not become a success until UCITSD III was adopted.[111] Although the EU and the US are similar in terms of GDP, the average UCITS was, until the introduction of UCITSD IV, five times smaller than its US counterpart (mutual fund).[112]

Post-FSAP, directives and regulations adopted at Level 1 have the nature of 'maximum harmonization'. Unsurprisingly, the tendency at the European level is to establish Level 1 instruments by means of a regulation that prevents 'goldplating' by national Member States.[113] Recent examples of product regulation established as a regulation include the ELTIFR, EuSEFR, EuVECAR and the MMFR.[114]

3.2.4 The Cornerstones of the European Passport for Financial Intermediaries: the 'Single Rulebook', 'Home Country Control' and the ESFS

'Mutual recognition', the underlying concept of the European passport, relies upon a 'single rulebook', i.e. detailed harmonized rules based upon the Lamfalussy procedure that governs the EU financial internal market and that allows host Member States to defer

---

111 U. Klebeck, *Interplay between AIFMD and the UCITSD* 96-97 (D.A. Zetzsche ed, Kluwer 2015).
112 European Commission, *Green Paper on the Enhancement of the EU Framework for Investment Funds*, 12 July 2005, (SEC(2005) 947), http://ec.europa.eu/finance/investment/docs/consultations/greenpaper-background_en.pdf.
113 *See also* the different implementations of the AIFMD: See D.A. Zetzsche, *Fondsregulierung im Umbruch – ein rechtsvergleichender Rundblick zur Umsetzung der AIFM-Richtlinie*, 1 ZBB 32 (2014); *Cf.* Voermans, *supra* note 44; Jans *et al, supra* note 44.
114 S.N. Hooghiemstra, *Wat is een beleggingsinstelling onder de AIFM-richtlijn?*, 3 Ondernemingsrecht 24 (2014).

supervision to home Member States.[115] The European passport for financial intermediaries is complemented by coordinated supervision through the concept of 'home state control' and the ESFS.[116] The so-called 'single rulebook' and ESFS together support sectoral European passports that allows for market access, removes host state control and prevents risks related to (cross-border) threats related to investor protection, financial stability and market integrity.[117]

3.2.4.1   The European Passport Substantive Legal Framework: 'The single rulebook'

The 'single rulebook concept' is applied to various types of European passports that are currently applied in the EEA, including passports for market infrastructures (CCPs), disclosure/information requirements (PR, PRIIPR), financial intermediaries (CRD IV, MiFID II) and financial products (IORPD II, UCITSD V).[118] Although the European passports of all these types are based upon the same principles, the focus of this section is on European passports for financial intermediaries.

Financial intermediaries, including credit institutions, UCITS ManCos, AIFMs and investment firms, all have a substantive legal framework, i.e. a thick dense 'single rulebook' with harmonized rules, on the basis of which they are allowed to 'passport' their services/products throughout the EEA. The general terminology for this 'single rulebook' that financial intermediaries have to comply with to obtain a European passport is 'intermediary regulation', i.e. the regulation of sectoral specific intermediaries that focusses on investor protection and market protection. Generally, 'intermediary regulation' is structured according to the four 'Lamfalussy levels'.

3.2.4.1.1   Level 1

At Level 1, the framework directive/regulation adopted usually includes provisions governing the:
–   object, definitions and scope;
–   authorization;
–   operational conditions;
–   cross-border activity (European Passport);
–   enforcement (ESFS vs. national Competent Authorities);
–   sanctions.

---

115 Moloney, *supra* note 71, 10.
116 M. Lehmann & C. Manger-Nestler, *Die Vorschläge zur neuen Architektur der europäischen Finanzaufsicht*, 3 Europäische Zeitschrift für Wirtschaftsrecht 87 (2010); M. Lamandini, *When More is Needed: the European Financial Supervisory Reform and its Legal Basis*, 6 European Company Law 197-202 (2009).
117 *Ibid.*
118 Zetzsche 2014, *supra* note 4, 101 et seq.

The object, definitions and scope of any Level 1 initiative set out the purpose, clarifies the definition of general terms, such as 'home and host Member States' and more specific terms related to the sector that the initiative intends to regulate, such as the definition of an 'AIF' and 'AIFM' under the AIFMD.[119]

The authorization of financial intermediaries depends upon the authorization conditions and the compliance of the intermediary with the operational conditions laid down in sectoral EEA legislation. Credit institutions, AIFMs, UCITS ManCos and depositaries/ custodians, for instance, have to comply with general (authorization and) organizational requirements that are common to financial intermediaries in European financial law and specific requirements aimed at the provision of financial services/activities and products.[120]

General organizational requirements require the establishment of an organizational structure that clearly assigns responsibilities, employ personnel with the right skills, knowledge and experience, establish adequate systems to safeguarding information and ensure business continuity.[121] General organizational requirements include:[122]

- fit and proper senior management;
- minimum capital requirements that vary upon the type of financial service/product provided;
- a business plan;
- adequate risk organization;
- sound third country relationships; and
- reliable significant shareholders.

Specific organizational requirements complement general requirements. These include, for example, compliance, risk management internal audit, complaints handling, personal transaction and delegation/outsourcing.[123]

By specifying certain common organizational and operational requirements upon authorization, the EEA legislature ensures that only fit and proper financial intermediaries are active on the European markets that are required by sectoral legislation to be

---

119 *See* for the definitions of an 'AIF' and 'AIFM' under the AIFMD: Arts. 4(1)(a) & (b) AIFMD.
120 European Commission, *Background Note accompanying Draft Commission Directive implementing Directive 2004/39/EC of the European Parliament and of the Council as regards record-keeping obligations for investment firms, transaction reporting, market transparency, admission of financial instruments to trading, and defined terms for the purposes of that Directive*, February 2006, 6 et seq.
121 *Ibid.*
122 Zetzsche 2015, *supra* note 15, 865.
123 C.M. Grundmann-van de Krol, *The Markets in Financial Instruments Directive and Asset Management* (D. Busch & D.A. DeMott eds, Oxford 2012).

highly specialized in the financial services/products they are, with certain exceptions in the asset management domain,[124] offering.[125]

Level 1 initiatives regulating financial intermediaries include a section 'cross-border activity'.[126] Once a financial intermediary has been authorized in a Member State, it may, on the basis of a so-called 'notification procedure', provide its products and services throughout the whole EEA by either 'acting on a cross-border basis' (providing services on a cross-border basis) or on the basis of the establishment of a branch without having to apply for any additional authorization.[127]

A European passport, thus, requires:[128]

–   an application of a financial intermediary under the authorization requirements to the Competent Authority of the home Member State;
–   a review of the European provisions by this Competent Authority;
–   a notification from the Competent Authority of the home state to the authorities of the host Member State;
–   and a minimum waiting period before the intermediary may provide services in the host Member State.

In addition, financial intermediaries that wish to establish a branch in another Member state would be required to:

–   show that it meets the organizational requirements to conduct business according to the rules in the host state; and
–   subject itself to supervision within a limited scope in the host Member State.

All Level 1 initiatives, thus, include a notification procedure of the home Member State in which the financial intermediary is authorized and the notification to host Member States in which the financial intermediary intends to provide its services.

The notification is the procedure that accommodates the 'cross-border activity' (the European passport) for financial intermediaries. Upon, for example, the authorization of

---

124 UCITS ManCos and AIFMs are allowed to discretionary manage IORPs and individual portfolio's under the AIFMD and UCITSD V. Nevertheless, MiFID II, AIFMD and UCITSD V all regulate the core business of 'investment management'. Exceptions are credit institutions that are 'automatically' recognized as investment firms under MiFID II. See Art. 1(3) MiFID II and Annex 1 CRD IV.
125 A legal entity that obtained an authorization as UCITS ManCo is, for example, for that reason prohibited from obtaining a license as an insurance undertaking. See Commission of the European Communities, *Toward a European Market for the Undertakings for Collective Investment in Transferable Securities – Commentary on the provisions of Council Directive 85/611/EEC of 20 December 1985* ('Van Damme Report'), 3, http://goo.gl/K0iUzv.
126 See Recital 19, Title V Provisions concerning the freedom of establishment and the freedom to provide services CRD IV; Art. 6(3) MiFID II; Recital 18, Arts. 145, 146 Solvency II; Arts. 16-21 UCITSD V (UCITS ManCo 'management passport'); Arts. 91-96 UCITSD V (UCITS ManCo 'marketing passport'. See on the 'rights of EU AIFMs to market and manage EU AIFs in the Union': Chapter VI AIFMD.
127 *Ibid.*
128 Zetzsche 2015, *supra* note 15, 865.

a UCITS, the UCITS ManCo sends a notification file that comprises all information necessary to be duly authorized to the Competent Authorities of the UCITS home Member State.[129] Upon being duly authorized, a UCITS ManCo may make use of its right to market UCITS to investors in other EEA Member States.[130] For that purpose, the UCITS ManCo must send a notification file, including all necessary information, to the Competent Authority of the UCITS home Member State.[131] This Competent Authority checks the completeness of the notification.[132] If the notification file is complete, the Competent authority adds an attestation (the so-called European passport) or informs the UCITS ManCo what is failing.[133] In addition to sending its notification file, the UCITS ManCo may indicate in what EEA Member States it wishes to market its UCITS. Within 10 days of receiving the notification letter of the UCITS ManCo, the Competent Authority of the home Member State is obliged to notify all Competent Authorities of the Member States in which the UCITS ManCo intends to market its UCITS.[134] After the Competent Authority of the home Member State informs the UCITS ManCo of the transmission date for the notification file, the marketing process may start immediately.[135] The host Member State may check ex post, but has to rely upon a cooperation mechanism between the home and host Member State in which, in non-accurate instances, the host Member State has to rely upon measures being taken by the Competent Authority of the home Member State.[136] The prudential and financial supervision of the business activities/financial products provided by a financial intermediary, thus, remains with the Competent Authority in the Member State that granted the initial authorization.

The Level 1 regimes, in addition, contain provisions related to enforcement that primarily requires the national Competent Authorities of the home Member State to take measures if financial intermediaries do not comply with the relevant sectoral EEA law.[137] Enforcement also addresses the cooperation between home and host Member States and the cooperation between national Competent Authorities and the ESAs.[138]

Sanctions include fines based upon administrative law and, in the worst case, a revocation of the European passport of a particular financial intermediary complement the Level 1 initiatives.[139]

---

129 *See, e.g.* Art. 32 AIFMD for the 'marketing passport' and Art. 33 AIFMD for the 'management passport'.
130 Art. 91 UCITSD V.
131 Art. 93(1) and (2) UCITSD V.
132 Art. 93(3) sub-para. 1 UCITSD V.
133 Art. 93(3) sub-para. 2 UCITSD V.
134 *Ibid.*
135 Art. 93(3) sub-para. 3 UCITSD V.
136 Art. 91(2) UCITSD V.
137 Art. 101(3) UCITSD V.
138 *See* Chapter XII and XIII UCITSD V.
139 *See* Art. 70 MiFID II.

3.2.4.1.2 Level 2

Level 1 could also include provisions delegating responsibilities to the European Commission to adopt directive/regulations clarifying the general framework set out in Level 1. UCITSD V, for example, sets out the details of the notification procedure, the KIID and master–feeder structures in Level 2 measures.[140]

3.2.4.1.3 Level 3

Guidelines issued by ESAs complement the Level 1 and 2 measures. These so-called 'Level 3 measures', for example under UCITSD V, determine risk management methods and the format in which a KIID is required to be presented.[141]

3.2.4.1.4 Level 4

At Level 4, the European legislation is implemented by the Member States and the European Commission ensures that the required secondary EEA law implementation is done correctly (Level 4). If necessary, the European Commission commences an infringement procedure pursuant to Article 258 TFEU.

3.2.4.2 The EEA Financial Supervisory Framework: Home Country Control and the ESFS

Financial supervision under a European passport is throughout sectoral EEA secondary legislation based upon (1) home country control and (2) the European System of Financial Supervision.

3.2.4.2.1 Home Country Control

Traditionally underpinning European (product) passport is the principle of home country control, i.e. the Member State where the financial product is being registered/authorized or the financial intermediary has its statutory/real seat is responsible for carrying out the supervision of the product or intermediary. The European passport requires that the Competent Authorities of the host Member State trust the supervision being carried out by the home Member State. Competent Authorities in host Member States, i.e. the Competent Authorities in Member States where the service provider may offer its products and services, have frequently expressed doubts regarding this equivalence.[142] Financial

---

140 *See* Art. 108 UCITSD V.
141 *See* Commission Regulation (EU) No 583/2010 of 1 July 2010 implementing Directive 2009/65/EC of the European Parliament and of the Council as regards key investor information and conditions to be met when providing key investor information or the prospectus in a durable medium other than paper or by means of a website, OJ L 176, 10 July 2010, 1 ('KIIDR').
142 Lannoo & Levin, *supra* note 87, 14.

crises and events, such as the Icesave scandal,[143] led to a larger degree of cooperation to supervise the activities of entities from other Member States by the establishment of the European System of Financial Supervision.

3.2.4.2.2   The European System of Financial Supervision

The European System of Financial Supervision[144] complements 'home country control' and consists of the ESRB carrying out macro-prudential supervision[145] and three ESAs (EBA, EIOPA and ESMA[146]) that carry out micro-prudential supervision on a sectoral basis. In 2011, the ESAs received more binding legal powers related to rulemaking, the implementation of EU law, emergency powers, conflict resolution and restricting certain financial products.[147]

ESAs have an advisory function in the rulemaking process for developing Level 1 directives or regulations. In addition, ESAs are involved in a preparatory and advisory capacity related to the Level 2 implementing acts that are adopted by the European Commission on the basis of Article 290 TFEU. The ultimate decision lies, however, in principle with the European Commission.

The second important competence relates to verifying compliance of the implementation of the directives and regulations in the national jurisdictions, including the Regulatory technical standards by ESAs.[148] Non-compliance is, based upon Article 258 TFEU, to be identified by the European Commission and to be brought before the CJEU. According to the ESA regulations, the identification is being attributed to ESAs that 'shall act' upon non-compliance and dialogues between ESAs and national Competent Authorities will take away most issues. After the dialogue, national Competent Authorities that continue to be non-compliant may receive a formal opinion of the European Commission that might be based upon the recommendation of the ESA and is subject to review by the CJEU.[149]

---

143 E. Wymeersch, *Europe's New Financial Regulatory Bodies*, 5, http://ssrn.com/abstract=1813811; E. Wymeersch, *The Institutional Reforms of the European Financial Supervisory System, An Interim Report*, https://ssrn.com/abstract=1541968.

144 N. Moloney, *The European Securities and Markets Authority and Institutional Design for the EU Financial Market. A Tale of Two Competences: Part (1) Rule Making*, 12 European Business Organization Law Review 41-86 (2011). *See also* N. Moloney, *The European Securities and Markets Authority and Institutional Design for the EU financial Market. A Tale of Two Competences: Part (2) Rules in Action*, 12 European Business Organization Law Review 177-225 (2011).

145 N. Kost – de Sevres & L. Sasso, *The New European Financial Markets Legal Framework: A Real Improvement? An Analysis of Financial Law and Governance in European Capital Markets from a Micro- and Macro-Economic Perspective*, 7 Capital Markets Law Journal 30 (2011).

146 D. Fischer-Appelt, *The European Securities and Market Authority: The Beginnings of a Powerful European Securities Authority?*, 1 Law and Financial Markets Review 21-32 (2011).

147 H. van Meerten & A.T. Ottow, *The Proposals for the European Supervisory Authorities (ESAs): The Right (Legal) Way Forward?*, 1/2 TvFR 5 (2010); E. Wymeersch, *Europe's Financial Regulatory Bodies* (H.S. Birkmose, M. Nevillie & K. E. Sørensen eds., Kluwer 2012).

148 J. Doelder & I.M. Jansen, *Een nieuw Europees toezichtraamwerk*, 1/2 TvFR 17 (2010).

149 E. Ferran, *Understanding the New Institutional Architecture of EU Financial Market Supervision*, Paper No. 29/2011 (2011).

Emergency situations, such as developments that jeopardize the orderly functioning and integrity of the financial markets, that are declared by the Council of ministers may be addressed 'decision' to the ESAs concerned. A recommendation or a request may be made by the ESRB or the ESA and ESAs may require national Competent Authorities to take action to ensure that the Level 1 measures are being complied with. In the absence of a Council decision, the ESA may also adopt emergency measures in exceptional circumstances when a serious danger arises to the orderly functioning of the markets or to financial stability. If the national authority does not respond to this request, ESAs may take direct actions that target the financial institutions in that Member State.[150]

Earlier experiences under European passport arrangements have shown that Competent Authorities sometimes experience difficulties in reaching agreements. The ESA regulations have provided a mechanism for dispute resolution between Competent Authorities to be settled by a decision of an ESA. This may, however, only be used for matters that are precisely expressed in a Level 1 document to be open for mediation and dispute resolution.[151] The procedure consists of a 'reconciliation phase' and a 'decision phase'. The decision made by ESAs are addressed to national Competent Authorities. In the case of non-compliance, however, ESAs may directly target financial institutions in individual Member State to ensure compliance with EU law.

ESAs on the basis of Article 9 of the ESA regulations are attributed with the power to prohibit or restrict certain 'financial activities', including financial products. This power is related to activities that threaten the 'orderly functioning and integrity of financial markets or the stability of whole or part of the financial system in the Union'. Decisions taken by ESAs directly affect the financial intermediaries conducting those financial activities without any intervention of national Competent authorities.

3.2.5   Conclusion

The so-called 'European passport' is at the heart of the EEA system for financial services. It is a general concept, which lays down the conditions for the 'mutual recognition' principle. The general idea is that financial products or services that are 'produced' (and marketed) in a 'home Member State' may, under conditions set out in European legislative acts, be marketed throughout the internal market without incurring further conditions imposed by 'host Member States'.[152] The concept is now widespread in European financial legislation as it is evidenced that it is effective in the development of an internal

---

150 van Meerten & Ottow, *supra* note 147.
151 E. Ferran & K. Alexander, *Can Soft Law Bodies be Effective? Soft Systemic Risk Oversight Bodies and the Special Case of the European Systemic Risk Board*, Paper No. 36/2011(2011).
152 Host Member State do have some competences: *See* Recital 2, 7, Art. 86 MiFID II, Recital 4 CRD IV, Recital 85 Solvency II and Art. 21 UCITSD V ('reporting requirement for UCITS ManCos').

market for financial intermediaries.[153] The underlying concepts of the European passport are 'risk asymmetry' and 'economies of scope and scale'.[154] To facilitate the 'mutual recognition' approach and overcome 'risk asymmetry', the European passport has to be based upon a harmonization of substantive law and financial supervision based upon positive integration and EU legal instruments.[155]

The European passport and the overarching principle of 'mutual recognition' are based upon two cornerstones: the 'single rulebook', i.e. a thick set of harmonized rules and a coordinated institutional framework for financial supervision comprising of 'home state control' and the ESFS that allows host Member States to defer supervision to home Member States and ESAs.[156] The so-called 'single rulebook' and ESFS together support sectoral European passports that allows for market access, removes host state control and prevents risks of (cross-border) threats related to investor protection, financial stability and market integrity.[157] The European passport as a regulatory tool is unique and not to be found in any other multilateral, regional or bilateral forms of cooperation at the international level.[158]

3.3   The External Dimension of the Cross-Border Provision of Financial Services

The regulation of TC financial intermediaries that want to offer cross-border financial services in the internal market is based upon the same 'law and economics' considerations as the regulation of EEA financial intermediaries. The 'external dimension', at the one hand, offers benefits in terms of market efficiency and economies of scale and scope. On the other hand, however, the possible 'risk asymmetry' externalities resulting from granting market access are even bigger than for EEA financial intermediaries.[159] TC financial intermediaries are not subject to the same centralized rulemaking and supervision as EEA financial intermediaries. In imposing regulation to these TC financial intermediaries in warding off externalities, international law obligations ensure that TC financial intermediaries are not treated on a discriminatory basis.

---

153 *See, e.g.* the considerations on the introduction of a European (product) passport in the upcoming PEPP initiative: EIOPA, *Final Report on Public Consultation No. CP-15/006 on the creation of a standardised Pan-European Personal Pension product (PEPP)*, 11 April 2016, EIOPA-16-341, 11.
154 Zetzsche 2014, *supra* note 4, 102-108, 110-111; Lehmann & Zetzsche, *supra* note 86; Zetzsche & Marte, *supra* note 25, 474 (D.A. Zetzsche ed, Kluwer 2015); J. Tegelaar & M. Haentjes, *Brexit: financieelrechtelijke gevolgen*, 74 Bedrijfsjuridische Berichten 257 (2016).
155 Lannoo & Levin, *supra* note 87, 4.
156 Moloney, *supra* note 71, 5.
157 *Ibid.*
158 Verdier, *supra* note 42.
159 *See* European Commission, *Europe a World partner: the External Dimension of the Single Market*, 21(10) Bulletin of the European Communities (1988), http://aei.pitt.edu/1770/1/World_partner_1988.pdf.

The 'prudential carve-out' under both the 'four freedoms' and GATS prevent the establishment of an 'internal market with external dimension' for financial services.[160] Already upon the introduction of the First Banking Directive, it was recognized that only market access conditions in EEA secondary law could lead to the establishment of an 'internal market with external dimension' on a non-discriminatory basis.

The tendency of adopting a TC approach in secondary law has several advantages. First, a coordinated approach strengthens the position of the EU in international financial governance.[161] The centralized and coordinated approach at the EU level ensures an influential position in negotiating financial regulation at the international level. Second, the centralized foreign commercial policy towards third country market access leads to a level playing field for small and big Member States.[162] Big Member States have a stronger position not only in international financial governance, but also could negotiate market access in third countries on better terms. Finally, a coordinated approach of the internal market as huge 'distribution target' for offshore financial centres reduces the regulatory gap between 'production' and 'distribution states'. EEA financial regulation, whether third countries are bound to it or not on a bilateral basis, has an extraterritorial effect on third countries as being regarded as 'non-equivalent' at the EEA level forecloses market access.

The EEA's equivalency concept in overcoming 'risk asymmetry' has, however, to abide by the rules related to the external dimension of the four freedoms and the obligations arising out of GATS in regulating:

– EEA financial intermediaries with an external dimension;
– TC financial intermediaries within the EEA; and
– EEA financial intermediaries within third countries.

This so-called EEA TC secondary legislation addressing the 'external dimension' will be addressed after a law and economics theory of this dimension has been introduced.

3.3.1   The External Dimension – A Law and Economics Theory

3.3.1.1   TC Financial Services and the EEA's External Dimension

The political economy of the internal market for financial services has a different approach towards the provision of cross-border financial services from and to third countries, i.e. the 'external dimension'.[163] Theoretically, the benefits of market efficiency and

---

160 J. Marchetti, *The GATS Prudential Carve-Out* 280-286 (P. Delimatsis & N. Herger eds., Kluwer 2011).
161 N. Moloney, *The EU in International Financial Governance*, 1 Russell Sage Journal of the Social Sciences 138-152 (2017).
162 Zetzsche 2014, *supra* note 4, 80 et seq.
163 Commission of the European Communities, *Commission Staff Working Document – The External Dimension of the Single Market Review Accompanying Document to the Communication from the Commission to*

scales of scope and economies for financial intermediaries also apply to an internal market with an 'external dimension'.[164] Allowing third country financial intermediaries to offer their financial services within the EEA leads to an internal market for financial services with an 'external dimension' leading to greater supply, competition and innovation.[165] The problem, however, is that TC firms are not subject to the EUs unique supranational rulemaking and enforcement system.[166] The deepening of the internal market in financial services has been characterized by detailed harmonization, centralized rulemaking and implementation at the European level under the Lamfalussy process.[167] In addition, the European Commission has the ability to monitor implementation and force Member States to comply with EEA regulatory standards through enforcement proceedings before the CJEU.[168] This is supplemented by a strong supranational ESFS system.[169] The enforcement of TC relationships, however, depends upon bilateral treaties. The problems related to the Icesave case have highlighted the potential problems that such relationships could face.[170] This suggests that EEA market access for TC financial intermediaries is only a viable option for intermediaries established in third countries with comparable levels of economic development and financial regulation.[171] Again, the concept of 'risk asymmetry' determines the EEA's approach towards the provision of cross-border financial services from and to third countries.

3.3.1.2 Risk Asymmetry, TC Financial Centres and the Concept of 'Production' and 'Distribution' States

The degree of 'risk asymmetry' is important for determining the EEA's regulatory approach towards the provision of cross-border financial services from and to a specific third country. 'Risk asymmetry' does not depend upon the size of States. Instead, it depends upon the supply and demand of certain types of financial products/services within a given State.[172]

---

the European Parliament, the Council, the European Economic and Social Committee and the Committee of the Regions, A single market for the 21st century Europe (COM(2007) 724 final) (SEC(2007) 1517) (SEC (2007) 1518) (SEC(2007) 1520) (SEC(2007) 1521), http://ec.europa.eu/citizens_agenda/docs/sec_2007_1519_en.pdf.

164 Zetzsche 2014, *supra* note 4, 60.

165 *Ibid.*, 60, 61.

166 Verdier, *supra* note 42.

167 Lannoo & Levin, *supra* note 87.

168 *See* Art. 258 TFEU.

169 H. Siekmann, H., *Das neue Europäische Finanzaufsichtssystem – Working Paper Series 40* (Institute for Monetary and Financial Stability 2010).

170 E.G. Gunnarsson, *supra* note 34; Benediktsdottir *et al*, *supra* note 34; Li, *supra* note 34, 110-115; Guðmundsson, *supra* note 34.

171 E.F. Greene, *Beyond Borders: Time To Tear Down the Barriers to Global Investing*, 48 HARV. INT'L L.J. 92 (2007).

172 Zetzsche 2014, *supra* note 4, 67 et seq.

For example, Singapore is a financial centre with a large fund industry. Nevertheless, the degree of 'risk asymmetry' is small as Singapore has many domestic professional investors with a large demand for investment funds. Singapore is, thus, a 'product' and a 'distribution' State for fund services. The degree in which the supply exceeds domestic demand determines the degree of 'risk (a)symmetry'. A TC State in which the supply exceeds domestic demand can be characterized as a 'production State'.[173] Such a TC State, de facto, has a higher 'export' than 'import' of specific financial services/products. TC States in which the demand exceeds supply can be labelled as a 'distribution State'. Due to the 'risk symmetry' in Singapore for fund services, Singapore has an incentive to protect its investors and subjects investment funds to a high degree of financial regulation and supervision. The degree of 'risk symmetry' of specific financial products/services in a third country determines the requirements EEA law requiresto be fulfilled upon granting access to the internal market. The concept of 'equivalency' functions as a substitute for 'risk asymmetry'.

3.3.1.3   Equivalency as a Substitute for Risk Asymmetry
The EEA internal market for financial services is built upon the principle of 'mutual recognition' that is facilitated by a harmonized substantive legal framework and a high degree of coordination in financial supervision. The TFEU as a multilateral treaty provides a strong basis for the highly centralized rulemaking and coordinated supervision at the EEA level in the financial services domain.[174] By the absence of such a multilateral framework in relation to third countries, the EEA relies upon various approaches in overcoming 'risk asymmetry' in relation to third countries. These approaches include 'national treatment', unilateral and multilateral (mutual) recognition and 'passporting'.[175] The latter two approaches are based upon the concept of 'equivalency'.

3.3.1.3.1   *The EEA's Third Country Rules Approaches*
EEA law has three approaches in regulating the 'external dimension' of the international market: national treatment, unilateral/multilateral (mutual) recognition and 'passporting'.

All EEA sectoral financial laws, such as CRD IV, the AIFMD, UCITSD V and Solvency II,[176] allow TC firms to enter the internal market based upon the concept of 'national treatment'. This approach essentially implies that TC firms are treated in the same manner as EEA entities in terms of market access and ongoing regulatory require-

---

173 *See* for 'production States' and 'distribution States: Zetzsche 2014, *supra* note 4, 60 and 61.
174 *Cf.* P. Schammo, *Equivalence-Based Regulation and EU/EEA Prospectus Law – The Shadow Regime* 493 (D. Prentice & A. Reisberg eds., Oxford University Press 2011).
175 IOSCO, *supra* note 73, 31 et seq.
176 Directive 2009/138/EC of the European Parliament and of the Council of 25 November 2009 on the taking-up and pursuit of the business of Insurance and Reinsurance (Solvency II) (recast), OJ L 335, 17 December 2009, 1 ('Solvency II').

ments.[177] The national treatment approach under the mentioned directives, essentially, allows subsidiaries of TC firms to be established and authorized under the same conditions as EEA entities. These subsidiaries are EEA legal entities and, thus, fall within the EEA centralized rulemaking and supervision framework.

Second, some types of TC firms are allowed EEA market access on the basis of unilateral/multilateral (mutual) recognition.[178] 'Recognition' is a regulatory tool on the basis of which a regulatory and supervisory regime of a specific third country is being assessed by the European Commission and/or another EU institution as being 'equivalent' and, thereupon, EEA market access is granted to the TC firm.[179] Depending upon the condition of 'reciprocity', i.e. the condition of 'mutual market access', the approach is to be labelled unilateral or mutual recognition.[180] An example of unilateral recognition at the EEA level is the TC regime for AIF depositaries.[181]

The mutual recognition approach was clearly observed in the First Banking Directive and the ISD.[182] 'Reciprocity' as a requirement of market access is, however, less applied nowadays.[183]

Finally, 'passporting' is a regulatory tool on which TC financial intermediaries may offer financial services/products throughout the EEA upon the authorization in a single Member State upon complying with a set of rules laid down in EEA law.[184] Examples of 'passporting', include the passport for TC-AIFMs under the AIFMD and TC investment firms under MiFID II.[185]

Under the approaches 'recognition' and 'passporting', TC firms may provide financial services within the EEA without the need of establishing legal entities (subsidiary) in the EEA. The cross-border provision of services and the establishment of branches is based upon the concept of 'equivalency'.

3.3.1.3.2   'Equivalency' and Risk Asymmetry

The concept of 'equivalency' is used in EEA as a substitute for 'risk asymmetry' to ward off any potential externalities of the 'external dimension' of the internal market.

'Equivalency' can be seen as a concept in which effectively conditions related to granting market access in the internal market depend upon the existence of an equivalent regulatory

---

177 See A. Mattoo, *National Treatment in the GATS. Corner-Stone or Pandora's Box?*, 31 Journal of World Trade 107 (1997).

178 IOSCO, *supra* note 73, 13 et seq.

179 *Ibid.*, 13.

180 L. Bruni, M. Gilli & V. Pelligra, *Reciprocity: theory and facts*, 55 International Review of Economics 1-11 (2008).

181 See Chapter 4. Section 4.5.

182 See *supra* 3.2.2.

183 See *supra* 3.2.1.

184 IOSCO, *supra* note 73, 31 et seq.

185 See *infra* 3.3.3.2.

and supervisory system in the home state.[186] Based upon this concept laid down in a variety of ways in sectoral financial EEA law, the EEA recognizes the adequacy of the regulation or supervision of an activity or financial intermediary as a substitute for its own.[187] The concept of equivalency, thus, reduces the risk resulting from risk asymmetries, i.e. the risk that regulatory failures originating in the home state will affect the investors in the internal market. Equivalency has, at least, three benefits.[188] First, it bypasses time-consuming harmonization efforts at the international level. Although an equivalency assessment procedure consumes time, it is easier than agreeing and implementing standards at the international level. Second, it fosters regulatory competition, innovation and allows for flexibility. Finally, market access granted upon a set of minimum standards under an equivalency assessment ensures that TC financial intermediaries in their home states will lobby for laxer financial regulation as this would lead to a withdrawal of market access in the EEA.

The EEA's third country rules approaches and the equivalency concept in overcoming 'risk asymmetry' have to abide by the rules related to the external dimension of the four freedoms and the obligations arising out of GATS in regulating:
–   EEA financial intermediaries with an external dimension;
–   TC financial intermediaries within the EEA; and
–   EEA financial intermediaries within third countries.

The equivalency approach in EEA law, however, appears in a variety of ways. These will now be subsequently discussed.

3.3.2   EEA Financial Intermediaries with an External Dimension

TC financial intermediaries, usually, enter the internal market by either establishing an EEA subsidiary or acquiring 'qualifying holdings'[189] and 'close links'[190] in EEA financial intermediaries.[191] EEA subsidiaries may then be authorized under the respective EEA sectoral legislative acts,[192] whereas EEA financial intermediaries in which a 'qualifying

---

186 Verdier, *supra* note 42.
187 IOSCO, *supra* note 73, 13 et seq.
188 Verdier, *supra* note 42.
189 'Qualifying holding' under various sectoral EEA legislative acts means a direct or indirect holding in an investment firm which represents 10 % or more of the capital or of the voting rights or a holding which makes it possible to exercise a significant influence over the management of the EEA financial intermediary in which that holding subsists; *See* for precise definitions: Art. 4(2) n. 12 MiFID II; Art. 4(1)(ah) AIFMD; *See* for a less detailed definition: Art. 2(1)(i) UCITSD V; Art. 13 n. 21 Solvency II; Art. 4 n. 36 CRR.
190 'Close links' under various sectoral EEA legislative acts means a situation in which two or more natural or legal persons are linked by participation in the form of ownership, direct or by way of control, of 20 % or more of the voting rights or capital of an undertaking; *See* Art. 2(1)(i), (4) UCITSD V; Art. 4(1)(e) AIFMD; Art. 4 n. 38 CRR; Art. 4(2) n. 26 MiFID II.
191 Zetzsche 2014, *supra* note 4, 81 et seq.
192 For example: the AIFMD, UCITSD V, MiFID II, CRD II or Solvency II.

holding' or 'close link' is acquired may have already done so. EEA law preserves the internal market by demanding compliance with EEA 'qualifying holding' and delegation requirements. EEA law also requires groups and conglomerates to comply with the EEA requirements related to consolidated supervision and conglomerates.

3.3.2.1 'Qualifying Holding' and 'Close Links' Requirements for Non-EEA Shareholders

Upon the authorization of EEA financial intermediaries, a common requirement in sectoral EEA financial legislation is the duty to inform the relevant Competent Authority of the identities of the shareholders or members that have 'qualifying holdings' and the amounts of those holdings.[193] Competent Authorities are required to refuse authorization of an EEA financial intermediary if, taking into account the need to ensure the sound and prudent management of an investment firm, they are not satisfied as to the suitability of the shareholders or members that have qualifying holdings.[194]

This duty also applies where 'close links'[195] exist between an EEA financial intermediary applying for authorization and other natural or legal persons.[196] 'Close links' include those natural or legal persons that are not direct shareholders of the EEA financial intermediary. Authorization to an EEA financial intermediary shall only be granted if those 'close links' do not prevent the effective exercise of the supervisory functions of the Competent Authority.[197] Competent Authorities shall also be notified of changes related to 'qualifying holdings'.[198]

3.3.2.2 Delegation

TC firms often establish a subsidiary within one of the EEA Member States in order to have EEA market access. TC firms, however, have their main resources in the third country in which they are established and authorized in. For this reason, TC firms often establish a subsidiary within the EEA to use an EEA European passport within a particular sector, whereas business activities are being delegated under sectoral delegation arrangements by the EEA subsidiary to the TC firm. Upon delegation of all critical or

---

193 *See* Art. 4(2) n. 12 MiFID II; Art. 4(1)(ah) AIFMD; *See* for a less detailed definition: Art. 2(1)(i) UCITSD V; Art. 13 n. 21 Solvency II; Art. 4 n. 36 CRR.
194 Art. 10(1) MiFID II; Art. 8(1)(d) AIFMD; Art. 14(1) CRD IV; Art. 24(1) Solvency II; Art. 8(1) UCITSD V.
195 Art. 7(2) UCITSD V (UCITS ManCos), Art. 29(1)(c) a.E. UCITSD V (UCITS Investment Companies); Art. 10(1) sub-para.3 MiFID II; Art. 8(3)(a) AIFMD; Art. 14(3) sub-para. 1 CRD IV; Art. 19(1) Solvency II.
196 *See* Art. 2(1)(i), (4) UCITSD V; Art. 4(1)(e) AIFMD; Art. 4 n. 38 CRR; Art. 4(2) n. 26 MiFID II.
197 Art. 10(1) sub-para. 3 MiFID II; Art. 7(2) UCITSD V (UCITS ManCos), Art. 29(1)(c) UCITSD V (Investment Companies); Art. 8(3)(a) AIFMD; Art. 14 (3) sub-para. 1 CRD IV; Art. 19(1) Solvency II.
198 Art. 14(3) CRD IV; Art. 7(2) UCITSD V (UCITS ManCo), Arts. 8, 10 AIFMD; Art. 19(3) Solvency II, Art. 11(1), (3) MiFID II.

important operational functions[199] by the EEA subsidiary to the TC firm, the relevant Competent Authority may under all EEA sectoral financial laws revoke the authorization of the EEA subsidiary.[200] The effect of this is, however, small as it 'punishes' the EEA subsidiary, whereas the TC firm received the majority of the fee income.

Several EEA UCITS ManCos as subsidiaries of Suisse asset managers are being established to enable EEA market access, for example in Liechtenstein.[201] Liechtenstein UCITS ManCos are, typically, responsible for fund administration and, in some cases, distribution, whereas investment and risk management is being delegated to the Suisse asset manager. Although the subsidiary is legally delegating these tasks to the Suisse asset manager, the asset manager is in practice a 'customer' that chooses its UCITS ManCo. The UCITS ManCo does not necessarily have to be a subsidiary, but may also by a 'third party' UCITS ManCo that is specialized in 'white-label funds'.[202] Again, revoking the authorization of the UCITS ManCo only 'punishes' the UCITS ManCo and not the Suisse asset manager as it is the 'client' that benefits.

For this reason, EEA sectoral financial laws require EEA financial intermediaries to comply with delegation/outsourcing requirements on an *ex ante* and ongoing basis to ward off externalities.

3.3.2.2.1   General Principles of EEA Delegation Rules

EEA sectoral financial laws do not prohibit[203] delegation as delegation also fosters efficiency.[204] EEA sectoral financial laws, however, increasingly regulate delegation arrangements.[205]

The main joint principle underlying EEA delegation rules is the 'letterbox company' prohibition.[206] Authorized financial intermediaries may not delegate their important operational function to such an extent that they are a, de facto, 'letterbox company'.[207]

---

199 *See* Art. 31 Commission Delegated Regulation (EU) 2017/565 supplementing Directive 2014/65/EU of the European Parliament and of the Council as regards organisational requirements and operating conditions for investment firms and defined terms for the purposes of that Directive, 25 April 2016 ('MiFID II (Commission) Directive II')).

200 Art. 70 MiFID II.

201 Zetzsche 2014, *supra* note 4, 97 et seq.

202 *See* R. Steyer, *White-Label Funds on Rise for DC Plans*, Pensions & Investments, October 27, 2014, www.pionline.com/article/20141027/PRINT/310279972/white-label-funds-on-rise-for-dc-plans.

203 *See* Recital 43 MiFID II (Commission) Directive II: "a general prohibition on the outsourcing of one or more critical or important functions. Investment firms should be allowed to outsource such functions if the outsourcing arrangements established by the firm comply with certain conditions."

204 P. Laaper, *Uitbesteding in de financiële sector – in het bijzonder van vermogensbeheer door pensioenfondsen* 57-60, 211 (Kluwer 2015).

205 *See, e.g.* the delegation requirements applicable to AIFMs: T. Partsch, *Delegation* (D.A. Zetzsche ed, Kluwer 2015).

206 *See* for a recent statement on 'letterbox companies' in relation to financial services and Brexit: IOSCO, *Opinion – General principles to support supervisory convergence in the context of the United Kingdom withdrawing from the European Union*, ESMA-42-110-433, 31 May 2017.

207 A. Lewis, R. Pretorius & E. Radmore, *Outsourcing in the Financial Services Sector*, 106 C.O.B. 1 (2013).

In this regard, European investment law requires that important functions may not be delegated in such a way that it impairs materially the quality of the internal control of the EEA financial intermediary concerned and the ability of the responsible Competent Authority to monitor the intermediary's compliance with all obligations.[208]

Other common principles of delegation rules to be found in European investment laws are:[209]

- notification (in some cases authorization) of the delegation arrangement to the relevant Competent Authority;[210]
- information on arrangements made for (sub-)delegation to third parties of functions is, when capable of constituting a material change of the conditions for the authorization of an EEA financial intermediary, shared with other relevant Competent Authorities;[211]
- an objective reason for delegation;[212]
- the delegate must dispose of sufficient resources and an appropriate organizational structure to perform the respective tasks. The EEA financial intermediary must be in a position to monitor effectively the delegated activity to give at any time further instructions to the delegate and to withdraw the delegation with immediate effect when this is in the interest of their clients;[213]
- delegates for authorized activities, generally, may only be undertakings that are authorized for carrying out that activity and subject to supervision regardless of whether established within or outside the EEA;[214]
- the delegate cooperates with the Competent Authorities of the EEA financial intermediary in connection with the delegated functions;[215]
- the responsibility and liability of EEA financial intermediaries is not affected upon delegating critical or important operational functions;[216]
- the delegation must not prevent the effectiveness of supervision of the relevant authorized/registered EEA financial intermediary.[217]

---

208 *See, e.g.* Art. 16(5) MiFID II.
209 Zetzsche 2014, *supra* note 4, 98-99.
210 Art. 20(1) sub-para. 1 AIFMD, Art. 81(2) AIFMD (Commission) Regulation; Art. 13(1)(a) UCITSD V; Art. 31(2) MiFID II (Commission) Directive II.
211 Recital 44 MiFID II (Commission) Directive II; Arts. 7(2)(e), 10(1) AIFMD; Art. 5(6) UCITSD V.
212 Art. 20(1) sub-para. 2(a) AIFMD, Art. 76 AIFMD (Commission) Regulation.
213 Art. 20(1) sub-para. 2(b) and (f) AIFMD, Art. 77 AIFMD(Commission) Regulation; Art. 13(1)(f)-(h) UCITSD V; Art. 16 MiFID II, Art. 31(1) MiFID II (Commission) Directive II.
214 Art. 20(1) sub-para. 2(c) AIFMD, Art. 78 AIFMD (Commission) Regulation; Art. 13(1)(c) UCITSD V; Art. 31(2) MiFID II (Commission) Directive II.
215 Art. 79(b) AIFMD (Commission) Regulation; Art. 31(2)(h) MiFID II (Commission) Directive II.
216 Arts. 31(1) MiFID II (Commission) Directive II.
217 Art. 20(1) sub-para. 2(e) AIFMD, Art. 79 AIFMD (Commission) Regulation; Art. 13(1)(b) UCITSD V; Art. 16 MiFID II, Arts. 31(2),(5), 32(1)(a) MiFID II (Commission) Directive II.

Sub-delegation arrangements under EEA sectoral financial laws are subject to the same delegation requirements as 'regular delegation arrangements' irrespective of whether the delegate is established in or outside the EEA.[218] In addition, financial intermediaries are required to inform the relevant Competent Authority about sub-delegations.[219]

Similar regulations applying to delegation arrangements are to be found for, amongst others, insurance undertakings under Solvency II and IORPs under IORPD II.[220]

3.3.2.2.2   'Equivalency' as Common Principle for TC Delegation Rules?
Upon delegation to TC firms, European investment laws stipulate a number of extra requirements to be complied with. For the delegation of portfolio- and risk management under the AIFMD and portfolio management under MiFID II to TC firms, for example, an appropriate cooperation agreement between the Competent Authority of the AIFM/ investment firm and the Supervisory Authority of the delegate is required.[221] Although formally no equivalency is being required for TC firms, the requirement that TC firm delegates under European investment law for authorized activity may only be undertakings that are authorized and subject to supervision[222] for carrying out that activity leads to a 'de facto' equivalency requirement.[223] TC firms are under delegation arrangements required to be subject to equivalent authorization and supervision requirements as EEA financial intermediaries.

3.3.2.3   Consolidated Supervision and Conglomerates
Since the introduction of the European passport, consolidated supervision, on a sectoral and cross-sectoral basis, has gradually emerged. This tendency responds to the accelerating consolidation in the financial industry and the development of (cross-)sectoral links between financial intermediaries in and outside of the EEA.[224] Credit institutions, investment firms and insurance companies increasingly carry on (parts of) their business through subsidiaries and affiliated entities on a sectoral or cross-sectoral basis. The ongoing consolidation in the financial industry resulting from increasing mergers and acquisitions leads to economies of scale and scope. At the same time, however, consolidation also leads to an increase of systematic risks.[225] For this reason, European banking

---

218 *See* for UCITS depositaries: Art. 22a UCITSD V; Art. 17(4) UCITSD V (Commission) Regulation.
219 *Ibid.*
220 Art. 13 n. 28, Art. 41(3) and Art. 49 Solvency II; Art. 31, 32 IORPD II.
221 Art. 113 AIFMD (Commission) Regulation; Art. 32(1)(b) MiFID II (Commission) Directive II.
222 Art. 20(1) sub-para. 2(c) AIFMD, Art. 78 AIFMD (Commission) Regulation; Art. 13(1)(c) UCITSD V; Art. 31(2) MiFID II (Commission) Directive II.
223 Zetzsche 2014, *supra* note 4, 99-100.
224 *See* Recital 2, 3 FiCOD.
225 T.H. Troeger, *Organizational Choices of Banks and the Effective Supervision of Transnational Financial Institutions*, 48 Texas International Law Journal 177 (2012).

and securities laws require credit institutions, investment firms and insurance companies to be both supervised on an individual and consolidated basis.[226]

CRD IV/CRR[227] and Solvency II regulate financial intermediaries on a sectoral basis. They cover solo and consolidated supervision applying on a sectoral basis to groups of credit institutions, investment firms, insurance companies and financial institutions.[228] On top of this, FiCOD[229] regulates groups of regulated entities that operate in more than one financial sector (conglomerates). FiCOD does not replace existing sectoral supervision. Instead, FiCOD applies as supplementary supervision of regulated entities. FiCOD primarily aims at coordinating the supervision of various supervisory authorities of different sectors of the financial industry so that a conglomerate can be prudentially supervised on a group-wide basis.[230]

This section, in particular, reflects the EEA approach towards sectoral group structures and conglomerates in which both EEA and TC financial intermediaries are involved.

3.3.2.3.1   Consolidated Supervision: Sectoral Groups

CRD IV/CRR and Solvency II regulate the consolidated supervision of EEA and TC financial intermediaries on a sectoral basis.

Credit Institutions and Investment Firms

Consolidated supervision under the CRD IV/CRR applies on a sectoral basis to groups of credit institutions, investment firms and financial institutions.[231]

CRD IV/CRR requires consolidated supervision of various requirements, including own funds, valuation and reporting of capital requirements, the monitoring of large exposures, liquidity coverage and the calculation of the leverage ratio at the group level.[232]

---

226 V. Peleckiene, K. Peleckis & G. Duzeviciute, *New Challenges of Supervising Financial Conglomerates*, 5 Intellectual Economics 298-311 (2011).

227 Regulation (EU) No. 575/2013 of the European Parliament and of the Council of 26 June 2013 on prudential requirements for credit institutions and investment firms and amending Regulation (EU) No 648/2012, OJ L 176, 27 June 2013, 1–337 ('CRR').

228 *See* M. Gruson, *Consolidated and Supplementary Supervision of Financial Groups in the European Union*, Der konzern, Teil 1, 65-93, Teil II, 249-265 (2004)

229 Directive 2002/87/EC of the European Parliament and of the Council of 16 December 2002 on the supplementary supervision of credit institutions, insurance undertakings and investment firms in a financial conglomerate and amending Council Directives 73/239/EEC, 79/267/EEC, 92/49/EEC, 92/96/EEC, 93/6/EEC and 93/22/EEC, and Directives 98/78/EC and 2000/12/EC of the European Parliament and of the Council, OJ L 35, 11 February 2003, 1 (FiCOD).

230 *See* Tripartite Group of Bank & Securities and Insurance Regulators, *The Supervision of Financial Conglomerates*, Bank for International Settlements, July 1995, 16.

231 Art. 111 CRD, Art. 11 et seq CRR. *See* M. Gruson, *Consolidated and Supplementary Supervision of Financial Groups in the European Union*, Institute for Law and Finance Johann Wolfgang Goethe- Universität Frankfurt, Working Paper Series No. 19 (2004), 66.

232 Arts. 11(1)-(3) CRR determine that Parts 2, 4, 6 and 7 should be consolidated.

The CRD IV group regimes applies supervision on a consolidated basis[233] to (1) parent credit institutions,[234] (2) parent financial holding companies [235] and (3) parent mixed financial holding companies.[236, 237]

Parent institutions are institutions (credit institutions or investment firms)[238] that have an institution or a financial institution[239] as a subsidiary[240] or hold a participation[241] in either of those institutions.[242] Parent institutions may not be a subsidiary of another institution authorized in the same Member State, or of a (mixed) financial holding company set up in the same Member State.[243]

Parent (mixed) financial holding companies are companies that are not itself a subsidiary of an institution, a financial holding company or mixed financial holding company set up in the same Member State.[244]

Financial holding companies are financial institutions that are not mixed financial holding companies that have subsidiaries that are exclusively or mainly institutions or financial institutions of which at least one of the subsidiaries qualifies as an institution.[245] A financial holding company may be a holding company that has only one credit institution or investment firm as a subsidiary.

On the contrary, mixed financial holding companies are parent undertakings, other than regulated entities, that together with their subsidiaries of which at least one is an EEA regulated entity and other entities constitute a financial conglomerate.[246]

Only credit institutions, investment firms and (mixed) financial holdings companies, can, thus, be the parent of a group that is subject to consolidated supervision.[247] Financial institutions are also part of a group subject to consolidated supervision if they are a

---

233 Art. 4(48) CRR: "Consolidated situation means the situation that results from applying the requirements of this Regulation in accordance with Part One, Title II, Chapter 2 CRR to an institution as if that institution formed, together with one or more other entities, a single institution." *See* Art. 4(47) CRR.
234 Art. 111(1) CRD IV.
235 Art. 111(2) CRD IV.
236 *Ibid.*
237 Art. 111 CRD IV and Art. 11 CRR; M. Gruson, *Supervision of Financial Holding Companies in Europe: The EEA Directive on Supplementary Supervision of Financial Conglomerates*, 36 The International Lawyer 1229-1260 (2002).
238 Art. 3(1)(24) CRD IV; Art. 4(1) n. 28 CRR.
239 A 'financial institution': 'an undertaking other than an institution, the principal activity of which is to acquire holdings or to pursue one or more activities' listed in points 2 to 12 and point 15 of Annex I to CRD IV, including a financial holding company or a mixed financial holding company. *See also* Art. 4(26) CRR).
240 Art. 2(10) FiCOD.
241 Art. 2(11) FiCOD.
242 Art. 4(28) CRR.
243 *Ibid.*
244 *See* for parent financial holding company: Art. 4(30) CRR; *See* for parent mixed financial holding company: Art. 4(32) CRR.
245 Art. 4(32) CRR.
246 Art. 4(21) CRR.
247 *See* Art. 2(15) FiCOD.

subsidiary of either one of those institutions. Consolidated supervision is not required for those institutions if they are merely subsidiaries of companies that are not credit institutions, investment firms or (mixed) financial holdings companies.

CRD IV and the CRR require Competent Authorities of EEA credit institutions and investment firms that are subsidiaries of TC parent undertakings[248] to verify whether the consolidated supervision carried out by the TC home state of that undertaking is equivalent to the standards and requirements set out in CRD IV and the CRR.[249] In the absence of equivalency, Member States may apply CRD IV and the CRR by analogy to the European credit institutions and investment firms involved.[250] Alternatively, the Competent Authorities responsible may apply other appropriate supervisory techniques to achieve the objectives of supervision on a consolidated basis of institutions.[251] The Competent Authority responsible for consolidated supervision must, however, after consulting other Competent Authorities involved, agree upon the method used.[252] Competent Authorities may, in particular, require the establishment of a (mixed) financial holding company in the EEA and apply the provisions on consolidated supervision to that (mixed) financial holding company.[253]

Article 48 CRD IV also grants the option to the European Commission, after having sent a proposal to the Council, to negotiate reciprocal bilateral agreements with one or more third countries related to consolidated supervision over credit institutions and investment firms that have a TC parent undertaking and TC investment firms and credit institutions that have an EEA parent undertaking.[254] Such agreements, in particular, have to ensure that the relevant EEA and TC Competent Authorities are able to obtain information necessary for the supervision of the CRD IV/CRR group on a consolidated basis.[255]

Insurance Undertakings

The Solvency II group supervision regime is applied at the level of the group of (re-) insurance undertakings that are part of a group.[256]

A group is under Solvency II defined as (non-)EEA (re-)insurance or (mixed-activity) holding company[257] with one or more participating interests in subsidiaries that are

---

248 Third country parent undertaking is required to be 'an institution, a financial holding company or mixed financial holding company'. *See* Art. 127(1) CRD IV; *See also* M. Gruson, *Foreign Banks and the Financial Holding Company* (M. Gruson & R. Reisner eds., Lexis Nexis Matthew Bender 4th ed. 2003).
249 Art. 127 CRD IV refers to Part One, Title II, Chapter 2 CRR.
250 Art. 127(3) CRD IV.
251 *Ibid.*
252 Art. 127(3) sub-para. 2 CRD IV.
253 Art. 127(3) sub-para. 3 CRD IV.
254 Art. 48(1) CRD IV.
255 Art. 48(2) CRD IV.
256 Art. 213(1) Solvency II.
257 *See* for a definition of an 'insurance holding company': Art. 212(1)(f) Solvency II; *See* for the definition of 'mixed-activity insurance holding company': Art. 212(1)(g) Solvency II.

primarily insurance or reinsurance firms.[258] Entities linked by a horizontal structure also qualify as a group.[259] The supervision of insurance and reinsurance undertakings relates to: the group solvency capital requirements,[260] risk concentration and intra-group transactions,[261] the group system of governance,[262] the group's own risk and solvency assessment (ORSA)[263] and disclosure and reporting requirements at the group level.[264] The Solvency II group supervision provisions supplements the supervision of the individual insurance firms in the group. The provisions of Solvency II is being applied to the group as a whole. In some cases, smaller parts of an insurance group may be supervised at the national or European level ('subgroup supervision').[265]

Group supervision applies to parent insurance companies or insurance holding companies.[266]

Insurance holding companies are parent undertakings, other than mixed financial holding companies,[267] that mainly acquire and hold participations in subsidiary undertakings, which are exclusively or mainly (non-)EEA insurance or reinsurance undertakings.[268]

A group headed by a non-insurance undertaking that carries out insurance activities as an 'ancillary' activity are referred to as 'mixed insurance holding companies'. Mixed-activity insurance holding companies are parent undertakings other than (non-)EEA insurance undertakings that have at least one insurance or reinsurance undertaking as a subsidiary although the core activity of the group is not insurance business.[269]

The approach towards the group supervision of insurance groups that are headed by TC parent undertakings depends upon an equivalency test.[270] Equivalency assessments

---

258 Referred to in the definition of 'group' under Art. 212 (c)(i) Solvency II as 'participating undertaking'. *See* a definition of 'participating undertaking' under Art. 212(1)(a) Solvency II.

259 Art. 212(c)(ii) Solvency II.

260 Art. 218-243 Solvency II.

261 Art. 244-245 Solvency II.

262 Art. 246 Solvency II.

263 Art. 45 Solvency II; *See also* EIOPA, *Final Report on Public Consultation No. 14/017 on Guidelines on own risk and solvency assessment*, 28 January 2015, EIOPA-BoS-14/259.

264 Art. 256 Solvency II; S.A. Lumpkin, *Risks in Financial Group Structures*, 2 OECD Journal: Financial Market Trends 105-136 (2010).

265 *See* for the provisions on the ultimate parent at EEA level: Art. 215 Solvency II. *See* for the ultimate parent undertaking at the national level: Art. 216 Solvency II.

266 Art. 213(1) and (2) Solvency II.

267 *See* Art. 2(15) FiCOD: "mixed financial holding company shall mean a parent undertaking, other than a regulated entity, which together with its subsidiaries, at least one of which is a regulated entity which has its head office in in the Union, and other entities, constitutes a financial conglomerate."

268 *See* Art. 212(1)(f) Solvency II.

269 *See* Art. 212(1)(g) Solvency II.

270 *See* Art. 260 Solvency II; *See* Title III Third Country Equivalence and Final Provisions, Commission Delegated Regulation (EEA) 2015/35 of 10 October 2014 supplementing Directive 2009/138/EC of the European Parliament and of the Council on the taking-up and pursuit of the business of Insurance and Reinsurance (Solvency II) Text with EEA relevance (hereafter: Solvency II Commission Delegated Regulation).

are undertaken by the European Commission and binding on all EEA Member States.[271] Group supervision may be (fully) left to the Competent Authority of the TC parent undertaking provided that an equivalent level of policyholder protection is in place and that there are strong mutual cooperation arrangements concluded between EEA insurance and TC Competent Authorities.[272]

By absence of equivalency, the Solvency II provisions may be applied to EEA (sub) groups or other methods may be applied that would ensure appropriate supervision of the group.[273]

3.3.2.3.2 Consolidated Supervision (FiCOD): Financial Conglomerates

FiCOD applies to EEA regulated entities, in addition to their sectoral supervision for solo firms or groups, provided that these EEA entities belong to a financial conglomerate.[274] Under Article 1 FiCOD, EEA regulated entities are defined as credit institutions, investment firms and insurance companies that have obtained an authorization under CRD IV, Solvency II or MiFID II.[275]

Subject to FiCOD is every regulated entity:[276]

– being at the head of a financial conglomerate;
– whose parent undertaking is an EEA mixed financial holding company;[277] and
– linked with another financial sector entity by a horizontal group relationship.[278]

EEA regulated entities that do fall outside this scope may be subject to the FiCOD TC regime if its parent undertaking is either a TC regulated entity or TC mixed financial holding company for which no equivalency decision has been taken in accordance with Article 18 FiCOD.[279]

---

271 See for specific country assessments the EC Delegated Decisions of 5 June 2015 on Australia, Bermuda, Brazil, Canada, Mexico, Switzerland and the USA: https://eiopa.EEAropa.EEA/external-relations/equivalence/overview-of-equivalence-decisions; See also J. Vinuales, *The International Regulation of Financial Conglomerates: A Case-Study of Equivalence as an Approach to Financial Integration*, 37 California Western International Law Journal 1-61 (2006); H. Holopainen, *Integration of financial supervision*, Bank of Finland Research Discussion Papers 12 (2007).
272 Arts. 261, 264 Solvency II.
273 Art. 262 and 263 Solvency II.
274 Joint Forum, *Principles for the Supervision of Financial Conglomerates*, Bank for International Settlements, September 2012.
275 Art. 1 FiCOD.
276 Art. 5(2) FiCOD.
277 Art. 5(2)(b) FiCOD.
278 Art. 5(2)(c) FiCOD; See also Art. 12(1) Seventh Council Directive 83/349/EEC of 13 June 1983 based on the Art. 54(3)(g) of the Treaty on consolidated accounts.
279 Art. 5(3) FiCOD.

Financial Conglomerate

For the scope of application of FiCOD, it is required that EEA regulated entities belong to a 'financial conglomerate'. The term financial conglomerate is pivotal in determining the personal scope of application of FiCOD. The term is being defined by FiCOD on the basis of the following criteria that apply on a cumulative basis:[280]

- the financial conglomerate must qualify as a group or subgroup;[281]
- the (sub)group must include an EEA regulated entity;[282]
- if the (sub)group is headed by an EEA regulated entity, that entity must at least be linked
  - with one entity in the financial sector;[283] or
  - have that entity as a subsidiary or as a participation.
  - non-EEA regulated entities at the head of the group must be operating mostly in the financial sector.[284]
- at least one of the entities in the group must be within the insurance sector and at least one within the banking or investment services sector;[285]
- the group must have significant cross-sectoral activities in both the banking, investment services and insurance sector.[286]

FiCOD distinguishes between groups that are headed by an EEA regulated entity and groups that are headed by TC regulated or a non-regulated entities.[287] Financial conglomerates that are headed by a non-regulated entity are mixed financial holding companies. Financial conglomerates may, thus, be headed by EEA regulated entities, non-EEA regulated entities and mixed financial holding companies. To all three entities that may be head of a financial conglomerate, the general criteria of the involvement of at least one EEA regulated entity and significant cross-sectoral activities must be fulfilled. Depending upon whether an EEA regulated or TC entity is the head of a group, specific criteria apply to those groups in order to meet the definition of a financial conglomerate. Before those criteria will be discussed in detail, first an inquiry will be made under what conditions an EEA regulated entity is part of a group.

A group is defined as a group of undertakings that consists of a parent–subsidiary relationship,[288] a relationship based upon participation[289] or a horizontal structure.[290]

---

280 Art. 2(14) FiCOD.
281 Art. 2(14) (a) FiCOD.
282 Art. 2(14) FiCOD.
283 Art. 12(1) Seventh Council Directive 83/349/EEC of 13 June 1983 based on the Art. 54 (3) (g) of the Treaty on consolidated accounts.
284 Art. 2 (14)(b)(i) FiCOD.
285 Art. 2(14) (a)(ii) and (b)(ii) FiCOD.
286 Art. 2(14)(a)(iii) and (b)(iii) FiCOD.
287 *See* V. De Vuyst, *Internal Governance bij financiële conglomeraten* (Intersentia 2010).
288 Art. 2(9) FiCOD.
289 *Ibid.*
290 *See* Art. 2(12) FiCOD; M. Gruson, *Supervision of Financial Conglomerates in the European Union*, 198 Journal of International Banking Law and Regulation 363-381, 364 (2004).

The parent–subsidiary relationship covered is being defined by the definition 'parent undertaking'. The definition in FiCOD includes both the definition of the term, according to Article 1 Directive 83/349/EEC, and every undertaking that, in the Competent Authorities' opinion, exercises a dominant influence on another undertaking.[291] Subsidiaries are an undertaking[292] and any undertaking, subject, in the Competent authorities' opinion, to the parent undertaking's dominant influence.[293] Participations include 'participations'[294] or the direct or indirect ownership of more of the voting rights or capital of an undertaking.[295] Non-equity relationships may also be covered if they are managed on a unified basis pursuant to a contract or charter provision or if the administration management or supervisory bodies of both undertakings consist of most of the same persons.[296]

To qualify as a financial conglomerate, FiCOD requires groups to include at least one EEA regulated entity irrespective of the parent–subsidiary relationship within the group. For that purpose, EEA regulated entities are defined as credit institutions, insurance undertakings and investment firms.[297] AIFMs[298] and asset management companies[299] are considered as 'regulated entities' provided that a group already qualified as a financial conglomerate[300] and that AIFMs or asset management companies are part of that group.[301]

All other categories of financial intermediaries than credit institutions, insurance undertakings and investment firms do not qualify as 'EEA regulated entity' even though they might be authorized at the European or the national level. The activities of those entities are only taken into account at the level of the parent undertaking if a group qualifies as a financial conglomerate. A group solely consisting of these types of entities, thus, does not qualify as a financial conglomerate.

The group must, to qualify as a financial conglomerate, have significant cross-sectoral activities in both the banking, investment services and insurance sector.[302] Irrespective of how a group is structured, at least one of its entities must be within the insurance sector and at least one within the banking or investment services sector.[303] FiCOD does not

---

291 Art. 2(11) FiCOD.
292 Art. 1 Seventh Council Directive 83/349/EEC of 13 June 1983 based on the Art. 54 (3) (g) of the Treaty on consolidated accounts.
293 Art. 2(9) FiCOD.
294 Art. 17 Fourth Council Directive 78/660/EEC of 25 July 1978 on the annual accounts of certain types of companies.
295 Art. 2(11) FiCOD.
296 Art. 12(1) Seventh Council Directive 83/349/EEC of 13 June 1983 based on the Art. 54 (3) (g) of the Treaty on consolidated accounts.
297 Art. 2(14)(a)(ii) FiCOD.
298 *See* for a definition of an 'alternative investment fund manager': Art. 2(5a) FiCOD.
299 *See* for a definition of an 'asset management company': Art. 2(5) FiCOD.
300 Art. 4 FiCOD.
301 *See* Art. 30 and 30a FiCOD.
302 Art. 2(14)(a)(iii) and (b)(iii) FiCOD.
303 Art. 2(14)(a)(ii) and (b)(ii) FiCOD.

require more than one of those entities to be authorized under MiFID II, Solvency II or CRD IV. In practice, however, almost all activities in these domains are fully harmonized under European law.[304] Article 2(14) FiCOD requires at least one regulated entity to have its legal seat within the EEA. All other (regulated) entities are, however, not required to be EEA entities.[305] Financial groups solely consisting of insurance undertakings do not satisfy the criterion 'cross-sectoral activities'.[306] They are subject to the sectoral group regulation under Solvency II. Groups that solely consist of investment firms and credit institutions do not qualify as 'financial conglomerate' and are, for that reason, solely within the scope of CRD IV.

The consolidated and aggregated activities of the entities in the (sub)group within the insurance sector and of the entity within the banking and investment services sector must also be 'significant'.[307] The assessment required is based upon quantitative criteria.

The activities of entities in both sectors[308] of financial conglomerates headed by an EEA, non-EEA regulated entity or mixed financial holding companies should represent at least 10% of the average ratio balance sheets and solvency ratio requirements of the group[309] or the smallest sector in the group must exceed 6 billion Euro.[310] Groups not headed by EEA regulated entities, on top of that, only qualify as a financial conglomerate if the group activities mainly occur in the financial sector.[311] Specific criteria apply to groups headed by EEA regulated or non-EEA regulated entities.

Groups or sub-groups headed by an EEA regulated entity must at least be linked with one entity in the financial sector[312] or have that entity as a subsidiary[313] or as a participation.[314] Irrespective of what category applies, the EEA regulated entity must be linked to another entity 'of the financial sector'.[315] The term 'financial sector' is defined by Article 2(8) FiCOD and includes regulated and non-regulated entities in the banking, insurance and investment services sector, including:

- credit institutions, financial institutions or ancillary services undertaking;[316]

---

304 *See* Art. 2(14) FiCOD. Art. 2(14)(a)(ii) and (b)(ii) FiCOD refer to 'entities' and not 'regulated entities'. Gortsos comes to the conclusion that on the basis of this the second entity may be unregulated. *See* Ch.V. Gortsos, *The Supervision of Financial Conglomerates under European Financial Law (Directive 2002/87/EC)*, 25 Banking & Financial Law Review 295-313 (2010).
305 Art. 2(14)(a)(ii) and (b)(ii) FiCOD do not refer to Art. 1 FiCOD.
306 Gruson, *supra* note 231.
307 Art. 2(14)(a)(iii) and (b)(iii) FiCOD.
308 The insurance sector, at the one hand, and the activities of the entities in the banking and investment services sector, at the other hand.
309 Art. 3(2) FiCOD.
310 Art. 3(3) and (3a) FiCOD.
311 Art. 2(8) FiCOD.
312 *Ibid.*
313 Art. 2(10) FiCOD.
314 Art. 2(11) FiCOD.
315 Defined in Art. 2(8)(a) FiCOD.
316 Art. 2(8)(a) FiCOD.

- insurance undertakings, reinsurance undertakings and insurance holding companies;[317] and
- investment firms.[318]

For that purpose, it is not important whether that entity in the financial sector is regulated, non-regulated[319] or established within the EEA.[320]

Non-EEA regulated entities at the head of the group must be operating mostly in the financial sector.[321] The balance sheet total of the (non-)regulated financial sector entities in the group should exceed 40% of the balance sheet total of the group.[322]

Supplementary Supervision

Supplementary supervision is exercised on a 'solo plus' basis. FiCOD supplements the sectoral solo supervision of individual entities by a quantitative assessment of the group and a quantitative assessment of the capital adequacy of the conglomerate.[323] FiCOD covers capital adequacy,[324] risk concentration,[325] intra-group transactions[326] and internal control mechanisms and risk management processes.[327]

Article 6 and Annex I FiCOD covers the capital adequacy of a financial conglomerate. The objective is to control risks arising from eliminating 'double gearing', i.e. intra-group creation of own funds and excessive leverage.[328] For that purpose, Annex I FiCOD sets forth different methods of the calculation of the solvency position for conglomerates and adequate capital policies at the level of the conglomerate.

Intra-group transactions may, in addition, lead to arbitrage where capital or other legal requirements are being evaded or risk concentrations where losses borne by one entity within a conglomerate may cause the insolvency of other regulated entities or the conglomerate as a whole.[329]

To prevent these risks that might arise from intra-group transactions and risk concentration, FiCOD requires adequate risk management and internal control mechanisms

---

317 Art. 2(8)(b) FiCOD; *See also* Arts. 13(1),(2),(4),(5) and 212(1)(f) Solvency II.
318 Art. 2(8)(c) FiCOD.
319 *See*, for instance, Art. 2(8)(a) FiCOD that refers to 'a financial institution or an ancillary services undertaking within the meaning of Directive 2006/48/EC (now replaced by CRD IV)'.
320 Gortsos, *supra* note 304.
321 Art. 2 (14) (b)(i) FiCOD.
322 Art. 3(1) FiCOD.
323 M. Gruson, *supra* note 290.
324 Art. 6 and Annex 1 FiCOD.
325 Art. 7 and Annex II FiCOD.
326 Art. 8 and Annex II FiCOD.
327 Art. 9 FiCOD.
328 European Commission, *Proposal for a Directive of the European Parliament and of the Council Amending Directives 98/78/EC, 2002/87/EC and 2006/48/EC as Regards the Supplementary Supervision of Financial Entities in a Financial Conglomerate*, 16 August 2010, COM(2010) 433 final, 2010/0232 (COD), 2.
329 Art. 2(19) FICOD.

– encompassing reporting and accounting procedures – at the level of the financial conglomerate.[330] On top of that, regulated entities or mixed financial holding companies are required on, at least, an annual basis to report significant risk concentration and intragroup transactions of regulated entities at the level of the conglomerate.[331]

These shall be reviewed by the coordinator Competent Authority that may act after having consulted other relevant Competent Authorities.[332] FiCOD requires the exchange of information of the entities within a financial conglomerate and the exchange of information and cooperation between all Competent Authorities supervising the regulated entities within a financial conglomerate.[333] For that purpose, FiCOD requires a coordinator. This coordinator is a Competent Authority that has been appointed among the authorities involved to coordinate the supervision conducted over the regulated entities within the conglomerate.[334] The coordinator has as its tasks, amongst others, to coordinate the gathering and disseminate relevant information concerning the conglomerate,[335] to assess the financial situation,[336] the compliance with the rules on capital adequacy[337] and of risk concentration and intra-group transactions[338] and to plan and coordinate supervisory activities conducted.[339]

The coordinator ensures the close cooperation between the authorities supervising the regulated entities within a financial conglomerate.[340]

Equivalent Supplemented Supervision for TC Parent Undertakings
FiCOD does not directly target groups headed by parent undertakings of conglomerates outside the EEA.[341] FiCOD applies, however, to TC parent undertakings that are not subject to equivalent standards and requirements as set out in FiCOD.[342] The equivalency assessment is carried out by the 'coordinator'.[343] Successful equivalency assessments result in conglomerates entirely being supervised by the home Competent Authority of the TC parent undertaking.[344]

---

330 Art. 9(1)-(3), (5) FiCOD.
331 Art. 7(2) sub-para. 2, Art. 8(2), Annex II FiCOD.
332 Art. 7(2), Art. 8(2) sub-para. 2 FiCOD.
333 Recital 13, Art. 12 FiCOD.
334 Art. 10(1) FiCOD.
335 Art. 11(1)(a) FiCOD.
336 Art. 11(1)(b) FiCOD.
337 Art. 11(1)(c) FiCOD.
338 Art. 11(1)(c) FiCOD.
339 Art. 11(1)(c) FiCOD.
340 Art. 12 FiCOD.
341 Art. 18 FiCOD.
342 Art. 18(2) FiCOD.
343 No coordinator needs to be appointed if FiCOD is not applicable. The Competent Authority that would be the coordinator if the FiCOD would be applicable to the conglomerate will carry out the equivalency assessment. This is being referred to in the literature as the 'hypothetical coordinator'.
344 Art. 18(3) FiCOD.

In the absence of equivalency, Member States may apply, like under CRD IV and the CRR, by analogy FiCOD to the EEA regulated entities involved.[345] Alternatively, the Competent Authorities responsible may apply other appropriate supervisory techniques to achieve the objectives of the supervision on a consolidated basis.[346]

The European Commission may submit proposals to the EEA Council for the negotiation of reciprocal bilateral agreements concerning the application of FiCOD of financial conglomerates that have regulated entities within the EEA that have their parent undertaking of outside the EEA.[347]

3.3.2.3.3   Conclusion

Since the introduction of the European passport, consolidated supervision, on a sectoral and cross-sectoral basis, has gradually emerged. This tendency responds to the accelerating consolidation in the financial industry and the development of (cross-)sectoral links between financial intermediaries in and outside of the EEA.[348] CRD IV/CRR and Solvency II regulate financial intermediaries on a sectoral basis. They cover solo and consolidated supervision applying on a sectoral basis to groups of credit institutions, investment firms, insurance companies and financial institutions.[349] On top of this, FiCOD regulates groups of regulated entities that operate in more than one financial sector (conglomerates).

Provided that requirements related to equivalence and exchange of information are complied with, the EEA regime on consolidation and conglomerates may allow the home state of a TC financial intermediary heading a group/conglomerate to perform 'consolidated supervision'.[350] The EEA consolidation and conglomerate regime (partly) substitutes the relevance of EEA sectoral delegation regimes.[351]

3.3.3   Financial Intermediaries within the EEA

Solely allowing EEA firms to be active within the internal market would be contrary to the GATS. For this reason, EEA law intends to offer a legal framework for TC firms that want to provide services within the EEA to avoid externalities that would put investor protection, the market integrity or the financial system in the EEA as a whole at risk. To this end, the EEA principle of 'mutual recognition' in the form of the equivalency of TC regulatory and supervisory frameworks is required by sectoral EEA secondary legislation to be in place in such a way that TC firms have access to the EEA. The TC regimes

---

345 Art. 56a sub-para. 4 FiCOD. *See also* Art. 127(3) CRD IV.
346 Art. 56a sub-para. 5 FiCOD.
347 Art. 10a FiCOD.
348 *See* Recital 2, 3 FiCOD.
349 *See* Gruson, *supra* note 228.
350 *See supra* 3.3.2.3.
351 Zetzsche 2014, *supra* note 4, 152.

regulating this vary from sector to sector as some sectors, such as banking and insurance, are harmonized to a larger extent at the international level than other sectors (e.g. asset management). For this reason, some EEA secondary laws require TC firms to comply with 'stand-alone authorizations', whereas others grant access to the EEA on the basis of the '(mutual) agreements solution' or even a European passport to TC financial intermediaries. These are now discussed in detail in this section.

3.3.3.1   'Stand-alone' Authorizations

Throughout the most recent European banking and securities laws, Solvency II, the AIFMD, CRD IV and MiFID II have TC regulations in which Member States may, under the minimum conditions set out in these directives, authorize TC firms to be active within their domiciles on the basis of a 'stand-alone' authorization regime.

3.3.3.1.1   Branch: Solvency II

Under Solvency II, TC insurance undertakings willing to carry out direct life and non-life insurance business within the EEA are subject to an authorization duty.[352] For that purpose, Solvency II imposes requirements to the TC insurance company[353] and a branch of the TC company is required to be established within a Member State of the EEA in which authorization is sought.[354]

TC insurance companies are required to:
- be entitled to pursue insurance business under its national law;[355]
- set up branch accounts specific to the business which it pursues there, and keep all records there related to the business transacted;[356]
- designate a general representative approved by the relevant supervisory authorities;[357]
- fulfil various minimum capital and solvency requirements;[358]
- appoint a claims representative in each Member State other than the Member State in which the authorization is sought.[359]

In addition, branches of TC insurance companies must:
- comply with certain Solvency II governance requirements;[360]

---

352 Art. 162(1) Solvency II; Arts. 162 to 171 refer only to direct life and non-life insurance business according to the first subparagraph of Art. 2(1) Solvency II. Reinsurers, therefore, do not fall under this provision but can access the EEA on the basis of Art. 172 et seq. Solvency II.
353 Art. 162(2) Solvency II.
354 Arts. 162(2)(b), 169 Solvency II.
355 Art. 162(2)(a) Solvency II.
356 Art. 162(2)(c) Solvency II.
357 Art. 162(2)(d) Solvency II.
358 Art. 162(2)(e) and (f) Solvency II.
359 Art. 162(2)(g) Solvency II.
360 Art. 162(2)(i) Solvency II. The governance requirements as laid down in chapter IV, Section 2 Solvency II.

- be established in the Member State in the territory of the Member State in which authorization is sought;[361]
- submit a scheme of operations;[362]
- separate non-life and life insurance business.[363]

Solvency II, thus, requires an authorization of a branch of a TC insurance company within the EEA.[364] Solvency II does not require TC insurance companies to comply with an equivalency test as Solvency II is partly applicable to the branch of the TC insurance company.[365]

Several advantages are granted to TC insurance companies that have authorized branches in more than one Member State.[366] The Solvency II capital requirements, for example, may be calculated in relation to the entire business. In addition, deposits are only required to be lodged in one of the Member States in which the TC insurance company has an authorized branch and assets representing the required minimum capital only has to be localized in any one of the Member States in which the TC insurance company pursues its activities.[367]

The application to benefit from the above-mentioned advantages has to be made by the TC insurance companies to the Competent Authorities of all the Member States in which it has an authorized branch.[368] Upon the reception of a positive reply or replies, only one of the Competent Authorities will be responsible to supervise the entire business of all the branches established within the EEA.[369] The advantages are, however, subjected to the veto right of all Competent Authorities of the Member States concerned.[370] If one of the Member States disagrees or requests a withdrawal, the advantages provided shall be withdrawn in all Member States concerned.[371]

The advantages of the authorization procedure for TC insurance companies branches under Article 162 et seq. Solvency II are, however, limited. The administrative hurdles and costs associated by requiring the establishment of a separate branch for each EEA Member State in which a TC insurance company wants to be active, de facto, only enables the big Member States to benefit from the increased supply of (re)insurance services

---

361 Art. 162(2)(b) Solvency II.
362 Art. 162(2)(h) Solvency II. Comply with the requirements as set out in Art. 163 Solvency II.
363 Art. 169 Solvency II.
364 Art. 162(1) Solvency II.
365 Zetzsche 2014, *supra* note 4, 100.
366 Art. 167, 169, 170 Solvency II.
367 Art. 169(1)(a)-(c) Solvency II.
368 Art. 169(2) Solvency II.
369 *Ibid.*
370 Art. 169(3) Solvency II.
371 Art. 169(4) Solvency II.

within the EEA of TC undertakings.[372] The latter poses hurdles to the objective of increasing market efficiency.[373]

For this reason, Solvency II gives European institutions the power to conclude mutual agreements with third countries on a reciprocal basis.[374] TC insurance undertakings may, if they are established in a third country with which an agreement is concluded, access the EEA without the establishment and authorization of branches within the Member States in which they are willing to be active.

The EU may, however, by means of agreements concluded with one or more third countries, agree to apply the Solvency II TC requirements differently. Recently, the EU institutions have increasingly made use of this option.[375]

3.3.3.1.2   National Private Placement Regimes under the AIFMD

The AIFMD provides for a national placement regime under which TC-AIFs marketed by EEA-AIFMs and AIFs marketed by TC-AIFMs are, for a transitional period, permitted to be authorized on a country-by-country basis.[376]

EEA-AIFMs may market TC-AIFs on a country-by-country basis as long as they comply with all AIFMD requirements except the provisions related to the appointment, delegation and liability of depositaries under Article 21 AIFMD.[377]

TC-AIFMs may market (TC-)AIFs on the basis of a national placement regime if they comply with a number of provisions of the AIFMD regarding investor information and reporting obligations to Competent Authorities.[378] The TC-AIFM is subjected to the AIFM regulation of the third country concerned. No equivalency requirement are imposed on the AIFM.

Member States may, however, impose stricter rules on the AIFM in respect of the marketing of units or shares of TC-AIFs within their territory. Not all Member States, for example, grant the 'depositary-lite' option.[379] In addition, to the general requirement of compliance with the AIFMD, AIFMs using the national placement regime must comply with two specific requirements under Articles 36 and 42 AIFMD.

The first of the two requirements is that a cooperation agreement related to information exchange for the purpose of systematic risk oversight must be signed between EEA and TC Competent Authorities.[380] Under Article 36 AIFMD, the cooperation arrangements must be in place between the Competent Authorities of the home Member State of

---

372 Zetzsche 2014, *supra* note 4, 108.
373 *See supra* 3.3.1.1.
374 *See* Art. 171, 175(2) Solvency II.
375 Art. 171 Solvency II.
376 Recital 85 AIFMD.
377 Art. 36(1)(a) AIFMD.
378 Art. 42 AIFMD.
379 *See* D.A. Zetzsche, *Fondsregulierung im Umbruch – ein rechtsvergleichender Rundblick zur Umsetzung der AIFM-Richtlinie*, ZBB 22 (2014). *See* Chapter 4, Section 4.3.1.6.
380 Art. 36(1)(b), Art. 42(1)(b) AIFMD.

the AIFM and the supervisory authorities of the third country where the TC-AIF is established.[381] Article 42 AIFMD requires the cooperation arrangement to be concluded between the Competent Authorities of the Member States where the AIFs are marketed, in so far as applicable, the Competent Authorities of the EEA-AIFs concerned and the Supervisory Authorities of the third country where the TC-AIFM is established, at the one, and, in so far as applicable, the Supervisory Authorities of the third country where the non-EU AIF is established, at the other hand.[382]

The second requirement is that the third country where the TC-AIF or TC-AIFM is established may not be listed as a non-cooperative country and territory by the FATF.[383] AIFMs making use of the national placement regime are, thus, at the one hand, required to fully or partially comply with the AIFMD and, at the other hand, with the two additional requirements regarding the cooperation agreements on information exchange and FATF compliance.

3.3.3.1.3   CRD IV

CRD IV does not contain any harmonized rules for the cross-border provision of services. Member States may on a country-by-country basis authorize branches of TC credit institutions.[384] Member States may, however, not treat the branches of TC credit institutions more favourably than branches of EEA credit institutions.[385] An authorization of a TC credit institution branch is, however, limited to the Member State in which a branch has been authorized.

3.3.3.1.4   The MiFID II Country-by-Country Branch Regime

Under MiFID I, the provision of investment services by TC firms was not harmonized.[386] TC firms seeking to do business in the EEA were subject to national regimes and requirements.[387] Each Member State could, thus, regulate the access in their domicile in its own way, subject to the principles laid down in GATS and under the condition that TC firms could not be given a more favourable treatment than EEA firms.[388]

This resulted in a highly fragmented regime for TC firms willing to do business in the EEA.[389] Moreover, TC firms authorized in accordance with the domestic TC regime of a single Member State could not make use of a European passport, i.e. they could not provide services and the right of establishment in Member States other than the one

---

381 Art. 36(1)(b) AIFMD.
382 Art. 42(1)(b) AIFMD.
383 See D.A. Zetzsche & T.F. Marte, AIFMD versus MiFID II/MIFIR: Similarities and Differences 455, 463 (D.A. Zetzsche ed, Kluwer 2015).
384 Recital 23 CRD IV.
385 Recital 23, Art. 47 CRD IV.
386 See R. Maggi, MiFID II: Marktzugang, Umsetzung, Handlungsoptionen (Zürich/Basel/Genf 2014).
387 Recital 41 MiFIR.
388 See U. Klebeck & J. Eichhorn, Drittstaatenregulierung der MiFID II und MiFIR, 3 RdF 1 (2014).
389 Recital 41 MiFIR.

where they were authorized.[390] TC firms willing to do business in more than one EEA Member State were under MiFID I required to obtain an authorization in every Member State that they would be willing to provide services in. In practice, TC firms could only obtain a European passport by establishing a newly created EEA legal entity (subsidiary) that was authorized under MiFID I.[391]

Under MiFID II/MiFIR, a harmonized legal regime for TC firms willing to provide investment services in the EEA has been introduced that ensures uniform treatment and a comparable level of protection of clients that are receiving services by TC firms.[392] For that purpose, a regime was designed that depends upon MiFID II client categorization. MiFID II TC approach differentiates between retail clients and elective professional investors,[393] on the one hand, and eligible counterparties and per sé professional clients on the other. The former relies on a country-by-country authorization basis, whereas a European TC passport under MiFID II is available for TC investment firms providing services to eligible counterparties and per sé professional clients. The 'country-by-country MiFID II authorization' is discussed here, while the MiFIR European TC passport is discussed in Section 3.3.3.2.2.

The provision of services by TC firms in the EEA to retail clients and elective professional clients in their domiciles under MiFID II still relies to a large degree on national regimes and requirements.[394]

Under MiFID II there is no European passport available for TC firms wishing to provide services to retail and certain professional clients.[395] The only way to obtain a European passport for these type of TC firms is by establishing a legal entity (subsidiary) that obtains an authorization as an EEA investment firm under MiFID II in one of the EEA Member States.[396]

Article 39 MiFID II grants Member States the option to require TC firms intending to provide investment services or perform investment activities with or without any ancillary services to retail clients or to eligible professional clients in its territory to establish a branch in that Member State.

Upon the establishment of a branch within a Member State under Article 39 MiFID II, TC firms do not enjoy passporting rights, i.e. they do not have the freedom to provide

---

390 Recital 31 MiFIR.
391 See T. Jutzi & C. Feuz, *MiFID II, AIFMD und UCITSD: Auswirkungen des EU-Vermögensverwaltungsrechts auf das grenzüberschreitende Geschäft Schweizer Finanzintermediäre*, Jusletter Next, 25. April 2016.
392 Recital 41 MiFIR.
393 See R. Sethe, *Das Drittstaatenregime von MiFIR und MIFID II*, 6 SZW 2014, 615 (2014).
394 Recital 109 MiFID II.
395 European Principal Traders Association, *Special Report Series: Third Country Firms under MiFID II*, 25. Juni 2014, www.futuresindustry.org/downloads/Special%20report%20seven%2025%20June%20-%20Third%20country%20firms%20under%20MiFID%20II.pdf.
396 See for authorization requirements of EEA investment firms under MiFID II: Zetzsche & Marte, *supra* note 383.

services and right of establishment in Member States other than the one in which they have established a branch.[397]

The requirements applicable to branches being established are subject to common harmonized EEA standards under MiFID II in light of the principle that TC firms should not be treated more favourably by Member States than EEA investment firms.[398]

According to Chapter IV MiFID II, various conditions would need to be met for the establishment of a branch. Member States in which a TC firms intends to establish a branch may only grant an authorization to those firms that fulfil (1) conditions for the establishment of a branch and (2) comply with certain MiFID II provisions.[399]

Pursuant to Article 39(2) MiFID II, an authorization for the establishment of branch shall only be granted by Competent Authorities of a Member State if the following conditions are fulfilled:

- the provision of services for which the TC firm requests authorization is subject to authorization and supervision in the TC where it is established, whereby the relevant Competent Authority pays due regard to:
  - FATCA recommendations; and
  - countering financing of terrorism.
- cooperation arrangements, including exchange of information for the purpose of enforcing regulatory compliance, are in place between the Competent Authorities of the Member State in which the branch is established and the Supervisory Authorities of the third country where the TC firm is established;
- sufficient initial capital is at free disposal of the branch;
- one or more persons are appointed and responsible for the management of the branch and compliance with MiFID II;[400]
- the third country where the TC firm is established has signed an agreement with the Member State where the branch is established with the standards laid down in Article 26 OECD Model Tax Convention;
- the TC firm belongs to an investor-compensation scheme authorized or recognized in accordance with Directive 97/9/EC.

Prior to obtaining authorization for the provision of any investment services, TC firms have, in accordance with Article 40 MiFID II, the obligation to provide information to the Competent Authority of the Member State in which they request authorization. They are required, amongst others, to provide the Competent Authority of that Member State with

---

397 Recital 109 MiFID II.
398 *See* for these EEA standards: J-P. Casey & K. Lannoo, *The MiFID Revolution*, ECMI Policy Brief No. 3 (November 2006); J-P. Casey & K. Lannoo, *The MiFID revolution* (Cambridge University Press 2009); J-P. Casey & K. Lannoo, *The MiFID Revolution: A Policy View*, 7 Competition and Regulation in Network Industries 519 (2006).
399 Art. 41 MiFID II.
400 *See* Art. 9(1) MiFID II.

the name of the third country Supervisory Authority by which they are supervised, relevant details of the firm, name of persons responsible for management of branch and information about the initial capital of the firm.[401] In addition to the conditions related to the authorization of the branch, the TC firm needs to comply with certain MiFID II provisions.[402]

In case Member States do not implement the branch requirement, the provision of services to retail clients and elective professional clients will remain to be subject to its national laws. It is unclear as to whether TC firms may provide services to retail clients in which a Member State does not require the establishment of a branch. MiFID II is silent on this point. In any case, however, TC firms may not be treated more favourably by individual Member States than EEA investment firms[403] under MiFID II. The requirements set out for EEA branches should, thus, be seen as minimum requirements applying to individual legal TC regimes of Member States for those Member States that allow TC firms to provide cross-border services within their domicile.[404]

3.3.3.2 European Passports for TC Financial Intermediaries

A recent legal innovation introduced in European investment law is the European passport for TC firms. TC-AIFMs and TC investment firms are the first TC intermediaries that are able to fully benefit from the cross-border provision of financial services throughout the EEA.

3.3.3.2.1 The TC-AIFM Passport Regime under the AIFMD

The third country passport for TC-AIFMs is modelled after the EEA-AIFM management and marketing passport.[405]

EEA-AIFMs may make use of the AIFMD management and marketing passport by means of cross-border activity. EEA-AIFMs may either rely on the freedom to provide services or the freedom of establishment (establishing a branch office in the host Member State).[406] The management passport entitles an AIFM to manage AIFs in a host Member State, whereas under the AIFMD marketing passport, an EEA-AIFM is allowed to market AIF units to professional investors.[407] The AIFMD management and marketing passport both require a notification procedure. A notification will be sent by the AIFM's Competent Authorities to the host Competent Authorities if the EEA-AIFM fully complies with the AIFMD and the relevant information is provided along the notification.[408]

---

401 Art. 41(2) MiFID II.
402 D. Busch & M. Louisse, *MiFID II/MiFIR's Regime for Third-Country Firms* (D. Busch & G. Ferrarini eds, Oxford 2017).
403 Recital 41 MiFIR.
404 Recital 109 MiFID II.
405 *See* ESMA/2011/270.
406 Arts. 32, 33 AIFMD; Similarly: Art. 16-21 UCITSD V.
407 *See* T. Jutzi & C. Feuz, *supra* note 391.
408 *See* Annex IV AIFMD for the AIFMD marketing passport and Art. 33(2) and (3) for the AIFMD management passport.

TC-AIFMs may under Articles 32, 33 and 37 AIFMD obtain a management and marketing passport. For this purpose, the AIFMD imposes additional requirements to the third country, in which the TC-AIFM has its registered and head office, and to the TC-AIFM itself.[409]

The third country in which the TC-AIFM is established:
- must have a cooperation agreement on information exchange in place between the Competent Authority of the 'Member State of reference',[410] the Competent authorities of the home Member State of the EEA-AIFs concerned and the Supervisory Authorities of the third country where the TC-AIFM is established.[411]
- may not be listed as a non-cooperating state by FATF and the third country where the TC-AIFM is established;[412] and
- has signed an agreement with the Member State of reference, which fully complies with the standards laid down in Article 26 of the OECD Model Tax Convention on Income and on Capital and ensures an effective exchange of information in tax matters, including any multilateral tax agreements.[413]

Apart from these requirements, the effective exercise by the Competent Authorities of their supervisory functions under the AIFMD may not be prevented by the laws, regulations or administrative provisions of a third country governing the TC-AIFM, nor by limitations in the supervisory and investigatory powers of that third country's Supervisory Authorities.[414]

A TC-AIFM that manages/markets AIFs using the EEA passport must fully comply with the AIFMD, including the EEA passporting requirements related to the EEA management and marketing passport with the exception of Chapter VI AIFMD that regulates AIFMs that manage specific types of AIFs.[415]

Under Article 37(2) AIFMD, a TC-AIFM is exempt from this requirement if it can demonstrate that compliance with one or more provisions of the AIFMD is 'incompatible with compliance with the law to which the TC-AIFM and/or the TC-AIF marketed in the EEA is subject'.[416] The TC-AIFM is, however, in that case required to demonstrate that

---

409 Zetzsche, & Marte, *supra* note 25, 474.
410 *Ibid.*, 465.
411 Art. 40(2)(c) AIFMD.
412 Art. 40(2)(b) AIFMD.
413 *See* for a definition of the 'Member State of reference': Art. 37(4) AIFMD.
414 Art. 37(7)(g) AIFMD.
415 Art. 37(2) AIFMD; R.E. Labeur, *Uniform derdelandenbeleid AIFMD: Nog een lange weg te gaan*, 10 TvFR 391-395 (2015); M. Bergervoet, *De impact van de AIFM Richtlijn voor derde landen en in het bijzonder voor Curaçao*, 4 TvFR 120 (2014).
416 Art. 37(2)(a) AIFMD; U. Klebeck & C. Meyer, *Drittstaatenregulierung der AIFM-Richtlinie*, Recht der Finanzinstrumente 95 (2012).

the third country rules the TC-AIFM is subjected to are equivalent and have 'the same regulatory purpose and offer the same level of protection to investors as the AIFMD'.[417] Following Article 37 AIFMD, TC-AIFMs have to be authorized in a 'Member State of reference' for the marketing or management of AIFs for which the TC-AIFM wants to use an EEA passport. The Member State in which the TC-AIFM is authorized is also the Member State that will supervise the TC-AIFM on an ongoing basis and ensures the TC-AIFM's compliance with the AIFMD.[418] The determination of the 'Member State of reference' depends upon the type of marketing or management that the TC-AIFM intends to undertake and can be extremely complex.[419] Factors considered in Article 37 AIFMD are, amongst others, the home Member State of the EEA-AIF, the total AuM managed and the development of effective marketing.[420]

The TC-AIFM is, thus, not obliged to establish a subsidiary or branch in the Member State of reference. Instead, the TC-AIFM must appoint a legal representative that acts as a contact person of the TC-AIFM for the investors of the relevant AIFs, ESMA and the Competent Authorities involved.[421]

Apart from this, the legal representative also needs to ensure compliance with the AIFMD for the management/marketing activities performed within the EEA under the AIFMD.[422]

3.3.3.2.2   The MiFIR European Passport for TC Investment Firms

MiFIR has also introduced a harmonized passporting regime for TC firms that want to provide services to eligible counterparties and per sé professional clients in the EEA.[423] This regime allows this type of TC firms to operate on a cross-border basis from outside the EEA or from an EEA-based branch. This harmonized regime allowing for passporting services throughout the EEA is, however, solely limited to eligible counterparties and per sé professional clients.[424] TC firms willing to provide services under MiFID II to retail clients and eligible professional clients have to comply with the Member State implementations of Article 39 MiFID II.

Following Article 46 MiFIR, TC firms may provide investment services on a cross-border basis to eligible counterparties and per sé professional clients without the establishment of a branch. Several conditions, however, need to be fulfilled. First, the European Commission has to adopt an equivalency decision, i.e. it must adopt a decision recognizing that the

---

417 Art. 37(2)(b) AIFMD; *See* for the vision of ESMA: ESMA/2016/1140 and ESMA/2011/270.
418 Art. 37(10) AIFMD.
419 *See* R.P. Raas, *De AIFM Richtlijn en derde landen* 59-69 (N.B. Spoor, M. Tausk, J.B. Huizink & R.P. Raas, Kluwer 2012).
420 *See* Art. 37(4)(g) AIFMD.
421 Art. 37(7)(c) AIFMD.
422 *See* Art. 38(3) AIFMD.
423 *See* Art. 46 et seq. MiFIR; R. Sethe, *supra* note 393; Maggi, *supra* note 386.
424 These professional clients are listed in Annex II, Section I MiFID II.

regulatory (prudential and business conduct requirements) and supervisory regime in which the TC firm is established and supervised achieves the same objectives as the EEA regime and with equivalent access to its markets.[425] Following Article 47 MiFIR, an equivalent regime is in place if, amongst others, the firm is subject to authorization and to effective supervision and enforcement on an ongoing basis,[426] subject to sufficient capital requirements and appropriate requirements applicable to shareholders and members of their management body,[427] the firm has adequate organization requirements in the area of internal control funds and subject to appropriate conduct of business rules.[428] Second, the firm must be subject to effective supervision and enforcement ensuring full compliance with regulatory requirements applicable in the third country.[429] Third, ESMA must have established cooperation arrangements with the Competent Authority of that third country.[430] Finally, ESMA has included the TC firm in a register that is publicly accessible.[431]

TC firms providing services must inform their EEA clients, prior to providing services to them, that they are not allowed to provide services to retail and elective retail clients.[432] Following Article 46(7) MiFIR, ESMA has developed RTS to specify information that TC firms must provide to ESMA regarding their application of registration and in what format the information should be delivered.[433]

Three years following the adoption of the equivalence decision, non-EEA firms have the choice either to register with ESMA or to continue to conduct investment services in compliance with Member States' national regimes.[434] The latter, however, implies that no European passport is available for the TC firm concerned.[435] Similarly, the national regimes are applicable to TC firms if the European Commission withdraws its equivalency decision or no equivalency decision has been adopted.[436]

Alternatively, TC firms may provide services to eligible counterparties or professional clients by means of a 'European passport' in all Member States through an EEA branch that has been authorized by a Competent Authority of a Member State pursuant to Article 39 MiFID.[437] TC firms must, however, for this purpose be established in a third

---

425 Art. 46 MiFIR; Klebeck & Eichhorn, *supra* note 388; Zetzsche & Marte, *supra* note 383.
426 Art. 47(1)(a) MiFIR.
427 Art. 47(1)(b) MiFIR; Busch & Louisse, *supra* note 402; A. Kern & A. Schmidt, *The Market in Financial Instruments Directive and Switzerland*, 1 GesKR45 (2012); R. Sethe, *Das Drittstaatenregime von MiFIR und MiFID II*, 6 SZW/ RSDA 615 (2014).
428 Art. 47(1)(c) and (d) MiFIR.
429 Art. 46 (1) (b) MiFIR.
430 Art. 46(2) (c) and Art. 47(2) MiFIR.
431 Art. 46(4), 48 MiFIR.
432 Art. 46(5) MiFIR.
433 ESMA, *Final Report -MiFID II/MiFIR Draft Technical Standards on Authorisation, Passporting, Registration of Third Country Firms and Cooperation between Competent Authorities*, 29 June 2015, ESMA/2015/1006.
434 Art. 54 MiFIR.
435 *Ibid.*
436 *See* Art. 49 MiFIR.
437 Art. 47 MiFIR.

country for which the European Commission has adopted an equivalence decision.[438] Finally, TC firms must also comply with the information requirements as laid down in Article 34 MiFID II.

3.3.3.3   The (Mutual) Agreements Solution

Access to the internal market is also granted to TC firms on the basis of (mutual) agreements concluded by the European institutions and their counterparts all over the world. Solvency II and CRD IV provide examples of this solution in the insurance and banking domain.

3.3.3.3.1   *Solvency II*

TC insurance undertakings may on the basis of Article 162 et seq. Solvency II obtain access to the EEA by establishing a branch that is subject to authorization.[439] In addition, Solvency II gives European institutions the power to conclude mutual agreements on a reciprocal basis.[440] TC insurance undertakings may, if they are established in a third country with which an agreement is concluded, access the EEA without the establishment and authorization of branches within the Member States in which they are willing to be active. Solvency II also contains a similar procedure for reinsurance undertakings. This type of undertakings are left outside the scope of the Solvency II third country 'branch regime'. Requirement however, differ for (non-)life insurance undertakings on the one hand and reinsurance undertakings on the other.[441] The differentiation between the third country regimes discussed stems from the fact that reinsurance undertakings may only access the EEA on the basis of an agreement concluded with third countries, whereas (non-)life insurance undertakings may either access the EEA by means of the establishment of an authorized branch in the EEA Member State in which they wish to be active or on the basis of any agreement concluded.

On behalf of (non-)life insurance undertakings, European institutions may, by means of agreements concluded on the basis of Article 218 TFEU, agree to grant access to third country insurance undertakings.[442] Agreements on the basis of Article 171 Solvency II, however, need to fulfil the condition of reciprocity and adequate protection for policy holders and insured persons in the EEA Member States.[443]

Under a predecessor of this provision,[444] European institutions have currently, for example, concluded an agreement with Switzerland regarding non-life insurance compa-

---

438 Art. 47(3) MiFIR.
439 Art. 162 Solvency II.
440 *See* Art. 171, 175(2) Solvency II.
441 This differentiation has evolved since the adoption of the first Non-life Insurance Directive (Art. 29), the Life Insurance Directive (Art. 32) and the Reinsurance Directive (Art. 50).
442 Art. 171 Solvency II.
443 *Ibid.*
444 *See* Art. 29 Non-life Insurance Directive.

nies.[445] The policy of reciprocity under this agreement implies that non-life insurance companies from Switzerland may establish direct branches in any EEA Member State on the same terms as non-life insurance companies from EEA Member States and vice versa.[446] The second requirement of adequate protection for policy holders and insured persons in the Member States is elaborated by the commitment of Switzerland to conform its insurance legislation, on the basis of the agreement, to the standards as set forth in Solvency II.[447] The harmonization of insurance legislation under Solvency II has, thus, been extended to Switzerland. The ambit of the agreement is, however, limited as Swiss non-life insurance undertakings do not benefit from the provisions of Solvency II with regard to cross-border services.[448]

The latter treaty does not prevent individual EEA Member States to conclude insurance agreements with third countries. Liechtenstein, for instance, has concluded a direct insurance agreement, including life and non-life insurances, that has been in force since 1997.[449] The agreement allows Swiss and Liechtenstein insurance companies freedom of establishment and services on a reciprocal basis. The agreement is based upon the pre-FSAP principles governing the single license, home country control and the supervision on solvency of the insurance companies. The ambit of this agreement does not include reinsurers and social insurance schemes.[450]

The European Council under Article 175(1) Solvency II may negotiate with one or more third countries agreements regarding the means of exercising supervision over reinsurance undertakings.[451] Agreements concluded grant, under the condition of market equivalence of prudential regulation and reciprocity, effective market access for reinsurance undertakings though establishment or the cross-border provision of services.[452] The criteria for the equivalence assessments under Article 172(1) and (3) Solvency II are

---

445 *See* agreement between the European Economic Community and the Swiss Confederation on direct insurance other than life insurance, in Official Journal of the European Communities L. 205. July 27, 1991.

446 *See* European Commission, *Proposal for a Council Decision on the conclusion of the Agreement between the Swiss Confederation and the European Economic Community concerning direct insurance other than life assurance,* 6 July 1989, COM (1989) 436 – 2; *See also* the European Commission, *Proposal for a Council Directive on the Implementation of the Agreement between the Swiss Confederation and the European Economic Community Concerning Direct Insurance Other Than life Assurance,* 28 February 1983, COM (83) 106 final.

447 *Supra* note 445.

448 *Ibid.*

449 Agreement between the Principality of Liechtenstein and the Swiss Confederation concerning Direct Insurance, Liechtenstein Law Gazette, 1998/129, 20 August 1998.

450 J. Gasser & M. Schwingshackl, *Asset Protection through Liechtenstein Annuities and Life Insurance,* (M. Gantenbein & M.A. Mata eds., John Wiley & Sons 2008).

451 H. Geiger, *Transnational Supervisory Recognition: a Macro-Jurisdictional Overview* 317, 318 (J. Burling, S.C. Chambers & K. Lazarus eds., Edward Elgar Publishing 2012).

452 Recital 89, Art. 172(2) Solvency II.

relevant for what third countries might be eligible to conclude an agreement.[453] The assessment criteria provide for a basis to assess the equivalence of prudential equivalence of third countries on a European-wide basis as to improve the liberalization of reinsurance services in third countries.[454] Under any agreement concluded, the contracting parties would be legally bound to recognize the prudential supervision being carried out by the home country, whereas the host country regulator would abandon its right to prudential supervision on the condition of information exchange.[455]

Under Article 175(1) Solvency II, the solvency regime of third countries, applying to reinsurance activities, may also be determined to be equivalent to the Solvency II Directive.[456] Following a positive equivalency decision, Member States are required to treat reinsurance contracts concluded with reinsurance undertakings in the relevant third country in the same manner as reinsurance contracts concluded with EEA undertakings that are authorized under Solvency II.[457] EEA Member States are prohibited from claiming the pledging of assets to cover unearned premiums and outstanding claims provisions[458] and the localization of assets within the EEA to cover risks in the EEA, nor assets that represent reinsurance recoverables.[459]

In the absence of treaties concluded under Article 175 Solvency II and an equivalence decision under Article 271 Solvency II, the treatment of reinsurance contracts remains to be subject to the laws of the individual EEA Member States. The national treatment of the individual EEA Member States, in such cases, are subject to the principle of non-discrimination. Article 174 Solvency II prohibits EEA Member States to treat TC undertakings more favourably than EEA undertakings.[460]

3.3.3.3.2   Credit Institutions

Similarly to Solvency II, CRD IV only grants a European passport to TC credit institutions on the basis of the conclusion of international treaties. CRD IV contains the legal basis on which the European Union may conclude agreements (Article 218 TFEU) with one or more third countries for branches of credit institutions to provide services on a cross-border basis throughout the EEA.[461] Till now, no agreements have been concluded.

Apart from this, the European Commission is on the basis of Article 48 CRD IV also entitled to submit proposals to the European Council for the negotiation of agreements with one or more third countries regarding the exercise of supervision of TC parent

---

453 H. Geiger, *Transnational Supervisory Recognition: a Macro-Jurisdictional Overview* 318 (J. Burling, S.C. Chambers & K. Lazarus eds., Edward Elgar Publishing 2012).
454 Recital 89 Solvency II.
455 Art. 172(2)(a) and (b) Solvency II.
456 Art. 172(1) Solvency II.
457 Art. 172(3) Solvency II.
458 *Ibid.*
459 Art. 134 Solvency II.
460 Art. 174 Solvency II Directive.
461 Art. 47(3) CRD IV.

undertakings or the parent undertakings of EEA conglomerates/groups on a consolidated basis.[462] The latter type of agreements shall, in particular, ensure that the Competent Authorities of Member States and the EBA are able to obtain information necessary for conducting financial supervision.[463]

3.3.4   EEA Financial Intermediary TC Market Access

Originally, the market access of EEA financial intermediaries in third countries was based upon bilateral and international treaties concluded by individual Member States or, to the extent there was an EEA legislative initiative with an 'external dimension', the European institutions.[464] A disadvantage of this was the fragmented landscape of market access for EEA financial intermediaries in third countries. Since an amendment of the Treaty of Nice, the EU common commercial policy became an exclusive competence of the EU.[465] To this end, various EEA secondary laws grant the European Commission a 'negotiation mandate' to ensure that EEA financial intermediaries are granted market access in third countries on a reciprocal basis.

3.3.4.1   The EU Commission Negotiation Mandate

The common commercial policy includes autonomous measures on the basis of which the European Parliament and Council may adopt measures to define the framework for implementing the common commercial policy.[466] In addition, they also have the competence to negotiate and conclude agreements with one or more third countries or internal organizations.[467]

The establishment of subsidiaries, branches and the provision of cross-border services by EEA financial intermediaries in third countries is, thus, an exclusive competence of the EU and Member States may not act unilaterally, unless European legislation allows them to do so.[468]

---

462 Art. 48(1) CRD IV.
463 Art. 48(2) CRD IV.
464 Zetzsche 2014, *supra* note 4, 67.
465 Art. 3(1)(e) TFEU.
466 Art. 207(2) TFEU.
467 Art. 207(3) TFEU.
468 Art. 2(1) TFEU.

3.3.4.2   The (Mutual) Agreements Solution under the Commission Negotiation Mandate

Upon the adoption of the First Banking Directive and the ISD, sectoral EEA financial laws began to grant the European Commission a 'negotiation mandate' to ensure effective market access, on a reciprocal basis, for TC firms willing to provide investment and banking services within the EEA. Under the First Banking Directive, for example, the European Commission could conclude agreements on the basis of the EEC Treaty with one or more third countries, on the basis of reciprocity, to grant branches of credit institutions from a certain third country 'national treatment' throughout the EEC.[469] By granting a 'negotiation mandate' to the European Commission, 'bargaining power' was being bundled to prevent EEA financial intermediaries from being discriminated in third countries.

Similar 'negotiation mandates' have been granted to the European Commission under, amongst others,[470] UCITSD V, AIFMD, Solvency II and the IDD.[471]

Article 9 UCITSD V regulates the 'relations with third countries'. Article 9(1) UCITSD V states that 'relations with third countries shall be regulated in accordance with Article 15 MiFID I'. Article 15 MiFID I required Member States to inform the European Commission of any general difficulties that investment firms face in establishing themselves or carrying out activities in any third country.[472] Under Article 15 MiFID I, the Council could grant a mandate to the European Commission to initiate negotiation to remedy the situation.[473] In the circumstance that EEA investment firms are not granted 'effective market access', the European Commission could even order national Competent Authorities to limit, suspend requests related to pending or future requests for authorization and the acquisition of holdings by direct or indirect parent undertakings governed by the law of the third country in question.[474] In addition, Article 9(2) UCITSD V requires Member States to inform any general difficulties that UCITS encounter in marketing their units in any third country.

Modern sectoral EEA financial laws, such as Article 67(2)(c) AIFMD, Article 177 Solvency II and Article 1(6) sub-paragraph 4 IDD, only require the latter approach. Under Article 67(2)(c) AIFMD, for example, ESMA shall base its opinion and advice on the application of the passport to the marketing of TC-AIFs by EEA-AIFMs in the Member States and the management and/or marketing of AIFs by TC-AIFMs in the Member States, inter alia, on

---

469 Art. 9(3) First Banking Directive.
470 *See also* Art. 15 MiFID I.
471 Directive (EU) 2016/97 of the European Parliament and of the Council of 20 January 2016 on insurance distribution (recast), OJ L 26/19, 2 February 2016, 19 ('IDD').
472 I.M. Hamstra, *Gedragsregels voor Nederlandse beleggingsondernemingen handelend met cliënten buiten de Europese Economische Ruimte*, 6 V&O 122-125 (2010).
473 Art. 15(2) MiFID I.
474 Art. 15(3) MiFID I.

the potential market disruptions and distortions in competition (level playing field) or any general or specific difficulties which EEA-AIFMs encounter in establishing themselves or marketing AIFs they manage in any third country.

The (mutual) agreements solution under the 'Commission negotiation mandate', thus, serves as to grant EEA financial intermediaries market access in third countries on a reciprocal basis.[475]

3.4   THE JOINT PRINCIPLES OF EEA TC FINANCIAL INTERMEDIARY REGULATION

The regulation of TC financial intermediaries that want to offer cross-border financial services in the internal market is based upon the 'internal dimension', i.e. the 'four free-doms', and the 'external dimension' that includes international law commitments and EEA secondary law. The equivalency of TC regulatory and supervision regimes to which TC financial intermediaries are subjected to serve the basis of 'equivalency' that is re-quired to be in place upon market access in the internal market. In addition, equivalency in EEA secondary law requires 'legal representation' in the EEA by means of subsidiaries, branches or 'legal representatives' to ensure compliance with EEA law. Both are comple-mented by cooperation and information exchange agreements that are required to be in place between the relevant Competent Authorities. Moreover, the European Commission and ESA's have a role in centralized rulemaking and supervision and, finally, TC financial intermediaries are subject to 'judicial control'.

3.4.1   Third Countries and EEA Secondary Law

Investor and market protection are the two primary goals of not only EEA, but also TC financial intermediary regulation.[476] EEA secondary law addressing third country rela-tionships are required to fulfil both legal requirements related to the EEA's internal and external dimension.

3.4.1.1   The Internal Dimension – The Four Freedoms
The internal market grants to EEA firms free access to the national market for goods, capital and cross-border services. The prerequisites for granting the principle of mutual

---

475 *See* Bruni *et al*, *supra* note 180.
476 D.A. Zetzsche, *Investment Law as Financial Law: From Fund Governance over Market Governance to Stake-holder Governance?* (H. S. Birkmose, M. Nevillie & K. E. Sørensen eds., Kluwer 2012).

recognition are (minimum) harmonization[477] and home state control.[478] The economic benefits of a European market resulting in more market efficiency and scale of economies benefitting both firms and their clients may only flourish when externalities resulting from risk asymmetry[479] can be avoided. EEA secondary laws prohibit that Member States treat TC firms more favourably than EEA firms.[480] TC firms that want to access the EEA are, therefore, required to comply with EEA secondary legislation.[481] Depending upon the specific sector, TC firms may access the EEA upon establishing a subsidiary, a branch or representative office that is required to wholly or partially comply with EEA secondary legislation. The 'four freedoms' and EEA secondary legislation are, thus, the minimum conditions for market entry for TC firms.[482]

3.4.1.2   The External Dimension: International Law Commitments and EEA Secondary Law

The EEA's 'external dimension' sets out the upper limit for what TC firms may be required to comply with upon EEA market access. The upper limit depends upon the international treaties to which the EU is bounded. In this regard, the most important commitment under the EU's common policy is the GATS. The EU, as a WTO member, is obliged to comply with the GATS when regulating and supervising their market for financial services with regard to activities of TC firms. Especially, the obligation of most-favoured-nation treatment and the commitment of national treatment are the two cornerstones that EEA secondary legislation needs a firm to comply with.

   Throughout EEA secondary law there are two types of regulations that comply with the EEA's internal and external dimension.[483] First, detailed market access requirements that apply to TC and EEA financial intermediaries equally (national treatment). Preferential arrangements, such as an eventual treaty regarding market access for financial intermediaries negotiated between the UK and the EU upon Brexit,[484] may be granted under the GATS 'economic integration' exception.[485] Under such an arrangement, the GATS allows the EU and UK to determine that the supervision over financial intermediaries entering both markets is, for example, carried out partly or fully by the home state. Clearly contrary to GATS would be any EEA market access requirements imposed on TC

---

477 In this regard, 'minimum harmonization' means a minimum level of harmonization. Not a limit degree of harmonization.
478 See Li, *supra* note 34, 110-115.
479 See *supra* 3.3.1.2.
480 See, for instance, Art. 41(2) MiFID II.
481 Cf. Art. 36, 42 AIFMD.
482 Zetzsche 2014, *supra* note 4, 141.
483 *Ibid.*, 142.
484 N. Moloney, *LSE Law Brexit Special #6: Negotiating a Financial Services Deal*, LSE Law – Policy Briefing Paper No. 25-2017, https://ssrn.com/abstract=2941373.
485 J.P. Trachtman, *Addressing Regulatory Divergence through International Standards: Financial Services* 27–41 (A. Mattoo & P. Sauvé eds., Oxford University Press, 2003).

firms that go far beyond what is required for EEA firms. A disadvantage of this approach, however, is that this approach does not offer a solution for difficulties that EEA firms encounter upon accessing third countries. For this reason, the equivalency assessment based (unilateral) 'recognition' approach is increasingly used.[486]

3.4.2 Equivalency in EEA Secondary Law

Equivalency of TC regulation and supervision regimes is more and more used as a precondition for EEA market access for TC firms.[487] The concept of equivalency in EEA secondary law is based upon three pillars: cooperation in exercising financial supervision, information exchange and 'representation in the EEA'.[488]

3.4.2.1 Equivalency of TC Regulatory and Supervision Regimes

The equivalency of substantive laws and enforcement is increasingly used as an underlying regulatory tool for unilateral/multilateral (mutual) recognition under EEA secondary law. Equivalency serves to create 'risk symmetry' prior to granting market access to TC firms. Equivalency may be granted in full or partially, for an indefinite period or with a time limit, to an entire supervisory framework of a TC state or to some of its supervisory authorities.[489]

The degree of 'recognition' granted by the EEA determines the scope of any equivalency assessment undertaken. 'Full recognition' of the EEA substantive laws and enforcement requires a larger equivalency assessment than 'partial recognition'.[490] Full recognition requires comparable levels of economic development and financial regulation.[491] The latter determines the level of risk asymmetry in a specific field of financial services and, therefore, the need to protect investors and prevent systematic risks.[492] The level of equivalency of the latter determines the risk of regulatory arbitrage, risk asymmetry and a possible *race to the bottom*.

Any equivalency assessment undertaken depends upon the international standards adopted in a specific field of financial services. In the past decades, the BCBS and IAIS, for example, have played a major role in developing international regulatory and super-

---

486 *See* Art. XXIX GATS.
487 T.B. Wei, *The Equivalence Approach to Securities Regulation*, 225 Northwestern Journal of International Law & Business 1 (2007).
488 Zetzsche 2014, *supra* note 4, 145.
489 *See* European Commission, *Recognition of non-EU financial frameworks (equivalence decisions)*, https://ec. europa.eu/info/business-economy-euro/banking-and-finance/international-relations/recognition-non-eu-financial-frameworks-equivalence-decisions_en.
490 *Cf.* ESMA/2014/1340, 7.
491 Verdier, *supra* note 42.
492 Zetzsche 2014, *supra* note 4, 61.

vision standards in the banking and insurance domain.[493] These standards require compliance with rules related to anti-money laundering, tax information exchange[494] and measures countering the financing of terrorism. The adoption of international standards has led to an increasing convergence of banking and insurance law at the international level that is also reflected in the EEA's insurance and banking TC regimes. Under both CRD IV and Solvency II, the internal market grants market access to TC firms on the basis of (mutual) agreements concluded by the European institutions and their counterparts all over the world.

On the contrary, no such degree of harmonization at the international level exists for investment law.[495] Until the AIFMD and the Dodd–Frank Act, many types of AIFs in the EEA and US were not regulated.[496] To date, this still holds true for, amongst others, private foundations and family offices.[497] This is also reflected in the TC regimes of, for example, the AIFMD and MiFID II. Under the AIFMD and the MiFID II TC 'retail regime', various requirements are imposed on TC intermediaries and third countries before market access is granted.[498] The AIFMD and MiFID II require TC-AIFMs and TC firms to fully or partially comply with the organizational and conduct of business requirements applying to EEA-AIFMs and investment firms.[499]

The extent to which a TC firm under MiFID II is being subjected to EEA legislation depends upon:

- the type of activity/service for which the intermediary seeks to access the EEA; and
- the type of investors to which financial services/products are offered (professional or non-professional investors).

---

493 Basel Committee on Banking Supervision, *Basel III: A global Regulatory Framework for More Resilient Banks and Banking Systems*, December 2010; IAS, *Insurance Core Principles*, November 2015.

494 OECD, *Commentary to the Model Double Taxation Convention on Income and on Capital* Art. 26 (OECD 2010); OECD, *Tackling Offshore Tax Evasion: The G20/OECD Continues to Make Progress* (June 2012), www.oecd.org/dataoecd/19/9/50630916.pdf.

495 Many areas of financial services do not have TC (equivalence) regimes. See O. Cherednychenko, The UK's Potential Withdrawal from the EU and Single Market Access under EU Financial Services Legislation, January 2017, www.europarl.europa.eu/RegData/etudes/IDAN/2016/595334/IPOL_IDA%282016%29595334_ EN.pdf.

496 *See* for a comparison in terms of investors protection between the investment funds regimes in the EEA and the US: H. Wegman, *Investor Protection. Towards Additional EU Regulation of Investment Funds?* (Kluwer 2015).

497 *See* for family office within the scope of the AIFMD: A.O. Kühne & M. Eberhardt, *Erlaubnispflicht eines 'Family Office' unter Berücksichtigung des neuen Finanzdienstleistungstatbestandes der Anlageberatung*, 8 Zeitschrift für Bank- und Kapitalmarktrecht 133 (2008); P. Schaubach, *Family Office: Ein Beitrag zur Begriffsfindung*, 51 Bank-Archiv: Zeitschrift für das gesamte Bank- und Börsenwesen 897 (2003); E. Waclawik, *Aufsichtsrechtliche Aspekte der Tätigkeit privater Family Offices*, Zeitschrift für Bankrecht und Bankwirtschaft 401 (2005); E. Waclawik, *Erlaubnispflicht privater Family Offices nach Umsetzung der MiFID?*, Zeitschrift für Wirtschaftsrecht 1341 (2007).

498 Art. 37 AIFMD; Art. 39 MiFID II.

499 Art. 37 AIFMD; Art. 41 MiFID II.

In addition, TC-AIFMs and TC firms (providing 'retail services') under the AIFMD and MiFID II are required to be 'legally represented'[500] in the EEA for supervisory purposes by means of a legal representative within a reference state,[501] a branch[502] or a subsidiary.

Apart from this, third countries are required:

- not to be listed at the FATF black list;[503]
- to have cooperation agreements in place between the relevant TC Supervisory Authorities and the EEA Member State Competent Authorities involved;[504] and
- to have tax information exchange agreements modelled after Article 26 OECD Model between the relevant third countries and EEA Member States in place.[505]

The AIFMD and MiFID II 'retail' third country regimes ensure 'equivalency' not by an equivalency assessment carried out by a European institution, but by laying down detailed requirements related to the TC-AIFM, TC firm and the third country in which these intermediaries are established.

The equivalency concept as regulatory tool based upon a centralized assessment and EEA secondary law are, thus, communicating vessels.[506] The more requirements TC firms and third countries are required to fulfil under EEA secondary law upon EEA market access, the less relevant is the equivalency of substantive laws and enforcement to which a TC intermediary is subjected to in its home state and vice versa.[507]

Depending upon the equivalency approach taken, reciprocity may also play a role. The third country approaches under the AIFMD and MiFID II 'retail regime' are based upon unilateral recognition in which 'equivalence' for TC-AIFMs and TC firms is given upon compliance with the EEA secondary law regime. In the past, 'reciprocity' was a precondition for EEA market access of TC intermediaries in EEA secondary law regimes.[508] Although Article 41(3) MiFID II proposal also contained such a requirement, it was removed in the final version.[509] Reciprocity, thus, seems to have lost its importance in equivalency regimes based upon EEA secondary law.

---

500 *Cf.* Art. 4(1)(u) AIFMD: "legal representative means a natural person domiciled in the Union or a legal person with its registered office in the Union, and which, expressly designated by a non-EU AIFM, acts on behalf of such non-EU AIFM vis-à-vis the authorities, clients, bodies and counterparties to the non-EU AIFM in the Union with regard to the non-EU AIFM's obligations under this Directive."
501 *See* Art. 37 AIFMD.
502 Art. 39 MiFID II.
503 Art. 40(2)(b) AIFMD; Art. 39(2)(a) MiFID II.
504 Art. 40(2)(a) AIFMD; Art. 39(2)(b) MiFID II.
505 OECD 2010, *supra* note 494; OECD 2012, *supra* note 494.
506 Zetzsche 2014, *supra* note 4, 149.
507 *Ibid.*
508 *See supra* Section 3.3.4.2.
509 Art. 41(3) MiFID II proposal ('third country provides for equivalent reciprocal recognition of the prudential framework applicable to investment firms authorised in accordance with this directive'); *See also* N. Moloney, *EC Securities Regulation* 403-405 (3rd edn., Oxford University Press 2014).

Reciprocity may, however, play a bigger role for the equivalency approach based upon a centralized assessment, such as TC-AIF depositaries and the MiFID II TC regime for 'professional investors'.[510] It may be a requirement for an equivalency assessment in the first place or European institutions may prioritize their equivalency assessment based upon reciprocity.[511] Recital 41 MiFIR, for example, states that:

> when initiating those equivalence assessments, the Commission should be able to prioritise among third country jurisdictions taking into account the materiality of the equivalence finding to Union firms and clients, the existence of supervisory and cooperation agreements between the third country and the Member States, the existence of an effective equivalent system for the recognition of investment firms authorised under foreign regimes as well as the interest and willingness of the third country to engage in the equivalence assessment process.

Equivalency is based upon the presumption that TC authorities are effectively supervising TC intermediaries. For this purpose, cooperation agreements are required to be in place.

3.4.2.2   Cooperation Agreements

A core element of the mutual recognition principle in the internal market for EEA financial intermediaries is the principle of home country control that is complemented by the ESFS.[512] The absence of an equivalent centralized supervision framework between third countries and EEA Member States requires bilateral cooperation agreements for effective supervision to be in place.[513]

Broadly speaking, there are two approaches related to the conclusion of cooperation agreements to be recognized at the EEA level.[514]

The first approach is that cooperation agreements are established as part of the equivalency decision between the relevant TC Competent Authority and one of the relevant ESAs. The equivalency decision has, de facto, no legal effect without a cooperation agreement being in place. This approach is, in particular, used for TC regimes where a centralized equivalency decision is required. Article 47(2) MiFIR, for example, requires ESMA to conclude cooperation arrangements with the relevant Competent Authorities

---

510 *See* for TC-AIF depositaries: Art. 21(6) AIFMD; Art. 84 AIFMD (Commission) Regulation.; *See* for MiFID II: Art. 46, 47 MiFIR; Klebeck & Eichhorn, *supra* note 388; Zetzsche & Marte, *supra* note 383.
511 Cherednychenko, *supra* note 495, www.europarl.europa.eu/RegData/etudes/IDAN/2016/595334/IPOL_I-DA%282016%29595334_EN.pdf.
512 Wymeersch, *supra* note 143.
513 *See, e.g.* Art. 40(2)(c) AIFMD.
514 Zetzsche 2014, *supra* note 4, 144; Cherednychenko, *supra* note 495, www.europarl.europa.eu/RegData/etudes/IDAN/2016/595334/IPOL_IDA%282016%29595334_EN.pdf.

of the third country whose legal and supervisory frameworks have been recognized as 'equivalent'. The cooperation agreement concluded is a mechanism for the exchange of information between the two authorities,[515] which requires the TC Competent Authority to promptly notify ESMA when the TC firm infringes the conditions of its authorization[516] and sets outs procedures related to the coordination of supervisory activities including, where appropriate, on-site inspections.[517]

The second approach is that cooperation agreements are a 'stand-alone' requirement as part of a TC (equivalency) regime.[518] An example is the AIFMD TC regime. Under the AIFMD, the TC-AIFM passport regime is built upon 'equivalence' that is embedded in the above-mentioned minimum requirements a TC-AIFM needs to comply with. As a consequence, cooperation agreements are concluded between TC Competent Authorities and individual Member States.[519] Compared to the first approach, this approach leads to a 'Big 5 Bias'. Small Member States, such as Liechtenstein, play such a minor role in international financial governance that they have little bargaining power. Cooperation agreements are, however, a constitutive requirement for the TC-AIFM passport regime. The first approach, thus, leads to a better outcome for the 'internal market with an external dimension' as it grants small Member States the same opportunities as bigger Member States.[520]

3.4.2.3   Information Exchange

Cooperation agreements are mainly concluded as a mechanism for the exchange of information. In this regard, the conclusion of cooperation agreements between Supervisory Authorities of third countries and Competent Authorities of EEA Member States traditionally, had a 'voluntary' nature. Under Article 66 Solvency II, for instance, Member States 'may' conclude cooperation agreements under the premise that any information disclosed is subject to guarantees of professional secrecy and information disclosed that originates in another Member State is not disclosed without the express agreement of the Competent Authority of that Member State.[521] Individual Member States had discretion for whether and to what extent they cooperated with third countries. Recently, Member States increasingly have a 'mandatory' duty to conclude cooperation arrangements. Under Article 115 CRD IV 'the consolidating supervisor and the other Competent Authorities *shall* have written coordination and cooperation arrangements in place'. This ten-

---

515 Art. 47(2)(a) MiFIR.
516 Art. 47(2)(b) MiFIR.
517 Art. 47(2)(c) MiFIR.
518 Zetzsche 2014, *supra* note 4, 144.
519 *See, e.g.* Art. 40(2)(a) AIFMD.
520 Zetzsche 2014, *supra* note 4, 144.
521 Art. 66 Solvency II.

dency is also observed in Article 19 FiCOD and Article 68 Solvency II regulating consolidated supervision.

3.4.2.4 'Legal Representation' in the EEA

TC regimes under secondary EEA legislation may require a 'legal presence' within the EEA for the purpose of 'effective supervision'. The 'legal presence' may be a natural or legal person within the EEA and acts on behalf of the TC financial intermediaries vis-à-vis the authorities, clients, bodies and counterparties to the TC financial intermediary in the EEA with regard to the obligations to be complied with under EEA law.[522] Depending upon the TC regime at hand, TC financial intermediaries may be 'represented' by means of a subsidiary, branch or a legal representative. The 'legal representation' required depends upon the degree of TC market access granted under sectoral EEA legislation and the design of the specific TC regime.

3.4.2.4.1 EEA Subsidiary

Under EEA secondary law that does not offer any TC regime, TC financial intermediaries may only establish or acquire an EEA subsidiary that obtains an authorization for the desired sector. UCITSD V is an example of an EEA legislative initiative that does not have a TC regime. Subsidiaries have to comply with EEA sectoral legislation as EEA legal entities. UCITS ManCos might, however, have TC relations due to TC shareholders, TC delegates or they might be part of a group structure/conglomerate that includes TC intermediaries. EEA legislation on 'qualifying holdings'[523] and 'close links',[524] delegation[525] and consolidation/conglomerates preserve the 'substance' of the subsidiary within the EEA.

Provided that requirements related to equivalence and exchange of information are complied with, the EEA regime on consolidation and conglomerates may allow the home state of a TC financial intermediary heading a group/conglomerate to perform 'consolidated supervision'.[526] Such 'consolidation' is allowed as such groups and conglomerates are considered to be a 'single entity' for financial law purposes.[527] This generally means that the head entity of the group/conglomerate is responsible for all or most of the obligations. The EEA consolidation and conglomerate regime (partly) substitutes the relevance of EEA sectoral delegation regimes.[528]

---

522 *Cf.* Art. 4(1)(u) AIFMD.
523 *See* Art. 8(1)(d) AIFMD.
524 *See* Art. 8(3)AIFMD.
525 *See* for AIFMs: Art. 20 AIFMD; *See* for depositaries: Art. 20(11) AIFMD.
526 *See supra* 3.3.2.3.2.
527 *Ibid.*
528 Zetzsche 2014, *supra* note 4, 152.

3.4.2.4.2   EEA Branch

The second type of 'legal presence' required under, for instance, Solvency II, CRD IV and the MiFID II 'retail regime' is the establishment of a branch.[529] The establishment of a branch may grant EEA market access on the basis of country-by-country authorization or a European passport.[530] A branch is not a legal entity, but ensures a certain degree of 'substance' of the TC intermediary by, for example under Solvency II, representatives within the EEA that carry out legal matters on behalf of the TC intermediary and the fulfilment of minimum capital/ solvency requirements.[531]

The requirement under EEA secondary legislation to establish an EEA branch that needs to fulfil certain requirements complements the relevant equivalency regime. The branch requirement, usually, compensates for a less stringent equivalency regime related to the TC regulatory and supervision regimes.[532]

3.4.2.4.3   EEA 'Legal Representation'

The TC regimes of reinsurance undertakings under Solvency II, TC-AIFMs under the AIFMD and the MiFID II 'professional regime' do not require the presence of a subsidiary nor a branch within the EEA. Instead, they grant a European passport for TC intermediaries on the basis of a centralized equivalency assessment complemented by cooperation agreements. The European passport granted is based upon a high degree of equivalency required under the assessment.[533] The cooperation agreements concluded have to ensure a flow of information between TC and Member State Competent Authorities preserving effective compliance of EEA law in the TC home state.[534] In addition, some EEA legal initiatives require the presence of a 'legal representative' of the TC intermediary within the EEA that is the contact point for any official correspondence between the Competent Authorities of the Member States and consumers.[535] Moreover, the legal representative is required to perform the compliance function related to EEA law.[536]

Apart from this, EEA law may require additional requirements to be fulfilled by the TC intermediary and the relevant TC state. Depending upon the comprehensiveness of the sectoral equivalency assessment, TC intermediaries may be (partly) subjected to the relevant sectoral EEA law. Finally, the third country in which the TC financial intermediary is established upon granting market access will need to comply with requirements

---

529 Art. 162(2) Solvency II; Recital 23, Art. 47 CRD IV, Art. 39 MiFID II.
530 Solvency II, CRD IV, the MiFID II 'retail regime' and the AIFMD private placement regime grant EEA market access, whereas the establishment of a branch under MiFIR under the 'professional regime' grants a European passport.
531 See, e.g. Art. 162(2)(e), (f) Solvency II.
532 Zetzsche 2014, supra note 4, 152.
533 See for a definition 'passporting': IOSCO, supra note 73, 31 et seq.
534 Zetzsche 2014, supra note 4, 153.
535 See, e.g. Art. 37(3) AIFMD.
536 Ibid.

related to anti-money laundering, the FATF blacklist[537] and the conclusion of a tax information agreement.[538]

3.4.3   The EEA's Centralized Rulemaking and Supervision

The European Commission and ESAs increasingly take a role in centralized rulemaking and supervision.

3.4.3.1   The Role of the European Commission in Centralized Rulemaking

In the TC domain, the European Commission has an ever-increasing role in 'centralized rulemaking'. Centralized equivalency assessments, for example, are typically initiated by the European Commission and the power to adopt such a decision is discretionary.[539] Equivalency decisions are most adopted after technical advice has been given by a relevant ESA. Decisions are made in the form of an implementing or delegated act depending upon the delegation provision in EEA secondary law.[540]

Recently, the equivalency process has been criticized for not being transparent.[541] The European Commission in a Report has been reviewing the equivalency process and made an attempt in improving the transparency related to the assessment procedure.[542]

The European Commission represents the collective interest not only in equivalency assessment procedures but also in concluding (mutual) agreements in 'reciprocity matters'.[543] This solution is favourable in cases of reciprocity negotiations as TCs cannot grant more favourable conditions under bilateral treaties to big 'distribution Member States', whereas market access may be disrupted for small 'production' Member States. Mutual agreements concluded on the basis of Article 218 TFEU prevent the fragmenta-

537 FATF, *International Standards on combating money laundering and the financing of terrorism*, The FATF Recommendations, February 2012, www.fatfgafi. org/media/fatf/documents/recommendations/pdfs/ FATF_Recommendations.pdf; FATF, *Methodology for assessing technical compliance with the FATF Recommendations and the Effectiveness of AML/CFT systems*, February 2013, www.fatfgafi.org/media/fatf/documents/methodology/FATF%20Methodology%2022%20Feb%202013.pdf; FATF, *Procedures for the FATF Fourth Round of AML/CFT mutual evaluations*, October 2013, www.fatf-gafi.org/media/fatf/documents/methodology/FATF-4th-Round-Procedures.pdf.
538 See D.A. Zetzsche & T.F. Marte, *The AIFMD's Cross-Border Dimension, TC Rules and the Equivalence Concept* 460 (D.A. Zetzsche ed., Kluwer 2015).
539 Moloney, *supra* note 71.
540 Cherednychenko, *supra* note 495, www.europarl.europa.eu/RegData/etudes/IDAN/2016/595334/IPOL_I-DA%282016%29595334_EN.pdf.
541 Moloney, *supra* note 71.
542 European Commission, *EU Equivalence Decisions in Financial Services Policy: An Assessment* (SWD (2017) 102) final, 27 February 2017.
543 See Art. 9(1) UCITSD V.

tion of market access EEA financial intermediaries at the expense of small Member States and adequately addresses investor and market protection concerns.[544]

In concluding (mutual) agreements, the bargaining power of the European Commission depends, however, upon the size of the EEA internal market compared to the size of the negotiation partner (e.g. the US, China). Despite a possible Brexit, the role of the European Commission and other European institutions is likely to increase in international financial governance due to ever-increasing centralized rulemaking and supervision in financial law.[545]

3.4.3.2 The Role of ESAs in TC Regimes

The ESAs also play various important roles related to third countries.

First, the ESAs play a role in international relations. The ESAs may develop contacts and enter into administrative arrangements with supervisory authorities, international organizations and the administrations of third countries.[546] They may, however, not create legal obligations on behalf of the EU and its Member States nor shall their role in international relations prevent Member States and their Competent Authorities from concluding (bilateral/multilateral) arrangements with those third countries.[547]

Second, ESAs shall assist in preparing equivalency decisions pertaining to supervisory regimes in third countries.[548]

Third, the ESAs are, in particular, under the 'centralized equivalency approach' responsible for concluding cooperation agreements with TC Competent Authorities of the TC whose legal and supervisory frameworks have been recognized as 'equivalent'.[549] The cooperation agreement is a mechanism for the exchange of information between the relevant ESA and TC Competent Authorities.[550] The ESAs are allowed to request the Competent Authorities of the Member States to deliver relevant information to them

---

544 Zetzsche 2014, *supra* note 4, 141.

545 Verdier, *supra* note 42; N. Moloney, *The EU in International Financial Governance*, 1 Russell Sage Journal of the Social Sciences 138-152(2017).

546 Art. 33 Regulation (EU) No. 1093/2010 of the European Parliament and of the Council of 24 November 2010 establishing a European Supervisory Authority (European Banking Authority), amending Dec. No. 716/2009/EC and repealing Commission Dec. 2009/78/EC, OJ L 331, 15 December 2010, 12 ('EBAR'); Art. 33 Regulation (EU) No. 1095/2010 of the European Parliament and of the Council of 24 November 2010 establishing a European Supervisory Authority (European Securities and Markets Authority), amending Dec. No 716/2009/EC and repealing Commission Dec. 2009/77/EC, OJ L 331, 15 December 2010, 84 ('ESMAR'); Art. 33 Regulation (EU) No. 1094/2010 of the European Parliament and of the Council of 24 November 2010 establishing a European Supervisory Authority (European Insurance and Occupational Pensions Authority), amending Dec. No 716/2009/EC and repealing Commission Dec. 2009/79/EC, OJ L 331, 15 December 2010, 48 ('EIOPAR').

547 *Ibid.*

548 Art. 33 sub-para. 2 EBAR, Art. 33 sub-para. 2 ESMAR, Art. 33 sub-para. 2 EIOPAR.

549 *See* Art. 47(2) MiFIR.

550 *See, e.g.* Art. 47(2)(a) MiFIR.

that is necessary in relation to their duties.[551] The information provided to ESAs is subject to professional secrecy obligations and the GDPR.[552]

Finally, TC Competent Authorities cooperating with ESAs are allowed to participate in the work of ESAs.[553] The rationale behind this is that ESAs are ought to foster dialogue and cooperation with TC Competent Authorities in the light of the globalization of financial services and the increased importance of international standards.[554] The participation is open to EEA Member States[555] and third countries that have been recognized as equivalent in the areas of competence of the respective ESA.[556] Third countries are allowed to participate in the work of the ESAs in accordance with the agreements concluded.[557] The nature, scope and procedural aspects of the involvement of the countries, including provisions relating to financial contributions and staff, are specified in those agreements.[558]

3.4.4   Judicial Control

The CJEU has jurisdiction over all EU acts. Judicial control includes the assessment of the validity of primary and secondary EU law. The CJEU is, thus, competent to adjudge actions for annulment or give preliminary rulings pertaining to EU market access in the light of EU directives or regulations establishing sectoral TC regimes.[559] In addition, any centralized equivalency decisions made by the European Commission on the basis of Article 263 TFEU is subject to the CJEU's jurisdiction. Member States, EU institutions, or, where the act is of direct and individual concern to them, EEA/TC natural/legal persons may challenge the legality of equivalence decisions made by the European Commission.[560] This could, for instance, be the revoking of a decision already made.[561] The validity of any inaction in taking equivalency decisions is, however, not challengeable.

---

551 Art. 35(1) EBAR, Art. 35(1) ESMAR, Art. 35 EIOPAR.
552 Regulation (EU) 2016/679 of the European Parliament and of the Council of 27 April 2016 on the protection of natural persons with regard to the processing of personal data and on the free movement of such data, and repealing Directive 95/46/EC, OJ L 119/1, 4 May 2016, 1 ('GDPR'). *Cf.* European Commission, *Commission Decisions on the Adequacy of the Protection of Personal Data in Third Countries*, http://ec. europa.eu/justice/policies/privacy/thridcountries/index_en.htm.
553 Recital 44 EBAR, Recital 44 ESMAR, Recital 44 EIOPAR.
554 *Ibid.*
555 Art. 75(1) EBAR, Art. 75(1) ESMAR, Art. 75(1) EIOPAR.
556 Art. 75(2) EBAR, Art. 75(2) ESMAR, Art. 75(2) EIOPAR.
557 Recital 65 EBAR, Recital 65 ESMAR, Recital 65 EIOPAR.
558 Art. 75(3) EBAR, Art. 75(3) ESMAR, Art. 75(3) EIOPAR.
559 In particular, related to Arts. 263, 265, 267 TFEU.
560 A. Duvillet-Margerit, M. Magnus, B. Mesnard & A. Xirou, *Third Country Equivalence in EU Banking Legislation*, 9 December 2016, www.europarl.europa.eu/RegData/etudes/BRIE/2016/587369/IPOL_BRI% 282016%29587369_EN.pdf.
561 P.P. Craig & G. De Búrca, *EU Law: Text, Cases, and Materials* 369 (6th edn., Oxford University Press 2015).

The EFTA court has jurisdiction over passporting rights that are extended to EEA countries.[562]

3.5   CONCLUSION

This chapter studied the EEA's approach towards the cross-border provision of financial services. In particular, the conditions under which European and TC European passports are granted to EEA and TC financial intermediaries have been studied to determine under what conditions a (cross-sectoral) European/TC passport could be granted to 'depositaries' and 'custodians'.

EEA law in regulating financial intermediaries has an 'internal' and 'external dimension'. The so-called 'internal dimension' is regulated by EEA secondary law that is based upon the four freedoms and regulates the cross-border provisions of financial services in the internal market by EEA financial intermediaries. The 'external dimension' regulates the cross-border provisions of financial services in the internal market by TC financial intermediaries and is based upon international law commitments and EEA secondary law.

EEA law in regulating both the 'internal' and 'external dimension' has as its purpose to establish an internal market for financial services that enhances market efficiency and leads to economies of scale and scope. Authorization and notification requirements under European passport arrangements, for example, only need to be fulfilled in one Member State while having a large market to offer their financial products and services without worrying about multiple authorization applications and the establishment of subsidiaries that would have led to a duplication of legal costs. Prices in an EEA internal market for financial services decline as fixed costs are shared amongst a larger client base.[563] Firms may organize themselves anywhere in the EEA, in small and big Member States and, as a result, have the potential to maximize their efficiency and become more competitive. In addition to reducing transaction costs, financial institutions from either smaller or bigger EEA Member States may market products and services to all of the European Union's 500 million citizens resulting in more revenue.

The market access that the internal market facilitates may create negative externalities, such as the insolvency of financial intermediaries or fraud that is particularly fuelled by 'risk asymmetry'.[564] In the past, this has led to a large degree of legal fragmentation posing hurdles to the cross-border provision of financial intermediaries that could not

---

562 See V. Skouris, *the ECJ and the EFTA Court under the EEA Agreement: A Paradigm for International Co-operation between Judicial Institutions* 123-129 (C. Baudenbacher, P. Tressel & T. Örlygsson eds., Hart Publishing 2005).

563 Zetzsche 2014, *supra* note 4, 56.

564 See Zetzsche 2016, *supra* note 16, 401-402.

be resolved by the 'four freedoms' due to the 'prudential carve-out' that justifies the infringements on the freedom movement of capital and establishment.

The 'European passport' is at the heart of the EEA system for financial services. It is a general concept that lays down the conditions for the 'mutual recognition' principle. The general idea is that financial products or services that are 'produced' (and marketed) in a 'home Member State' may, under conditions set out in European legislative acts, be marketed throughout the internal market without incurring further conditions imposed by 'host Member States'. The concept of the European passport is now widespread and commonly used to enhance the development of the EEA internal market for financial intermediaries that are active in a wide range of sectors. The European passport and the overarching principle of 'mutual recognition' are based upon two cornerstones: the 'single rulebook', i.e. a thick set of harmonized rules and a coordinated institutional framework for financial supervision comprising of 'home state control' and the ESFS that allows host Member States to defer supervision to home Member States and ESAs.[565] The European passport as regulatory tool is unique and not to be found in any other multilateral, regional or bilateral forms of cooperation at the international level.[566] The reason for this is the degree of centralized rulemaking and supervision at the EEA level on which the regulatory tool is based.[567]

Along the development of the European passport as primary regulatory concept for EEA financial intermediaries, the EEA developed its 'external dimension', i.e. the conditions under which TC financial intermediaries may provide financial services in the internal market. TC financial intermediaries are not subject to the same centralized rulemaking and supervision as EEA financial intermediaries. Moreover, the harmonization of financial regulation at the international level varies from sector to sector. Banking and insurance legislation are harmonized to a large degree, whereas other sectors, such as asset management, are hardly harmonized. For this reason, the EEA determines in EEA secondary legislation whether and to what extent TC financial intermediaries may provide certain services within the EEA.

The regulation of TC financial intermediaries that want to offer cross-border financial services in the internal market is based upon the 'internal dimension', i.e. the 'four freedoms', and the external dimension that includes international law commitments and EEA secondary law. The equivalency of TC regulatory and supervision regimes to which TC financial intermediaries are subjected to serve as the basis for 'equivalency' that is required to be in place upon market access in the internal market. In addition, equivalency in EEA secondary law requires 'legal representation' in the EEA by means of subsidiaries, branches or 'legal representatives' to ensure compliance with EEA law. Both are complemented by cooperation and information exchange agreements that are required to

---

565 Moloney, *supra* note 71, 5.
566 Verdier, *supra* note 42.
567 IOSCO, *supra* note 73, 31 et seq.

be in place between the relevant Competent Authorities. Moreover, the European Commission and ESAs have a role in centralized rulemaking and supervision and, finally, TC financial intermediaries are subject to 'judicial control'.

Depositaries are 'custodians', i.e. financial intermediaries performing the safekeeping and administration of financial instruments, that perform additional 'controlling/monitoring' duties. This additional task could justify the difference in treatment for the purpose of introduction of a European/TC passport between AIF/UCITS depositaries, on the one hand and MiFID II/CRD IV 'custodians', on the other. This will be studied in detail in Part III.

Part III
Depositaries vs. Custodians

4   The AIFMD and UCITSD V Depositary Regulation

4.1   Introduction

Since the mandatory appointment of depositaries was adopted in the UCITSD I in 1985, the appointment of a depositary for AIFs remained a subject left to Member States. This lack of harmonization left room for diverging interpretations of AIF's/UCITS' depositary duties and liabilities.[1] As a result, different depositary regimes have been developed providing investors with different levels of investor protection in various European jurisdictions. The potential consequence was highlighted in the course of the financial crisis. Huge amounts of assets of collective investment schemes that were entrusted to Lehman Brothers Internal Europe vanished into thin air after its collapse in 2008. In addition, the asset management business of Bernard Madoff turned out to be a giant Ponzi scheme.[2] These two events stirred up a number of questions as to whether the European legal framework for depositaries needed to be further harmonized and strengthened to ensure a level playing field in terms of investor protection measures across all Member States.[3]

Following the Madoff fraud and Lehman Brothers bankruptcy, the European Commission developed a strong desire to clarify, harmonize and strengthen the depositary function. In 2009 and 2010, the European Commission launched two public consultations on the role of UCITS depositaries.[4] These consultations have been taken into con-

---

1   Earlier versions of the AIFMD depositary regime have been published in: S.N. Hooghiemstra, *Depositary Regulation* (D.A. Zetzsche ed., Kluwer 2015) and S.N. Hooghiemstra, *Depositary Regulation* (D.A. Zetzsche ed., Kluwer 2012).

2   *See* L. Fortado, *Lehman Segregated Accounts Appeal May delay Payouts*, www.canadianhedgewatch.com/content/news/general/?id=5643; G.N. Gregoriou, & F.S. Lhabitant, Madoff, *A Riot of Red Flags*, EDHEC (2009); S. Gene, *Luxembourg Called on to "Brush Up" Governance*, Financial Times, Fund Management Supplement, (26 January 2009); P. Skypala, *UCITS Victory Soured by Madoff Scandal*, Financial Times, Fund Management Supplement (19 January 2009), 6; P. Hollinger, B. Hall & N. Tait, *Grand Duchy Hits Back at Madoff*, Financial Times (14 January 2009), 23; P. Hollinger & J. Chung, *Madoff Affair Sparks Demand for Revamp of Investment Fund Rules*, Financial Times, (13 January 2009), 15.

3   N. Amenc, S. Focardi, F. Goltz, D. Schröder, & L. Tang, *EDHEC-Risk European Private Wealth Management Survey*, EDHEC (2010).

4   European Commission, *Consultation Paper on the UCITS Depositary Function, Markt/G4 D* (2010) 950800; European Commission, *Working Document of the Commission Services (DG Markt), Consultation Paper on the UCITS Depositary Function*, July 2009; *Summary of Responses to UCITS Depositary's Consultation Paper – Feedback Statement; Working Document of the Commission Services (DG Markt), Consultation Paper on the UCITS Depositary Function and on the UCITS Managers' Remuneration* (December 2010), *MARKT/G4 D* (2010) 950800; *Feedback on public consultation on UCITS V* (February 2011).

sideration when adopting the depositary provisions in the AIFMD.[5] By means of the AIFMD and UCITSD V, legal clarity and certainty concerning the responsibilities of depositaries within the AIF and UCITS domain have been created amongst Member States.[6]

This chapter focuses on the AIFMD and UCITSD V depositary framework. Section 4.2 discusses the obligation to appoint a depositary, Section 4.3 which entities are eligible, Section 4.4 what general requirements apply to depositaries and Section 4.5 what additional requirements apply to third country depositaries. Section 4.6 focuses on the functions and role of depositaries in relation to investors and AIFM s/UCITS ManCos. In particular, this part seeks to define the safekeeping and oversight duties of depositaries under the AIFMD and UCITSD V. Section 4.7 analyses the AIFMD's (sub-)delegation requirements for depositary functions, Section 4.8 the AIFMD/UCITSD V depositary liability regime and Section 4.9 the 'lex specialis' depositary provisions laid down in the AIFMD/UCITSD V 'product regulations'. Section 4.10 concludes.

4.2   THE SCOPE OF THE AIFMD AND UCITSD V WITH REGARD TO DEPOSITARIES

The AIFMD and UCITSD V harmonize the law applicable to depositaries by requiring, with a few exemptions under the AIFMD, a depositary to be appointed for all AIFs and UCITS.

4.2.1   The Obligation to Appoint a Depositary under the AIFMD

The appointment of a depositary under the AIFMD

		EEA-AIF	TC-AIF
EEA-AIFM	Private Placement	AIFMD Depositary	Depositary-lite
	AIFMD Marketing Passport	AIFMD Depositary	Depositary-lite
TC-AIFM	Private Placement	None- MS Law	None- MS Law
	AIFMD Marketing Passport	AIFMD Depositary	AIFMD Depositary

---

5   Most of the AIFMD depositary framework provisions that are discussed in this chapter applies to UCITS depositaries as well. *See* Arts. 22-26b UCITSD V.

6   I. Riassetto, *Dépositaires – Quelles différences entre la directive OPCVM V et la directive AIFM?*, 4 RD Bancaire et Financier (2014); K. Lachgar, *From the UCITS Directive to the Transposition of AIFMD: Exegesis of Evolutions's Depositary Activity in Europe*, Joly Bourse (2014); I. Riassetto, *La clarification des obligations et de la responsabilité des dépositaires par la directive OPCVM V*, 98 Revue Lamy Droit des Affaires 31 (2014); I. Riassetto, *Le nouveau régime applicable aux dépositaires issu de la directive OPCVM V*, 3 Bulletin Joly Bourse 113 (2015).

4.2.1.1   General Rule

Prior to the AIFMD, managers of European AIFs were in several Member States not required to appoint a depositary.[7] The AIFMD ended up this inconsistency amongst Member States by requiring AIFMs to appoint a single depositary for each AIF it manages.[8]

4.2.1.2   The Retail-AIF Depositary

The obligation to appoint a depositary applies to AIFMs regardless of whether units or shares of AIFs are marketed to professional or retail investors. Member States are only left the discretionary choice whether they allow AIFMs to market AIFs to retail investors in their territory, which are managed in accordance with the AIFMD or not.[9] For that purpose, Member States may determine:[10]

- the types of AIFs that AIFMs are allowed to market to retail investors in their territory;[11]
- any additional requirements that the Member State imposes for the marketing of AIFs to retail investors.[12]

Stricter (depositary) requirements may be imposed on the AIFM or the AIF by Member States than the requirements applicable to professional-AIFs provided that these are not stricter than those imposed on AIFs marketed domestically.[13]

Germany[14] and Luxembourg[15] have made use of this opportunity as they are of the opinion that a higher degree of protection should be offered to retail-AIF investors compared to professional-AIFs.[16] Both Member States limit the eligible entities of retail-AIFs

---

7   In the Netherlands, for instance, many AIFs were not subjected to regulatory law and, thus, did not have to appoint a depositary at all. *See* S.N. Hooghiemstra, *The AIFM's Transposition in the Netherlands* (D.A. Zetzsche ed., Kluwer 2015); M. Tausk, *De verplichting om een bewaarder te benoemen: alles gaat veranderen* 22-43 (N.B. Spoor, M. Tausk, J.B. Huizink & R.P. Raas eds., Kluwer 2012).

8   Art. 21(1) AIFMD; K. Lachgar, *Le rôle du dépositaire dans l'ère AIFM: 'business as usual' ou opportunité de différenciation?*, 749 Revue Banque (2012).

9   This applies to all managed AIFs, irrespective of whether such AIFs are marketed on a domestic or cross-border basis or whether they are EEA or TC-AIFs. *See* Art. 43(1) AIFMD.

10   Art. 43(2) AIFMD.

11   Art. 43(2)(a) AIFMD.

12   Art. 43(2)(b) AIFMD.

13   Art. 43(1) AIFMD.

14   § 87 KAGB.

15   Art. 15 law of 17 December 2010 relating to undertakings for collective investment.

16   Germany: Gesetzentwurf der Bundesregierung Entwurf eines Gesetzes zur Umsetzung der Richtlinie 2014/91/EU des Europäischen Parlaments und des Rates vom 23 Juli 2014 zur Änderung der Richtlinie 2009/65/EG zur Koordinierung der Rechts- und Verwaltungsvorschriften betreffend bestimmte Organismen für gemeinsame Anlagen in Wertpapieren (OGAW) im Hinblick auf die Aufgaben der Verwahrstelle, die Vergütungspolitik und Sanktionen, Drucksache 18/6744, 18 November 2015, 35-36; Luxembourg: *See* the commentary on Art. 3 and 15 Projet de loi du portant transposition- de la directive 2014/86/UE du Conseil du 8 juillet 2014 modifiant directive 2011/96/UE, Session ordinaire 2014-2015, 05 August 2015.

depositaries to credit institutions.[17] On top of that, both Germany and Luxembourg extend the stricter retail investor protection depositary provisions offered under UCITSD V and the UCITSD V (Commission) Regulation[18] to retail-AIF depositaries that relate to the;[19]

- requirement to provide an inventory of assets;[20]
- independence of the management/investment company and the UCITS depositary;[21]
- prohibition on the right of reuse/rehypothecation of assets;[22]
- client asset protection on insolvency of the depositary or a sub-custodian;[23]
- strict liability for a loss of custody assets;[24] and
- redress of investors against the depositary.[25]

Similarly, Austria[26] applies its UCITSD V implementation to two types of retail-AIFs, including Special Funds[27] and Other Funds.[28] Unlike Germany and Luxembourg, Austria has, however, not specified whether the UCITSD V (Commission) Regulation applies to these retail-AIFs. Given the extension of the UCITSD V depositary regime to these types of retail-AIFs, the UCITSD V (Commission) Regulation should be applied analogously.

Ireland[29] and the UK[30] impose a few additional tasks upon retail-AIF compared to professional-AIF depositaries.[31] They do, however, not extend the UCITSD V depositary requirements to retail-AIFs.

France,[32] Liechtenstein,[33] Malta[34] and the Netherlands[35] have implemented the UCITSD V but do not require stricter requirements for depositaries of retail-AIFs compared to professional-AIFs.

---

17 Germany: § 87 KAGB; Luxembourg: Art. 15 law of 17 December 2010 relating to undertakings for collective investment.
18 Commission Delegated Regulation (EU) 2016/438 of 17 December 2015 supplementing Directive 2009/65/EC of the European Parliament and of the Council with regard to obligations of depositaries, OJ L 78/11, 24 March 2016, 11 ('UCITSD V (Commission) Regulation')).
19 T. Dolan, *UCITS V Brings Convergence of the Depositary Role with AIFMD*, 1 JIBFL 64B (2015).
20 Art. 22(6) UCITSD V.
21 *See* Art. 26b UCITSD V; Art. 21 UCITSD V (Commission) Regulation.
22 Art. 22(7) UCITSD V.
23 Art. 22(8) UCITSD V.
24 Art. 24 UCITSD V.
25 Art. 24 UCITSD V.
26 § 164(2), § 167(1) InvFG 2011.
27 § 164(2) InvFG 2011.
28 § 167(1) InvFG 2011.
29 *See, e.g.* Central Bank of Ireland, Chapter 1 – Retail Investor AIF Requirement, Part I. General Rules, 2. Supervisory Requirements, v. Replacement of Depositary, 56.
30 The UK has retained pre-AIFMD existing standards for retail authorized funds ('NURS'); *See* COLL 6.6.
31 *See, e.g.* Central Bank of Ireland, *supra* note 29; UK: COLL 6.6.
32 Arts. L214-10 et seq. CMF.
33 Art. 32 et seq. UCITSG.
34 Investment Services Act (custodians of collective investment schemes) Regulations 2016.
35 Art. 4:62l-4:62w Wft.

Member States are, thus, not allowed to derogate the mandatory depositary appointment for AIFs that are (solely) marketed to retail investors. Instead, Art. 43 AIFMD allows them impose stricter depositary rules to retail-AIFs.

4.2.1.3   Exemptions from the Depositary Obligation

The AIFMD provides several exemptions from the general depositary obligation. EEA-AIFMs managing TC-AIFs that are marketed outside of the EEA are not required to appoint a depositary as they fall outside the scope of the AIFMD.[36] The same holds true for:

- AIFs which are managed by 'small' AIFMs;
- (non-)EEA-AIFs that are managed by third country AIFMs[37] and marketed in the EEA on a private placement basis.[38]

4.2.1.3.1   'Small' AIFMs

The AIFMD contains a *de minimis* exemption for 'small' AIFMs.[39] Although the AIFMD exempts these AIFMs from the scope of the AIFMD, Member States are allowed to adopt stricter rules with respect to 'small' AIFMs.[40] As a result, whether a depositary needs to be appointed or not for an AIF that is either marketed to professional and/or retail investors by a 'small' AIFM depends upon the AIFMD implementation laws of the individual Member States. For this purpose, various Member States differentiate between 'small' AIFMs that market AIFs to retail and professional investors, whereas others apply a depositary regime to AIFs managed by 'small' AIFMs regardless of whether the AIF is being marketed to professional or retail-AIFs.

'Small' AIFMs that are managing professional-AIFs in Austria,[41] Germany,[42] Luxembourg[43] and the Netherlands[44] are solely subject to the minimum registration requirement laid down in the AIFMD. Consequently, Austria,[45] Germany[46] and the Netherlands do not require a depositary for professional-AIFs to be appointed. Luxembourg exempts

---

36 *See* Art. 42(1)(a) AIFMD. The same applies to AIFs that are marketed to retail investors. *See* Art. 43 AIFMD.
37 TC-AIFMs refers to AIFMs that are established outside of the EEA.
38 Art. 42 AIFMD.
39 This exemption refers to AIFMs managing (i) AIFs whose AuM do not exceed a threshold of EUR 100 million, irrespective of whether such AuM are wholly or partly acquired through the use of leverage, or (ii) AIFs whose AuM in total do not exceed a threshold of EUR 500 million, provided that such AuM are unleveraged and investors are not granted redemption rights for a period of five years. AIFMs wishing to rely on these exemptions are subject to a duty to register themselves with the Competent Authorities of the AIF's home Member State. *See* Art. 3 AIFMD.
40 D.A. Zetzsche & C.D. Preiner, *Scope of the AIFMD* (D.A. Zetzsche ed., Kluwer 2015).
41 § 1(5) Austrian AIFM Law.
42 § 2(4), § 2(5), § 44(1), (3)-(7), § 45-48 KAGB.
43 Art. 3(3) Luxembourg AIFM Law.
44 Art. 2:66a Wft.
45 § 1(5) Austrian AIFM Law.
46 § 2(4), § 2(5), § 80-90 KAGB.

professional-AIFs from the AIFMD depositary requirement as well. Nevertheless, Luxembourg requires a depositary to be appointed in its national product regulation for SICARs and SIFs that are managed by 'small' AIFMs.[47] For these SIFs/SICARs an amended depositary regime is applicable, which is based upon both the AIFMD and the pre-AIFMD depositary regime.[48]

Austria[49] and the Netherlands[50] require 'small' AIFMs that market AIFs to retail investors to obtain a full authorization under the AIFMD.[51] For these AIFs, a depositary needs to be appointed. In Germany, it depends upon the type of AIF whether a depositary needs to be appointed or not.[52] Closed-end AIFs that do not exceed the EUR 100 million AIFMD threshold (including leverage) and are not exclusively marketed to professional investors are only subject to a registration requirement.[53] All closed-end retail-AIFs that are not managed by a 'small' internally managed AIFM[54] that does not manage more than EUR 5 million (including leverage) and does not have more than five natural persons as investors must, amongst others,[55] appoint a depositary.[56] The same applies to internally managed closed-end retail-AIFs that are being established as a cooperative[57] and do not manage more than EUR 100 million (incl. leverage).[58] Similar as for SIFs and SICARs, Luxembourg exempts retail-AIFs (UCIs) managed by 'small' AIFMs from the AIFMD depositary requirement. Luxembourg requires, however, a depositary to be appointed in its national product regulation for UCIs that are managed by 'small' AIFMs.[59] Similar as for SIFs and SICARs, the pre-AIFMD depositary regime is, to a large extent,

---

47 *See* Art. 16-19 SIF Law; Art. 8-10 SICAR Law; For SIFs, and SICARs Luxembourg delineates between Part I and Part II of the SIF and SICAR Law. Part I of the SIF/SICAR law applies to (1) SIFs/SICARs that do not qualify as AIFs, and (2) SIFs and SICARs benefitting from the 'small' AIFM regime.

48 Part I SICAR and SIF depositaries do not have to exercise any controlling duties under the Luxembourg depositary regime. The AIFMD delegation and liability regimes are for these depositaries also not applicable. Part II SIFs and Part II SICARs fall entirely within the AIFMD and, thus, have to apply the AIFMD depositary rules; *See* Arts. 16-19 SIF Law and Arts. 8-10 SICAR Law.

49 § 2(5) Austrian AIFM Law.

50 Extra requirements apply to the organization of the AIFMs that is marketing AIFs to retail investors. *See* § 10.3.1.1. Besluit Gedragstoezicht financiële ondernemingen Wft.

51 Member States have, however, different interpretations of what constitutes a 'retail investor' under the AIFMD; *See* D.A. Zetzsche, *Fondsregulierung im Umbruch – ein rechtsvergleichender Rundblick zur Umsetzung der AIFM-Richtlinie*, ZBB 22 (2014).

52 § 80-90 KAGB.

53 § 2(5), 80-90 KAGB.

54 § 2(4a) KAGB.

55 § 1-17, 26-28, 42 and 44 KAGB.

56 § 2(4a) KAGB, § 80-90 KAGB.

57 § 53-64c Genossenschaftgesetz.

58 § 2(4b) KAGB.

59 Art. 90(2) UCI Law; Some adjustment to the pre-AIFMD depositary regime were made. Both credit institutions and investment firms are in the post-AIFMD era allowed to be appointed as a depositary. Under the UCI Law, depositaries remained to be partly exempted of their obligations. For contractual funds this concerns the valuation controlling duty and the AIFMD depositary liability. Furthermore, SICAVs and UCIs which have not been constituted as common funds or are not subject to the valuation and AIFM instruction controlling duty. *See* Art. 95(1b), 99(6bis) UCI Law.

maintained in Luxembourg for UCIs marketed to retail investors managed by 'small' AIFMs.[60]

Ireland and France do not differentiate between professional and retail investors and require all types of 'small' AIFMs to obtain a full-fledged AIFM authorization.[61] Both Ireland and France, however, dispense from certain AIFMD requirements.[62] France, for example, does not require the 'small' AIFMs managing professional-AIFs to appoint a depositary.[63] Ireland, however, does require a depositary.[64] In Liechtenstein 'small' AIFMs are subjected to a 'light authorization'. The appointment of a depositary is mandatory irrespective of whether the AIF is marketed to professional or retail investors.[65]

The UK does not differentiate between professional and retail-AIFs managed by 'small' AIFMs for the purpose of depositary regulation either. Unlike France and Ireland, however, a full-fledged AIFM authorization is not required.[66] 'Small' AIFMs, including 'small authorized AIFMs'[67] and 'small registered AIFM s',[68] both do not have to abide by the AIFMD depositary rules irrespective of whether they manage professional or retail-AIFs. The application of the COLL depositary requirements in the UK is applicable to AIFs depending upon whether the 'small' AIFM managing them is a small authorized AIFM or a small registered AIFM. The COLL depositary regulation does not apply to (unauthorized) AIFs managed by small registered AIFMs.[69] The application of the COLL depositary rules to a small authorized AIFM depends on whether it manages an authorized AIF or an unauthorized AIF.[70] A small authorized AIFM that manages an authorized AIF will be subject to the requirements in COLL, but a small authorized UK AIFM of

---

60   Art. 90(2), Art. 95(1b), 99(6bis) UCI Law.
61   France: L 214-24 III CMF and Art. 532-9 CMF, that refer to L214-24 II CMF; *See also* AMF, Guide des mesures de modernisation apportées aux placements collectifs français (Julliet 2013), 3 et seq., 21 et seq.; Ireland: Central Bank of Ireland, AIF Rulebook, July 2013, Chapter 2 – Qualifying Investor AIF Requirements, Part. III. Additional Provisions Applicable to Qualifying Investor AIFs which have a registered AIFM.
62   *See also* AMF, *Guide des mesures de modernisation apportées aux placements collectifs français* (Julliet 2013), 3 et seq., 21 et seq.;
63   Central Bank of Ireland, *supra* note 61.
64   France: Art. L 214-24 III. Code monétaire et financier. *See also* L. 532-9 Code monétaire et financier; Ireland: Central Bank of Ireland, *supra* note 61.
65   Also other provisions of the AIFMD partly apply to these AIFMs. Apart from the mandatory appointment of an authorized administrator, Liechtenstein requires, amongst others, the appointment of an auditor/ accountant, the AIFMD's rules of conduct and valuation to be applied. *See* Art. 3(1), (4)-(6) Liechtenstein AIFM Law. Several provisions, such as the minimum capital requirement, the securitization provisions and the AIFMD remuneration requirements do not apply.
66   *See* J.R. Siena & D. Eckner, *The AIFM's Transposition in the United Kingdom* 805 (D.A. Zetzsche ed., Kluwer 2015).
67   FUND 1.3.6 G.
68   *Ibid.* The small registered AIFM is limited to three types of AIFMs for which registration is possible: the small internal AIFM, the small property AIFM and managers of EuSEFs and EuVECAs; *See* Siena & Eckner, *supra* note 66.
69   COLL 6.1 and COLL 6.6.
70   COLL 6.6.

an unauthorized AIF is not subjected to COLL.[71] The specific depositary requirements under COLL depend on whether the authorized AIF qualifies as an NURS or a QIS.[72]

The mandatory duty to appoint a depositary for 'small' AIFMs that manage professional and retail investors, thus, varies from Member State to Member State.

4.2.1.3.2 Private Placement Regime – AIFs Managed by TC-AIFMs

Member States may, for AIFs managed by TC-AIFMs and marketed within their domicile, decide to extend the AIFMD depositary laws to AIFs that do not use the AIFMD marketing passport in their respective private placement regimes. The approaches taken by Member States that decided to implement Article 42 AIFMD differ significantly. Austria[73] requires an AIFMD depositary to be appointed, whereas Ireland,[74] Luxembourg,[75] the Netherlands[76] and the UK[77] do not impose a depositary requirement to TC-AIFMs that wish to market (non-)EEA-AIFs to professional investors within their domiciles.

Denmark,[78] France,[79] Germany[80] and Liechtenstein[81] take a position in the middle. They do not require TC-AIFMs that are permitted to market (non-)EEA-AIFs to professional investors on a private placement basis in their domiciles to appoint a depositary that complies with Article 21 AIFMD nor do they exempt them from appointing a depositary fully. Instead, they make use of the option to require stricter rules regarding the marketing of non-EEA funds managed by TC-AIFMs by extending the Article 36 AIFMD 'depositary-lite' requirement to their Article 42 AIFMD implementation.[82] It is,

---

71 COLL 6.1 and COLL 6.6.
72 *See* for non-UCITS retail schemes: COLL 6.6. *See* for Qualified Investor Schemes: COLL 8.5.4.
73 Section 47(1) Austrian AIFM Law.
74 The Irish implementation grants by means of Art. 43(4) AIFM Regulations the Central Bank of Ireland the power to impose additional conditions or requirements, such as the appointment of a depositary, where it considers it necessary for the proper and orderly regulation and supervision of AIFMs. No such conditions or restrictions have been made to date.
75 Art. 45 Luxembourg AIFM Law.
76 Art. 1:13b(1), (2) FSMA; *See* C.M. Grundmann-van de Krol, *Regulering beleggingsinstellingen en icbe's in de Wft* 166-170 (Den Haag: Boom Juridische Uitgevers 2013); *See* on the general implementation of the implementation of Art. 42 AIFMD in the Netherlands: Hooghiemstra, *supra* note 7.
77 Art. 57 Alternative Investment Fund Managers Regulations, 2013, S.I. (2013) No. 1773 as implemented in: FUND 10.5.9-10.5.11A; PERG 8.37 AIFMD Marketing.
78 In Denmark, the depositary-lite provision is only required for TC-AIFMs marketing TC-AIFs. No depositary-lite requirement exists for EEA-AIFs being marketed on the basis of national private placement rules by TC-AIFMs in their domicile. *See* s. 130(5) Alternative Investment Fund Managers Etc. Act (Act No. 598 of the 12 June 2013); s. 4. Executive Order on authorization for alternative investment fund managers to market the alternative investment fund established in third country in Denmark (EO No. 798 of the 26 June 2014).
79 Art. D 214-32 CMF.
80 Paragraph 330(1) sub-para. 1, (2) KAGB.
81 TC-AIFMs willing to market (non-)EEA AIFs in Liechtenstein without making use of the AIFM marketing passport need to be authorized according to Art. 128, 150 Liechtenstein AIFM Law. *See* Art. 133(1)(a) Liechtenstein AIFM Law.
82 *See infra* 4.2.1.4.

however, possible that the private placement regime will be phased out in 2018 and that this 'exemption' from the depositary requirements under the private placement regime may not be available after that date. Compliance with the depositary requirements is, however, in any case required by the AIFMD when an AIF is marketed to professional investors on the basis of the pan-European passport for both EEA- and TC-AIFMs.

4.2.1.4   Depositary-Lite Regime

Article 36 AIFMD provides an option for Member States to relax the AIFMD depositary regime with respect to TC-AIFs that are managed by EEA-AIFMs and marketed to professional investors in their domiciles on the basis of a private placement regime (referred to in practice as 'depositary-lite'). This option may only be granted by Member States to EEA-AIFMs provided that:[83]

- appropriate cooperation arrangements providing for information exchange between the Competent Authorities of both the home Member State of the AIFM and the supervisory authorities of the TC-AIF should be in place;[84]
- the country where the TC-AIF is established is not listed as a Non-Cooperative Country and Territory by FATF;[85] and
- the (EEA) AIFM complies with all the AIFMD requirements with the exception of the mandatory appointment of a depositary under Article 21 AIFMD.[86]

Member States that exempt EEA-AIFMs from appointing an Article 21 AIFMD depositary should, however, instead require EEA-AIFMs to ensure that one or more entities are appointed to carry out depositary duties mentioned under Article 21(7)–(9) AIFMD.[87] The depositary duties to be performed by these entities include: the monitoring of cash,[88] the safekeeping of assets[89] and the performance of oversight duties.[90] Unless Member States have chosen to impose stricter rules on such entities,[91] the AIFMD depositary eligibility criteria, the AIFMD delegation and liability regime are not applicable. The AIFM managing and marketing the TC-AIF may not at the same time perform those

---

83 Recital 63, Art. 36(1) AIFMD.
84 Art. 36(1)(b) AIFMD.
85 Art. 36(1)(c) AIFMD.
86 Art. 36(1)(a) AIFMD.
87 Art. 36(1)(a) AIFMD.
88 The monitoring of the TC-AIFs cash flows includes the reconciliation of the cash accounts with the records of third parties. *See infra* at 4.6.3.7.
89 The safekeeping function comprises of either holding financial instruments assets in custody, where such assets can be held in custody, or verifying the fund's ownership for assets that cannot be held in custody. *See infra* 4.6.2.
90 The performance of oversight function includes, amongst others, the calculation of distributions made to investors and checking compliance with investment restrictions.
91 Art. 36(2) AIFMD.

depositary functions for this AIF.[92] The AIFM shall provide its supervisory authorities with the information about the identity of the entities responsible for carrying out the depositary functions.[93]

Several Member States have adopted the depositary-lite model under their Article 36 AIFMD implementation.[94] The safekeeping of financial instruments may in all Member States only be performed by investment firms, credit institutions or other domestic entities that have obtained an authorization to provide custody services.[95] The regulatory approach taken regarding the entities performing the monitoring of cash and the performance of oversight duties differs from Member State to Member State. Ireland, for instance, does only require entities providing the safekeeping function, including both the custody as the record-keeping tasks, to be authorized under the Investment Intermediaries Act 1995.[96] Entities that are only providing the cash monitoring, regulatory oversight or both functions will not need to obtain authorization. To the contrary, both Malta[97] and the UK[98] require entities appointed to carry out one of the latter two functions to obtain an authorization as a depositary/custodian.

4.2.2 The Obligation to Appoint a Depositary under the UCITSD V

A UCITS ManCo has to ensure that for each UCITS a single depositary is appointed in accordance with UCITSD V.[99] UCITSD V requires a depositary to be appointed irrespective of the legal form of the UCITS and whether or not the UCITS is listed.[100] Unlike under the AIFMD, no exemptions from this requirements are available. This can be explained by the fact that UCITS are undertakings for collective investment that are man-

---

92 Art. 36(1)(a) AIFMD.
93 *Ibid.*
94 Austria: Art. 38(1) sub-para. 1, (2) Austrian AIFM Law; Germany: para. 329(1)(2) KAGB; Ireland: Art. 37(2) (a) SI 257 of 2013- European Union (Alternative Investment Fund Managers) Regulations 2013 (AIFM Regulation); Liechtenstein: Art. 128(1)(a) Liechtenstein AIFM Law; Luxembourg: Art. 37 Luxembourg AIFM Act; Malta: Art. 7(1)(a) Investment Services Act (Alternative Investment Fund Manager) (Third Country) Regulations; UK: FUND 3.11.33.
95 Central Bank of Ireland, *Consultation on Carrying Out Depositary Duties in Accordance with Article 36 of the AIFMD*, 2014; Central Bank of Ireland, *Feedback Statement on CP78: Consultation on carrying out depositary duties in accordance with Article 36 of the AIFMD*, Consultation Paper CP 78, 2014.
96 *Ibid.*
97 SLC 1.03, Part BIV: Part BIV: *Standard Licence Conditions Applicable to Investment Services Licence Holders which Qualify as Custodians, Investment Services Rules* for *Investment Services Licence Holders*; See MFSA, Feedback statement further to industry responses to MFSA Consultation Document dated 18 September 2013 on the introduction of the depositary lite provisions, 2.1.1. [I]. Feedback Statement.
98 *See* FCA, *Frequently Asked Questions: Q9—Does an Article 36 custodian require a Part 4A permission for acting as depositary of an AIF?*, www.fca.org.uk/firms/markets/international-markets/aifmd/depositaries; FCA, *Implementation of the Alternative Investment Fund Managers Directive*, PS 13/5, 39 (2013).
99 Art. 22(1) UCITSD V.
100 Recital 32 UCITSD V; J.E. Klerk & R. Slange, *UCITS V and beyond*, 1/2 TvFR 34-39 (2015).

datorily open-end and are required by the UCITS product regulation to invest mainly in liquid financial assets.

4.3   ENTITIES ELIGIBLE AS A DEPOSITARY AND ITS ORGANIZATIONAL REQUIREMENTS

Since the creation of the EEA legal framework for UCITSD I, the depositary became, alongside the fund and the UCITS ManCo, the third pillar of the investment fund.[101] Depositaries were, however, subject to a very limited number of principles and duties at EEA level, leaving Member States free to regulate many aspects of depositaries. The AIFMD and UCITSD V harmonize the law applicable to entities that are eligible as depositaries and its organizational requirements. In this regard, the AIFMD diverges from UCITSD V due to the larger variety of undertakings of collective investment that fall under the scope of the AIFMD compared to the UCITSD V.[102]

4.3.1   *Entities Eligible as a Depositary under the AIFMD*

The depositary of an AIF must be: (1) a credit institution; (2) an investment firm; (3) an eligible entity under the UCITSD V; (4) a prime broker or (5) an equivalent non-EEA entity.[103] In addition, the AIFMD allows discretion for Member States to appoint a person or entity as depositary for certain closed-end funds.

4.3.1.1   Credit Institution

Under Article 21(3)(a) AIFMD, credit institutions eligible to be appointed must have their registered office in the EEA and be authorized in accordance with CRD IV. Unlike investment firms, the AIFMD does not require credit institutions to obtain an authorization to provide the 'ancillary service' of safekeeping and administration of securities[104] to be eligible as a depositary.[105] The mere authorization of credit institutions for deposit-taking activities suffices.[106]

---

101 *See* D.A. Zetzsche, '*Investment Law as Financial Law: From Fund Governance over Market Governance to Stakeholder Governance?*' 337–355 (Birkmose, Neville & K. Sørensen eds., Kluwer Law International 2012).
102 Zetzsche & Preiner, *supra* note 40.
103 A prime broker can also be appointed as a depositary and is, in particular, subject to the requirements of Art. 21(4) AIFMD. *See* D.A. Zetzsche, *(Prime) Brokerage* (D.A. Zetzsche ed., Kluwer 2015).
104 Annex I n. 12 CRD IV.
105 *See* for a more detailed explanation of credit institutions providing the ancillary service of safekeeping and administration of securities: Chapter 6, Section 6.2.
106 Art. 3(1) point 1 CRD IV/Art. 4(1) point 1 CRR.

4.3.1.2   Investment Firm

Under Article 21(3)(b) AIFMD, investment firms eligible to be appointed must have their registered office in the EEA. Compared to credit institutions, eligible investment firms have to be subject to capital adequacy requirements in accordance with Article 95(1) CRR, including capital requirements for operational risks and authorized in accordance with MiFID II. Only those investment firms are eligible that provide the ancillary service of safekeeping and administration of financial instruments for the account of clients in accordance with Section B Annex I MiFID II.[107] This implies that the safekeeping and administration of financial instruments for the account of clients is not an investment service or activity and can only be provided by investment firms in connection with investment services and activities, such as, amongst others, portfolio management and investment advice.[108] Unlike credit institutions under CRD IV, obtaining an authorization for one of the investment services and activities under MiFID II does not suffice to be eligible as a depositary under the AIFMD. Investment firms that provide this ancillary service shall not have less initial capital than EUR 730.000 referred to in Article 28 CRD IV.

4.3.1.3   Other Eligible Institutions

Besides investment firms and credit institutions, the AIFMD allows other institutions that were on 21 July 2011 eligible under the UCITSD IV to be appointed as a depositary.[109]

The recently adopted UCITSD V creates in Member States uncertainty regarding the question of whether these institutions other than credit institutions and investment firms that were eligible under UCITSD IV may from March 2016 onwards be appointed as a depositary for AIFs.

Under the original UCITSD V proposal, the appointment of 'other eligible institutions' as depositaries for AIFs would effectively only be allowed during a transitional period. The UCITSD V proposal provided an exhaustive list of eligible entities, including credit institutions and investment firms that would be allowed to be appointed as depositaries. After entry into force, the UCITSD V would have set aside this 'grandfathering clause'[110] under the AIFMD.[111] Except for TC-entities and the carve-out for private equity, commodity and real estate funds,[112] no entities other than credit institutions and investment firms would be eligible under the AIFMD.

---

107 *See* P.J. van Zaal, *Aanhouden van gelden door beleggingsondernemingen en betaaldienstverleners*, 9 TvFR 226-237 (2010).

108 Annex I s. A MiFID II.

109 Art. 21(3)(c) AIFMD.

110 European Commission, *Working Document of the Commission Services (DG Internal Market and Services) – Consultation Paper on the UCITSD Depositary Function and on the UCITS Managers' Remuneration*, MARKT/G4 D (2010) 950800, 14 December 2010, 16.

111 Art. 23a(2) UCITSD V Draft proposal.

112 *See infra* at 4.3.1.6.

The final UCITSD V text, however, finally settled on an extension of eligible institutions compared to the originally proposed UCITSD V.[113] Depositaries under the UCITSD V may be a credit institution, a national central bank or another legal entity that is authorized by Member States to carry on depositary activities[114] that are subject to ongoing supervision as well as minimum capital, prudential and organizational requirements.[115]

UCITSD V nor its preparatory documents have provided any clarity on whether and to what extent these other eligible institutions will be allowed to be appointed under the AIFMD as an AIF depositary.[116] The UCITSD V 'other legal entities' eligible as depositaries are subjected to minimum harmonization on the European level regarding capital, prudential and organizational requirements.[117] Additional minimum requirements regarding these other legal entities apply in relation to infrastructure, experience, administrative and accounting procedures internal control mechanisms, risk management procedures and arrangements to prevent conflicts of interest.[118] These entities are, thus, offering more investor protection than some of the institutions that Member States determined to be eligible as a depositary under UCITSD IV.[119] By interpreting the AIFMD 'grandfathering provision' dynamically, entities complying with these requirements can both be determined by Member States to be appointed as a depositary for UCITS and AIFs.[120] Apart from this, it prevents that in some Member States entities are excluded from the AIFMD depositary market that fulfil similar minimum capital, prudential and organizational requirements as credit institutions and investment firms.[121] Taken into account that for TC-AIFs it is under the AIFMD possible for a depositary not only to be a credit institution or investment firm, but also any other entity of the same nature as this dynamic interpretation should be acceptable for these entities.[122]

---

113 *See* Art. 23(2) UCITSD V.
114 Art. 23(2) UCITSD V.
115 Art. 23(2)(c) sub-para. 1 UCITSD V.
116 *See* the Explanatory Memorandum of the UCITSD V Draft proposal, 4 and 5.
117 Art. 23(2)(c) sub-para. 1 UCITSD V.
118 Art. 23(2)(c) UCITSD V.
119 Dutch UCITS IV depositaries, for instance, were only subject to an own funds requirement of EUR 112,500, which is sufficiently lower than the EUR 730,000 required by Art. 23(2)(c) UCITSD IV. *See* Art. 48(1)(n) Prudential Rules Decree of 12 October 2006 (Besluit prudentiële regels, Bpr).
120 European Commission, Undertakings for collective investment in transferable securities – amended Directive (UCITS V): Frequently asked questions, MEMO/14/198, 15 April 2014, Question 7. What is the link between the provisions on depositaries in the Alternative Investment Fund Managers Directive and the amended UCITS Directive?
121 European Commission, *Impact Assessment – Proposal for a Directive of the European Parliament and of the Council amending Directive 2009/65/EC on the coordination of laws, regulations and administrative provisions relating to undertakings for collective investment in transferable securities (UCITS) as regards depositary functions, remuneration policies and sanctions* (COM(2012) 350) (SWD(2012) 186), 32, 33.
122 Recital 34 AIFMD; this dynamic interpretation is applied in practice by the Dutch AIFMD and UCITSD V implementation. The eligible entities for both (Dutch) AIF and UCITS depositaries has been completely harmonized under Art. 4:62n Wft.

4.3.1.4 Prime Broker

The AIFMD recognizes the fact that many AIFs, such as hedge funds, make use of a prime broker.[123] Under the AIFMD, the prime broker may, in addition to its role as counterparty to an AIF, be appointed as a depositary (and as a sub-custodian).[124]

4.3.1.4.1 The Prime Broker as Counterparty

Under Article 4(1)(af) AIFMD the prime broker is being defined as

> a credit institution, a regulated investment firm or another entity subject prudential regulation and ongoing supervision, offering one or more services to professional investors primarily to finance or execute transactions in financial instruments as counterparty and which may also provide other services such as clearing and settlement of trades, custodial services, securities lending, customized technology and operational support facilities.

Following this definition, prime brokers under the AIFMD are primarily counterparties to AIFs. Prime brokers are 'offering one or more services to professional investors *primarily* to finance or execute transactions in financial instruments as *counterparty*'.[125] In its capacity as counterparty, prime brokers, when offering 'core' services, may also provide 'ancillary' services, including the clearing and settlement of trades, custodial services, securities lending, customized technology and operational support facilities Prime brokers may, however, only provide 'custodial services' as 'ancillary' service to AIFs[126] by being appointed as a depositary (or a sub-custodian) under the AIFMD provided that certain conditions preventing conflicts of interest are in place.[127]

4.3.1.4.2 The Prime Broker as Depositary

Under Article 21(4)(b) AIFMD, prime brokers acting as counterparty to an AIF may only be appointed as a depositary for that AIF provided that:
- it has functionally and hierarchically separated the performance of its depositary functions from its tasks as prime broker; and
- the potential conflicts of interest that may arise from the fact that the depositary is also acting as prime broker are identified, managed, monitored and disclosed to the investors of the AIF.

---

123 Recital 43 AIFMD.
124 *See* Zetzsche, *supra* note 103, 580–590.
125 Art. 4(1)(af) AIFMD. *See* on the counterparty function and its risks: M.R. King & P. Maier, *Hedge Funds and Financial Stability: Regulating Prime Brokers will Mitigate Systemic Risks*, 5 Journal of Financial Stability 283–297 (2009); N. Tuchschmid, E. Wallerstein & A. Zanolin, *Hedge Funds and Prime Brokers: The Role of Funding Risk*, http://ssrn.com/abstract=1343673.
126 Recital 43 AIFMD.
127 Art. 21(4)(b) AIFMD.

The rationale behind this mandatory segregation of depositary from prime broker functions is that there is an inherent conflict of interest between prime brokers acting as counterparties to AIFs and, therefore, the prime broker in its capacity as counterparty cannot at the same time act in the best interest of the AIF as is required of a depositary.[128]

Prime brokers acting as a counterparty for an AIF may, thus,, only be appointed as a depositary for that AIF provided that Chinese walls are in place.[129]

4.3.1.5   Eligible Non-EEA Entities

For TC-AIFs, either a credit institution or any other entity of the same nature as an EEA investment firm may be appointed. The depositary, however, shall be subject to effective prudential regulation, including minimum capital requirements and supervision, which has the same effect as EU law and is effectively enforced.[130] In addition, TC depositaries underlie the requirements discussed in Section 4.5.

4.3.1.6   Option for Private Equity Funds, Venture Capital Funds and Real Estate AIFs

Member States may authorize both TC- and EEA-AIFs to appoint a person or entity as depositary (e.g. a lawyer, trustee, notary or registrar) not belonging to the eligible entities as discussed above.[131]

Such persons or entities are required to:
– carry out the depositary functions as part of their professional or business activities;
– be subject to mandatory professional registration recognized by law or to statutory or regulatory provisions or rules of professional conduct; and
– furnish sufficient financial and professional guarantees to be able to effectively perform the relevant depositary functions and meet the commitments inherent to those functions.

Member States may allow this for AIFs:
– that have no redemption rights exercisable during a period of five years from the date of their initial investments and which, according to their core investment policy, generally do not invest in financial instruments that must be held in custody; or
– generally invest in issuers or non-listed companies in order to potentially acquire control over such companies.[132]

---

128 *See* Recital 43 AIFMD.
129 Art. 21(4)(b) AIFMD
130 Art. 21(3)(c) sub-para. 2 AIFMD.
131 O. Schröder & A. Rahn, *Das KAGB und Private-Equity-Transaktionen – Pflichten für Manager von Private-Equity-Fonds und deren Verwahrstellen*, GWR 49 (2014).
132 Art. 21(3)(c) sub-para. 3 AIFMD.

This option is designed for closed-end AIFs, such as private equity, venture capital and real estate funds, that generally do not invest in financial instruments. Credit institutions and investment firms have little expertise in safekeeping such assets as real estate, partnership shares, ships and physical assets (e.g. pure gold).[133] Moreover, these assets cannot be held in bank accounts. As this option requires significant private law and corporate law expertise, the AIFMD allows specialists to carry out the safekeeping of these types of assets.

The implementation of this option diverges from Member State to Member State. France has chosen not to implement this option. Only the 'regular depositaries', including credit institutions, investment firms and UCITSD IV/V depositaries may be appointed under the AIFMD implementation in France.[134]

To the contrary, Ireland and the Netherlands subject their 'PE-depositary' to the minimum requirements under Article 21(3)(c) sub-para. 3 AIFMD.[135] Both Ireland and the Netherlands do not specify what professionals or entities may perform this function. All persons and entities as indicated under the AIFMD may be appointed as a 'PE-depositary'. Ireland, however, requires professionals and entities to have a minimum capital of at least EUR 125.000.[136] For entities and professionals that undertake business activities riskier than, for example, safekeeping of assets other than financial instruments that can be held in custody, more minimum capital is required.[137]

In Austria and Liechtenstein only professional trustees are eligible as a 'PE-depositaries' to carry out depositary functions as part of their professional activities.[138] Liechtenstein trustees are subject to the professional conduct rules as laid down in the Liechtenstein Trustee Act.[139] In addition, the trustee is required to have a mandatory liability insurance.[140] Trustees appointed as a 'PE-depositaries' depositary' in Austria are also required to conclude a liability insurance contract.[141] Moreover, trustees in Austria have to notify the financial market authority of the duration of the insurance contract and the conditions under which the contract may be terminated in case an insurance company is covering the financial guarantees of the trustee.[142] Similarly, Germany also

---

133 Zetzsche, *supra* note 51.
134 *See* Art. L214-24-5 CMF.
135 Ireland: n. 22(3)(a)(iii) AIFM Regulations; Central Bank of Ireland, AIF Rulebook, July 2013, Chapter 6 – AIF Depositary Requirements, Annex I Minimum Capital Requirement Report – Notes on Compilation (Depositary); The Netherlands: Art. 115g BfGO.
136 N. 22(3)(a)(iii) AIFM Regulations; Central Bank of Ireland, *supra* note 135.
137 Central Bank of Ireland, *supra* note 135.
138 Referred to as 'treuhänder'. *See* in Austria: § 19(18) Austrian AIFM Law.; *See* in Liechtenstein: Art. 57 Liechtenstein AIFM Law.
139 Art. 57 Liechtenstein AIFM Law.
140 Art. 5-11 Treuhändergesetz.
141 § 19(18) Austrian AIFM Law.
142 *Ibid.*

allows trustees to be appointed as a depositary for illiquid assets.[143] A different regime applies depending upon whether the trustee is appointed for professional or retail-AIFs.[144] Trustees acting for retail-AIFs need to obtain an authorization, whereas trustees action for professional-AIFs are exempted from this obligation.[145] The authorization procedure for retail-AIF trustees requires trustees to be 'fit and proper' and to furnish sufficient financial and professional guarantees. Trustees are not allowed to safekeep any financial instruments that should be held in custody or any funds belonging to an AIF. In addition, a liability insurance contract and enough financial resources are required.[146] Finally, a depositary contract needs to be concluded between the trustee and the AIFM.[147]

Luxembourg and the UK have taken another approach by introducing a specific type of 'national investment firm' that needs to obtain an authorization as a 'PE-depositary'. In Luxembourg a new category of investment firm had been introduced that is authorized to act as a 'professional depositary of assets other than financial instruments'.[148] This depositary is authorized to safekeep assets other than financial instruments for SIFs, SICARs and Part II UCIs. Only legal entities having a minimum subscribed and paid-up share capital of EUR 500.000 may be authorized to act as professional depositary of assets other than financial instruments. 'PE depositaries' in Luxembourg may, additionally, be authorized for other investment services/activities, such as fund administration.[149] Similarly, 'PE depositaries' in the UK have to be authorized as a specific type of 'national investment firm'.[150] Unlike Luxembourg, the 'PE-depositary' is not restricted to only safekeep other assets than financial instruments that can be held in custody. Instead, the UK requires substantially more own capital for 'PE-depositaries' that undertake activities with a higher risk, such as the safekeeping of financial instruments that can be held in custody.[151]

Most Member States in the EEA, thus, have implemented the option of the 'PE-depositary' in their national laws. There are, however, considerable differences in how Member States have implemented this option. The main differences in the national im-

---

143 § 80(3) KAGB; *See also* BaFin, a Guidance Notice on the requirements for trustees acting as depositary (Merkblatt zu den Anforderungen an Treuhänder als Verwahrstelle nach para. 80 Absatz 3 KAGB, Geschäftszeichen WA 41-Wp 2137-2013/0080); J. Kobbach & D. Anders, *Umsetzung der AIFM-Richtlinie aus Sicht der Verwahrstellen*, NZG 1170 (2012).

144 BaFin, *supra* note 143. Bafin, a Guidance Notice on the requirements for trustees acting as depositary ('Merkblatt zu den Anforderungen an Treuhänder als Verwahrstelle nach § 80 Absatz 3 KAGB, Geschäftszeichen WA 41-Wp 2137-2013/0080').

145 § 69(1), (2) and (4), § 87 KAGB.

146 § 80(3) sub-para. 2 KAGB. BaFin, *supra* note 143. BaFin, *Merkblatt zu den Anforderungen an Treuhänder als Verwahrstelle nach § 80 Absatz 3 KAGB*, WA 41-Wp 2137-2013/0080, 18 July 2013.

147 § 80(1), (2) and (3); *See also* Art. 83 AIFMD (Commission) Regulation.

148 Art. 26-1 Law of 5 April 1993 on the financial sector, as amended on 12 June 2013.

149 D.A. Zetzsche, *supra* note 51.

150 FUND 3.11.12 R; FUND 3.11.12 R; FUND 3.11.14 R: *See also* the Glossary Definition FCA: 'Part 4a Permission' and 'acting as trustee or depositary of an AIF' and 'own funds' (FUND 3.11.12-14).

151 FUND 3.11.15, 3.11.16 and 3.11.17 R.

plementations relate to (1) the entities that are allowed to serve as a 'PE-depositary', (2) the conduct of business rules and (3) prudential regulation. Given the AIFMD depositary liability regime, the different implementation of the 'PE-depositary' in the national laws of Member States are unsurprising. Under Article 21 AIFMD, the professionals/entities under the national Member State laws safekeep financial instruments that can be held in custody are subjected to the 'guarantor liability' under the AIFMD depositary liability regime. This liability also applies to 'PE-depositaries' that do not have the organizational structure to safekeep financial instruments that can be held in custody and, in practice, fully delegate this safekeeping task to sub-custodians. It would have been more logical that the AIFMD would have required a 'prime custodian' either being a credit institution or investment firm to be appointed that would be responsible for safekeeping financial instruments that can be held in custody. Credit institutions and investment firms have the organizational structure to grant access to settlement systems and have a better overview of the custody holding chain than 'PE-depositaries' and, apart from this, would be better suited to bear the AIFMD 'guarantor liability' under the AIFMD depositary liability regime.

In short, it can be concluded that the special depositary option for closed-end AIFs funds has been warmly welcomed in Europe. Considerable differences exist in the implementation laws of the national Member States and it can, therefore, be questioned whether the purpose of increasing competition amongst professionals to minimize depositary costs can be obtained.

4.3.2   Entities Eligible as a Depositary under UCITSD V

UCITSD IV provided little clarity on the entities eligible as a UCITS depositaries.[152] Under Article 23(3) UCITSD IV, Member States had the sole discretion to determine the entities eligible provided that they were subject to prudential regulation and ongoing supervision.[153] This discretion led to differences regarding the entities eligible as UCITS depositaries throughout the EEA.[154] The UCITSD V proposal sought to introduce a closed list of eligible entities comprising credit institutions and investment firms addressing the issue of non-harmonized minimum capital requirements, effective regulation and supervision that were present under UCITSD IV.[155] Although harmonization in this area

---

152 European Commission, *Consultation Paper on the UCITS Depositary Function and on the UCITS Managers 'Remuneration* (December 2010), MARKT/G4 D (2010) 950800; European Commission, *Communication from the Commission to the Council and to the European parliament – Regulation of UCITS Depositaries in the Member States: Review and Possible Developments*, 30 March 2004, COM(2004) 207 final; FEFSI, *supra* note 105, *Position Paper on Depositaries*, 4-5 (6 November 2002).
153 *See* Art. 23(2) UCITSD IV.
154 UCITSD V proposal, 4, 5; European Commission, *supra* note 152.
155 European Commission, *supra* note 121, 32.

was warmly welcomed in the UCITSD V consultation responses[156] and industry position papers,[157] the proposal also received criticism that in common law countries such a limited list would disregard an entire sector of depositary services providers that were under UCITSD IV active in at least ten different Member States.[158] Eliminating other entities than credit institutions and investment firms from being eligible as a UCITS depositary was found to go beyond what is reasonable in order to ensure a proper level playing field without undermining the protection of UCITS investors.[159] EFAMA and the EBF proposed that other entities authorized in Member States to act as depositaries under UCITSD IV should remain eligible to act as depositaries as long as they are subject to prudential regulation and ongoing supervision and provide sufficient guarantees in terms of capital requirements, investor protection, conflicts of interests and risk management.[160]

Article 23(2) UCITSD V adopted this criticism by determining that national central banks, credit institutions and other legal entities complying with additional prudential, organizational and capital requirements to provide sufficient guarantees are allowed to be eligible as UCITS depositaries. The UCITSD V leaves Member States discretion to determine in their national Member State laws which of the three categories of institutions shall be eligible to be UCITS depositaries.[161]

4.3.2.1   National Central Bank

Under Article 23(2)(a) UCITSD V, national central banks are eligible as UCITS depositaries. Adopting national central banks as eligible entity remains to be somewhat surprising as very few Member States allowed them to be UCITS depositaries under UCITSD IV.[162] The UCITSD V nor its preparatory documents explain why this, to the contrary of the UCITSD V proposal, has been adopted in the final version UCITSD V version. Taken the suggestion of EFAMA in its position paper, the merit of extending the categories of eligible institutions to national central banks is that they might play a useful role of 'last resort in exceptional circumstances'.[163] UCITSD V does not explicitly require central

---

156 *See* Art. 23(2) UCITSD V proposal.
157 EBF, *EBF Position on UCITS V*, 5, www.ebf-fbe.eu/uploads/D1425F-2012-Final%20EBF%20position%20on %20UCITS%20V.pdf; EFAMA, *EFAMA Position Paper on the legislative proposal of the Commission amending Directive 2009/65/EC ("UCITS V")*, 3,4, www.efama.org/Publications/Public/UCITS/12-4040_EFAMA position paper on UCITS V.pdf.
158 European Commission, *supra* note 121, 33.
159 EBF, *supra* note 157; EFAMA, *supra* note 157, 3 and 4.
160 Art. 23(2)(c) UCITSD V.
161 Art. 23(3) UCITSD V.
162 *See, e.g.* in Belgium: Art. 50 § 2 2° Wet betreffende de instellingen voor collectieve belegging die voldoen aan de voorwaarden van Richtlijn 2009/65/EG en de instelling voor belegging in schuldvorderingen, Belgisch Staatsblad, 19 oktober 2012, Opschrift vervangen bij artikel 414 van de wet van 19 april 2014 – BS 17 juni 2014.
163 EFAMA *supra* note 157, 4.

banks to fulfil a specific organizational, prudential or additional capital requirements.[164] UCITSD V, thus, deems that national central banks provide in any case sufficient guarantees to be eligible as a UCITS depositary. Nevertheless, few Member States have implemented this option under their UCITSD V implementation laws.[165]

4.3.2.2 Credit Institutions

Article 23(2)(b) UCITSD V allows credit institutions to be appointed as a UCITS depositary.

The European Commission in its UCITSD V Impact Assessment considered credit institutions (and investment firms) to be the most suitable entities to perform the UCITS depositary task. According to the European Commission, credit institutions (and investment firms) are subjected to sound conduct of business rules, have expertise in investment services and safekeeping and are subject to strong EEA mechanisms that protect clients' interests in case of a default.[166]

All Member States have adopted credit institutions in their UCITSD V implementation laws.[167] This is unsurprising given that all major UCITS jurisdictions under UCITSD IV already required a depositary to be a credit institution (or an investment firm).[168]

By adopting credit institutions it has been acknowledged that they fulfil in any case sufficient guarantees in terms of minimum capital requirements, effective regulation and supervision.

---

164 Art. 23(2)(a) UCITSD V.

165 *See* France: Art. L214-10-1 I.(a) n. 1 CMF. France also allows la Caisse des dépôts et consignations to be appointed under Art. L214-10-1 I.(a) n. 1 CMF; Malta: Art. 13(2)(a) Investment Services Act (CAP 370) (Custodians of Collective Investment Schemes) Regulations, 2016; *See* in the UK: COLL 6.6A.8R.

166 European Commission, *Impact Assessment – Commission Delegated Regulation supplementing Directive 2009/65/EC of the European Parliament and of the Council with regard to obligations of depositaries* {C (2015) 9160 final}, 82.

167 Austria: § 41(1) Investmentfondsgesetz 2011 (InvFG 2011); Croatia: Art. 4(7) Act on Open-Ended Investment Funds with a Public Offering (Official Gazette 44/16); Cyprus:Art. 88(I)(2) Open-Ended Undertakings for Collective Investment (UCI) Law of 2012 Consolidated with Law 88(I)/2015; Czech republic: § 69 (1)(a) and (b) 240/2013 Sb.ZÁKON ze dne 3. července 2013 o investičních společnostech a investičních fondech; Denmark: Art. 2 (1) n. 11 Act n. 597 of 12 June 2013 on investment associations; Germany: § 68 (2) and (3) KAGB; France: Art.L214-10-1 I.(a) n. 3 CMF; Ireland: Art. 35 (2) (*a*) and (*b*) (Undertakings for Collective Investment in Transferable Securities) Regulations 2011 (S.I. No. 352 of 2011); Liechtenstein: Art. 32(2)(a) and (b) UCITSG; Luxembourg; Art. 17(3) OPC law 2010; Malta: Art. 13(2)(b) Investment Services Act (custodians of collective investment schemes) Regulations 2016; the Netherlands: Art. 4:62n(b) Wft; UK: COLL 6.6A.8R (2).

168 *See* CESR/09-175; European Commission *supra* note 121, 32 and 33; European Commission, *Impact Assessment – Commission Delegated Regulation supplementing Directive 2009/65/EC of the European Parliament and of the Council with regard to obligations of depositaries* {C(2015) 9160 final}, 81.

4.3.2.3   Another Legal Entity

Apart from national central banks and credit institutions, Member States may under Article 23(2)(c) UCITSD V determine which kind of other legal entities are eligible to carry out the UCITS depositary function provided that a certain amount of requirements are met.[169] Similar as investment firms under the AIFMD,[170] 'another legal entity' should be subject to capital adequacy requirements as laid down in Art. 315 or 317 CRD IV and have own funds of not less than 730.000 Euro. Unlike under the AIFMD, 'another legal entity' under UCITSD V is not required to be authorized for the ancillary service of safekeeping and administration of financial instruments as this would effectively restrict the eligible entities to investment firms and credit institutions. Instead, only those entities are allowed to be eligible by Member States that satisfy the minimum requirements regarding infrastructure, experience, administrative and accounting procedures, internal control mechanisms, risk management procedures and arrangements to prevent conflicts of interest.[171]

Member States, thus, have discretion whether or not 'other entities' are eligible in their domicile as UCITSD V depositaries. Member States have taken different approaches by not implementing at all this option,[172] allowing all legal entities fulfilling these criteria to be appointed[173] or to specify the types of legal entities, such as investment firms,[174] CSDs,[175] prime brokers[176] or eligible legal entities authorized under national law[177] fulfilling the additional UCITSD V criteria, to be appointed as a UCITS depositary.

---

169 Art. 23(2)(c) UCITSD V.

170 Art. 21(3)(b) AIFMD.

171 Art. 23(2)(c) UCITSD V

172 The following Member States, *e.g.* only allow credit institutions to be appointed as a UCITSD V depositary: Austria: § 41(1) Investmentfondsgesetz 2011 (InvFG 2011); Croatia: Art. 4(7) Act on Open-Ended Investment Funds with a Public Offering (Official Gazette 44/16); Denmark: Art. 2 (1) n. 11 Act n. 597 of 12 June 2013 on investment associations; Germany: § 68 (2) and (3) KAGB; Luxembourg; Art. 17(3) OPC law 2010.

173 Cyprus: Art. 88(I)(2) Open-Ended Undertakings for Collective Investment (UCI) Law of 2012 Consolidated with Law 88(I)/2015; Liechtenstein: Art. 32(2)(c) UCITSG; the Netherlands: Art. 4:62n(a) Wft.

174 Czech republic: § 69(1)(c) 240/2013 Sb. ZÁKON ze dne 3. července 2013 o investičních společnostech a investičních fondech; France: Art. L214-10-1 I.(a) n. 5 CMF; Liechtenstein: Art. 32(2)(a) and (b) UCITSG; the Netherlands: Art. 4:62n(c); Malta: Art. 13(2)(e) Investment Services Act (custodians of collective investment schemes) Regulations 2016; UK: COLL 6.6A.8R(3)(b)(i).

175 Finland: Finnish Government Bill, draft legislation for Managers of Alternative Investment Funds, 5 September 2013, 218; *See also* §16, Chapter 2 of the Act amending the Clearing Operations Act; *See also* Chapter 14, Section 3 Finnish Law on Alternative Investment Funds; Poland: Art. 71(3) Act of 27 May 2004 on Investment Funds.

176 *See* CSSF, Circular 14/587, as amended by Circular CSSF 15/608, Sub-Chapter 7.3. Organisational arrangements at the level of the depositary and the UCITS in case of the appointment of a prime broker.

177 Ireland: Art. 35(2)(c) (Undertakings for Collective Investment in Transferable Securities) Regulations 2011 (S.I. No. 352 of 2011); Malta: Art. 13(2)(e) Investment Services Act (custodians of collective investment schemes) Regulations 2016; UK: COLL 6.6A.8R(3)(b)(i).

4.3.2.3.1   Investment Firms as Per Sé Depositaries – A Missed Opportunity?
The UCITSD V proposal was based on the approach of establishing a closed list of entities that could be appointed as depositaries. Apart from credit institutions, investment firms authorized under MiFID II to provide safekeeping and administration of financial instruments for the account of clients and subject under the capital adequacy and own funds requirements under CRD IV were proposed to be eligible under the UCITSD V proposal.[178] The eligibility of this closed list of entities was based upon the European Commission UCITSD V Impact Assessment that considered credit institutions and investment firms on the basis of its conduct of business rules, expertise in investment services and safekeeping the protection of clients' interests in case of default to be the most suitable entities to perform the UCITS depositary task.[179]

Article 23(2) UCITSD V has not listed investment firms, amongst national central banks and credit institutions, as 'per sé depositaries', i.e. depositaries that are in any case considered by UCITSD V to fulfil the additional criteria required for the eligibility of 'other legal entities' under Article 23(2)(c) UCITSD V as a depositary. Instead, investment firms qualify as 'another legal entity'. This is highly surprising as under the AIFMD investment firms qualify as 'per sé depositaries'[180] and the UCITSD V Impact Assessment also considered investment firms to be addressing the issue of minimum capital requirements, effective regulation and supervision that were under UCITSD IV not harmonized for UCITS depositaries.[181] In Member States that limit UCITSD V eligible entities to, for example, credit institutions this leads to discrepancies with the AIFMD as investment firms qualify as 'per sé depositaries' under the AIFMD.[182]

Investment firms authorized under MiFID II to provide safekeeping and administration of financial instruments for the account of clients qualify as 'another legal entity' and are, formally, required to comply with the prudential regulation and ongoing supervision minimum requirements under Article 23(2)(c) UCITSD V. In various Member States, including the Czech Republic, Liechtenstein and the Netherlands, investment firms are considered to be 'per sé UCITSD V depositaries'.[183] In France, Malta and the UK, investment firms are eligible provided that they (formally) fulfil the Article 23(2)(c) UCITSD V minimum requirements related to prudential regulation and ongoing supervision.[184] Given the view of the European Commission in its UCITSD V Impact Assessment, invest-

---

178 Art. 23(2) UCITSD V proposal.
179 European Commission, *supra* note 121, 32.
180 Art. 21(3)(b) AIFMD.
181 European Commission, *supra* note 121, 32.
182 Member States may under Art. 43 AIFMD require stricter requirements for retail-AIF depositaries by limiting the entities eligible to, for instance, credit institutions.
183 Czech republic: § 69(1)(c) 240/2013 Sb.ZÁKON ze dne 3. července 2013 o investičních společnostech a investičních fondech; Liechtenstein: Art. 32(2)(a) and (b) UCITSG; the Netherlands: Art. 4:62n(c);
184 France: Art. L214-10-1 I. (a) n. 5 CMF; Malta: Art. 13(2)(e) Investment Services Act (custodians of collective investment schemes) Regulations 2016; UK: COLL 6.6A.8R(3)(b)(i).

ment firms in Member States, such as Cyprus,[185] that allow any legal entity fulfilling the Article 23(2)(c) UCITSD V minimum requirements should in any case be deemed to be eligible as a UCITSD V depositary.[186]

4.3.2.3.2   CSDs

Considering that various Member States under the AIFMD[187] allowed CSDs to be eligible as a (UCITSD IV) depositary, the question is relevant whether CSDs may qualify as 'another legal entity' within the meaning of Article 23(2)(c) UCITSD V. UCITSD V nor the CSDR provides a straightforward answer to this question.

Recital 21 UCITSD V mentions that CSDs[188] that are initially recording the securities of a UCITS in a book-entry system through initial crediting and maintaining those securities in an account at the top tier level[189] are not considered sub-custodians of that UCITS.[190] Entrusting the custody of securities of a UCITS by a UCITS depositary to any CSD, or to any TC CSD is, however, considered a delegation of custody functions.[191]

Under Section B Annex CSD Regulation, CSDs may on top of the core services of CSDs under Section A

> establish CSD links, provide, maintain or operate securities accounts in relation to the settlement service, collateral management, other ancillary services.[192]

This includes the opening of 'lower tier' securities accounts, either in direct holding systems or when the CSD acts as 'investor CSD' [193] by maintaining for its customers securities issued in 'issuer CSDs'.[194]

---

185 Cyprus: Art. 88(I)(2) Open-Ended Undertakings for Collective Investment (UCI) Law of 2012 Consolidated with Law 88(I)/2015.
186 European Commission, *supra* note 121, 32 and 33.
187 Finland: Finnish Government Bill, draft legislation for Managers of Alternative Investment Funds, 05.09.2013, 218; *See also* §16, Chapter 2 of the Act amending the Clearing Operations Act; *See also* Chapter 14, Section 3 Finnish Law on Alternative Investment Funds; Poland: Art. 71(3) Act of 27 May 2004 on Investment Funds.
188 *See* Art. 2(1) CSDR.
189 *See* Section A Annex CSDR.
190 Recital 21 UCITSD V.
191 *Ibid.*
192 *See* on investor CSDs: Chapter 6, Section 6.3.
193 Art. 2(1) n. (29) CSDR: "CSD link means an arrangement between CSDs whereby one CSD becomes a participant in the securities settlement system of another CSD in order to facilitate the transfer of securities from the participants of the latter CSD to the participants of the former CSD or an arrangement whereby a CSD accesses another CSD indirectly via an intermediary. CSD links include standard links, customised links, indirect links, and interoperable links."
194 European Commission, *Commission Staff Working Document of 07 March 2012 (SWD(2012) 22) accompanying the Proposal for the CSDR: Impact Assessment* (COM(2012) 73) (SWD(2012) 23), 7, http://ec.europa. eu/internal_market/investment/docs/alternative_investments/fund_managers_impact_assessment.pdf ('CSDR Impact Assessment').

The European Commission in its CSDR Impact Assessment confirms that CSDs may combine

> the core function 'central safekeeping' with 'non-central safekeeping' (from ancillary services) on the basis that the related prudential and conduct of business rules (e.g. on protection of customer assets) should in principle be the same.[195]

CSDs under the CSDR may in the view of the European Commission, thus, provide 'custody' under the UCITS depositary's safekeeping function.

Unclear is whether and to what extent CSDs are suitable to perform UCITS depositary oversight[196] and cash management[197] services. The author takes the view that these can be considered 'other ancillary services' under Section B Annex CSDR. The oversight and cash management function are of a similar 'administrative' nature as the other non-banking-type ancillary services that are listed under Section B CSDR and do not entail credit or liquidity risks. CSDs are, thus, able to be determined by individual Member States as 'another legal entity' carrying out the UCITS depositary function. CSDs eligible as a UCITS depositary may perform banking-types of ancillary services[198] under the CSDR, such as the provision of cash accounts and accepting deposits provided that the CSD either:[199]

- has obtained an authorization as a credit institution itself; or
- establishes a separate legal entity, authorized as a credit institution under CRD IV which is located either within or outside the group of which the CSD is a part.

In practice, CSDs not entitled to provide commercial bank money services are likely to play a minor role in exercising the depositary function as they would be restricted in the reuse of assets. The credit institution authorization under CRD IV necessary for providing these services would, however, directly or indirectly entitle such CSDs already to be eligible as a depositary. Investor CSDs are, thus, subject to sufficient capital, organizational and prudential requirements that may, along acting as a sub-custodian, by individual Member States be determined to be a UCITS depositary within the meaning of Article 23(2)(c) UCITSD V. CSDs, in practice, however, might already be directly or indirectly entitled to be eligible as a depositary based upon an authorization as a credit institution obtained under CRD IV.

---

195 See also European Commission, supra note 194, 7 and 90.
196 Art. 21(9) AIFMD.
197 Art. 21(7) AIFMD.
198 See Section C Annex CSDR.
199 Art. 54 CSDR.

4.3.2.3.3   Prime Brokers as UCITS Depositaries?

Unlike the AIFMD, UCITSD V does not regulate prime brokers and the prime brokerage relationship between UCITS ManCos, depositaries and prime brokers. This leaves the question whether prime brokers under UCITSD V are allowed as a depositary and/or sub-custodian.

In its FAQ, the European Commission answered the question 'what is a UCITS depositary?' by indicating that the UCITS depositary must be an 'entity that is independent from the UCITS fund and the UCITS funds investment manager'.[200] In addition, the European Commission clarified that 'neither the fund manager nor any prime brokers that act as so-called 'counterparties' to a fund may also act as a UCITS depositary'.[201] Finally, the European Commission pointed out that the independence of a depositary is necessary because the depositary by exercising its controlling duties is the 'legal conscience' of a UCITS and oversees the UCITS' assets. By referring to 'prime brokers that act as counterparties' instead of prime brokers in general, the European Commission confirms the view that prime brokers can have the same roles, i.e. act as a counterparty, a depositary or a sub-custodian, under the UCITSD V as under the AIFMD. The FAQ, however, does not answer the question whether prime brokers may be appointed as a UCITS depositary if they, as under Article 21(4)(b) AIFMD, functionally and hierarchically separate its counterparty and depositary function and conflicts of interests are remedied.[202]

Luxembourg has clarified that prime brokers are eligible as depositaries (and sub-custodians) provided that prime brokers functionally and hierarchically separate its counterparty and depositary function and that conflicts of interests are remedied.[203] UCITS depositaries in Luxembourg may, however, only be credit institutions.[204] Only prime brokers that are authorized as a credit institution are, thus, allowed to be appointed as a depositary.[205] In addition, Luxembourg has extended the AIFMD prime broker definition,[206] the provisions related to the selection and appointment of the prime broker[207]

---

200 European Commission, *supra* note 120, Question 2. What is a UCITS depositary?

201 *Ibid.*

202 The UCITSD V leaves open the question whether the restriction on the 'reuse' of assets by the depositary or a sub-custodian for own account prohibits prime brokers from being appointed as a depositary or a sub-custodian under the UCITSD V; *See* T. Moroni & L. Wibbeke, *OGAW V: Die Sprunglatte für OGAW-Verwahrstellen liegt höher*, 3 Recht der Finanzinstrumente 187 (2015).

203 Essentially, Luxembourg extends Art. 21(4)(b) AIFMD to its UCITS depositaries. *See* CSSF, Circular 14/587, as amended by Circular CSSF 15/608, Sub-Chapter 7.3. Organisational arrangements at the level of the depositary and the UCITS in case of the appointment of a prime broker.

204 Luxembourg; Art. 17(3) OPC law 2010.

205 Under Art. 4(1)(af) AIFMD a 'prime broker' may be a credit institution, a regulated investment firm or another entity subject to prudential regulation and ongoing supervision. Prime brokers under the UCITSD V may be established as these entities as well. Luxembourg, however, restricts its UCITSD V eligible entities to credit institutions. This effectively limits prime brokers willing to act as UCITS depositaries to those authorized as a credit institution.

206 CSSF, *supra* note 203, 7 and 8; *See* for the prime broker definition under the AIFMD: Art. 4(af) AIFMD.

207 *Ibid.*

and the functions of the AIFM,[208] depositary[209] and prime broker[210] in the prime brokerage relationship to UCITS. The Luxembourg view makes sense as it is the only way how 'Newcits'[211] could operate. Prohibiting prime brokers as UCITS depositaries or sub-custodians would imply that UCITS would be severally restricted in employing leverage at all.[212] Prime brokers may in Luxembourg, thus, be appointed as a UCITS depositary provided that they are established as a credit institution and abide to the AIFMD conflict of interest rules.

4.3.2.3.4   Other Legal Entities Eligible under UCITSD V Member State Laws

Cyprus, Ireland, Malta, the Netherlands and the UK, along the eligible UCITSD V depositaries mentioned above, allow under their UCITSD V implementation laws other legal entities than investment firms, CSDs and prime brokers to be eligible as a depositary.

Cyprus,[213] Liechtenstein[214] and the Netherlands[215] do not specify the types of legal entities and allow under their national implementation laws all legal entities that comply with Article 23(2)(c) UCITSD V to be appointed as a UCITS depositary. In the Netherlands, this option has, in particular, been implemented to continue to allow the traditional Dutch 'safekeeping entity' (bewaarentiteit) that was traditionally appointed as a UCITSD IV depositary to be eligible under UCITSD V.[216] In the Netherlands, this safekeeping entity is traditionally a legal person that has the legal title of the UCITS' assets.[217] All legal persons can be appointed as a safekeeping entity provided that the sole object of its articles of association is the holding of assets and administering the goods in which the UCITS invests.[218] This safekeeping entity is not a depositary as under the UCITSD IV commonly

---

208 Extended the AIFM functions, including (1) risk management duties, (2) compliance duties and (3) reporting and disclosure duties to UCITS ManCos; Art. 15(4), 24, 27 AIFMD; See ESMA 2011/379, 49-51.

209 CSSF, supra note 203, Chapter 7. Specific organisational arrangements at the level of the depositary in view of the investment policy of the UCITS or the techniques that the UCITS employs.

210 See for the reporting obligations towards the Depositary: Art. 91 AIFMD (Commission) Regulation.

211 EDHEC Risk Institute, Are Hedge Fund UCITS the Cure-All? (EDHEC-Position Paper 2010).

212 Moroni & Wibbeke, supra note 202.

213 Art. 88(I)(2) Open-Ended Undertakings for Collective Investment (UCI) Law of 2012 Consolidated with Law 88(I)/2015.

214 Art. 32(2)(c) UCITSG.

215 Art. 4:62n(a) Wft.; C.J. Groffen, UCITS V implementatie in Nederland, 3 TvFR 114 (2016); C.M. Grundmann-van de Krol, Consultatiewetsvoorstel implementatie UCITS V in de Wft, 49 Ondernemingsrecht 262 (2015).

216 See explanatory notes (Memorie van Toelichting), UCITSD Amendment Act (Implementatiewet wijziging richtlijn icbe's), 2,3; See for the role of the pre-AIFMD safekeeping company: Hooghiemstra, supra note 1; See for the role of the safekeeping company post-AIFMD: Hooghiemstra, supra note 1; R.K.Th.J., Smits, De AIFMD-bewaarder; praktische gevolgen voor Nederlandse beleggingsinstellingen, 11 V&O 200-204 (2012).

217 This tradition applies to both AIFs and UCITS. See J. W. P. M. van der Velden, Hoofdstuk 25 Beleggingsinstelling en aansprakelijkheid in het zicht van de nieuwe regelgeving, in Aansprakelijkheid in de Financiële Sector 976-977 (D. Busch, C.J.M. Klaassen & T.M.C. Arons eds., Kluwer Law 2013); Grundmann-van de Krol, supra note 76, 223-228; J.W.P.M. Van der Velden, Beleggingsfondsen naar Burgerlijk recht 129-185 (Kluwer 2008).

218 Art. 4:44(1) Wft.

understood in the EEA. Dutch non-corporate legal forms, including limited partnerships and funds for joint account, were only established on the basis of private law and do not provide for limited liability and asset segregation.[219] For this purpose, the mandatory appointment of a legal entity (the safekeeping entity) that holds the legal title of the UCITS' assets covers for the absence of these two corporate elements under Dutch private law.[220] Under the Dutch UCITSD IV implementation, the safekeeping entity could act as a 'depositary' as it was assigned for performing oversight duties. The safekeeping of financial instruments that can be held in custody was, however, delegated to credit institutions as sub-custodians.[221] This was necessary as safekeeping companies traditionally do not have the resources to act as a 'custodian' and are unlikely to fulfil the prudential regulation and ongoing supervision requirements under UCITSD V. Under UCITSD V they remain, however, required to be mandatorily appointed for non-corporate UCITS.[222]

Unlike the above-mentioned Member States, Ireland, Malta and the UK allow, along credit institutions (and investment firms),[223] legal entities authorized under national law under their Article 23(2)(c) UCITSD V implementation laws to be appointed as a UCITS depositary.[224] Ireland allows Irish companies to be eligible as 'other eligible institution' provided that the company is wholly owned by either an EEA/TC credit institution[225] or an equivalent EEA/TC institution[226] that guarantees the liabilities of the company and that have a paid-up share capital of at least EUR 5 million.[227] Similarly, Malta allows Maltese companies to be appointed as a depositary that are wholly owned by an EEA credit institution provided that the liabilities of the company are guaranteed by that credit institution.[228] In the UK, 'another legal entity' may be an investment management firm to

---

219 This ranking of claims preserves the segregation of the UCITS' assets from the estate of the participants, the UCITS ManCo and the safekeeping company as SPV itself. *See* Art. 4:44 Wft. The requirement that the safekeeping company must be a legal entity ensures limited liability for investors.

220 *See* for possible liability arising for investors when the depositary is not the legal owner of the assets: D. Busch & J.W.P.M. van der Velden, *Aansprakelijkheid en verhaal bij Fondsen voor Gemene Rekening*, 9 TvFR 161-162 (2009).

221 In the Netherlands this is being referred to as a 'Babylonian confusion of tongues'. *See* J.W.P.M. van der Velden, *Babylonische bewaarders*, 17 Ondernemingsrecht 173(2009).

222 Art. 4:44(1) Wft.

223 Malta and the UK also allow investment firms. Ireland does not allow this. *See* for Malta: Art. 13(2)(e) Investment Services Act (custodians of collective investment schemes) Regulations 2016 and for the UK: COLL 6.6A.8R(3)(b)(i).

224 Ireland: Art. 35 (Undertakings for Collective Investment in Transferable Securities) Regulations 2011 (S.I. No. 352 of 2011); Malta: Art. 13 Investment Services Act (CAP 370) (Custodians of Collective Investment Schemes) Regulations, 2016; UK: COLL 6.6.A8R.

225 Art. 35(2)(c) (Undertakings for Collective Investment in Transferable Securities) Regulations 2011 (S.I. No. 352 of 2011).

226 This is assessed by the Irish Central Bank. *See* Art. 35(2)(c)(iii) (Undertakings for Collective Investment in Transferable Securities) Regulations 2011 (S.I. No. 352 of 2011).

227 Art. 35(2)(c) (Undertakings for Collective Investment in Transferable Securities) Regulations 2011 (S.I. No. 352 of 2011). *See* for similar depositaries under the AIFMD: Art. 22(3)(iii) AIFM Regulations.

228 Art. 13(2)(d) Investment Services Act (CAP 370) (Custodians of Collective Investment Schemes) Regulations, 2016.

which IPRU(INV) 5 applies and that satisfies the UCITSD V prudential regulation and ongoing supervision requirements.[229] These are firms whose permitted activities include designated investment business other than, amongst others, credit institutions and investment firms. The designated investment business is to act as a trustee or depositary of a UCITS.[230] Various Member States, thus, allow under their UCITSD V implementation other legal entities than investment firms, CSDs and prime brokers to be eligible as a depositary.

4.4   EEA-AIF AND UCITS DEPOSITARIES – GENERAL REQUIREMENTS

The AIFMD and UCITSD V impose a general duty of loyalty and a duty to prevent conflicts of interest to all (non-)EEA-AIF and UCITS depositaries.

4.4.1   Duty of Loyalty

The AIFMD and UCITSD V set out an overarching rule of conduct.[231] In the context of the respective roles of the AIFM, UCITS ManCo and the depositary, the depositary shall act honestly, fairly, professionally, independently and in the interest of the AIF/UCITS and the investors of the AIF/UCITS. This duty applies to all depositary functions under the AIFMD and UCITSD V. The depositary may, for instance, not offer or accept payments or any other inducements, if such payments or inducements would be detrimental to the interests of its clients.

4.4.2   Conflicts of Interest

The AIFMD and UCITSD V try to prevent conflicts of interest by requiring depositaries not to carry out activities with regard to the AIF/UCITS (or the AIFM/UCITS ManCo on behalf of the AIF/UCITS) that may create conflicts of interest between the AIF/UCITS, its investors, the relevant AIFM/UCITS ManCo and itself, unless the depositary has functionally and hierarchically separated its depositary tasks from its other potentially conflicting tasks.[232] The AIFMD and UCITD V impose a general duty on depositaries to identify, manage and ultimately disclose conflicts of interest to the investors of the AIF/UCITS.[233] This duty applies to depositaries in addition to the general requirement to act

---

229 COLL 6.6.A8R(3)(b)(c)(ii).
230 *See* Art. 40 and 42a Financial Services and Markets Act 2000; *See also* Art. 51ZB Financial Services and Markets Act 2000 (Regulated Activities) Order 2001.
231 Art. 21(10) AIFMD; Art. 25(2) sub-para. 1 UCITSD V.
232 Art. 21(10) sub-para. 2 AIFMD; Art. 25(2) sub-para. 2 UCITSD V.
233 *Ibid.*

in the AIFs/UCITS and its investors' best interests. The duties referred to are in addition to the general duty of loyalty under the depositary contract, as well as the general duty of loyalty.[234]

4.4.3   The Third Party Depositary Requirement

The AIFMD and UCITSD V, on top of the general duty of care and prevention of conflict of interests, require the depositary to be a 'third party'. In order to avoid conflicts of interest between the depositary, the AIFM, AIF and its investors,[235] Article 21(4)(a) AIFMD requires that 'an AIFM shall not act as a depositary'. Similarly, Article 25 UCITSD V sets out that 'no company shall act as both management company and depositary' and 'no company shall act as both investment company and depositary'. The reference to 'company' under the UCITSD V and the definition of 'AIFMs' under the AIFMD that requires 'an AIFM to be a legal person whose regular business is managing one or more AIFs'[236] seem to indicate that the AIFMD and UCITSD V require the depositary to be a separate legal entity from the AIFM/UCITS ManCo.[237] This can be explained by (1) the controlling tasks to the AIF and UCITS depositary and (2) the entities eligible as a depositary under the AIFMD and UCITSD V.

First, the AIFMD assigns controlling tasks to the AIF and UCITS depositary. For this reason, MiFID II does not require investors nor investment firms to appoint a third party custodian. The difference can be explained by the collective investment nature of AIFs and UCITS as opposed to the individual investment nature under MiFID II. Investment firms that perform portfolio management or investment advice perform investment services/activities and ancillary services relate to individual portfolios.[238] The law demands individual investors to monitor the investment firm themselves by, for example, giving investment instructions or terminating their service agreement based upon the MiFID II information that is being provided to them. The collective investment nature of AIFs and UCITS implies that AIFMs and UCITS ManCos invest on behalf of multiple investors that are sharing 'pooled risks' as they are bound by the terms of a single legal form. The plurality of investors leads to investor passivity as a result of collective action problems.[239] Instead, the AIFMD and UCITSD V require the depositary to performing controlling tasks on behalf of the plurality of investors based upon the economic principle of 'cheap-

---

234 Art. 21(10) sub-para. 1 AIFMD; Art. 25(2) sub-para. 1 UCITSD V.
235 Art. 21(4) AIFMD.
236 Art. 4(1)(b) AIFMD.
237 D.A. Zetzsche, *Prinzipien der kollektiven Vermögensanlage* § 21 (Mohr Siebeck 2015).
238 *See* for portfolio management: Art. 4(1) n. 8 MiFID II.
239 M. Olsen, *The Logic of Collective Action: Public Goods and the Theory of Groups* (Harvard University Press 1971) ('describing that the free rider problem results in a disincentive to act because any shareholder may decide to save itself the cost of acting in the belief that other shareholders will do so'); R. Hardin, *Collective Action* (Routledge 1982).

est cost avoider' efficiency.[240] Given the existence of transaction costs,[241] the optimal legal solution is to assign the depositary to perform controlling tasks as the depositary is the party that is able to minimize negative externalities, the sum of the cost of (preventing) accidents for the plurality of investors, most efficiently.[242] The depositary for the performing of the controlling tasks, thus, needs to be a separate legal entity from the AIFM and UCITS ManCo.[243] Second, the third party depositary requirement can be explained by the entities eligible as a depositary under the AIFMD and UCITSD V. Investment firms are allowed to perform the safekeeping and administration of financial instruments for investors along their core investment services/activities.[244] Investment firms are merely subjected to client assets protection requirements and under MiFID II not required to establish a separate legal entity for performing the safekeeping and administration of financial instruments.[245] Contrary to AIFMs and UCITS ManCos under the AIFMD and UCITSD V, only credit institutions and investment firms may be authorized under MiFID II.[246] AIFMs nor UCITS ManCos are necessarily credit institutions or investment firms. Credit institutions and investment firms are, thus, required as third party depositary as (1) they can safekeep all of the AIF and UCITS assets, (2) they are less prone to insolvency as they are both subjected to the CRR and have 'stronger balance sheets' than AIFMs and UCITS ManCos, and (3) investment firms and credit institutions are generally accepted as CSDs participants allowing for effective segregation and protection of assets upon an insolvency of the AIFM/UCITS ManCo.[247] To prevent conflicts of interests, the depositary needs to be a separate legal entity from the AIFM and UCITS ManCo.[248] Depositaries may, however, be independent or part of a financial conglomerate that might comprise AIFMs/UCITS ManCos, brokers and custodians. For this reason, the third party depositary requirement is under the UCITSD V (Commission) Regulation complemented by additional 'independence requirements'. Various Member States require similar 'independence requirements' for their AIFs.[249]

---

240 K.D. Logue & J.B. Slemrod, *Of Coase, Calabresi, and Optimal Tax Liability*, Law & Economics Working Papers Law & Economics Working Papers Archive: 2003-2009, University of Michigan Law School Year 2009, 3, http://repository.law.umich.edu/cgi/viewcontent.cgi?article=1097&context=law_econ_archive; G. Calabresi, *The Costs of Accidents: A Legal and Economic Analysis* (Yale University Press 1970).

241 R.H. Coase, *The Problem of Social Cost*, 3 Journal of Law and Economics 1 (1960).

242 Logue & Slemrod, *supra* note 240.

243 Art. 21(4)(a) AIFMD; Art. 25 UCITSD V.

244 Annex I s. A MiFID II.

245 Individual Member States may, however, require a separate legal entity to be established. *See* for the safekeeping company established by credit institutions in the Netherlands: Art. 4:87 Wet op het financieel toezicht; § 6.5 Regels met betrekking tot de bescherming van de rechten, financiële instrumenten of gelden van de cliënt (Arts. 7:14-7:20); P. Rank, *Vermogensscheiding* (D. Busch & C.M. Grundmann-van de Krol eds., Kluwer 2009).

246 *See* for AIFMs: Arts. 6 et seq. AIFMD; *See* for UCITS ManCos: Arts. 6 et seq. UCITSD V.

247 Zetzsche, *supra* note 237.

248 Art. 21(4)(a) AIFMD; Art. 25 UCITSD V.

249 *See* for research conducted by ESMA in this regard: ESMA/2014/1417, ESMA/2014/1183.

4.4.4   *Independence Requirements under UCITSD V*

Despite the third party depositary requirement, the independence of the management/ investment company and the UCITS depositary can still be jeopardized by the existence of links related to the common management/supervision and cross-shareholdings/group inclusion between these parties.[250] For that purpose, Article 25(2) UCITSD V and Chapter 4 UCITSD V (Commission) Regulation[251] require, on top of the duty of loyalty and conflict of interest provisions, UCITS ManCos and the depositary to be independent in carrying out their respective functions.[252]

4.4.4.1   Common Management/Supervision

Upon introducing UCITSD V, the European Commission and ESMA considered that the independence of the depositary could be eroded if the management/investment company and the depositary, by means of executive power or supervision, could control the actions of each other.[253] For this reason, the management bodies of these entities should be kept separate.[254] UCITSD V has introduced limitations to the possibility for members of the body in charge of the supervisory functions of one of the entities to be also members of the management body, the body in charge of the supervisory functions or employees of the other entity. In particular:

- no person may at the same time be both members of the management body of the UCITS ManCo (investment company) and a member of the management body of the depositary;[255]
- no person may at the same time be both members of the management body of the UCITS ManCo (investment company) and an employee of the depositary;[256] and
- no person may at the same time be both a member of the management body of the depositary and an employee of the UCITS ManCo or the investment company.[257]

Where the management body of the UCITS ManCo or depositary is not in charge of the supervisory functions, up to one-third of the members of the body in charge of the supervisory functions of the other entity may also be members of the management body, the body in charge of the supervisory functions or employees of that other entity.[258] For

---

250 *See* Art. 26b UCITSD V; *See also* ESMA/2014/1183, 18; ESMA/2014/1417,
251 These are not intended to replicate: Chapter III-Obligations regarding management companies and Chapter V – Obligations regarding investment companies, *See* ESMA/2014/1183, 17.
252 *See also* ESMA/2014/1183, 17.
253 ESMA/2014/1183, 18.
254 *See* for the meaning of 'management body': Art. 2(1) UCITSD V.
255 Art. 21(a) UCITSD V (Commission) Regulation; ESMA/2014/1183, 22.
256 Art. 21(b) UCITSD V (Commission) Regulation.
257 Art. 12(c) UCITSD V (Commission) Regulation.
258 Art. 21(d) and (e) UCITSD V (Commission) Regulation; ESMA/2014/1183, 22.

UCITS ManCos and depositaries that have a two-tier board structure[259] less stringent rules for the members of the body in charge of the supervisory functions apply.[260] The reason for introducing this less stringent regime for two-tier board structures is that for entities that have a two-tier board structure strong safeguards should already be in place at the level of the body carrying out the managerial function.

4.4.4.2   Cross-Shareholdings/Group Inclusion

The European Commission and ESMA upon introducing UCITSD V considered that the independence of the UCITS ManCo (investment company) and the depositary could also be prejudiced if either of them could control the other by means of voting or if both are part of the same group.[261] To this end, the independence requirements under Chapter 4 UCITSD V (Commission) Regulation require measures and arrangements to be taken by the UCITS ManCo (investment company) and the depositary if these entities are having a (1) link or a (2) group link. The UCITS ManCo and the depositary are deemed to be 'linked' if they are in a situation that either entity has by a direct or indirect holding of 10% or more capital or voting rights or which makes it possible to exercise a significant hold over the management of the undertaking in which that holding subsists.[262] Both are considered to be having a 'group link' if they are included in the same group under the Consolidated Accounts Directive, as defined in Directive 2013/34/EU, or in accordance with recognized international accounting rules.[263] Chapter 4 UCITSD V (Commission) Regulation imposes measures and arrangements to management companies and depositaries having a link or a group link (cross-shareholdings).[264] In addition, specific governance and organizational arrangements have to be put in place to UCITS ManCos and depositaries that are part of the same group to preserve the independence of both (group inclusion).[265]

The UCITS ManCo and the depositary that have a link or a group link are obliged to justify the choice of the depositary/sub-custodian and put in place conflict of interest policies to avoid conflict arising from the qualifying shareholding or group structure.[266] The UCITS ManCo shall put in place a decision-making process for appointing a depositary that is based upon objective pre-defined criteria and at the same time meets the exclusive interests of the UCITS and its investors.[267] UCITS ManCos appointing a de-

---

259 *See* ESMA/2014/1183, 19.
260 *Ibid.*
261 *Ibid.*, 20.
262 Art. 1(a) UCITSD V (Commission) Regulation; The definition of link is based upon the definition of 'qualifying holding' in Art. 2(1)(j) UCITSD V; *See* ESMA/2014/1183, 20.
263 Art. 1(b) UCITSD V (Commission) Regulation; ESMA/2014/1183, 20-21.
264 *See* Art. 22 and 23 UCITSD V (Commission) Regulation.
265 *See* Art. 24 UCITSD V (Commission) Regulation.
266 ESMA/2014/1183, 23.
267 Art. 22(1) UCITSD V (Commission) Regulation; ESMA/2014/1183, 23.

positary to which it has a link[268] or a group link[269] have to keep documentary evidence of:[270]

- an assessment comparing the merits of the appointment of a depositary with and without a cross-shareholding with the UCITS ManCo, taking into account the costs, expertise, financial standing and the quality of services provided by the depositaries assessed;[271]
- a report based upon the assessment describing the way in which the appointed depositary meets the objective pre-defined criteria and that the appointed is made in the sole interest of the UCITS and the investors of the UCITS.[272]

The UCITS ManCo has to demonstrate the Competent Authority of the UCITS home Member State that it is satisfied with the choice of the depositary and that the appointment is in the sole interest of the UCITS and its investors.[273] For this purpose, the UCITS ManCo shall make the documentary evidence available to the Competent Authority.[274] The UCITS ManCo also has to justify to investors the choice of the depositary upon request.[275] Finally, the depositary has to have a decision-making process in place for choosing sub-custodians to whom it may delegate safekeeping functions[276] that is also based upon objective pre-defined criteria that meet the sole interest of the UCITS and its investors.

UCITS ManCos and depositaries that are either having a link or group link are required to ensure[277] that they identify all conflicts of interest arising from that link[278] and that they take all reasonable steps to avoid those conflicts of interest.[279] Where conflicts of interest, however, cannot be avoided, the UCITS ManCo and depositary are required to manage, monitor and disclose that conflict of interest in order to prevent adverse effects on the interests of the UCITS and of the investors of the UCITS.[280]

For group structures consisting of both the management and the depositary, additional arrangements should be put in place. The management bodies of UCITS ManCos and depositaries of one-tier structures are required to have at least one-third of the members of the management body or two persons, whichever is lower, to be independent that

---

268 Art. 1(a) UCITSD V (Commission) Regulation.
269 Art. 1(b) UCITSD V (Commission) Regulation.
270 Art.22(2) UCITSD V (Commission) Regulation.
271 Art.22(2)(a) UCITSD V (Commission) Regulation.
272 Art.22(2)(b) UCITSD V (Commission) Regulation.
273 Art.22(3) UCITSD V (Commission) Regulation.
274 Art.22(3) UCITSD V (Commission) Regulation.
275 Art.22(4) UCITSD V (Commission) Regulation.
276 Safekeeping functions are being referred to the functions as set out in Art. 22a UCITSD V.
277 Art. 23 sub-para. 1 UCITSD V (Commission) Regulation.
278 Art. 23 sub-para. 1(a) UCITSD V (Commission) Regulation.
279 Art. 23 sub-para. 1(b) UCITSD V (Commission) Regulation.
280 See also for the general conflict of interest duty: Art. 25(2) UCITSD V.

are in charge of the supervisory functions of the above companies on the management body.[281] The management bodies of UCITS ManCos and depositaries of two-tier structures shall be the same amount of independent members on the body in charge of the supervisory functions with the UCITS ManCo and depositary.[282] Independence within the group structure, for this purpose, is understood as requiring that independent directors may not be members of the management body, the supervisory body nor employees of any of the undertakings within the group.[283] Nor may they have any of those functions in the undertakings between which a group link exists and should the members be free of any business, family or other relationship with the UCITS ManCo and depositary or any other undertaking within the group that gives rise to a conflict of interest.[284] The independence requirement for management boards and supervisory functions is put in place as to prevent an impaired judgment of its members.[285]

UCITSD V, thus, complements the third party depositary requirement that targets the independence of the UCITS Manco (investment company) and the UCITS depositary, whereas equivalent measures are being left over to the Member States under the AIFMD.[286]

4.5 AIFMD THIRD-COUNTRY DEPOSITARIES

4.5.1 Additional Requirements for TC Depositaries

The AIFMD extends the European 'mutual recognition' approach to TC-AIFs and TC-AIFMs that are willing to benefit from a European passport within the EEA. The appointment of a depositary established in a third country is subject to the following requirements:

- cooperation and exchange of information agreements must be concluded between: (1) the supervisory authority of the depositary, and (2) the supervisory authorities of the AIFM and (3) all the supervisory authorities of the Member State in which the AIFM intends to market its AIFs;[287]
- the third country where the depositary is established must not be listed as a non-cooperative country and territory by the FATF;[288]
- tax information exchange arrangements complying with Article 26 of the OECD Model Tax Convention must be in place between: (1) the country in which the de-

---

281 Art. 24(1)(a) UCITSD V (Commission) Regulation.
282 Art. 24(1)(b) UCITSD V (Commission) Regulation.
283 ESMA/2014/1183, 24.
284 Art. 24(2) UCITSD V (Commission) Regulation.
285 Art. 24(2) UCITSD V (Commission) Regulation.
286 See Art. 26b UCITSD V; See also ESMA/2014/1183, 18.
287 Art. 21(6)(a) AIFMD.
288 Art. 21(6)(c) AIFMD.

positary is established; (2) the AIFM home Member State and (3) all Member States in which the AIF is intended to be marketed;[289]

– the depositary is subject to 'effectively enforced' prudential regulation (including minimum capital requirements) and supervision, which have the same effect as EU law;[290]

– the depositary must contractually subject itself to the AIFMD depositary liability regime and commit itself to comply with the AIFMD rules on delegation duties and appointment of sub-custodians.[291]

4.5.2   The Third-Country Depositary and 'Effective Prudential Regulation'

Pursuant to Article 21(6)(b) AIFMD, the depositary must be subject to 'effectively enforced' prudential regulation (including minimum capital requirements) and 'supervision equivalent' to that applicable under EEA law. On the basis of these criteria, the European Commission adopts implementing acts stating the third countries in which depositaries are deemed to be equivalent.[292]

4.5.2.1   Effectively Enforced Prudential Regulation

The AIFMD (Commission) Regulation[293] sets out that prudential regulation, supervision and its effective enforcement shall be assessed by the EC against the following criteria:[294]

– the depositary has to be subject to authorization and ongoing supervision by a public Competent Authority with adequate resources to fulfil its tasks;[295]

– the law of the third country shall set out criteria for authorization as a depositary that have the same effect as those set out for the access to the business of credit institutions or investment firms within the European Union;[296]

– the capital requirements imposed on the depositary in the third country shall have the same effect as those applicable in the European Union, depending on whether the depositary is of the same nature as an EEU credit institution or investment firm.[297]

---

289 Art. 21(6)(d) AIFMD.
290 Art. 21(6)(b) AIFMD.
291 Art. 21(6)(e) AIFMD.
292 Art. 21(6) sub-para. 3 AIFMD.
293 Commission Delegated Regulation (EU) No. 231/2013 of 19 December 2012 supplementing Directive 2011/61/EU of the European Parliament and of the Council with regard to exemptions, general operating conditions, depositaries, leverage, transparency and supervision, OJ L 83, 22 March 2013, 1 ('AIFMD (Commission) Regulation').
294 Art. 84 AIFMD (Commission) Regulation.
295 Art. 84(a) AIFMD (Commission) Regulation.
296 Art. 84(b) AIFMD (Commission) Regulation.
297 Art. 84(c) AIFMD (Commission) Regulation.

- the operating conditions applicable to a depositary in the third country have the same effect as those set out for credit institutions or investment firms within the European Union, depending on the nature of the depositary;[298]
- the requirements regarding the performance of the specific duties as AIF depositary established in the law of the third country shall have the same effect as those provided for in Article 21(7)–(15) AIFMD and its implementing measures and the relevant national laws;[299]
- the law of the third country shall provide for the application of sufficiently dissuasive enforcement actions in case of breach by the depositary of the requirements of the AIFMD and its implementing measures.[300]

The assessment of whether there is 'supervision which has the same effect as Union law' should be made by comparing: (1) the authorization criteria, and (2) the ongoing operating conditions (including capital requirements) applicable to the third country depositary against the corresponding requirements that the AIFMD imposes on credit institutions or investment firms within the EEA for authorization.[301]

Under third country legislation, other entities comparable to EEA credit institutions or investment firms are eligible. In that case, such entities must also be subject to prudential oversight and be licensed under a local category, whereas those local criteria should have the same effect as those for credit institutions or investment firms under the AIFMD.[302]

4.5.2.2   'Supervision under Equivalent' to That Applicable under EEA Law

This equivalent with the AIFMD can only be achieved if the depositary established in a third country is subject to prudential supervision performed by a 'Competent Authority'. The exact nature of a Competent Authority is not clarified by the AIFMD (Commission) Regulation. According to ESMA's Final Report, this can be understood as oversight by a public authority that can 'effectively enforce' a depositary established in a third country to comply with the third country's prudential regulation.[303] A third country authority is considered competent if it is compliant with Part II ('The Regulator') of the IOSCO Objectives and Principles for Securities Regulation[304] and relevant methodology,[305] and

---

298 Art. 84(d) AIFMD (Commission) Regulation.
299 Art. 84(e) AIFMD (Commission) Regulation.
300 Art. 84(f) AIFMD (Commission) Regulation.
301 Recital 96 AIFMD (Commission) Regulation.
302 Recital 95, 96 AIFMD (Commission) Regulation. *See also* ESMA/2011/379, 145-146.
303 ESMA/2011/379, 145.
304 IOSCO, *Objectives and Principles of Securities Regulation*, Part II 'The Regulator' (2003).
305 IOSCO, *Methodology – For Assessing Implementation of the IOSCO Objectives and Principles of Securities Regulation*, FR 08/11 (2011).

the Basel Committee Core Principles[306] and its relevant methodology.[307] However, according to ESMA, this does not imply that the authority itself needs to be a member of this organization.[308] The oversight of the third country should merely mean being able to 'effectively enforce' its prudential regulation, meaning that the third country authority should, at least, have the power to request information, intervene and sanction the depositary as regards the relevant requirements under its domestic legislation.[309]

4.6   THE DEPOSITARY AND ITS FUNCTIONS

Since the creation of the UCITS framework,[310] depositaries are one of the three fundamental pillars of European collective investment law, alongside the fund (the joint investors) and its manager.[311] Upon the introduction of the AIFMD, both AIFMs and UCITS ManCos are required to ensure that a single depositary is appointed for each AIF/UCITS they manage. The AIFMD, thus, extended the tripartite structure, which may be called the 'investment triangle'[312] to AIFs.[313] The question of how a depositary relationship is established under the AIFMD and UCITSD V will now be addressed, and the particulars of the depositary's safekeeping and control function will then be discussed.

4.6.1   The Particulars of the Written Contract

The AIFM and UCITS ManCo must ensure that a depositary is appointed for each AIF/UCITS it manages.[314] The AIFMD and UCITSD V require that each AIF/UCITS must have one single depositary, meaning that the functions of a depositary (safekeeping and control) must be carried out by one and the same entity.[315]

The evidenced written contract appointing the depositary shall be drawn up between the depositary on the one, and the AIFM/UCITS ManCo and/or the AIF/UCITS or other entity acting on behalf of the AIF/UCITS, on the other hand.[316] In particular, the written

---

306 Basel Committee on Banking Supervision, *Core Principles for Effective Banking Supervision* (2006). In December 2011 a revised version was issued for consultation.

307 Basel Committee on Banking Supervision, *Core Principles Methodology* (2006).

308 ESMA/2011/379, 145.

309 *Ibid.*, 144–145.

310 Directive 85/611/EEC.

311 Arts. 22 et seq. UCITSD V; Art. 21 AIFMD; Art. 16(8)-(10) MiFID II and Arts. 2-8 MiFID II (Commission) Directive; Art. 35 IORPD II.

312 K. Ohl, *Die Rechtsbeziehungen innerhalb des Investment-Dreiecks* (1989); Zetzsche, *supra* note 237; N. Seegebarth. *Stellung und Haftung der Depotbank im Investment-Dreieck* (2004).

313 *See* D.A. Zetzsche, *The AIFMD and the Joint Principles of European Asset Management Law* (D.A. Zetzsche ed., Kluwer 2015).

314 Art. 21(1) AIFMD; Art. 22(1) UCITSD V.

315 *Ibid.*

316 Art. 21(2) AIFMD; Art. 22(2) UCITSD V.

contract regulates the flow of information, which is necessary for a depositary and its sub-custodians to appropriately perform its safekeeping, as well as for the proper compliance of the depositary's oversight functions[317] with relevant laws, regulations or administrative provisions.[318] It is possible for the AIFM/UCITS ManCo and the depositary to enter into a framework agreement that applies to several AIFs/UCITS managed by that AIFM/UCITS ManCo, unless otherwise provided by relevant national laws.[319]

The specific rights and obligations that are required to be set out in the written contract can be found in the AIFMD and UCITSD V (Commission) Regulation.[320]

4.6.1.1 Eligible Assets

The depositary contract has to contain a description of the depositary services and the particular procedures to be adopted for each type of asset in which the AIF/UCITS is allowed to invest.[321] In order to allow the depositary to assess and monitor custody risk, the contract shall provide a description of the assets in which the AIF/UCITS can invest so that the depositary knows upon its appointment what procedures it shall set up to allow the appropriate safekeeping of the assets of the AIF/UCITS as well as procedures for the oversight functions that the depositary will exercise over them.[322] With respect to custody duties, the description of the categories of assets shall not necessarily contain all assets and sub-categories of financial instruments to be subject to safekeeping. It must, however, include country lists, as well as procedures for adding and withdrawing countries from the list so that the depositary can assess and monitor custody risks.[323] This shall be consistent with the information provided in the AIF/UCITS rules, instruments of incorporation and offering documents regarding the assets in which the AIF/UCITS may invest.[324]

---

317 Recital 94 AIFMD (Commission) Regulation; Recital 20 UCITSD V (Commission) Regulation.
318 Art. 83(6) AIFMD (Commission) Regulation and Art. 2(5) UCITSD V (Commission) Regulation require the national laws applicable to the contract appointing the depositary and any subsequent agreements to be specified. Although this contract might contain confidentiality obligations applicable to the parties that signed the depositary contract, this shall not impair the ability of the relevant Competent Authorities to have access to all relevant documents and information related to the depositary contract.
319 Art. 83(5) AIFMD (Commission) Regulation; Art. 2(4) UCITSD V (Commission) Regulation.
320 Art. 83 AIFMD (Commission) Regulation; Art. 2 UCITSD V (Commission) Regulation.
321 ESMA/2011/379, 142.
322 Ibid.
323 Art. 83(1)(b) AIFMD (Commission) Regulation; Art. 2(2)(b) UCITSD V (Commission) Regulation.
324 Ibid.

4.6.1.2   Flow of Information

The core aim of the depositary contract is, amongst other things, to regulate the flow of information.[325] In particular, the AIFM/UCITS ManCo is required[326] to ensure that the depositary receives all information it needs to perform its safekeeping[327] and oversight duties,[328] including information to be provided directly by third parties, such as prime brokers and third parties where bank accounts have been opened in the name of the AIF/UCITS or the AIFM/UCITS ManCo acting on behalf of the AIF/UCITS.[329] The depositary can check the quality of the information provided by enquiring into the conduct of the AIFM/UCITS ManCo and/or the AIF/UCITS, by accessing the books of the AIF/UCITS and/or AIFM/UCITS ManCo, or by way of on-site visits.[330] On the other hand, procedures have to be established that ensure that the AIFM/UCITS ManCo and/or the AIF/UCITS can review the performance of the depositary with regard to its duties.[331]

4.6.1.3   Escalation Procedure

Details of escalation procedures shall be included in the depositary contract.[332] For example, the depositary has the obligation to alert the AIFM/UCITS ManCo if it has identified any material risk in a particular market's settlement system.[333] This includes the

---

325 The contract does, for instance, also contain elements on information on the obligations related to the prevention of money laundering and the financing of terrorism (Art. 83(1)(m) AIFMD(Commission) Regulation; Art. 2(2)(k) UCITSD V (Commission) Regulation)) and the procedures to be followed when a modification to the AIF rules, instruments of incorporation or offering documents is considered (Art. 83 (1)(i) AIFMD (Commission) Regulation; Art. 2(2)(g) UCITSD V (Commission) Regulation)).

326 Art. 83(1)(g) AIFMD (Commission) Regulation and Art. 2(2)(f) UCITSD V (Commission) Regulation set out that the contract shall include the means and procedures by which the AIFM/UCITS ManCo or the AIF/UCITS will transmit all relevant information or will ensure that the depositary has access to all the information it needs to fulfil its duties, including ensuring that the depositary will receive information from any relevant third parties appointed by the AIF/UCITS or the AIFM/UCITS ManCo.

327 See Art. 83(1)(b) AIFMD (Commission) Regulation and Art. 2(2)(b) UCITSD V (Commission) Regulation. See Art. 83(1)(h) AIFMD (Commission) Regulation and for the obligation to whether the depositary and its sub-custodians to which it has delegated safekeeping function is allowed or not to reuse the AIF's assets and, where relevant, the conditions related to the potential reuse. See also the obligation of the depositary under Art. 83(1)(p) AIFMD (Commission) Regulation and Art. 2(2)(n) UCITSD V (Commission) Regulation to notify the AIFM/UCITS ManCo when the segregation of assets is not or no longer sufficient to protect assets from insolvency of a sub-custodian to whom assets have been delegated.

328 See on necessary information to be exchanged between the AIF/UCITS, AIF/UCITS and a third party acting on behalf of the AIFM/UCITS ManCo, AIF/UCITS or the depositary upon subscriptions/redemptions Art. 83(1)(j) AIFMD (Commission) Regulation and Art. 2(2)(h) UCITSD V (Commission) Regulation, upon the AIFM's/UCITS ManCo's instructions Art. 83(1)(k) AIFMD (Commission) Regulation and Art. 2(2)(i) UCITSD V (Commission) Regulation, and upon exercising any rights attached to assets Art. 83(1)(f) AIFMD (Commission) Regulation and Art. 2(2)(e) UCITSD V (Commission) Regulation.

329 See Art. 83(1)(f) and Art. 83(1)(n) AIFMD (Commission) Regulation; Art. 2(2)(e) and Art. 2(2)(l) UCITSD V (Commission) Regulation,

330 Art. 83(1)(q) AIFMD (Commission) Regulation; Art. 2(2)(o) UCITSD V (Commission) Regulation.

331 Art. 83(1)(r) AIFMD (Commission) Regulation; Art. 2(2)(p) UCITSD V (Commission) Regulation.

332 Art. 83(1)(o) AIFMD (Commission) Regulation; Art. 2(2)(m) UCITSD V (Commission) Regulation.

333 Recital 94 AIFMD (Commission) Regulation; Recital 2 UCITSD V (Commission) Regulation.

identification of the persons to be contacted within the AIF/UCITS and/or the AIFM/
UCITS ManCo by the depositary when it launches such a procedure.[334]

4.6.1.4   Third Parties

The contract must take into account the details of, and steps taken to monitor, sub-
custodians.

Depositary contracts concluded by both AIFMs and UCITS ManCo contains provisions that the depositary, AIF/UCITS and relevant AIFM/UCITS ManCo exchange information on a regular basis and, upon request, information on the criteria used to select
third parties and the steps undertaken to monitor the activities carried out by the selected
third party. In addition, the depositary contract concluded by AIFMs includes a statement that the depositary's liability is not affected by any delegation of its custody functions, unless it has discharged itself contractually of its liability in accordance with Article
21(13) and (14) AIFMD. In particular, the contract has to set out in detail the conditions
under which the depositary can transfer its liability to a sub-custodian.

4.6.1.5   Termination of the Contract

The contract should include situations that could lead to the termination of the contract
as well as details regarding the termination procedure.[335] Following the depositary's liability regime with regard to the custody of assets, this would be the ultimate recourse for
the depositary if it is not satisfied with how assets are protected.[336] This possibility should
prevent moral hazards whereby AIFMs/UCITS ManCos make investment decisions irrespective of custody risks on the basis that the depositary would be liable in these
cases.[337]

By using the principles-based approach and not providing a model agreement, there
seems to be a balance between, on the one hand, ensuring the flow of information that a
depositary needs to fulfil its safekeeping and oversight functions and, on the other hand,
sufficient freedom for the industry to adapt their contracts to a wide range of AIFs/
UCITS, investment strategies and different national legal frameworks.

4.6.2   Safekeeping

Safekeeping the assets of an AIF/UCITS is the *raison d'être* of a depositary. The AIFMD
and UCITSD V seek to clarify the understanding of this safekeeping duty by making

---

334 Art. 83(1)(o) AIFMD (Commission) Regulation; Art. 2(2)(m) UCITSD V (Commission) Regulation.
335 Art. 83(1)(d) AIFMD (Commission) Regulation; Art. 2(2)(c) UCITSD V (Commission) Regulation.
336 Recital 94 AIFMD (Commission) Regulation; Recital 2 UCITSD V (Commission) Regulation.
337 *Ibid.*

reference to the type of assets held by the AIF/UCITS. In doing so, it makes a distinction between 'financial instruments that can be held in custody', on the one hand, and 'other assets', including financial instruments that cannot be held in custody, on the other.

4.6.2.1   Financial Instruments That Should Be Held in Custody

Depending on the type of assets, the depositary's safekeeping functions can take the form of custody, for financial instruments that can be held in custody, or record-keeping for other assets.[338] According to the AIFMD and UCITSD V, the depositary shall hold in custody all *financial instruments* that:[339]

– can be registered in a financial instruments account opened in the depositary's book; and

– can be physically delivered to the depositary.

Financial instruments, which cannot be physically delivered to the depositary, fall within the scope of the depositary's custody obligation when they are either: (1) transferable securities, or (2) capable of being registered or held in an account directly or indirectly in the name of the depositary. The definition of transferable securities includes certain types of derivatives,[340] money market instruments and units of collective investment undertakings.[341] The definition is broad and captures certain instruments, such as derivatives, in Annex I Section C of MiFID II that were in some jurisdictions traditionally not being considered as assets to be held in custody.[342] Beyond the AIFMD and UCITSD V (Commission) Regulation, the EMIR[343] provides a list of derivatives that have to be cleared via central counterparties.[344] This list has brought more legal certainty as to what types of financial instruments are considered transferable securities and, thus, fall within the scope of the depositary's custody obligation.[345] The custody obligation includes financial instruments that are provided to a third party, or by a third party to the AIF/UCITS as collateral, as long as they are owned by the AIF/AIFM or UCITS/UCITS ManCo on behalf of the AIF/UCITS.[346] This is also valid for financial instruments

---

338 Art. 21(8)(b) AIFMD; Art. 22(5)(b) UCITSD V.

339 Art. 21(8)(a); Art. 22(5)(a) UCITSD V.

340 These derivatives have to be in accordance with Art. 51(3) UCITS IV. *See* Art. 88(1)(a) AIFMD (Commission) Regulation and Art. 12(1)(a) UCITSD V (Commission) Regulation.

341 Art. 88(1)(a) AIFMD (Commission) Regulation and Art. 12(1)(a) UCITSD V (Commission) Regulation.; *See* on the status of derivate contracts and holdings in collective investment undertakings: ESMA/2015/850, 22.

342 ESMA/2011/379, 157.

343 *See*, in particular: Art. 6 Regulation (EU) No 648/2012 ('EMIR') of the European Parliament and of the council of 4 July 2012 on OTC derivatives, central counterparties and trade repositories, L 201/1, 27 July 2012.

344 Art. 88(1) AIFMD (Commission) Regulation; Art. 12(1) UCITSD V (Commission) Regulation.

345 *Ibid.*

346 Recital 100 AIFMD (Commission) Regulation; Recital 12 UCITSD V (Commission) Regulation.

for which the AIFM/UCITS ManCo has given its consent to the depositary to reuse as long as the right of reuse has not been exercised.[347]

The definition of financial instruments is designed to capture all financial instruments the depositary is in a position to control and retrieve. Following the AIFMD and UCITSD V (Commission) Regulation,[348] this excludes all securities that are directly registered with the issuer itself or its agent (i.e. a registrar or a transfer agent) in the name of the AIF/UCITS, except in the situation where financial instruments can be physically delivered to the depositary[349] or are registered/held in an account directly or indirectly in the name of the depositary (through a subsidiary or sub-custodian).[350]

Financial instruments that can be held in custody fall within the scope of the depositary liability regime that is defined by the AIFMD and UCITSD V, which obliges depositaries to return the financial instrument or an identical type or the corresponding amount in case of a loss of a financial instrument held in custody by the depositary.[351] This liability is clearly linked to assets for which only the depositary can instruct a transfer, including where it is the registered owner in the issuer's register.[352] Instruments that do not comply with the requirements above for satisfying the definition of 'financial instruments' should be considered 'other assets' within the meaning of the AIFMD/UCITSD V and are subject to record-keeping duties.[353]

4.6.2.2 Safekeeping Duties with regard to Assets Held in Custody

Financial instruments that can be held in custody include transferable securities, money market instruments and units in collective investment undertakings.[354] Financial instruments held in custody should be subject to due care and protection at all times.[355] The meaning of 'due care' is clarified in the AIFMD and UCITSD V (Commission) Regulation.[356] This obligation requires the depositary to ensure that custody risk is properly assessed. In doing so, 'due care' obliges the depositary to know which custodians are a

---

347 In contrast to ESMA/2011/379, 158, the final text of Art. 88 AIFMD (Commission) Regulation and Art. 12 UCITSD V (Commission) Regulation brings more uncertainty with respect to the issue of collateral provided by the AIF or AIFM on behalf of the AIF.

348 Recital 100 AIFMD (Commission) Regulation; Recital 12 UCITSD V (Commission) Regulation.

349 Art. 88(3) AIFMD (Commission) Regulation; Art. 12(3)UCITSD V (Commission) Regulation.

350 Art. 88(1)(b) AIFMD (Commission) Regulation. Art. 12(1)(b) UCITSD V (Commission) Regulation.

351 Art. 21(12) AIFMD; Art. 24 UCITSD V; *See* C. Clerc, *The AIF Depositary's Liability for Lost Assets* (D.A. Zetzsche ed., Kluwer 2015).

352 *See* explanation ESMA/2011/379, 157.

353 Art. 21(8)(b) AIFMD; Art. 22(5)(b) UCITSD V.

354 *See* Annex I s. C Financial Instruments MiFID II. Please note that not all financial instruments within Annex I s. C are financial instruments that can be held in custody under Art. 21(8) AIFMD and Art. 22 (5) UCITSD V. By contrast, assets that cannot be held in custody are: real estate, physical assets (gold, coal), non-tradeable partnership shares and ships.

355 Art. 89 AIFMD (Commission) Regulation; Art. 13 UCITSD V (Commission) Regulation.

356 Recital 101 AIFMD (Commission) Regulation; Recital 13 UCITSD V (Commission) Regulation.

part of the custodian chain. In order to comply with this obligation, the AIFMD and UCITSD (Commission) Regulation require the depositary to ensure that:[357]
- financial instruments shall be properly registered in a segregated financial instruments account;[358]
- its sub-custodians maintain records and segregated accounts for cash and financial instruments held for AIFs/UCITS;[359]
- it regularly reconciles the internal accounts and records of the depositary and the sub-custodian;[360]
- due care is exercised and all relevant custody risks throughout the custody chain are monitored;[361]
- custody risks throughout the custody chain are assessed and monitored and material risks reported to the AIFM/UCITS ManCo;[362]
- adequate organizational arrangements are introduced to minimize the risk of the loss, diminution of financial instruments, or the rights in connection with those financial instruments;[363]
- the AIF's/UCITS' ownership right over the assets or of the AIFM/UCITS ManCo acting on behalf of the AIF/UCITS are verified.[364]

The depositary has to ensure that financial instruments are subject to due care and protection at all times.[365] To that extent, the depositary has to properly assess the custody risk throughout the custody chain.[366] In exercising due care, the depositary identifies all sub-custodians, ensures that due diligence and segregation obligations are maintained throughout the custody chain and that it has access to the books and records of third parties to whom custody functions have been delegated.[367]

In order to avoid circumvention of these strict requirements, the AIFMD (Commission) Regulation requires a 'look-through approach' regarding the depositary's safekeeping duties.[368] This implies that whenever the AIF has set up a legal structure between itself and the assets in which it wishes to invest, the depositary must apply the above-mentioned safekeeping rules to the underlying assets of financial and/or legal structures

---

357 Art. 89 AIFMD (Commission) Regulation; Art. 13 UCITSD V (Commission) Regulation.
358 Art. 89(1)(a) AIFMD (Commission) Regulation; Art. 13(1)(a) UCITSD V (Commission) Regulation.
359 Art. 89(1)(b) AIFMD (Commission) Regulation; Art. 13(1)(b) UCITSD V (Commission) Regulation.
360 Art. 89(1)(c) AIFMD (Commission) Regulation; Art. 13(1)(c) UCITSD V (Commission) Regulation.
361 Art. 89(1)(d) AIFMD (Commission) Regulation; Art. 13(1)(d) UCITSD V (Commission) Regulation.
362 Art. 89(1)(e) AIFMD (Commission) Regulation; Art. 13(1)(e) UCITSD V (Commission) Regulation.
363 Art. 89(1)(f) AIFMD (Commission) Regulation; Art. 13(1)(f) UCITSD V (Commission) Regulation.
364 Art. 89(1)(g) AIFMD (Commission) Regulation; Art. 13(1)(g) UCITSD V (Commission) Regulation.
365 Recital 101, Art. 89(2) AIFMD (Commission) Regulation; Recital 13, Art. 13(2) UCITSD V (Commission) Regulation.
366 Ibid.
367 Art. 89(2) AIFMD (Commission) Regulation; Art. 13(2) UCITSD V (Commission) Regulation.
368 Art. 89(3) AIFMD (Commission) Regulation.

that are controlled directly or indirectly by the AIF or the AIFM acting on behalf of the AIF.[369] The UCITSD V (Commission) Regulation does not require a similar 'look-through approach' regarding the UCITS depositary's safekeeping duties.[370]

4.6.2.2.1   Insolvency Protection of UCITS Assets

Article 22(8) UCITSD V requires Member States to ensure that in the event of an insolvency of the depositary and or sub-custodian located in the EEA to which custody of UCITS assets has been delegated, the assets of a UCITS held in custody shall be unavailable for distribution among, or the realization for the benefit of, creditors of such a depositary/sub-custodian.[371]

4.6.2.3   'Other Assets'

All assets that do not fall under the definition of financial instruments constitute 'other assets'.[372] These include:

– physical assets (non-financial assets) that do not qualify as financial instruments or cannot be physically delivered to the depositary (e.g. real estate, commodities, ships);
– financial instruments that can neither be held in book-entry form nor be physically delivered to the depositary (e.g. financial contracts), such as (OTC) derivatives other than those embedded in the transferable securities definition within Article 21(8)(a) AIFMD and Article 22(5)(a) UCITSD V, in particular, derivatives are other assets that are important for prime broker settings;[373]
– cash deposits;[374]
– financial instruments issued in nominative form and registered with an issuer or a registrar.[375]

The last category refers to assets that are not intermediated and where the ownership derives from direct registration in the register held by the issuer itself (or a registrar agent acting on its behalf). Examples include investments in privately held companies, or participation interest in funds with a capital call structure, such as real estate or private equity funds. Also, assets of the AIF/UCITS provided as collateral in general will be subject to safekeeping duties related to 'other assets'.[376]

---

369 See Recital 102 AIFMD (Commission) Regulation.
370 See Art. 13 UCITSD (Commission) Regulation.
371 Art. 22(8) UCITSD V. See also infra 4.7.3.3. for extra requirements preserving insolvency protection on the sub-custodian level for UCITS assets.
372 Art. 21(8)(b) AIFMD; Art. 22(5)(b) UCITSD V.
373 See Zetzsche, supra note 103.
374 Recital 103 AIFMD (Commission) Regulation and Recital 14 UCITSD V (Commission) Regulation. See also ESMA/2011/379, 161.
375 See Art. 88(2) AIFMD (Commission) Regulation and Art. 12(2) UCITSD V (Commission) Regulation.
376 ESMA/2011/379, 162.

The depositary should have a comprehensive overview of all assets that are not finan-cial instruments to be held in custody.[377] These assets are subject to the obligation of the depositary to verify that the relevant 'other assets' effectively belong to the AIF/UCITS itself or to the AIFM/UCITS ManCo acting on behalf of the AIF/UCITS ManCo.[378] The ownership verification must be based on information or documents provided by the AIF/UCITS or the AIFM /UCITS ManCo and, where available, external evidence.[379] External evidence could be a copy of an official document showing that the AIF/UCITS is the owner of the asset(s) or any formal and reliable evidence that the depositary considers appropriate.[380] If necessary, the depositary should request additional evidence from the AIF/UCITS or AIFM/UCITS ManCo or, as the case may be, from a third party.[381] A broad range of evidence could potentially prove ownership. The parameters of the ver-ification obligation are, however, uncertain. The official document clarifies whether this obligation covers both the legal and equitable or beneficial title. The verification obliga-tion of the depositary is also unclear insofar as, for instance, the enforceability of deriva-tives or share borrowing contractual arrangements are concerned. A record of those assets shall be maintained and regularly updated.[382]

4.6.2.4   Safekeeping Duties regarding Ownership Verification and Record-keeping

For 'other assets', the AIFM/UCITS ManCo is obliged to provide the depositary on an ongoing basis with all relevant information that the depositary needs to comply with its obligations.[383] In doing so, it ensures that the depositary is also provided with all relevant information by any third parties.[384] In order for a depositary to comply with ownership verification and record-keeping duties, it shall meet the following requirements:[385]

- it shall access without undue delay the relevant information it needs to perform its ownership verification and record-keeping duties, including information to be pro-vided by third parties;[386]
- it shall make sure it possesses sufficient and reliable information to satisfy the AIF/AIFM's and UCITS'/UCITS Manco's ownership rights over the AIF's/UCITS' as-sets;[387]

---

377 Financial instruments within the meaning of Art. 21(8)(a) AIFMD and Art. 22(5)(a) UCITSD V.
378 Art. 21(8)(b) AIFMD; Art. 22(5)(b) UCITSD V.
379 Art. 21(8)(b)(ii) and (iii) AIFMD; Art. 22(5)(b)(i) and (ii) UCITSD V.
380 Recital 104 AIFMD (Commission) Regulation. *See also* ESMA/2011/379, 162.
381 *Ibid.*
382 Art. 21 (8)(b)(i) AIFMD; Art. 22(5)(b)(i) UCITSD V; Recital 105 AIFMD (Commission) Regulation and Recital 16 UCITSD V (Commission) Regulation.
383 Art. 90(1) AIFMD (Commission) Regulation and Art. 14(1) UCITSD V (Commission) Regulation.
384 *Ibid.*
385 Art. 90(2) AIFMD (Commission) Regulation and Art. 14(2) UCITSD V (Commission) Regulation.
386 Art. 90(2)(a) AIFMD (Commission) Regulation and Art. 14(2)(a) UCITSD V (Commission) Regulation.
387 Art. 90(2)(b) AIFMD (Commission) Regulation and Art. 14(2)(b) UCITSD V (Commission) Regulation.

– it shall maintain a record of the assets of which the AIF holds the ownership and it shall: (1) register in its record the name of the AIF's/UCITS' assets,[388] (2) be able to provide at any time a comprehensive and up-to-date inventory of an AIF's/UCITS' assets.[389]

To that end, the depositary has to ensure that:[390]
– the procedures are in place so that assets registered cannot be assigned, transferred, exchanged or delivered without the depositary or its delegate being informed of such transactions; or
– it has access without undue delay to documentary evidence of each transaction and positions of relevant third parties.

Regarding the last requirement, AIFMs/UCITS ManCos are obliged to ascertain that relevant third parties provide depositaries with certificates or other documentary evidence without undue delay every time there is a sale, acquisition of assets or a corporate action resulting in the issue of financial instruments. This must happen at least once a year.

Depositaries have to ensure that AIFMs/UCITS ManCos implement the appropriate procedures to verify that the assets being acquired by the AIF/UCITS are appropriately registered in the name of the AIF/UCITS or AIFM/UCITS ManCo acting on behalf of the AIF/UCITS. The depositary's duty is to check consistency between the positions in the AIFM's/UCITS ManCo's records and assets for which the depositary has satisfied that the AIF/UCITS or the AIFM/UCITS ManCo has ownership. In addition, the AIFM/UCITS ManCo has to send all instructions and relevant information related to the AIF's/UCITS' assets to the depositary so that the depositary can carry out its own verification or reconciliation procedure.[391]

If an anomaly is detected, depositaries shall set up and implement an escalation procedure. This procedure shall include a notification of the AIFM/UCITS ManCo, and, if the situation cannot be clarified, to the Competent Authority.[392]

Equivalent to the safekeeping requirements for assets to be held in custody, the AIFMD (Commission) Regulation applies a 'look-through' approach to the record-keeping obligations of a depositary that apply vis-à-vis assets that are, for example, held by the AIF via intermediary companies. The duties of a depositary do not stop at the level of a

---

388 Art. 90(2)(c)(i) AIFMD (Commission) Regulation and Art. 14(2)(c)(i) UCITSD V (Commission) Regulation.
389 Art. 90(2)(c)(ii) AIFMD (Commission) Regulation and Art. 14(2)(c)(ii) UCITSD V (Commission) Regulation.
390 Art. 90(2)(c) sub-para. 2 AIFMD (Commission) Regulation and Art. 14(2)(c) sub-para. 2 UCITSD V (Commission) Regulation.
391 Art. 90(3) AIFMD (Commission) Regulation and Art. 14(3) UCITSD V (Commission) Regulation.
392 Art. 90(4) AIFMD (Commission) Regulation and Art. 14(4) UCITSD V (Commission) Regulation.

top holding company.[393] Again, the UCITSD V (Commission) Regulation does not apply a 'look-through approach' to the UCITS depositary's record-keeping obligations.[394]

4.6.3   Control

Besides the safekeeping of assets, the AIFMD and UCITSD V impose on depositaries the additional duty to control the AIF's/UCITS' compliance with the applicable national laws and its rules or instruments of incorporation. The oversight duties require depositaries to ensure compliance with applicable law and AIF/UCITS rules in relation to:
- subscriptions/redemptions;
- valuations of share/unit pricing;
- duties relating to the carrying out of the AIFM's/UCITS ManCo's instructions;
- timely settlement of transactions;
- distribution of income;
- cash management.

These will now be subsequently discussed.

4.6.3.1   Oversight Duties – General Requirements
General requirements relating to the depositary's oversight duties are laid down in the AIFMD and UCITSD V (Commission) Regulation to ensure that the depositary is able to carry out its duties.[395] These general requirements relate to *ex ante* verification and *ex post* controls to be undertaken by the depositary.[396]

4.6.3.1.1   Ex Ante Verification
The depositary should set up procedures and processes to define *ex ante* oversight procedures which are proportionate to the estimated risks of an AIF/UCITS and the assets in which it invests.[397] Upon its appointment, the depositary is, therefore, required to assess the risk associated with the nature, scale and complexity of the AIF's/UCITS' strategy and the AIFM's/UCITS ManCo' organization. In doing so, the depositary has to take into account various factors, such as the size of the AIF/UCITS and of the AIFM/UCITS ManCo, the type of assets, the procedures in place at the AIF/UCITS, the AIFM/UCITS ManCo, a third party and the AIF's/UCITS' trading frequency.[398] This is in line with the

---

393 Art. 90(5) AIFMD (Commission) Regulation.
394 *See* Art. 14 UCITSD (Commission) Regulation.
395 Art. 92 AIFMD (Commission) Regulation; Art. 3 UCITSD V (Commission) Regulation.
396 Recital 106 AIFMD (Commission) Regulation/Recital 4 UCITSD V (Commission) Regulation.
397 Art. 92(1) AIFMD (Commission) Regulation; Art. 3(1) UCITSD V (Commission) Regulation.
398 ESMA/2011/379, 165.

rationale behind the *ex ante* risk assessment that it should make sure that appropriate processes are in place rather than double-checking every single event.[399]

4.6.3.1.2   Ex Post Controls

The depositary shall conduct *ex post* verification and procedures that are the responsibility of the AIFM/UCITS ManCo, the AIF/UCITS or an appointed third party.[400] The third parties involved can, for example, be an administrator or accountant working with the appropriate procedures control led by the depositary[401] that are frequently reviewed. In addition, the AIFM/UCITS ManCo must send all instructions related to the AIF's/ UCITS' assets and operations to the depositary so that it is able to perform its own verification or reconciliation procedure.

The depositary should have its own clear and comprehensible escalation procedure to address and detect irregularities in order to ensure that it is able to carry out its duties.[402] Such a procedure shall include a notification of Competent Authorities in case of any material breaches.[403] Moreover, the depositary must make available the details of the escalation to Competent Authorities upon request.[404]

The AIFM/UCITS ManCo also to ensure that the depositary is able to have access to the books and perform on-site visits on its own premises and of those of any service provider appointed by the AIF/UCITS or the AIFM/UCITS ManCo, such as administrators or external valuers, and/or to review reports and statements of recognized external certifications by qualified independent auditors or other experts to ensure the adequacy and relevance of the procedures in place.[405]

4.6.3.2   Subscriptions/Redemptions

Depositaries have the duty to check that the sale, issue, re-purchase, redemption and cancellation of units or shares of the AIF/UCITS are carried out in accordance with the applicable national laws and the AIF/UCITS rules or instruments of incorporation.[406]

In doing so, the depositary shall ensure that the AIF/UCITS, the AIFM/UCITS ManCo or the designated entity establishes, implements and applies an appropriate procedure to:[407]

– reconcile:

---

399 *Ibid.*, 164.
400 Art. 92(2) AIFMD (Commission) Regulation; Art. 3(2) UCITSD V (Commission) Regulation.
401 ESMA/2011/379, 165.
402 Art. 92(3) AIFMD (Commission) Regulation; Art. 3(3) UCITSD V (Commission) Regulation.
403 ESMA/2011/379, 165.
404 Art. 92(3) AIFMD (Commission) Regulation; Art. 3(3) UCITSD V (Commission) Regulation.
405 Art. 92(4) AIFMD (Commission) Regulation; Art. 3(4) UCITSD V (Commission) Regulation.
406 Art. 21(9)(a) AIFMD; Art. 22(3)(a) UCITSD V.
407 Art. 93(1) AIFMD (Commission) Regulation; Art. 4(1) UCITSD V (Commission) Regulation.

- the subscription/redemption orders with the subscription proceeds/redemptions paid;[408] and
- the number of units or shares issued/cancelled with the subscription proceeds received/redemptions paid by the AIF/UCITS.[409]
- verify on a regular basis that the reconciliation procedure is appropriate.[410]

To that end, the depositary has the obligation to verify that the number of units or shares in the AIF's/UCITS' account matches the number of outstanding units or shares in the AIF's/UCITS' register.[411]

The depositary has to ascertain and regularly check the subscription/redemption of the AIF/UCITS with the applicable national laws, the AIF/UCITS rules and/or instruments of incorporation and verify that these procedures are effectively implemented.[412]

The frequency of the depositary's checks shall be consistent with the frequency of subscriptions and redemptions.[413] This implies that the depositary is expected to adapt its procedures taking into account the frequency of subscriptions and redemptions.[414] The frequency of these controls could be defined at the time of the depositary's appointment.[415]

In this regard, it should be noted that the duties regarding subscription and redemptions are relevant for open-end AIFs and UCITS. The AIFMD itself makes no distinction between open-end and closed-end AIFs relating to the oversight duties with respect to subscriptions and redemptions.[416] The AIFMD and UCITSD V (Commission) Regulation, however, requires that the frequency of the depositary's checks is proportionate to

---

408 Art. 93(1)(i) AIFMD (Commission) Regulation; Art. 4(1) sub-para. 1(a) UCITSD V (Commission) Regulation.
409 Art. 93(1)(ii) AIFMD (Commission) Regulation; Art. 4(1) sub-para.1(b) UCITSD V (Commission) Regulation.
410 Art. 93(1)(iii) AIFMD (Commission) Regulation; Art. 4(1) sub-para.1(c) UCITSD V (Commission) Regulation.
411 Art. 93(1)(iii) sub-para. 2 AIFMD (Commission) Regulation; Art. 4(1) sub-para.1(c) UCITSD V (Commission) Regulation.
412 In ESMA/2011/379, 158, 167, ESMA clarifies that this requirement should be seen as limited to the sales of units of shares by the AIF or the AIFM. ESMA argues that it would be materially impossible for a depositary to check the compliance with applicable law and AIF rules regarding the sales on a secondary market. Such a situation would entail that if an AIF sets out in its rules that units of an AIF shall not be distributed to investors of a certain country for tax purposes, the depositary would have the obligation to ensure no units/shares would be sold by any unit-/shareholder to such an investor.
413 Art. 93(3) AIFMD (Commission) Regulation; Art. 4(3) UCITSD V (Commission) Regulation.
414 ESMA/2011/379, 166. *See also* Recital 107 AIFMD (Commission) Regulation; Recital 5 UCITSD V (Commission) Regulation.
415 ESMA/2011/379, 166.
416 *Ibid.*

the frequency of subscriptions and redemptions.[417] This clause provides for flexibility for the depositary to adapt its oversight duties to, for instance, closed-end AIFs.[418]

4.6.3.3   Valuation of Shares/Units

The depositary must ensure that the value of the units or shares of the AIF/UCITS is calculated in accordance with the applicable national laws, the AIF/UCITS rules or instruments of incorporations and the procedures with regard to valuation.[419]

To comply with this requirement the depositary shall:[420]

– verify on an ongoing basis that appropriate and consistent valuation policies and procedures for the assets of the AIF/UCITS are effectively implemented, and periodically reviewed;
– ensure that the valuation policies and procedures are effectively implemented and periodically reviewed.

This implies that the AIFM/UCITS ManCo is responsible for the valuation process and that the depositary is not expected to systematically recalculate the NAV.[421]

The depositary's procedures shall be conducted at a frequency consistent with the frequency of the AIF's[422]/UCITS' valuation policy and its implementing measures.[423] In order to comply, the depositary will have to ascertain that the valuation process procedures are appropriate, taking into account the nature, scale and complexity of the AIF/UCITS, and that the valuation of shares/units provided to investors is appropriate.[424] Compliance with these requirements could be achieved by performing sample checks, where appropriate, or by comparing the consistency of the evolution of the NAV calculation over time with that of a benchmark.[425]

When the depositary establishes valuation procedures, it shall have a clear understanding of the valuation methodologies that are used by the AIFM or the external valuer to value the AIF's/UCITS' assets. If NAV valuation takes place on a daily basis, the depositary is not required to check the valuation every day. It shall, however, define a frequency of enquiries consistent with the frequency to asset valuation of the AIF/UCITS.[426]

---

417 Art. 93(3) AIFMD (Commission) Regulation; The same applies to UCITS. *See* Art. 4(3) UCITSD V (Commission) Regulation.
418 *Ibid.*
419 For the AIF depositary this shall be compliant with the AIFMD valuation rules as laid down in Art. 19 AIFMD. *See* Art. 21(9)(b) AIFMD; *See also* Art. 22(3)(b) UCITSD V.
420 Art. 94(1) AIFMD (Commission) Regulation; Art. 5(1) UCITSD V (Commission) Regulation.
421 ESMA/2011/379, 168.
422 *See* Art. 19 AIFMD on valuation.
423 Art. 94(2) AIFMD (Commission) Regulation; Art. 5(2) UCITSD V (Commission) Regulation.
424 ESMA/2011/379, 168.
425 Recital 108 AIFMD (Commission) Regulation; ESMA/2011/379, 168; Recital 6 UCITSD V (Commission) Regulation.
426 Recital 108 AIFMD (Commission) Regulation; Recital 6 UCITSD V (Commission) Regulation.

The depositary is obliged to notify the AIFM/UCITS ManCo and monitor the changes to the valuation process if the depositary considers the valuation procedure not to be appropriate or effectively implemented.[427] This duty shall ensure that corrective measures are being taken in time for the safekeeping of the interests of the investors.[428] In addition, the depositary shall check, where an external valuer has been appointed, that the appointment is in accordance with the legislation and its implementing measures.[429]

4.6.3.4   AIFM's/UCITS ManCo Instructions

The depositary has to carry out the instructions of the AIFM/UCITS ManCo, unless they conflict with the applicable national laws, the AIF/UCITS rules or instruments of incorporation.[430]

The AIFMD and UCITSD V (Commission) Regulation clarify that this general duty of the depositary to carry out ongoing oversight entails at least:[431]

– the set up and implementation of appropriate procedures to verify the compliance of the AIF/UCITS and AIFM /UCITS ManCo with applicable laws and regulations as well as with the AIF's/UCITS' rules and instruments of incorporation;[432] and

– the set up and implementation of an escalation procedure if the AIF/UCITS has breached one of the limits or restrictions referred to above.[433]

The depositary has to verify on an *ex post* basis, by virtue of its oversight obligation, the compliance of the AIF/UCITS with applicable laws, regulations and the AIF/UCITS rules and instruments of incorporation.[434] In particular, the depositary has to monitor the AIF's/ UCITS' transactions and investigate any that are 'unusual',[435] and check the AIF's/UCITS' compliance with the investment restrictions and leverage limits defined in the AIF's/UCITS' offering documents.[436] This involves a general check on whether the AIFM/UCITS ManCo applies the investment policy described in the constituting documents.

The depositary shall set up and implement an escalation procedure.[437] Should any breach be identified, the depositary shall obtain from the AIFM/UCITS ManCo the instruction to reverse the transaction that is in breach at its own cost.[438] Although these

---

427 Art. 94(3) AIFMD (Commission) Regulation; Art. 5(3) UCITSD V (Commission) Regulation.
428 ESMA/2011/379, 168.
429 Again this shall be for AIFs compliant with the valuation rules set out in Art. 19 AIFMD. *See* Art. 94(4) AIFMD (Commission) Regulation.
430 Art. 21(9)(c) AIFMD; Art. 22(3)(c) UCITSD V.
431 Art. 95 AIFMD (Commission) Regulation; Art. 6 sub-para.1 UCITSD V (Commission) Regulation.
432 Art. 95(a) AIFMD (Commission) Regulation; Art. 6 sub-para.1(a) UCITSD V (Commission) Regulation.
433 Art. 95(b) AIFMD (Commission) Regulation; Art. 6 sub-para. 1(b) UCITSD V (Commission) Regulation.
434 Recital 109 AIFMD (Commission) Regulation; Recital 7 UCITSD V (Commission) Regulation.
435 *Ibid.*
436 Art. 95(a) AIFMD (Commission) Regulation; Art. 6 sub-para1(a) UCITSD V (Commission) Regulation.
437 Art. 95(b) AIFMD (Commission) Regulation; Art. 6 sub-para1(b) UCITSD V (Commission) Regulation.
438 Recital 109 AIFMD (Commission) Regulation; Recital 7 UCITSD V (Commission) Regulation.

duties have to be carried out by a depositary on an *ex post* basis, this does not prevent the depositary from adopting an *ex ante* approach where it seems appropriate.

4.6.3.5   The Timely Settlement of Transactions

The depositary must ensure that, in transactions involving the AIF's/UCITS' assets, any consideration is remitted to the AIF/UCITS within the usual time limits.[439]

Compliance with this duty entails that at least the following requirements are met:

- the depositary shall set up a procedure to detect any situation where consideration involving the AIF's/UCITS' assets is not remitted to the AIF/UCITS within the usual time limits.[440] In such a case, the depositary shall notify the AIFM /UCITS ManCo and, if the situation has not been remedied, request the restitution of the financial instruments from the counterparty;[441]
- where the transactions do not take place on a regulated market, the usual time limits shall be assessed with regard to the conditions, attached to the transaction (OTC derivative contracts, investments in real estate assets or in privately held companies).[442]

The duty relating to the timely settlement of transactions is relatively clear in situations concerning open-end AIF's and UCITS that trade in liquid markets.[443] However, where the transactions do not take place on a regulated market the 'usual time limit' shall be assessed with regard to the conditions attached to the transactions. In these cases the 'usual time limit' could be determined by referring to the relevant contract by which the AIF/UCITS has secured its investment.[444]

4.6.3.6   AIF's Income Distribution

Once an income distribution is declared by an AIFM/UCITS ManCo, the depositary must:

- ascertain that the AIF's/UCITS' income is being applied in accordance with the applicable national laws and the AIF/UCITS rules or instruments of incorporation;[445]
- take the appropriate steps and monitor where auditors have expressed reserves on the AIF's annual accounts to ensure that such reserves will not be reiterated.[446] The AIF/

---

439 Art. 21(9)(d) AIFMD; Art. 22(3)(d) UCITSD V.
440 Art. 96(1) AIFMD (Commission) Regulation; Art. 7(1) UCITSD V (Commission) Regulation.
441 *Ibid.*
442 Art. 96(2) AIFMD (Commission) Regulation; Art. 7(2) UCITSD V (Commission) Regulation.
443 ESMA/2011/379, 170.
444 *Ibid.*
445 Art. 21(1)(9) (e) AIFMD; *See also* Art. 97(1)(a) AIFMD (Commission) Regulation; Art. 22(3(e) UCITSD;
   See also Art. 7(2) UCITSD V (Commission) Regulation.
446 ESMA/2011/379, 171.

UCITS or the AIFM/UCITS ManCo provides the depositary with all information on reserves expressed on the financial statements;[447]
–   check the completeness and accuracy of dividend payments, once declared by the AIFM/UCITS ManCo, and, where relevant, of the carried interest.[448]

The depositary's role is to ensure that the income distribution is appropriate, and, where an error has been identified, ensure that the AIFM /UCITS ManCo takes the appropriate remedial action.[449] The net income calculation can be performed by the AIFM/UCITS ManCo itself or another entity appointed to provide that calculation.[450] The depositary verifies the completeness and accuracy of the income distribution once it has ensured that the net income calculation (primarily of dividend payments) is correct.[451]

4.6.3.7   Monitoring of the AIF's/UCITS' Cash Flows

The depositary must ensure that the AIF's/UCITS' cash flows are properly monitored. In particular, it must ensure that all payments made by or on behalf of investors upon the subscription of units or shares of an AIF/UCITS have been received and that all the AIF's/UCITS' cash has been booked into cash accounts.[452]

The AIF's/UCITS' cash must be booked in one or more cash accounts opened in the name of either:[453]
–   the AIF/UCITS itself; or
–   the AIFM/UCITS ManCo acting on behalf of the AIF/UCITS; or
–   the depositary acting on behalf of the AIF/UCITS.

The depositary ensures that all the AIF's/UCITS' cash is booked in accounts opened at:[454]
–   a central bank;[455]

---

447 Art. 97) (b) AIFMD (Commission) Regulation; Art. 8(1)(b) UCITSD V (Commission) Regulation.
448 Art. 97(1)(c) AIFMD (Commission) Regulation; Art. 8(1)(c) UCITSD V (Commission) Regulation.
449 Art. 97(2) AIFMD (Commission) Regulation; Art. 8(2) UCITSD V (Commission) Regulation.
450 ESMA/2011/379, 171.
451 *Ibid.*
452 Although Art. 21(7) AIFMD, Art. 86 AIFMD (Commission) Regulation; Art. 22(4) UCITSD V, Art. 10 UCITSD V (Commission) Regulation; These provisions only refer to the cash flow monitoring regarding the subscription moneys received. This obligation should be interpreted as covering all relevant AIF/UCITS cash flows, such as cash flows resulting from transactions, corporate actions and, where relevant, redemptions.
453 Art. 21(7) AIFMD; Art. 22(4)(a) UCITSD V.
454 Art. 21(7) AIFMD and Art. 22(4)(b) UCITSD V refer for the depositing of clients funds to Art. 4(1)(a)-(c) MiFID II (Commission) Directive. Compared to the MiFID I and II (Commission) Directive, qualifying money market funds are not eligible.
455 Art. 4(1)(a) MiFID II (Commission) Directive.

- an EEA credit institution;[456] or
- a non-EEA bank.[457]

Where the cash accounts are opened in the name of the depositary acting on behalf of the AIF/UCITS, no cash from the entity and none of the depositary's own cash shall be booked on such accounts, as will be the usual case when depositary banks are involved.[458]

When depositing third country clients' funds, the depositary must also ensure that the third country entity makes adequate arrangements to safeguard the AIF's/UCITS' funds, especially in the case of insolvency. When doing so, the depositary should take into account the third country's legal regime, which could affect the AIF's/UCITS' rights. The requirements for safeguarding the AIF's/UCITS' funds encompass the obligation for a depositary to ensure that client funds deposited in such third country entities are held in an account or accounts identified separately from any accounts used to hold funds belonging to third party entities.[459]

4.6.3.7.1 Cash Monitoring – General Requirements

The depositary should ensure that the AIF's/UCITS' cash flows are properly monitored. As a prerequisite, the AIFM/UCITS ManCo is required to ensure that the depositary has access to all information it needs to perform its cash management function. This obligation on the part of the AIFM/UCITS ManCo encompasses the duty to provide this information upon commencement of the depositary's duties as well on an ongoing basis.[460] The AIFM and UCITSD V (Commission) Regulation leave open who must provide this information. According to ESMA's Advice, such information can be either provided directly by the AIF/UCITS, the AIFM/UCITS ManCo acting on the AIF's/UCITS' behalf or by any other entity appointed by the AIF/UCITS or AIFM/UCITS ManCo, such as prime brokers, third party banks or administrators.[461]

The AIFMD and UCITSD V (Commission) Regulation take into account various situations that can occur under the AIFMD and UCITSD V relating to cash accounts and their impact on the depositary's ability to monitor.[462] The AIFMD and UCITSD V distinguish between the situations in which:[463]

---

456 Art. 4(1)(b) MiFID II (Commission) Directive.
457 Art. 4(1)(c) MiFID II (Commission) Directive. The AIFMD allows cash accounts to be opened at 'another regulated entity of the same nature' in the relevant (non-EEA) market where cash accounts are provided. Such an entity has to be subjected to 'effectively enforced' prudential regulation (including segregation rules) and supervision which have the same effect as Union law and are effectively enforced in accordance with Art. 2 MiFID II (Commission) Directive.
458 Art. 21(7) sub-para. 2 AIFMD. Art. 22(4) sub-para. 2 UCITSD V.
459 Art. 2(1)(e) MiFID II (Commission) Directive.
460 Art. 85(1) AIFMD (Commission) Regulation; Art. 9(1)UCITSD V (Commission) Regulation.
461 ESMA/2011/379, 151.
462 Ibid.
463 Art. 85(1) AIFMD (Commission) Regulation; Art. 9(1) UCITSD V (Commission) Regulation.

- the account is opened by the depositary itself;
- the account is opened by a third party in the name of the depositary;
- the account is opened by a third party in the name of the AIF/UCITS or in the name of the AIFM/UCITS ManCo on behalf of the AIF/UCITS.

In the first two situations, the depositary has complete knowledge of all inflows and out-flows and there cannot be a transfer without its knowledge. However, in the last situation, the depositary has clearly to rely upon information provided by third parties.

To that extent, the AIFMD and UCITSD V (Commission) Regulation require the depositary to be informed upon its appointment of all existing cash accounts opened in the name of the AIF/UCITS or the AIFM/UCITS ManCo acting on behalf of the AIF/U-CITS.[464] Moreover, the depositary must be informed when any new cash account is opened by either the AIF/UCITS or the AIFM/UCITS ManCo acting on its behalf,[465] and, for cash accounts opened by a third party, those third parties shall provide the depositary directly with all such information.[466]

4.6.3.7.2   Proper Monitoring of All AIF's/UCITS' Cash Flows

The depositary must ascertain that the AIF's/UCITS' cash flows are properly monitored. To that end, the depositary's obligation is to verify that there are procedures effectively implemented to appropriately monitor the AIF's/UCITS' cash flows and that these pro-cedures are reviewed periodically.[467]

The depositary shall ensure effective and proper monitoring of the AIF's/UCITS' cash flows by ascertaining that all the AIF's/UCITS' cash is booked into accounts opened with entities as referred to above.[468] Where the cash accounts are opened by the depositary, this could be done by the depositary itself. In other cases, this could be performed by the AIFM/UCITS ManCo, its accountant/administrator or another service provider.[469]

When monitoring, the depositary should in particular establish reconciliation proce-dures for all cash flow movements and ensure that these procedures are verified at an appropriate interval taking into account the nature, scale and complexity of the AIF/U-CITS.[470] Such a reconciliation procedure should compare each cash flow individually, as reported in the bank accounts statements with the cash flows recorded in the AIF's/UCITS' accounts.[471] Accordingly, the depositary must define its own verification pro-

---

464 Art. 85(2)(a) AIFMD (Commission) Regulation; Art. 9(2) UCITSD V (Commission) Regulation.
465 Art. 85(2)(b) AIFMD (Commission) Regulation; Art. 9(2) UCITSD V (Commission) Regulation.
466 Art. 85(2)(c) AIFMD (Commission) Regulation; *See also* ESMA/2015/850, 20; Art. 9(2) UCITSD V (Com-mission) Regulation.
467 Recital 98 AIFMD (Commission) Regulation.
468 Art. 86(a) AIFMD (Commission) Regulation.
469 ESMA/2011/379, 152.
470 Art. 86(b) AIFMD (Commission) Regulation.
471 Recital 98 AIFMD (Commission) Regulation.

cess.[472] For example, if reconciliation is performed daily, as it is for most open-end AIF's/ UCITS', the depositary would be expected to perform its verifications also on a daily basis.

The depositary's verification procedures with respect to cash management should consist of:

- conducting a full review of the reconciliation procedures at least once a year, i.e. checking that cash accounts opened by third parties in the name of the AIF/UCITS, AIFM/UCITS ManCo or depositary are included in an appropriate and effectively implemented reconciliation process;[473]
- monitoring on an ongoing basis the discrepancies detected by the reconciliation procedures and the corrective measures taken in order to notify the AIFM/UCITS ManCo of any anomaly that has not been remedied without undue delay.[474]

In addition, the depositary must ensure that significant cash flows, which could be inconsistent with the AIF's/UCITS' investment policy, are identified on a timely basis.[475] This monitoring consists of checking the changes of: (1) positions in the AIF's/UCITS' assets, or (2) subscriptions/redemptions with the periodic cash account statements and the consistency of its own records of cash positions with those of the AIFM/UCITS ManCo.[476] The AIFM/UCITS ManCo, on its behalf, shall ensure that all instructions and information related to the cash accounts opened by third parties are sent to the depositary. Without the appropriate information, the depositary is not able to carry out its own verification or reconciliation procedures.

4.6.3.8   UCITS Mergers and Master–Feeder Structures

The UCITS depositary under UCITSD V has been assigned as a 'third party monitor' for UCITS mergers[477] and has got extended obligations to fulfil its controlling duties of feeder UCITS in master–feeder structures.

4.6.3.8.1   UCITS Mergers

UCITSD IV introduced (cross-border) mergers to allow UCITS to exploit economies of scale.[478] Mergers are under the UCITSD V subject to prior authorization by the Compe-

---

472 *Ibid.*
473 Art. 86(d) AIFMD (Commission) Regulation.
474 Art. 86(e) AIFMD (Commission) Regulation.
475 Art. 86(c) AIFMD (Commission) Regulation.
476 Art. 86(f) AIFMD (Commission) Regulation.
477 Recital 29 and 31, Art. 39 UCITSD V.
478 Cross-border mergers between all types of UCITS (contractual, corporate and unit trusts) are permitted. *See* Recital 27 UCITSD V; *See also* Appendices to the report on Investment Fund Market Efficiency, *Facilitating UCITS Mergers*, 9, http://ec.europa.eu/internal_market/investment/docs/other_docs/reports/annex_efficiency_en.pdf; European Commission, *White Paper of on Enhancing the Single Market Framework for In-*

tent Authorities of the merging UCITS (home Member State).[479] For this purpose, common draft terms of the proposed merger are prepared and agreed by the UCITS ManCos of the merging UCITS and the receiving UCITS. The common draft terms of merger must set out the particulars under the UCITSD V.[480] Once prepared, the common draft terms of merger must be reviewed and be satisfied by the depositaries of the merging and receiving UCITS as a 'third party monitor'.[481] The depositary of the merging and receiving UCITS shall review and be satisfied that the common draft terms of the merger are in conformity with the law and with the merging UCITS fund rules or instruments of incorporation.[482] The role of the depositary is, thus, not to verify whether the proposed merger is in the interest of the investors but rather to verify whether the common draft terms comply with all legal requirements.[483] The compliance check involves, in particular, the criteria adopted in the common draft terms related to valuing the assets and liabilities of each UCITS, the exchange ratio in relation to shares in each UCITS, and the cash payment per unit/share.[484] The compliance has to be completed by the depositary (or the Competent Authority) of either the merging or the receiving UCITS in advance of the merger.[485] Each of the depositaries would have to inform the merging UCITS and the receiving UCITS in writing of its approval to the proposed common draft terms of merger so as to enable the UCITS to include such information in its application file for regulatory approval.[486] Reports of the depositary statements shall be provided on request to investors in the merging and receiving UCITS and their respective Competent Authorities.[487]

The Competent Authorities of the merging UCITS, additionally, require an up-to-date version of the prospectus and the KIID of the merging UCITS and information on the proposed merger that the merging funds intend to provide to their respective investors.[488] Investors of both the merging UCITS and the receiving UCITS have the right to request the repurchase or redemption of their units or to convert their units into units in other UCITS with similar investment policies managed by the same UCITS ManCo.[489]

---

vestment Funds, 15 November 2006, (COM (2006) 686 final), 10-16, http://ec.europa.eu/internal_market/securities/docs/ucits/whitepaper/whitepaper_en.pdf.

479 See Recitals: 27-33, Arts: 37-49 UCITSD V.
480 Arts. 39(2)(a), 40 UCITSD V.
481 Recital 31 UCITSD V.
482 Art. 41 UCITSD V.
483 European Commission, *Exposure Draft – Initial Orientations for Discussion on Possible Adjustments to the UCITS Directive: Merger*, 14, http://ec.europa.eu/finance/investment/docs/ucits-directive/poolingexposurel_en.pdf.
484 Recital 31, Art. 42(1)(a)-(c) UCITSD V.
485 Art. 41 UCITSD V.
486 Art. 39(2)(c) UCITSD V.
487 Art. 42(3) UCITSD V.
488 Arts. 39(2)(b), 43 UCITSD V.
489 Recital 30, Art. 45(1) UCITSD V.

Once the Competent Authorities have received the complete file, they will consider the potential impact of the proposed merger on unit-holders of the merging and the receiving UCITS respectively to assess whether authorization should be granted or not.[490]

4.6.3.8.2   Master–Feeder Structures

The master–feeder structure introduced under UCITSD IV[491] offers another solution for UCITS ManCos seeking to achieve economies of scale across their existing fund structures.[492] Feeder UCITS are under UCITSD V allowed to invest at least 85% of its assets in a single master UCITS.[493] Feeder UCITS may invest up to 15% of its assets in ancillary liquid assets and financial derivate instruments that are used for hedging purposes.[494] Master UCITS are under UCITSD V prohibited from simultaneously acting as a feeder fund.[495]

This so-called 'entity pooling' makes it more difficult for the depositary to monitor the UCITS ManCo of a feeder UCITS since its investment policy depends on that of the master UCITS.[496] The problem may be accentuated when the master and feeder UCITS are established in different Member States.[497] Feeder and master UCITS that are established in different Member States are, however, obliged to appoint a depositary in the Member State in which they are established.[498] The requirements that feeder UCITS must at least invest 85% of its assets in a master UCITS creates a 'strong link' between the feeder UCITS and the master UCITS.[499] In the case where the master and feeder UCITS appoint two different depositaries, the depositary of the feeder UCITS can only comply with its controlling tasks if it 'looks through' into the master UCITS.[500]

For this purpose, UCITSD V imposes two additional requirements to ensure that the depositary of the feeder UCITS can comply with its controlling duties. First, UCITSD V

---

490 Art. 39(3) and (4) UCITSD V.

491 Recitals 51-57, Arts. 58-68 UCITSD V.

492 Establishing multiple 'local' feeders in specific EEA Member States that (almost) exclusively invest in a master UCITS based in a European financial centre may be used for tax or marketing reasons. Entity pooling be used to achieve economies of scale and cost efficiencies; See IMA, *Pooling: How Can Fund Managers Respond Efficiently to Different Investor Needs?*, www.theinvestmentassociation.org/assets/files/research/20050701pooling.pdf; European Commission, *Green Paper on the Enhancement of the EU Framework for Investment Funds*, 12 July 2005 (SEC(2005) 947), 33 and 54, http://ec.europa.eu/finance/investment/docs/consultations/greenpaper-background_en.pdf; European Commission, *supra* note 478.

493 Art. 58(1) UCITSD V.

494 Art. 58(2) UCITSD V.

495 Art. 58(3)(b) UCITSD V.

496 See Appendices to the report on Investment Fund Market Efficiency, *Pooling for Investment-Funds*, 24, http://ec.europa.eu/internal_market/investment/docs/other_docs/reports/annex_efficiency_en.pdf.

497 *Ibid.*

498 See Art. 23 UCITSD V.

499 European Commission, *Exposure Draft - Initial orientations for discussion on possible adjustments to the UCITS Directive: Pooling*, 17, http://ec.europa.eu/finance/investment/docs/ucits-directive/poolingexposurel_en.pdf.

500 *Ibid.*

requires that where the depositaries of the master and feeder UCITS are different entities, they must enter into a depositary information sharing agreement in order to ensure the fulfilment of their respective duties.[501] The information sharing agreement is the legal basis for information request of the feeder UCITS' depositary that allows the depositary to have timely access to all relevant information and documents to meet its obligations.[502] Second, the master UCITS depositary is required to immediately inform the Competent Authorities of the master UCITS home Member State, the feeder UCITS or, where applicable, the UCITS ManCo and the depositary of the feeder UCITS about any irregularities it detects with regard to the master UCITS, which are deemed to have a negative impact on the feeder UCITS.[503] Given the 'strong link' between feeder UCITS and master UCITS, this enables both Competent Authorities and the feeder UCITS depositary to check whether a master UCITS complies its legal obligations and to take the appropriate decisions to protect the interests of their investors.[504]

4.7   DELEGATION IN THE DEPOSITARY CHAIN

Delegation in the depositary chain concerns the appointment of a sub-custodian to which a depositary may delegate its safekeeping function.[505] The AIFMD and UCITSD V allow a depositary to delegate neither its cash management[506] function nor its oversight duties [507] to third parties. By allowing depositaries to delegate its safekeeping duties, the AIFMD and UCITSD V recognize that the vast majority of securities are held in indirect holding systems involving a large and complex chain of intermediaries that record the rights of securities as book-entries at the various levels of the intermediaries in the chain of holdings.

The appointment of a sub-custodian is subject to numerous requirements. For the purpose of the AIFMD and UCITSD V, all 'sub-custodians' are considered delegates of the AIF's/UCITS' depositary.

The term 'sub-custodian' is not being defined under the AIFMD and UCITSD V. The Recitals in the AIFMD and UCITSD V, however, provide some guidance in answering the question what 'delegates' should be regarded as 'sub-custodians'.

Recital 41 AIFMD provides that

---

501 Art. 61(1) UCITSD V.
502 European Commission, *supra* note 499.
503 Art. 61(2) UCITSD V.
504 European Commission, *supra* note 499.
505 Art. 21(11) AIFMD; Art. 22a UCITSD V.
506 Art. 21(7) AIFMD; Art. 22(4) UCITSD V.
507 Art. 21(9) AIFMD; Art. 22(3) UCITSD V.

entrusting the custody of assets to the operator of a securities settlement system as designated for the purposes of Directive 98/26/EC of the European Parliament and of the Council of 19 May 1998 on settlement finality in payment and securities settlement systems or entrusting the provision of similar services to third country securities settlement systems should not be considered a delegation of custody functions.

Recital 21 UCITSD V states the following:

> when a Central Securities Depositary (CSD), as defined in point (1) of Article 2 (1) CSDR, or a third country CSD provides the services of operating a securities settlement system as well as at least either the initial recording of securities in a book-entry system through initial crediting or providing and maintaining securities accounts at the top tier level, as specified in Section A of the Annex to that Regulation, the provision of those services by that CSD with respect to the securities of the UCITS that are initially recorded in a book-entry system through initial crediting by that CSD should not be considered to be a delegation of custody functions. However, entrusting the custody of securities of the UCITS to any CSD, or to any third country CSD should be considered to be a delegation of custody functions.

Entrusting the custody of assets to 'operators of a securities settlement systems' is, thus, not considered a delegation of custody functions under the AIFMD, whereas under UCITSD V entrusting the custody of assets to 'issuer CSDs'[508] is not considered a 'delegation of custody functions'. In light of UCITSD V, confusion arose under the AIFMD whether both 'issuer' and 'investor CSDs' or only 'issuer CSDs' qualify as 'operators of a securities settlement system'. Against this background, ESMA has published an opinion that argues in favour of convergence between UCITSD V and the AIFMD. For this purpose, ESMA suggests that the AIFMD also should refer to 'issuer CSDs' instead of 'securities settlement systems'.[509] With this taken into account, 'sub-custodians' under the AIFMD and UCITSD V are entities to which the custody of assets are being entrusted, with the exception of 'issuer CSDs'. 'Investor CSDs' are, thus, also seen as 'sub-custodians' under the AIFMD and UCITSD V.

Sub-custodians may further delegate the safekeeping duties assigned to them subject to similar conditions as applicable to the appointment of sub-custodians themselves.[510]

---

508 *See* Chapter 6, Section 6.2.2.3.
509 ESMA/2017/34-45-277, 28 et seq.
510 Security settlement systems operators are not considered as delegates within the meaning of the AIFMD. *See* Art. 21(11) sub-para. 2 (b) AIFMD; Art. 22a(2) (b) UCITSD V.

4.7.1   Avoiding Requirements

The depositary may not delegate (or sub-delegate) safekeeping functions to a sub-custodian with the intention of avoiding the requirements of the AIFMD and UCITSD V.[511] The AIFMD/UCITSD V and AIFMD/UCITSD V (Commission) Regulation do not specify this requirement. In line with the 'letter-box entity' approach of delegating AIFM functions under Article 20 AIFMD, one can understand this requirement as follows. Depositaries must obtain an authorization before they may take up any of the functions under the AIFMD and UCITSD V. When successfully applying for authorization, the depositary has to ensure it complies with a number of organizational requirements, such as fit-and-proper tests, conflict of interest rules and numerous operating conditions (conduct of business rules). For that purpose, the AIFMD and UCITSD V impose a general duty on the depositary not to delegate its safekeeping function to the extent that, in essence, it undermines the conditions for which the depositary is authorized to carry out its duties in accordance with the AIFMD and UCITSD V.[512]

4.7.2   Objective Reason

The depositary has to demonstrate that there is an objective reason for the delegation.[513] Unlike the delegation of AIFM/UCITS ManCo functions, neither the AIFMD/UCITSD V nor the AIFMD and UCITSD V (Commission) Regulation specify this obligation in the context of delegation. The depositary may assess the criteria of the objective reasons for the contractual discharge of liability for guidance.[514] Objective reasons could be that a certain depositary has expertise related to certain assets or a specific region.

   The depositary has the obligation to provide further explanations and/or provide documents to the Competent Authorities, if requested, to prove that the delegation structure is based on objective reasons.[515] The objective reasons may also be included in the delegation contract concluded with the sub-custodian.

4.7.3   Due Diligence

The depositary may only delegate to a third party its safekeeping function if it has exercised all due skill, care and diligence in the selection and appointment of the third party

---

511 Art. 21(11) sub-para. 2 (a) AIFMD; Art. 22a(2) (a) UCITSD V.
512 See Recital 111 AIFMD (Commission) Regulation; Recital 18 UCITSD V (Commission) Regulation.
513 Art. 21(11) sub-para. 2 (b) AIFMD; Art. 22a(2) (b) UCITSD V.
514 See infra 4.8.1.3.
515 Art. 21(11) sub-para. 2(b) AIFMD; Art. 22a(2) (b) UCITSD V.

to whom it wants to delegate parts of its tasks, and continues to exercise such diligences on an ongoing basis.[516]

The AIFMD and UCITSD V distinguish between, on the one hand, a due diligence obligation by the depositary when appointing a sub-custodian and, on the other hand, the diligence to perform on an ongoing basis as part of monitoring the sub-custodian.[517] This difference is reflected in the AIFMD and UCITSD V (Commission) Regulation.[518]

4.7.3.1   Due Diligence upon Appointment of the Sub-custodian

Compliance with the due diligence duties requires a depositary to be responsible for the implementation and an appropriately documented (due diligence) procedure for the selection and ongoing monitoring of the sub-custodian.[519]

When selecting and appointing a sub-custodian, the depositary shall exercise all due skill, care and diligence to ensure that entrusting financial instruments to a sub-custodian provides an adequate level of protection.[520] Such a process of selecting and appointing a sub-custodian to whom financial instruments that can be held in custody can be delegated, requires the depositary to assess whether the risk of delegating the tasks to a sub-custodian is acceptable by ensuring that the following requirements are met:[521]

- in the process of appointing a sub-custodian, the depositary must assess the regulatory and legal framework, including country risk, custody risk and the enforceability of the third party's contracts.[522] This analysis is done to evaluate the potential implications of insolvency of the sub-custodian. In particular, it shall take into account the assets and rights of the AIF/UCITS and notify the AIFM/UCITS ManCo immediately if it becomes aware that the segregation of assets is not protected sufficiently from insolvency[523];
- the depositary shall conduct an assessment as to whether the sub-custodian's practice, procedures and internal controls ensure that the financial instruments belonging to the AIF/UCITS are subject to a high standard of care and protection[524];
- the sub-custodian's financial strength and reputation shall be assessed.[525] This assessment shall be based on information provided by the sub-custodian, as well as other data and information where available;[526]

---

516 Art. 21(11) sub-para. 2(c) AIFMD; Art. 22a(2) (c) UCITSD V.
517 Art. 21(11) sub-para. 2(c) AIFMD. See ESMA/2011/379, 173; Art. 22a(2) (c) UCITSD V.
518 Art. 98(1) and (2) AIFMD (Commission) Regulation; Art. 15(1) and (2) UCITSD V (Commission) Regulation.
519 Art. 98(1) AIFMD (Commission) Regulation; Art. 15(1) UCITSD V (Commission) Regulation.
520 Art. 98(2) AIFMD (Commission) Regulation; Art. 15(2) UCITSD V (Commission) Regulation.
521 *Ibid.*
522 Art. 98(2)(a) AIFMD (Commission) Regulation; Art. 15(2)(a) UCITSD V (Commission) Regulation.
523 *Ibid.*
524 Art. 98(2)(b) AIFMD (Commission) Regulation; Art. 15(2)(b) UCITSD V (Commission) Regulation.
525 Art. 98(2)(c) AIFMD (Commission) Regulation; Art. 15(2)(c) UCITSD V (Commission) Regulation.
526 *Ibid.*

– the depositary shall make sure that the sub-custodian has the operational and technological capabilities to perform the delegated custody tasks with a satisfactory degree of protection and security.[527]

4.7.3.2   Ongoing Monitoring Diligence Sub-custodian
Ongoing monitoring mainly consists of verifying that the sub-custodian performs all of its tasks correctly and complies with the elements specified in the contract. The depositary ensures that the sub-custodian meets certain conditions at all times during the performance of the tasks delegated to it.[528]

4.7.3.2.1   Adequate Structures and Expertise
The depositary must ensure that the sub-custodian has the structures and expertise that are adequate and proportionate to the nature and complexity of the AIF/UCITS or the AIFM/UCITS ManCo acting on behalf of the AIF/UCITS that has been entrusted to it.[529] Pursuant to the AIFMD and the UCITSD V, the depositary has to perform this due diligence duty irrespective of the type of assets (including record-keeping tasks).[530] The delegation of record-keeping tasks is likely to concern administrative functions in most cases.[531]

Where the depositary decides to delegate safekeeping functions related to 'other assets', it is only required to implement an appropriate and documented procedure to ensure that the sub-custodian complies with the ongoing monitoring requirements.[532]

4.7.3.2.2   Effective Prudential Regulation
For financial instruments to be held in custody, the sub-custodian should be subject to effective prudential regulation, including minimum capital requirements and supervision in the jurisdiction concerned. Moreover, the sub-custodian has to be subject to an external periodic audit to ensure that the financial instruments are in its possession.[533] It might, however, be the case that the law of a third country requires certain financial instruments to be held in custody by a local entity and that none of such entities satisfies these additional requirements related to the delegation to third country entities. In that case, the AIFMD and UCITSD V allows the depositary to delegate its functions to such an entity only to the extent required by the law of the third country and only as long as

---

527 Art. 98(2)(d) AIFMD (Commission) Regulation; Art. 15(2)(d) UCITSD V (Commission) Regulation. Where the sub-custodian decides to further delegate any of the function delegated to it, the same conditions apply.
528 Art. 21(11) sub-para.2 (d) AIFMD; Art. 22a(3) (a) UCITSD V.
529 Art. 21(11) sub-para.2 (d)(i) AIFMD; Art. 22a(3) (a)(i) UCITSD V.
530 Art. 21(11) AIFMD; Art. 22a UCITSD V; ESMA/2011/379, 173 and seq.
531 Recital 111 AIFMD (Commission) Regulation; Recital 18 UCITSD V (Commission) Regulation.
532 ESMA/2011/379, 173 and seq.
533 Art. 21(11) sub-para. 2 (d)(ii) AIFMD; Art. 22a(3) (b) UCITSD V.

there is no local entity available that satisfies the delegation requirements under the AIFMD and UCITSD V. This exemption is subject to two requirements:

- investors of the relevant AIF/UCITS have to be duly informed that such delegation is required due to legal constraints in the law of the third country and of the circumstances prior to their investment; and
- the AIF/UCITS, or the AIFM/UCITS ManCo acting on behalf of the AIF/UCITS, have instructed the depositary to delegate the custody of such financial instrument to such local entity.

4.7.3.2.3 Segregation of Assets

The depositary must ensure that the sub-custodian segregates the assets of the depositary's clients, its own assets and the assets from the depositary in such a way that they can be clearly identified as belonging to clients of a particular depositary.

When safekeeping functions are delegated partly or wholly to a sub-custodian, the depositary has to make sure that the requirements of Article 21(11)(d)(iii) AIFMD and Article 22a(3) UCITSD V are fulfilled and that the assets of the AIF/UCITS clients of the depositary are properly segregated.[534] These segregation obligations apply to both financial instruments held in custody and to assets subject to record-keeping.[535] The objective of the segregation requirements in the depositary chain is to prevent the loss of assets as a result of the insolvency of a sub-custodian when safekeeping tasks are delegated.[536] This requirement should be seen in conjunction with the due diligence requirements regarding the appointment of sub-custodians and its ongoing monitoring.

By verifying whether sub-custodians have appropriate segregation of assets in place, the depositary assesses certain requirements. The sub-custodian has to keep such records and accounts so that it can without delay distinguish the assets of the depositary's clients from:[537]

- its own assets;
- assets of its own clients;
- assets held by the depositary for its own account; and
- assets held for clients of the depositary, which are not AIFs/UCITS.[538]

Records and accounts are maintained by the sub-custodian in a way that ensures their accuracy, and in particular their correspondence to the assets under safekeeping for the depositary's clients.[539] The sub-custodian conducts, on a regular basis, reconciliations between its internal accounts and records and any other parties to whom it may have

---

534 Recital 112 AIFMD (Commission) Regulation; Recital 21 UCITSD V (Commission) Regulation.
535 ESMA/2011/379, 176.
536 *Ibid.*
537 *See* for considerations made by ESMA: ESMA/2014/1326.
538 Art. 99(1)(a) AIFMD (Commission) Regulation; Art. 16(1)(a) UCITSD V (Commission) Regulation.
539 Art. 99(1)(b) AIFMD (Commission) Regulation; Art. 16(1)(b) UCITSD V (Commission) Regulation.

delegated safekeeping functions.[540] Adequate organizational arrangements are introduced by the sub-custodian to minimize the risk of loss or diminution of financial instruments or of rights in connection with those financial instruments as a result of misuse
of the financial instruments, fraud, poor administration, inadequate record-keeping or
negligence.[541]

The depositary shall take the necessary steps to ensure that the AIF's/UCITS' cash is
held in an account,[542] as discussed above, if the delegate is a:[543]
- central bank;
- credit institution; or
- bank authorized in a third country, which is subject to effective prudential regulation
  and supervision that has the same effect as EU law and is effectively enforced.

The segregation requirements should particularly ensure that the assets of the AIF/
UCITS are not lost due to insolvency of the sub-custodian, to whom safekeeping functions are delegated.[544] However, if for reasons of applicable law, including the law relating
to property or insolvency, the effect of segregation is not recognized, the depositary shall
take additional steps.[545] These steps include:[546]
- making a disclosure to AIF/UCITS and AIFM/UCITS ManCo so that this aspect of
  custody risk is properly taken into account in the investment decision;
- taking such measures as possible in the local jurisdictions to make the assets as 'in-
  solvency-proof' as possible based on local legal advice;
- using buffers;
- prohibiting temporary deficits in client assets;
- putting in place arrangements prohibiting the use of a debit balance for one client to
  offset a credit balance for another.

However, while taking into account these additional measures when delegating safekeeping functions, they do not alter the obligation to return the financial instruments or pay
the corresponding amount where these are lost if the depositary can be held liable based
on the fulfilled criteria of the depositary liability regime.[547]

If sub-custodians further delegate a part or all of the safekeeping functions, the above
segregation requirements shall apply to that delegate.[548]

---

540 Art. 99(1)(c) AIFMD (Commission) Regulation; Art. 16(1)(c) UCITSD V (Commission) Regulation.
541 Art. 99(1)(d) AIFMD (Commission) Regulation; Art. 16(1)(d) UCITSD V (Commission) Regulation.
542 An account in accordance with the requirements of Art. 21(7) AIFMD and Art. 22(4) UCITSD V.
543 Art. 99(1)(e) AIFMD (Commission) Regulation; Art. 16(1)(e) UCITSD V (Commission) Regulation.
544 Recital 112 AIFMD (Commission) Regulation; Recital 21 UCITSD V (Commission) Regulation.
545 Art. 99(2) AIFMD (Commission) Regulation; Art. 16(2) UCITSD V (Commission) Regulation.
546 Recital 112 AIFMD (Commission) Regulation; Recital 21 UCITSD V (Commission) Regulation.
547 See Art. 21(12) AIFMD and Art. 24 UCITSD V.
548 Art. 99(3) AIFMD (Commission) Regulation; Art. 16(2)UCITSD V (Commission) Regulation.

4.7.3.2.4 Asset Inventories for UCITS Assets

UCITSD V, to the contrary of the AIFMD, contains the (additional) requirement for depositaries to provide the UCITS ManCo, on a regular basis, with a comprehensive inventory of all of the assets of the UCITS.[549] This inventory relates both to assets that can and cannot be held in custody.[550]

4.7.3.2.5 Rehypothecation

Rehypothecation rights allow a firm to treat a client's assets as its own and may involve outright title transfer or a security interest accompanied by a right of reuse.[551] Both the AIFMD and UCITSD V impose restrictions on depositaries and its sub-custodians that want to reuse the assets safekept by the depositary.

Under the AIFMD, the AIF's assets may only be used (rehypothecated) if the depositary has received the prior consent of the AIF (or of the AIFM acting on its behalf).[552] To the contrary of the AIFMD, the UCITSD V prohibits the depositary or its sub-custodian to reuse UCITS for their own account.[553] Reuse is defined as any transaction of assets that can be held in custody including, but not limited to, transferring, pledging, selling and lending.[554] Reuse of assets held in custody by the depositary is allowed if it is for the account of the UCITS[555] and subject to certain conditions, including:[556]

- the depositary is carrying out the instructions of the UCITS ManCo;[557]
- the reuse is for the benefit of the UCITS and in the interest of the unit-holders;[558] and
- the transaction is covered by high-quality and liquid collateral received by the UCITS under a title transfer arrangement.[559]

The market value of the collateral is required to amount, at all times, to at least the market value of the reused assets plus a premium.[560]

The reuse of assets under UCITSD V is, thus, restricted compared to the AIFMD.

---

549 Art. 22(6) UCITSD V.
550 *Ibid.*
551 M. Singh & J. Aitken, *The (sizeable) Role of Rehypothecation in the Shadow Banking System* (IMF Working Paper 2010).
552 Art. 21(11)(d)(iv) AIFMD.
553 Art. 22(7) UCITSD V.
554 *Ibid.*
555 Art. 22(7)(a) UCITSD V.
556 Art. 22(7) UCITSD V.
557 Art. 22(7)(b) UCITSD V.
558 Art. 22(7)(c) UCITSD V.
559 Art. 22(7)(d) UCITSD V.
560 Art. 22(7) sub-paragraph 2 UCITSD V.

4.7.3.2.6   General Obligations

The sub-custodian needs to take into account all the general obligations related to the safekeeping of assets,[561] as well as a general duty of loyalty to act in the best interests of the AIF/UCITS, its investors and the duty not to carry out activities with regard to the AIF/UCITS or AIFM/UCITS ManCo acting on its behalf that might create conflicts of interest without establishing Chinese walls.[562]

4.7.3.2.7   Ongoing Monitoring and Periodic Review

When monitoring, the depositary shall exercise all due skill, care and diligence in the periodic review and monitoring to ensure that the sub-custodian continues to comply with the implemented and documented procedures as prescribed by the depositary and the ongoing diligence conditions as discussed above.[563] To this end, the depositary shall at least:

- monitor the sub-custodian and its compliance with the depositary's standards;[564]
- ensure that the sub-custodian exercises a high standard of care, prudence and diligence in the performance of its custody tasks and, in particular, effectively segregates financial instruments;[565]
- review the risks associated with delegating the safekeeping of assets to a third party. If, based on the information it has from sub-custodians as well as other data, there is any potential risk it shall promptly notify the relevant AIF/UCITS or AIFM/UCITS ManCo.[566]

Ongoing monitoring mainly consists of verifying that the sub-custodian correctly performs all of the duties mentioned above and that it complies with the delegation contract.[567] In this regard, ESMA clarified this obligation in its advice by giving the example that regular reviews can take the form of mutual visits and/or conference calls between the depositary and the sub-custodian.[568]

The frequency of the review should be adapted by the depositary so as to remain consistent with market conditions and associated risks.[569] For instance, during market turmoil or when risks have been identified, the frequency and scope of the review should be increased. If the segregation of assets is no longer sufficient to ensure that the AIF's/UCITS' assets are protected from insolvency due to the legislation of the country where the sub-

---

561 These are set out in Art. 21(8) AIFMD and Art. 22(5) UCITSD V.
562 Chinese walls might be established based upon Art. 21(10) AIFMD and Art. 25(2) UCITSD V.
563 Art. 98(3) AIFMD (Commission) Regulation; Art. 15(3) UCITSD V (Commission) Regulation.
564 Art. 98(3)(a) AIFMD (Commission) Regulation; Art. 15(3)(a) UCITSD V (Commission) Regulation.
565 Art. 98(3)(b) AIFMD (Commission) Regulation; Art. 15(3)(b) UCITSD V (Commission) Regulation.
566 Art. 98(3)(c) AIFMD (Commission) Regulation; Art. 15(3)(c) UCITSD V (Commission) Regulation.
567 Recital 111 AIFMD (Commission) Regulation; Recital 17, 18 UCITSD V (Commission) Regulation.
568 ESMA/2011/379, 174.
569 Art. 98(3)(c) AIFMD (Commission) Regulation; Art. 15(3)(c) UCITSD V (Commission) Regulation.

custodian is located, the depositary shall immediately inform the relevant AIFM/UCITS ManCo.[570] In any case, a depositary should effectively be prepared to respond to the possible insolvency of a sub-custodian by having designated contingency plans for each market in which it appoints a sub-custodian.[571] Such contingency planning shall include the designation of alternative strategies and the possible selection of alternative providers if relevant.[572] It should be noted, however, that such a plan does not alter the obligation to return the financial instruments or pay the corresponding amount should any financial instruments be lost and the criteria under the depositary liability regime be fulfilled.[573]

Given the introduction of the liability regime under the AIFMD and UCITSD V, the depositary is liable for a loss of financial instruments held in custody by itself or any of its sub-custodians. The depositary has, thus, a vested interest in monitoring the sub-custodian.[574]

In any case, the depositary shall ensure that any conflicts of interest are avoided by ensuring that sub-custodians neither sub-delegate safekeeping functions to the relevant AIFM/UCITS ManCo nor sub-delegate any of these functions to a prime broker that is acting as an counterparty to an AIF, unless it has functionally and hierarchically separated the performance of its depositary functions from its tasks as a prime broker.[575] However, if the relevant conditions under Article 21(11) AIFMD and Article 22a UCITSD V are met and all potential conflicts of interest are properly identified, managed, monitored and disclosed to investors of the AIF/UCITS, delegation to such a prime broker is allowed.

4.7.3.3   Insolvency Protection of UCITS Assets

UCITSD V requires the insolvency protection of UCITS assets when safekeeping is delegated by depositaries to sub-custodians.[576] Article 17 UCITSD V (Commission) Regulation imposes obligations to both the sub-custodian and the depositary. Article 17 UCITSD V (Commission) Regulation applies to the sub-custodian to which custody is delegated a non-exhaustive list of measures, arrangements and tasks to be put in place and performed on an ongoing basis.[577] This non-exhaustive list takes into the account whether the sub-custodian is operating inside or outside the EEA, its insolvency laws and relevant jurisprudence.[578] Depositaries, in the case of the delegation of safekeeping duties, are required to take measures to ensure that the sub-custodian fulfils its obligations.[579]

---

570 *Ibid.*
571 Art. 98(6) AIFMD (Commission) Regulation; Art. 15(5) UCITSD V (Commission) Regulation.
572 Recital 111 AIFMD (Commission) Regulation Recital 17, 18 UCITSD V (Commission) Regulation.
573 *Ibid.*
574 *See also* in this regard: ESMA/2011/379, 174.
575 Art. 98(5) AIFMD (Commission) Regulation; Art. 15(3)(e) UCITSD V (Commission) Regulation.
576 Art. 22(3)(e) UCITSD V.
577 ESMA/2014/1183, 8.
578 *Ibid,* 8 and 10.
579 *Ibid.,* 8.

4.7.3.3.1   Sub-custodian

To ensure insolvency protection of UCITS assets, a depositary has to ensure that the sub-custodian, to whom custody has been delegated,[580] takes 'all necessary steps' to 'protect UCITS assets' upon its insolvency.[581] Protecting UCITS assets requires steps by the sub-custodian that ensure, in the event of an insolvency of the sub-custodian, that the assets of the UCITS held by the sub-custodian in custody are unavailable for distribution among or for the realization of benefit of creditors of that sub-custodian.[582] The 'necessary steps' to be taken by the sub-custodian depends upon whether the sub-custodian is located in a third country or within the EEA.[583] This differentiation is based upon the premise that the applicable insolvency laws and jurisprudence within the EEA are expected to have implemented Article 22(8) UCITSD V that require that assets of UCITS cannot be distributed to the creditors of a sub-custodian in case of its insolvency.[584]

Sub-custodians located in a third country are required to receive independent legal advice, to verify that the applicable insolvency laws and jurisprudence:[585]

–   recognize the segregation of the UCITS' assets from the own assets of the sub-custodian and from the assets of the depositary; and

–   the UCITS' segregated assets do not form part of the sub-custodian's estate in case of insolvency and are unavailable for distribution among or realization for the benefit of creditors of the third party.

The sub-custodian has to ensure that the above-mentioned steps are taken at the moment of the conclusion of the delegation arrangement with the depositary and on an ongoing basis for the entire duration of the contract.[586] During the life of the delegation agreement with the sub-custodian, the conditions may no longer be met or amended due to modifications of insolvency laws and/or jurisprudence. In such an occasion, the sub-custodian is required to inform the depositary when any of the above-mentioned conditions is no longer met.[587] To ensure that the depositary receives appropriate information on the insolvency laws applicable to the UCITS assets, sub-custodians are required to adequately inform the depositary about the rules and conditions applicable.[588] For that purpose, Article 17(2)(d)-(f) UCITSD V (Commission) Regulation requires the sub-custodian to:

---

580 Art. 22a UCITSD V.
581 Art. 17(1) UCITSD V (Commission) Regulation; In its consultation, ESMA spoke of 'reasonable' efforts. *See* ESMA/2014/1183, 14.
582 Art. 22(3)(e) UCITSD V; Art. 17(1) UCITSD V (Commission) Regulation.
583 *See* Art. 17(1) and (3) UCITSD V (Commission) Regulation.
584 *See* ESMA/2014/1183, 10.
585 Art. 17(2)(a) UCITSD V (Commission) Regulation.
586 Art. 17(2)(b) UCITSD V (Commission) Regulation.
587 Art. 17(2)(c) UCITSD V (Commission) Regulation; *See* ESMA/2014/1183, 10.
588 *See* ESMA/2014/1183, 10.

- maintain accurate and up-to-date records and accounts of the UCITS' assets on the basis of which the depositary is able to make an inventory of UCITS assets held with the sub-custodian;[589]
- provide, on a regular basis, and in any case whenever a change occurs, a statement to the depositary detailing the assets of the depositary's UCITS clients;[590]
- inform the depositary about changes of applicable insolvency law and of its effective application.[591]

EEA sub-custodians are deemed to be subject to insolvency laws that do not allow UCITS assets to be distributed to personal creditors in case of insolvency.[592] The duty of EEA sub-custodians are reduced to merely providing on a regulator basis a statement to each depositary that gives an overview of the UCITS' assets held for or on behalf of such a depositary.[593] The requirements applying to EEA and non-EEA sub-custodians are required to be applying *mutatis mutandis* to third parties to whom all or parts of its safe-keeping functions have been sub-delegated.[594]

4.7.3.3.2   Depositary

Before and during the delegation of safekeeping functions, the depositary has to ensure that the sub-custodian takes measures and puts in place arrangements to ensure the insolvency protection of UCITS assets.[595] The depositary has to ensure, by means of (pre-) contractual arrangements, that the UCITS assets are protected from distribution among or realization for the benefit of creditors of the sub-custodian.[596] For this purpose, the UCITSD V deems the insolvency laws of EEA Member States to be already in line with this requirement.[597] Depositaries, however, in case of delegation of safekeeping duties to non-EEA sub-custodians, are required to take extra due diligence measures to ensure that the sub-custodian fulfils its obligations.[598] These extra measures serve as extra protection against an insolvency of a sub-custodian and in general, require the depositary to understand the insolvency law of the third country in which the sub-custodian is established and ensures that the sub-custodian contract concluded is enforceable. Before the selection and appointment of any non-EEA sub-custodians, the depositary[599] has to obtain inde-

---

589 Art. 17(2)(d) UCITSD V (Commission) Regulation. *See also* Art. 22(6) UCITSD V.
590 Art. 17(2)(e) UCITSD V (Commission) Regulation.
591 Art. 17(2)(f) UCITSD V (Commission) Regulation.
592 *See* ESMA/2014/1183, 10.
593 Art. 17(3) UCITSD V (Commission) Regulation.
594 Art. 17(4) UCITSD V (Commission) Regulation; *See also* Art. 22a UCITSD V.
595 Recital 22 and Art. 17(1) UCITSD V (Commission) Regulation.
596 *Ibid.*
597 Recital 22 UCITSD V (Commission) Regulation.
598 *Ibid.*
599 ESMA/2014/1183, 15.

pendent information about the applicable insolvency laws and case law of a third country where the UCITS' assets are required to be held to assess:[600]
- the material effects of the provisions of the delegation arrangement governing the relationship with the sub-custodian on the UCITS' rights in respect of its assets;
- how the provisions of the delegation arrangement would operate in the jurisdictions where the assets are held, including the event of insolvency of the sub-custodian.

The contractual arrangement between the depositary and sub-custodian should allow the depositary to terminate the contractual relationship without undue delay in case:[601]
- the applicable insolvency laws and jurisprudence do no longer guarantee the segregation of UCITS' assets in the event of an insolvency of the sub-custodian; or
- the conditions under the laws and jurisprudence are no longer fulfilled.[602]

In those cases, the depositary is obliged to inform the UCITS ManCo.[603] The UCITS ManCo has to notify the Competent Authorities about the increased custody and insolvency risk to UCITS' assets in a third country. The depositary nor the UCITS ManCo are upon such a notification discharged from their duties and obligations under UCITSD V.[604]

UCITSD V requires the insolvency protection of UCITS assets when safekeeping is delegated by depositaries to sub-custodians.[605] Article 17 UCITSD V (Commission) Regulation imposes obligations on both the sub-custodian and the depositary. There is a natural link between this provision and the segregation of assets requirements under Article 22a(3)(d) UCITSD V. The segregation of assets requirement ensures that assets held by a sub-custodian, upon an insolvency of the sub-custodian, do not form part of the estate of the sub-custodian under insolvency proceedings[606] since those assets would be solely identified as being assets of a UCITS.[607] For the purpose of insolvency protection of UCITS assets, the depositary has to ensure that in the event of insolvency of the sub-custodian, UCITS assets held in custody by that sub-custodian are unavailable for distribution among or realization for the benefit of the creditors of the sub-custodian.[608]

---

600 Recital 22 UCITSD V (Commission) Regulation; The opinions on the applicable insolvency laws and case law of third countries may be combined, as the case may be, or issued for each jurisdiction by relevant industry federations or law firms for the benefit of several depositaries; See Recital 19 UCITSD V (Commission) Regulation; ESMA/2014/1183, 16.
601 Recital 20 UCITSD V (Commission) Regulation; ESMA/2014/1183, 16.
602 Ibid.
603 Recital 20 UCITSD V (Commission) Regulation.
604 Ibid.
605 Art. 22(3)(e) UCITSD V.
606 Art. 22a(3) (e) and 26b (e) UCITS V.
607 ESMA/2014/1183, 9.
608 Art. 22(3)(e) UCITSD V.

4.7.4   Lex Specialis – The Prime Broker as a Sub-custodian under the AIFMD

Under Recital 43 AIFMD, depositaries may delegate custody tasks to one or more prime brokers or other third parties. In addition to being appointed as a sub-custodian, prime brokers are allowed to provide prime brokerage services as a counterparty to AIFs.[609] This is logical as entities under the AIFMD that qualify as a prime broker primarily perform prime brokerage services as a counterparty to AIFs. Apart from their function as counterparty providing prime brokerage services, prime brokers may under certain conditions be appointed as a depositary [610] and/or a sub-custodian.[611] Prime brokers, thus, provide services to AIFs as counterparties, depositaries and sub-custodians.[612]

Under Article 21(4)(b) AIFMD depositaries are, in accordance with Article 21(11) AIFMD, allowed to delegate *custody tasks* to one or more prime brokers provided that relevant conditions are met.[613] Article 21(4)(b) AIFMD applies as a *lex specialis* for prime brokers that are appointed as a sub-custodian. Article 21(4)(b) AIFMD amends the general conditions for delegation by AIFMD depositaries to prime brokers laid down under Article 21(11) AIFMD in various ways.

Article 21(4)(b) AIFMD limits the delegation of functions by depositaries to prime brokers as sub-custodians to *custody tasks*.[614] Like under Article 21(11) AIFMD, Article 21(4)(b) AIFMD allows depositaries to delegate neither its cash management[615] function nor its oversight duties [616] to prime brokers.[617] Under Article 21(11) AIFMD, however, the delegation of functions to all other types of sub-custodians than prime brokers concerns the appointment of a sub-custodian to which a depositary may delegate its *safekeeping function*.[618] The safekeeping function is under Article 21(8) defined as the safekeeping of assets concerning 'financial instruments that can be held in custody' and the safekeeping of 'other assets' that include financial instruments that cannot be held in custody. Article 21(4)(b) AIFMD as *lex specialis*, however, effectively limits the delegation of the *safekeeping function* under Article 21(11) AIFMD by the depositary to a prime broker as a sub-custodian to *custody tasks*.[619] Following, various provisions of the

---

609 Recital 43 AIFMD; Art. 21 (4) (b) AIFMD restricts the safekeeping of prime brokers also to 'counterparties'. This term is not defined by the AIFMD. Following Art. 20(2) AIFMD (Commission) Regulation 'counterparties' should be understood as 'counterparties of an AIFM or an AIF in an OTC derivatives transaction, in a securities lending or in a repurchase agreement'.
610 *See supra* 4.3.1.4.
611 *See* Art. 21(10) and (11) AIFMD.
612 Zetzsche, *supra* note 103, 580-590.
613 Recital 43 AIFMD.
614 Art. 21 (4)(b) AIFMD.
615 Art. 21(7) AIFMD.
616 Art. 21(9) AIFMD.
617 Prime brokers should be, in this regard, understood as prime brokers solely acting as counterparty to an AIF.
618 Art. 21(11) AIFMD.
619 *See* Recital 43 AIFMD.

AIFMD, 'custody tasks' refer to the safekeeping of 'financial instruments that can be held in custody' under Article 21(8)(a) AIFMD.[620] Depositaries are, thus, not allowed to delegate the safekeeping of 'other assets' under Article 21(4)(b) AIFMD to a prime broker as sub-custodian.[621] To the contrary of 'financial instruments that can be held in custody', depositaries may, thus, deliver 'other assets', such as cash and derivatives on behalf of an AIF to prime brokers acting as counterparties without being obliged to appoint the prime broker as a sub-custodian under the AIFMD. At the same time, the depositary remains to be subject to ownership verification and record-keeping rules to 'other assets' that are being delivered to the prime broker as a counterparty. Depositaries, thus, have to ensure that these assets cannot be assigned, transferred, exchanged or delivered by the prime broker without the depositary or a sub-custodian that has been informed of such transactions and the depositary shall also have access to documentary evidence of each transaction from the relevant prime broker.[622]

Depending upon the legal status of financial instruments (that can be held in custody) they qualify as 'other assets' and may be held by prime brokers without the regulatory duty of the depositary under Article 21(4)(b) AIFMD to appoint the prime broker holding these financial instruments as a sub-custodian.

Financial instruments may be unencumbered, encumbered, i.e. subject to a security interest or right of rehypothecation in favour of the depositary/prime broker,[623] or on a title transfer.[624] The holding of financial instruments that can be held in custody on an unencumbered basis is clearly within the scope of the definition of financial instruments that can be held in custody. Prime brokers may under Article 21(4)(b) AIFMD not hold these assets without being appointed as a sub-custodian. The same holds true for financial instruments owned by the AIF (or the AIFM on its behalf) for which the AIF (or the AIFM on its behalf) has given its consent to a right of reuse of assets for the depositary. These financial instruments remain to be held 'in custody' as long as the right of reuse[625] has not been exercised.[626] Financial instruments that are provided as collateral to a prime broker or are provided by a third party to a prime broker for the benefit of the AIF have to be held in custody too by the depositary itself or the prime broker as sub-custodian as long as they are owned by the AIF or the AIFM acting on behalf of the AIF.[627] Financial instruments, thus, do not fall outside of the scope of 'financial instruments that can be held in custody' simply because they are subject to particular business transactions such

---

620 See Recital 34, 37, 44, 45, 47 and Art. 21 (11) (d)(ii), (13), (14) and (17)(c)(i) AIFMD.
621 See supra 4.6.2.1.
622 Art. 90(2)(c) para. 2 AIFMD (Commission) Regulation.
623 Zetzsche, supra note 103, 586.
624 Allen & Overy, Alternative Investment Fund Managers Directive: Allen & Overy Briefing Paper No. 7 Impact on Prime Brokers, www.allenovery.com/archive/Documents/Legacy/62666.pdf.
625 T.R.M.P. Keijser, A Custodian's Right of Use under Dutch Law? 40-42 (T. Keijser ed., Report on A 'Right of use' for collateral takes and custodians, Presented to the UNIDROIT Secretariat (2003)).
626 Recital 100 AIFMD (Commission) Regulation; Recital 12 UCITSD V (Commission) Regulation.
627 Ibid.

as financial collateral arrangements. The prime brokerage relationship between depositaries and prime brokers related to unencumbered and encumbered financial instruments that can be held in custody can under the AIFMD be arranged in several ways:[628]

- the prime broker as collateral taker is appointed as the depositary of the AIF or is appointed by the AIF's depositary as sub-custodian over the AIF's collateralized assets;
- the AIF's depositary appoints a sub-custodian that acts for the prime broker as collateral taker; or
- the collateralized assets remain with the AIF's depositary and are 'earmarked' in favour of the prime broker as collateral taker.

Financial instruments that are provided to a prime broker by way of title transfer do not qualify under the AIFMD as 'financial instruments that can be held in custody'. Upon a title transfer, the AIF loses its proprietary claim to the financial instruments in return for a contractual claim on the prime broker as collateral taker, for re-delivery.[629] Assets for which a TTCA is concluded are, thus, considered 'other assets' that may be delivered to the prime broker without the obligation for depositaries to appoint them as a sub-custodian within the meaning of Article 21(4)(b) AIFMD.

Under Article 21(4)(b) AIFMD depositaries are allowed to delegate custody tasks to one or more prime brokers.[630] Upon appointing a prime broker as a sub-custodian, the depositary needs to make sure that upon appointment and on an ongoing basis the prime-broker fulfils the depositary delegation requirements as set out in Article 21(11) AIFMD. In particular, the depositary needs to make sure that the prime broker as sub-custodian complies with the obligations and prohibitions concerning its safekeeping (custody) task. These concern Article 21(8)(a) AIFMD and the related provisions laid down in the AIFMD (Commission) Regulation.[631]

Under Article 21(4)(b) AIFMD depositaries fulfilling the requirements under Article 21(11) AIFMD may only delegate custody tasks to prime brokers provided that relevant conditions are met.[632] These relevant conditions are laid down in Article 21(10) and (11) AIFMD. Article 21(10) and (11) AIFMD do not only require the depositary but also its sub-custodian to act honestly, fairly, professionally and in the interests of the AIF or the investors in the AIF. Article 21(10) AIFMD also imposes a requirement to prime brokers acting as a counterparty to an AIF that are appointed as a sub-custodian for that AIF not to carry out activities with regard to the AIF or the AIFM that may create conflicts of interest between the AIF, its investors, the AIFM and the depositary unless there is due separation of function and management of conflicts. Such prime brokers, thus, are re-

---

628 Recital 98 AIFMD (Commission) Regulation; Recital 10 UCITSD V (Commission) Regulation.
629 Allen & Overy, *supra* note 624.
630 Recital 43 AIFMD.
631 *See supra* 4.6.2.1.
632 Art. 21(4)(b) AIFMD.

quired to functionally and hierarchically separate its sub-custodian tasks from its tasks as a counterparty to that AIF.[633] In addition, prime brokers are under Article 21(10) AIFMD required to properly identify, manage, monitor and disclose potential conflicts of interest to the investors of an AIF.[634] Finally, any assets kept by the prime broker as a sub-custodian may not be reused by the prime broker without the prior consent of the AIF or the AIFM acting on behalf of the AIF.[635]

The latter three conflicts of interests requirements are derived from the fact that, in addition to being a delegate of custody tasks, prime brokers are allowed to provide prime brokerage services to the AIF. Prime brokerage (counterparty) services do not form part of the delegation arrangement.[636] The AIFM, thus, remains to be responsible for appointing the prime broker and prime brokerage management (counterparty, i.e. prime brokerage services), whereas the depositary is responsible for the due diligence upon the appointment and the ongoing due diligence of the prime broker as sub-custodian. The depositary remains to be responsible for carrying out its controlling functions, cash monitoring and its safekeeping task comprising record-keeping.

The delegation of custody tasks by the depositary to prime brokers is, in accordance with Article 21(11) AIFMD, thus, allowed if relevant conditions related to mitigating conflicts of interest are met.[637]

4.8   THE DEPOSITARY'S LIABILITY REGIME UNDER THE AIFMD AND UCITSD V

One of the most debated issues in the field of depositary regulation that has had a large impact on the industry is the depositary liability regime under the AIFMD and UCITSD V.[638]

After the Madoff-fraud[639] it became clear that a lack of harmonization has led to different depositary liability regimes in Europe.[640] In France, for example, depositaries were acting as a guarantor of financial instruments being safekept.[641] Lost financial in-

---

633 Recital 43 and Art. 21(10) AIFMD; This requirement is similar for prime brokers appointed as depositaries. *See* Art. 21(4)(b) AIFMD.

634 Art. 21(10) and (11) (d) (v) AIFMD.

635 *Ibid.*

636 Recital 43 AIFMD.

637 *Ibid.*

638 An earlier version of this paragraph that targeted the AIFMD depositary liability regime has been published in: S.N. Hooghiemstra, *De AIFM-richtlijn en de aansprakelijkheid van de bewaarder*, 6 TvFR 178 (2013).

639 Gene, *supra* note 2; Skypala, *supra* note 2; Hollinger *et al*, *supra* note 2; Hollinger & Chung, *supra* note 2; D. Schwartz, *European banks tally losses linked to Madoff*, New York Times (17 December 2008), www.nytimes.com/2008/12/17/business/worldbusiness/17iht-17exposure.18747038.html?pagewanted=1&_r=1.

640 CESR/09-175.

641 *See* S. Dussart, F. Rodriguez et M. Thouch, *La restitution des actifs par le dépositaire*, Joly Bourse 542 (2008); I. Riassetto & A. Prüm, *La fonction de conservation du dépositaire, source de responsabilité civile, note sous Paris, 1ère Ch., Section H, 8 avril 2009, no. 2008/22218*, 3 Joly Bourse 191, §I-A-2 (2009); I. Riassetto, *Obligation de restitution du dépositaire d'OPCVM*, 4 RD Bancaire et Financier Comm. 161, point 1-B (July 2010); S. Gaouaoui, *Conservation d'actifs, la Cour d'appel entérine la responsabilité des dépositaires,*

struments that were subject to a custody duty would trigger a strict liability for the depositary, unless an Act of God was proven.[642] At the other hand, most European countries only held depositaries for lost assets to be held in custody liable to the extent that the loss could be attributed to culpable conduct of the depositary itself or its sub-custodian.[643] Following the French example,[644] the AIFMD introduced, a 'guarantor liability' for lost assets to be held by depositaries, which has led to many questions at the political and industry level.[645] UCITSD V introduced a depositary liability regime that is to a large extent the same for UCITS depositaries.[646] This section discusses the AIFMD and UCITSD V depositary liability regime, its consequences for AIF and UCITS depositaries and the rights of the AIFM/UCITS ManCo and investors against the AIF/UCITS depositary.

4.8.1   The Depositary's Liability under the AIFMD and UCITSD V

The AIFMD and UCITSD V deviate between liability of the depositary for the loss of financial instruments that can be held in custody and other losses. The depositary is under the AIFMD and UCITSD V liable to the AIF/UCITS or to the investors for losses of financial instruments held in custody either by the depositary itself or sub-custodians to whom custody has been delegated.[647] Upon a loss, the depositary shall return a financial instrument of identical type or the corresponding amount to the AIF/UCITS, or the AIFM/UCITS ManCo, without undue delay.[648] The depositary shall not be liable if it can

---

1025 Option finance 10 (2009); Ph. Goutay, *Obligation de restitution des dépositaires: les arrêts du 8 avril 2009 de la Cour d'appel de Paris*, 2 RD Bancaire et Financier 166 (2009).

642 Also referred to as an obligation of results, i.e. a strict obligation to return all assets entrusted to a depositary. *See* J.R. Siena, *Depositary Liability: A Fine Mess and How to Get Out of It* (D.A. Zetzsche ed., Kluwer 2015), 568-569; M. Pierrat, *De la distinction entre obligations de moyens et obligations de resultat: pile ou face?* 15 Journal des Tribunaux 61 et seq (2011); Clerc, *supra* note 351, 528.

643 This standard of liability is being referred to in practice as an obligation of means, i.e. a standard of care to act without negligence or willful failure to execute one's responsibilities. *See* Siena, *supra* note 642, 568-569; *See also* H. Hövekamp & G. Hugger, *Die Reichweite der Haftung der Depotbanken vor dem Hintergrund des Madoff-Skandals* 2015-2028 (S. Grundmann, B. Haar & H. Merkt eds., De Gruyter 2010).

644 Letter from French Finance Minister Christine Lagarde to Charlie McCreevy, European Commission, Jan. 2009.

645 A. Maffei, *Controverse autour des obligations du dépositaire*, 1 RD Bancaire et Financier étude 8 (2011); Siena, *supra* note 642, 541-544; R. Weber & S. Grünewald, *UCITS and the Madoff Scandal: Liability Depositary Banks?*, www.zora.uzh.ch/20149/.

646 I. Riassetto, *Dépositaires – Quelles différences entre la directive OPCVM V et la directive AIFM?*, 4 RD Bancaire et Financier (2014); I. Riassetto, *La clarification des obligations et de la responsabilité des dépositaires par la directive OPCVM V*, 98 Revue Lamy Droit des Affaires 31 (2014).

647 Art. 21(12) AIFMD; Art. 24(1) UCITSD V.

648 I. Riassetto, *L'obligation de restitution du dépositaire d'OPC en droit Luxembourgeois*, 30 Journal des Tribunaux Luxembourg 167 (2013).

prove in a private law case that the loss has arisen as a result of an external event beyond its reasonable control, the consequences of which would have been unavoidable despite all reasonable efforts to the contrary.[649] This strict liability regime is not applicable to real estate and any other assets than financial instruments that can be held in custody. With regard to losses for these assets, the depositary is liable to the AIF/UCITS, or the investors of the AIF/UCITS, if the loss is the result of the depositary's negligent or intentional failure to properly fulfil its obligations under the AIFMD/UCITSD V.[650] Determining liability will, regarding these assets, solely be based upon the private law standards of the individual Member States. In civil law jurisdictions claims are likely to be based upon a breach of contract or a general tort law provision.[651] The AIFMD and UCITSD V does not assign for these losses the burden of proof to the depositary, but to the AIF/ UCITS, the AIFM/UCITS ManCo or investors involved. To the contrary, the AIFMD and UCITSD V (Commission) Regulation regulate in detail (1) when a financial instrument that can be held in custody is considered to be lost, (2) what exactly constitutes an external event beyond the reasonable effort, the consequences of which would have been unavoidable despite reasonable efforts so that the depositary can be discharged from liability and under the AIFMD (Commission) Regulation (3) whether and to what extent the depositary may contractually discharge itself from liability. This will now be discussed in detail.

4.8.1.1   Loss of Financial Instruments That Can Be Held in Custody

The depositary's liability is triggered in the event of a 'loss of financial instruments held in custody' by the depositary itself or by a sub-custodian to whom safekeeping has been delegated.[652] The definition of loss is important as it determines the scope of the liability of a depositary. A loss of a financial instruments held in custody only gives rise to a depositary's liability if the loss is definitive and there is no prospect of recovering the financial asset.[653] Situations where financial instruments are only temporarily unavailable do not count as a loss.

A 'loss of financial instruments held in custody' should be distinguished from an investment loss that investors face as a result from a decrease in value of assets as a consequence of an investment decision.[654]

Following the AIFMD and UCITSD V (Commission) regulation, a 'loss' of a financial instrument held in custody shall be deemed to have taken place when:[655]

---

649 Art. 21(12) AIFMD; Art. 24(1) UCITSD V.
650 I. Riassetto, *Responsabilité de la société de gestion et du dépositaire d'un OPC envers les actionnaires d'une société cible, note sous Cass. com. fr. 27 mai 2015*, 4 RD Bancaire et Financier (2015).
651 *See, e.g.* in the Netherlands: Art. 6:162 and Art. 6:74 BW.
652 Art. 21(12) AIFMD; Art. 24(1) UCITSD V.
653 Recital 114 AIFMD (Commission) Regulation; Recital 24 UCITSD V (Commission) Regulation.
654 Recital 113 AIFMD (Commission) Regulation; Recital 24 UCITSD V (Commission) Regulation.
655 Art. 100(1) AIFMD (Commission) Regulation; Art. 18(1) UCITSD V (Commission) Regulation.

- a stated right of ownership of the AIF/UCITS is demonstrated not to be valid because it either ceased to exist or never existed;[656]
- the AIF/UCITS has been definitively deprived of its right of ownership over the financial instrument;[657] or
- the AIF/UCITS is definitively unable to directly or indirectly dispose of the financial instrument.[658]

The situation in which financial instruments no longer exist or never existed is the most obvious type of situation in which the loss of the financial instrument should be deemed to be 'definitive'.[659] A financial instrument is, for example, deemed no longer to exist when it has disappeared following an accounting error that cannot be corrected or if it never existed, when the AIF's/UCITS' ownership was registered on the basis of falsified documents.[660] All situations where the loss of financial instruments is caused by fraudulent conduct should be deemed a loss.[661]

In the other two situations set out in the AIFMD and UCITSD V (Commission) regulation, it will need to be ascertained that the financial instruments are lost without any prospect of recovering the financial assets in question.[662] There is only a loss in those situations if the AIF/UCITS has been permanently deprived of its ownership right over the financial instruments or is permanently unable to dispose of them.[663] Financial instruments are only deemed to be lost when the financial instrument exists but the AIF/UCITS has *definitively* lost its right of ownership over it and where the AIF/UCITS has the ownership right but can no longer transfer title of or create property rights over the financial instrument on a permanent basis.[664]

No loss can be ascertained when a financial instrument has been substituted by or converted into another financial instrument, for instance, in situations where shares are cancelled and replaced by the issue of new shares in a company reorganization.[665] Situations where financial instruments are only temporarily unavailable or frozen do not count as a loss. If, for instance, a depositary can temporarily not dispose of financial instruments as a result of an insolvency procedure[666] of a sub-custodian or as a consequence of an error in a settlement system, the financial instruments shall not be deemed to be lost.[667]

---

656 Art. 100(1)(a) AIFMD (Commission) Regulation; Art. 18(1)(a) UCITSD V (Commission) Regulation.
657 Art. 100(1)(b) AIFMD (Commission) Regulation; Art. 18(1)(b) UCITSD V (Commission) Regulation.
658 Art. 100(1)(c) AIFMD (Commission) Regulation; Art. 18(1)(c) UCITSD V (Commission) Regulation.
659 Recital 114 AIFMD (Commission) Regulation; Recital 24 UCITSD V (Commission) Regulation.
660 Recital 115 AIFMD (Commission) Regulation; Recital 25 UCITSD V (Commission) Regulation.
661 *Ibid.* See also ESMA/2011/379, 181.
662 Recital 114 AIFMD (Commission) Regulation; Recital 24 UCITSD V (Commission) Regulation.
663 ESMA/2011/379, 178.
664 Recital 114 AIFMD (Commission) Regulation; Recital 24 UCITSD V (Commission) Regulation.
665 Recital 116 AIFMD (Commission) Regulation; Recital 26 UCITSD V (Commission) Regulation.
666 ESMA/2011/379, 181; *See also* Art. 101(4) and (5) AIFMD (Commission) Regulation.
667 Art. 100(4) AIFMD (Commission) Regulation; Art. 18(4) UCITSD V (Commission) Regulation.

According to ESMA, financial instruments upon an insolvency of a sub-custodian should be considered to be permanently lost:[668]

- where the sub-custodian failed to apply the AIFMD/UCITSD V segregation rules;
- where the law of the country where the financial instruments are being held does not recognize the AIFMD/UCITSD V segregation rules; and
- in the event a small percentage of the assets are lost in the insolvency procedure due to the disruption in the entity's activity in relation to its default.

Following the AIFMD and UCITSD V (Commission) Regulation, the second situation might, however, be considered an external event beyond the control of the depositary. For the other two situations, the depositary is only not held liable if it can prove that the loss resulted from an external event beyond its reasonable control, the consequences of which would have been unavoidable despite all reasonable efforts to the contrary.[669]

4.8.1.2 The AIFMD and UCITSD V Liability Discharge

Depositaries can only avoid to be held liable under the AIFMD and UCITSD V in the case of an external event beyond the reasonable control of the depositary, the consequences of which are unavoidable despite all reasonable efforts to the contrary.[670] The depositary should prove that it cumulatively fulfils the conditions of the liability discharge.[671] The AIFMD and UCITSD V (Commission) Regulation lays down a procedure that needs to be followed by the depositary for that purpose. To be discharged of liability, the depositary would first need to prove that the event that led to the loss of the financial instruments held in custody was 'external'.[672] Then, the depositary should prove that the event was 'beyond its reasonable control', which is understood by the AIFMD and UCITSD V (Commission) Regulation as an event that the depositary could not have prevented by reasonable efforts.[673] Finally, the depositary should prove that the loss could not have been prevented by the depositary with reasonable efforts.[674] These requirements will now be discussed in detail.

---

668 Recital 27 UCITSD V (Commission) Regulation; *See also* ESMA/2011/379, 180-181.
669 *Ibid.*, 181.
670 Art. 21(12) AIFMD; *See* Recital 117 AIFMD (Commission) Regulation; Art. 24(1) UCITSD V; Recital 27 UCITSD V (Commission) Regulation.
671 *Ibid.*
672 Recital 118, Art. 101(1)(a) AIFMD (Commission) Regulation; Recital 28, Art. 19(1)(a) UCITSD V (Commission) Regulation.
673 Recital 118, Art. 101(1)(b) AIFMD (Commission) Regulation; Recital 28, Art. 19(1)(b) UCITSD V (Commission) Regulation.
674 Recital 119, Art. 101(1)(c) AIFMD (Commission) Regulation; Recital 28, Art. 19(1)(c) UCITSD V (Commission) Regulation; ESMA/2011/379, 179.

4.8.1.2.1 External Event

The depositary would first need to prove that the event that led to the loss of the financial instruments held in custody was 'external'[675] The rationale behind this is that the depositary's liability under the AIFMD and UCITSD V may not be affected by delegation.[676] An event is deemed to be external if it does not occur as a result of any act or omission of the depositary or sub-custodian to which custody of financial instruments has been delegated.[677] Depositaries may, for example, not be able to rely on internal situations such as a fraudulent acts by employees or an accounting error to discharge itself from liability.[678] Depositaries may also not rely upon these 'internal situations' that occur at the level of one of the depositary's sub-custodians to discharge itself from liability. A technical failure at the level of the CSD or a settlement system are examples that would be considered 'external'.

4.8.1.2.2 Beyond Reasonable Control

Any external events that are proven by a depositary only lead to a discharge of liability if the event is considered to be beyond the reasonable control of the depositary.[679] For this purpose, the depositary would have to prove that it could have done nothing to be a more 'prudent depositary' in preventing the occurrence of the event.[680] Depositaries that have adopted all precautions incumbent on a diligent depositary as reflected in common industry practice that has conducted rigorous and comprehensive due diligence to prevent a loss are considered to be a 'prudent depositary'.[681]

The AIFMD and UCITSD V (Commission) Regulation set out a non-exhaustive list of circumstances that can be seen as 'external events beyond the reasonable control of the depositary'.[682] Deemed as external events beyond reasonable control would be the following circumstances:

- natural events beyond human control or influence;[683]
- war, riots or other major upheavals;[684] and

---

675 Recital 118, Art. 101(1)(a) AIFMD (Commission) Regulation; Recital 28, Art. 19(1)(a) UCITSD V (Commission) Regulation.
676 Recital 118 AIFMD (Commission) Regulation; Recital 28 UCITSD V (Commission) Regulation.
677 Art. 101(1)(a) AIFMD (Commission) Regulation; Art. 19(1)(a) UCITSD V (Commission) Regulation; *See also* ESMA/2011/379, 184.
678 Recital 44 AIFMD; Art. 101(3) AIFMD (Commission) Regulation; Art. 19(3) UCITSD V (Commission) Regulation.
679 ESMA/2011/379, 185.
680 Recital 118, Art. 101(1)(b) and (c) AIFMD (Commission) Regulation; Recital 28, Art. 19(1)(b) and (c) UCITSD V (Commission) Regulation.
681 *Ibid.*
682 Recital 118, Art. 101(2) AIFMD (Commission); Recital 28, Art. 19(2) UCITSD V (Commission) Regulation.
683 Art. 101(2)(a) AIFMD (Commission) Regulation; Art. 19(2)(a) UCITSD V (Commission) Regulation.
684 Art. 101(2)(b) AIFMD (Commission) Regulation; Art. 19(2)(b) UCITSD V (Commission) Regulation.

- the adoption of any laws, decrees, regulation, decision or any orders issues by governmental body, including any court or tribunal which impacts the financial instruments held in custody.[685]

4.8.1.2.3 'Reasonable Efforts'

Finally, the depositary should prove that the loss could not have been avoided despite all reasonable efforts to the contrary. For this purpose, the depositary has (1) to ensure that they have the appropriate means to identify and monitor events that are deemed beyond its control and could lead to a loss, (2) the depositary should regularly update its assessment of such events and (3) take appropriate action when needed.[686]

This would be deemed to be fulfilled under AIFMD and UCITSD V (Commission) Regulation when the depositary could not have prevented the loss despite rigorous and comprehensive due diligence as documented by:[687]

- establishing, implementing, applying and maintaining structures and procedures and insuring expertise that are adequate and proportionate to the nature and complexity of the assets of the AIF/UCITS in order to identify in a timely manner and monitor on an ongoing basis external events that may result in loss of a financial instrument held in custody; [688]
- assessing on an ongoing basis whether any of the events identified under the first indent presents a significant risk of loss of a financial instrument held in custody;[689]
- informing the AIFM/UCITS ManCo of the significant risks identified and taking appropriate actions, if any, to prevent or mitigate the loss of financial instruments held in custody, where actual or potential external events have been identified that are believed to present a significant risk of loss of a financial instrument held in custody.[690]

The depositary should inform the AIFM/UCITS ManCo and take appropriate action depending on the circumstances.[691] This can, for example, be the case in a situation where the depositary believes that the only appropriate action is the disposal of the financial instruments held in custody. The AIFM/UCITS ManCo must, in turn, instruct the depositary in writing whether the financial instruments should be continued to be held or to dispose of them.[692] Any such instruction to continue to hold the financial

---

685 Art. 101(2)(c) AIFMD (Commission) Regulation; Art. 19(2)(c) UCITSD V (Commission) Regulation.
686 ESMA/2011/379, 185.
687 Art. 101(1)(c) AIFMD (Commission) Regulation; Art. 19(1)(c) UCITSD V (Commission) Regulation.
688 Art. 101(1)(c)(i) AIFMD (Commission) Regulation; Art. 19(1)(c)(i) UCITSD V (Commission) Regulation.
689 Art. 101(1)(c)(ii) AIFMD (Commission) Regulation; Art. 19(1)(c)(ii) UCITSD V (Commission) Regulation.
690 Art. 101(1)(c)(iii) AIFMD (Commission) Regulation; Art. 19(1)(c)(iii) UCITSD V (Commission) Regulation.
691 Recital 119 AIFMD (Commission) Regulation; Recital 29 UCITSD V (Commission) Regulation.
692 Ibid.

instruments should be reported to the AIF's/UCITS' investors. Informing the AIFM/ UCITS ManCo by the depositary, however, does not discharge the depositary of its liability.[693] When the standard of protection of the financial instruments held in custody remains to be insufficient despite repeated warnings, the depositary might consider to take other actions, such as transferring the liability contractually to a sub-custodian or the termination of the depositary contract concluded with the AIFM/UCITS ManCo.[694]

4.8.1.3   The AIFMD Contractual Discharge of Liability

The depositary's liability is not affected by any delegation of the safekeeping task to a sub-custodian.[695] The AIFMD, to the contrary of UCITSD V,[696] provides the possibility for depositaries to contractually discharge itself of liability if the depositary complies with a number of strict requirements.[697] First, the depositary must be able to prove that all requirements for the delegation of its custody tasks set out in the AIFMD are met.[698] Second, the sub-custodian must accept the transfer of liability of the depositary to that sub-custodian by means of a written contract concluded between the depositary and the sub-custodian. The written contract should include that it is possible for the AIF or the AIFM to make a claim against the sub-custodian in respect of the loss of financial instruments or for the depositary to make such a claim on their behalf.[699] Finally, the written contract between the depositary and the AIF (or AIFM) should expressly allow a discharge of the depositary's liability and establish an 'objective reason'[700] to contract such a discharge.[701] The objective reason for contracting such discharge should be accepted by both the depositary and the AIF (or AIFM).[702] For each discharge of liability[703] an objective reason should be established that takes into account the concrete circumstances in which custody has been delegated.[704] The objective reason established should also be consistent with the depositary's policies and decisions.[705] When considering an objective reason, careful considerations should be made to ensure that the contractual discharge can be effectively relied upon by the depositary if needed and that sufficient safeguards are put in place to avoid any misuse.[706] Under no circumstances the contractual dis-

---

693 ESMA/2011/379, 185.
694 Recital 119 AIFMD (Commission) Regulation; Recital 29 UCITSD V (Commission) Regulation.
695 Art. 21(13) AIFMD; Art. 24(2) UCITSD V.
696 Art. 24(3) UCITSD V.
697 Art. 21(13) AIFMD.
698 See Recital 45, Art. 21(13) sub-para. 2 AIFMD; Art. 24(2) UCITSD V.
699 Recital 45 AIFMD.
700 Recital 122, Art. 102 lid 1 AIFMD (Commission).
701 Art. 21(13) (c) AIFMD.
702 Recital 121 AIFMD (Commission) Regulation.
703 Recital 121, Art. 102(2) AIFMD (Commission) Regulation.
704 Art. 102(1)(a) AIFMD (Commission) Regulation.
705 Art. 102(1)(b) AIFMD (Commission) Regulation.
706 Recital 122 AIFMD (Commission) Regulation.

charge of liability may be used to circumvent the depositary's liability requirements under the AIFMD. Contracting a discharge will always be in the best interest of the AIF (or AIFM acting on its behalf) and its investors. The depositary should be able to demonstrate that it was forced by the specific circumstances to delegate custody to a sub-custodian[707] In particular, the AIFMD (Commission) Regulation considers this to be the case where:[708]

- the law of a third country requires that certain financial instruments shall be held in custody by a local entity and local entities exist that satisfy the delegation criteria laid down in Article 21(11) AIFMD; or
- the AIFM insists on maintaining an investment in a particular jurisdiction despite warnings by the depositary as to the increased risk this presents.

Where the law of a third country requires certain financial instruments to be held by a local entity and no local entities satisfy the criteria as laid down in the AIFMD,[709] the depositary may only discharge itself of liability provided that:[710]

- the rules or instruments of incorporation of the AIF concerned expressly allow for such a discharge;[711]
- the investors of the relevant AIF have been duly informed of that discharge and of the circumstances justifying the discharge prior to their investment;[712]
- the AIF (or AIFM) instructed the depositary to delegate the custody of such financial instruments to a local entity;[713]
- the written contract between the depositary and the AIF (or the AIFM) expressly allows such a discharge;[714] and
- the written contract between the depositary and the third party expressly transfers the liability of the depositary to that local entity and makes it possible for the AIF (or AIFM) to make a claim against that local entity in respect of the loss of financial instruments or for the depositary to make such a claim on their behalf.[715]

4.8.2   *The Impact of the AIFMD/UCITSD V Liability Regime for Depositaries*

The AIFMD and UCITSD V depositary liability regime upon its implementation has had a major impact in Europe. A 'guarantor liability' was introduced for safekeeping financial

---

707 *Ibid.*
708 Art. 102(3) AIFMD (Commission) Regulation.
709 *See* Art. 21(11)(d)(ii) AIFMD, Art. 22a(3) (b) UCITSD V.
710 Art. 21(14) AIFMD.
711 Art. 21(14) (a) AIFMD.
712 Art. 21(14) (b) AIFMD.
713 Art. 21(14) (c) AIFMD.
714 Art. 21(14) (d) AIFMD.
715 Art. 21(14) (e) AIFMD.

instruments that can be held in custody that triggers a liability for depositaries to restitute the lost assets, unless an Act of God discharges them.[716]

First, the broad definition of 'financial instruments to be held in custody' under the AIFMD and UCITSD V results in a broad scope of financial instruments for which depositaries have become guarantors.[717] The definition includes all financial instruments that can be registered in a financial instruments account opened in the depositary's books and all financial instruments that can be physically delivered to the depositary. The definition, however, also includes financial instruments that are capable of being registered or held in an account directly or indirectly in the name of the depositary.[718] This includes financial instruments, such as non-listed units of collective investment undertakings, that are not traded on a regulated or an equivalent market and are not lodged or registered in an issuer CSD. Therefore, these financial instruments fall outside the scope of the certainty of settlement that 'delivery versus payment' systems of CSDs provide. For financial instruments that are capable of being registered or held in an account directly or indirectly in the name of the depositary, the depositary and not the (investors of the) AIF/UCITS are owner of the financial instruments, whereas either the investors or the AIF/UCITS have a contractual claim to the (balance sheet of the) depositary. This is not in line with the international accepted standards in which financial instruments can only be held in custody[719] if in rem property rights exist for financial instruments in the holding chain that are being kept by the depositary in custody with taking into account the rules of asset segregation[720] on behalf of (the investors of) an AIF/UCITS.[721] The AIFMD and UCITSD V depositary liability regime, thus, also holds the depositary liable for financial instruments for which no rights in rem exist in the holding chain and the depositary lacks the means to control.

Second, the vast scope of the depositary guarantor liability is not only the result of the broad definition of financial instruments, but also due to a very broad interpretation of the financial instruments subject to financial collateral arrangements that are considered to be held 'in custody'. The key question during the consultation of the AIFMD was whether the holding of assets that are encumbered, but have not been transferred[722] to

---

716 Siena, *supra* note 642, 450-551.
717 *Ibid.*
718 Art. 88(2) AIFMD (Commission) Regulation; Art. 12(2) UCITSD V (Commission) Regulation.
719 *See* D. Frase, *Custody* (D. Frase ed., Sweet & Maxwell 2011), 274.
720 In practice, depositaries use, for instance, earmarking to administratively segregate assets held on behalf of (the investors of an) AIF/UCITS from the assets of the depositary itself and other clients of the depositary.
721 The AIFMD and UCITSD V are based upon the concept in which (the investors of an) AIF/UCITS are legal or beneficial owner of the assets safekept by the depositary. The transfer of custody laws in some Member States attribute legal ownership to (the investors of an) AIF/UCITS by granting a deemed 'continued ownership of assets', whereas other Member States deem (the investors of an) AIF/UCITS to be beneficial owners that have a 'preferential creditor status'; *See also* M. Haentjes, *Harmonisation of Securities Law: Custody and Transfer of Securities in European Private Law* 131-172 (Kluwer 2007).
722 T.R.M.P. Keijser, *Financiële zekerheidsovereenkomsten*, 11 Ars Aequi 835-840 (2006).

a collateral taker by way of title transfer, falls within the depositary's custody function or not.[723] In this regard, the AIFMD/UCITSD V determines that financial instruments subject to a security financial collateral arrangement[724] should be considered as being held in custody as long as they are owned by the AIF/UCITS (or AIFM/UCITS ManCo on its behalf) whether that arrangement includes a transfer of the financial instruments to a third party for that purpose or not.[725] The final position taken in the AIFMD/UCITSD V was surprising as ESMA in its advice considered to exclude all encumbered financial instruments from the scope of the depositary's custody duty as encumbered financial instruments are often not any more in the 'possession or control' of the AIF/UCITS, but of the collateral taker.[726] The AIFMD/UCITSD V has as a consequence that collateral takers of AIFs/UCITS, such as (prime) brokers, may not hold encumbered financial instruments without being a depositary or sub-custodian. This does not prevent a prime broker from vesting security interests over assets held in custody with the depositary or a sub-custodian, but the absence of control of the assets could give rise to operational and legal barriers to enforcement.[727] Given the additional risks faced by prime brokers, the holding of encumbered assets in the division performing prime broker functions have been prohibited.[728] Instead, prime brokers have required an increasing amount of title-transferred assets for providing credit to compensate for the additional credit risk borne. The position of the AIFMD/UCITSD V towards encumbered financial instruments has, thus, led to a change in the way assets in prime brokerage relationships are being kept in the hedge fund domain.[729]

Third, pursuant to the AIFMD and UCITSD V, a 'loss' of a financial instrument held in custody by a depositary or any of its sub-custodians triggers directly an obligation for the depositary to return a financial instrument of an identical type or the corresponding amount to be triggered.[730] The depositary can only be discharged from liability if it can demonstrate that the loss resulted from an external event beyond its reasonable control, the consequences of which would have been unavoidable despite all reasonable efforts to the contrary.[731] The depositary's liability regime has been an important issue upon the introduction of the AIFMD and UCITSD V.[732] It has established a practice that has led to important changes of the depositary's liability regime in many Member States. Prior to the AIFMD and UCITSD V, depositaries were in most Member States only liable for a loss of financial instruments in the event of failure or negligence that could be attributed to the depositary

---

723 ESMA/2011/379, 148, 158.
724 Keijser, *supra* note 722.
725 Recital 100 AIFMD (Commission) Regulation; Recital 12 UCITSD V (Commission) Regulation.
726 ESMA/2011/379, 148, 158; Siena, *supra* note 642, 544.
727 Allen & Overy, *supra* note 624.
728 *Ibid.*
729 Art. 21(4)(b) AIFMD; *See* Zetzsche, *supra* note 103, 600-605.
730 Art. 21(12) AIFMD; Art. 24(1) UCITSD V.
731 *Ibid.*
732 ESMA/2011/379, 178.

itself or any of its sub-custodians.[733] After the introduction of the AIFMD and UCITSD V, only acts of State, acts of God[734] are considered an 'external event beyond reasonable control'. In addition, a depositary can only in limited circumstances contractually transfer liability to any of its sub-custodians. Depositaries have been made responsible for all internal events of sub-custodians, including events in which there is not any event of failure or negligence at the depositary level that are not under the absolute control of the depositary.

During the consultation phase of the AIFMD and UCITSD V, the industry has brought forward the argument that depositaries do not delegate the custody of assets to circumvent liability, but that the appointment of a sub-custodian is necessary to have access to a large variety of markets to serve their clients.[735] This might, for example, be the case if certain financial instruments in certain markets are registered at local CSDs (not Euroclear or Clearstream) whereas foreign global custodians are not allowed to open any financial instruments account. In addition, the contractual discharge of liability leads to legal complexities. The AIFMD and UCITSD V require that, in order to successfully transfer contractually liability, the AIF/UCITS or its AIFM/UCITS ManCo have to be able to hold the sub-custodian liable. This implicates that in practice the written agreement between the depositary and sub-custodian needs to contain a 'third party clause'. Unclear is how this could be established in the case of omnibus-accounts.[736] Practically it is almost impossible for a depositary to include such a clause in all written agreements that are being concluded for each individual AIF/UCITS.

Finally, the 'guarantor liability'[737] introduced under the AIFMD and UCITSD V has been argued to lead to increased systemic risk.[738] The AIFMD and UCITSD V limit not only the type of entities that are able to be appointed as a depositary, but also impose a liability on depositaries for which the depositary can hardly (contractually) discharge itself.[739] Triggering such a liability on depositaries might lead, in the case of huge amounts of assets being safekept by the depositary, to an insolvency of the depositary. This insolvency can be systematic, i.e. the failure of a depositary can trigger a chain reaction of bankruptcies of investors that have contracted with the depositary.[740] This effects both secured creditors of the depositary,

---

733 CESR/09-175.
734 Siena, *supra* note 642, 450-551.
735 *Ibid.*, 541-544.
736 An omnibus account is an account opened in the name of a depositary as account provider in which securities are credited that belong to several clients of the depositary. The depositary maintains the interests of the clients in respect of the financial instruments that are credited to the account in the name of the depositary on his own books and records. Omnibus accounts may contain the depositary's own and clients' assets. See http://ec.europa.eu/internal_market/financial-markets/docs/certainty/background/31_8_5_turing_en.pdf; The CSDR refers to 'omnibus client segregation'. See Recital 42, Art. 38(3) CSDR: "A CSD shall keep records and accounts that enable any participant to hold in one securities account the securities that belong to different clients of that participant."
737 J.R. Siena, *supra* note 642, 450-551.
738 ESMA/2011/379, 178.
739 N. Moloney, *EC Securities Regulation* 298 (3rd edn., Oxford University Press 2014).
740 Financial Services Authority, *Implementation of the Alternative Investment Fund Managers Directive*, DP 12/1 (January 2012), 70, www.fsa.gov.uk/static/FsaWeb/Shared/Documents/pubs/discussion/dp12-01.pdf.

as well as, investors of AIFs/UCITS. On top of that, depositaries and investors increasingly share beneficial rights in assets safekept by depositaries leaving AIFs/UCITS investors not with an in rem, but an in personam right against the depositary. In the depositary contract, the depositary often negotiates a right of reuse. This creates uncertainty whether the creditors of the depositary, in the event of bankruptcy, may claim against all assets or merely the assets in which the depositary has an interest that increases the costs for investors to transact with the depositary and may discourage transactions altogether.[741]

The AIFMD/UCITSD V leads, thus, to the consequence that depositary under the AIFMD and UCITSD V serve as a liability guarantor for all financial instruments that can be held in custody.[742] For other losses the depositary is only liable towards the AIF or its investors in the event of failure or negligence.

4.8.3   Rights of the AIFM/UCITS ManCo and Investors against the Depositary

The depositary is under the AIFMD/UCITSD V liable to the AIF/UCITS or to the investors[743] for the loss of financial instruments. With regard to other losses, the depositary is liable to the AIF/UCITS or the investors if the loss is the result of the depositary's negligent or intentional failure to properly fulfil its obligations under the AIFMD/UCITSD V.[744] In case the depositary does not lawfully perform its tasks damages based on either a breach of contract or tort law. An important issue concerns the 'direct' or 'indirect' rights of investors to raise claims against the depositary. The AIFMD and the UCITSD V provide different regimes to invoke liability for investors.

4.8.3.1   AIFMD
Under Article 21(15) AIFMD,

> liability to the investors of the AIF may be invoked directly or indirectly through the AIFM, depending on the legal nature of the relationship between the depositary, the AIFM and the investors.

Article 21(15) AIFMD provides an option for Member States to grant AIFMs and/or its investors to opt for legal standing against the depositary based upon regulatory and/or private laws.[745]

---

741 S.L. Schwarcz, *Systemic Risk*, 1 Georgetown Law Journal (2008).
742 Maffei, *supra* note 645.
743 M. Reiss, *Pflichten der Kapitalanlagegesellschaft und Depotbank gegenüber dem Anleger und die Rechte des Anlegers bei Pflichtverletzungen* (Duncker & Humblot 2006), 279 et seq.
744 Art. 21(12) AIFMD; Art. 24(1) UCITSD V.
745 D.A. Zetzsche, *Aktivlegitimation gemäß § 78, 89 KAGB im Investment-Drei-und – Viereck* 691 (M. Casper, L. Klöhn, W.H. Roth & C. Schmies eds., RWS Verlag 2016).

Article 21(15) AIFMD is based upon Article 24 sub-para. 2 UCITSD IV, which states that

> liability to unit-holders may be invoked directly or indirectly through the management company, depending on the legal nature of the relationship between the depositary, the management company and the unit-holders.

Under UCITSD IV, Member States established different regimes for UCITS investors depending on the legal form of the UCITS. The reference in Article 24 sub-para. 2 UCITSD IV to 'unit-holders' under Article 24 UCITSD IV indirectly referred to UCITS established as unit trust and common contractual funds that do not have legal personality. UCITSD IV did not regulate the legal standing of 'shareholders', i.e. investors investing in investment companies, towards depositaries. UCITSD IV, thus, allowed Member States to grant only legal standing to UCITS ManCos to the depositary or to both UCITS ManCos and investors. UCITSD IV, however, did not require Member States to hold depositaries liable to both UCITS ManCos and investors at the same time. In addition, Member States could implement this option by regulating liability solely based upon regulatory law or a combination of regulatory and private law. The latter option was provided by Article 24 sub-para. 2 UCITSD IV that referred to "the legal nature of the relationship between the depositary, the management company and the unit-holders."

Member States could, thus, not only determine in their regulatory law whether solely UCITS ManCos have legal standing towards depositaries but could also differentiate in this regard for UCITS established in different legal forms.[746] A court in Luxembourg, for example, held that shareholders in a UCITS established as a SICAV had no right to directly invoke liability against the depositary as they were shareholders of the SICAV and had no direct contractual relationship with the depositary and UCITS ManCo.[747] Luxembourg, however, granted direct legal standing to investors of common contractual funds as not the SICAV but the investors themselves suffer damages and could, therefore, directly invoke liability.[748]

By amending the reference to 'unit-holders' to 'investors' under Article 21(15) AIFMD, investors have the right to claim in relation to the liabilities of depositaries either directly or indirectly through the AIFM, irrespective of the legal form of the AIF. Article 21(15) AIFMD continues, however, to refer to the 'legal nature of the relationship between the depositary, the AIFM and the investors'. Article 21(15) AIFMD refers to "liability to the investors of the AIF may be invoked *directly or indirectly through the AIFM,*

---

746 *See*, for examples of private law standing for investor investing in UCITS established as common contractual fund, unit trust and investment company: Zetzsche, *supra* note 745.

747 V. Naveaux & R. Graas, *Direct Action by Investors against a UCITS Depositary – A Short-Lived Landmark Ruling?*, 7 Capital Markets Law Journal 455 (2012).

748 *Ibid.*

depending on the legal nature of the relationship between the depositary, the AIFM and the investors." The latter suggests that all investors, i.e. unit-holders and shareholders, have to be granted legal standing towards the depositary. Article 21(15) AIFMD, however, does not preclude Member States from restricting shareholders to invoke liability indirectly through the AIFM.[749] The AIFMD, thus, seems not to offer more protection to investors in invoking depositary liability compared to UCITSD IV.

4.8.3.2   UCITSD V

UCITSD V grants the right to every investor in a UCITS to invoke claims relating to the liability of its depositary directly or indirectly through the UCITS ManCo or the investment company.[750] To the contrary of the AIFMD, UCITSD V provides legal standing against the depositary that does not depend on the legal form of the UCITS (corporate or contractual) or the legal nature of the relationship between the depositary, the UCITS ManCo and the unit-holders.[751] The right of unit-holders is, however, limited as it may not lead to a duplication of redress or to unequal treatment of the unit-holders.[752]

The right of unit-holders to invoke depositary liability under the UCITSD V differs in three respects from the right under the AIFMD. First, the UCITSD V refers to 'unit-holders' instead of 'investors'. The term 'unit-holder' is likely 'copy-pasted' from Article 24 sub-para. 2 UCITSD IV without realizing the legal implications it had under UCITSD IV. This view is supported by Recital 28 UCITSD V, which confirms the view of the UCITSD V consultation in 2010 that

> UCITS units-holders and UCITS shareholders should have the same rights regardless of the legal structure of the UCITS they invest in.[753]

---

749 In Germany, the AIFM/UCITS ManCo is obliged to invoke liability of the depositary by means of claiming damages for the account of the investors. Invoking liability by the AIFM/UCITS ManCo on behalf of the investors does not preclude investors to claim damages on their own behalf. *See* § 78(2) and § 89(2) KAGB. *See also* Reiss, *supra* note 743; In Luxembourg, AIF and UCITS investors of common contractual funds may only invoke the liability of the depositary if the AIFM/UCITS ManCo has during a period of three months refrained from doing so. *See* Art. 19 sub-para. 3 OPC Law 2010; Art. 19(15) sub-para. 2 Luxembourg AIFM Law. AIF and UCITS shareholders of investment companies may, however, not directly invoke liability of a depositary. *See* Naveaux & Graas, *supra* note 747; In the Netherlands, all written depositary contracts concluded by either AIFMs or UCITS ManCo and the depositary need to mandatorily contain a clause that stipulates that the contract is being concluded on behalf of not only the AIF/UCITS, but also its investors ('third party clause'). In case the depositary does not lawfully perform its tasks, the AIFM/UCITS ManCo, AIF/UCITS and its investors may claim damages based on either a breach of contract or tort law. *See* Art. 4:62m(2)Wft, Art. 6:74 BW and Art. 6:162 BW.
750 Recital 28, Art. 28(5) UCITSD V.
751 Recital 28 UCITSD V.
752 Recital 28, Art. 28(5) UCITSD V.
753 European Commission, *supra* note 152, 15.

Second, investors under UCITSD V have the right to claim liability of the depositary regardless of the legal form. The term 'unit-holders', thus, needs to be interpreted as 'investors' that have the right to claim in relation to the liabilities of depositaries either directly or indirectly through the UCITS ManCo, irrespective of the legal form of the fund.[754]

Third, the UCITSD V approach diverges from the AIFMD approach by having mandatory legal standing for investors. Member States, thus, do not have the option to grant UCITS ManCos and/or its investors legal standing against the depositary based upon regulatory and/or private laws.[755] Instead, investors always have, directly or indirectly, the right to invoke liability based upon regulatory law.

Finally, the 'direct or indirect' investor right to invoke liability under UCITSD V is limited, as opposed to the AIFMD, as it may not lead to a duplication of redress or to unequal treatment of the unit-holders.[756] This provision has to be explained in such a way that investors may not directly and indirectly invoke liability to receive 'double damages' (ni perte, ni profit).[757] In claiming damages, investors are, from a procedural law perspective, not limited in their right to claim both damages directly and indirectly through the UCITS ManCo.[758] The duplication of redress and unequal treatment of unit-holders only refers to the damages ultimately received by the investor.

To the contrary of the AIFMD, the UCITSD V, thus, does not give any Member States discretion to grant UCITS ManCos and/or its investors a legal standing against the depositary based upon regulatory and/or private laws.[759] Under UCITSD V, investors always have the right to directly and indirectly claim damages through the UCITS ManCo provided that this does not lead to a duplication of redress or to unequal treatment of the unit-holders.[760]

4.8.4   Conclusion

The Madoff fraud made painfully clear that a lack of harmonization has led to many different depositary liability regime in Europe. Prior to the AIFMD and UCITSD V, France treated the depositary as a liability guarantor for lost financial instruments that can be held in custody, whereas in most other European countries depositaries were only liable towards the AIF/UCITS or its investors in the event of failure or negligence of either the depositary and/or its sub-custodian. The AIFMD and UCITSD V (partly) har-

---

754 *Ibid.*
755 Zetzsche, *supra* note 745.
756 Recital 28, Art. 28(5) UCITSD V.
757 Zetzsche, *supra* note 745.
758 *Ibid.*, 694.
759 *Ibid.*, 691.
760 Recital 28, Art. 28(5) UCITSD V.

monizes the lack of harmonization of the depositary's liability in Europe by, in accordance with the French example, determining that a 'loss' of a financial instrument held in custody by a depositary or any of its sub-custodians triggers directly an obligation for the depositary to return a financial instrument of an identical type or the corresponding amount to be triggered. This is the case unless it can prove that the loss has arisen as a result of an 'external event beyond its reasonable control, the consequences of which would have been unavoidable despite all reasonable efforts to the contrary'.

Following the AIFMD and UCITSD V (Commission) Regulation, it has become clear that the exoneration is only accepted in exceptional cases and that the depositary may only under strict conditions contractually transfer its liability to a sub-custodian. This strict depositary liability, however, is not applicable to all 'other losses'. The depositary is for these losses only liable towards the AIF/UCITS and its investors in the event of failure or negligence.

An important issue in this regard concerns the 'direct' or 'indirect' rights of investors to raise liability claims against the depositary. The AIFMD and UCITSD V provide different regimes to invoke liability for investors. The AIFMD provides an option for Member States to grant AIFMs and/or its investors to opt for legal standing against the depositary based upon regulatory and/or private laws.[761] Under the UCITSD V, investors always have the right to directly and indirectly claim damages through the UCITS ManCo provided that this does not lead to a duplication of redress or to unequal treatment of the unit-holders.[762]

Having analysed the AIFMD and UCITSD V, it becomes clear that the AIFMD and UCITSD V have introduced a strict liability for lost financial instruments that can be held in custody that, de facto, is a guarantor liability that has a big impact on depositaries serving AIFs/UCITS in practice.

4.9   THE DEPOSITARY UNDER THE 'AIFMD/UCITSD V PRODUCT REGULATIONS'

The 'AIFMD/UCITSD V Product Regulations' have wholly or partly introduced depositary legislation that applies on top of the AIFMD and UCITSD V depositary regimes or (partly) replaces these regimes.

---

761 Zetzsche, *supra* note 745.
762 Recital 28, Art. 28(5) UCITSD V.

4.9.1 The ELTIFR Depositary Regime

EEA-AIFMs authorized under the AIFMD (full-AIFM s) may apply for an authorization for an ELTIF.[763] ELTIFRs are, thus, in the first place AIFs that are subject to the Article 21 AIFMD depositary regime. In addition to the AIFMD, Article 29 ELTIFR applies certain UCITSD V depositary provisions concerning the eligible entities that are allowed to act as a depositary,[764] the 'no contractual discharge of liability' rule[765] and the reuse of assets [766] to ELTIFs. The ELTIFR is, however, unclear whether the additional (UCITSD V) depositary regulation applies to ELTIFs marketed to retail investors, professional investors or both.[767] Recital 45 ELTIFR suggests that only ELTIFs that are marketed to retail investors should comply with the UCITSD V requirements, whereas ELTIFs that are solely marketed to professional investors merely have to comply with Article 21 AIFMD. This view seems to be confirmed by the heading of Article 29 ELTIFR that reads: "specific provisions concerning the depositary of an ELTIF marketed to retail investors." Article 29 ELTIFR, however, seems to suggest another view. Article 29(1)–(4) ELTIFR all specifically refer to being applicable to retail ELTIFS by referring to 'ELTIFs being marketed to retail investors',[768] whereas Article 29(5) ELTIFR refers to the reuse of 'assets held in custody by the depositary of an ELTIF'. A grammatical interpretation of this provision would imply that Article 29(5) ELTIFR is applicable to all ELTIFs, regardless of whether the ELTIF is marketed to only professional or to both professional and retail investors. The conditional reuse of assets is copied from UCITSD V that offers retail investor protection.[769] The fact that AIFs that are not authorized as ELTIF and solely marketed to professional investors are subjected to a more lenient rehypothecation provision under the AIFMD seems to confirm the view that all provisions under Article 29 ELTIFR only apply to 'ELTIFs marketed to retail investors',[770] ELTIFs that are marketed to retail investors should comply with the UCITSD V requirements concerning the entities eligible to act as a depositary, the 'no discharge of liability' rule, and the reuse of assets.[771] The depositary of retail ELTIFs are required to be an entity of the type permitted under UCITSD V.[772] De facto, Article 29(1) ELTIFR prohibits retail ELTIFs, regardless of its investment policy and closed-end nature, to appoint a 'PE-depositary'.

---

763 Recital 8, Art. 5(2) ELTIFR; D.A. Zetzsche, *Verordnung über europäische langfristige Investmentfonds (EL-TIF-VO) – Langfristigkeit im Sinne der Kleinanleger?*, 6 ZBB 362 (2015); T. Bühler, *ELTIF – eine neue Säule der Finanzierung der Europäischen Realwirtschaft*, 3 Recht der Finanzinstrumente 196 (2015).
764 Art. 23(2) UCITSD V.
765 Art. 24(3) UCITSD V.
766 Art. 22(7) UCITSD V.
767 *See* D.A. Zetzsche & C.D. Preiner, *ELTIFR versus AIFMD* 149- 150 (D.A. Zetzsche ed., Kluwer 2015).
768 Art. 29(1)-(4) ELTIFR.
769 *See* Art. 22(7) UCITSD V.
770 *See* for a different view: Zetzsche & Preiner, *supra* note 767.
771 Recital 45 ELTIFR.
772 Art. 29(1) ELTIFR.

ELTIFs that are, however, marketed to professional investors remain to be entitled to appoint a 'PE-depositary' under national Member States laws if they fulfil the AIFMD criteria related to the redemption rights exercisable (closed-end nature) and having a core investment policy of investing in illiquid assets.[773] Professional ELTIFs not fulfilling these 'PE-depositary' criteria or are established in a Member State that has not implemented this option are under the AIFMD required to appoint a credit institution, investment firm or an UCITSD V[774] depositary.[775] The depositary of retail ELTIFs is, in any case, required to be an entity of the type permitted under UCITSD V.[776]

Apart from this, depositaries of retail ELTIFs may under Art. 29 ELTIFR not apply the AIFMD 'contractual discharge of liability' provision.[777] Like under UCITSD V, the retail ELTIF depositary's liability cannot be excluded or limited by agreement nor is a depositary allowed to discharge itself of liability in the event of a loss of financial instruments held in custody by a third party.[778] Any agreement that contravenes this provision is void.[779] Finally, ELTIF assets held in custody are prohibited to be reused[780] for the own account by the depositary or any sub-custodian.[781] Like under UCITSD V, assets held in custody may only be reused by the ELTIF's depositary provided that[782] the depositary is carrying out the instruction of the AIFM,[783] the reuse is for the account,[784] the benefit[785] and the interests[786] of the ELTIF and covered by high-quality and liquid collateral received under a title transfer arrangement.[787] The market value of the collateral is at all times required to amount to at least the market value of the reused assets plus a premium.[788] The ELTIFR depositary regime, thus, seems to be consistent with the professional investor nature under the AIFMD and the retail investor nature under UCITSD V.

---

773 *See* Art. 26 AIFMD.
774 This is an dynamic interpretation UCITSD IV depositaries eligible under Art. 21(3) AIFMD of the author. *See supra* Section 4.3.1.3.
775 Art. 21(3) AIFMD.
776 Art. 29(1) ELTIFR.
777 Art. 29(2) ELTIFR.
778 Art. 29(3) ELTIFR.
779 Art. 29(4) ELTIFR.
780 'Reuse' comprises any transaction of assets held in custody including, but not limited to, transferring, pledging, selling and lending; Art. 29(5) sub-para. 1 ELTIFR; *See also* Art. 22(7) UCITSD V.
781 Art. 29(5) sub-para. 1 ELTIFR.
782 Art. 29(5) sub-para. 2 ELTIFR.
783 Art. 29(5) sub-para. 2(b) ELTIFR.
784 Art. 29(5) sub-para. 2(a) ELTIFR.
785 Art. 29(5) sub-para. 2(c) ELTIFR.
786 Art. 29(5) sub-para. 2(c) ELTIFR.
787 Art. 29(5) sub-para. 2 ELTIFR.
788 Art. 29(5) sub-para. 3 ELTIFR.

4.9.2 The MMFR Depositary Regime

Consistent with the AIFMD and UCITSD V, the MMFR requires the UCITSD V depositary regime to be applied for UCITS-MMFs and the AIFMD depositary regime for AIF-MMFs marketed to professional investors.[789] Like under the AIFMD, the depositary regime for MMFs established as retail-AIFs depends upon the private placement regimes of the individual Member States implementing Article 43 AIFMD.[790] Similar as for UCITS,[791] however, MMFs authorized as AIF-MMF both marketed to retail and professional investors must upon authorization obtain approval for the choice of their depositary.[792]

4.9.3 The EuVECAR/EuSEFR 'Depositary Regime'

'Small' AIFMs managing and marketing EuVECAs/EuSEFs are under the EuVECAR/EuSEFR not required to appoint a depositary. Instead, an auditor of the EuVECA/EuSEF must be appointed to conduct, at least annually, an audit of the EuVECA/EuSEF confirming that (1) money and assets are held in name of the qualifying EuVECA/EuSEF and (2) records are adequately kept by the EuVECA/EuSEF manager. For two reasons this 'depositary' regime is logical and fits in the AIFMD depositary regime.

First, EuVECAs and EuSEFs may only be managed and marketed by 'small' AIFMs. Only full-AIFMs managing and marketing EuVECAs/EuSEFs are subjected to the compulsory depositary requirement under the AIFMD.[793] AIFs managed and marketed by 'small' AIFMs under the AIFMD are exempted from the depositary appointment and individual Member States may decide whether they extend the compulsory depositary requirement to AIFs managed by these AIFMs.[794]

Second, closed-end AIFs managed by full-AIFMs that are similar to EuVECAs/EuSEFs are under the AIFMD Member State implementations allowed to appoint a 'PE depositary' if they fulfil the AIFMD criteria related to the redemption rights exercisable. EuVECAs/EUSEFs have a core investment policy of investing in illiquid assets that, at all times, complies with the 'PE depositary' requirements under the AIFMD.[795] The mandatory investment policy under the EuVECAR/EuSEFR for these types of AIFs requires at least 70% of their investment portfolio to be invested in non-liquid assets. The qualifying portfolio companies in which they are required to invest must be directly held by the

---

789 Art. 4(2), 4 MMFR.
790 *See supra* Section 4.2.1.2.
791 Art. 5(1) MMFR.
792 *Ibid.*
793 *See supra* Section 4.2.1.
794 *See supra* Section 4.2.1.3.1.
795 *See* Art. 26 AIFMD.

EuVECA/EuSEF and may, therefore, not be listed on a regulated market. The (quasi-) equity instruments invested in may be financial instruments, but on many occasions do not qualify as financial instruments that can be held in custody. In practice, the 70% qualifying investments are, thus, not invested in transferable securities, MMFs and CIUs that can be directly registered or held in an account on behalf of a depositary. The assets would under the AIFMD qualify as 'other assets', which would require a re-cord-keeping requirement on behalf of the depositary that requires the verification of ownership and the keeping of records. The 30% assets that are other than qualifying investments might be financial instruments that can be held in custody. The EuVECAs/EuSEFs may, but are not required to, appoint (non-)EEA custodians that might be authorized under CRD IV, MiFID II or equivalent non-EEA regulations.

Considering these two reasons, it is logical that an audit is merely required to confirm whether money and assets are held in the name of the qualifying EuVECA/EuSEF and records are adequately kept by the EuVECA/EuSEF manager. The 'small' AIFM manag-ing EuVECAs/EuSEFs and illiquid nature of the investments invested in, however, do not explain why an auditor is allowed under the EuVECAR/EuSEFR to perform the safekeep-ing function related to 'other assets' of an AIF depositary. Under the AIFMD, the PE-depositary, being a lawyer, notary or specialized financial intermediary, appointed is re-quired to be subjected to mandatory professional registration recognized by law or to legal or regulatory provisions or rules of professional conduct. From this perspective, the choice for an auditor as a 'depositary' under the EuVECAR/EuSEFR seems to be remarkable as auditors are under most Member State laws not allowed to perform the function of 'PE depositary'.[796] The choice for the auditor may, however, be explained on the basis of the AIFMD depositary liability regime. AIFs managed by 'small' AIFMs fall outside the scope of the AIFMD depositary regime and its strict liability rules on the loss of financial instruments that can be held in custody. The EuVECAR/EuSEFR does not contain such a strict depositary liability rule. Under the AIFMD, the PE-depositary is subjected to the strict depositary liability regime related to financial instruments that can be held in custody. Even if financial instruments that can be held in custody are not safekept by the PE-depositary but by a sub-custodian appointed by them, the liability regime applies to them as they are deemed to be a depositary und the AIFMD. This is remarkable as, in particular professionals, such as lawyers and notaries, do not have the resources to conduct due diligence over financial instruments that can be held in custody as they have in the first place not the technical infrastructure to perform the safekeeping of these assets by themselves. Many Member States are aware of the potential conse-quences of the AIFMD depositary liability regime applying to these types of depositaries. As a result, Member States that allow professionals to be appointed as PE-depositaries require these professionals to have an indemnity insurance and to comply with own

---

796 *See supra* Section 4.3.1.6.

capital requirements, whereas Member States that only allow financial intermediaries to be appointed as PE-depositaries require these intermediaries to comply with strict organizational and conduct of business requirements.[797] The absence of the strict liability rules on the loss of financial instruments that can be held in custody is, thus, the explanation for the EuVECAR/EuSEFR to require an auditor to be appointed to substitute the appointment of a depositary.

4.9.4 The AIFMD Product Regulation Depositary Regimes versus the AIFMD/UCITSD V

The 'AIFMD Product Regulations' differ from the AIFMD and UCITSD V for three reasons. First, AIFMs may be 'small' AIFMs or full-AIFMs. Full-AIFMs are subjected to the compulsory depositary requirement, whereas small AIFMs under the AIFMD are exempted from depositary appointment and it is left over to the individual Member States whether they extend the compulsory depositary requirement to AIFs managed by these AIFMs.[798] This criterion is reflected in the ELTIFR and MMFR that applies to full-AIFMs and the EuVECAR and EuSEFR that solely applies to 'small' AIFMs. Under the MMFR only authorized UCITS and full-AIFMs managing AIFs may apply for MMFR authorizations.[799] Depositaries may be UCITSD V or AIFMD depositaries depending upon whether an MMF is a UCITS or an AIF. Similarly, only full-AIFMs may apply for retail-ELTIF authorization that requires 'patch-up' depositary provisions under the ELTIFR to be complied with on top of the provisions set out under the AIFMD.[800]

Second, the regulations are different in terms of depositary regulation due to the different type of investors to which they may be marketed.[801] EuSEFs and EuVECAs may only be marketed to professional investors and HNWIs.[802] The MMFR requires the UCITSD V depositary regime to be applied for MMFs that are established as UCITS. UCITS are allowed to be marketed to both retail and professional investors.[803] The AIFMD depositary regime applies to MMFs registered as professional-AIFs.[804] The depositary regime for MMFs established as retail-AIFs depends upon the private placement regimes of individual Member States implementing Article 43 AIFMD. Similarly, the

---

797 *Ibid.*
798 *See supra* Section 4.2.1.3.1.
799 Arts. 4(2) and 5(1) MMFR.
800 Recital 45, Art. 29 ELTIFR.
801 This is exemplified by Recital 47 AIFMD that states that the AIFMD depositary regime is without prejudice to any future legislative measures with respect to the depositary in the UCITSD (UCITSD V was later adopted), because UCITS and AIFs are different in terms of the investment policy that they may pursue and the type of investors to which they may be marketed. Recital 2 UCITSD V (Commission) Regulation also states that the UCITSD V takes into account the retail investor nature of a UCITS.
802 Art. 6 EuVECAR/EuSEFR.
803 Art. 4(2) MMFR.
804 Art. 5(1) MMFR.

ELTIFR requires the AIFMD depositary regime to be applied to ELTIFs being marketed to professional investors, whereas retail ELTIFRs are, on top of the AIFMD, required to be applying the additional UCITSD V depositary provisions.[805]

Finally, the difference in terms of the investment policy pursued by UCITS and different types of AIFs in terms of investment policy is also reflected under the 'AIFMD Product Regulations'. EuSEFs/EuVECAs are required to invest at least 70% of their assets in illiquid assets and would, if managed and marketed by a full-AIFM, all be allowed to appoint a 'PE-depositary' under the AIFMD. The MMFR requires the depositary regimes applying to 'liquid AIFs' and UCITS under the AIFMD and UCITSD V to apply. The ELTIFR seems in this regard to be a bit inconsistent. Professional ELTIFs may under the applicable AIFMD depositary regulation appoint a 'PE-depositary', whereas retail-ELTIFs are at all times required to appoint an eligible entity under UCITSD V that excludes this option. In sum, the 'AIFMD/UCITSD V Product Regulations' seem to be consistent with the depositary regimes under UCITSD V and the AIFMD.

4.10 CONCLUSION

Prior to adopting the AIFMD and UCITSD V, Member States enjoyed significant discretion as to whether the appointment of a depositary was required and as to which entities were allowed to act as a depositary. This led to divergent approaches in Member States regarding the duties and responsibilities depositaries had and under which conditions these responsibilities could be delegated to a sub-custodian, which caused legal uncertainty and different levels of investor protection in the EEA. The introduction of the AIFMD and UCITSD V depositary framework has provided clarification on these points by requiring a single depositary to be appointed for each AIF/UCITS that an AIFM/UCITS ManCo manages. The depositary of an AIF must be: (1) a credit institution, (2) an investment firm, (3) an eligible entity under UCITSD V, (4) prime brokers or (5) an equivalent non-EEA entity.[806] In addition, the AIFMD allows discretion for Member States to appoint professionals as depositaries for certain closed-end funds. National central banks, credit institutions and other legal entities complying with additional prudential, organizational and capital requirements to provide sufficient guarantees may all be provided for by the implementing laws of the individual Member States as eligible depositaries under UCITSD V.[807] Besides clarifying the eligible entities, both the AIFMD and UCITSD V clarify the safekeeping and controlling functions of a depositary, set out the conditions under which delegation of safekeeping may take place and clarifies the

---

805 Art. 4(2), 5(1) MMFR.
806 A prime broker can also be appointed as a depositary, but is in particular subject to the requirements of Art. 21(4) AIFMD. For details see Zetzsche, *supra* note 103.
807 Art. 23(3) UCITSD V.

liability of depositaries for both financial instruments that can be held in custody and 'other assets'.

Depositary regulation under both the AIFMD and UCITSD V is, thus, largely the same. This is unsurprising given the fact that UCITS are 'liquid AIFs'. The larger scope of the AIFMD that includes not only liquid, but also illiquid and highly leveraged AIFs and the retail investor nature of UCITSD V, however, have led to some differences related to, in particular, the eligible entities, the practical application of functions, the UCITSD V depositary delegation and liability regime.

Following the new (cross-sectoral) consistent regime for depositaries under both the AIFMD and the UCITSD V, one can clearly conclude that by clarifying the appointment, eligible entities, the depositary's functions, delegation and liability, a level playing field in depositary regulation for AIFs and UCITS in the EEA is achieved.

5   THE IORPD II DEPOSITARY REGIME

5.1   INTRODUCTION

IORPD I was originally enacted to harmonize the regulation across the EEA regarding IORPs while promoting the cross-border provision of occupational pensions to a larger extent by allowing the plan sponsor, the IORP, its asset manager and depositary to be located in different countries of the EEA. By introducing an European passport for IORPs, the European Commission sought to increase economies of scale by allowing the pooling of schemes of companies operating in several EEA Member States. The rules set out by IORPD I and the harmonization it accomplished were minimal.[1] Given the diversity in national securities laws requirements and social and labour laws,[2] IORPD I has had very limited success. In 2015, there were only 88 cross-border IORPs out of approximately 120,000 schemes.[3] After carrying out a review of IORPD I and after having sought the advice of EIOPA, IORPD II contains a large amount of amendments in comparison to IORPD I. The amendments in IORPD II aim at:[4]

- removing remaining prudential barriers to cross-border IORPs;
- ensuring good governance and risk management in relation to IORPs;
- providing clear and relevant information to members and beneficiaries; and
- ensuring supervisors have the necessary tools to effectively supervise IORPs.

IORPD II harmonizes the legal framework applicable to IORPs and their depositaries to a much larger extent. IORPD II leaves the decision of making the appointment of a depositary compulsory to each individual Member State to avoid unjustified changes to their pension system.[5] Nevertheless, an IORPD II depositary has been established to promote convergence for the depositaries that are required to be appointed by individual Member States.[6] The depositary legal regime is based on the preparatory work that has been done under the AIFMD and UCITSD V[7] and harmonizes the entities eligible, the depositary's duties and liabilities.

---

1   CEIOPS-OP-03-08 final, concludes, based on the questionnaire on custodians/depositaries, that there are differences across Member States in relation to the appointment of a custodian, the eligible entity which is appointed to fulfil this role and the function that custodians perform.
2   H. Van Meerten, *Pension Reform in the European Union*, 14 Pensions Int J 259-272 (2009); H. Van Meerten & B. Staring, *Cross-Border Obstacles and Solutions for Pan-European Pensions*, 1 EC Tax Rev 30-41 (2011).
3   EIOPA-BoS-15/144 09, 11.
4   EIOPA, *Call for Advice from EIOPA (EIOPA) for the Review of Directive 2003/41/EC (IORP II)*, https://eiopa.europa.eu/Publications/Requests%20for%20advice/20110409-CfA-IORPII-final.pdf.
5   EIOPA-BOS-12/015, 463.
6   *See* EIOPA-CP-11/006.
7   *See* EIOPA-BOS-12/015, 451-459, 467-469.

5.2   THE APPOINTMENT OF DEPOSITARIES UNDER IORPD II

In EIOPA's Final Advice, the most prominent question to be answered was whether Member States should be required to make the appointment of an IORP depositary compulsory.[8] EIOPA considered that a more consistent approach among Member States in relation to the appointment of a depositary was necessary. Given the heterogeneity of IORPs throughout the EEA, EIOPA considered that convergence in relation to the appointment of depositaries was difficult to achieve.[9] IORPs in one Member State may show resemblance to investment funds, whereas in other Member States IORPs have more features in common with pension funds and insurance companies.[10] Apart from this, it was an important consideration that many IORPs do not have a depositary and it was considered that in those Member States alternative measures were in place that offer a similar level of protection for members and beneficiaries.[11] In particular, it was considered that requiring the compulsory requirement for the appointment of an IORP depositary would not fit in the existing legal regimes of all Member States and could lead to an increase in costs.[12]

Taking into account the considerations of EIOPA and its stakeholders, IORPD II leaves the decision of making the appointment of a depositary compulsory to each individual Member State to avoid unjustified changes to their pension system.[13] IORPD II differentiates between full DC and other types of IORPs in the degree in which IORP home Member States are left the discretion for making the appointment of IORP depositaries compulsory. The difference in degree of discretion for these different types of IORPs will now be discussed.

5.2.1   The Appointment for Full DC and Other Types of IORPs

For the purpose of the appointment of a depositary, IORPD II differentiates between IORPs in which members and beneficiaries fully bear and do not fully bear investment risks.

---

8   *Ibid.*, 460.
9   *Ibid.*, 463.
10 N. Kortleve et al., *European Supervision of Pension Funds: Purpose, Scope and Design*, Netspar Design Papers No. 4 (Oct. 2011), 15-18; H. Van Meerten, *The Scope of the EU 'Pensions' – Directive: Some Background and Solutions for Policymakers* 413-431 (U. Neergaard, E. Szyszczak, J.W. van de Gronden & M. Krajewski eds., Springer 2013).
11 EIOPA-BOS-12/015, 463.
12 *Ibid.*, 460.
13 *Ibid.*, 463.

5.2.1.1   Full DC IORPs

Member States *may* require IORPs, where members and beneficiaries fully bear investment risks, to appoint one or more depositaries for the safekeeping of assets *and* oversight duties in accordance with the IORPD II depositary regime.[14]

The discretional choice of IORP home Member States[15] not to require a full DC IORP to appoint one or more depositaries is, however, limited by the national laws of host Member States.[16] Host Member States[17] *may* require full DC IORPs that carry out cross-border activity[18] to appoint one or more depositaries for the safekeeping of assets and oversight duties[19] under the condition that such an appointment is required under its national law. DC IORPs that carry out cross-border activity in one or more host Member States that requires a depositary in accordance with the IORPD II depositary regime to be appointed have to appoint such a depositary regardless of the discretionary choice made under the national law of the IORP home Member State. The limitation in the discretion of the depositary appointment under the national law of the home IORP Member State only applies to IORPs that carry out a cross-border activity under Article 11 IORPD II. Under Article 11 IORPD II, home Member States have to allow IORPs that are registered or authorized[20] to carry out cross-border activities. Under Article 6(19) IORPD II a cross-border activity is defined as the operating of a pension scheme[21] by an IORP that is governed by the social labour law of another Member State than the home Member State. The pension scheme might be a contract, agreement, trust deed or rules (other legal form) that stipulates which retirement benefits are granted and under which conditions[22]

---

14 Art. 33(1) IORPD II.
15 Art. 6(10) IORPD II: "home Member State means the Member State in which the IORP has been registered or authorised and in which its main administration is located in accordance with Art. 9." Following Art. 9 sub-para. 1 IORPD II, the location of the main administration is the place where the main strategic decisions of an IORP are made.
16 Art. 33(1) IORPD II.
17 Art. 6(11) IORPD II: "host Member State means the Member State whose social and labour law relevant to the field of occupational pension schemes is applicable to the relationship between the sponsoring undertaking and members or beneficiaries."
18 Art. 6(19) IORPD II: "cross-border activity means operating a pension scheme where the relationship between the sponsoring undertaking, and the members and beneficiaries concerned, is governed by the social and labour law relevant to the field of occupational pension schemes of a Member State other than the home Member State."
19 A depositary that performs the duties in accordance with Art. 34 and 35 IORPD II; See Art. 33(1) IORPD II.
20 See Art. 9 IORPD II.
21 Art. 6(2) IORPD II: "pension scheme means a contract, an agreement, a trust deed or rules stipulating which retirement benefits are granted and under which conditions."
22 Art. 6(4) IORPD II: "retirement benefits means benefits paid by reference to reaching, or the expectation of reaching, retirement or, where they are supplementary to those benefits and provided on an ancillary basis, in the form of payments on death, disability, or cessation of employment or in the form of support payments or services in case of sickness, indigence or death. In order to facilitate financial security in retirement, these benefits may take the form of payments for life, payments made for a temporary period, a lump sum, or any combination thereof."

these are being granted in the relationship between the sponsoring undertaking[23] and the members[24] and beneficiaries.[25] Following Recital 5 IORPD II, the cross-border activity is determined by the applicability of the social labour laws of the IORP host Member State without prejudice to the national social and labour laws that applies to the IORP pension scheme to the relationship between the sponsoring undertaking and members and beneficiaries of the host Member State. The mere fact that the members and beneficiaries of an IORP pension scheme reside in another Member State than the Member State where the sponsoring undertaking and the IORP are located does not constitute a cross-border activity. It is, thus, decisive that the social and labour laws of another Member State than the home Member state[26] applies to the relationship between the sponsoring undertaking and members or beneficiaries to constitute a cross-border activity.

Full DC IORPs carrying out a cross-border activity that are both not required to appoint a depositary have to ensure under Article 34 and 35 IORPD II that equivalent protections are in place for the performance of the safekeeping and oversight duties.[27] Full DC IORPs that do not have equivalent protections in place for either of these functions are, thus, de facto, compulsorily required to appoint a depositary for the safekeeping or the safekeeping and oversight function.[28]

5.2.1.2   Other Types of IORPs

For IORPs in which the members and beneficiaries do not fully bear the investment risk, the IORP home Member State may require an IORP to appoint a depositary for safekeeping of assets or for safekeeping of assets and oversight duties in accordance with the IORPD II depositary regime.[29] There are two differences between the appointment of a depositary for full DC IORPs and other types of IORPs.

First, IORP home Member States have the full discretion to decide whether a depositary is required to be appointed for this type of IORP.[30] DB and hybrid IORPs carrying out cross-border activity that are not required by their IORP home Member State to

---

23 *See* Art. 6(3) IORPD II: "any undertaking or other body that acts as an employer or in a self-employed capacity or any combination thereof and which offers a pension scheme or pays contributions to an IORP. Sponsor undertakings may include or consist of one or more legal or natural persons."

24 *See* Art. 6(5) IORPD II: 'members' means "a person, other than a beneficiary or prospective members, whose past or current occupational activities entitle or will entitle him/her to retirement benefits in accordance with the provisions of a pension scheme."

25 *See* Art. 6(6) IORPD II: "a person that receives retirement benefits."

26 *See* Art. 6(11) IORPD II.

27 *See infra* 5.4.

28 Recital 45 Proposal for a Directive of the European Parliament and of the Council on the activities and supervision of institutions for occupational retirement provision (recast), /* COM/2014/0167 final – 2014/0091 (COD) */ ('Initial Draft IORPD II'): "only institutions operating schemes where members and beneficiaries bear all the risks and where equivalent protections are not already in place, should be required to appoint a depositary."

29 Art. 33(2) IORPD II.

30 *Ibid.*

appoint a depositary may not be 'forced' by any of their host Member States to appoint a depositary.

Second, Article 33(2) IORPD II allows home Member States the choice for DB and hybrid IORPs to require a depositary for the safekeeping of assets or for the safekeeping of assets and oversight duties or not to require anything in this regard at all and leave it completely up to market practice. In practice, there will, however, in this regard not be any difference with full DC IORPs. Home Member States have the discretion not to require a depositary for the safekeeping of assets *and* oversight duties. The discretion being left to the home Member State to require a depositary for both functions at all in itself leaves the possibility open to IORP home Member States to require merely a depositary to be appointed for the safekeeping of assets function. Article 34(5) IORPD II leaves this open as 'equivalent protections' only need to be provided for the situation 'where no depositary is appointed for the safekeeping of assets'. Article 34(5) IORPD II does not prevent home Member States from doing so. Full DC IORPs that carry out cross-border activities are, however, still obliged to appoint a depositary for both functions if a host Member State requires this under their national laws regardless of the implementation of the IORPD II depositary regime under the national laws of the IORP home Member State.

Home Member States are, thus, the only Member State that determine whether a depositary and what type of depositary should be appointed for DB and hybrid IORPs that are authorized or registered in their domiciles. The appointment of the depositary for full DC IORPs depends upon the national implementation of Article 33(1) IORPD II under the home Member State laws and, if carrying out cross-border activities, also upon implementation of the host Member States in which that particular IORP operates.

The crucial question for IORPs whether and to what extent to apply the IORPD II appointment of a depositary regime is, thus, whether members and beneficiaries of an IORP fully bear investment risk. For this purpose, it should be clarified what 'fully bearing investment risks' means.

5.2.2   Investment Risks – Full DC, Hybrid and/or Full DB IORPs?

For the purpose of the appointment of a depositary, IORPD II differentiates between IORPs in which members and beneficiaries fully and do not fully bear the investment risk.[31] IORPD II leaves the decision of making the appointment of a depositary compulsory to each individual Member State to avoid unjustified changes to their pension system.[32] For this purpose, however, IORPD II differentiates between full DC and other types of IORPs in the degree in which IORP home Member States are left the discretion

---

31   *See* Art. 33(1) and (2) IORPD II.
32   EIOPA-BOS-12/015, 463.

for making the appointment of depositaries compulsory. The compulsory appointment of the depositary for full DC IORPs depends upon the national implementation of the IORPD II depositary provision under the home Member State laws and, for IORPs carrying out a cross-border activity, also upon the national laws of the host Member States in which an IORP operates.

The rationale behind this differentiation lies in EIOPA's IORPD II preparatory work. EIOPA, in considering the need for having a (compulsory) depositary appointed, reviewed the depositary practices under UCITSD I/IV, the AIFMD and Solvency II.[33] While in the first two directive a depositary is to be appointed, the latter directive does not contain such a requirement. This is mainly because IORPs showing resemblance to insurance companies (full DB and hybrid IORPs) manage assets and, generally, the employer and/or IORP bears the costs of any operational failures associated with the safeguarding of assets and investment operations. Therefore, the need for safekeeping and oversight functions to be performed by a depositary to protect members/beneficiaries was not being seen as imperative. The situation, however, is different for IORPs showing resemblance to AIFs and UCITS in which members/beneficiaries bear investment risk (full DC IORPs). The external appointment of a depositary that safekeeps assets and oversees the activities of an IORP was considered to ensure due care of assets and mitigate the risk of fraud.[34] This consideration ultimately led to the difference in the appointment of a depositary requirements between IORPs in which members and beneficiaries fully and do not fully bear the investment risk. IORPD II does not contain a definition of IORPs in which members and beneficiaries fully and do not fully bear investment risk. The actuarial function under Article 28 IORPD II provides some guidance on this point. Under this provision an actuary is required for IORPs that 'provides cover against biometric risks or guarantees either an investment performance or a given level of benefits'.[35] Article 33(1) IORPD II, thus, seems to suggest that members fully bear the investment risk if an IORP does not guarantee either an investment performance or a given level of benefits.

Whether the appointment of a depositary depends upon the national laws of merely the home Member State or also upon the national laws of host Member States for IORPs carrying out a cross-border activity, thus, depends on whether a scheme's plan is a full DC, a DB or a hybrid plan. Full DC IORPs, plan sponsors and/or insurance companies/asset manager do not bear any of the financial (or biometric risks) that are related to the IORP's pension plan.[36] Instead, the benefits paid to its members are purely determined on the basis of the investment result yielded. The eventual cost of operational failures that

---

33 EIOPA-BOS-12/015, 460,
34 *Ibid.*
35 Art. 6(h) IORPD II defines biometric risks as: "[...] risks linked to death, disability and longevity."
36 F. Stewart & J. Yermo, *Pension Fund Governance: Challenges and Potential Solutions*, OECD Working Papers on Insurance and Private Pensions No. 18 (June 2008), 3.

are stemming from the management of the plan's assets by an asset manager, such as administration risks, including contributions and investment returns allocated to an incorrect account,[37] are fully borne by members/beneficiaries of full DC IORPs.[38] In DB and hybrid plans, on the contrary, the plan sponsor, the insurance company or the asset manager insures the plans' members against financial or biometric risks.[39] Any of these actors may guarantee the plan's members a guaranteed minimum rate of return on investments or annuitization rate or a formula is specified through which the guarantee will be calculated based upon the employee's past earnings.[40] DB and hybrid schemes, thus, bear (to some extent) the cost of potential failures that are related to managing and safeguarding assets.[41]

EIOPA in its Final Advice considered a similar appointment of a depositary as for full DC IORPs not appropriate for hybrid schemes as there are many different types of hybrid schemes within the EEA. EIOPA stated that further clarification of the function of depositaries for these schemes would be necessary before imposing a similar requirement.[42] The appointment of a depositary that both exercises the safekeeping and oversight functions, thus, depends, upon the national laws of the home and host Member States for IORPs carrying out a cross-border activity for IORPs in which no investment guarantee at all is given by the pension plan sponsor and/or the IORP. IORPD II leaves it up to the home Member States to decide whether or not a depositary is required for other types of IORPs (hybrid and DB IORPs).

5.2.3   The Definition of a 'Depositary' under IORPD II

The IORPD II eligible entities requirement applies to 'depositaries'. Article 33(1) and (2) IORPD II defines a depositary as both being a depositary for safekeeping of assets or for safekeeping of assets *and* oversight duties in accordance with the IORPD II. The wording is different compared to IORPD I. Under Article 19(2) IORPD I, IORP home Member States were required not to

> restrict institutions from appointing, for the custody of their assets, custodians established in another Member State and duly authorized in accordance with Directive 93/22/EEC or Directive 2000/12/EC, or accepted as a depositary for the purposes of Directive 85/611/EEC.

---

37 EIOPA-BOS-12/015, 462.
38 *Ibid.*
39 Stewart & Yermo, *supra* note 36.
40 *Ibid.*
41 EIOPA-BOS-12/015, 461.
42 *Ibid.*, 462.

Member States could require either a depositary or a custodian to be compulsory appointed.[43] Article 19(2) IORPD I referred to 'custodians' established in another Member State and duly authorized in accordance with the ISD (predecessor of MiFID I/II) or CRD I (predecessor of CRD IV) or accepted as a 'depositary' for the purpose of UCITSD V. Article 33(3) IORPD II requires Member States not to restrict IORPs from appointing, depositaries *established in another Member State* and duly authorized in accordance with CRD IV or MiFID (II), or accepted as depositaries for the purposes of UCITSD IV/V or the AIFMD.[44] In conjunction with Article 33(1) and (2) IORPD II, the 'IORPD I custodian' has, thus, been replaced by a 'depositary for the safekeeping of assets' and the 'IORPD I depositary' by a depositary appointed for the safekeeping of assets and oversight duties in accordance with IORPD II.

EIOPA stated in its IORPD II Final Advice that the terms 'custodian' and 'depositary' might correspond to different types of functions that would depend upon the jurisdiction and the type of IORP.[45] EIOPA found it, for that purpose, relevant to establish a common and harmonized understanding of 'custodians' and 'depositaries' and their functions. The term 'depositary' under the AIFMD was being taken as a 'benchmark' as it was the most 'advanced piece of legislation' and taken as a template for the role of the depositary under UCITSD V. According to the AIFMD and UCITSD V, being referred to by EIOPA, the depositary has two core functions: the safekeeping assets and the compliance with fund rules and applicable law.[46] Further, EIOPA, without making reference to CRD IV, MiFID II or the CSDR, stated that the 'custodian function' only relates to the 'safekeeping of assets'.[47]

Despite the fact that EIOPA recognized that both terms imply different functions, EIOPA advised to always refer to the word 'depositary', as is the case under the AIFMD and UCITSD V.[48] This advice was followed up in the final legal text of IORPD II and creates major confusion about the (compulsory or optional) appointment of depositaries and the mandatory duties to be performed.[49]

Article 33(1) IORPD II regulates for full DC IORPs the appointment of one or more depositaries for the safekeeping of assets *and* oversight duties. On the contrary, Article 33 (2) IORPD II refers, for all other types of IORPs, to the appointment of a depositary for the safekeeping of assets or for the safekeeping of assets and performance of oversight duties. Under Article 33(1) IORPD II, the requirement of the appointment of a deposi-

---

43 Art. 19(2) sub-para. 2 IORPD I; *See also* CEIOPS-OP-03-08 final, 12-13, 56-58.
44 Art. 33(3) IORPD II.
45 *See* EIOPA-BOS-12/015, 451.
46 *Ibid.*, 451.
47 European Commission, *Communication from the Commission to the Council and to the European parliament – Regulation of UCITS Depositaries in the Member States: Review and Possible Developments*, 30 March 2004, COM(2004) 207 final, 7, 14, and 26.
48 EIOPA-BOS-12/015, 471.
49 *Ibid.*

tary for full DC IORPs seems to have a similar meaning as depositaries within the meaning of the AIFMD and UCITSD V. Member States for other types of IORPs may under their national laws, thus, require the appointment of 'custodians' or 'depositaries'.

The difference of the meaning of a depositary under Article 33(1) and (2) IORPD II does, however, de facto not exist. Home Member States *may* require an IORP under Article 33(1) IORPD II to appoint one or more depositaries for the safekeeping of assets *and* oversight duties in accordance with the IORPD II depositary regime. The phrase 'may require' under Article 33(1) IORPD II suggests that home Member States may also choose to not require a 'depositary' for the safekeeping of assets *and* oversight duties to be appointed. Taken a grammatical approach, the discretion given by 'may require' leaves open the choice for home Member States to require, instead, a depositary to be appointed for the safekeeping of assets *or* for the safekeeping of assets and oversight duties in accordance with the IORPD II depositary regime. This discretion, again, is limited for full DC IORPs that carry out cross-border activity and are required by one or more host Member States to appoint a depositary for the safekeeping of assets *and* oversight duties in accordance with the IORPD II depositary regime. The preference of EIOPA to always use the word 'depositary' for both 'custodians' and 'UCITSD V/AIFMD depositaries' required to be appointed might be explained by the fact that Member States in their national laws have the discretion to require both a 'custodian' or a 'depositary' for both full DC IORPs and other types of IORPs to be appointed. The meaning of a depositary under both Article 33(1) and (2) IORPD II for both full DC and other types of IORPs should, thus, be read as either a 'custodian' or a 'AIFMD/UCITSD V depositary'. The limitation provided under Article 33(1) IORPD II by a possible requirement to appoint a depositary for host Member States for full DC IORPs carrying out cross-border activity is an exception to the main rule and solely refers to 'AIFMD/UCITSD V depositaries'.

IORPD II has, thus, made the political choice to regulate both 'MiFID II/CRD IV custodians' and 'AIFMD/UCITSD V depositaries' as 'depositaries' under IORPD II.

5.2.4   *The Appointment of a Single Depositary versus Multiple Depositaries*

The ambiguous meaning of the word 'depositary' used in Article 33 IORPD II leads to inconsistency with the single depositary requirement under the AIFMD/UCITSD V and lack of clarity in the application of various IORPD II depositary provisions.

5.2.4.1   The Inconsistency of the 'Depositary' Terminology under IORPD II
Throughout the IORPD II consultation process, it has been debated whether IORPs should be required to appoint a *single* depositary or not. The Initial Draft IORPD II

required the compulsory appointment of a *single* depositary for full DC IORPs.[50] Article 35(2) Initial Draft IORPD II proposed to allow Member States in their national laws to require an IORP to appoint either a single depositary or multiple depositaries for other types of IORPs.[51] Unlike the Initial Draft IORPD II, the final IORPD II text does not differentiate for this purpose between 'one or more' 'custodians' or 'depositaries'. The main rule is that the terminology 'depositaries' under Article 33(1) and (2) IORPD II leaves discretion to (host) Member States to require either a 'MiFID II/CRD IV custodian' or an 'AIFMD/UCITSD V depositary' to be appointed for full DC and other types of IORPs. Leaving the option open to individual Member States to require one or more 'depositaries' to be appointed can be explained on the basis of this. Under MiFID II and CRD IV, one or more 'MiFID II/CRD IV custodians' may be appointed, whereas under the AIFMD and UCITSD V only a single depositary may be appointed. This requirement, thus, suits both 'MiFID II/CRD IV custodians' and 'AIFMD/UCITSD V depositaries'. The discretion left to Member States may, however, lead to inconsistencies. Leaving the decision to the Member States to allow an IORP to appoint multiple depositaries that perform both safekeeping and oversight duties is at odds with the compulsory appointment of a single depositary for these duties under the AIFMD and UCITSD V.[52] Similarly, allowing Member States to appoint a single depositary for other IORPs for merely the safekeeping of assets would be at odds with CRD IV and MiFID II that both do not require the appointment of a single depositary for safekeeping of assets (custodian).[53]

The Final Advice of EIOPA clearly advised to leave the decision of requiring the appointment of one or more compulsory depositaries to each Member State in order to avoid unjustified changes to their pension systems.[54] The final IORPD II text followed up this advice.

The requirement of a single compulsory depositary was also discussed prior to the introduction of the 'single depositary rule'[55] under the AIFMD and UCITSD V. During the UCITSD V consultation, it was pointed out that the UCITSD I-IV did not expressly mention that a UCITS may only have a single depositary and clarification on this point was desirable.[56]

The outcome of the UCITSD V consultation was that the compulsory appointment of a single depositary was the only way to guarantee that the depositary has an exhaustive and complete overview of the fund's assets (e.g. a single depositary for an umbrella struc-

---

50 Art. 35(1) Initial Draft IORPD II.
51 Art. 35(2) Initial Draft IORPD II.
52 Art. 21(1) AIFMD and Art. 22(1) UCITSD V.
53 *See* Annex I Section A MiFID II.
54 EIOPA-BOS-12/015, 463.
55 European Commission, *Consultation Paper on the UCITS Depositary Function and on the UCITS Managers 'Remuneration (December 2010)*, MARKT/G4 D (2010) 950800, 19 and 20.
56 European Commission, *Summary of Responses to UCITS Depositary's Consultation Paper - Feedback Statement*, 9.

ture or a single fund).[57] This principle was considered to be essential to ensure that the depositary keeps an overview of all the assets and cash transaction of the AIF/UCITS portfolios and, therefore, be in a proper position to perform its oversight duties (such as to control that, for instance, a UCITS complies with the applicable regulatory ratios).[58]

Requiring a single depositary both ensures a complete overview of all the IORP assets and allows both asset managers and investors to have a single point of reference in the event that problems occur in relation to the safekeeping of assets or the performance of oversight functions.[59] In light of these considerations, Member States should require a *single depositary* for both full DC and other IORPs that are appointed for the safekeeping of assets and oversight duties. Depositaries appointed for merely the safekeeping of assets should, in line with CRD IV and MiFID II, not be required to appoint a single depositary, but one or more depositaries. For that purpose, Article 34(1) IORPD II should clarify that a single depositary shall be entrusted for the safekeeping of assets for those depositaries that are entrusted with both the safekeeping and oversight task. This is in line with namely the rationale of a single compulsory depositary assigned for both tasks, resolving collective action issues based upon the cheapest cost avoider theory.[60] Nonetheless, such type of depositaries shall not be prevented from delegating its safekeeping to sub-custodians.[61] Such a requirement should not be put in place for depositaries that are merely performing the safekeeping task as these depositaries do not perform oversight duties and do not need to have an overview of all the assets of an IORP throughout the custody holding chain. Instead, they should be required to merely have a comprehensive and up-to-date inventory of all assets that they are safekeeping by themselves.[62]

5.2.4.2 The Unclear 'Depositary' definition under IORPD II

The ambiguous meaning of the word 'depositary' used in Article 33 IORPD II also leads to lack of clarity in the application of various IORPD II depositary provisions.

First, a grammatical interpretation of Article 33(3) IORPD II seems to suggest that the entities eligible as a depositary are limited for Member States that choose the appointment of either a single depositary or multiple depositaries. Article 33(3) IORPD II refers to the appointment of *depositaries* established in another Member State and duly authorised in accordance with CRD IV or MiFID II, or accepted as *a depositary* for the

57 European Commission, *supra* note 55.
58 European Commission, *Working Document of the Commission Services (DG Markt), Consultation Paper on the UCITS Depositary Function,* July 2009, 9; European Commission, *Commission Staff Working Document of 3 July 2012* (SWD(2012) 185 final): accompanying the Proposal for the UCITSD V: Impact Assessment, Question 9, http://eur-lex.europa.eu/legal content/EN/TXT/PDF/?uri=CELEX:52012SC0185&from=EN.
59 *See* Recital 12 UCITSD V.
60 *See* D.A. Zetzsche, *Prinzipien der kollektiven Vermögensanlage* § 21 (Mohr Siebeck 2015).
61 *See* for considerations regarding the 'single depositary rule' under UCITSD V: European Commission, *Summary of Responses to UCITS Depositary's Consultation Paper – Feedback Statement,* 9.
62 *See* EIOPA-BOS-12/015, 465.

purpose of UCITSD IV/V or the AIFMD. The wording 'accepted as *a depositary*' could be interpreted as a compulsory single depositary requirement that Member States are o-bliged to apply when adopting 'AIFMD/UCITSD IV/V depositaries' in their national IORPD II implementation laws. In the context of IORPD II it could, however, lead to the confusion that only depositaries under UCITSD IV/V and the AIFMD are eligible to be appointed in those Member States that choose a *single* 'AIFMD/UCITSD V depositary' or 'custodian' to be appointed. On the contrary, a grammatical interpretation of 'the appointment of *depositaries*' under Article 33(3) IORPD II could suggest that only enti-ties under CRD IV or MiFID II would be eligible for those Member States that would allow one or more depositaries to be appointed. This confusion has either way no prac-tical relevance as credit institutions and investment firms are also eligible under the AIFMD if a grammatical interpretation of this provision would be applied.

Similar confusion is to be observed in applying Article 34 and 35 IORPD II related to the safekeeping of assets and the exercise of the oversight duties of IORPD II depositaries. Article 34 IORPD II, for the purpose of applying the safekeeping of assets provisions, refers to assets being 'entrusted to *a depositary* (emphasis added by the author) for safe-keeping'. Article 34 IORPD II is unclear whether a single or multiple depositaries are required to appointed for the safekeeping function. This is relevant as Article 33 IORPD II allows multiple 'custodians' and 'AIFMD/UCITSD V depositaries' to be appointed, but does not clarify whether the safekeeping function may be carried out by a single or by multiple depositaries. A grammatical interpretation of Article 34 IORPD II would restrict Member States to only allow a single depositary to be appointed for the safekeeping function. Such an interpretation of both provision, however, leads to confusion as Mem-ber States under their national laws may require 'one or more' 'custodians' or 'AIFM-D/UCITSD V depositaries' to be appointed. Again, not differentiating between 'AIFM-D/UCITSD V depositaries' and 'custodians' leads to an unsatisfactory result. Full DC IORPs that show larger resemblance to AIFs and UCITS, for which a single depositary for safekeeping of assets and oversight duties is required, may appoint either a single or multiple depositaries for performing the safekeeping task.[63] On the contrary, Member States may compulsorily require a *single* 'custodian' to be appointed for the safekeeping task, whereas the appointment of a *single* custodian is not required under CRD IV and MiFID II.

Article 35 spreads similar confusion about whether or not multiple depositaries may be appointed for performing oversight duties.

Article 35(1) IORPD II requires 'the depositary appointed for oversight duties' to carry out oversight duties. An earlier draft version of this Article required 'at least one of the depositaries' appointed under the IORPD II to carry out oversight duties. IORPD II, thus, allows IORPs to appoint multiple 'AIFMD/UCITSD V depositaries' to be ap-

---

63 Art. 33(1) and (2) IORPD II.

pointed for IORPs. This is inconsistent with the single depositary requirement under the AIFMD and UCITSD V. Safekeeping and oversight duties may, thus, both be carried out by multiple depositaries irrespective of whether a Member State requires a 'AIFMD/UCITSD V depositary' or a 'custodian' to be appointed.

Allowing multiple depositaries for these tasks prevents a (single) depositary from keeping a complete overview of all the assets that is necessary to perform its oversight duties. Multiple depositaries being appointed by an IORP for performing the oversight duties could lead to coordination problems. The appointment of multiple depositaries for both the safekeeping and oversight duties would make the performance of both functions even harder. Member States are, thus, well suggested to implement IORPD II by requiring a single depositary to be appointed for 'AIFMD/UCITSD V depositaries' performing both tasks, whereas they could leave it open for 'custodian s' being appointed. The confusing wording used in Article 33(3), Article 34 and Article 35 IORPD II should, thus, be seen as to accommodate the intention to leave a large room for discretion to individual Member States to require the appointment of either a 'custodian' or a 'AIFMD/UCITSD V depositary'.

5.2.5   The Discretionary Choice of Member States for a 'Depositary' or 'Custodian' under IORPD II

Member States are left the choice whether or not to compulsorily require a depositary for the safekeeping of assets or for the safekeeping of assets and oversight duties for full DC, hybrid or DB IORPs in accordance with the IORPD II depositary regime.[64] IORPs not required to appoint a depositary at all are required to adhere to 'equivalent protections' for performing the safekeeping and oversight duties under Articles 34 and 35 IORPD II.

The Initial Draft IORPD II contained a mandatory requirement for full DC IORPs to appoint a depositary for both safekeeping and oversight duties.[65] The appointment of a third party depositary that safekeeps assets and oversees the activities of full DC IORP was considered by EIOPA to ensure due care of assets and mitigate the risk of fraud as members/beneficiaries bear full investment risk.[66] This consideration ultimately led to the difference in the appointment of a depositary requirements between IORPs in which members and beneficiaries fully and do not fully bear investment risk under IORPD II.

It is, however, unclear whether this differentiation between full DC IORPs and other types of IORPs will be followed up by the IORPD II Member States. None of the Member States upon implementing IORPD I in their national laws delineated for the purpose of the compulsory appointment of a depositary/custodian between full DC and other types

---

64   Arts. 33(1), 34 and 35 IORPD II.
65   Art. 35(1) Initial Draft IORPD II.
66   EIOPA-BOS-12/015, 460.

of IORPs.[67] Liechtenstein and Luxembourg, for example, required for IORPs that may operate DC, hybrid and DC IORPs a depositary for both tasks to be appointed.[68] Belgium, France and Malta required for all types of IORPs a custodian to be appointed,[69] whereas other Member States, including Denmark, Finland and the Netherlands, did not require a mandatory depositary or custodian for any type of IORP at all.[70] Under the IORPD I Member State implementation laws the compulsory appointment of depositaries for IORPs varied from Member State to Member State for different reasons. First, the nature of the IORPs varied from Member State to Member State. Essentially, the choice whether and to what extent investment guarantees are provided determines the attribution of risks. The larger the insurance element is, the less risk will be borne by members/beneficiaries and vice versa.

Second, the interpretation of Member States as to whether members and beneficiaries bear investment risks may differ from Member State to Member State. The members and beneficiaries of (full) DB and hybrid IORPs may only have a residual interest in a slight sense as investment guarantees may be partially or fully given. Almost all IORPs of the latter type, however, only provide a conditional investment guarantee, i.e. the investment guarantee is only being granted if the regulatory funding ratio of an IORP allows such a guarantee to be given. Regardless of whether IORPs are full DC, hybrid or full DB IORPs, members and beneficiaries of all types of IORPs bear, thus, at least an 'indirect investment risk'. Depending upon the funding ratio of a hybrid or DB IORP, investment losses may lead to non-indexation of pension benefits or another form of benefit cut. Member States may be of the opinion that members /beneficiaries in their domicile bear (indirectly) the cost of any operational failures associated with investment operations and, therefore, require a compulsory depositary to perform safekeeping and oversight duties for all types of IORPs in order to protect policyholders' interest.[71]

Finally, Member States may, regardless of their interpretation of 'investment risk', be of the opinion that equivalent measures for oversight duties are already in place. Based upon this consideration, Member States may decide not to require any compulsory de-

---

67 *See also* CEIOPS-OP-03-08 final, 12-13, 56-58.
68 Liechtenstein: Art. 12 Gesetz vom 24. November 2006 betreffend die Aufsicht über Einrichtungen der betrieblichen Altersversorgung (Pensionsfondsgesetz; PFG); Luxembourg: Arts. 18 (1) and 42 (1) Loi du 13 juillet 2005 relative aux institutions de retraite professionnelle sous forme de société d'épargne-pension à capital variable (sepcav) et d'association d'épargne-pension (assep) et portant modification de l'article 167, alinéa 1 de la loi modifiée du 4 décembre 1967 concernant l'impôt sur le revenu.
69 Belgium: Art. 92 Law of 27 October 2006 on the supervision of institutions for occupational retirement provision; France: Art. L.143-4 du Code des Assurances; Malta: B.6 Custody of Retirement Fund's Assets, B.6.1 General Conditions, Directives for Occupational Retirement Schemes, Retirement Funds and related Parties under the Special Funds (Regulation) Act, 2002.
70 Denmark: Consolidated Supervision of Company Pension Funds Act (Consolidated Act n. 1017 of 24 October 2005); Pensions Act (Consolidated Act n. 939 of 15 September 2004); Finland: Act on Employment Pension Insurance Companies, 25 April 1997/354, Netherlands: Wet van 7 december 2006 houdende regels betreffende pensioenen (Pensioenwet).
71 Art. 33(1) and (2) IORPD II.

positary at all for any type of IORPs. Instead, the IORP governing body may be given the full discretion to decide to appoint a depositary exercising safekeeping and oversight duties or a depositary for exercising the safekeeping function or, if allowed by the national regulation applicable, to perform self-custody.[72] Member States, thus, varied in their compulsory depositary requirement for all types of IORPs under their IORPD I implementation laws and, for the three reasons mentioned above, this is unlikely to change under their IORPD II Member State implementation laws.

5.3 THE IORPD II SUBSTANTIVE DEPOSITARY REGIME

IORPD II leaves the decision of making a depositary compulsory, to a large extent, to each Member State.[73] Nevertheless, IORPD II seems to have established a more consistent approach with regard to eligible institutions, its organizational requirements, the safekeeping and oversight duties rules of IORP depositaries regardless of whether Member States require depositaries to be compulsorily appointed by IORPs or not. Moreover, the substantive IORPD II depositary standards also raised for IORPs the standards of alternative mechanisms applied to the safekeeping of IORP assets and the exercise of oversight duties for which no depositary is appointed.[74] These will now be subsequently discussed.

5.3.1 The Scope of the IORPD II 'Substantive' Depositary Regime

The discretion left to Member States to require a compulsory depositary under Art. 33(1) and (2) IORPD II has created confusion for Member States whether they should implement Articles 33-35 IORPD II or not. In particular, Member States, such as the Netherlands, indicated during the IORPD II implementation phase that the implementation of Articles 33-35 was not necessary as they opted in for not requiring a compulsory depositary for IORPs. The Netherlands considered that alternative mechanisms that offer a similar level of protection to members and beneficiaries are already in place[75] and that for this reason Articles 33(1)-(7), 34(1)-(4) and Art. 35(1), (2) IORPD II did not have to be implemented.[76] IORPD II is unclear on this point. Taking a grammatical and teleological interpretation of Arts 33-35 IORPD, it seems, however, that the 'substantive deposi-

---

72 OECD, *OECD Recommendation on Core Principles of Occupational Pension Regulation*, Principle 6.8.
73 EIOPA-BOS-12/015, 463.
74 *Ibid.*, 464.
75 *Ibid.*, 463.
76 *See* Arts. 33-35 IORPD II Transponeringstabel implementatie Richtlijn 2016/2341/EU van het Europees Parlement en de Raad van 14 december 2016 betreffende de werkzaamheden van en het toezicht op instellingen voor bedrijfspensioenvoorziening (IBPV's) (PbEU 2016, L 354/37) in de Pensioenwet, Wet verplichte beroepspensioenregeling en daarop gebaseerde regelgeving; *See also* Kamerbrief resultaat onderhandelingen

tary regime' is applicable to depositaries appointed by IORPs regardless of whether Member States require in their implementation laws a compulsory depositary for the purpose of performing the safekeeping task or the safekeeping task and oversight duties to be appointed. The decisive criterion seems to be that Articles 33 and 34 IORPD II are applicable to depositaries *appointed by IORPs* for safekeeping purposes and Articles 33, 34 and 35 IORPD II to depositaries appointed for safekeeping and oversight duties. The obligation to comply with these provisions seems to be based upon the decision by IORPs to appoint a depositary and not upon the decision of individual Member States to introduce a compulsory obligation for IORPs to appoint a depositary.

Article 34(1) IORPD II, for example, refers to "where the assets of an IORP [...] are entrusted to a depositary for safekeeping" and Article 35(1) IORPD II refers to "in addition to the tasks referred to in Article 34(1) and (2) IORPD II, the depositary appointed for oversight duties shall." Other examples are to be found in Articles 34(5) and 35(3) IORPD II. Article 34(5) IORPD II refers to "where no depositary is appointed for the safekeeping of assets, *the IORP* shall." Similarly, Article 35(3) IORPD II refers to "where no depositary is appointed for oversight duties." None of these provisions relates to the optional compulsory obligation to require the appointment of a depositary by Member States under Article 33(1) and (2) IORPD II. Instead, all four provisions target the appointment of a depositary by an IORP. The question remains whether and to what extent Article 33(1) and (2) IORPD II have a function in determining the application of the 'substantive IORP regime'. Article 33(1) and (2) IORPD II both read that

> [...] the home-Member State may require the IORP to appoint one or more depositaries for the safekeeping of assets and oversight duties in accordance with Articles 34 and 35.

Article 33(1) and (2) IORPD II refer, however, to Article 34 and 35 to define what a depositary is for the purpose of the compulsory depositary appointment under Art. 33(1) and (2) IORPD II. Most likely this provision is based upon an equivalent provision in UCITSD V.[77] The sole purpose of the discretion seems to be to let Member States determine whether IORPs should appoint an 'AIFMD/UCITSD V depositary' or a 'CRD IV/-MiFID II custodian'. A grammatical interpretation of Article 34(1), (4) and Article 35(1), (3) IORPD II suggests that the substantive safekeeping and oversight tasks are directed to depositaries that are appointed to perform these duties. The substantive requirements of Article 33, 34 and 35 IORPD II, thus, apply to depositaries appointed by IORPs regardless

---

herziening IORP-richtlijn, 24 june 2016, https://www.rijksoverheid.nl/documenten/kamerstukken/2016/06/24/kamerbrief-resultaat-onderhandelingen-herziening-iorp-richtlijn.
77 Art. 2(1)(a) UCITSD V.

of whether Member States require such an appointment in their implementation laws or not. This is logical for three reasons.

First, not applying Article 33, 34 and 35 IORPD II to depositaries that are deliberately appointed by IORPs in Member States in which no compulsory obligation exists would jeopardize a level playing field for IORP depositaries in Europe. Under such an interpretation, depositaries appointed by IORPs that are required to appoint a compulsory depositary would have to comply with the requirements laid down in Article 33, 34 and 35 IORPD II, whereas the same depositaries that are deliberately appointed by IORPs, 'custodians' in particular, would be exempted from doing so. This would be very problematic as, in practice, all IORPs need to appoint custodians to be able to access (settlement) services provided by CSDs regardless of whether the legislator required them to be appointed compulsorily or not.

Second, requiring all depositaries appointed by IORPs to apply the IORPD II substantive depositary regime would ensure consistency with the depositary regimes under the AIFMD and UCITSD V on the basis of which the regime is inspired.[78] Many IORP depositaries and Member States requiring compulsory depositaries are likely following the practice laid down in the AIFMD and UCITSD V (Commission) Regulation related to the safekeeping and oversight duties tasks to be performed by depositaries.[79]

Finally, such an interpretation is contrary to the purpose and meaning of the IORPD II depositary regime. Following EIOPA's Final Advice to the European Commission regarding IORPD II in 2012, the aim of IORPD II was to create a 'more consistent approach' for depositaries on the EEA level.[80] In this regard, EIOPA stated in its advice that

> Taking into account the previous considerations, EIOPA advices to leave the decision of making the appointment compulsory to each Member State, in order to avoid unjustified changes to their pension systems and increase of costs that will ultimately be pass on to members and beneficiaries. This does not however prevent the creation of a more consistent approach from a supervisory perspective in relation to the eligible institutions, the liability regime, the duties of a depositary in case it is appointed to perform oversight functions, the rules regarding conflicts of interest or incompatibility, etc.[81]

EIOPA seems, thus, to point out a 'substance over form' approach in which a consistent approach for, amongst others, eligible institutions, the liability regime and the duties of depositaries is being applied regardless of whether a Member State requires a compulsory

---

78   EIOPA studied the AIFMD and UCITSD V depositary regimes extensively in its Final Advice to the EC. *See* EIOPA-BOS-12/015, 460-461.

79   *See* Chapter 4, Sections 4.6.2 and 4.6.3.

80   EIOPA-BOS-12/015, 463.

81   *Ibid.*, 463.

appointment of depositaries in the form of 'AIFMD/UCITSD V depositaries' or 'custodians'. The substantive provisions of Article 33, 34 and 35 IORPD II, thus, apply to depositaries appointed by IORPs regardless of whether they have a compulsory obligation under the IORPD II national implementation laws of Member States to do so.

Not implementing Articles 33-35 IORPD II in national legislation by Member States that do not require a compulsory depositary is, thus, contrary to the grammatical and teleological interpretation of these provisions under IORPD II.

5.3.2 Entities Eligible as a Depositary and Its Organizational Requirements

5.3.2.1 Entities Eligible

Under Article 33(3) IORPD II, Member States may not restrict IORPs from appointing depositaries established in another Member State and duly authorized in accordance with CRD IV or MiFID II, or accepted as a depositary for the purposes of UCITSD V or the AIFMD.

5.3.2.1.1 National versus European Depositaries

The wording of Article 33(3) IORPD II suggests that Member States in their national laws under all circumstances have to allow depositaries authorized under CRD IV, MiFID II, UCITSD V and the AIFMD to be appointed by IORPs that appoint depositaries in another Member State. Article 33(3) IORPD II, however, does not explicitly prohibit individual Member States from allowing entities other than the ones listed in either of these European directives and authorized under national regulatory law to be appointed by IORPs within their domicile.

Allowing IORPs to appoint any of the above-mentioned depositaries in another Member State leads to a de facto harmonization of eligible entities under IORPD II. IORP depositaries under the national laws of the individual Member States are, likely, not able to compete with the depositaries regulated under European law that are able to exploit both vertical and horizontal economies of scale. Vertical economies of scale as they may be appointed as a depositary on a cross-border basis for all EEA IORPs and national IORP depositaries are only eligible to the extent that an individual Member State allows it. Horizontal economies of scale as the listed 'European depositaries' are not only eligible as an IORP depositary, but also as a depositary under the AIFMD and UCITS or as a custodian under the CRD IV and MiFID II. This explains why Member States had almost exclusively decided under their IORPD I implementation laws to allow for 'European depositaries', i.e. credit institutions and investment firms, to be appointed not only on a cross-border basis but also within their national domiciles itself. This is likely to be maintained by Member States under the IORPD II implementation laws.

5.3.2.1.2   The Expanding List of Heterogeneous Eligible Entities under IORPD II
The heterogeneous list of entities eligible to be appointed as an IORP depositary seems under IORPD II to be expanded in comparison to IORPD I.[82] EIOPA considered in its Final Advice that there was no need to include a more detailed list of institutions eligible under IORPD II as a depositary.[83] A regulatory update of the references to the predecessors of the MiFID II, CRD IV and UCITSD IV/V were considered to be sufficient. The final categories of eligible entities under the IORPD II have, however, been expanded by referring for both IORPD I custodians and depositaries to the term depositaries under IORPD II and including AIFMD depositaries in the eligible entities list. On top of that, the amendments of both UCITSD V and MiFID II have led to an ever bigger expansion of eligible entities to be appointed under IORPD II.

5.3.2.1.3   The Impact of 'Custodians' and 'Depositaries' Being IORPD II Depositaries
Under IORPD I, Member States could require the appointment of either a depositary or a custodian to be compulsory.[84] Article 19(2) IORPD I referred to 'custodians' established in another Member State and duly authorized in accordance with the ISD (predecessor MiFID I/II) or CRD I (predecessor CRD IV) or accepted as a 'depositary' for the purposes of the UCITSD I-IV. Taken a grammatical interpretation, Member States could, thus, restrict the eligible entities under IORPD I for custodians to investment firms under the ISD and CRD I, whereas only those entities eligible under UCITSD IV could be restricted to be eligible as depositaries under IORPD I. Article 33(3) IORPD II, however, requires Member States not to restrict IORPs from appointing depositaries *established in another Member State* and duly authorized in accordance with CRD IV or MiFID II, or accepted as depositaries for the purposes of UCITSD IV/V or the AIFMD.[85] The eligible entities under IORPD II do not depend anymore upon whether a 'custodian' or an 'AIFMD/U-CITSD V depositary' is appointed. Credit institutions and investment firms were, however, under the IORPD I Member State implementation laws in many Member States already eligible as both UCITSD I-IV depositaries and ISD custodians. De facto, the change of referring to 'depositaries' under IORPD II instead of differentiating between 'custodians' and 'depositaries' under IORPD I, thus, in practice does not affect the entities eligible under IORPD II much.

---

82 EIOPA-BOS-12/015, 450-451.
83 *See* EIOPA-BOS-12/015, 464.
84 Art. 19(2) sub-para. 2 IORPD I.
85 Art. 33(3) IORPD II.

5.3.2.2 The AIFMD Depositaries Eligible

The inclusion of AIFMD depositaries as eligible entities for IORP depositaries seems not to be well considered.[86] The AIFMD not only allows credit institutions and investment firms, but also UCITS depositaries (UCITSD IV/V), eligible non-EEA entities, prime brokers (subject to a functional and hierarchical separation of functions) and 'PE depositaries' to be appointed. De facto, the inclusion of the AIFMD depositaries, thus, only added the latter three types of eligible entities to the list as credit institutions, investment firms and UCITS depositaries were already under the other listed European directives eligible as an IORP depositary. Although formally eligible, non-EEA entities are not eligible as IORP depositaries as the entities eligible under IORPD II are restricted to 'depositaries established in another Member State'.[87] Although this has not been clarified under the IORPD II, the AIFMD provides guidance on this point. Article 21(5) AIFMD requires a depositary for EEA-AIFs to be established in the home Member State of the EEA-AIF. Following Article 4(1)(j)(iii) AIFMD, 'established' means that depositaries of EEA-AIFs should have their registered office or branch in the same country as the EEA-AIF. Non-EEA entities are, thus, excluded from being appointed as an IORP depositary. Prime brokers and 'PE depositaries' established in another Member State, however, fulfil this criterion. The utility of including both types of eligible entities under IORPD II seems to be questionable.

5.3.2.2.1 The AIFMD Prime Broker

Prime brokers are under the AIFMD credit institutions, regulated investment firms or other entities subject to prudential regulation and ongoing supervision offering 'prime brokerage services'.[88] Prime brokers are the main counterparty for substantially leveraged AIFs that have a clear overview of all AIF assets that serve as collateral for underlying obligations.[89] Allowing prime brokers to be appointed as a depositary, thus, leads to cost reductions. IORPs are, however, by means of the prudent person rule prohibited from acting as a 'substantially leveraged AIF'. Allowing a prime broker to be a depositary for IORPs seems to be of no use.

---

86 EIOPA nor the European Commission prior to the Initial Draft IORPD II considered to include IORP depositaries in the list of eligible entities; See Art. 35(3) Initial Draft IORPD II; See also EIOPA-BOS-12/015, 464.

87 Art. 33(3) IORPD II.

88 Art. 4(1)(af) AIFMD defining a prime broker defines these 'prime brokerage services' as "services to professional investors primarily to finance or execute transactions in financial instruments as counterparty and which may also provide other services such as clearing and settlement of trades, custodial services, securities lending, customised technology and operational support facilities."

89 See D.A. Zetzsche, D.A., (Prime) Brokerage (D.A Zetzsche ed, Kluwer 2015), 574-578; D.P. Delmont, Managing Hedge Fund Risk and Financing – Adapting to a New Era 7 (Wiley 2011).

5.3.2.2.2   The AIFMD 'PE Depositary'

'PE depositaries', persons or entities carrying out the AIFMD depositary functions as part of their professional or business activities are allowed to be appointed for AIFs that have no redemption rights exercisable during a period of five years from the date of their initial investments and which, according to their core investment policy, generally, do not invest in financial instruments that must be held in custody.[90] IORPs have, due to their 'occupational' nature, not any redemption rights. Their core investment policy is, however, required to be very diversified and includes liquid, illiquid, as well as (substantially) leveraged assets to fulfil their short- and long-term duty of balancing IORP funding requirements and paying out the benefits due to its beneficiaries.[91] IORPs do not fulfil the investment policy requirement under the AIFMD and may, thus, not be appointed as an IORP depositary.

5.3.2.2.3   UCITSD V Depositaries

Depositaries under the UCITSD V may, apart from being a credit institution, also be a national central bank or another legal entity that is authorized by Member States to carry on depositary activities[92] that are subject to ongoing supervision as well as minimum capital, prudential and organizational requirements.[93] Other legal entities are subjected to requirements that go beyond UCITSD IV. UCITS IV only required depositaries to be an institution that was subject to prudential and ongoing supervision and furnished sufficient financial and professional guarantees to be able to pursue its business as a depositary.[94] Member States had under UCITSD IV a lot of discretion to determine the types of eligible entities fulfilling this requirement.[95]

Prudentially regulated intermediaries that were eligible under UCITSD V still qualify as 'other legal entities' under UCITSD V if they are subject to the minimum harmonization requirements set out under UCITSD V regarding capital, prudential and organizational requirements.[96] IORP investment policies contain liquid, illiquid and (substantially) leveraged assets. Depositaries eligible under UCITSD V are suitable to perform depositary functions related to these assets and are, therefore, suitable as IORP depositary.

5.3.2.2.4   Investment Firms under MiFID II

The list of heterogeneous eligible entities has been significantly expanded by MiFID II. Under MiFID II a third country regime has been introduced that allows TC-investment

---

90 Art. 21(3)(c) sub-para. 3 AIFMD.
91 Art. 19 IORPD II.
92 Art. 23(2) UCITSD V.
93 Art. 23(2) sub-para. 1 UCITSD V.
94 Art. 23(2) UCITSD IV.
95 Art. 23(2) and (3) UCITSD V.
96 Art. 23(2) sub-para. 1 UCITSD V.

firms to provide safekeeping and the administration of financial instruments, including custodianship in the EEA by means of the establishment of a branch or on a cross-border basis.

Article 33(3) IORPD II requires Member States not to restrict IORPs from appointing, depositaries 'established in another Member State' and duly authorized in accordance with MiFID II. Unlike the AIFMD, IORPD II does not clarify what 'established in another Member State' means. Following Article 4(1)(j)(iii) AIFMD 'established' means that depositaries of EEA-AIFs should have their registered office or branch in the same country as the EEA-AIF. Article 21(3)(b) AIFMD, however, merely allows investment firms that have their registered office in the EEA to act as a depositary for EEA-AIFs.[97] Only EEA investment firms that have a branch in the same country as the EEA-AIF may, thus, act as a depositary for EEA-AIFs. IORPD II, on the contrary, does not explicitly restrict IORPs from appointing non-EEA investment firms from being appointed as a depositary provided that they are duly authorized in accordance with MiFID II and established in another Member State.[98]

Contrary to the AIFMD, TC investment firms are not subject to additional TC depositary requirements as discussed under the AIFMD. Pursuant to Article 21(6)(b) AIFMD, TC depositaries must be subject to 'effectively enforced' prudential regulation, including minimum capital requirements and 'supervision equivalent' to that applicable under EEA law. This seems to be justified as MiFID II TC investment firms are mandatorily subject to authorization and supervision in the EEA.[99] There are, thus, no additional requirements for TC investment firms necessary to determine whether these investment firms are subjected to regulation that has the same effect as those for investment firms in that third country.[100] This is already done upon authorizing a branch of a TC investment firm within the EEA.

Both EEA investment firms and TC investment firms that have a branch or are established in a Member State and are duly authorized for providing safekeeping and the administration of financial instruments are under IORPD II suitable to be appointed as a depositary.

5.3.2.2.5 Conclusion

The heterogeneous list of entities eligible to be appointed as an IORP depositary has been under IORPD II expanded in comparison to IORPD I.[101] Allowing AIFMD depositaries to be appointed have allowed prime brokers and 'PE-depositaries' to become eligible IORP depositaries. The upgrade from UCITSD IV to UCITSD V allows depositaries,

---

97 Art. 21(4)(a) AIFMD.
98 *See* Art. 33(3) IORPD II.
99 Art. 39-43 MiFID II; Recital 41-43, Arts. 46-49 MiFIR.
100 *See* for the conditions under which TC investment firms are allowed to perform depositary services under MiFIR: Art. 47 MiFIR.
101 *See* EIOPA-BOS-12/015, 451.

apart from being a credit institution, also to be a national central bank or 'another legal entity' that is authorized by Member States to carry on depositary activities[102] that are subject to minimum capital, prudential and organizational requirements.[103] Finally, the introduction of MiFID II allows both EEA investment firms and TC investment firms that have a branch in another Member State and are duly authorized for providing safe-keeping and the administration of financial instruments to be appointed as a depositary under IORPD II.

5.3.3   IORP Depositaries – General Requirements

IORPD II introduces a general duty of loyalty and a duty to prevent conflicts of interests for IORP depositaries.[104] Both are modelled after Article 21(10) AIFMD as EIOPA was of the opinion that "potential conflicts of interest or incompatibility could be an obstacle for the appropriate performance of the safekeeping and oversight duties and, therefore, should be avoided."

5.3.3.1   The Duty of Loyalty

Article 33(6) IORPD II sets out an overarching rule of conduct. It requires IORPs and depositaries to act honestly, fairly, professionally, independently and in the interest of the scheme's members and beneficiaries.[105] According to EIOPA, this is crucial for deposi-taries which do not only safekeep, but also exercise oversight duties over the investment process.[106]

5.3.3.2   Conflicts of Interest

IORPD I was both silent on the rules regarding conflicts of interests or incompatibility. EIOPA in its Final Advice was of the opinion that potential conflicts of interest or in-compatibility could be an obstacle for depositaries in performing the safekeeping and oversight duties and that this should be avoided.[107] Especially, a general conflicts of inter-est rule was considered to be very crucial for depositaries both carrying out these func-tions.[108] For this reason, IORPD II has introduced a general rule that intends to prevent conflicts of interest by requiring depositaries not to carry out activities with regard to the IORP that may create conflicts of interest between the IORP, the scheme's members,

---

102 Art. 23(2) UCITSD V.
103 Art. 23(2) sub-para. 1 UCITSD V.
104 *See* Art. 33(6) and (7) IORPD II.
105 Art. 33(6) IORPD II.
106 EIOPA-BOS-12/015, 466.
107 *Ibid.*
108 *Ibid.*, 467.

beneficiaries and itself.[109] Carrying out activities that lead to conflict of interests are, however, allowed when the depositary has functionally and hierarchically separated the performance of its depositary tasks from its other potentially conflicting tasks.[110] Moreover, potential conflicts of interest have to be properly identified, managed, monitored and disclosed to the IORP and the scheme members/beneficiaries and to the governing body of the IORP.[111]

EIOPA advised not to prevent Member States from laying down more detailed rules on conflicts of interest or incompatibility.[112] IORPD II does not indicate whether this is allowed or not. Given that a large amount of discretion is being given to Member States, introducing more detailed conflicts of interest rules, such as extending the UCITSD V independence requirements [113] to IORP depositaries, should be acceptable.[114]

Where no depositary is appointed, IORPs shall make arrangements to prevent and resolve any conflict of interest in the course of tasks otherwise performed by a depositary and an asset manager.[115] The latter refers to the situation that a Member State does not require a compulsory depositary for either tasks, but, de facto, allows an IORP governing body to either act both as an asset manager and a depositary, or appoint an investment firm that acts as both an asset manager and a depositary for a specific IORP. The MiFID II safeguarding client assets regime[116] that aims at preventing conflicts of interests between both conflicting tasks does, in general, not apply to IORPs as they are left out of the scope of the MiFID II.[117] Article 33(8) IORPD II, de facto, requires that IORPs within their risk management organization[118] or any investment firms both tasks would need to implement similar procedures as would be otherwise performed under the safeguarding client assets regime by an investment firm acting as both a depositary and an asset manager under MiFID II.

The overarching conflicts of interest rule under Article 33(8) IORPD II, where no depositary is appointed, apply, in addition to, the conflicts of interest rules that apply to IORPs where 'no depositary is appointed for the safekeeping of assets'.[119] Article 34(5)(c) IORPD II, however, specifies that it only applies in relation to the safekeeping of assets.

---

109 Art. 33(7) IORPD II.
110 Art. 33(7) IORPD II is based upon Art. 21(10) AIFMD and Art. 25(2) sub. para. 2 UCITSD V; *See* EIOPA-BOS-12/015, 466; Art. 25(2) sub-para. 2 AIFMD/UCITSD V.
111 Art. 33(7) IORPD II.
112 *See also* EIOPA-BOS-12/015, 467.
113 The independence requirements under UCITSD V, include Art. 25(2) and 26(b) (8h) UCITSD V that are further elaborated in provisions on common management/supervision (Art. 20, 21, and 24 UCITSD V (Commission) Regulation)) and on cross-shareholdings/group inclusion (Art. 22 and 23 UCITSD V (Commission) Regulation)).
114 *See* Chapter 4, Section 4.4.4.
115 Art. 33(8) IORPD II.
116 *See* Chapter 6, Section 6.4.
117 *See* Art. 16(8)-(10) MiFID II.
118 *See infra* 5.4.2.1.1.
119 Art. 34(5) IORPD II.

Article 33(8) IORPD II, thus, seeks to introduce an overarching conflicts of interest rule for IORPs where no depositary is appointed for both the safekeeping and oversight duties.

5.3.4   The IORPD II Depositary and Its Functions

IORPD II harmonizes the depositary function for DC or other types of IORPs that are by individual Member States required to be appointed for performing the safekeeping or the safekeeping and controlling function. The particulars of the written contract governing the relationship between the IORP and depositary, the safekeeping and the control function under IORPD II will now be discussed.

5.3.4.1   Particulars of the Written Depositary Contract

The appointment of the depositary by an IORP must by evidenced by a written contract.[120] Although not specified by IORPD II, the written contract has to be concluded by the depositary and the IORP. EIOPA considered the written contract to be relevant as strengthening the relationship between the depositary and the IORP would improve the protection of pension scheme members and beneficiaries.[121]

The written contract shall stipulate the transmission of the information necessary for the depositary to perform its duties as set out in IORPD II.[122] Unlike the AIFMD and UCITSD V, IORPD II does not specify the elements of the written contract nor does it include a delegation provision for the European Commission to specify any elements.[123] EIOPA, however, considered in its Final Report that Article 21(2) AIFMD for the purpose of IORPD II should be adopted.[124] EIOPA related to the fact that the written contract has a wider scope under the AIFMD and is, therefore, more appropriate for strengthening the relationship between the depositary and the IORP than the written contract under UCITSD IV.[125]

Considering this, it is likely that the elements of the written contract in the AIFMD (Commission) Regulation text will be adopted by Member States in their IORPD II implementation laws. This argument finds support in the elements of the written contract under UCITSD V that are almost the same. Furthermore, the safekeeping and oversight tasks of depositaries under IORPD II are also inspired by these two directives. Based

---

120 Art. 33(5) IORPD II.
121 EIOPA-BOS-12/015, 464.
122 Art. 33(5) IORPD II.
123 *See* for the delegation provisions under the AIFMD and UCITSD: Art. 21(17) AIFMD and Art. 26b UCITSD V.
124 EIOPA-BOS-12/015, 468.
125 *Ibid.*

upon this, it is reasonable to be expected that the required written contract regulates, amongst others:[126]

- a description of the depositary services and the particular procedures to be adopted for each type of asset in which an IORP invests;
- the flow of information ensuring that the depositary receives all information necessary to perform its safekeeping or its safekeeping and oversight function;
- details and steps taken to monitor sub-custodians;
- escalation procedures; and
- conditions related to the termination of the depositary contract.

Unlike the AIFMD and UCITSD V, however, depositaries under IORPD II are both appointed for the safekeeping of assets or for the safekeeping of assets and oversight duties.[127] The question that remains is to what extent the elements of the written contract should be adopted in depositary contracts for depositaries that are only appointed for the safekeeping of assets. MiFID II, for example, does not require custodians to enter into a written contract with either the investor or the asset manager at all.

A solution could be to require the above-mentioned element to be proportionally applied on the basis of whether a depositary is solely appointed for the safekeeping of assets or for the safekeeping of assets and oversight duties. The leading principle of the written contract is to transmit the information necessary for the depositary to perform its duties as set out in IORPD II. Of all written contract elements only the flow of information ensuring that the depositary receives all information necessary to perform its safekeeping or its safekeeping and oversight function seems relevant to be proportionally applied depending upon the type of IORP for which the depositary is appointed.

5.3.4.2 Safekeeping

IORPD II introduced the AIFMD/UCITSD V safekeeping of assets provision in the IORPD II depositary regime.[128] The European Commission took the same approach to overcome the differences that became apparent under the IORPD I Member State implementation laws and to ensure cross-sectoral consistency on the European level related to the safekeeping function. Depending on the type of assets, IORPD II distinguishes between safekeeping duties with regard to financial instruments that can be held in custody and record-keeping duties for all other assets. Financial instruments that can be held in custody are defined as all financial instruments that can be registered in a financial instruments account opened in the depositary's books or can be physically delivered to the depositary.[129]

---

126 *Ibid.*, 464, 468.
127 *See* Art. 33(1) and (2) IORPD II.
128 Art. 21(8) AIFMD and Art. 22(5) UCITSD V.
129 Art. 34(1) sub-para. 1 IORPD II; *See also* 21(8)(a)(i) AIFMD and Art. 22(5)(a)(i) UCITSD V.

For this type of assets, the depositary has the duty to ensure that these are properly registered in the depositary's books within segregated accounts at credit institutions in order to be identified at all times.[130] The depositary has a record-keeping duty applying to all other assets of an IORP pension scheme than financial instruments that can be held in custody.[131] The record-keeping duty requires IORP depositaries to verify that the IORP is the owner of such assets and to maintain a record of those assets.[132] The verification has to be carried out by the depositary on the basis of information or documents provided by the IORP and, where available, on the basis of external evidence.[133] The depositary has to ensure that its records shall be up-to-date.[134]

The extensive set of depositary safekeeping duties are under the AIFMD and UCITSD V complemented by an AIFMD and UCITSD V (Commission) Regulation that clarifies the definition of 'financial instruments to be held in custody'[135] and specifies the safekeeping duties with regard to assets held in custody[136] and safekeeping duties regarding ownership verification and record-keeping.[137]

IORPD II does not contain any similar delegation provision for the European Commission to adopt similar measures.[138] The safekeeping task is, thus, not harmonized to the same degree under IORPD II as under the AIFMD and UCITSD V. Considering that the safekeeping task has been copied from the AIFMD and UCITSD V, it is, however, likely that national Member States, Competent Authorities and legal practice will interpret the definition of financial instruments held in custody and the safekeeping duties in the same way as under the AIFMD and UCITSD V (Commission) Regulation.

5.3.4.3 Control

IORPD II introduced oversight duties for depositaries under its depositary regime to overcome the differences that became apparent under the IORPD I Member State implementation laws and to ensure cross-sectoral consistency on the European level. Full DC and other IORPs are only required to appoint a depositary for the safekeeping of assets *and* oversight duties if the national law of the home Member States requires such a depositary to be appointed.[139] Host Member States may require full DC IORPs that

---

130 Art. 34(1) sub-para. 2 IORPD II; *See also* 21(8)(a)(ii) AIFMD and Art. 22(5)(a)(ii) UCITSD V.

131 Art. 34(2) IORPD II; *See also* 21(8)(b) AIFMD and Art. 22(5)(b) UCITSD V.

132 Art. 34(2) IORPD II; *See also* 21(8)(b)(i) AIFMD and Art. 22(5)(b)(i) UCITSD V.

133 Art. 34(2) IORPD II; *See also* 21(8)(b)(ii) AIFMD and Art. 22(5)(b)(ii) UCITSD V.

134 Art. 34(2) IORPD II; *See also* 21(8)(b)(iii) AIFMD and Art. 22(5)(b)(ii) UCITSD V.

135 Art. 21(8)(a) AIFMD and Art. 22(5)(a) UCITSD V; Art. 88 AIFMD (Commission) Regulation and Art. 12 UCITSD V (Commission) Regulation.

136 Art. 21(8)(a) AIFMD and Art. 22(5)(a) UCITSD V; Art. 89 AIFMD (Commission) Regulation and Art. 13 UCITSD V (Commission) Regulation.

137 Art. 21(8)(b) AIFMD and Art. 22(5)(b) UCITSD V; Art. 90 AIFMD (Commission) Regulation and Art. 14 UCITSD V (Commission) Regulation.

138 *See* Art. 21 (17) AIFMD and Art. 26b UCITSD V.

139 Art. 33(1) and (2) IORPD II.

carries out cross-border activity to appoint a depositary for both tasks if the home Member State does not require the appointment of such a depositary under its national law.[140] Article 35(1) IORPD II requires depositaries appointed for oversight duties to carry out these duties, in addition to, the safekeeping of assets under Article 34(1) and (2) IORPD II.[141] Member States under its national laws are, thus, prohibited from solely requiring a depositary to be appointed for oversight duties.

Contrary to the safekeeping task, IORPD II has only partly based the required oversight duties on the AIFMD and UCITSD V. IORPD II distinguishes between mandatory and optional oversight duties.

IORPD II mandatorily requires depositaries appointed for oversight duties to:[142]

- carry out instructions of the IORP, unless they conflict with the applicable national law or the IORP rules;[143]
- ensure that in transactions involving an IORP or pension scheme's assets any consideration is remitted to it within the usual time limits;[144]
- ensure that income produced by assets is applied in accordance with the applicable national law and the IORP rules.[145]

These oversight duties are based upon the AIFMD and UCITSD V. The oversight duties related to subscriptions/redemptions and the valuation of units under the AIFMD and UCITSD V are not mandatorily required for IORPs.[146] These two duties were considered to be inappropriate as IORPs have an occupational nature and only supports schemes that are limited to certain employees. Under the IORPD II, no subscriptions and redemptions take place.[147] Instead, new employees may upon signing their employment contract be automatically enrolled in their scheme and receive benefits upon retirement. It could, however, be argued that some types of IORPs, such as full DC IORPs, resemble open-end AIFs/UCITS. Unsurprisingly, some Member States required (full DC) IORPs to perform oversight duties regarding subscriptions/redemptions and the valuation of units under their IORPD I implementation laws to be performed.

Notwithstanding the 'mandatory' oversight tasks under IORPD II, home Member States of IORPS may require other oversight duties to be performed by their depositaries.[148] The optional oversight duties are provided under IORPD II to accommodate the ambiguous nature of the IORP. EIOPA mentioned in its Final Advice that Member

---

140 *Ibid.*
141 Art. 35(1) IORPD II reads: "in addition to the tasks referred to in Art. 34(1) and (2), the depositary appointed for oversight duties shall."
142 Art. 35(1) IORPD II.
143 Art. 35(1)(a) IORPD II.
144 Art. 35(1)(b) IORPD II.
145 Art. 35(1)(c) IORPD II.
146 EIOPA-BOS-12/015, 468.
147 *Ibid.*
148 Art. 35 (2) IORPD II.

States should have the opportunity to introduce 'whistle-blowing duties' for depositaries.[149] According to EIOPA, depositaries having a 'whistle-blowing duty' would be required to inform Competent Authorities in case a breach of national law or IORP rules is identified.[150] Examples of other oversight duties to be adopted are to be found under the AIFMD and UCITSD V. The oversight duties regarding subscriptions/redemptions and the valuation of units for full DC IORPs could, for example, be considered by Member States for full DC IORPs.[151] Finally, a cash flow monitoring duty would be an option as this duty has been mandatory for depositaries under several IORPD I Member State implementation laws and Member States could choose to maintain their current regimes.

Member States have, thus, the option under their IORPD II implementation laws to adopt the mandatory oversight duties and maintain any other oversight duties to be performed by the depositary as an option.[152]

The extensive set of depositary oversight duties are under the AIFMD and UCITSD V complemented by an AIFMD and UCITSD V (Commission) Regulation that specifies the general requirements related to oversight duties,[153] including the carrying out of the AIFM's/UCITS' instructions,[154] the timely settlement of transactions[155] and the AIF's/UCITS' income calculation and distribution.[156] The absence of a delegation provision under IORPD II for the European Commission to adopt the same measures and the discretion for Member States to include optional oversight tasks leads to less harmonization of the oversight duties as compared to the AIFMD and UCITSD V. This is enhanced by the likelihood of less Member States requiring oversight tasks for depositaries under Article 35 IORPD II as compared to merely the safekeeping task under Article 34 IORPD II.

Similar as for the safekeeping task, the mandatory oversight duties have been copied from the AIFMD and UCITSD V and, therefore, it is likely that national Member States, Competent Authorities and legal practice interpret these duties in the same way. The same might hold true for optional oversight duties regarding subscriptions/redemptions and the duties regarding the valuation of units that might be imposed upon depositaries by Member States. For other optional oversight duties no interpretation is available on

---

149 EIOPA-BOS-12/015, 466.
150 *Ibid.*
151 *See, e.g.* Art. 21(9)(a) and (b) AIFMD and Art. 23(a) and (b) UCITSD V.
152 Art. 35(2) IORPD II.
153 Art. 21(9) AIFMD and Art. 22(3) UCITSD V; Art. 92 AIFMD (Commission) Regulation and Art. 3 UCITSD V (Commission) Regulation.
154 Art. 21(9)(c) AIFMD and Art. 22(3)(c) UCITSD V; Art. 95 AIFMD (Commission) Regulation and Art. 6 UCITSD V (Commission) Regulation.
155 Art. 21(9)(d) AIFMD and Art. 22(3)(d) UCITSD V; Art. 96 AIFMD (Commission) Regulation and Art. 7 UCITSD V (Commission) Regulation.
156 Art. 21(9)(e) AIFMD and Art. 22(3)(e) UCITSD V; Art. 97 AIFMD (Commission) Regulation and Art. 8 UCITSD V (Commission) Regulation; M. van der Westen, *Survey: More than 83% of Dutch pension assets Under Fiduciary Management*, IPE 3 January 2014, www.ipe.com/survey-more-than-83-of-dutch-pension-assets-under-fiduciary-management/10000711.fullarticle.

the European level. The interpretation of comparable optional duties are for these duties likely to vary from Member State to Member State.

5.3.5   Delegation in the Depositary Chain

Article 34(4) IORPD II requires Member States to ensure that a depositary's liability shall not be affected by the fact that it has entrusted to a third party all or some of the assets in its safekeeping. The depositary liability regime introduced under IORPD II has been taken from the general and very broad UCITSD I-IV depositary delegation provisions. The UCITSD I-IV depositary delegation/liability regime received after the Madoff affair a lot of criticism and was, consequently, being replaced by a very detailed depositary delegation regime under the AIFMD and UCITSD V.[157]

Similar to UCITSD I-IV, IORPD I did not provide any rules in relation to the delegation of functions by IORP depositaries either. Quite some Member States did not impose any conditions on the delegation of the depositary.[158] The regulatory landscape of the Member States that unilaterally adopted an IORP depositary delegation regime was fragmented. Some of the Member States that imposed conditions restricted the use of delegation to certain depositaries, whereas others imposed various conditions that needed to be fulfilled before depositaries were allowed to delegate tasks.[159]

IORPD II is, however, unlikely to significantly change the approach of Member States taken under IORPD I. The experience with UCITSD I-IV has shown that the introduction of the UCITSD IV regime under IORPD II may lead to a similar variety of depositary delegation regimes under Member State laws. IORPD II only requires those Member States that did not provide for any depositary delegation regime to introduce in their national legislation that

> a depositary's liability shall not be affected by the fact that it has entrusted to a third party all or some of the assets in its safekeeping.

IORPD II, thus, requires depositaries not to be able to absolve themselves of their responsibilities by delegating to sub-custodians all or some of the assets in its safekeeping.[160] Article 34(4) IORPD II, however, does not clarify the duties that are allowed to be delegated and the conditions under which depositaries may delegate their duties. Article 34 (4) IORPD II only refers to the delegation of safekeeping duties. Under UCITSD I-IV, Member States had implemented this provision in various ways. Some Member States

---

157 Art. 21(11) AIFMD and Art. 22(a) UCITSD V; Art. 98, 99 AIFMD (Commission) Regulation and Art. 15, 16 UCITSD (Commission) Regulation on due diligence and the segregation obligation.
158 *See also* CEIOPS-OP-03-08 final, 12-13, 56-58.
159 *Ibid.*
160 *See also* EIOPA-BOS-12/015, 464.

allowed other duties than safekeeping, such as oversight duties, to be delegated, whereas other Member States prohibited the delegation of all duties other than safekeeping.[161] In between these extreme examples, the approaches differed from Member State to Member State.[162] On the contrary, the AIFMD and UCITSD V introduced detailed conditions in their depositary delegation regimes, on the basis of which safekeeping duties can be entrusted to a delegate. Safekeeping and all other depositary duties, except oversight duties (including cash management),[163] are allowed to be delegated. A depositary may, however, only delegate the safekeeping tasks to sub-custodians that are subject to equivalent levels of regulation and supervision.[164] In the aftermath of the Madoff affair, this regime would have been more suitable for IORPD II depositaries.

Adopting the UCITSD I-IV depositary regime in IORPD II is unlikely to significantly change the approach of Member States taken under IORPD I. Member States will, as was the case under UCITSD IV, continue to impose depositaries to a large variety of delegation provisions in their IORPD II implementation laws.

5.3.6   The Depositary Liability Regime

Article 34(3) IORPD II requires Member States to ensure that a depositary is liable to the IORP or the members and beneficiaries for any loss suffered by them as a result of its unjustifiable failure to perform its obligations or its improper performance of them. Similar as for the delegation of depositary tasks, Article 34(3) IORPD II introduces the UCITSD I-IV liability regime for IORPD II depositaries. IORPD I did not contain any depositary liability regime and the different approaches taken by Member States in their national IORPD I implementations were similar as for UCITS under UCITSD I-IV. The UCITSD I-IV depositary liability regime received after the Madoff case even more criticism than the UCITSD I-IV delegation regime. Similarly, the UCITSD IV regime was being replaced by a very detailed depositary liability regime under the AIFMD and UCITSD V.[165] Nevertheless, the UCITSD I-IV liability regime was introduced in IORPD II after EIOPA in its advice set out that the liability regime under the AIFMD was too burdensome.[166] The introduction of this depositary liability regime is, however, likely to be implemented in Member States in the same way as was the case under UCITSD I-IV.

---

161 European Commission, *supra* note 47, 8.

162 S.N. Hooghiemstra, De AIFM-richtlijn en de aansprakelijkheid van de bewaarder, 6 TvFR 178 (2013).

163 IORPD II does not contain a mandatory duty related to cash management. *See* Art. 35 IORPD II.

164 *See* CESR/09-781, 7; *See* S.N. Hooghiemstra, *Depositary Regulation* 511-518 (D.A. Zetzsche ed, Kluwer 2015).

165 Art. 21(12) AIFMD and Art. 24 UCITSD V; Art. 100 AIFMD (Commission) Regulation and Art. 18 UCITSD V (Commission) Regulation related to a loss of a financial instrument held in custody; Art. 101 and 102 AIFMD (Commission) Regulation related to a liability discharge and objective reasons for the depositary to contract a discharge of liability.

166 EIOPA-BOS-12/015, 468.

The preparatory works leading to the AIFMD and UCITSD V have proven that the UCITSD I-IV liability regime had resulted in different approaches taken by Member States regarding:[167]
- the interpretation of what is considered to be 'improper performance';
- who should be liable for any loss of assets?;
- the scope of depositary liability (when assets are lost by a sub-custodian);
- the burden of proof; and
- the rights of the IORP, members and beneficiaries against the IORP depositary.

The introduction of the UCITSD I-IV liability regime in IORPD II may lead to some Member States applying a 'strict' liability regime, whereas others would consider a loss of assets not necessarily to be 'unjustifiable'.[168] IORPD II is, thus, unlikely to significantly change the approach of Member States taken under IORPD I.

5.4 'EQUIVALENT PROTECTION' FOR IORPs WITHOUT A DEPOSITARY APPOINTED

IORPD II introduces minimum requirements for the internal organization for IORPs that either do not appoint a depositary at all or appoint only for the safekeeping of assets. In its Final Advice, EIOPA considered that many IORPs do not have a depositary and that in those Member States a similar level of protection to members and beneficiaries are in place that offers a sufficient level of protection.[169] In particular, EIOPA was of the opinion that requiring the compulsory requirement for the appointment of a depositary would not fit in all Member States and could lead to an increase in costs.[170] For this purpose, the IORPD II has introduced 'equivalent protection' rules for IORPs that are not required to appoint a depositary for full DC IORPs and other types of IORPs.

The laws of the IORP home Member State has to provide for protection for safekeeping assets *and* oversight duties equivalent to the IORPD II depositary regime.[171] This duty applies to Member States regardless of whether they do not require a depositary to be appointed at all or a depositary is only required to be appointed for performing the safekeeping of assets.[172] Essential for Member States is to clarify whether and to what extent their implementation laws provide for equivalent protection for the safekeeping of assets *and* oversight duties under Article 34(5) and Article 35(3) IORPD II.

---

167 Derived from: CESR/09-781, 12-15.
168 *See* on the UCITSD V: CESR/09-781, 14; *See also* EIOPA-BOS-12/015, 453-454.
169 *See also* EIOPA-BOS-12/015, 463.
170 *Ibid.*, 460.
171 *See* Arts. 34(5) and 35(3) IORPD II.
172 *See* Arts. 33(1), 34 and 35 IORPD II.

5.4.1   IORPs without a Depositary Appointed for Safekeeping

Member States under their national IORPD II implementation laws have to provide for equivalent protection for the safekeeping of assets 'where no depositary is appointed for the safekeeping of assets'.[173]

Member States that under Article 33(1) and (2) IORPD II require one or more depositaries to be appointed for the safekeeping function (and oversight function) that comply with the IORPD II depositary safekeeping requirements under Article 34(1)-(4) IORPD II are exempted from applying these requirements.

Article 34(5) IORPD II indicates what is considered to be equivalent protection provided by the IORPD II implementation laws of Member States for exercising the IORPD II safekeeping duties. The provision has as its objective to ensure that appropriate procedures/controls are in place for cases where there is no appointment of a depositary in relation to the risk of a loss of assets or rights related to those assets as a result of fraud, inadequate record-keeping and other operational risks within the IORP.[174] When no depositary is appointed for the safekeeping of assets, IORPs are, at least, required to:[175]

- ensure that financial instruments are subject to due care and protection;
- keep records to identify all IORP assets at all times and without delay;
- take the necessary measures to avoid conflicts of interest in relation to the safekeeping of assets;
- inform the Competent Authorities, upon request, about the manner in which assets are kept.

5.4.1.1   Financial Instruments Subject to Due Care and Protection

The OECD Guidelines for pension fund governance allows the custody of the IORP assets to be carried out by the pension entity (self-custody IORP), the financial institution that manages the pension fund or by an independent custodian (both third party custody).[176] Article 34(5) IORPD II implements this rule.

5.4.1.1.1   Third Party Custody

The OECD Guidelines for pension fund governance allows third party custody to be carried out either by the financial institution that manages the pension fund or by an independent custodian.[177]

IORPD II allows a 'financial institution managing the pension fund' to act as a third party custodian. A financial institution managing the pension fund may in the IORP

---

173 Art. 34(5) IORPD II.
174 *See also* EIOPA-BOS-12/015, 465.
175 Art. 34(5) IORPD II.
176 OECD, *supra* note 72.
177 *Ibid.*

context be either an external IORP governing board for contractual IORPs or an external asset manager to which the governing board has fully or partly delegated asset management. Considering the conflicts of interest requirement discussed below, such a financial institution would need to be an investment firm, credit institution subjected to the safeguarding of client assets regime under MiFID II or an equivalent financial institution regulated on the national level that is subject to this or an equivalent safeguarding of client assets regime.[178]

A compulsory requirement for the appointment of an independent custodian, other than the IORP or 'the financial company managing the IORP' is an effective way to safeguard the physical and legal integrity of the IORP assets.[179] In addition, independent custodians may provide additional services, such as securities lending, cash management, investment accounting, reporting and performance measurement. The latter is a huge advantage of an independent custodian in comparison to IORP performing self-custody.[180] Member States in various ways already require financial instruments that are allowed to be held by third parties to be subject to due care and protection by means of requiring an authorization for operating as an independent custodian.[181] At the European level, credit institutions and investment firms authorized for the ancillary service to operate as a custodian under MiFID II may be required to be appointed by Member States to fulfil this requirement. Similarly, the appointment of custodians regulated under national law that are required to fulfil similar conduct of business, prudential requirements and have access to a CSD may be deemed to 'ensure that financial instruments are subject to due care and protection' as well. Examples of this type of national custodians are to be found in Austria,[182] Germany[183] and Liechtenstein[184] where all custodians are required to be credit institutions. Apart from this, national custodians in Ireland,[185] Lux-

---

178 *See, for instance,* the UK: Section 19, Schedule 2 Part I Clause (5)(1) FSMA 2000.The Financial Conduct Authority (FCA) has adopted rules on client assets (CASS).; *See* for Ireland: Central Bank of Ireland, Guidance on Client Asset Regulations For Investment Firms, March 2015.

179 *See* OECD, *supra* note 72.

180 *Ibid.*

181 According to the European Commission, a custodian is "an entity entrusted with the safekeeping and administration of securities and other financial assets on behalf of others, and may moreover provide additional services, including clearing and settlement, cash management, foreign exchange and securities lending." *See* European Commission, *supra* note 47, 14.

182 § 1(1) n. 5 BWG.

183 § 1(1) sub-para. 2 n. 5. KWG; BaFin, *Merkblatt Depotgeschäft – Hinweise zum Tatbestand des Depotgeschäfts*, 6 January 2009 (Stand: February 2014).

184 Art. 3(1) and (2) (c) BankG.

185 *See* Section 2(1) 'investment business firm' and Section (2) 'investment business services' (*h*) custodial operations involving the safekeeping and administration of investment instruments; Part IV and Part VII Investment Intermediaries Act 1995; *See also* Central Bank of Ireland, *Guidance Note on Completing and Submitting an Application for Authorisation Under Section 10 of the Investment Intermediaries Act,1995 (as amended) excluding Restricted Activity Investment Product Intermediaries*, January 2012.

embourg[186] and the UK[187] that are required to fulfil similar criteria as credit institutions and investment firms under MiFID II should be deemed to be eligible as well.

5.4.1.1.2   Self-Custody

Some Member States, such as Germany, allow certain assets to be kept in a safe inside the resident building of the IORP (this is, e.g. common practice for registered bonds, so-called 'Namenspapiere' in Germany, or German mortgage loans).[188] To fulfil the criterion that financial instruments are subject to due care and protection, Member States might require that these safes are complying with certain security criteria. This ensures that the practice of keeping certain kinds of assets in self-custody that would otherwise lead to unnecessary additional costs for IORPs can be continued.[189]

5.4.1.1.3   Record-Keeping IORP Assets

In the absence of a depositary, IORPs are explicitly required to provide a comprehensive and up-to-date inventory at any time of all assets safe-kept.[190]

5.4.1.1.4   Measures to Avoid Conflicts of Interest

Depositaries and third party custodians appointed are all subjected to conflicts of interest rules as part of their authorization.[191] The same measures to avoid conflicts of interest in relation to self-custody are not in place. For that purpose, the Member State IORP implementation laws have to ensure that, for instance, people administering the IORP do not have sole and uncontrolled access to the safes where assets are held in self-custody.[192]

5.4.1.1.5   Notification Competent Authorities

Competent Authorities are to be informed, upon request, about whether and to what extent assets are being safe-kept by means of self-custody or a third party custodian. This requirement enables Competent Authorities to check whether IORPs comply with the rules catering for the security of the self-custody of assets.

---

186 Art. 26 Law of 5 April 1993 on the financial sector on 'Professional depositaries of financial instruments'.

187 The UK Financial Services and Markets Act 2000 (FSMA 2000) classifies the "safeguarding and administering assets belonging to another which consist of or include investments" as a regulated activity. *See* Section 19, Schedule 2 Part I Clause (5)(1) FSMA 2000.

188 Pensions Europe, *Position Paper on the proposal for an IORP II Directive*, 6 October 2014, 19, 20, www.pensionseurope.eu/system/files/PensionsEurope%20position%20paper%20IORP%20II.pdf.

189 *Ibid.*, 19.

190 *See also* EIOPA-BOS-12/015, 465.

191 *See* for custodians under MiFID II: Chapter 6, section 4; *See* for AIF/UCITS depositaries: Chapter 4, Section 4.2.

192 Pensions Europe, *Position Paper on the proposal for an IORP II Directive*, 6 October 2014, p. 20; EIOPA-BOS-12/015, 467.

5.4.1.2   'Equivalency Protection' Criticism

The 'equivalency provision' under Article 34(5) IORPD II indicating what is considered to be equivalent protection provided by the implementation laws of Member States for exercising the IORPD II depositary regime safekeeping duty is remarkable. EIOPA and the OECD have clearly indicated the advantages of having an independent depositary for the safekeeping of assets to be appointed. EIOPA sees, the following advantages of requiring *at least* a (single) depositary to be appointed for the purpose of the safekeeping of IORP assets:[193]

-   depositaries can provide at any time a comprehensive and up-to-date overview of all assets held under its safekeeping;
-   information of safe-kept assets is centralized;
-   risk of fraud and other operational risks of an IORP are reduced;
-   depositaries can play a whistleblowing role in alerting an IORP to a material risk identified in a specific market settlement system;
-   depositaries may make it easier for the supervisory authorities to limit or prohibit the free disposal of assets.

In addition, the OECD sees the appointment of an independent depositary for the safekeeping of assets as an effective way to safeguard the physical and legal integrity of the assets of an IORP.[194] Custodians do not only hold the IORP assets and ensure their safekeeping, but also provide additional services, such as securities lending, cash management, investment accounting, reporting and performance measurement.[195] It is, thus, highly questionable whether allowing the custody of IORP assets to be carried out by the IORP itself can be considered to be an equivalent way of safeguarding the physical and legal integrity of IORP assets.

5.4.2   *IORPs without a Depositary Appointed for Oversight Duties*

Member States may under Article 33(1) and (2) IORPD II require IORPs to appoint one or more depositaries for the safekeeping *and* oversight function that comply with the IORPD II depositary oversight duties.[196] IORPs for which no depositary is appointed for oversight duties are under Article 35(3) IORPD II required to implement procedures that ensure that the tasks, otherwise subject to oversight by depositaries, are being duly performed within the institution.

---

193 *See also* EIOPA-BOS-12/015, 465.
194 OECD, *supra* note 72.
195 *Ibid.*
196 Arts. 35(1) and (2) IORPD II.

5.4.2.1 Oversight Duties Duly Performed within the IORP

Article 35(3) IORPD II does not clarify what 'implementing procedures to perform oversight tasks within the IORP' means. This could be interpreted twofold. First, this could mean that the internal risk management organization of the governing body of the IORP[197] would have to implement procedures to ensure the tasks otherwise subject to oversight by depositaries are being duly performed within the institution. Second, Article 35(3) IORPD II could imply that the board of directors, trustees or the independent oversight committees of the legal form in which the IORP is established would be suitable to perform these oversight tasks. These options will both have to be reviewed in order to assess how Member States could comply with Article 35(3) IORPD II.

5.4.2.1.1 Risk Management Organization within the IORP Governing Body

Taken a grammatical interpretation, 'procedures for oversight duties duly performed within the IORP' would indicate that the risk management organization of the IORP governing board would need to implement procedures for oversight functions otherwise performed by depositaries. This interpretation seems to be unlikely intended by IORPD II as operational/internal control is already mandatorily performed by the compliance, internal audit and risk management function required under the IORPD II for all governing bodies of IORPs, regardless of the legal form employed.[198]

This view seems to be confirmed by EIOPA in its Final Report. EIOPA is of the view that depositaries can play an important oversight role.[199] EIOPA, however, stresses in its report that the appointment of a depositary with oversight duties is not aimed to duplicate any task. In particular, no task is aimed to be duplicated related to operational/internal control already performed by the IORP itself. Instead, the depositary would act as an additional external and independent control mechanism. Taken this into consideration, Article 35(3) IORPD II likely requires the trustees, board of directors or independent oversight committees of the legal form in which IORPs are established to implement procedures to ensure that the tasks otherwise subject to oversight by depositaries are being duly performed within the institution.

5.4.2.1.2 Trustees, Board of Directors and Independent Oversight Committees

The question remains whether and to what extent trustees, board of directors and independent oversight committees could be considered by Member States to comply with the requirements laid down in Article 35(3) IORPD II.[200]

---

197 Governing body is being referred to as "management or supervisory body of the IORP that has the ultimate responsibility under national law for compliance." *See* Art. 21(1) IORPD II.
198 Art. 24-26 IORPD II.
199 EIOPA-BOS-12/015, 465, 469.
200 Art. 35(3) IORPD II.

EIOPA considered that the compulsory appointment of a depositary is already seen as a widespread risk mitigation mechanism among Member States for pure DC IORPs.[201] For that purpose, EIOPA proposed to make a depositary compulsory for these full DC IORPs, regardless of the legal form employed by the IORP. EIOPA, however, stated that it should be taken into account that in some Member States additional requirements may be in place to ensure that the activities of the IORP are being properly monitored. In this regard, EIOPA mentioned the example of a trust-based system, employed in Ireland and the UK, in which trustees are required to perform an oversight function and that, therefore, appointing a depositary with oversight duties would lead to a duplication of role/cost without extra benefits in terms of member/beneficiary protection.

EIOPA in its IORPD II consultation considered whether IORPD II should comprise of different depositary regimes depending upon the legal form of the IORP.[202] More specifically, EIOPA asked respondents in its consultation to consider the compulsory appointment of a depositary for trust- and contractual-based IORPs and leave the appointment to the discretion of the individual Member States for IORPs with legal personality. EIOPA ultimately came to the conclusion that a legal form dependent depositary regime should not be considered as this would lead to minimum harmonization because the majority of Member States have IORPs with legal personality.[203] This is the reason why the appointment of a depositary was being left to the discretion of the individual Member States for all types of IORPs regardless of the legal form in which the IORP is established.

Article 35(3) IORPD II is, thus, clearly inspired by the legal form based approach that EIOPA pursued in its consultations. The fact that EIOPA explicitly mentioned trust-based systems as an example[204] and referred to alternative mechanisms being in place for the performance of oversight duties implies that trustees, board of directors and independent oversight committees within the legal form of the respective IORPs are considered by EIOPA to be providing 'equivalent protection'. The question that remains to be answered is to what extent trustees, board of directors and independent oversight committees could be considered by Member States to fulfil the criterion of duly performing within the IORP 'oversight duties that are otherwise subject to oversight by depositaries'.[205]

---

201 EIOPA-BOS-12/015, 462.
202 *Ibid.*
203 *Ibid.*, 463.
204 *Ibid.*, 462.
205 Spain: Art. 13 Real Decreto Legislativo 1/2002, de 29 de noviembre, por el que se aprueba el texto refundido de la Ley de Regulacila de los Planes y Fondos de Pensiones; Portugal: Art. 53 Decreto-Lei n.o 12/2006 de 20 de Janeiro.

5.4.2.2   Equivalent Protection for Oversight Duties?

Member States seem not necessarily to have a consistent practice in requiring a compulsory depositary to be employed for IORPs with a specific legal form. However, it remains unclear whether Member States have the discretion to require the appointment of trustees, separate oversight committees or board of directors under the legal form of an IORP in their national laws as to fulfil the criteria

> "tasks, otherwise subject to oversight by depositaries" that are "duly performed within the IORP".

The wording 'duly performed within the IORP' is not clarified in IORPD II and spreads confusion in this regard. A grammatical interpretation would exclude a trustee for trust-based and a separate oversight committee for contractual IORPs from performing 'tasks, otherwise subject to oversight by depositaries'. Both can be considered to be an external and independent control mechanism but are not 'duly performed within the IORP'. If both would be seen as providing 'equivalent protection' as a board of directors for IORPs with legal personality, it would have been better to replace 'duly performed within the IORP' by 'equivalent protection for the performance of oversight duties'.[206] The large room for discretion under wording of Article 33(1) and (2) IORPD II leaves it up to individual Member States to decide whether or not the roles played by trustees, separate oversight committees, as well as a board of directors under the legal form of an IORP in their national laws are being regarded as providing for 'tasks, otherwise subject to oversight by depositaries' that are 'duly performed within the IORP'.

5.4.2.3   Tasks Subject to Oversight by Depositaries

Where no depositary is appointed for oversight duties, the board of directors, trustees or separate oversight committees have to implement procedures to ensure that the tasks are being duly performed within the IORP. Article 35(3) IORPD II refers for this to tasks that are 'otherwise subject to oversight by depositaries'. These oversight duties involve the mandatory oversight duties as laid down in Article 35(1) IORPD II and other oversight duties otherwise to be performed by the depositary that individual Member States may optionally establish.[207]

---

206 'Equivalent protection' was being referred to under Art. 35(1) Proposal for a Directive of the European Parliament and of the Council on the activities and supervision of institutions for occupational retirement provision (recast), /* COM/2014/0167 final – 2014/0091 (COD) */ (version February 2016).
207 Art. 35(1) and (2) IORPD II.

5.5   CONCLUSION

Prior to IORPD II, Member States enjoyed discretion as to whether to require the appointment of a 'depositary' or 'custodian'. Similar as under UCITSD I-IV, this led to considerable differences across Member States in relation to whether or not a depositary or custodian being appointed, was of the type of entities that can fulfil this role and the duties the depositary/custodian was required to perform.[208] The divergent practices caused legal uncertainty and different levels of investor protection.[209]

Despite considerable joint efforts of EIOPA and the European Commission, the IORPD II depositary framework is not likely to lead to the same degree of harmonization as for UCITS and AIF depositaries. IORPD II leaves the decision of making the appointment of a 'depositary' or 'custodian' compulsory for both full DC and other IORPs to each individual Member State to avoid unjustified changes to their pension system.[210] IORPD II only requires the compulsory appointment for full DC IORPs if an IORP carries out cross-border activity and the appointment of one or more depositaries for safekeeping and oversight duties is compulsory under the national laws of a host Member State and not compulsory under the law of the home Member State.

The IORPD II 'substantive depositary regime', nevertheless, seems to have established a more consistent approach with regard to, amongst others, eligible institutions, its organizational requirements, the safekeeping and oversight duties rules of IORP depositaries. Although there is lack of clarity in the implementation process on several counts, the IORPD II 'substantive depositary regime' seems to be applicable to all 'depositaries' and 'custodians' that are appointed by IORPS regardless of whether Member States require a compulsory appointment of 'depositaries' and 'custodians'. Compared to UCITS and AIF depositaries, the IORPD II depositary regime is not as much harmonized. IORPs that do not appoint 'depositaries' or 'custodians' may, for instance, use 'alternative mechanisms' for the safekeeping of IORP assets and the exercise of oversight duties under IORPD II. These provisions seek to ensure 'equivalent' investor protection. It is questionable, however, whether the conditions set out in IORPD II will achieve this objective.[211] In addition, the 're-introduction' of the former non-harmonized UCITSD I-IV delegation and liability regime for IORPs under IORPD II will not bring any harmonization compared to the depositary regimes of Member States under IORPD I.

Finally, the level 2 measures applicable to depositaries under the AIFMD and UCITSD V are not being extended to IORP depositaries. Whether or not the same interpretation will be followed under IORPD II for the provisions copied from the AIFMD and UCITSD V, such as the safekeeping and oversight duties, will be completely left over

---

208 EIOPA-BOS-12/015, 451.
209 *Ibid.*, 460.
210 *Ibid.*, 463.
211 *Ibid.*, 464.

to the individual Member States. The non-harmonization of the appointment of 'depositaries' and 'custodians', the 'alternative mechanisms' ensuring 'equivalent protection' for IORPs without a 'depositary' appointed and the UCITSD I-IV delegation and liability regime for IORPs under IORP D II leaves, thus, the considerable differences in investor protection amongst Member States under IORPD I to be unresolved. Only a fully harmonized approach under future amendments of IORPD II that addresses these issues would likely change this.

6 THE CRD IV, MIFID II AND THE CSDR 'CUSTODIAN REGIME'

6.1 INTRODUCTION

No definition is found in European law of what is a 'custodian'.[1] The European Commission in a Commission Communication reviewing possible developments on the regulation of UCITS depositaries defined custodians as

> an entity entrusted with the safekeeping and administration of securities and other financial assets on behalf of others, and may moreover provide additional services, including clearing and settlement, cash management, foreign exchange and securities lending.

Although not directly targeted, CRD IV and MiFID II regulate credit institutions and investment firms that provide the service of 'safekeeping and administration of securities/financial instruments' as an ancillary service.[2] The 'ancillary service' nature under CRD IV and MiFID implies that credit institutions and investment firms are only regulated for providing 'custodianship' if they are authorized for 'core services' that are for credit institutions' deposit-taking[3] and investment firms' investment services/activities.[4] Similarly to depositaries under the UCITSD V, AIFMD and IORPD II, this leaves a 'regulatory gap'[5] for Member States to regulate their own national custodians. Furthermore, 'investor CSDs' under the CSDR are allowed to maintain securities accounts in relation to the settlement service, collateral management and other ancillary services.[6] Investor CSDs are, thus, performing similar services as investment firms and credit institutions acting as custodians. Nevertheless, MiFID II explicitly excludes CSDs from its scope.

The question to be answered in this chapter is what custodians are and whether and to what extent custodians are regulated in the EEA. By reviewing credit institutions, investment firms, 'investor CSDs' and the MiFID II client asset requirements, this chapter seeks to answer this and to highlight to what extent custodians differ from depositaries under the AIFMD, UCITSD V and IORPD II.

---

1   European Commission, *Communication from the Commission to the Council and to the European Parliament – Regulation of UCITS Depositaries in the Member States: Review and Possible Developments*, 30 March 2004, COM(2004) 207 final, 7, 14, 26.
2   Annex I n. 12 CRD IV.
3   Arts. 8, 9 CRD IV.
4   Annex I s. A MiFID II.
5   Legal Certainty Group, *Second Advice of the Legal Certainty Group – Solutions to Legal Barriers Related to Post-Trading within the EU*, August 2008, 46.
6   Annex – List of Services, S. B, n. 4 CSDR.

6.2 THE 'CUSTODIAN' UNDER CRD IV AND MiFID II

Credit institutions and investment firms acting as 'custodians' are under CRD IV and MiFID II indirectly regulated. This section seeks to answer what 'custodianship' under both legislative acts is, to what extent the definition of the ancillary services allowed to be performed under both acts differ and to what extent national Member States may diverge from the European standards.

6.2.1 *'Safekeeping and Administration Services' as an 'Ancillary Service'*

6.2.1.1 Credit Institutions under CRD IV

CRD IV[7] contains an authorization obligation and requirements for credit institutions. Pursuant to the CRD IV, a 'credit institution' is an undertaking, the business of which is to take deposits or other repayable funds from the public and to grant credits for its own account.[8]

Credit institutions must obtain an authorization before conducting business. Credit institutions may, in addition to deposit-taking and lending, engage in any of the activities of Annex I CRD IV within the EEA on a cross-border basis (European passport).[9] The most relevant activity regarding the exercise of depositary functions is listed under Number 12 (safekeeping and administration of securities).[10] In addition to this list, credit institutions may provide the investment services/activities and ancillary services under Annex I MiFID II,[11] in particular the

> safekeeping and administration of financial instruments for the account of clients, including custodianship and related services such as cash/collateral management and excluding maintaining securities accounts at the top tier level.[12]

Unlike investment firms, credit institutions are authorized under the CRD IV and do not need to obtain authorization under MiFID II in order to provide safekeeping and admin-

---

7 Arts. 8, 9 CRD IV.

8 Art. 3(1) n. 1 CRD IV/Art. 4(1) n. 1 CRR.

9 Arts. 8, 9 CRD IV grants each Member State the option to decide for itself whether one or more of the activities listed in Annex I are regulated businesses requiring authorization, with the exception of Number 1 of Annex I (acceptance of deposits and other repayable funds), which may only be conducted by authorized credit institutions. In this regard, it should, however, be noted that such credit institutions being authorized on a 'private placement' basis do not benefit from the European passport as discussed below. *See also* Art. 33, 34 CRD IV.

10 Annex I n. 12 CRD IV.

11 *See* for the investment services/activities and the ancillary services which credit institutions are able to provide: Annex I s. A and B MiFID II.

12 This ancillary service includes custodianship and related services, such as cash/collateral management and excludes maintaining securities accounts at the top tier level. *See* Annex I s. B MiFID II.

istration of securities. Credit institutions that, in addition, provide any of the MiFID II investment services/activities and ancillary services are, however, required to comply with certain MiFID II provisions, such as the general organizational requirements, operational conditions (conduct of business rules), safeguarding of client financial instruments and funds.[13] Like investment firms, credit institutions are required under MiFID II to be members of authorized investor compensation schemes.[14]

6.2.1.2   Investment Firm under MiFID II

Under MiFID II, the provision of investment services or activities, with or without ancillary services, requires authorization. Authorization must be granted by Competent Authority. Before authorization may be granted, an investment firm must fulfil a number of conditions. *Inter alia*, the investment firm has to be a member of an authorized investor compensation scheme.[15]

The safekeeping and administration of financial instruments for the account of clients is an ancillary service under Section B Annex I MiFID II. This implies that the safekeeping and administration of financial instruments for the account of clients is not an investment service or activity and can only be provided by credit institutions and investment firms in connection with investment services and activities, such as, amongst others, portfolio management and investment advice.[16]

Under the original MiFID II proposal, the safekeeping and administration of financial instruments for the account of clients was proposed to be upgraded to a full-fledged investment service.[17] Following this proposal, any firm providing the service of safekeeping and administration of financial instruments for the account of clients would have been on a stand-alone basis subject to a separate authorization duty.[18] This would have implied that under MiFID II, compared to MiFID I, not every investment firm,[19] but merely those entities with an authorization for safekeeping, would have been eligible as a custodian. This proposal was, however, not adopted in the final version of MiFID II. Under MiFID II the safekeeping and administration of financial instruments for the account of clients, thus, remained to be an ancillary service. Member States are, however, free to specify the types of entities that can be authorized for purely providing safekeeping/custodian services within their domiciles.[20] The non-harmonization in this area will, thus, also in the future remain to raise a number of questions as to whether the European

---

13 *See* Recital 38, Art. 1(3) MiFID II.
14 Art. 14 MiFID II.
15 *Ibid.*
16 Annex I s. A MiFID II.
17 *See* Annex 1 s. A MiFID II proposal.
18 *Ibid.*
19 Generally speaking, the MiFID custody rules apply to all 'MiFID investment firms', such as brokers, dealers, asset managers and advisers. *See* D. Frase, *Custody* 276 (D. Frase ed., Sweet & Maxwell 2011).
20 Legal Certainty Group, *supra* note 5, 25 and 32.

legal framework for custodians needed to be further harmonized and strengthened to ensure a level playing field in terms of investor protection measures across all Member States.[21]

6.2.2 The MiFID II versus CRD IV Definition of 'Safekeeping and Administration Services'

The MiFID II and CRD IV definition of 'safekeeping and administration services' differs in various respects. MiFID II relates to 'financial instruments' being defined under Section C Annex I MiFID II, whereas the CRD IV refers to 'securities' that has not been further elaborated. In addition, the MiFID II definition includes the wording 'for the account of clients' and 'custodianship and related services such as cash/collateral management'.[22] Finally, the MiFID II version, in comparison to MiFID I, has clarified that this ancillary service excludes 'maintaining securities accounts at the top tier level'.[23] The meaning of both definitions have not been further defined on the European level. Given the fact that CRD IV has been adopted in 2013 and MiFID II in 2014, the narrow definition of 'safekeeping and administration of securities' under CRD IV has to be interpreted dynamically in the light of MiFID II. A dynamic interpretation holds water as the original purpose of the introduction of the ISD, the predecessor of MiFID II, was to provide a level playing field in terms of investor protection for banking and investment services provided to clients.[24]

6.2.2.1 The Safekeeping and Administration of Financial Instruments for the Account of Clients

6.2.2.1.1 Safekeeping
Under MiFID II and CRD IV, investment firms (custodians) may be, additionally, authorized for safekeeping on behalf of investors. Firms that obtained authorization are allowed to hold financial instruments and cash.[25] Financial instruments can either be held in book-entry form or physically. Following the dematerialization and immobilization trend,[26] fi-

---

21 Question 3, Bank of New York Mellon response to the MiFID/MiFIR II questionnaire of MEP Markus Ferber – 12 January 2012.
22 *Ibid.*
23 *See* Annex 1 s. B MiFID II proposal.
24 *See* S.J. Key, *Financial Integration in the European Community*, Board of Governors of the Federal Reserve System – International Finance Discussion Papers, No. 349 (April 1989), 105-106.
25 *See* on depositing client financial instruments: Art. 3(1) sub-para. 1 MiFID II (Commission) Directive; *See* on depositing client funds: Art. 16(10) MiFID II.
26 M. Haentjes, *Harmonisation of Securities Law: Custody and Transfer of Securities in European Private Law* 131-172 (Kluwer 2007).

nancial instruments are mainly held in book-entry form, i.e. a dematerialized form in which financial instruments are held electronically with no physical certificate issued.[27] Issuers may issue electronic financial instruments through a CSD that are the central service providers that provide the definitive record of ownership and facilitate the central settlement of securities.[28]

CSDs maintain accounts for participating intermediaries (custodians) and provide the service of clearing and settlement of securities to them.[29] Upon a transfer of securities, CSDs credit/debit the amount of securities to the accounts of the intermediaries held at the CSD (book-entry settlement).[30] These intermediaries (custodians) maintain accounts for their investors/intermediaries. The latter, may again hold accounts for their investors/intermediaries, etc. CSDs, thus, centralize the custody of security certificates.

CSDs and national laws typically differ in what type of securities[31] and intermediaries are admitted to a CSD and whether investors may hold an account with a CSD.[32] As a result, the length of a holding chain depends upon the laws applicable to the accounts held by the custodians and CSDs involved.[33] For this purpose, securities that are held across national borders typically involve a chain of intermediaries in which custodians hold the securities of their investors and need to maintain an account through, for example, a second account, which holds an account with a CSD in a foreign market that is keeping the securities of an issuer centrally.[34] Custodians have to segregate their client

---

27   D. Einsele, *Wertpapier als Schuldrecht: Funktionsverlust von Effektenurkunden, international Rechtsverkehr* (Tübingen: Mohr Siebeck 1995).

28   *See* K.M. Löber, *The Developing EU Legal Framework for Clearing and Settlement of Financial Instruments*, European Central Bank – Legal Working Paper Series, No. 1 (February 2006), 8.

29   Under the SLD proposal, it was suggested that account providers in the first place be responsible for effectively safeguarding clients' book-entry securities; *See* H. Motani, *The Proposed EU legislation on Securities Holding*, 68-73.

30   M. Haentjes, *Clearing and Settlement – Ways Forward*, 5 Journal of International Banking Law and Regulation (2011); L. Thévenoz, *Transfer of Intermediated Securities*, 135-159. (H.P. Conac, U. Segna & L. Thévenoz eds, Cambridge 2013).

31   E. Micheler, *The Legal Nature of Securities: Inspirations from Comparative Law*, 131-149. (L. Gullifer & J. Payne eds, Hart Publishing 2010).

32   L. Thévenoz, *Intermediated Securities, Legal Risk, and the International Harmonization of Commercial Law*, 13 Stanford Journal of Law, Business & Finance (2008), 384-452; L. Thévenoz, *Who holds (Intermediated) Securities? Shareholders, Account Holders, and Nominees?*, 3-4 Uniform Law Review (2010), 845-859.

33   P. Paech, *Cross-Border Issues of Securities Law – European Efforts to Support the Securities Market with a Coherent Legal Framework, Study Prepared for the European Parliament*, www.europarl.europa.eu/document/activities/cont/201106/20110606ATT20781/20110606ATT20781EN.pdf; P. Paech, *Market Needs as Paradigm – Breaking up the Thinking on EU Securities Law*, 22-64. (H.P. Conac, U. Segna & L. Thévenoz eds, Cambridge 2013); E. Micheler, *Custody Chains and Asset Values: Why Crypto Securities are Worth Contemplating*, 3 Cambridge Law Journal 1-6 (2015); E. Micheler, *Intermediated Securities and Legal Certainty*, LSE Law, Society and Economy Working Papers No. 3 (2014), 3-7; E. Micheler, *Custody Chains and Asset Values*, http://ssrn.com/abstract=2539074; P. Dupont, *Rights of the Account Holder Relating to Securities Credited to Its Securities Account*, 90-104. (H.P. Conac, U. Segna & L. Thévenoz eds, Cambridge 2013); H.P. Conac, *Rights of the Investor*, 105-134. (H.P. Conac, U. Segna & L. Thévenoz eds, Cambridge 2013).

34   H. De Vaplane & J.P. Yon, *The Concept of Integrity in Securities Holding Systems*, 193-214. (H.P. Conac, U. Segna & L. Thévenoz eds, Cambridge 2013).

securities from securities that are held for their own account, i.e. their own securities and the securities held for clients are booked into distinct accounts with the account provider[35] of the custodian.

Generally, there are two account types that are used: omnibus and segregated accounts. Omnibus accounts are accounts in which the custodian holds financial instruments on behalf of all its clients in a single ('omnibus') account at a CSD. Segregated securities account structures, i.e. accounts held for a specific (sub-category) of end-investors may also be held. The latter is the preference in the market as it is less complex and more cost-effective to operate.[36] Data, for example, only needs to be stored, maintained and updated in one place so that updates do not need to be processed through multiple accounts leading to less operational risks that it will not be processed in the same manner or at the same time.[37] Omnibus accounts are, however, associated with asset protection, asset servicing and operational issues.[38] Asset protection issues might arise as some legal systems recognize the intermediary (i.e. a nominee), and not the end-investor as the legal owner of a specific financial instrument. Asset servicing may be used for end-investors, for example, to effectuate their voting rights. Operational issue might be generated by the different requirements regarding the CSD account structure.[39]

For that purpose, the proposed SLD, which so far has not been adopted, sets out a core role for account providers being, amongst others, custodians.[40] It is proposed that account providers in the first place are responsible for effectively safeguarding clients' book-entry securities.[41] Custodians as account providers would be responsible for correctly crediting and debiting account-held securities related to the acquisitions and dispositions of account-held securities.[42] They would make sure that they hold enough securities to cover the corresponding number of securities credited to clients' accounts.[43] Errors should be avoided by appropriate remedies.[44] Account providers must follow the instructions of the account holder or any other person entitled to give instructions[45] and process

---

35 Principle 22(c) European Commission, *EU Consultation Document 'Legislation on Legal Certainty of Securities Holding and Dispositions'. DG Markt G2 MET/OT/acg D(1010) 768690*, http://ec.europa.eu/finance/consultations/2010/securities/docs/consultation_paper_en.pdf: 'account provider' means a person who maintains securities accounts for account holders and is authorized in accordance with MiFID II) or is a CSD as defined in the CSDR and, in either case, is acting in that capacity.

36 Association for Financial Markets in Europe, *Post Trade explained – The role of post-trade services in the financial sector*, February 2015, 13.

37 *Ibid.*, 9.

38 *Ibid.*, 5.

39 *Ibid.*, 12.

40 Principle 22(c) European Commission, *supra* note 35.

41 Legal Certainty Group, *supra* note 5, 36.

42 *See* Principle 4 Methods for acquisition and disposition' European Commission, *supra* note 35: Principle 4.2 sets out the methods for acquisition and dispositions. Six methods are recognized and categorized based upon book-entry and non-book-entry methods.

43 *Ibid.*, Principle 7, 22(c).

44 *Ibid.*, Principle 4.

45 *Ibid.*, Principle 11.

corporate actions[46] exclusively in accordance with the account agreement. Account providers would be required to report on securities movements and holdings in a manner with a scope and regularity as prescribed by the applicable law.[47] Other duties of account providers would be subject to contract.

Custodians, thus, hold their clients' financial instruments through the custody holding chain, i.e. accounts that are held at CSDs established in each market or through (sub-) custodians that are clients of such a CSD.

6.2.2.1.2 Administration

The provision of administration by custodians has its roots in the physical safekeeping of securities by banks.[48] The safekeeping of financial instruments and the holding of cash led to the development of additional services that were related to settlement and asset servicing. This development can be explained by the fact that custodians developed economies of scale in providing these services as they were the exclusive provider of physical safekeeping and other assets that were deposited in their vaults.[49] Custodians in the dematerialized and immobilized custody environment still cater for delivering and receiving financial instruments on behalf of clients against the negotiated amount of cash referred to as 'settlement'.[50]

Furthermore, custodians generally provide services related to the benefits, rights and obligations of an investor portfolio held by the custodian on behalf of their clients. Examples of asset-related services include, amongst others, the collection of income receivable (e.g. dividends and interest), corporate actions and the reclaiming of tax refunds.[51]

6.2.2.1.3 For the Account of Clients

Custodians are safekeeping and administrating assets on behalf of eligible counterparties, professional and retail clients. The provision of the safekeeping and administration of financial instruments does not include the safekeeping of the financial instruments that belong to the legal property of the investment firm itself.[52]

---

46 *Ibid.*, Principle 15.
47 *Ibid.*, Principle 16.
48 *See* Löber, *supra* note 28, 6.
49 *Ibid.*
50 Art. 2(1) n. 7 CSDR: "settlement means the completion of a securities transaction where it is concluded with the aim of discharging the obligations of the parties to that transaction through the transfer of cash or securities, or both."
51 European Commission, *Commission Staff Working Document of 12 July 2005* (SEC(2005) 947) Annex to the Green Paper on the enhancement of the EU Framework for Investment Funds, 22 and 23, http://ec.europa.eu/finance/investment/docs/consultations/greenpaper-background_en.pdf.
52 In general investment activities/services and ancillary services need to be provided for the account of clients in order to fall within the scope of MiFID II. *See* Art. 4(1) n. 1 MiFID II.

6.2.2.2   Custodianship and Related Services Such As Cash and Collateral Management

The safekeeping and administration of financial instruments is under MiFID II generally referred to as 'custodianship'.[53] The definition of the ancillary service, in addition, refers to the provision of 'related services' such as cash/collateral management'. The latter indicates that custodians under MiFID II are allowed to provide other value-added services, in addition to, the 'core service' of the safekeeping and administration of securities. Adding 'such as' refers to other value-added services that may be provided apart from cash/collateral management. Examples of value-added services include: investment reporting, fund accounting, performance measurement, foreign exchange transactions, fiduciary and trust services.[54]

6.2.2.3   Exclusion: Securities Accounts at Top Tier Level

The safekeeping and administration of financial instruments ancillary service under MiFID II excludes providing and maintaining securities accounts at the top tier level ('central maintenance service').[55] The CSDR refers to the central maintenance service as 'providing and maintaining securities accounts at the top tier level'.[56]

A 'top tier securities account' has not been defined by the CSDR. The European Commission in its impact assessment considering the proposal for the CSDR held that 'top tier securities accounts' are securities accounts that are placed at the top of the holding chain and are the accounts into which securities are being recorded in book-entry form for the first time.[57] The safekeeping and administration service under CRD IV and MiFID II, thus, aims at those credit institutions and investment firms that act as 'account keepers' by maintaining securities accounts that are not held at the top tier level, i.e. hold accounts with a CSD. CSDs, however, may, besides acting as an 'issuer CSD', also act as an 'investor CSD'. CSDs, however, fall outside of the scope of the ancillary safekeeping and administration service under CRD IV and MiFID II. The question that remains is whether 'investor CSDs' that maintain securities accounts with other CSDs on behalf of investors are to be seen as a 'custodian'.

---

53 *See* Annex I s. B MiFID II. Annex I CRD IV, however, does not include the term 'custodianship'.

54 *See* for 'other valued-added services' Annex – List of Services, s. C CSDR. Association for Financial Markets in Europe, *Post Trade explained – The Role of Post-Trade Services in the Financial Sector*, February 2015, 14; Oxera, *The Role of Custody in European Asset Management*, 13, www.oxera.com/Latest-Thinking/Publications/Reports/2002/The-role-of-custody-in-European-asset-management.aspx.

55 The definition of safekeeping and administration services under Annex 1 s. B MiFID II was replaced by Art. 71(3) CSDR.

56 Annex – List of Services, S. A, n. 2 CSDR.

57 *See* for 'top tier securities account': Annex 14 – Glossary of terms, European Commission, *Commission Staff Working Document of 7 March 2012 (SWD(2012) 22 final) Accompanying the Proposal for a Regulation of the European Parliament and of the Council on Improving Securities Settlement in the European Union and on Central Securities Depositories (CSDs) and Amending Directive 98/26/EC(COM(2012) 73 final): Impact Assessment*, http://eur-lex.europa.eu/legal-content/EN/TXT/PDF/?uri=CELEX:52012SC0022&from=EN.

6.2.3   Conclusion

Credit institutions and investment firms may act as 'custodian s' under the CRD IV and MiFID II. Both may perform 'safekeeping and administration services' as an ancillary service, in addition to the 'core services' for which they have obtained a 'stand-alone' authorization. The ancillary service status leaves a regulatory gap as for the activity itself credit institutions nor investment firms have to obtain an authorization under the CRD IV and MiFID II. National Member States are, thus, free to regulate their own national custodians. Moreover, the ancillary service nature of 'safekeeping and administration services' has led to diverging and unclear definitions of the activity under CRD IV and MiFID II. The CRD IV definition defines the activity as the 'safekeeping and administration of securities', whereas the MiFID II definition is more extended. The CRD IV ancillary service definition, however, has to be interpreted in the light of the MiFID II definition. The nature of MiFID II is to prevent regulatory arbitrage between MiFID II and CRD IV.[58] In addition, credit institutions performing investment services are investment firms that fall under the scope of MiFID II and MiFID II has been adopted at a later stage. The definition of the CRD IV ancillary service has, thus, to be interpreted dynamically in the light of MiFID II. The MiFID II definition, however, excludes CSDs, including CSDs that act as 'investor CSDs'. The question remains what CSDs are, to what extent they are different from CRD IV and MiFID II 'custodians' and what the difference is between 'investor CSDs' and 'issuer CSDs'.

6.3   THE (INVESTOR) CSD

During the MiFID I and II discussions regarding the possible update from custodianship to a full-fledged investment service, one of the arguments for not introducing a 'custodian passport' was that it was unclear whether and to what extent CSDs would fall within the scope of MiFID II.[59] The 'investor CSD' is similar as a custodian.[60] For cross-border transactions investors can access securities in an issuer CSD by using either a custodian bank or an investor CSD that has an account with the issuer CSD (investor CSD).[61] Furthermore, (investor) CSDs may perform the same ancillary services as custodians.

---

58 *See Key, supra note 24.*

59 European Commission, *Preliminary Orientations for Revision of the Investment Services Directive (ISD)*, IP/01/1055, July 2011, Annex 1: Definition and Scope of Investment Services Directive, 6-7; *See* for 'non-central safekeeping of financial instruments for the account of clients': European Commission, *Public Consultation on Central Securities Depositaries (CSDs) and on the Harmonisation of Certain Aspects of Securities Settlement in the European Union, DG Markt G2 D(201)8641*, 9, http://ec.europa.eu/finance/consultations/2011/csd/docs/consultation_csd_en.pdf.

60 *See B.J.A. Zebregs, De CSD-verordening in het licht van de Capital Markets Union, Ondernemingsrecht* 2017/18.

61 European Commission, *supra* note 57, 9.

Some CSDs, especially those licensed as credit institution under CRD IV, compete with custodians regarding certain administration services and value-added services provided to custodians. Delineating custodians from CSDs has been for a long time uncertain as regarding the duties and tasks employed. The CSDR has clarified this issue as it has introduced a definition of what is a CSD and, in particular, an 'investor CSD' under the CSDR.

6.3.1 CSDs under the CSDR

Under the CSDR, a CSD means a legal person that operates a settlement service and the notary and/or central maintenance service ('core services').[62] In addition, CSDs are permitted to perform certain 'ancillary' services, which are mostly related to the core services.[63] These can either be 'non-banking-type' or 'banking-type' ancillary services.[64]

6.3.1.1 Core Services

The CSDR sees the operation of the settlement service, and notary and/or central maintenance service as 'core services' for which CSDs need to be authorized. An authorized CSD may provide services across the EEA provided that those services are covered by its authorization.[65] These core services determine whether a CSD needs to be authorized under the CSDR as in practice the vast majority of CSDs in the pre-CSDR era performed these three services.

6.3.1.1.1 Settlement Service

The operation of a securities settlement system has been defined under Article 2(a) Settlement Finality Directive as "being a formal arrangements allowing transfers of securities between three or more participants, governed by the law of a Member State chosen by the participants, and designated as a system and notified as such to the European Commission."[66] De facto, this means the operation of the settlement service through which securities are initially delivered to investors or are exchanged between buyers and sellers.[67] CSDs, in this regard, operate IT platforms that provide the settlement of securities transactions.[68] Transactions, are, typically, 'settled' in a process called 'delivery versus pay-

---

62 Recital 26 CSDR; Annex – List of Services, S. A CSDR.
63 Annex – List of Services, S. A CSDR.
64 Annex – List of Services, S. B, C CSDR.
65 Recital 21, Art. 23 CSDR.
66 European Commission, *Proposal for a Regulation of the European Parliament and of the Council on improving securities settlement in the European Union and on central securities depositories (CSDs) and amending Directive 98/26/EC /*, COM/2012/073 final – 2012/0029 (COD) */ ('CSDR Proposal'), 7.
67 *See* for the settlement function: http://ecsda.eu/facts/faq.
68 European Commission, *supra* note 59, 7 and 8.

ment' by CSDs through crediting the purchased securities and debiting the corresponding cash amount of the accounts of the buyer, whereas the seller's securities account will be debited and its corresponding cash account credited.[69]

6.3.1.1.2   Notary Service

The 'notary' function refers to the function of CSDs in relation to the securities issuance process. CSDs are the 'first entry point' for the recording of securities into a book-entry system. Securities issued by issuers are in practice deposited into a CSD, referred to as 'issuer CSD'.[70] The notary service of CSD is characterized by a 'central register' that is being kept for a particular issue of securities in order to enable the settlement of the corresponding securities.[71] The CSD makes sure that the number of securities issued equals the securities the securities booked in the accounts of investors. CSDs, thus, ensure the integrity of the issue by ascertaining the existence of the securities when the reimbursement upon maturity takes place.[72] The CSD notary function should be distinguished from the keeping of the central register for the issuer. The latter is being performed by registrars and serves a different purpose namely the provision of information to shareholders.

6.3.1.1.3   Central Maintenance Service

The 'central safekeeping' function means the maintenance of 'top tier' accounts in a book-entry system.[73] CSDs performing this function are the central account provider for the entire market of the relevant financial instrument. The participants of the CSD may, thus, deposit their securities in securities accounts provided to them by the CSD on which transfers resulting from transactions are debited/credited.[74] All rights and obligations linked to the securities are managed under the central maintenance service. The central maintenance of securities includes, for example, the processing of corporate actions, such as dividend and interest payments and voting rights in the case of shares.[75] The central maintenance service is carried out related to securities at the 'top tier level', i.e. all holdings in a given financial instrument that is ultimately being kept in a securities account at a CSD.[76]

---

69 ECB, *T2S Framework Agreement*, https://www.ecb.europa.eu/paym/t2s/pdf/csd_FA/T2S_Framework_Agreement_Schedules.pdf.
70 *See* for the notary function: http://ecsda.eu/facts/faq.
71 European Commission, *supra* note 59, 6.
72 European Commission, *supra* note 66.
73 European Commission, *supra* note 59, 7.
74 European Commission, *supra* note 66.
75 *See* for the central maintenance function: http://ecsda.eu/facts/faq.
76 *See* http://ecsda.eu/facts/faq.

6.3.1.1.4   Ancillary Services

CSDs authorized to carry out the core services may additionally provide non-banking and banking-type of ancillary services. The CSDR differentiates between the two as for non-banking ancillary services the CSDR does not take principal risks (credit or liquidity risks). Banking ancillary services are those ancillary services provided for which CSDs that have, simultaneously, obtained a license as credit institution. CSDs must obtain such a license as they do take principal risks, such as credit and/or liquidity risks.

6.3.1.2   Non-banking-type Ancillary Services of CSDs

Non-banking-type ancillary services of CSDs are services that may be performed, in addition to, the core services for which a CSD is authorized. On top of that, there are two extra categories, including the function of 'investor CSD' and 'any other service'.[77]

6.3.1.2.1   Operation of Settlement System

Ancillary services allowed to be provided along the notary function are: organizing a securities lending mechanism,[78] providing collateral management services and settlement matching,[79] order routing and trade confirmation/verification.[80]

6.3.1.2.2   Central Safekeeping/Notary Function

Ancillary services that may be provided linked to the central maintenance service, the safekeeping of securities and the notary function are: services related to shareholder registers,[81] the processing of 'corporate actions'[82] and the new issue services, such as the allocation and management of ISIN codes.[83]

6.3.1.2.3   'Investor CSDs'

Regardless of the core services provided, CSDs may maintain securities accounts in relation to the settlement service, collateral management and other ancillary services.[84] CSDs are under this ancillary service allowed to open 'lower tier' securities accounts, either in direct holding systems or by acting as an 'investor CSD' by maintaining securities accounts for its customers for securities issued in 'issuer CSDs'.[85] The investor CSD is, thus, similar as a custodian. For cross-border transactions, investors can access securities in an

---

77 Annex – List of Services, S. B, n. 3(a) CSDR.
78 Annex – List of Services, S. B, n. 1(a) CSDR.
79 Annex – List of Services, S. B, n. 1(b) CSDR.
80 Annex – List of Services, S. B, n. 1(c) CSDR.
81 Annex – List of Services, S. B, n. 2(a) CSDR.
82 Annex – List of Services, S. B, n. 2(b) CSDR.
83 Annex – List of Services, S. B, n. 2(c) CSDR.
84 Annex – List of Services, S. B, n. 4 CSDR.
85 European Commission, *supra* note 66.

issuer CSD by using either a custodian bank or an investor CSD that has an account with an issuer CSD.[86] CSDs may also perform the same ancillary services as custodians.

6.3.1.2.4   Any Other Service
On top of this, CSDs may provide general ancillary services referred to as 'any other service' supporting the core services, including the provision of general collateral management services as agent,[87] regulatory reporting[88] and providing data and statistics to market/census bureaus.[89] The list of non-banking-ancillary services is indicative. CSDs are not restricted in performing other ancillary services than the services explicitly mentioned in Section B Annex List of Services CSDR.

6.3.1.3   Banking-type Ancillary Services
CSDs may be authorized under Title 14 CSDR to provide banking-type ancillary services. CSDs may, however, only be 'limited purpose credit institutions'. They are restricted to a legal framework that governs the provision of commercial bank money settlement by CSDS to their participants. An example of an ancillary service allowed to be provided is the provision of cash accounts and accepting deposits from its participants.[90] CSDs may either obtain such a license by themselves[91] or a separate legal entity may obtain the license belong to the group of which both entities are ultimately controlled by the same parent entity.[92]

6.3.2   Conclusion

Under the CSDR, a CSD is a legal person that operates a settlement service and notary and/or central maintenance service ('core services').[93] In addition, CSDs are permitted to perform certain 'ancillary' services, which are mostly related to the core services.[94] These 'ancillary' services can be 'non-banking-type ancillary services of CSDs'[95] and 'banking-type ancillary services'.[96] Under MiFID II and the CRD IV, CSDs are excluded that are authorized for providing and maintaining securities accounts at the top tier level ('central

---

86   Ibid., 8.
87   Annex – List of Services, S. B, n. 4(a) CSDR.
88   Annex – List of Services, S. B, n. 4(b) CSDR.
89   Annex – List of Services, S. B, n. 4(c) CSDR.
90   Annex – List of Services, S. C(a) CSDR.
91   Art. 54(3) CSDR.
92   Art. 54(4) CSDR.
93   Recital 26 CSDR; Annex – List of Services, S. A CSDR.
94   Annex – List of Services, S. A CSDR.
95   Annex – List of Services, S. B CSDR.
96   Annex – List of Services, S. C CSDR.

maintenance service').[97] Regardless of the core services provided, CSD may, as a non-banking ancillary service, maintain securities accounts in relation to the settlement service, collateral management and other ancillary services.[98] CSDs are under this ancillary service allowed to open 'lower tier' securities accounts, either in direct holding systems or by acting as an 'investor CSD' by maintaining securities accounts for its customers for securities issued in 'issuer CSD s'.[99] Investor CSDs, thus, partly provide similar services as 'custodians' under CRD IV and MiFID II. The core services provided under the CSDR, however, delineate 'investor CSDs' from 'custodians'.

6.4   THE MiFID II CLIENT ASSET REQUIREMENTS

MiFID II requires general and specific organizational requirements to ensure the safeguarding of client assets. These specific organizational requirements related to the safeguarding of client assets applies to (non-bank) investment firms. For credit institutions these requirements are only applicable to the extent that they provide investment services/activities and, therefore, fall within the scope of MiFID II. Considering the regulation to which CSDs are subjected to for providing their core services under the CSDR, CSDs are not required to comply with MiFID II for the provision of the non-banking ancillary service to maintain 'lower tier' securities accounts.[100] These requirements do also not apply to custodians regulated under national law. As the regulation of these 'national custodians' is largely based upon the CRD IV/MiFID II, various Member States, such as Ireland,[101] have decided to apply these requirements on an unilateral basis to their 'national custodians'.

6.4.1   General and Specific Organizational Requirements

Upon authorization, an investment firm must comply with many organizational requirements that MiFID II imposes on investment firms. General and specific organizational requirements apply. The basic provision covering general organizational requirements is Article 13(2) MiFID II. This provision requires a firm to establish adequate policies and procedures sufficient to ensure compliance of the firm, including its managers, employees, tied agents and appropriate rules governing personal transactions by such persons. In

---

97 The definition of safekeeping and administration services under Annex 1 s. B MiFID II was replaced by Art. 71(3) CSDR.
98 Annex – List of Services, S. B, n. 4 CSDR.
99 European Commission, *supra* note 66.
100 *Ibid.*
101 Central Bank of Ireland, *Guidance on Client Asset Regulation for Investment Firms*, March 2015 https://www.centralbank.ie/press area/pressreleases/Documents/150330%20Guidance%20on%20Client%20Asset%20Regulations%20for%20Investment%20Firms.pdf.

addition, specific organizational features are required regarding risk management, internal audit, outsourcing, conflicts of interest and the safeguarding of client assets. These procedures aim to avoid operational risks, conflict of interest and adequate protection of clients assets.[102]

6.4.2   Safeguarding of Client Financial Instruments and Funds

MiFID II lays down specific organizational requirements to investment firms that concern the safeguarding of client assets that are elaborated in detail in the MiFID II (Commission) Directive.[103] Organizational requirements imposed by MiFID II relate to the safeguarding of client financial instruments[104] and funds,[105] the use of client financial instruments,[106] the inappropriate use of TTCA [107] and reports by external auditors.[108] Article 16(2) MiFID II requires investment firms to establish adequate policies and procedures to ensure compliance of the investment firm with the governance arrangements concerning the safeguarding of client assets.[109] The protection of investor ownership and other similar rights in respect of securities and funds entrusted to an investment firm are an important part of the MiFID II investor protection regime.[110] For this purpose, an investment firm shall, when holding financial instruments and funds belonging to clients, have in place adequate arrangements to safeguard investor ownership and rights with respect to the securities and funds entrusted to an investment firm.[111] In particular, those rights should be kept distinct from those of the investment firm.[112] Investments firms, when holding financial instruments belonging to clients, are required to make adequate arrangements to safeguard the ownership rights[113] of clients in the event of the investment firm's insolvency and to prevent the use of a client's instruments on own account, except for cases where the client has given its express consent.[114] Similarly, investment

---

102 See Art. 16(2)-(10) MiFID II.
103 Commission Delegated Directive (EU) 2017/593 of 7 April 2016 supplementing Directive 2014/65/EU of the European Parliament and of the Council with regard to safeguarding of financial instruments and funds belonging to clients, product governance obligations and the rules applicable to the provision or reception of fees, commissions or any monetary or non-monetary benefits, C(2016) 2031 final, 7 April 2016 ('MiFID II (Commission) Directive').
104 Art. 16(8) MiFID II; Art. 2 and 3 MiFID II (Commission) Directive.
105 Art. 16(9) MiFID II; Art. 2 and 4 MiFID II (Commission) Directive.
106 Art. 16(8) and (9) MiFID II; Art. 5 MiFID II (Commission) Directive.
107 Art. 16(10) MiFID II; Art. 6 MiFID II (Commission) Directive.
108 Art. 16(8), (9) and (10) MiFID II; Art. 5 MiFID II (Commission) Directive.
109 Art. 16(2) MiFID II; Art. 7 and 8 MiFID II (Commission) Directive.
110 Recital 51 MiFID II; Recital 1 and 2 MiFID II (Commission) Directive.
111 Recital 2 MiFID II (Commission) Directive.
112 Recital 51 MiFID II.
113 Art. 1(2), (3) and (4) MiFID II determines that this provision is applicable to both investment firms and credit institutions.
114 Art. 16(8) MiFID II; See Löber, supra note 28, 27.

firms, when holding funds belonging to clients, are required to make adequate arrangements to safeguard clients' rights.[115] Investment firms, except in the case of credit institutions, are additionally required to prevent the use of client funds for their own account.[116] The safeguarding of client financial instruments and funds, however, does not prevent investment firms from doing business in their own name but on behalf of the investor, where that is required by the nature of the transaction and the investor agrees, for example for securities lending.[117]

6.4.2.1 General Regime

Article 2 MiFID II (Commission) Directive requires investment firms, for the purpose of safeguarding client financial instruments and funds, to:
- keep records and accounts as are necessary to enable them at any time and without delay to distinguish assets held for one client from assets held for any other client and from their own assets (asset segregation);[118]
- maintain records and accounts in a way that ensures their accuracy and, in particular, their correspondence to the financial instruments and funds held for clients that may be used as an audit trail;[119]
- introduce adequate organizational arrangements to minimize the risk of the loss or diminution of client assets or of rights in connection with those assets, as a result of misuse of the assets, fraud, poor administration, inadequate record-keeping or negligence.[120]

Investment firms that deposit client financial instruments and funds must:
- conduct reconciliations, on a regular basis, between their internal accounts, records and those of any third parties by whom those assets are held;[121]
- take the necessary steps to ensure that client instruments deposited with a third party are identifiable separately from the financial instruments belonging to the investment firm and from financial instruments belonging to that third party, by means of differently titled accounts on the books of the third party or other equivalent measures that achieve the same level of protection;[122]
- take the necessary steps to ensure that client funds (client money) are deposited in a central bank, a credit institution or a bank authorized in a third country or a qualify-

---

115 Art. 16(10) MiFID II.
116 *Ibid.*
117 Recital 51 MiFID II.
118 Art. 2(1)(a) MiFID II (Commission) Directive.
119 Art. 2(1)(b) MiFID II (Commission) Directive.
120 Art. 2(1)(f) MiFID II (Commission) Directive.
121 Art. 2(1)(c) MiFID II (Commission) Directive.
122 Art. 2(1)(d) MiFID II (Commission) Directive; Art. 3 MiFID II (Commission) Directive, discussed below, lay down the specific steps to be taken for depositing client financial instruments.

ing money market fund[123] that are held in an account or accounts identified separately from any account used to hold funds belonging to the investment firm.[124]

6.4.2.2   Equivalent Measures Achieving the Same Level of Protection

Member States are required to put in place arrangements to ensure that client' assets are safeguarded to meet the objectives of the safeguarding of client financial instruments and funds. MiFID II recognizes that there can be situations where applicable national law,[125] in particular the law relating to property or insolvency, may prevent investment firms from complying with the requirements related to the depositing of client financial instruments and funds.[126] In such cases, Member States shall require investment firms to put in place arrangements to ensure that the objectives of safeguarding client assets laid down in Article 2(1) MiFID II (Commission) Directive are being met.[127] If national law prevents investment firms from complying with the requirements related to the depositing of client financial instruments and funds, Member States shall require equivalent requirements in terms of safeguarding clients' rights.[128]

When relying on such equivalent requirements, Member States have to ensure that investment firms inform clients that they do not benefit from provisions related to the depositing of client financial instruments and funds under MiFID II.[129]

If applicable law[130] prevents investment firms from complying[131] with the requirements related to the depositing of client financial instruments and funds, Member States shall prescribe requirements that have an equivalent effect on the safeguarding of clients' rights.[132] Investment firms have to inform clients in the circumstance that they rely on equivalent requirements and not on the MiFID II regime related to the depositing of client financial instruments and funds.[133]

---

123 *See* for a definition of 'qualifying money market fund': Art. 1(4) MiFID II (Commission) Directive.
124 Art. 2(1)(e) MiFID II (Commission) Directive; Art. 4 MiFID II (Commission) Directive, discussed below, lay down the specific steps to be taken for depositing client funds.
125 The applicable law, for instance, related to property or insolvency, may prevent investment firms established in a particular Member State to comply with any of the requirements discussed in this paragraph. *See* Art. 2 (2) MiFID II (Commission) Directive.
126 Art. 2(2) MiFID II (Commission) Directive; ESMA/2014/549, 61.
127 Art. 2(2) MiFID II (Commission) Directive.
128 Art. 2(3) sub-para. 1 MiFID II (Commission) Directive.
129 Art. 2(3) sub-para. 2 MiFID II (Commission) Directive.
130 The applicable law, for instance, related to property or insolvency, may prevent investment firms established in a particular Member State to comply with any of the requirements discussed in this paragraph. *See* Art. 2 (2) MiFID II (Commission) Directive.
131 Art. 2(2) MiFID II (Commission) Directive; ESMA/2014/549, 61.
132 Art. 2(3) sub-para. 1 MiFID II (Commission) Directive.
133 Art. 2(3) sub-para. 2 MiFID II (Commission) Directive.

6.4.2.3 Inappropriate Custody Liens over Clients Assets

MiFID II explicitly prohibits investment firms to grant security interests, liens or rights of set-off over financial instruments or funds that allows third parties to dispose these in order to recover debts that do not relate to the clients or the provision of services to the client.[134] MiFID II has introduced this general prohibition as liens of a general and wide-ranging nature were allowed under MiFID I.[135] Examples of liens were identified after the 2008 Lehman insolvency in which investment firms granted third parties the right to dispose of the (client') financial instruments in the event of a default insolvency of the investment firm itself or any of its affiliated group entities to satisfy the investment firm's obligations towards that party.[136] A general prohibition of these type of transactions is embedded in MiFID II as clients are not party to these type of agreements and the risks they face are, thus, not obvious for them until an insolvency of an investment firm occurs. The holding of client assets in some third country jurisdictions, however, may require general and wide-ranging liens to be granted. For this purpose, MiFID II exempts investment firms of this general prohibition when security interests, liens or rights of set-off of this nature are required by the applicable law in a third country jurisdiction in which the client funds or financial instruments are held.[137] Investment firms on such an occasion are exempted from the provision provided that the investment firm has disclosed this information to his clients indicating to them the risks associated with those arrangements.[138] Liens, security interests or other encumbrances over client funds/financial instruments that are in accordance with these requirements are valid.[139] Such security interests, where granted by an investment firm or where the firm has been informed that they are granted, should be kept in the firm's own record so that the ownership status of client assets are clear upon an insolvency of the firm.[140]

6.4.2.4 Information and Record-keeping

Investment firms are required under MiFID II to hold basic information and information under record-keeping requirements related to the safeguarding of client assets that can be easily accessed by insolvency practitioners, Competent Authorities and those responsible for the resolution of failed institutions.[141] This requirement resulted from relevant parties

---

134 Art. 2(4) sub-para. 1 MiFID II (Commission) Directive; ESMA/2014/1570, 60, 66.
135 An investment firm was permitted to conclude such liens under Art. 13(7) and (8) MiFID I.
136 ESMA/2014/1570, 60.
137 Recital 14, Art. 2(4) sub-para. 1 MiFID II (Commission) Directive.
138 Art. 2(4) sub-para. 2 MiFID II (Commission) Directive; ESMA/2014/1570, 48, 60; IOSCO, *Report of the IOSCO Technical Committee – Client Asset Protection*, August 1996, Principle 3, https://www.iosco.org/library/pubdocs/pdf/IOSCOPD57.pdf.
139 Recital 14 MiFID II (Commission) Directive; ESMA/2014/1570, 60, 61.
140 Art. 2(4) sub-para. 3 MiFID II (Commission) Directive; ESMA/2014/1570, 60, 61, 66, 67.
141 ESMA /2014/1569, 74; C.A. Rooke, *MiFID en custodians: let op extra informatieverplichtingen!*, 1/2 TvFR 43-46 (2008).

having difficulties in timely accessing information to return these to clients to take appropriate action, for example, to request freezing orders or the immediate return of funds.[142]

Making information easily available to insolvency practitioners and relevant authorities by holding information under record-keeping requirements related to the safeguarding of client assets reduces this risk and helps to increase the speed of return of client' assets after an insolvency.[143] For this purpose, investment firms are required to make the following information readily available:

- related internal accounts and records that readily identify the balances of funds and instruments held for each client (reconciliations, client ledgers, cash books etc.);[144]
- details of the third party accounts where client financial instruments/funds are held and the relevant agreements with those entities;[145]
- details of third parties carrying out any related outsourced tasks and the details of those tasks;[146]
- the key employees of the investment firm that are responsible for related processes, including those responsible for compliance with the requirements related to the safeguarding of client assets[147] and
- agreements relevant to establish client ownership over assets.[148]

6.4.3 Depositing Client Financial Instruments

MiFID II allows investment firms to deposit financial instruments held by them on behalf of their clients into an account or accounts opened with a sub-custodian. Depositing client financial instruments is only allowed if such an investment firm performs *ex ante* and ongoing due diligence upon appointing a sub-custodian. This obligation recognizes the fact that depositing client financial instruments to a sub-custodian reduces the protection of clients' financial instruments.[149] To ensure that financial instruments are subject to due care and protection at all times, an investment firm has to exercise all due skill, care and diligence in the selection, appointment and periodic review of any sub-custodian they deposit client' financial instruments with, as well as, in the choice of the arrangements for the holding and safekeeping of those instruments.[150] In addition, investment firms have to take into account the expertise and market reputation of the third party

---

142 ESMA/2014/549, 62.
143 *Ibid.*, 60.
144 Art. 2(5)(a) MiFID II (Commission) Directive.
145 Art. 2(5)(b) and (c) MiFID II (Commission) Directive.
146 Art. 2(5)(d) MiFID II (Commission) Directive.
147 Art. 2(5)(e) MiFID II (Commission) Directive.
148 Art. 2(5)(f) and (c) MiFID II (Commission) Directive.
149 IOSCO, *Report of the IOSCO Technical Committee – Client Asset Protection*, August 1996, 20, https://www.iosco.org/library/pubdocs/pdf/IOSCOPD57.pdf.
150 Recital 11, Art. 3(1) sub-para. 1 MiFID II (Commission) Directive.

custodian, as well as, legal requirements or market practices related to the holding of those financial instruments that could adversely affect clients' rights.[151] This is intended to protect the client by requiring the firm to use as a custodian a firm that is subject to specific regulation and supervision of safekeeping of financial instruments for the account of other persons.[152] Investment firms that deposit client' financial instruments with a sub-custodian in a third country that does not regulate and supervise the holding and safekeeping of financial instruments for the account of another person is only allowed if:[153]

- the nature of the financial instruments or of the investment services connected with these instruments requires them to be deposited with a safekeep in that particular country;[154] or
- a professional client requests in writing to deposit financial instruments with a sub-custodian in such a third country.[155]

The *ex ante* and ongoing due diligence requirements set out by Article 3 MiFID II (Commission) Directive also apply if a sub-custodian has sub-delegated any of its functions concerning the holding and safekeeping of financial instruments. Article 3 MiFID II (Commission) Directive only applies to investment firms that provide the ancillary service of safekeeping and administration of financial instruments for the account of clients. This is clear from Article 3(1) sub-paragraph 1 MiFID II (Commission) Directive that applies to investment firms that deposit 'financial instruments held by them'. Investment firms that only perform investment services and activities for a particular client, such as portfolio management,[156] but do not provide the specific ancillary service of safekeeping and administration of financial instruments for the account of that particular client, are not subjected to the due diligence requirements set out in Article 3 MiFID II (Commission) Directive. No due diligence obligation, thus, applies to such investment firms for financial instruments held by third party custodians[157] or self-custody, if allowed by the specific laws of the Member State concerned.

---

151 Recital 11, Art. 3(1) sub-para. 2 MiFID II (Commission) Directive.
152 Art. 3(2) MiFID II (Commission) Directive.
153 Art. 3(3) MiFID II (Commission) Directive.
154 Art. 3(3)(a) MiFID II (Commission) Directive.
155 Art. 3(3)(b) MiFID II (Commission) Directive.
156 *See* Annex I s. A, n. 4 MiFID II.
157 Third-party custodians may, however, be subjected to this requirement if they are investment firms within the scope of MiFID II or the requirements applying to the depositing of client financial instruments set out in Art. 3 MiFID II (Commission) Directive are being extended by their national legislation to custodians that are merely authorized as a custodian under national law.

6.4.4   Depositing Client Funds

Investment firms, when holding funds belonging to clients, are required to make adequate arrangements to safeguard clients' rights.[158]

6.4.4.1   Eligible Entities for Depositing Client Funds

Investment firms are required, on receiving any client funds,[159] to promptly place those funds into one or more accounts opened with:[160]

–   a central bank;
–   a credit institution within the meaning of CRD IV;
–   a bank authorized in a third country; and
–   a qualifying money market fund.[161]

Credit institutions are exempted from this requirement in relation to deposits within the meaning of CRD IV. The rationale behind this is that deposits received by credit institutions are protected by the regulatory requirements laid down in CRD IV, the DGSD and other European (banking) regulations that are directly and indirectly protecting deposits. Credit institutions receiving client funds in the course of providing investment services are exempt from mandatory placing funds into one or more accounts opened with any of the above-mentioned entities when providing investment services to the extent that client funds can be considered to be deposits within the meaning of CRD IV.[162] Deposits are defined by Annex I Nr. 1, Recital 14 and Article 9(1) CRD IV. Annex I Nr. 1 CRD IV refers to 'taking deposits and other repayable funds'. Recital 14 CRD IV refers to deposit-taking business as 'to receive repayable funds from the public, whether in the form of deposits or in other forms'. Article 9(1) CRD IV prohibits 'persons or undertakings that are not credit institutions from carrying out the business of taking deposits or other repayable funds from the public'. Deposits can, thus, under the respective provisions under the CRD IV be defined as a form of repayable funds received from the public. Credit institutions receiving funds that qualify as deposits are, thus, not considered to

---

158 Art. 16(10) MiFID II.
159 In Ireland and the UK 'client funds' are often being referred to as 'client money'. *See* for Ireland: Central Bank of Ireland, *Guidance on Client Asset Regulation for Investment Firms*, March 2015 https://www.centralbank.ie/pressarea/pressreleases/Documents/150330%20Guidance%20on%20Client%20Asset%20Regulations%20for%20Investment%20Firms.pdf; *See* for the UK: CASS 7.
160 Art. 16(9) MiFID II.
161 A qualifying money market fund means in this regard a UCITS or a collective investment undertaking which is subject to supervision and authorized by an (Competent) Authority that is satisfying additional conditions and, therefore, qualifies as a 'high quality' money market fund. *See* for the definition of a qualifying money market fund and any of the additional conditions for collective investment undertakings other than UCITS: Art. 1 MiFID II (Commission) Directive.
162 IOSCO, *Report of the IOSCO Technical Committee – Client Asset Protection*, August 1996, 25, https://www.iosco.org/library/pubdocs/pdf/IOSCOPD57.pdf.

be 'client funds' and, therefore, credit institutions are not mandatorily required to deposit these funds with an eligible entity and to comply with any other requirements applying to the depositing of client funds.

6.4.4.2 Depositing Client Funds – Due Diligence Requirements

General due diligence requirements apply to investment firms when depositing client funds at eligible entities other than central banks.[163] Investment firms are required upon depositing client funds to such entities to exercise all due skill, care and diligence in the selection, appointment and periodic review of the credit institution, bank or money market fund where the funds are placed and the arrangements for the holding of those funds. In appointing eligible entities other than central banks, investment firms have to take into account the expertise and market reputation of such institutions, as well as, legal requirements or market practices related to the holding of those financial instruments that could adversely affect clients' rights.[164] Clients have the right to oppose the placement of their funds in a qualifying money market fund. To ensure their right to be effective, investment firms are required to inform clients that funds placed with qualifying money market funds are not in accordance with the requirements for safeguarding client funds as set out in MiFID II.[165]

6.4.4.3 Due Diligence – The Diversification of Client Funds

MiFID II has introduced a requirement to consider the diversification of investment firm's holding of client funds as part of the depositing client fund due diligence requirements.[166] This is to prevent that an investment firm places all client funds at a single institution and is prone to the misuse and possible loss of the funds upon an insolvency of such an institution.[167] Investment firms may not circumvent their duty to consider diversification by requiring clients to waive protection.[168] The diversification requirement does, however, not apply to credit institutions in relation to deposits[169] and to investment firms that do not hold the money.[170] Examples of situations in which investment firms do not hold money are, for example, where clients have their own bank account and the investment firm has received mandate from its client to instruct the bank.[171]

---

163 Art. 4(2) sub-para. 1 MiFID II (Commission) Directive.
164 *Ibid.*
165 Art. 4(2) sub-para. 3 MiFID II (Commission) Directive.
166 Art. 4(2) sub-para. 1 MiFID II (Commission) Directive; ESMA/2014/1570, 57, 58.
167 Recital 12 MiFID II (Commission) Directive; ESMA/2014/1570, 66, 67.
168 Recital 12 MiFID II (Commission) Directive.
169 Art. 4(1) sub-para. 2 MiFID II (Commission) Directive;
170 Art. 4(2) sub-para. 1 MiFID II (Commission) Directive; ESMA/2014/1570, 57.
171 *Ibid.*

Investment firms are expected to conduct due diligence as if they were considering to place their own funds.[172] No specific criteria for consideration are laid down by MiFID II as factors could vary significantly between different investment firms. Investment firms are, therefore, allowed to determine their own factors of consideration.[173] The judgment should be proportionate and may include factors, such as the size of the firm and the diversity of its clients base. The diversification requirement is not intended to interfere with operational necessities of undertaking transactions for clients. Funds that have been transferred to a transaction account to make a specific transaction are, therefore, not subject to the MiFID II diversification of client funds requirement.[174] Funds transferred to a clearing house (CCP) or exchange to pay margin calls are examples of funds that are not intended to be subjected to a diversification requirement.[175]

6.4.4.4   Intra-Group Deposits of Client Funds

The portion of client funds deposited outside/inside the group are subject to the general due diligence requirements related to the diversification of funds.[176] The placing of funds within the same group as the investment firm may, similar to the placement of client funds with one single institution, lead to concentration and contagion risk.[177] Concentration risks are created when placing all client funds in a single institution and contagion risk in the sense that when one firm in a group fail, the other firms will also fail.[178]

When considering the need for diversification, investment firms have to take into account various factors to avoid concentration risks, such as the total balance of client funds held, the operational risks of using more than one institution and the credit worthiness of the institution where client funds are deposited.[179] When considering contagion risk, investment firms have to consider the extent to which funds are deposited at an intra-group entity or outside of the group.[180]

Extra requirements apply, in addition to, the general diversification requirements of client funds for intra-group deposits of client funds.[181] Investment firms that are depositing client funds with a credit institution, bank or money market fund of the same group

---

172 ESMA/2014/1570, 57.
173 *Ibid.*, 57, 58.
174 *Ibid.*, 58.
175 Recital 12 MiFID II (Commission) Directive; ESMA/2014/1570, 58.
176 ESMA/2014/1570, 59.
177 European Commission, *Request to ESMA for Technical Advice on possible Delegated Acts and Implementing Acts concerning the Regulation on Markets in Financial Instruments and amending Regulation [EMIR] on OTC Derivatives, Central Counterparties and Trade Repositories [MiFIR((EC) No XX/2014] and the Directive on Markets in Financial Instruments in repealing Directive 2004/39/EC (MiFID (EC) No XX/2014)*, 23 April 2014, 19.
178 ESMA/2014/1570, 59.
179 Recital 13 MiFID II (Commission) Directive; ESMA/2014/1570, 59.
180 *Ibid.*
181 Art. 4(3) MiFID II (Commission) Directive.

as the investment firm are required to comply with a deposit limit of 20% if client funds are placed with an intra-group entity.[182] Group entities or a combination of group entities are considered intra-group entities.[183]

An investment firm may choose not to comply with this limit if it is able to demonstrate that the limit is not proportionate.[184] The limit may not be proportionate in the view of the nature, scale and complexity of the business, the small balance of client funds the investment firm holds or the safety offered by third party institutions considered.[185] Investment firms are required to periodically review the proportionality assessment made and notify their initial and reviewed assessments to their national Competent Authorities.[186]

The deposit limit does in any case not apply where investment firms are not receiving client funds, for instance, where it only has a mandate over the client bank account. The deposit limit does also not apply to credit institutions receiving deposits that are exempt from Article 4(1) MiFID II (Commission) Directive and are considered to be subject to appropriate prudential regime and oversight addressing banking risks.[187]

6.4.5   The Use of Client Financial Instruments

6.4.5.1   General Regime

Article 16(8) MiFID II contains a general prohibition on using client financial instruments without client consent. Article 5 MiFID II (Commission) Directive sets out the conditions related to client consent for using client financial instruments. Investment firms may not enter into arrangements concerning SFT in respect of financial instruments held by them on behalf of a client, or otherwise use such financial instruments for their own account or the account of another person or client of the firm, unless;[188]

– the client has given his prior express consent evidenced in writing to the use of the instruments on specified terms;[189] and
– the use of that client's financial instruments is restricted to the specified terms to which the client consents.[190]

---

182 Art. 4(3) sub-para. 1 MiFID II (Commission) Directive; ESMA/2014/1570, 65.
183 Art. 4(3) sub-para. 1 MiFID II (Commission) Directive.
184 Art. 4(3) sub-para. 2 MiFID II (Commission) Directive; ESMA/2014/1570, 65.
185 Recital 13, Art. 4(3) sub-para. 2 MiFID II (Commission) Directive.
186 *Ibid.*
187 ESMA/2014/1570, 59.
188 Art. 5(1) MiFID II (Commission) Directive; MiFID II, in comparison with MiFID I, has extended the written evidence requirement of the express consent to both professional and retail clients. Under MiFID I this was only required for retail clients.
189 Art. 5(1)(a) MiFID II (Commission) Directive.
190 Art. 5(1)(b) MiFID II (Commission) Directive.

Recital 10 MiFID II (Commission) Directive requires that prior express consent should be given and recorded by investment firms so that the investment firm is able to demonstrate what the client agreed to and the status of client assets can be clarified.[191] MiFID II does not set out legal requirements in respect of the form in which the consent may be given, as long as it is clear that the client has consented to the use of his securities.[192]

Investment firms may, in addition, not enter into arrangements for SFTs in respect of financial instruments that are held on behalf of a client in an omnibus account maintained by a third party, or otherwise use financial instruments held in such an account for their own account or of another client unless, in addition to the criteria set out above:[193]

– each client has expressed his prior consent;[194]
– the investment firm has in place systems and controls that ensure that only financial instruments belonging to clients that have given prior express consent are used.[195]

The investment firm shall hold in the records details of the client on whose instructions the use of the financial instruments has been effected, as well as, the number of financial instruments that are used belonging to each client who has given his consent.[196] The latter is to enable to correct allocations of any loss.[197]

6.4.5.2   Unintended use of Client Financial Instruments

MiFID II introduced additional measures that aim to strengthen the organizational requirements of investment firms to prevent the unintended use of client financial instruments and supplement the measures discussed above.[198]

ESMA gave a clear example of one situation that may lead to the unintended use of client financial instruments.[199] This example relates to automated settlement systems and omnibus accounts that are opened at a CSD where fungible securities in a company are held for several of the investment firm's clients in omnibus accounts. ESMA referred to the risk that a sales transaction is executed whereas instruments are not available on the account of the client. Delivery and settlement of the securities on the clients' account in such a case could occur at some point of time in the future on an automated basis, and, therefore, the instruments of an unrelated client are used to settle the transaction. Investment firms are required by MiFID II to prevent these situations by taking measures that may include:[200]

---

191 Recital 10 MiFID II (Commission) Directive.
192 *Ibid.*
193 Art. 5(2) MiFID II (Commission) Directive.
194 Art. 5(2)(a) MiFID II (Commission) Directive.
195 Art. 5(2)(b) MiFID II (Commission) Directive.
196 Art. 5(2) sub-para. 2 MiFID II (Commission) Directive.
197 *Ibid.*
198 ESMA/2014/1570, 61.
199 *Ibid.*
200 Art. 5(3) MiFID II (Commission) Directive.

- the conclusion of arrangements with clients on the measures to be taken by the firm in case the client does not have the required instruments on its account on the settlement date (e.g. borrowing of securities or unwinding the position);
- the close monitoring of the projected ability to deliver the instruments on the settlement date and implementing remedial measures if this cannot be done; and
- the monitoring and prompt requesting of undelivered securities that are outstanding on the settlement date and beyond.

6.4.5.3   SFTs and Collateralization

Investment firms have to make sure that specific arrangements are adopted for all clients to ensure that the borrower of client financial instruments provide appropriate collateral, irrespective of whether it concerns arrangements for retail or non-retail clients.[201] Firms are expected to monitor on an ongoing basis the appropriateness of such collateral and to take the necessary steps to maintain the balance with the value of client assets.[202] The duty of investment firms to monitor collateral applies when they are party to an SFT agreement. The monitoring duty also applies to investment firms that act as an agent for the conclusion of a SFT or in the case of a tripartite agreement between the external borrower, the client and the investment firm.[203]

6.4.6   SFTs and TTCA

Article 5(5) MiFID II (Commission) Directive ensures that investment firms do not enter into arrangements that are prohibited under Article 16(10) MiFID II.[204] Article 16(10) MiFID II precludes the use of TTCAs by any party for retail clients. Article 5(1) (Commission) Directive, however, allows investment firms to enter into arrangements for SFTs if retail client's consent has been given for the use of their assets by any party. Article 16 (10) MiFID II does not explicitly affect the use of retail client instruments under Article 5 (1) (Commission) Directive.[205] Some types of transactions that fall under the definition of a 'securities financing transaction',[206] such as securities lending, require the transfer of title in some jurisdictions.[207] The use of retail client financial instruments is allowed when all the requirements under Article 5(1) (Commission) Directive would be met.[208]

---

201 Art. 5(4) MiFID II (Commission) Directive; ESMA/2014/1570, 64.
202 Art. 5(4) MiFID II (Commission) Directive.
203 Recital 9 MiFID II (Commission) Directive.
204 *See also* Recital 8 MiFID II (Commission) Directive.
205 ESMA/2014/1570, 56.
206 'Securities financing transactions' are defined in: Art. 3(11) Regulation 2015/2365 on the transparency of securities financing transactions and of reuse; *See* Art. 1(3) MiFID II (Commission) Directive; *See also* S.L. Schwarcz, *Systemic Risk*, 1 Georgetown Law Journal (2008).
207 ESMA/2014/1570, 56.
208 *Ibid.*

Under Article 16(10) MiFID II such a transaction requiring the transfer of title would qualify as a collateral arrangement concluded with a retail client for the purpose of securing or otherwise covering present or future, actual or contingent or prospective obligations that are prohibited under Article 16(10) MiFID II. Article 5(5) MiFID II (Commission) Directive, thus, ensures that investment firms do not enter into TTCAs on the basis of Article 5(1) (Commission) Directive that are prohibited under Article 16(10) MiFID II.

6.4.7   Inappropriate Use of TTCA

MiFID II requires investment firms to safeguard client assets. Under TTCAs investment firms can take full ownership of client financial instruments and funds for the purpose of securing or covering present or future, actual or contingent or prospective obligations of any client.[209] Clients lose their legal title to the instruments and funds subjected to the TTCA and, instead, receive a contractual claim that entails the investment firm's promise to repay funds or (equivalent) financial instruments. The loss of legal entitlement to the client instruments and funds implies that those client assets do not benefit from the MiFID II client asset protection regime that would otherwise apply if a TTCA would not have been concluded. Under TTCAs concluded, the nature of the risks involved for the client alter from having full ownership to a contractual claim resulting in a counterparty risk that could materialize upon an insolvency of the investment firm.[210] TTCAs may be used for transactions, such as repos or rehypothecation in prime brokerage.[211] Considering the risks with TTCAs, Article 16(10) MiFID II prohibits investment firms to conclude TTCA with retail clients for the purpose of securing or covering present or future, actual or contingent or prospective obligations for clients.[212] MiFID II, however, does not prohibit investment firms from concluding TTCAs with non-retail (professional and eligible counterparties) clients under MiFID II. Non-retail clients could also be exposed to risks resulting from TTCAs that undermine the effectiveness of the segregation of client assets requirements.[213] This could lead to the indiscriminate use of TTCAs with regard to non-retail clients. In light of the effects of TTCAs on investment firms' duties towards clients and in ensuring that the MiFID II safeguarding and segregation rules are not undermined, MiFID II, thus, regulates the indiscriminate use of TTCAs.[214]

---

209 *See* Recital 52 MiFID II. *See also* European Commission, *Review of the Markets in Financial Instruments Directive (MiFID)* (Public Consultation), 8 December 2010, 70.
210 Recital 6 MiFID II (Commission) Directive.
211 ESMA/2014/1570, 55.
212 *See* Recital 6 MiFID II (Commission) Directive.
213 European Commission, *Review of the Markets in Financial Instruments Directive (MiFID)* (Public Consultation), 8 December 2010, 18.
214 Recital 6, Art. 6 MiFID II (Commission) Directive.

6.4.7.1 TTCA

Recital 52 MiFID II refers to the Financial Collateral Directive for a definition of 'title transfer financial collateral arrangement'. Under Article 2(1)(b) FCD[215] a 'title transfer financial collateral arrangement' means:

> an arrangement, including repurchase agreements, under which a collateral provider transfers full ownership of financial collateral to a collateral taker for the purpose of securing or otherwise covering the performance of relevant financial obligations.

6.4.7.2 Appropriateness of TTCAs

Investment firms are allowed to use TTCA if they demonstrate the appropriateness of TTCA in relation to the client obligations and disclose the risks involved, as well as, the effect of the TTCAs on client assets.[216] When considering and documenting the appropriateness of the use of TTCAs, investment firms shall take into account whether:[217]
- there is only a very weak connection between the client's liability or consideration to the firm and the use of TTCAs, including where the likelihood of a liability arising is slow or negligible;
- the amount of client funds or financial instruments that are subject to TTCAs far exceeds the client's liability, or is even unlimited if the client has any liability at all to the firm; or
- the firm insist that all clients' assets must be subject to TTCAs, without considering what obligation each client has to the firm.

Investment firms in demonstrating a connection under TTCAs and client's liability do not preclude taking appropriate security against client obligations.[218] Investment firms under MiFID II may require sufficient collateral and, where appropriate, so by a TTCA.

The obligation to demonstrate a 'robust link' does not prevent the compliance of an investment firm with the obligations under EMIR and does not prohibit the use of appropriate TTCAs for concluding contingent liability transactions or repos for non-retail clients.[219] Investment firms are required to have a documented process of their use of TTCAs.[220] The ability of investment firms to enter into TTCAs does not exempt firms

---

215 Directive 2002/47/EC of the European Parliament and of the Council of 6 June 2002 on financial collateral arrangements, OJ L 146, 10 June 2009, 37 ('Financial Collateral Directive; FCD').
216 Recital 6, Art. 6(1) MiFID II (Commission) Directive; ESMA/2014/1570, 63.
217 Art. 6(2) MiFID II (Commission) Directive.
218 Recital 7 MiFID II (Commission) Directive.
219 Ibid.
220 Recital 6, Art. 6(1) MiFID II (Commission) Directive.

from the need to obtain clients' prior express consent to use client assets.[221] Provided that the above-mentioned conditions are met, investment firms still may make use of TTCAs, if besides the appropriateness of the TTCA, they ensure that their non-retail clients are properly informed of the risks involved and the effect of the TTCA on the assets of the client when concluding a TTCA.[222]

6.4.8   Governance Arrangements Concerning the Safeguarding of Client Assets

Article 16(2) MiFID II requires investment firms to establish adequate policies and procedures to ensure compliance of the investment firm with the governance arrangements concerning the safeguarding of client assets.[223] Notwithstanding the existing requirements relating to the compliance function, investment firms are required by MiFID II to appoint a single officer of sufficient skill and authority with specific responsibility for matter relating to the compliance by firms with their obligations regarding the safeguarding of client financial instruments and funds.[224] The appointment of such an officer reduces fragmented responsibility across various departments and prevents the occurrence of insufficient seniority and oversight within the organization of an investment firm to solve issues related to client assets.[225] The single officer is not only required to possess sufficient skills and authority, they also have the duty to report to the investment firm's senior management in respect of compliance with the safeguarding of client assets requirements.[226] MiFID II allows the single officer to carry out additional roles where this does not prevent the officer from fulfilling his duties related to the safeguarding client financial instruments and funds effectively.[227] Article 7 MiFID II (Commission) Directive, thus, allows investment firms to decide whether full compliance with this regime is done by a single appointed officer solely dedicated to this task or whether the officer has additional responsibilities.[228]

6.4.9   Reports by External Auditors

Investment firms are required to ensure that external auditors report, at least, annually to the Competent Authority of the home Member State of the investment firm on the adequacy of the safeguarding of client financial instruments and funds.[229]

---

221 Recital 6 MiFID II (Commission) Directive.
222 Art. 6(3) MiFID II (Commission) Directive; ESMA/2014/1570, 56, 64.
223 Art. 16(2) MiFID II; Arts. 7 and 8 MiFID II (Commission) Directive.
224 Art. 7 sub-para. 1 MiFID II (Commission) Directive.
225 Recital 5 MiFID II (Commission) Directive.
226 *Ibid.*
227 Recital 5, Art. 7 sub-para. 2 MiFID II (Commission) Directive; ESMA/2014/1570, 55.
228 Art. 7 sub-para. 2 MiFID II (Commission) Directive.
229 Art. 8 MiFID II (Commission) Directive.

6.5   CONCLUSION

The European Commission in a Commission Communication reviewing possible developments on the regulation of UCITS depositaries defined custodians as

> an entity entrusted with the safekeeping and administration of securities and other financial assets on behalf of others, and may moreover provide additional services, including clearing and settlement, cash management, foreign exchange and securities lending.

Although not directly targeted, CRD IV and MiFID II regulate credit institutions and investment firms that provide the service 'safekeeping and administration of securities/financial instruments' as an ancillary service.[230] The CRD IV definition defines the activity as 'safekeeping and administration of securities', whereas the MiFID II definition is more extended. The CRD IV ancillary service definition, however, has to be interpreted in the light of the MiFID II definition. The nature of MiFID II is to prevent regulatory arbitrage between MiFID II and CRD IV.[231] In addition, credit institutions performing investment services are investment firms that fall under the scope of MiFID II and MiFID II has been adopted at a later stage. Under MiFID II and the CRD IV, CSDs are excluded that are authorized for providing and maintaining securities accounts at the top tier level ('central maintenance service'). Regardless of the core services provided, CSDs may, as a non-banking ancillary service, maintain securities accounts in relation to the settlement service, collateral management and other ancillary services.[232] CSDs are under this ancillary service allowed to open 'lower tier' securities accounts, either in direct holding systems or by acting as an 'investor CSD' by maintaining securities accounts for its customers for securities issued in 'issuer CSD s'.[233] Investor CSDs, thus, partly provide similar services as 'custodians' under CRD IV and MiFID II. The core services provided under the CSDR, however, delineate 'investor CSDs' from 'custodians'.

The ancillary service status leaves a regulatory gap as for the activity itself credit institutions nor investment firms have to obtain an authorization under the CRD IV and MiFID II. National Member States are, thus, free to regulate their own national custodians. Nevertheless, 'national custodians'[234] in most Member States have to be authorized according to national legislation that is largely based upon CRD IV/MiFID II. The question to be answered in this chapter was what custodians are and whether and to what extent custodians are regulated in the EEA. Custodians within the meaning of the Com-

---

230 Annex I n. 12 CRD IV.
231 *See* Key, *supra* note 24.
232 Annex – List of Services, S. B n. 4 CSDR.
233 European Commission, *supra* note 66.
234 Legal Certainty Group, *supra* note 5, 25.

munication of the European Commission are entrusted with the safekeeping and administration of securities and other financial assets on behalf of others, including various ancillary services.[235] By reviewing credit institutions, investment firms, 'investor CSDs' and the MiFID II client asset requirements, this chapter highlighted that credit institutions, investment firms and 'national custodians' based upon MiFID II and CRD IV are to be seen as 'custodians'.

---

235 European Commission, *supra* note 1.

7   DEPOSITARY VERSUS CUSTODIAN REGULATION

The previous chapters have shown that the core activity under the AIFMD, UCITSD V and IORPD II for which a depositary is required to be appointed is the safekeeping of assets.[1] The safekeeping function includes the custody function for financial instruments that can be held in custody and record-keeping of ownership of 'other assets' that cannot be held in custody.[2] Under CRD IV and MiFID II, a 'custodian'[3] is a credit institution or an investment firm entrusted with the safekeeping and administration of securities on behalf of others.[4] Both depositaries and custodians also provide additional (ancillary) services such as securities lending, brokerage and the execution of foreign exchange trades.[5] The core activity for both depositaries and custodians under the respective investment law directives is the safekeeping and administration of assets on behalf of others. Depositaries are, thus, custodians. Under the AIFMD and UCITSD V, the notion of 'depositary' is wider than the notion of a pure 'custodian'.[6] UCITSD V and the AIFMD, for example, require the depositary to perform additional oversight functions.[7] The viewpoint that depositaries are custodians that, on top of the safekeeping function, perform oversight duties is confirmed by IORPD II that refers to both entities that are pure 'custodians' and 'AIFMD/UCITSD V depositaries' performing both safekeeping and oversight functions. Depending upon the IORPD II Member State implementation, 'depositaries'[8] may be required to perform merely the safekeeping function or both safekeeping and oversight duties.[9] Unsurprisingly, the same 'global custodians' provide as a 'depositary' safekeeping services to UCITS, AIFs, IORPs, whereas, at the same time, they act as a 'custodian' under MiFID II, CRD IV or national Member State laws to investors,

---

1   Art. 21(8) AIFMD; Art. 22(5) UCITSD V; Art. 34 IORPD II.
2   *Ibid.*
3   Both CRD IV and MiFID II do not make reference to this term. *See* Chapter 6.
4   European Commission, *Communication from the Commission to the Council and to the European parliament – Regulation of UCITS depositaries in the Member States: review and possible developments*, 30 March 2004, COM(2004) 207 final; *See* Annex I s. B MiFID II. Annex I CRD IV.
5   *See* Annex I s. B MiFID II; *See* Annex I CRD IV; European Commission, *Impact Assessment – Commission Delegated Regulation supplementing Directive 2009/65/EC of the European Parliament and of the Council with regard to obligations of depositaries*, {C(2015) 9160 final}, 5, Annex 4: Impact Assessment refers to activities/services that are not considered as depositary functions under UCITS, including, amongst others, fund accounting/administration, transfer agency, foreign exchange management, prime brokerage, treasury and securities lending, collateral management, banking services and the performance of investment (ancillary) services under MiFID II.
6   European Commission, *supra* note 5, 5, Annex 4.
7   Art. 21(9) AIFMD; Art. 22(3) UCITSD V; Art. 35 IORPD II.
8   Note that the IORPD II refers to both 'depositaries' and 'custodians': Chapter 5, section 5.4.1.
9   *See* Art. 33, 35 IORPD II.

such as pension funds, insurance companies and individual investors.[10] The regulation and oversight for depositaries and custodians relate to the performance of the safekeeping function, thus, both direct to risks related to, for instance, the misappropriation of assets and the prevention of a loss of assets as a result of the insolvency of the depositary/custodian. The AIFMD, UCITSD V and IORPD II, however, apply additional conduct of business rules to depositaries to target risks that relate to the depositary's oversight functions.[11]

7.1   AUTHORIZATION

7.1.1   Credit Institutions, Investment Firms and 'Equivalent Other Legal Entities'

In essence, both depositaries and pure 'custodians' are, at least, performing the safekeeping function as a custodian. This is also reflected in the authorization requirements and the supervision of intermediaries that are allowed to be eligible as a custodian under MiFID II and CRD IV and as a depositary under the AIFMD, UCITSD V and IORPD II.[12] The AIFMD, UCITSD V and IORPD II do not contain a separate authorization regime for depositaries as is the case for AIFMs, UCITS ManCos and IORPs. Instead, these three directives reflect the 'Custody Plus' nature of the depositary, i.e. the depositary as a custodian performing additional oversight duties, by (partly) referring to credit institutions, investment firms or equivalent 'other legal entities' as eligible depositaries/custodians that are regulated in other European legislative acts.

Under the AIFMD, eligible 'per sé depositaries' are credit institutions authorized under CRD IV and investment firms authorized under MiFID II for the performance of the ancillary service of safekeeping and administration of financial instruments for the account of clients in accordance with MiFID II.[13] Article 21(3) AIFMD further refers to Non-EEA Entities,[14] prime brokers[15] and UCITSD IV/V depositaries[16] as eligible AIFMD depositaries. De facto, the latter three types of eligible entities are legal entities subject to equivalent prudential regulation and ongoing supervision as credit institutions and investment firms under CRD IV and MiFID II. Depending upon the locational restrictions under the AIFMD, AIFMs may either appoint a credit institution or any other entity of the same nature as an EEA investment firm may be appointed as a 'TC deposi-

---

10 European Commission, *supra* note 5, 5.
11 J. de Larosière, *The High-Level Group on Financial Supervision in the EU*, 25 February 2009, http://ec. europa.eu/internal_market/finances/docs/de_larosiere_report_en.pdf.
12 Art. 21(3) AIFMD; Art. 23(2) UCITSD V; Art. 33(3) IORPD II.
13 Art. 21(3)(a) and (b) AIFMD.
14 Art. 21(3)(c) sub-para. 2 AIFMD.
15 Art. 21(4)(b) AIFMD.
16 *See* Chapter 4, Section 4.3.1.3.

tary'. The 'TC depositary' shall, however, be subject to effective prudential regulation, including minimum capital requirements and supervision, that has the same effect as EU law and is effectively enforced.[17] Prime brokers allowed to be appointed may under Article 4(1)(af) AIFMD be credit institutions, investment firms or 'another entity subject to prudential regulation and ongoing supervision'.[18] Article 4(1)(af) AIFMD, however, refers to the appointment of a credit institution as a counterparty. Prime brokers that are eligible as a depositary, in addition to 'the conflicts of management rule',[19] need to fulfil the eligible entities and location restriction provisions under the AIFMD. Apart from credit institutions[20] and investment firms,[21] only prime brokers that would qualify as eligible 'TC depositaries' for TC-AIFs or UCITSD V depositaries would be eligible as a depositary.

'PE depositaries' are an exception to the 'Custody Plus' model of depositaries under the AIFMD. Depending upon the Member State implementation of the 'PE depositary option',[22] 'PE depositaries' that are eligible under the AIFMD for closed-end AIFs cannot be seen as 'custodians' that are performing safekeeping and oversight duties. 'PE depositaries' are professionals or investment firms regulated under national law that may be appointed for AIFs that mainly do not invest in financial instruments that can be held in custody.[23] The AIFMD formally treats 'PE depositaries' as custodians by assigning both the custody task for financial instruments that can be held in custody and the record-keeping task for 'other assets' to these type of depositaries. In addition, 'PE depositaries' also fall within the scope of the 'guarantor liability regime' of Article 21(12) AIFMD. In practice, however, various Member States in their national implementations limit the safekeeping task of 'PE depositaries' to merely the record-keeping task for 'other assets' under Article 21(8)(b) AIFMD. It, thus, depends upon the Member State implementation of national Member States whether or not the professionals and 'national investment firms'[24] eligible as 'PE depositary' can be seen as a custodian performing additional oversight duties.

Under UCITSD V, an exhaustive list of entities is eligible to be appointed as a depositary.[25] Those entities are limited to national central banks,[26] credit institutions[27] and other legal entities authorized under the laws of individual Member States to carry out

---

17 Art. 21(3)(c) sub-para. 2 AIFMD.
18 The latter reference is similar to the appointment of non-EEA entities as depositaries under the AIFMD. Art. 21(3)(c) sub-para. 2 AIFMD allows for TC-AIFs, either a credit institution or 'any other entity of the same nature as an EEA investment firm' to be appointed.
19 Art. 21(4)(b) AIFMD.
20 Art. 21(3)(a) AIFMD; Art. 23(2)(b) UCITSD V.
21 Art. 21(3)(b) AIFMD; Art. 23(2)(c) UCITSD V.
22 *See* Chapter 4, Section 4.3.1.6.
23 *Ibid.*
24 Art. 21(3)(c) sub-para. 3 UCITSD V.
25 Recital 25, Art. 23 UCITSD V.
26 Art. 23(2)(a) UCITSD V.
27 Art. 23(2)(b) UCITSD V.

depositary activities.[28] These 'other entities' must be subject to 'equivalent' prudential and ongoing supervision regulation as investment firms under MiFID II.[29] Examples include investment firms,[30] (investor) CSDs,[31] prime brokers[32] and various other legal entities eligible under national UCITSD V Member State implementation laws.[33] Member States, however, remain to have discretion to identify which entities in the exhaustive list of entities are eligible to act as UCITS depositaries.[34]

Under Article 33 IORPD II, Member State implementation laws decide whether an 'AIFMD/UCITSD V depositary' or 'custodian' is compulsory to be appointed for IORPs. Similar as to the AIFMD and UCITSD V, Article 33(3) IORPD II requires Member States not to restrict IORPs from appointing, a 'custodian' established in another Member State and duly authorized in accordance with CRD IV or MiFID II, or accepted as a depositary for the purpose of UCITSD V or the AIFMD.[35] Similar as for the AIFMD, IORPD II and UCITSD V, thus, treat their depositaries as 'custodians' performing additional oversight duties and allow credit institutions, investment firms and other eligible entities providing equivalent investor protection as credit institutions and investment firms to be appointed as depositaries and custodians.

CRD IV and MiFID II regulate the safekeeping and administration of securities on behalf of others as 'ancillary service'.[36] As a consequence, Member States may in their national laws also allow other entities to be authorized as custodian. There are, thus, not only European custodians regulated under CRD IV and MiFID II but also 'national custodians'.[37] Member States, generally, require similar authorization, prudential and business organizational requirements to national custodians that are fully or partly based upon CRD IV and MiFID II.[38]

Depositaries and custodians under the various European investment law directives may be credit institutions, investment firms or 'equivalent other legal entities'. Most depositaries and custodians operating in Europe are authorized as credit institution under CRD IV.[39] Investment firms account for a small portion of the market. In comparison to credit institutions, investment firms have, however, significantly fewer assets in cus-

---

28 Art. 23(2)(c) UCITSD V.
29 *See* Chapter 4, Section 4.3.2.3.
30 *See* Chapter 4, Section 4.3.2.3.1.
31 *See* Chapter 4, Section 4.3.2.3.2.
32 *See* Chapter 4, Section 4.3.2.3.3.
33 *See* Chapter 4, Section 4.3.2.3.4.
34 Art. 23(3) UCITSD V.
35 Art. 33(3) IORPD II; By referring to 'not restricting IORPs from appointing', Art. 33(3) IORPD II leaves it up to Member States to allow other eligible entities to be appointed as an IORP custodian or depositary. Member States in practice, however, do not make use of this option. *See* Chapter 5, Section 5.3.2.
36 European Commission, *supra* note 4; *See* Annex I s. B MiFID II. Annex I CRD IV.
37 Legal Certainty Group, *Second Advice of the Legal Certainty Group – Solutions to Legal Barriers related to Post-Trading within the EU*, August 2008, 25.
38 *Ibid.*
39 European Commission, *supra* note 5, 81 and 82.

tody.[40] Equivalent other legal entities are effectively 'single market' depositaries/custodians that have in practice, as a result of the absence of an European passport, lost the race in competing with credit institutions and investment firms on both service and cost.[41] Nevertheless, the authorization, conduct of business rules, prudential regulation, supervision and enforcement of credit institutions, investment firms and 'equivalent other entities' are considered under the various European investment law directives to be appropriately addressing the risks related to the safekeeping function of custodians and depositaries. The notion of 'depositary' under IORPD II, UCITSD V and the AIFMD is wider than the notion of pure 'custodian'.[42] For this reason, IORPD II, UCITSD V and the AIFMD require additional conduct of business rules to be fulfilled for depositaries that in their capacity of acting as a custodian perform oversight duties. Depositary law is, thus, a separate area of law applying on top of the 'general law' applying to credit institutions, investment firms or 'other equivalent legal entities' authorized to act as a custodian.

7.1.2   Authorization Requirements

Eligible depositaries and custodians that are regulated under CRD IV, MiFID II and equivalent (national) regulation are required to comply with the same general authorization requirements in reducing risks related to the safekeeping function. Examples of risks mitigated include the loss of investor' assets caused by negligent or fraudulent practices and the insolvency risk of depositaries/custodians as financial intermediaries.

Some of the authorization requirements to be found in MiFID II, CRD IV and 'equivalent legal entities' to which depositaries/custodians are subjected include:[43]
– fit and properness requirements for senior management;[44]
– (minimum) capital requirements;[45]
– a business plan;[46]
– an adequate risk organization;[47]
– an adequate and appropriate business organization;[48]
– reliable significant shareholders.[49]

---

40 *Ibid.*
41 K.M. Löber, *The Developing EU Legal Framework for Clearing and Settlement of Financial Instruments*, European Central Bank – Legal Working Paper Series, No. 1 (February 2006), 21; European Commission, *supra* note 5, 115-116.
42 European Commission, *supra* note 5, Annex 4.
43 *See* D.A. Zetzsche, *The AIFMD and the Joint Principles of European Asset Management Law* (D.A. Zetzsche ed., Kluwer 2015), 749.
44 Art. 9 MiFID II; Art. 91 CRD IV.
45 Art. 15 MiFID II; Art. 12 CRD IV.
46 Art. 7 MiFID II; Art. 8 CRD IV.
47 Art. 16(2) MiFID II; Art. 74 CRD IV.
48 Art. 16(3) MiFID II; Art. 74 CRD IV.
49 Art. 10 MiFID II; Art. 14 CRD IV.

Authorization requirements set out the conditions for entering the depositary/custodian market. The fit and properness, business plan, adequate/appropriate business organizational and reliable significant shareholders requirements ensure that depositaries/custodians participating in the market have enough knowledge, resources, skills and the right 'ethical attitude'.[50] Initial and ongoing capital requirements ensure that only solvent depositaries/custodians offer their services, whereas requiring an adequate and appropriate business organization prevents both fraudulent and financially instable depositaries/custodians from being active. By requiring these conditions to be fulfilled, regulation for both depositaries and custodians set out similar conditions of entry complemented by conduct of business rules and prudential regulation.

7.2   BUSINESS ORGANIZATIONAL REQUIREMENTS

Conduct of business rules have as its purpose to protect investors and to preserve market integrity.[51] The need for this has been highlighted by the Madoff affair.[52] Similar as for authorization requirements, the business organizational requirements for eligible depositaries and custodians under the European investment law directives show common principles as they are all regulated under CRD IV MiFID II and equivalent (national) regulation.[53] CRD IV, MiFID II and equivalent (national) regulation lay down general organizational requirements that custodians and depositaries as financial intermediaries need to comply with. The general conduct of business requirements under CRD IV, MiFID II and equivalent (national legislation) contain similar rules that include, *inter alia*:[54]

- the commitment to fairness, honesty and acting in the investor's best interest;[55]
- conflict of interests rules;[56]
- rules on the intermediary's remuneration;[57] and
- the prohibition of letter-box entities.[58]

---

50 IOSCO, *Objectives and Principles of Securities Regulation*, Part II The Regulator (2003), 33, www.legco.gov. hk/yr04- 05/english/panels/fa/papers/fa0217cb1-880-9e.pdf.

51 *Ibid.*, 35.

52 S. Gene, *Luxembourg Called On to "Brush Up" Governance*, Financial Times, Fund Management Supplement, (26 January 2009); P. Skypala, *UCITS Victory Soured by Madoff Scandal*, Financial Times, Fund Management Supplement, (19 January 2009), 6; P. Hollinger, B. Hall & N. Tait, *Grand Duchy Hits Back at Madoff*, Financial Times (14 January 2009), 23; P. Hollinger & J. Chung, *Madoff Affair Sparks Demand for Revamp of Investment Fund Rules*, Financial Times, (13 January 2009), 15.

53 Zetzsche, *supra* note 43.

54 *Ibid.*, 749.

55 Recital 86, Art. 24(1) MiFID II; Art. 91(8) CRD IV.

56 Art. 16(3) MiFID II; Art. 88 CRD IV.

57 Art. 9(3)(c) MiFID II; Art. 92 CRD IV.

58 Art. 16(5) MiFID II.

These general requirements imposed on depositaries and custodians are equivalent to those of other financial intermediaries [59] regulated on the European level. Specific requirements are laid down in MiFID II for investment firms entrusted with the ancillary service[60] of providing safekeeping and administration of securities on behalf of others.[61] Custodians regulated under CRD IV are not subject to any specific requirements other than the general authorization and conduct of business requirements. In addition, the AIFMD, IORPD II and UCITSD V, on top of that, require specific conduct of business rules to be fulfilled that relate to the depositary's safekeeping and oversight functions.[62]

In discussing the conduct of business rules applying to both depositaries and custodians, there is an 'internal' and an 'external dimension'. The internal dimension relates to rules that prevent risks related to the depositary/custodian and its sub-custodians. The external dimension to rules imposed on depositaries/custodians that function as a risk-mitigation mechanism for operation risks that do not relate to the depositary/custodian itself.

7.2.1   *The Internal Dimension: Depositaries versus Custodians – Key Risks*

Conduct of business rules not only protect investors and preserve market integrity in serving as 'external risk mitigating mechanism' but also prevent the risks related to the use of (third party) depositaries/custodians and their sub-custodian network.[63]

7.2.1.1   The Segregation of Assets and Third Party Custody

Depositaries/custodians are required to segregate assets.[64] There is, however, a risk that these 'client assets' in the depositary's/custodian's care may become co-mingled with:
– the assets of the investment firm, AIFM, UCITS ManCo or IORP (governing body);[65]
– the assets of the depositary/sub-custodian throughout the custody chain; or
– the assets of other investors of the depositary/custodian, unless held in a permissible omnibus account.[66]

---

59   *See, for instance,* insurance companies under Solvency II.
60   *See* Annex I s. B MiFID II. Annex I CRD IV.
61   European Commission, *supra* note 4.
62   De Larosière, *supra* note 11.
63   Oxera, *The Role of Custody in European Asset Management,* 20, www.oxera.com/Latest-Thinking/Publications/Reports/2002/The-role-of-custody-in-European-asset-management.aspx.
64   *See* Art. 21(11)(d)(iii) AIFMD; Art. 22a(3) UCITSD V; Art. 2(1)(a) MiFID II (Commission) Directive; IORPD II and CRD IV do not explicitly refer to asset segregation related to the safekeeping function. Although no statutory asset segregation duty applies, this principle is also applied by custodians and depositaries under IORPD II and CRD IV.
65   *See* Art. 21(11)(d)(iii) AIFMD; Art. 22a(3) UCITSD V.
66   *See, e.g.* Art. 5(2) MiFID II (Commission) Directive.

The co-mingling of assets could result in the ownership of the assets belonging to investors, AIFs, UCITS or IORPs to be called in question upon an insolvency of the depositary/custodian.[67] As a result, the difficulties in verifying ownership of assets could result in client assets being used to fulfil the claims of personal creditors of depositary/custodians.

The AIFMD and UCITSD V require a third party depositary to be appointed.[68] In addition, MiFID II allows 'self-custody' for investment firms under the condition that the safeguarding of client assets regime is being applied.[69] In this way, the AIFMD, UCITSD V and MiFID II try to curb conflicts of interest. CRD IV does not contain specific, but general conflicts of interest rules that require conflicts between their custodian department and other functions to be remedied. Regardless of the third party depositary/custodian requirement, almost all depositaries/custodians appointed are credit institutions, investment firms or equivalent entities.[70] Credit institutions and investment firms may not be authorized for 'custody services' on a stand-alone basis. Instead, their provision of these services is under CRD IV and MiFID II always an 'ancillary service'.[71] For these entities there are, thus, always conflicts of interest present that will need to be remedied. The safety and integrity of assets may, thus, be at risk if the depositary/custodian or any of its sub-custodians fail to address conflicts of interest in a way that minimizes conflicts between its custody department and other functions.[72]

7.2.1.2 Safekeeping

Most risks conduct of business rules aim to resolve relate to the 'custody task' of depositaries and custodians. The risks related to the record-keeping of 'other assets' and oversight duties are less prominent.

The custody task of depositaries/custodians is characterized by multiple tiers of holding. Financial instruments that can be held in custody are for the largest part dematerialized and immobilized in a CSD that constitute the first tier of holding. Since investors are not usually members of the CSD, they will have accounts at depositaries/custodians that is a member of the CSD creating at least two tiers in the custody holding chain.[73] There may be many more tiers, with each depositary/custodian concluding agreements with sub-custodians. Risks depositary and custodian regulation intend to mitigate with conduct of business rules, thus, relate to risks (1) at the level of the depositary/custodian

---

67 IOSCO, *Standards for the Custody of Collective Investment Schemes' Assets – Final Report*, FR 25/2015, November 2015, 6, https://www.iosco.org/library/pubdocs/pdf/IOSCOPD512.pdf.
68 Art. 21(1) AIFMD; Art. 22(1) UCITSD V.
69 *See* Art. 13(2) MiFID II.
70 Art. 21(9) AIFMD; Art. 22(3) UCITSD V; Art. 35 IORPD II; Annex I s. B MiFID II. Annex I CRD IV.
71 Annex I s. B MiFID II; Annex I CRD IV.
72 IOSCO, *supra* note 67, 7.
73 Oxera, *supra* note 63, 14.

and (2) at the level of the sub-custodian. Although there are also risks in the custody holding chain at the CSD level, these risks are being regulated by the CSDR.[74]

Main risks being targeted by conduct of business rules at the level of the depositary/custodian involve the risk of fraud or theft and information technology risk.

The inevitable risk related to the custody function is that the assets could be lost or misappropriated by (an employee of) the depositary/custodian. This could be possible by falsified records or the stealing from accounts belonging to clients.[75] In addition, financial instruments that can be held in custody are held in book-entry form in the accounts opened with the depositary/custodian. There could be fraud, a loss of data, human error or system failures that could result in, for example, incorrectly calculated NAV.[76]

Delegation of custody tasks to sub-custodians may adversely affect the protection of financial instruments that can be held in custody. Clients and depositaries/custodians conclude independent (depositary) contracts.[77] Depositaries/custodians on their turn conclude independent contracts between themselves and a sub-custodian. Clients, such as AIFMs, UCITS ManCos, individual investors or IORP governing bodies do not have any rights under the sub-custodian contract except under the depositary/custodian contract concluded with the depositary/custodian.[78] Delegation, thus, dilutes investor protection as their protection depends upon the sub-custodian contract concluded further down the chain and also the legal insolvency and regulatory laws of the jurisdictions in which those sub-custodians are established.[79] There is no limitation on delegation in the intermediary holding chain. Custody chains make it difficult for AIFMs, UCITS ManCos, individual investors or IORP governing bodies to enforce their claims towards the assets further down the custody holding chain.[80] This risk is further exacerbated by incompatible national securities laws and conflict of law regimes that apply to the different levels of the securities holding chain.[81]

The AIFMD and UCITSD V have introduced a guarantor liability for depositaries that holds depositaries/custodians fully responsible for lost financial instruments that can be

---

74 *See* Chapter 6, Section 6.3.

75 IOSCO, *Report of the IOSCO Technical Committee – Client Asset Protection*, August 1996, 6, https://www.iosco.org/library/pubdocs/pdf/IOSCOPD57.pdf.

76 The AIFMD/UCITSD V liability regime addresses this. *See* Art. 21(12) AIFMD; Art. 24(1) UCITSD V.

77 *See* for the written agreement: Art. 21(1) AIFMD; Art. 22(1) UCITSD V; Art. 33(5) IORPD II.

78 E. Micheler, *Custody Chains and Asset Values*, http://ssrn.com/abstract=2539074.

79 E. Micheler, *Custody Chains and Asset Values: Why Crypto Securities are Worth Contemplating*, 3 Cambridge Law Journal (2015), 1-6.

80 Micheler, *supra* note 78.

81 of Law, Business & Finance (2008), 384-452; L. Thévenoz, *Who holds (Intermediated) Securities? Shareholders, Account Holders, and Nominees?*, 3-4 Uniform Law Review (2010), 845-859; E. Micheler, *Intermediated Securities and Legal Certainty*, LSE Law, Society and Economy Working Papers No. 3 (2014), 3-7; P. Dupont, *Rights of the account holder relating to securities credited to its securities account*, 90-104. (H.P. Conac, U. Segna & L. Thévenoz eds, Cambridge 2013); H.P. Conac, *Rights of the investor*, 105-134. (H.P. Conac, U. Segna & L. Thévenoz eds, Cambridge 2013).

held in custody throughout the entire securities holding chain. Equivalent liability protection does not exist under CRD IV, MiFID II and IORPD II.[82]

Depositaries/custodians often agree in their agreements with clients on the 'right of reuse'.[83] Reuse is defined as any transaction of assets that can be held in custody including, but not limited to, transferring, pledging, selling and lending.[84] AIFs, UCITS, IORPs and individual investors may hold large amounts of (liquid) financial instruments and may reuse these assets through securities lending or as collateral to finance their investment strategies.[85] On the other side, depositaries and custodians may agree upon the reuse the assets of their clients and/or collateral received to fund their balance sheets or to generate additional revenues through collateral management services.

Rehypothecation rights allow a depositary/custodian to treat client's assets as its own and may involve outright title transfers or a security interest accompanied by a right of use.[86] Rights of reuse are inherent in TTCAs (because the ownership of the property actually changes), whereas under, for example, a pledge, the collateral taker will only enjoy rights of rehypothecation if the parties have expressly agreed to this in their written pledge agreement.[87] Rehypothecation is standard market practice allowing depositaries and custodians to offer reduced fees for its services through a reduction in operating costs as a result of access to client' collateral.

For TTCAs and rights of reuse that have been exercised, depositaries/custodians take full ownership of client' instruments and funds. Due to the resulting loss of ownership, clients will no longer benefit from the safekeeping protections under the AIFMD, CRD IV, UCITSD V, IORPD II and MiFID II that would otherwise apply.[88] Instead, clients upon agreeing to a right of reuse accept the depositary's/custodian's promise to repay the funds or (equivalent) financial instruments.[89] The nature of the risks involved for the client is therefore significantly altered as clients do not have a 'proprietary right'[90] (right in rem)[91] towards the assets but instead receive a claim on the depositary/custodian facing counterparty risks (rights in personam).[92] The 2007–2008 crisis, such as the Lehman Brothers bankruptcy,[93] has shown

---

82 *See* Chapter 5, Section 5.3.6 and Chapter 6.
83 *See* for a definition under the right of reuse: Art. 22(7) UCITSD V.
84 *See, e.g.* Art. 22(7) UCITSD V.
85 Art. 21(11)(d)(iv) AIFMD; Art. 22(7) UCITSD V; Art. 16(8) MiFID II and Art. 5 MiFID II (Commission) Directive.
86 M. Singh & J. Aitken, *The (sizeable) Role of Rehypothecation in the Shadow Banking System* (IMF Working Paper 2010).
87 Art. 16(8) MiFID II and Art. 5 MiFID II (Commission) Directive.
88 ESMA/2014/549, 55.
89 *Ibid.*
90 *See* IOSCO, *supra* note 75, 12 and 13; *See also* M. Haentjes, *Harmonisation of Securities Law: Custody and Transfer of Securities in European Private Law* 131-172 (Kluwer 2007).
91 *See* D. Frase, *Custody* (D. Frase ed., Sweet & Maxwell 2011), 274.
92 J.R. Siena, *Depositary Liability: A Fine Mess and How to Get Out of It* (D.A. Zetzsche ed., Kluwer 2015), 450-551.
93 ESMA/2014/549, 60.

the impact of rights of reuse by both the counterparty risks being borne by investors and the systematic implications on the financial system as a whole.[94] In addition, the erosion of client asset protection under the depositary's/custodian's safekeeping obligation was exacerbated by the:

- indiscriminate use of TTCAs;
- inappropriate custody liens on client financial instruments and funds of a too general and wide-ranging nature; and
- the unintended use of client financial instruments.

To prevent the indiscriminate use of the rights of reuse eroding investor protection, the AIFMD, UCITSD V and MiFID II have adopted extra measures. Both the AIFMD and UCITSD V impose restrictions on depositaries and its sub-custodians that want to reuse the assets safekept by the depositary. Under the AIFMD, the AIF's assets may only be used (rehypothecated) if the depositary has received the prior consent of the AIF (or of the AIFM acting on its behalf).[95] To the contrary of the AIFMD, UCITSD V prohibits the depositary or its sub-custodian to reuse UCITS for their own account and reuse is, therefore, only allowed under certain conditions.[96]

Article 16(8) MiFID II contains a general prohibition on using client financial instruments without client consent. Investment firms may not enter into arrangements concerning SFTs in respect of financial instruments held by them on behalf of a client, or otherwise use such financial instruments for their own account or the account of another person or client of the firm, unless:[97]

- the client has given his prior express consent evidenced in writing to the use of the instruments on specified terms;[98] and
- the use of that client's financial instruments is restricted to the specified terms to which the client consents.[99]

Under MiFID II, this general prohibition is complemented by specific rules on:
- the indiscriminate use of TTCAs;[100]
- SFT, TTCA and collateralisation;[101]

---

94 J. Mackintosh, *Lehman Collapse Puts Prime Broker Model in Question*, Financial Times (24 September 2008); G.O. Aragon & P. E. Strahan, *Hedge Funds as Liquidity Providers: Evidence from the Lehman Bankruptcy* (August 2009), www.nber.org/papers/w15336.
95 Art. 21(11)(d)(iv) AIFMD.
96 Art. 22(7) UCITSD V.
97 Art. 5(1) MiFID II (Commission) Directive; MiFID II, in comparison with MiFID I, has extended the written evidence requirement of the express consent to both professional and retail clients.
98 Art. 5(1)(a) MiFID II (Commission) Directive.
99 Art. 5(1)(b) MiFID II (Commission) Directive.
100 Recital 6, Art. 6 MiFID II (Commission) Directive; ESMA/2014/549, 55.
101 Art. 5(5) MiFID II (Commission) Directive; ESMA/2014/549, 56.

- inappropriate custody liens on client financial instruments and funds;[102] and
- prevents the unintended use of client financial instruments.[103]

The same risks applying to depositaries/custodians apply at the level of the sub-custodian.[104] For that reason, the AIFMD and UCITSD V require:
- safekeeping not to be delegated with the intention to avoid the requirements under the AIFMD/UCITSD V;[105]
- an objective reason;[106] and
- due diligence upon the appointment and on an ongoing basis of the sub-custodian, including:[107]
    - adequate structures and expertise;[108]
    - effective prudential regulation;[109]
    - the segregation of assets;[110] and
    - restrictions related to the right of reuse.[111]

MiFID II requires investment firms to firm perform *ex ante* and ongoing due diligence upon depositing of client financial instruments /funds with a custodian.[112] IORPD II allows depositaries/custodians to delegate their safekeeping task while remaining responsible to investors.[113]

Investors holding assets with 'investor CSDs' face additional risks that are regulated by the CSDR.[114] These risks include: asset-commitment risks, the risk that insufficient securities/funds are available to meet commitments (liquidity risk), counterparty risk and the risk of CSDs acting as an 'investor-CSD' ('CSD-on-CSD risk').[115]

Those of the risks involved that are related to 'other assets', such as physical gold and wine, are less complex given the fact that these assets fall outside the intermediary holding chain. Typically, there are only two tiers of 'safekeeping' (recordkeeping) involved. 'PE depositaries' that are almost exclusively safekeeping 'other assets' are, therefore, subject to less stringent conduct of business rules and prudential regulation.[116] Risks related

---

102 Art. 16(10) MiFID II; Art. 6 MiFID II (Commission) Directive; ESMA/2014/549, 60.
103 Art. 5(3) MiFID II (Commission) Directive; ESMA/2014/549, 61.
104 Oxera, *supra* note 63, 20 and 21.
105 Art. 21(11) AIFMD; Art. 22a UCITSD V.
106 Art. 21(11) sub-para. 2 (b) AIFMD; Art. 22a(2)(b) UCITSD V.
107 Art. 21(11) sub-para. 2(c) AIFMD; Art. 22a(2)(c) UCITSD V.
108 Art. 21(11) sub-para.2 (d)(i) AIFMD; Art. 22a(3)(a)(i) UCITSD V.
109 Art. 21(11) sub-para. 2 (d)(ii) AIFMD; Art. 22a(3)(b) UCITSD V.
110 Art. 21(11)(d)(iii) AIFMD and Art. 22a(3) UCITSD V.
111 Art. 21(11)(d)(iv) AIFMD; Art. 22(7) UCITSD V.
112 Recital 11 MiFID II; Art. 16(10) MiFID II; Art. 3 and 4 MiFID II (Commission) Directive.
113 Art. 34(4) IORPD II.
114 Annex – List of Services, S. B, n. 4 CSDR.
115 Oxera, *supra* note 63, 21.
116 *See* on the 'PE depositary': Art. 21(3)(c) sub-para. 3 AIFMD.

to these 'other assets' involve 'inadequate record-keeping' and additional operational risks.[117] The segregation of 'other assets' depends on depositaries/custodians maintaining appropriate records of ownership.[118] Inadequate record-keeping involves the risk that the title of client' assets is lost or incorrect due to inadequate record-keeping.[119] In addition, the holding of 'other assets' might face additional risks depending upon the nature of these 'other assets'. The safekeeping of physical gold requires, for example, a depositary/(sub-)custodian with appropriate vault facilities. Depositaries/custodians would need to care, for instance, for the physical security of physical gold or other proper storage.[120] If the depositary/custodian cannot offer appropriate services to safekeeping these 'other assets', they are obliged to delegate the safekeeping of these assets to specialized custodians. The conduct of business rules related to the depositary's/custodian's safekeeping and delegation duties regulate this safekeeping task.

7.2.1.3 Oversight Duties

AIFs, UCITS and IORP investors/members face legal and compliance risks where a depositary fails to comply with its oversight duties. Negligence or breaches of depositaries with regard to its oversight duties may lead to investor losses. The AIFMD, UCITSD V and IORPD II, therefore, require depositaries to comply with conduct of business rules related to these oversight duties.[121]

7.2.2 External Dimension: Depositaries versus Custodians as Risk-Mitigation Mechanism

The conduct of business rules applicable have to be understood in light of the 'external dimension' of the role and responsibilities that depositaries and custodians have.

7.2.2.1 Segregation of Assets and Third party Custody

The segregation of assets is a general principle related to the safekeeping task to be applied by depositaries and MiFID II custodians.[122] Both depositaries and custodians are required to segregate assets belonging to, for instance, investors, AIFs, UCITS or IORPs from:

– the assets of the investment firm, AIFM, UCITS ManCo or IORP governing body;[123]
– the assets of the depositary/sub-custodian throughout the custody chain; and

---

117 IOSCO, *supra* note 50.
118 Art. 21(8)(b) AIFMD; Art. 22(5)(b) UCITSD V.
119 IOSCO, *supra* note 50.
120 *Ibid.*, 7.
121 Art. 21(9) AIFMD; Art. 22(3) UCITSD V; Art. 35 IORPD II.
122 *See* Art. 21(11)(d)(iii) AIFMD; Art. 22a(3) UCITSD V; Art. 2(1)(a) MiFID II (Commission) Directive.
123 *See* Art. 21(11)(d)(iii) AIFMD; Art. 22a(3) UCITSD V.

- the assets of other investors of the depositary of the depositary/custodian, unless held in a permissible omnibus account.[124]

Asset segregation is applied by depositaries and custodians to 'safeguard client assets' in the course of ordinary business of investment firms, asset managers, AIFMs, UCITS ManCos and IORP governing bodies. The use of depositaries and custodians prevents misappropriation of client funds[125] by these firms to meet their own expenses. It also prevents the use of client assets to settle claims of the personal creditors of investment firms, AIFMs, UCITS ManCos and IORP governing bodies.[126] In addition, asset segregation prevents a loss of assets if those firms default. Instead, investors are exposed to the risk of misappropriation of assets by the depositary/custodian itself.

Asset segregation is complemented by the insolvency and regulatory law that preserve client' assets in insolvency.[127] Client assets of insolvent depositaries/custodians are receiving differential treatment to prevent the use of these assets to settle claims of the personal creditors of the depositary/custodian. For this purpose, two mechanisms are generally used in the insolvency and regulatory law of Member States. First, insolvency regimes may grant a 'preferential creditor status', i.e. the creditors of the client held by the depositary/custodian are treated as preferred creditors that rank ahead of the creditors of the depositary/custodian upon an insolvency of the latter.[128] Second, regimes provide the 'continuing client ownership of client assets'.[129] This mechanism provides that, although assets are held or controlled by depositaries/custodians, they are not property of the depositary/custodian and available for distribution to the depositary's/custodian's creditors in the event of their insolvency.[130] Under this mechanism, the depositary/custodian may hold the assets through a sub-custodian, but the client retains the title to the assets and can assert title against the depositary/custodian and its creditors.[131] Member States are, for instance, obliged under IORPD II and UCITSD V to implement this mechanism for assets safekept by IORPD II and UCITSD V depositaries and their sub-custodians.[132]

Both mechanisms may be achieved under the private laws of Member States in various ways. In common law jurisdictions, assets under both mechanisms are generally held in trust that requires assets to be able to be 'traced'.[133] In Member States having the con-

---

124 See, e.g. Art. 5(2) MiFID II (Commission) Directive.
125 Art. 2(1)(f) MiFID II (Commission) Directive.
126 Oxera, supra note 63, 17.
127 IOSCO, supra note 75, 12.
128 Ibid., 13.
129 Art. 22(3)(e) and 22(8) UCITSD V; Art. 17 UCITSD V (Commission) Regulation; See ESMA/2014/1183, 14; Art. 33(4) IORPD II.
130 IOSCO, supra note 75, 13.
131 Ibid.
132 Art. 22(3)(e) and 22(8) UCITSD V; Art. 17 UCITSD V (Commission) Regulation; See ESMA/2014/1183, 14; Art. 33(4) IORPD II.
133 R.H. Sitkoff, An Agency Costs Theory of Trust Law, 89 Cornell Law Review 621 (2004).

tinental legal tradition, the same effect is achieved by laws that require assets that are held by providers to (1) be subject to a mandatory ranking of claims[134] or (2) stipulate that client assets are not available to meet the depositary's/custodian's creditor claims.[135] Both mechanisms are only effective if they are supported by asset segregation to distinguish client assets from the assets of the investment firm, AIFM, UCITS ManCo or IORP governing body,[136] the assets of the depositary/sub-custodian, and the assets of other investors of the depositary/custodian, unless held in a permissible omnibus account.[137] These two mechanisms, however, only protect 'counterparty risks' of depositaries/custodians for financial instruments that can be held in custody. The record-keeping obligation for 'other assets' also leads to asset segregation. Clients, however, do not always have a proprietary interest in 'other assets'. Cash is an example of 'other assets' that are merely a claim. Upon the insolvency of a depositary/custodian, clients become an ordinary creditor of the depositary in receivership or liquidation.[138] To the contrary, a loss of financial instruments that can be held in custody do enjoy this protection and the risk of clients related to these assets upon a default of an depositary/custodian are limited to the disruption and inconvenience from the freezing of assets during insolvency proceedings that only lead to loss in terms of liquidity and opportunity costs.

The appointment of a third party depositary/custodian may reduce the risk of misappropriation of client assets by investment firms, AIFMs, UCITS ManCos and IORP governing bodies.[139] In particular, client assets held in a discretionary portfolio may still be moved at the manager's discretion.[140] Asset segregation requirement do not preclude that these parties have control over client accounts.[141] Any of these intermediaries providing (discretionary) management services along the safekeeping function may be tempted to use cash to meet their own expenses or sell assets to settle claims of personal creditors. The risk of misappropriation and other operational risks may be mitigated if assets are held by a third party depositary/custodian.

The AIFMD and UCITSD V require that assets are strictly segregated from the AIFM and UCITS ManCo by requiring the appointment of a mandatory third party depositary. In addition, UCITSD V recognizes that the third party depositary requirement can still be jeopardized by the existence of links related to the common management/supervision and cross-shareholdings/group inclusion between these parties.[142] For this reason, inde-

---

134 *See* Dutch UCITS: 4:37j Wft; *See* for Dutch IORPs: 4:71a Wft.
135 Art. 22(3)(e) and 22(8) UCITSD V; Art. 17 UCITSD V (Commission) Regulation; *See* ESMA/2014/1183, 14; Art. 33(4) IORPD II.
136 *Ibid.*
137 *See* Art. 5(2) MiFID II (Commission) Directive.
138 Oxera, *supra* note 63, 17.
139 Art. 2(1)(f) MiFID II (Commission) Directive/
140 Oxera, *supra* note 63, 17.
141 *Ibid.*
142 *See* Art. 26b UCITSD V; *See also* ESMA/2014/1183, 18; ESMA/2014/1417,

pendence of the UCITS ManCo (investment company) and the UCITS depositary is required.[143]

No similar third party depositary/custodian is available under IORPD II. Member States may require IORPs to appoint a third party depositary, custodian and may even perform self-custody.[144] When no depositary/custodian is appointed for the safekeeping of assets, IORPs are, at least, required to:[145]

- ensure that financial instruments are subject to due care and protection;[146]
- keep records to identify all IORP assets at all times and without delay;[147]
- take the necessary measures to avoid conflicts of interest in relation to the safe-keeping of assets;[148]
- inform the Competent Authorities, upon request, about the manner in which assets are kept.[149]

CRD IV does not contain similar third party custodian requirements. Credit institutions that do not provide any investment services/activities under MiFID II are apparently considered to be subject to conduct of business rules, prudential regulation and supervision of such a nature that a third party custodian requirement is not deemed to be necessary.

Under MiFID II, self-custody performed by credit institutions and investment firms that provide safekeeping and administration of financial instruments for others as an ancillary service is allowed.[150] Under MiFID II, self-custody is possibly allowed as investment firms and credit institutions are, due to its principal risk-taking activities, subject to more stringent conduct of business rules, capital requirements and supervision compared to, for example, AIFMs and UCITS ManCos that do not take principal risks when providing their discretionary investment management services. Self-custody is, however, only allowed under the condition that they employ adequate arrangements to safeguard client assets.[151] The safeguarding of client assets regime is to ensure that investor protection and public confidence is maintained for clients that are dependent on investment firms that provide various investment services/activities to them.[152] In particular, investment firms may hold and control client assets, transfer client assets and use assets, such as cash, to acquire securities in the course of providing their services to clients.[153] The

---

143 See Art. 26b UCITSD V; Art. 21 UCITSD V (Commission) Regulation.
144 See Chapter 5, Section 5.4.1.1.2.
145 Art. 34(5) IORPD II.
146 Art. 34(5)(a) IORPD II.
147 Art. 34(5)(b) IORPD II.
148 Art. 34(5)(c) IORPD II.
149 Art. 34(5)(d) IORPD II.
150 See Chapter 6, Section 6.3.2.
151 See Chapter 6, Section 6.4.
152 IOSCO, *supra* note 75, 7.
153 *Ibid.*

MiFID II safeguarding of client assets regime ensures client asset protection.[154] Adequate arrangements need to be in place to safeguard ownership right of clients, especially in the event of the investment firm's insolvency.[155] The investment firm shall not use the client's financial instruments on own account, except with the consent of the client.[156] In addition, investment firms, when holding client funds, have to make adequate arrangements to safeguard the rights of clients and, except in the case of credit institutions, prevent the use of client funds for its own account.[157] Finally, investment firms shall not conclude any TTCAs with retail clients for the purpose of securing or covering present or future, actual or contingent or prospective obligations of clients.[158] Despite MiFID II allowing self-custody by credit institutions and investment firms providing safekeeping of securities and administration for others, various Member States, however, limit self-custody to credit institutions or specific types of investment firms.[159]

7.2.2.2 Safekeeping, Administration and 'Other Value-added Services'

Both depositaries and custodians have as key objective to protect the physical and legal integrity of assets by means of safekeeping.[160] The safekeeping of assets reduces the risk of theft and accidental destruction of investments.

The safekeeping task for depositaries and custodians applies under the AIFMD, UCITSD V and IORPD II to both financial instruments that can be held in custody[161] and 'other assets'.[162] Although, CRD IV and MiFID II refer to the safekeeping and administration of securities for others, the safekeeping duty of credit institutions and investment need to be considered equivalent.[163]

Under these directives, the 'custody task' is a key risk-mitigation mechanism of the depositary's and custodian's safekeeping task. Mostly financial instruments that can be held in custody are recorded in book-entry systems that are held through accounts with CSDs, thus, avoiding the risk of loss or destruction of the assets upon effecting a transfer of ownership.[164] Custodians act as settlement agents on behalf of others and reduce settlement errors due to their expertise in dealing with CSDs, cash-payment systems and central counterparties. In addition, they have invested in information technology that

---

154 *See* Art. 16(2)-(10) MiFID II.; *See* S.J. Key, *Financial Integration in the European Community*, Board of Governors of the Federal Reserve System – International Finance Discussion Papers, No. 349 (April 1989), 105-106.
155 Art. 16(8) MiFID II.
156 *Ibid.*
157 Art. 16(9) MiFID II.
158 Art. 16(10) MiFID II.
159 Chapter 6, section 4.2.
160 *See* IOSCO, Chapter 7, section 7.2.1.1. *supra* note 67, 3.
161 Art. 21(8)(a) AIFMD; Art. 22(5)(a) UCITSD V.
162 Art. 21(8)(b) AIFMD; Art. 22(5)(b) UCITSD V.
163 *See* Chapter 6, Section 6.2.1.
164 Oxera, *supra* note 63, 17.

identifies problems related to trades, simplifies the collection of client entitlements, responses to corporate actions, identifies large or risky trades and verifies trade information.[165] This, in addition to the regular and independent reconciliation of assets, may bring to light both errors and fraudulent activities.

To the contrary, all other assets that by their nature cannot be held in custody (e.g. derivate instruments or physical gold) are subject to the record-keeping obligation of the depositary/custodian, i.e. the depositary/custodian needs to maintain and keep up-to-date a record of all 'other assets'.[166] The risk mitigation role of depositaries and custodians is less pronounced for these 'other assets'. Financial instruments that can be held in custody are recorded in book-entry systems that are held through accounts with CSDs, thus, creating a minimum of two tiers of custody. This intermediary holding chain is necessary as investors are not usually allowed to be members of CSDs.[167] 'Other assets', to the contrary, do not fall within the scope of the 'intermediary holding chain' and, therefore, no tiers of custody are involved.[168]

Additional investor protection offered by depositaries/custodians depend upon 'administration' and 'other value-added services' that are concluded in the depositary/custodian agreement, in addition to the safekeeping task.

7.2.2.3   Oversight Duties

Although the safekeeping task of depositaries and custodians prevent operational failures, the safekeeping task of depositaries/custodians alone does not mitigate the agency costs resulting from the actions of, in particular (collective) asset managers, related to those assets.

Under the AIFMD and UCITSD V, depositaries are, therefore, required to ensure compliance of the AIFM's and UCITS ManCo's actions with applicable law and AIF/ UCITS rules related to:[169]

- subscriptions/redemptions;
- valuations of share/unit pricing;
- duties relating to the carrying out of the AIFM's instructions;
- timely settlement of transactions;
- distribution of income;
- cash management.

Similarly, IORPD II requires depositaries appointed for both safekeeping and oversight duties to:[170]

---

165 *Ibid.*, 18.
166 Art. 21(8)(b) AIFMD; Art. 22(5)(b) UCITSD V.
167 Oxera, *supra* note 63, 14.
168 *Ibid.*
169 *See* Chapter 4, Section 4.6.3.
170 Art. 35(1) IORPD II.

- carry out instructions of the IORP, unless they conflict with the applicable national law or the IORP rules;
- ensure that in transactions involving an IORP or pension scheme's assets any consideration is remitted to the depositary within the usual time limits;
- ensure that income produced by assets is applied in accordance with the applicable national law and the IORP rules.

The AIFMD, UCITSD V and IORPD II in requiring the explicit obligation to monitor (collective) asset managers, in particular, prevent:[171]

- the breach of investment policy guidelines, i.e. the (collective) asset manager purchases assets that are not permitted under the investment policy guidelines, law and regulations;
- unintentional errors by (collective) asset managers in issuing orders to brokers (misdealing);
- the incorrect valuation of fund assets (mispricing);
- the misappropriation of fund' assets by the (collective) asset manager, including its employees and its delegates; and
- failure in best execution.

In short, the oversight duties of depositaries under the AIFMD, UCITSD V and IORPD II prevent the (collective) asset manager's misuse of fund' assets and fraud. In particular, depositaries are entrusted with the task of checking whether the holding and disposition of fund' assets is in compliance with investment policy guidelines.[172]

CRD IV, MiFID II and national equivalent regulations do not contain such an explicit obligation for custodians. This can be explained by the agency costs borne by AIF/UCITS investors and IORP Members in relation to (collective) asset managers compared to individual investors under MiFID II. The AIFMD, UCITSD and IORPD II regulate collective investments in which the (collective) asset manager–investor/member relationship is of a fiduciary nature, i.e. investors/members may not give investment instructions or individually agree upon the investment policy. In contrast, investment firms may offer execution only, investment-based advice or discretionary portfolio management services that have an agency nature, i.e. investors may give investment directions and have the final decision related to the purchase of their investments. The monitoring and oversight functions performed by depositaries in preventing agency costs, thus, distinguish depositaries from custodians that merely perform a safekeeping task.

---

171 Oxera, *supra* note 63, 18 and 19.
172 *Ibid.*

7.3   Prudential Requirements

The protection of investors and stability of the financial system are preserved by an adequate supervision of prudential requirements.[173] Typically, clients, including AIFs/ UCITS /IORPs and individual investors, are exposed to the credit risk of the depositary/custodian and the risk that is default if it becomes insolvent to the extent that depositaries/custodians are acting as a counterparty.

7.3.1   The Depositary/Custodian as a Counter-party

Assets safe-kept by depositaries/custodians include cash, 'financial instruments held in custody' and 'other assets'.

7.3.1.1   Cash

Depositaries/custodians that are authorized as a credit institution are allowed to receive deposits from the public.[174] This includes cash belonging to investment firm's clients, AIFs, UCITS and IORPs.[175] Cash deposits may be considerations from transactions and any cash held on an ancillary basis or as collateral, for example, in the context of SFTs. The counterparty risk is that upon an insolvency credit institutions may be unable to return deposited cash amount to the extent that these exceed the DGSD[176] guarantee threshold of EUR 100,000.[177]

Depositaries/custodians established as credit institutions may, but are not required to, hold cash itself. Investment firms and other legal entities are prohibited from holding cash itself.[178] Under the AIFMD/UCITSD V, the depositary is entrusted with the cash-flow monitoring task.[179] This includes the monitoring of AIF's/UCITS' cash that is booked with third party eligible entities.[180] Depositaries may open accounts in their own name on behalf of the AIF/UCITS. No cash belonging to the depositary or a third party entity may, however, be booked on such an account.[181] A depositary's counterparty risk may be mitigated by open-

---

173 IOSCO, *supra* note 50.
174 Art. 3(1) n. 1 CRD IV/Art. 4(1) n. 1 CRR.
175 Art. 21(7) AIFMD; Art. 22(4)(a) UCITSD V; Art. 2, 4(1) MiFID II (Commission) Directive; Art. 54 CSDR.
176 Directive 2014/49/EU of the European Parliament and of the Council of 16 April 2014 on deposit guarantee schemes (recast), OJ L 173/149, 12 June 2014 ('DGSD').
177 Art. 6 DGSD.
178 Art. 2, 4(1) MiFID II (Commission) Directive.
179 Art. 21(7) AIFMD, Art. 86 AIFMD (Commission) Regulation; Art. 22(4) UCITSD V, Art. 10 UCITSD V (Commission) Regulation.
180 Art. 21(7) AIFMD and Art. 22(4)(b) UCITSD V refer for the depositing of clients funds to Art. 4(1)(a)–(c) MiFID II (Commission) Directive.
181 Art. 21(7) AIFMD, Art. 86 AIFMD (Commission) Regulation; Art. 22(4) UCITSD V, Art. 10 UCITSD V (Commission) Regulation.

ing cash account with eligible third parties in the name of the depositary by being clearly identifiable as cash belonging to the AIF/UCITS.[182] Thus, the protection of cash belonging to AIFs/UCITS against the insolvency of a depositary may be achieved by opening cash accounts with eligible third party in the name of the AIF/UCITS or the AIFM/UCITS Man-Co on behalf of the AIF/UCITS. Cash segregation is required to avoid the risk of commingling and preserve segregation of cash booked on such an account as clearly belonging to AIFs/UCITS in case of insolvency of the depositary.

Similarly, non-bank investment firms are required, upon receiving any client funds,[183] to promptly place those funds into one or more accounts opened with:[184]
- a central bank;
- a credit institution within the meaning of CRD IV;
- a bank authorized in a third country; and
- a qualifying money market fund.

Investment firms have a general due diligence duty upon depositing client' funds.[185] Specific due diligence duties apply to the diversification[186] and intra-group deposits of client funds.[187]

IORPD II does not contain any provisions related to cash. Unclear is whether the AIFMD/UCITSD V or the MiFID II provisions related to cash would need to be applied in analogy. The safekeeping task has, however, been copy-pasted from the AIFMD and UCITSD V.[188] Similar depositary counterparty protection, thus, should, as a minimum, under IORPD II be deemed to be available for IORPs appointing depositaries for both the safekeeping and oversight task under IORPD II.

7.3.1.2 Financial Instruments That Can Be Held in Custody
Financial instruments that can be held in custody are mostly in book-entry form and registered on the depositary's/custodian's book in segregated accounts, so that they can be clearly identified as belonging to client's and the client' rights are safeguarded upon the depositary's/custodian's insolvency.[189] In the case of delegation under the AIFMD and

182 Art. 21(7) sub-para. 2 AIFMD; Art. 22(4) UCITSD V.
183 In Ireland and the UK 'client funds' are often being referred to as 'client money'. See for Ireland: Central Bank of Ireland, Guidance on Client Asset Regulation for Investment Firms, March 2015, 58, https://www.centralbank.ie/pressarea/pressreleases/Documents/150330%20Guidance%20on%20Client%20Asset%20Regulations%20for%20Investment%20Firms.pdf; See for the UK: CASS 7; 'Client money' are funds being deposited in a bank account that are legally owned by the investment firm and beneficially owned by the investment firm's clients.
184 Art. 16(9) MiFID II; Art. 4(1) MiFID II (Commission) Directive.
185 Art. 4(2) MiFID II (Commission) Directive.
186 Art. 4(2) sub-para. 1 MiFID II (Commission) Directive; ESMA/2014/1570, 57, 58.
187 Art. 4(3) MiFID II (Commission) Directive.
188 Art. 34 IORPD II.
189 Art. 85(1) AIFMD (Commission) Regulation; Art. 9(1) UCITSD V (Commission) Regulation; Art. 4(1)(a)–(c) MiFID II (Commission) Directive.

UCITSD V, sub-custodians are required to segregate such financial instrument from its own assets and the assets of the depositary so that these financial instruments can be identified as belonging to the AIF/UCITS and not to the AIFM/UCITS ManCo, depositary, the sub-custodian or other clients.[190] AIFs/UCITS, however, may bear counterparty risk for unencumbered financial instruments that can be held in custody of a depositary that faces 'guarantor liability' for the loss of financial instruments on the sub-custodian level.[191]

In depositing client' financial instruments, investment firms under MiFID II have to take into account the expertise and market reputation of institutions other than central banks, as well as, legal requirements or market practices related to the holding of those financial instruments that could adversely affect clients' rights.[192] Sub-custodians are under CRD IV, MiFID II and IORPD II not required to hold clients' financial instruments in segregated accounts. Omnibus accounts are, thus, also allowed. Clients generally do not face counterparty risks of depositaries/custodians for unencumbered financial instruments that can be held in custody. Counterparty risk may, however, arise upon a loss of financial instruments at the depositary/custodian or the sub-custodian level.

For encumbered financial instruments and those on title transfer, financial instruments are under the AIFMD and UCITSD V not considered to be in custody anymore if the legal title has been lost by the AIF/UCITS.[193] The loss of title is also under the national implementation laws of MiFID II considered to be resulting in counterparty risk, whereas for encumbered assets it depends upon the individual Member State under what conditions encumbered assets fall within the MiFID II safeguarding of client assets regime.[194] The same holds true for custodians regulated under CRD IV and depositaries under IORPD II.[195]

7.3.1.3 'Other Assets'

Assets other than financial instruments held in custody and cash that qualifies as 'other assets' do not result in counterparty risk. Such assets are not lost due to the depositary's's/custodian's insolvency as they are subject to ownership verification and record-keeping and do not fall under the custody task.[196] If there is a segregation of clients' 'other assets', the depositary/custodian is, thus, a 'pure investment service provider'.[197]

---

190 Art. 21(11)(d)(iii) AIFMD and Art. 22a(3) UCITSD V; Art. 4(1)(a)–(c) MiFID II (Commission) Directive.
191 Art. 21(12) AIFMD; Art. 24(1) UCITSD V.
192 Art. 4(2) sub-para. 1 MiFID II (Commission) Directive.
193 Recital 114 AIFMD (Commission) Regulation; Recital 24 UCITSD V (Commission) Regulation.
194 *See also* S.L. Schwarcz, *Intermediary Risk in a Global Economy*, 6 Duke Law Journal 1541 (2001); S.L. Schwarcz, *Indirectly Held Securities and Intermediary Risk*, 2 Uniform Law Review 283 (2001).
195 *See* D. Frase, *Custody* (D. Frase (ed.), Sweet & Maxwell 2011), 274.
196 Art. 21(8) AIFMD; Art. 22(5) UCITSD V; Art. 34 IORPD II.
197 Oxera, *supra* note 63, 22.

7.3.2   *Prudential Requirements related to Credit Institutions, Investment Firms and 'Equivalent Other Legal Entities'*

Depositaries and custodians are mostly credit institutions, investment firms or 'equivalent other legal entities'.

7.3.2.1   Credit institutions and Investment Firms

Credit institutions and investment firms are regulated under the so-called 'banking union'[198] that sets out a common financial regulatory framework ('single rulebook') and is complemented by a Single Supervisory Mechanism and a Single Resolution Mechanism.[199] The 'single rulebook' is the name of a single set of harmonized prudential rules which credit institutions and investment firms must comply with. The term 'single rulebook' refers to the aim of a unified regulatory framework for the EEA financial sector that would complete the single market in financial services.[200] The 'single rulebook' consists of three main legislative acts, including CRD IV/CRR, the DGSD and the BRRD.[201] CRD IV/CRR implements Basel III under which credit institutions (and investment firm s) are required to hold better and more own capital, conservation buffers and counter-cyclical buffers. CRD IV and the CRR aim to avoid the impact of possible financial meltdown and mitigate factors addressing systematic risk.[202] CRD IV/CRR also apply to investment firms. Depending upon the business model of investment firms taking more or less 'principal risk', investment firms are required to hold more own capital and abide to capital adequacy rules.[203] The banking union has sought to improve the existing European legislation on the protection of depositors in cases of the failure of credit institutions. The DGSD regulates deposit insurance in case of a credit institution's inability to pay its

---

198 K. Lannoo, *The Great Financial Plumbing: From Northern Rock to Banking Union* 40 (Rowman and Littlefield International 2015).

199 D. Busch & G. Ferrarini, *A Banking Union for a Divided Europe: An Introduction* (D. Busch & G. Ferrarini, Oxford 2015); E. Ferran, *European Banking Union: Imperfect, But it Can Work* (D. Busch & G. Ferrarini, Oxford 2015); N. Moloney, *Banking Union and the Implications for Financial Market Governance in the EU: Convergence or Divergence* (D. Busch & G. Ferrarini, Oxford 2015); E. Wymeersch, *The European Banking Union, a First Analysis*, Financial Law Institute Working Paper Series WP 2012-07 (2012).

200 G. Ferrarini & F. Recine, *The Single Rulebook and the SSM: Should the ECB Have More Say in Prudential Rule-making?* (D. Busch & G. Ferrarini, Oxford 2015).

201 Directive 2014/59/EU of the European Parliament and of the Council of 15 May 2014 Establishing a Framework for the Recovery and Resolution of Credit Institutions and Investment Firms and Amending Council Directive 82/891/EEC, and Directives 2001/24/EC, 2002/47/EC, 2004/25/EC, 2005/56/EC, 2007/36/EC, 2011/35/EU, 2012/30/EU and 2013/36/EU, and Regulations (EU) No 1093/2010 and (EU) No 648/2012, *OJ L 173*, 12 June 2014 ('BRRD'); E. Ferran, *European Banking Union: Imperfect, But It Can Work*, University of Cambridge Faculty of Law Research Paper No. 30/2014 (2014).

202 P. Mülbert & A. Wilhelm, *CRD IV Framework for Banks' Corporate Governance* (D. Busch & G. Ferrarini eds., Oxford 2015).

203 C.P. Buttigieg, *The Development of the EU Regulatory and Supervisory Framework applicable to UCITS: A Critical Examination of the Conditions and Limitations of Mutual Recognition*, 40, http://sro.sussex.ac.uk/48285/1/Buttigieg%2C_Christopher_P.pdf.

debts.[204] For that purpose, the DGSD reimburses a limited amount of deposits (EUR 100,000) to depositors.[205] From a financial stability perspective, this promise prevents depositors from making panic withdrawals from their credit institutions, thereby preventing severe economic consequences.[206] This is necessary for the overall financial stability in the single market.[207] The BRRD is part of the second pillar of the Banking Union. It is considered to be a cornerstone in the EEA setting out of measures dealing with the failures of banking and certain investment firms ('financial institutions').[208] The BRRD provides various resolution tools to prevent insolvency of financial institutions or, when insolvency occurs, to minimize damage and loss to investors and the financial system as a whole by preserving the systemically important functions of financial institutions.[209]

The Single Resolution Mechanism is a pillar of the Banking Union that implements the BRRD in participating Member States and establishes a Single Resolution Fund to finance their restructuring.[210] The Single Resolution Fund, essentially, requires credit institutions to pay for resolution so that taxpayers will be protected from having to bail out credit institutions if they fail.[211] The Single Resolution Mechanism is complemented by the 'Single Supervisory Mechanism' that grants the ECB a supervisory role to monitor the financial stability of credit institutions that are based in participating states.[212] Eurozone Member States are obliged to participate, whereas Member States that are not in the eurozone may voluntarily participate.[213] The Single Supervisory Mechanism' functions in conjunction with the Single Resolution Mechanism as the two pillars underlying the 'single rulebook'.[214]

---

204 F. Arnaboldi, *Deposit Guarantee Schemes – A European Perspective* (Springer 2014).

205 Art. 6 DGSD.

206 Muelbert & Wilhelm, *supra* note 202.

207 Proposal for a Directive .../.../EU of the European Parliament and of the Council on Deposit Guarantee Schemes [recast]/* COM/2010/0368 final – COD 2010/0207 */.

208 V. Seriere, *Recovery and Resolution Plans of Banks in the Context of the BRRD and the SRM: Some Fundamental Issues* (D. Busch & G. Ferrarini, Oxford 2015).

209 E. Wymeersch, *Banking Union: Aspects of the Single Supervisory Mechanism and the Single Resolution Mechanism Compared*, ECGI – Law Working Paper No. 290/2015 (2015).

210 E. Ferran & V.S.G. Babis, *The European Single Supervisory Mechanism*, University of Cambridge Faculty of Law Research Paper No. 10/2013 (2013); D. Busch, *Governance of the Single Resolution Mechanism* (D. Busch & G. Ferrarini, Oxford 2015).

211 Council Implementing Regulation (EU) 2015/81 of 19 December 2014 specifying uniform conditions of application of Regulation (EU) No 806/2014 of the European Parliament and of the Council with regard to ex-ante contributions to the Single Resolution Fund; European Commission, *Press release- Single Resolution Mechanism to come into effect for the Banking Union*, 31 December 2015; R.Z. Wiggins, M. Wedow & A. Metrick, *European Banking Union B: The Single Resolution Mechanism*, Yale Program on Financial Stability Case Study 2014-5B-V1 (2014).

212 E. Wymeersch, *The Single Supervisory Mechanism: Institutional Aspects* (D. Busch & G. Ferrarini eds., Oxford 2015).

213 T.H. Troeger, *The Single Supervisory Mechanism – Panacea or Quack Banking Regulation?*, SAFE Working Paper No. 27 (2013).

214 E. Wymeersch, *The Single Supervisory Mechanism or 'sSM'*, Part One of the Banking Union, European Corporate Governance Institute (ECGI) – Law Working Paper No. 240/2014 (2014).

7.3.2.2   'Equivalent Other Legal Entities'

'Equivalent other legal entities' are required under the AIFMD, UCITSD V and IORPD II to fulfil minimum prudential regulation standards under CRD IV and the CRR.[215] Prudential regulation for 'national custodians' is normally based upon MiFID II, CRD IV and the CRR.[216] Usually, these concern only various provisions from the CRD IV/CRR and other prudential regulation under the 'single rulebook', 'Single Resolution Mechanism' and 'Single Supervisory Mechanism'.[217] This is acceptable as 'national custodians' are under Member State regulation only allowed to provide safekeeping and administration of securities for others. 'National custodians' are pure investment service providers as they are not authorized to provide 'other value-added services'[218] and, thus, do not bear principal risk. The safekeeping and administration of securities for others is a low margin business.[219] Most fees are earned through 'other value-added services' that lead to 'principal risk' for which only credit institutions and investment firms are authorized. Domestic custodians do not have any systematic impact and, therefore, a minimum set of prudential regulation is considered to be acceptable.

7.4   SUPERVISION

The regulatory framework is complemented by the initial and ongoing supervision of depositaries/custodians on the national and European level. Credit institutions and investment firms are being supervised on a macro- and micro-prudential level by the so-called 'European Supervisory Architecture'. Equivalent other legal entities are only supervised at the national level.

7.4.1   The European Supervisory Architecture

The ESFS involves both macro- as well as micro-prudential supervision. Four bodies together form the ESFS that complement 'Home Member State Control', i.e. prudential supervision on the Member State level in which the depositary/custodian is established'.[220]

The ESRB carries out macro-prudential supervision. Its primary task is the prevention/mitigation of systematic risks.[221] For that purpose, the ESRB determines, collects

---

215 Art. 23(2)(c) UCITSD V.
216 Legal Certainty Group, *supra* note 37, 25 and 32.
217 G. Ferrarini & L. Chiarella, *Common Banking Supervision in the Eurozone: Strengths and Weaknesses*, ECGI – Law Working Paper No. 223/2013 (2013).
218 Legal Certainty Group, *supra* note 37, 25 and 32.
219 European Commission, *supra* note 5, 5, Annex 4.
220 E. Wymeersch, Eddy, *Europe's New Financial Regulatory Bodies*, 5, http://ssrn.com/abstract=1813811.
221 Art. 3(1) EBAR.

and analyses information.[222] On the basis of that the ESRB issues warnings and recommendations.[223] The ESRB has no legal personality and no binding powers.[224] All its recommendations have to be implemented by Member States on a 'comply-or-explain' basis.[225]

Micro-prudential supervision is being carried out by the three 'ESAs'. The three ESA's are EBA, EIOPA and ESMA. Depending upon whether depositaries/custodians act under the AIFMD, UCITSD V, CRD IV, IORPD II or MiFID II, one or more ESA's are involved in supervising depositaries/custodians.

First, ESAs have 'rulemaking powers'. They advise the European Commission on new legislation to be adopted on both Level 1 initiatives and more detailed advice for Level 2 measures. The advisory function is mandatory for cases expressly stated in Level 1 instruments. ESAs may be involved in preparing and advising on delegated and implementing acts. However, the ultimate decision has to be made by the European Commission.

Apart from the rulemaking powers, the ESAs also play a role in ensuring the consistent application of European (investment) law. ESAs are empowered to prevent inconsistent application by Member States of European law by entering into a dialogue with the Competent Authority of the Member State concerned. By absence of adequate measures, ESAs issue a recommendation of non-compliance with the European Commission. The European Commission is entitled to start an infringement procedure before the CJEU against Member States.[226]

ESAs have also emergency powers in situations that have to be formally declared as an 'emergency situation' by the Council of Ministers. ESAs may also adopt emergency measures in absence of a Council decision when otherwise danger would arise to the orderly functioning of the financial markets or financial stability.[227] Further, ESAs are entitled to settle cross-border disagreements between national Competent Authorities. They may assist in conflict resolution in the college of supervisors.[228] This may be exercised in cases expressively declared open for mediation by a Level 1 instrument. Finally, ESAs are entitled to prohibit or restrict 'financial activities' in case of emergency.[229]

---

222 Art. 3(1)(a) EBAR.

223 Art. 3(1)(c)-(d), 16-18 EBAR.

224 J. Doelder & I.M. Jansen, *Een nieuw Europees toezichtraamwerk*, 1/2 TvFR 17 (2010).

225 H. van Meerten & A.T. Ottow, *The proposals for the European Supervisory Authorities (ESAs): the right (legal) way forward?*, 1/2 TvFR 5 (2010).

226 E. Ferran & K. Alexander, *Can Soft Law Bodies be Effective? Soft Systemic Risk Oversight Bodies and the Special Case of the European Systemic Risk Board*, Paper No. 36/2011(2011).

227 N. Kost – de Sevres & L. Sasso, *The New European Financial Markets Legal Framework: A Real Improvement? An Analysis of Financial Law and Governance in European Capital Markets from a Micro- and Macro-Economic Perspective*, 7 Capital Markets Law Journal 30 (2011).

228 E.J. van Praag, *Het grensoverschrijdend financieel toezicht loopt tegen grenzen aan*, 9 TvFR 259 (2011).

229 Art. 11 EBAR, EIOPA and ESMA.

7.4.2   *Equivalent Other Legal Entities*

Equivalent other legal entities are only supervised on the national level. Equivalent other legal entities are under the AIFMD, UCITSD V and IORPD II only subject to minimum European standards.[230] Remarkably, 'equivalent other legal entities' may be appointed as 'UCITSD V depositary' on a cross-border basis (a de facto European passport) under the IORPD II although the European Supervisory Architecture does not (fully) apply to these entities.

7.5   CONCLUSION

Depositaries under the AIFMD/UCITSD V perform a safekeeping and oversight role and custodians under CRD IV, MiFID II and on the national level merely a safekeeping role. In spite of this, the same entities that within individual Member States act as a depositary perform mainly safekeeping under MiFID II and safekeeping (and oversight duties) under IORPD II. At the same time, they are subjected to the same custody transfer laws that determine the legal scope of the safekeeping function. The author holds that this is the case because depositary law is a specialized area of custody law. The depositary is, thus, a 'specialized custodian'.

The authorization, conduct of business rules, prudential regulation, supervision and enforcement of credit institutions, investment firms and 'equivalent other entities' are considered under the various European investment law directives to be appropriately addressing the investor and market protection risks related to the safekeeping function of custodians and depositaries. The notion of 'depositary' under IORPD II, UCITSD V and the AIFMD is wider than the notion of pure 'custodian'.[231] Although the safekeeping task of depositaries and custodians prevent operational failures, the safekeeping task of the depositary/custodians alone does not mitigate the agency costs resulting from the actions of, in particular, (collective) asset manager's related to those assets. To this end, depositaries under sectoral 'depositary laws' are required to perform oversight duties towards these (collective) asset managers. CRD IV, MiFID II and national equivalent regulations do not contain such an explicit obligation for custodians. This can be explained by the agency costs borne by AIF/UCITS investors and IORP Members in relation to (collective) asset managers compared to individual investors related to investment firms. For this reason, IORPD II, UCITSD V and the AIFMD require additional conducts of business rules to be fulfilled for depositaries that in their capacity of custodian perform oversight duties. Depositary law is, thus, a separate area of law applying on top of the 'general law' targeting credit institutions, investment firms or 'other equivalent legal entities' authorized to act as a custodian.

---

230 Art. 23(2)(c) UCITSD V.
231 European Commission, *supra* note 5, Annex 4.

PART IV
TOWARDS A CROSS-SECTORAL
DEPOSITARY PASSPORT

8 Towards the Introduction of a Cross-Sectoral European Depositary Passport in European Investment Law

Part I set out the current 'depositary passport paradox'. Part II clarified the conditions under which European/TC passports are granted to EEA and TC financial intermediaries. Part III explained the differences between 'depositaries', on the one hand, and 'custodians', on the other hand, throughout European investment law. This chapter, on the basis of the outcome of the preceding parts, advocates in favour of introducing not only an AIF/UCITS depositary but a 'cross-sectoral European depositary passport' in European investment law. To this end, this chapter takes into account the differences between 'depositaries' and 'custodians', the problems and inconsistencies related to the 'European depositary passport paradox' and 'investor protection concerns' in setting out the conditions for introducing such a passport under a proposed 'Custody Plus' solution. Depositaries are regarded as 'custodians' that in addition to the safekeeping of financial instruments also perform 'controlling/monitoring duties'. For this reason, the 'safekeeping task' of 'custodians' and 'depositaries' is proposed to be regulated on a 'cross-sectoral' basis under a MiFID II 'stand-alone' regime, whereas the 'controlling/monitoring tasks' and the particularities of 'depositaries' are left over to sectoral legislation. A proposal is made in this chapter to achieve 'cross-sectoral consistency' for these sectoral depositary regimes.

8.1 A Cross-Sectoral Passport for European Depositaries and Custodians – The 'Custody Plus' Solution

The introduction of a (full) passport for AIF/UCITS depositaries would imply that several separate legal regimes applying to custodians and depositaries would exist that would entitle a custodian/depositary to provide the safekeeping of assets (and controlling duties) on a cross-border basis. Depositaries/custodians would, however, comply with different legal standards, whereas the core activity of safekeeping assets in the intermediary holding chain and its corresponding risks are the same.[1] A streamlined cross-sectoral European passport for depositaries/custodians willing to provide cross-border services to IORPs, UCITS, AIFMs and investment firm clients (MiFID II) could, therefore, lead to

---

1 *See* Chapter 7, Section 7.2.

a further reduction of operational costs and achieve economies of scale.[2] Such a passport could be modelled after the 'cross-sectoral investment management passport' currently in place. The basic foundation of the passport would be a 'stand-alone' custodian that would be regulated under MiFID II. This would restrict eligible depositaries/custodians to credit institutions/investment firms and allow for cross-sectoral consistency of the intermediary regulation applying to all depositaries/custodians appointed under European investment law.

8.1.1   The 'EEA Cross-Sectoral Investment Management Passport' as an Example

Recently, UCITSD IV, the AIFMD and MiFID II have introduced legislation that allows a single 'asset manager' complying with a proportional set of legal standards to manage AIFs, individual portfolios, UCITS and IORPs on the basis of a 'cross-sectoral management passport'.[3]

The 'cross-sectoral investment management passport' is based upon the rationale that 'asset managers' under the above-mentioned sectoral legislation all perform investment/ portfolio and risk management as core tasks. For this reason, 'asset manager s' willing to exploit economies of scope and scale by operating several business lines simultaneously are, under specific conditions, not required to comply with all sectoral requirements in full. Instead, the 'cross-sectoral management passport' is built upon a proportional system in which the authorization for the provision of 'portfolio management' of AIFMs/UCITS Man-Cos under the AIFMD or UCITSD V substitutes for a full-fledged 'portfolio management' authorization under MiFID II. Moreover, AIFMs complying with a couple of UCITS ManCo related requirements may have a 'dual license' under which they have an AIFM and UCITS ManCo 'management passport'.[4] The AIFM, MiFID II and UCITS ManCo authorizations are also recognized under IORPD II. The proportional regime is designed upon the two 'core functions' of asset managers. The AIFMD, UCITSD V and MiFID II, however, vary in the scope and, therefore, in the type of 'asset managers' that are to be authorized under these directives.[5] MiFID II is primarily focused on 'financial instruments', UCITSD V on financial instruments and liquid financial assets, whereas the AIFMD captures liquid, illiquid and leveraged AIFs. For this reason, the proportional 'cross-sectoral investment management

---

2   C.P. Buttigieg, *The Development of the EU Regulatory and Supervisory Framework applicable to UCITS: A Critical Examination of the Conditions and Limitations of Mutual Recognition*, March 2014, 66, http://sro.sussex.ac.uk/48285/1/Buttigieg%2C_Christopher_P..pdf.

3   Portfolio management and risk management are both considered to be 'investment management'. *See* Point 1(a) and (b) Annex I and Art. 4(1)(w) AIFMD and Annex II, Art. 6(2) UCITSD V. *See also* Allen & Overy, *Alternative Investment Fund Managers Directive: Allen & Overy Briefing Paper No. 9 AIFMD, UCITSD and MiFID: Interactions and Overlaps*, www.allenovery.com/archive/Documents/Legacy/62666.pdf.

4   U. Klebeck, *Interplay between AIFMD and the UCITSD* (D.A. Zetzsche ed, Kluwer 2015).

5   D.A. Zetzsche & T.F. Marte, *AIFMD versus MiFID II/MIFIR: Similarities and Differences* (D.A. Zetzsche ed, Kluwer 2015).

passport' does not allow UCITS ManCos and MiFID II portfolio managers to manage
AIFMs without applying for a full-fledged AIFM authorization.

Modelled after this concept, indeed, a proportional 'cross-sectoral depositary passport'
could be built upon the core activities of the safekeeping of assets and the performance of
oversight duties. All depositaries and custodians perform at least the safekeeping of assets at
a minimum. Essentially, depositaries are custodians that perform, in addition to the safekeeping of assets, oversight duties.[6] For this reason, a 'cross-sectoral depositary passport'
could be built on the basis of an harmonized authorization regime for custodians based on
the regulatory activity 'safekeeping of assets', whereas on the sectoral level a cross-sectoral
consistent set of legislation applies, on top of that, for custodians that act as depositaries.
This solution is being referred to in this book as 'Custody Plus' as this terminology is used in
practice for custodians that are appointed as AIF/UCITS/IORP depositaries.

8.1.2   *The Basic Foundation of the Cross-Sectoral Depositary Passport: The MiFID
II 'Stand-Alone' Custodian*

8.1.2.1   Considerations on a Cross-Sectoral European/TC Depositary Passport
Currently, MiFID II and CRD IV allow Member States to regulate 'custodians' as 'stand-
alone' regulatory activity.[7] Consistent with the general principles of the European passport, these 'stand-alone' custodians regulated on the national level are not allowed to
make use of the European passport granted under MiFID II or CRD IV.[8] The safekeeping
and administration of securities /financial instruments may as an 'ancillary service' only
be passported along 'core' investment services/activities.[9]

On the contrary, IORPD II grants a 'de facto' European depositary passport[10] to
'UCITSD V depositaries' that may, depending upon the UCITSD V Member State implementations, be credit institutions, central banks or 'another legal entity'.[11] These 'other
legal entities' may, amongst others,[12] be entities that are regulated under national law.[13]
IORPD II, thus, facilitates a 'de facto' European IORP depositaries passport for entities
regulated on the national level 'through the backdoor'.[14] Allowing TC and national regu-

---

6   *See* Chapter 7, Section 7.2.2.3.
7   *See* Chapter 6, Section 6.2.1.
8   *See* Chapter 3, Section 3.2.
9   *See* Chapter 6, Section 6.2.1.
10 *See* Chapter 2, Section 2.1.3.
11 *See* Chapter 5, Section 5.3.2.2.3.
12 *See* for 'another legal entity': Chapter 4, Section 4.3.2.3.
13 *See* Chapter 4, section 4.3.2.3.4.
14 This includes UCITSD V depositaries under Irish and Maltese law that are full subsidiaries of TC parent
    undertakings and only fulfil the minimum conditions set out under UCITSD V. *See* Chapter 2, Section
    2.1.2.1.

lated entities to provide services on a cross-border basis is contrary to the joint principles of the European passport.[15] Under EEA secondary law, the European passport and the overarching principle of 'mutual recognition' are based upon two cornerstones: the 'single rulebook', i.e. a thick set of harmonized rules of a specific sector and a coordinated institutional framework for financial supervision comprising of 'home state control', and the ESFS that allows host Member States to defer supervision to home Member States and ESAs.[16]

In order to establish a 'cross-sectoral European depositary passport', the entities allowed to be appointed as custodian and depositary would, thus, need to be limited to entities regulated under EEA secondary law. For this purpose, either a 'stand-alone regime' or an 'existing regime' could be used. The existing MiFID II regime seems to be the most appropriate regime. This would be logical as most depositaries/custodians currently used are credit institutions and investment firms.[17] Introducing a 'cross-sectoral depositary passport' with MiFID II as 'basic foundation' under the 'Custody Plus' solution would lead to 'vertical' and 'horizontal consistency'. It would lead to 'vertical consistency' as limiting custodians and depositaries to be appointed to credit institutions and investment firms under MiFID II leads to consistency throughout sectoral legal initiatives. Under UCITSD V, for instance, Germany and Luxembourg restrict eligible entities to 'credit institutions',[18] whereas in the Netherlands credit institutions, investment firms and 'other legal entities' are allowed to be appointed as a UCITS depositary.[19] It would also lead to horizontal consistency. In Austria and Germany, for instance, credit institutions and investment firms may be appointed as AIF depositaries, whereas credit institutions may only be appointed as 'custodians' and UCITS depositaries.[20] Limiting custodians and depositaries, with the exception of 'PE-depositaries',[21] to credit institutions and investment firms, thus, leads to vertical and horizontal consistency that would be a solid foundation of a 'cross-sectoral depositary passport'.[22] The 'custody' part of 'Custody Plus' regulating the safekeeping of assets of depositaries and custodians could be regulated in MiFID II, whereas the 'plus' part regulating the oversight duties and related governance could be regulated on a sectoral basis. Obviously, this solution would lead to many ad-

---

15 Chapter 3, Section 3.2.
16 N. Moloney, *Brexit, the EU and its Investment Banker: Rethinking 'Equivalence' for the EU Capital Market*, LSE Legal Studies Working Paper No. 5/2017, 5, https://ssrn.com/abstract=2929229.
17 European Commission, *Impact Assessment – Proposal for a Directive of the European Parliament and of the Council amending Directive 2009/65/EC on the coordination of laws, regulations and administrative provisions relating to undertakings for collective investment in transferable securities (UCITS) as regards depositary functions, remuneration policies and sanctions*, (COM(2012) 350) (SWD(2012) 186), 32, 33.
18 Germany: § 87 KAGB; Luxembourg; Art. 17(3) OPC law 2010.
19 Art. 4:62n(b) Wft.
20 Austria: § 164(2), § 167(1) InvFG 2011; Germany: § 87 KAGB.
21 Chapter 4, Section 4.3.1.6.
22 *Cf.* C.P. Buttigieg, *The Alternative Investment Fund Managers Directive in Malta: Past, Present … What Next?*, https://ssrn.com/abstract=2602750.

vantages. As almost all depositaries and custodians are credit institutions or investment firms a 'cross-sectoral depositary passport' could be introduced at little cost. Moreover, the harmonization of the 'custodian' part and only leaving the 'depositary' over to sectoral legislation would lead to lower compliance costs for those entities seeking to offer depositary/custody services on a cross-sectoral basis. Finally, no considerations on a TC regime would need to be made as simply the MiFID II TC regime would apply to 'custodians' and the current TC regimes for depositaries under the sectoral regulations would remain to be in place.[23]

Upgrading the safekeeping and administration to a 'full-fledged' MiFID II investment service/activity and limiting eligible depositaries to these entities is not a new idea. The European Commission already made an attempt with its MiFID II and UCITSD V proposal and the AIFMD. Ultimately, however, this idea was under the MiFID II and UCITSD V proposal being revoked. This leaves us the question why this idea has been revoked and what could be done to overcome the problems related to such an introduction.

8.1.2.2   Credit Institutions and Investment Firms as Full-Fledged MiFID II Custodians

Under the original MiFID II proposal, the safekeeping and administration of financial instruments for the account of clients was proposed to be upgraded to a full-fledged investment service/activity.[24] Following this proposal, any firm providing the service of safekeeping and administration of financial instruments for the account of clients would be on a stand-alone basis subject to a separate authorization procedure.[25] This would have implied that under MiFID II, compared to MiFID I, not every investment firm,[26] but merely those entities with an authorization for safekeeping, would have been eligible as a depositary. This proposal was, however, not adopted in the final version of MiFID II. This was the result of mixed responses from various industry players to a questionnaire on MiFID II and MiFIR. The respondents that argued against the upgrade mainly argued that a reclassification would in any case not enhance investor protection for the following main reasons.[27] First, the safekeeping and administration of financial instruments for the account of clients carried out by entities holding securities accounts for their clients,

---

23   See for the AIFMD TC depositary regime: Chapter 4, section 4.5.
24   See Annex I s. B MiFID II proposal.
25   Ibid.
26   Generally speaking, the MiFID II custody rules apply to all 'MiFID II investment firms', such as brokers, dealers, asset managers and advisers. See D. Frase, Custody 276 (D. Frase ed., Sweet & Maxwell 2011).
27   Safekeeping should remain an 'ancillary service' under MiFID II: CSD services, including safekeeping, should be regulated under the upcoming CSD regulation instead; Position paper, CSDA response to the MiFID/MiFIR II questionnaire of MEP Markus Ferber – 12 January 2012; Question 3, EBF response to the MiFID/MiFIR II questionnaire of MEP Markus Ferber – 12 January 2012.

whether custodians or CSDs, are already regulated under EEA legislation.[28] Most custodian banks within the EEA are subject to authorization either as investment firms or as credit institutions under MiFID II and CRD IV, whereas CSDs are regulated under the CSDR.[29] Second, various respondents argued that the safekeeping and the provision of custody services differ significantly from the trading and distribution of financial instruments targeted by MiFID II.[30] A few respondents mentioned, for instance, that applying the suitability,[31] assessment of appropriateness[32] or the best execution duty[33] to custody services would be inappropriate.[34]

These arguments, however, rather seem to be a product of the lobbying industry. Indeed, almost all custodians are already regulated under MiFID II and CRD IV. This is, however, not a valid argument for not upgrading the safekeeping and administration of financial instruments for the account of clients to an investment activity/service. Under the ISD, 'ancillary' services were introduced as these services were not yet harmonized on the European level. It was under the ISD decided that, until valid considerations for the harmonization of those services were made, a European 'ancillary' passport would be granted for these services under the condition that investment firms were authorized for 'core' investment services/activities. De facto, the MiFID II prudential regime was, thus, seen as a sufficient degree of harmonization to grant these services an ('ancillary') European passport. In fact, the 'ancillary passport' for custodians introduced upon the adoption of the Second Banking Directive and the ISD has led to market consolidation of custodians in Europe.[35] Credit institutions and investment firms have pushed custodians that were merely regulated on the national level out of the market.[36] Credit institutions

---

28 Question 3, CSDA response to the MiFID/MiFIR II questionnaire of MEP Markus Ferber – 12 January 2012; Question 3, EBF response to the MiFID/MiFIR II questionnaire of MEP Markus Ferber – 12 January 2012.

29 *See* Chapter 6.

30 Question 3, EBF response to the MiFID/MiFIR II questionnaire of MEP Markus Ferber – 12 January 2012.

31 Art. 19(4) MiFID I/ Art. 25 MiFID II; *See* for ESMA Guidelines on certain aspects of the MiFID suitability requirements: ESMA/2012/387 and on the consultation: ESMA/2011/445; Question 3, British Banker's Association response to the MiFID/MiFIR II questionnaire of MEP Markus Ferber – 12 January 2012; Blackrock response to the MiFID/MiFIR II questionnaire of MEP Markus Ferber – 12 January 2012.

32 Art. 19(5) MiFID I/ Art. 25(2) of MiFID II; *See also* question 3, EFAMA response to the MiFID/MiFIR II questionnaire of MEP Markus Ferber – 12 January 2012; Question 3, Bundesverband Investment and Asset Management response to the MiFID/MiFIR II questionnaire of MEP Markus Ferber – 12 January 2012; Question 3, Investment Management Association response to the MiFID/MiFIR II questionnaire of MEP Markus Ferber – 12 January 2012.

33 Art. 27 MiFID II; Question 3, British Banker's Association response to the MiFID/MiFIR II questionnaire of MEP Markus Ferber – 12 January 2012.

34 Question 3, CSDA response to the MiFID/MiFIR II questionnaire of MEP Markus Ferber – 12 January 2012; Question 3, ALFI response to the MiFID/MiFIR II questionnaire of MEP Markus Ferber – 12 January 2012.

35 *See* European Commission, *supra* note 17.

36 *See* European Commission, *Communication from the Commission to the Council and to the European Parliament – Regulation of UCITS Depositaries in the Member States: Review and Possible Developments*, 30 March 2004, COM(2004) 207 final, 6.

and investment firms were under the 'ancillary passports' able to exploit economies of scope and scale in the market for 'custodians'. These 'ancillary custodian passports' led to competitive advantages arising from operational and cost benefits and, therefore, credit institutions and investment firms increasingly dominated not only the 'custodian' market but also the 'depositary market'. Credit institutions, investment firms and 'local custodians' were all facing the same restrictions and obstacles under the UCITSD I-V and the (pre-)AIFMD depositary regimes. Credit institutions and investment firms were, however, able to obtain cost advantages in horizontally integrating their business activities as they benefitted from the 'ancillary passports' in which they could act throughout Europe as a 'custodian'.[37] This gradually emerged business practice is also currently to be observed throughout the EEA Member State laws. Most Member States do not regulate 'custody' as 'stand-alone' activity under national laws as almost all custodians/depositaries are investment firms and credit institutions under MiFID II and CRD IV.[38] Those Member States that do so regulate these entities as 'national investment firms' based upon their MiFID II implementations.[39]

It would, thus, make sense to regulate the safekeeping and administration of financial instruments for the account of clients under MiFID II. MiFID II would be better suited to regulate this compared to CRD IV as both investment firms and credit institutions fall within its scope.[40] Upgrading of the safekeeping and administration of financial instruments for the account of clients under MiFID II to an investment service/activity, thus, ensures a level playing field in terms of investor protection measures across all Member States.[41]

8.1.2.3   Credit Institutions and Investment Firms as ('Cross-Sectoral') Eligible Depositary Entities

The planned MiFID II upgrade of 'custodianship' was also reflected in the AIFMD and the UCITSD V proposal. The AIFMD and the UCITSD V planned to introduce a 'closed list of eligible entities' that together with the MiFID II upgrade of 'custodianship' would provide the foundation for a European depositary passport for AIFs and UCITS to be introduced in the future.[42] The considerations made upon limiting the eligible entities were separately discussed from the MiFID II upgrade of 'custodianship'. Despite the fact that the upgrade politically failed, UCITSD V still could have limited the eligible entities to credit institutions and investment firms. A MiFID II upgrade of 'custodianship' would

---

37 Chapter 6, Section 6.2.1.
38 Legal Certainty Group, *Second Advice of the Legal Certainty Group – Solutions to Legal Barriers related to Post-Trading within the EU*, August 2008, 25, 32.
39 *Ibid.*
40 Recital 38, Art. 1(3) MiFID II.
41 Question 3, Bank of New York Mellon response to the MiFID/MiFIR II questionnaire of MEP Markus Ferber – 12 January 2012.
42 *See, e.g.* Recital 36 AIFMD.

not have been constitutional for this. Despite of this, the European Commission decided for different reasons otherwise.

Under the original plan to slowly pave the way towards an AIF/UCITS depositary passport, (liquid) AIFs were under the AIFMD allowed to appoint credit institutions, investment firms and 'UCITSD IV depositaries'.[43] The latter was a 'grandfathering clause' that was planned to be phased out under UCITSD V by limiting eligible UCITS depositaries to credit institutions and investment firms.[44] Under this approach, the (liquid) AIFs and UCITS would both only be allowed to appoint credit institutions and investment firms as depositaries. After having received Position Papers of EFAMA and the EBF during the UCITSD V consultation, the European Commission decided, however, not to introduce a 'closed list of eligible entities' under UCITSD V.[45] Although the European Commission did not officially published its considerations, the reasons set out in these Position Papers may serve as a guideline.

EFAMA stated in its Position Paper that

> the eligibility to provide depositary services should not be restricted to credit institutions and MiFID firms subject to CRD requirements but should also remain open to other types of institutions which are currently authorized to act as depositaries in their jurisdiction provided that they are subject under their national law to similar conditions, in particular in terms of prudential regulation and ongoing supervision.[46]

In addition, the EBF held that the majority of its members in civil law countries were in favour of the 'closed list of entities', whereas EBF members of common law countries believed that UCITSD I-IV depositaries should continue to be allowed to be appointed as UCITSD V depositaries.[47]

Not adopting the 'closed list of entities' under UCITSD V, however, had a large impact on the fragmented sectoral depositary landscape. Under a dynamic interpretation of UCITSD V,[48] some Member States in their AIFMD implementation still allow UCITS depositaries to be appointed. In addition, the IORPD II depositary regime also allows

---

43 For illiquid and highly leveraged AIFs also 'PE-depositaries' and prime brokers that classify under one of the eligible entities are allowed.

44 European Commission, *Working Document of the Commission Services (DG Internal Market and Services) – Consultation Paper on the UCITSD Depositary Function and on the UCITS Managers' Remuneration*, MARKT/G4 D (2010) 950800, 14 December 2010, 16.

45 EBF, *EBF Position on UCITS V*, 5, www.ebf-fbe.eu/uploads/D1425F-2012-Final%20EBF%20position%20on %20UCITS%20V.pdf.

46 EFAMA, *EFAMA Position Paper on the Legislative proposal of the Commission Amending Directive 2009/65/ EC ("UCITS V")*, 4, www.efama.org/Publications/Public/UCITS/12-4040_EFAMA position paper on UCITS V.pdf.

47 EBF, *supra* note 45.

48 *See* Chapter 4, Section 4.3.1.3.

UCITSD V depositaries to be appointed.[49] Under IORPD II, UCITSD V depositaries regulated on the national level do have a 'de facto' European passport. This is contrary to the principle of the European passport concept in which financial intermediaries are required to be subject to the 'single rulebook' and the European coordinated approach towards financial supervision.[50]

Recently literature also considers credit institutions and investment firms to be the most suitable eligible entities for several reasons.[51] The structural separation required between AIFMs and UCITS ManCos and depositaries required under the AIFMD and UCITSD V is based upon the idea that managerial risks related to fraud and insolvency are being mitigated by requiring a third party depositary to be appointed. The third party depositary requirement, however, only makes sense when a depositary is able to safekeep the fund's assets, depositaries are less prone to insolvency than UCITS ManCos and AIFMs and the AIF/UCITS' assets are properly segregated from all other assets.[52] Credit institutions and investment firms are, in particular, the most suitable eligible depositary entities as the EEA-regulated CRR capital requirements to which they are subjected to significantly reduce the insolvency risks of these entities. Although UCITSD V requires 'another legal entity' regulated under the national level also to comply with the 'own funds' requirement under the CRR, they fall outside of the scope of the CRR capital requirements.[53] In addition, they are only subject to minimum requirements regarding infrastructure, experience, administrative and accounting procedures, internal control mechanisms, risk management procedures and arrangements to prevent conflicts of interest.[54] These requirements, however, do not constitute a 'single rulebook' that is commonly required under sectoral legislation upon granting an European passport. Apart from this, these 'another legal entities' regulated on the national level also do not fall under any coordinated institutional framework for financial supervision comprising of 'home state control' and the ESFS that allows host Member States to defer supervision to home Member States and ESAs.[55] For that reason, limiting depositaries to credit institutions and investment firms would ensure a level playing field in terms of investor protection measures across all sectoral depositary regimes.[56]

---

49   See for 'depositaries' under IORPD II: Chapter 5, Section 5.3.2.2.
50   See Chapter 3, Section 3.2.
51   D.A. Zetzsche, *Prinzipien der kollektiven Vermögensanlage* § 24 C.I. 2. (Mohr Siebeck 2015).
52   *Ibid.*
53   See Chapter 4, Section 4.3.2.3.
54   Art. 23(2)(c) UCITSD V.
55   Moloney, *supra* note 16.
56   Question 3, Bank of New York Mellon response to the MiFID/MiFIR II questionnaire of MEP Markus Ferber – 12 January 2012.

8.1.3   The Depositary as 'Custody plus' under Sectoral Regulations

Depositaries are, apart from 'PE-depositaries',[57] custodians that safekeep assets and per-form oversight duties. The MiFID II 'stand-alone' custodian regime would adequately address investor and market protection concerns related to the safekeeping task.

Nevertheless, the additional monitoring task assigned to depositaries reflects that the role of a depositary goes beyond that of a mere custodian.[58] The monitoring task is the result of the fiduciary and collective investment nature of the AIF, UCITS and IORPs. Custodians are mainly appointed for investment relationships with an agency and indi-vidual investment nature, such as 'execution only' services, discretionary portfolio man-agement and investment advice-based investment relationships.[59] In terms of govern-ance, custodians mainly cater for asset segregation and limited liability, whereas depositaries play a more prominent role in 'fiduciary governance' under the common concept of the investment triangle.[60] Depositary regulation can, thus, be seen as a sepa-rate area of law. For this reason, depositary regulation has on the national and (partly) the European level always been based upon a reference to eligible entities that were usually the entities authorized to act as a custodian, whereas 'lex specialis' rules addressed the 'fiduciary governance' role of depositaries. The AIFMD, for instance, makes reference to credit institutions and investment firms that may be authorized as a 'custodian' under European law.[61] Similarly, many Member States historically on the national level referred to credit institutions (and investment firms) for depositaries appointed for AIFs, UCITS and IORPs. On top of this, sectoral depositary regulation requires 'lex specialis' provi-sions to be fulfilled related to:

- the mandatory appointment of a single depositary;[62]
- the legal independence of the depositary, AIFM, UCITS ManCo, the IORP (governing board) and related requirements;[63]
- the eligible entities required to be appointed and the organizational requirements applicable to them (depending upon the UCITSD V Member State implementation: credit institutions, investment firms and 'other legal entities');[64]
- the reuse of assets; [65]

---

57 *See* Chapter 4, section 7.3.1.6.
58 *See* Chapter 7, section 7.1.1.
59 *See* Chapter 6.
60 *See* D.A. Zetzsche, *The AIFMD and the Joint Principles of European Asset Management Law* (D.A. Zetzsche ed, Kluwer 2015).
61 Art. 21(3) AIFMD.
62 Art. 22(1) UCITSD V; Art. 21(1) AIFMD; Art. 33(1) and (2) IORPD II.
63 *See* Arts. 25, 26b UCITSD V; Art. 21 UCITSD V (Commission) Regulation; Art. 33(7) IORPD II.
64 Art. 23(2) UCITSD V; Art. 21(3) AIFMD; Art. 33(3) IORPD II.
65 Art. 21(11)(d)(iv) AIFMD; Art. 22(7) UCITSD V.

- the safekeeping duties;[66]
- the oversight duties;[67]
- the delegation regime;[68] and
- the depositary's liability regime.[69]

The 'Custody Plus' solution proposed is, thus, consistent with how depositaries till now have been regulated on the national and European level.

The 'fiduciary governance' role of depositaries varies from sector to sector as investor protection concerns slightly differ throughout these sectors. For this reason, the 'Custody Plus' solution suggested in this book proposes to introduce a common legislative framework for custodians under MiFID II, whereas specific depositary provisions reflecting the fiduciary governance of a specific sector remain to be regulated on the sectoral level under the AIFMD, UCITSD V and IORPD II. To increase the efficiency and lower the compliance burden, depositary provisions on the sectoral level should be 'horizontally' harmonized wherever possible. Only such an approach could ensure an effective introduction of a 'cross-sectoral depositary passport'.

8.2   'Custodianship', a Stand-Alone Investment Service/Activity under MiFID II

The 2011 MiFID II proposal may serve as guidance for how 'custodianship' as 'stand-alone' investment service/activity could be defined and what authorization/operational requirements such investment firms would be required to fulfil.

8.2.1   Defining 'Custodianship' as Stand-Alone Investment Service/Activity

The proposed MiFID II already showed in 2011 how 'custodianship' as a 'stand-alone' investment service/activity could be regulated. The MiFID II proposal inserted the following definition under Annex I Section A under the list of investment services/activities:

> safekeeping and administration of financial instruments for the account of clients, including custodianship and related services such as cash/collateral management.[70]

---

66 Art. 22(5) UCITSD V; Art. 21(8) AIFMD; Art. 34 IORPD II.
67 Art. 22(3) UCITSD V; Art. 21(9) AIFMD; Art. 35 IORPD II.
68 Art. 22a UCITSD V; Art. 21(11) AIFMD; Art. 34(4) IORPD II.
69 Art. 24(1) UCITSD V; Art. 21(12) AIFMD; Art. 34(4) IORPD II.
70 This ancillary service includes custodianship and related services, such as cash/collateral management, and excludes maintaining securities accounts at the top tier level. *See* Annex I s. B MiFID II.

This definition is the same definition that was adopted in the final MiFID II with the exception of the exclusion of the 'maintaining securities accounts at the top tier level'. The current definition used defines the 'safekeeping and administration of financial instruments' as an 'ancillary service' that could be used as an overall broad definition on which the stand-alone investment service/activity could be based. During the consultation phase, a revised MiFID II version stated in Recital 113a that

> the Commission should put forward a proposal for a regulation on securities law further specifying the definition of safekeeping and administration of financial instruments.[71]

Apparently, the 'safekeeping and administration of financial instruments' was desired to be defined to a larger extent. For that purpose, the safekeeping definition, as defined in detail under the AIFMD, UCITSD V and IORPD II could be used.[72] Based upon this, 'safekeeping' can take the form of custody, for 'financial instruments that can be held in custody' or record-keeping for 'other assets'.[73] Depending upon the political desirability of the Member States, the MiFID II 'stand-alone' investment service/activity could include only the 'safekeeping of financial instruments that can be held in custody' or the safekeeping of both 'financial instruments that can be held in custody' and 'other assets'. The first approach would fit in the profile of a custodian and fits in better with the scope of MiFID II that applies to 'financial instruments'. The second approach fits in better with the depositary regimes under sectoral regulation and the approach taken by Ireland, Malta and the UK in implementing the 'depositary-lite model'[74] under Article 36 AIFMD. Member States may on the basis of Article 36 AIFMD for a transitional period of time exempt EEA-AIFMs from appointing an Article 21 AIFMD depositary.[75] Instead, however, Article 36 AIFMD obliges Member States to require EEA-AIFMs to ensure that one or more entities are appointed to carry out depositary duties mentioned under Article 21(7)-(9) AIFMD.[76] For this purpose, Ireland, for instance, requires entities providing the safekeeping function, including both the custody as the record-keeping task, to be

---

71 See www.europarl.europa.eu/sides/getDoc.do?pubRef=-//EP//TEXT+TA+P7-TA-2012-0406+0+DOC+XML+V0//EN#top.
72 *See* Zetzsche & Marte, *supra* note 5.
73 Art. 22(5) UCITSD V; Art. 21(8) AIFMD; Art. 34 IORPD II.
74 *See* Chapter 4, section 4.2.1.4.
75 *Ibid.*
76 Art. 36(1)(a) AIFMD.

authorized under the Investment Intermediaries Act 1995.[77] Malta[78] and the UK[79] take the same approach. In either approach taken, the 'safekeeping' definition chosen could benefit from definitions of, amongst others, 'financial instruments that can be held in custody' and 'other assets' as defined in detail under the AIFMD and UCITSD V.[80]

8.2.2   Authorization Requirements and Operational Conditions

'Custodians' will be required to comply with the regular MiFID II authorization require-ments, and general and specific organizational requirements. Under Article 13(2) MiFID II 'custodians' are required to establish adequate policies and procedures sufficient to ensure compliance of the firm, including its managers, employees and tied agents and appropriate rules governing personal transactions by such persons. In addition, specific organizational features are required regarding risk management and internal audit, out-sourcing, conflicts of interests and the safeguarding of client assets.[81] These procedures aim to avoid operational risks, conflict of interest and adequate protection of client as-sets.[82] Currently, the 'safeguarding of client assets regime' applies to all investment firms regardless of whether they are authorized for providing 'custodianship' as an 'ancillary' service or not. The safeguarding of client assets regime will, thus, under this proposal continue to apply to investment firms regardless of whether the firm is authorized as a 'stand-alone' 'custodian' or not.

During the MiFID II proposal consultation phase a few respondents mentioned that applying the suitability[83] of the assessment of appropriateness[84] and the best execution

---

77 Ibid.
78 SLC 1.03, Part BIV: *Standard Licence Conditions applicable to Investment Services Licence Holders* which *qualify* as *Custodians*, *Investment Services Rules* for *Investment Services Licence Holders; See* MFSA, Feed-back statement further to industry responses to MFSA Consultation Document dated 18 September 2013 on the introduction of the depositary lite provisions, 2.1.1. [I]. Feedback Statement.
79 *See* FCA, *Frequently Asked Questions: Q9: Does an Article 36 custodian require a Part 4A permission for acting as depositary of an AIF?*, www.fca.org.uk/firms/markets/international-markets/aifmd/depositaries; FCA, *Implementation of the Alternative Investment Fund Managers Directive*, PS 13/5, 39 (2013).
80 *See* Chapter 4, Section 4.6.2.
81 C.W.M. Lieverse, C.W.M., *The Scope of MiFID II* (D. Busch & G. Ferrarini eds, Oxford 2017).
82 *See* Art. 16(2)-(10) MiFID II.
83 Art. 25 MiFID II; *See* for ESMA Guidelines on certain aspects of the MiFID suitability requirements: ESMA/2012/387 and on the consultation: ESMA/2011/445; Question 3, British Banker's Association response to the MiFID/MiFIR II questionnaire of MEP Markus Ferber – 12 January 2012; Blackrock response to the MiFID/MiFIR II questionnaire of MEP Markus Ferber – 12 January 2012.
84 Art. 25(2) of MiFID II; *See also* question 3, EFAMA response to the MiFID/MiFIR II questionnaire of MEP Markus Ferber – 12 January 2012; Question 3, Bundesverband Investment and Asset Management response to the MiFID/MiFIR II questionnaire of MEP Markus Ferber – 12 January 2012; Question 3, Investment Management Association response to the MiFID/MiFIR II questionnaire of MEP Markus Ferber – 12 Jan-uary 2012.

requirements[85] to stand-alone custodians would be inappropriate.[86] MiFID II could, indeed, include a provision that exempts 'stand-alone' investment firms from complying with these requirements. This should, however, not be considered in great detail. Almost all custodians that will be authorized under MiFID II will combine this authorization with the authorization of one or more other investment and ancillary services/activities. This will be the case as 'custodianship' in itself is a low-margin business.[87]

The sectoral depositary regime will provide 'lex specialis' provisions that may fully or partially substitute the general and specific organizational requirements to which 'MiFID II custodians' are subjected to.

8.3   The Depositary as 'Custody Plus' under Sectoral Regulations

'Depositaries' may play a slightly different role under the various sectoral regulations. For this reason, the specifics of depositaries as compared to mere custodians are suggested to be left over to regulation at the sectoral level. Nevertheless, a 'cross-sectoral depositary passport' is only cost effective if sectoral regulations are aligned to the extent that the role played by the depositary on the sectoral level is similar. For this reason, this section makes suggestions to align the AIFMD, UCITSD V and IORPD II depositary regimes.

8.3.1   The AIFMD and UCITSD V Depositary Regime – Towards Alignment?

The AIFMD and UCITSD V depositary regimes are based upon the same 'post-Madoff' considerations and constitute the most sophisticated regimes.[88] For the purpose of the introduction of a cross-sectoral depositary passport, both regimes are, apart from the current eligible entities available, sufficiently harmonized. The UCITSD V depositary regime, however, was adopted a couple of years later. This is reflected in the slightly different approach taken under UCITSD V. UCITSD V, in comparison to the AIFMD, contains stricter (retail investor protection) depositary provisions related to, in particular, the:[89]

– requirement to provide an inventory of assets; [90]
– independence of the management/investment company and the UCITS depositary;[91]

---

85   Art. 27 MiFID II; Question 3, British Banker's Association response to the MiFID/MiFIR II questionnaire of MEP Markus Ferber – 12 January 2012.

86   Question 3, CSDA response to the MiFID/MiFIR II questionnaire of MEP Markus Ferber – 12 January 2012; Question 3, ALFI response to the MiFID/MiFIR II questionnaire of MEP Markus Ferber – 12 January 2012.

87   European Commission, *supra* note 17.

88   *See* Chapter 4, section 4.1.

89   T. Dolan, *UCITS V Brings Convergence of the Depositary Role with AIFMD*, 1 JIBFL 64B (2015).

90   Art. 22(6) UCITSD V.

91   *See* Art. 26b UCITSD V; Art. 21 UCITSD V (Commission) Regulation.

- prohibition on right of use/rehypothecation of assets;[92]
- client asset protection on insolvency of the depositary or a sub-custodian; [93]
- strict liability for a loss of custody assets;[94] and
- redress of investors against the depositary.[95]

In the light of a 'cross-sectoral depositary passport', it is desirable to aim for the approximation of depositary laws on a sectoral (vertical harmonization) and cross-sectoral (horizontal harmonization) basis. Apart from the stricter liability for a loss of custody assets and the prohibition on the right of use, the differences in depositary provisions between the AIFMD and UCITSD V seem not to be justified on the basis of retail protection. Extending considerations made under UCITSD V to AIFMD could be considered for the provisions under UCITSD V related to the:[96]

- requirement to provide an inventory of assets;[97]
- investor insolvency protection;[98]
- independence of the management/investment company and the UCITS depositary;[99]
- client asset protection on insolvency of the depositary or a sub-custodian;[100] and
- redress of investors against the depositary.[101]

This would lead to more cross-sectoral consistency. Moreover, a couple of other considerations could be made. Prime brokers, for instance, should be continued to be allowed to be appointed as a depositary under the AIFMD. Only those prime brokers would, however, under the proposal made in this chapter be allowed that are authorized under MiFID II as a custodian.[102] In addition, the AIFMD prime broker provisions targeting the prime broker as a counterparty and depositary should apply *mutandis mutatis* to UCITS.[103] UCITS, compared to AIFs, are restricted in applying leverage. Nevertheless, so-called 'Newcits'[104] are appointing prime brokers and, for that reason, cross-sectoral

---

92 Art. 22(7) UCITSD V.
93 Art. 22(8) UCITSD V.
94 Art. 24 UCITSD V.
95 *Ibid.*
96 T. Dolan, *UCITS V Brings Convergence of the Depositary Role with AIFMD*, 1 JIBFL 64B (2015).
97 Art. 22(6) UCITSD V.
98 ESMA, Opinion – *Asset Segregation and Application of Depositary Delegation Rules to CSDs*, 20 July 2017, ESMA34-45-277.
99 *See* Art. 26b UCITSD V; Art. 21 UCITSD V (Commission) Regulation.
100 Art. 22(8) UCITSD V.
101 Art. 24 UCITSD V.
102 Currently, prime brokers appointed as depositary under the AIFMD are also required to be an 'eligible entity'; *See* Chapter 4, Section 4.3.1.4.2.
103 *See* for more considerations made in this domain: Chapter 4, section 4.3.2.3.3.
104 EDHEC Risk Institute, *Are Hedge Fund UCITS the Cure-All?* (EDHEC-Position Paper 2010).

consistency would be desirable.[105] Furthermore, the 'PE-depositary' lex specialis provisions could be considered to remain in place.[106] In this regard, the large variety of Member State implementations would make it desirable to require a MiFID II 'investment firm-light' to be appointed.[107] Under the AIFMD, a couple of lex specialis provisions for 'PE-depositaries' could be inserted that would require the appointment of a MiFID II custodian that is exempted from complying with 'onerous' MiFID II provisions related to the CRR capital requirements and conduct of business rules. Such an exemption could be based upon the Luxembourg and UK 'PE-depositary regimes'. The Luxembourg regime would serve as an example of the 'investment firm-light', whereas the UK regime related to 'proportional capital requirements' could be considered.[108] Depending upon the extent that 'PE-depositaries' safekeep 'financial instruments that can be held in custody' such an investment firm-light is subject to a lesser or larger part of the CRR capital requirements. 'PE-depositaries' exclusively safekeeping 'other assets' could be exempted from applying most CRR capital requirements. Finally, the AIFMD TC regime would remain in place.[109] TC MiFID II custodians as eligible entities would be required to be assessed in the light of the provisions adopted. No such a regime would need to be considered for UCITS depositaries as a TC regime for UCITS is not (yet) in place.

By taking into account these considerations, the AIFMD and UCITSD V could be approximated to a larger extent lowering compliance costs for those custodians seeking to use the 'cross-sectoral depositary passport'.

8.3.2 The IORPD II Depositary Regime – A Proposal

The IORPD II 'depositary regime' is not as sophisticated as the AIFMD and UCITSD V regimes. The reason for this is that the IORPD II regime aims to target both 'custodians' and AIFMD/UCITSD V 'depositaries'. The different roles of both in 'fiduciary governance' render a consistent regime integrating both an impossible task. This is reflected in the quality of the regime currently in place.[110] In the light of the introduction of a cross-sectoral depositary passport, considerations would have to be made to ensure consistency of the IORPD II regime with the AIFMD and UCITSD V depositary regimes.

---

105 *See also* T. Moroni & L. Wibbeke, *OGAW V: Die Sprunglatte für OGAW-Verwahrstellen liegt höher*, 3 Recht der Finanzinstrumente 187 (2015).

106 Chapter 4, Section 4.3.1.6.

107 *Ibid.*

108 Luxembourg: Art. 26-1 Law of 5 April 1993 on the financial sector, as amended on 12 June 2013; UK: FUND 3.11.12 R; FUND 3.11.12 R; FUND 3.11.14 R: *See also* the Glossary Definition FCA: 'Part 4a Permission' and 'acting as trustee or depositary of an AIF' and 'own funds'. (FUND 3.11.12-14); *See also*: D.A. Zetzsche, *Fondsregulierung im Umbruch – ein rechtsvergleichender Rundblick zur Umsetzung der AIFM-Richtlinie*, ZBB 22 (2014).

109 Chapter 4, Section 4.5.

110 *See* for an overview and criticism: Chapter 5.

The primary reason for the current inconsistent IORPD II 'depositary' regime is that the IORP itself is broadly defined and can take the form of an 'investment fund', insurance company or 'pension fund'. For this reason, large discretion is given to Member States in compulsorily requiring depositaries and custodians to be appointed.[111] It could be considered, as was the case under the original IORPD II proposal, that Member States have to require a compulsory depositary for 'full DC IORP s' in which members bear full investment risk.[112] This would be consistent with AIFs and UCITS as most full DC IORPs are, de facto, occupational 'investment funds'. Full DC IORPs could, however, also offer (occupational) unit-linked insurances in which an AIF or UCITS is embedded that already requires the appointment of a depositary. As was suggested in the IORPD II proposal amendments, the adverse effect of any possible 'duplication' of the depositary requirement for these unit-linked insurances exclusively investing in an AIF/UCITS could be prevented by inserting an 'IORP pooling structure exemption'.[113] All other IORPs than full DC IORPs are under the CJEU VAT case law not considered to be comparable with AIFs and UCITS as members do 'not fully bear investment risk'.[114] Considerations regarding a compulsory depositary/custodian requirement for these IORPs should, therefore, be left over to the individual Member States.

A hybrid depositary/custodian sectoral IORPD II regime would need to be considered. The UCITSD V depositary regime should be considered for IORPs that (are required to) appoint a depositary and the MiFID II 'stand-alone' custodian regime for IORPs appointing custodians. This would lead to consistency between MiFID II custodians, on the one hand, and the AIFMD and UCITSD V, on the other hand.

The UCITSD V depositary regime should be considered due to its 'retail investor protection nature'.

Applying the UCITSD V depositary regime to all IORPs for which a depositary is required to be appointed ensures a level playing field related to, amongst others:

- the mandatory appointment of a single depositary;[115]
- the legal independence of the depositary and the IORP (governing board) and related requirements;[116]
- the eligible entities required to be appointed and the organizational requirements applicable to them (depending upon the UCITSD V Member State implementation: credit institutions, investment firms and 'other legal entities');[117]
- the safekeeping duties;[118]

---

111 Art. 33(1), (2) IORPD II.
112 See R.M.J.M de Greef, *Herziening IORP richtlijn – Een verbetering?*, 50 TPV 27 (2016).
113 See EIOPA-BOS-12/015, 460-461.
114 See, e.g. CJEU (Judgement 13 March 2014), Case C-464/12, ATP Pension Service, ECLI:EU:C:2014:139, para. 57, 59.
115 Art. 22(1) UCITSD V; Art. 21(1) AIFMD.
116 See Arts. 25, 26b UCITSD V; Art. 21 UCITSD V (Commission) Regulation.
117 Art. 23(2) UCITSD V; Art. 21(3) AIFMD.
118 Art. 22(5) UCITSD V; Art. 21(8) AIFMD.

- the oversight duties;[119]
- the delegation regime;[120] and
- the depositary's liability regime.[121]

The oversight duties would be allowed to be proportionally applied. In particular, the duties related to subscriptions/redemptions, the valuations of share/unit pricing and cash management could be irrelevant for IORPs.[122] No 'equivalency regimes' would be in place for IORPs that do not appoint a custodian/depositary for the safekeeping of assets nor for IORPs that do not have appointed a depositary for oversight duties.[123] The reason for this is that IORPs do not have the same prudential standards to safekeep assets as professional custodians/depositaries.[124] In addition, IORPs for which no depositary for oversight duties is appointed do not have to have a specific obligation to 'ensure that the tasks, otherwise subject to oversight by depositaries, are being duly performed within the IORP'.[125] Such a task is already part of the IORP's risk management organization required under IORPD II.

The proposed hybrid depositary/custodian regime would fit in under the sectoral AIFMD and UCITSD V depositary regimes.

8.4   Conclusion

This chapter, on the basis of the outcome of the preceding parts, advocates in favour of the case for introducing not only an AIF/UCITS depositary but a 'cross-sectoral European depositary passport' in European investment law.

The introduction of a (cross-sectoral) depositary passport would, thus, enable depositaries to offer their services on the European level and to consolidate services on a cross-sectoral and cross-border basis.

Notwithstanding the benefits of introducing an AIF/UCITS depositary passport, a European passport for UCITS and AIF depositaries has so far been multiple times considered, but not introduced due to investor protection concerns.[126] MEP Perreau de Pinninck in 1993 after the introduction of the 'ancillary European passport' under the ISD and Second Banking Directive considered that a European depositary passport for UCITS

---

119 Art. 22(3) UCITSD V; Art. 21(9) AIFMD.
120 Art. 22a UCITSD V; Art. 21(11) AIFMD.
121 Art. 24(1) UCITSD V; Art. 21(12) AIFMD.
122 *See* Chapter 5, Section 5.3.4.3.
123 *See* for the 'equivalency' regime for IORPs that do not have appointed a 'depositary' for the safekeeping of assets: Chapter 5, section 5.4.; *See* for the 'equivalency' regime for IORPs that do not have appointed a 'depositary' for oversight duties: Chapter 5, section 5.4.2.
124 *See* for the criticism on this regime: Chapter 5, section 5.4.1.2.
125 *See* Art. 35(3) IORPD II.
126 *See* Chapter 2, Section 2.1.2.

should not be introduced for two reasons.[127] First, it was considered that the depositary function was going beyond mere performing the 'custodian' function under the ISD and Second Banking Directive. Second, the depositaries in the UCITS domain had not been harmonized to effectively perform the controlling function.

Prior to introducing an AIF/UCITS or cross-sectoral depositary passport the question would, thus, need to be answered whether the differences between depositaries and custodians justify the locational restriction applicable to AIF/UCITS depositaries. Furthermore, it should be verified whether AIF, UCITS and IORPs are sufficiently harmonized or what should be done to make the introduction of a cross-sectoral passport acceptable.

A 'de facto European depositary passport' is granted to IORP depositaries, whereas this is not available for AIF/UCITS depositaries. This is highly remarkable as depositaries perform the same functions with the same underlying investor protection objective. This inconsistency can be rightfully called an 'European depositary passport paradox' as the eligible entities and, in particular, the depositary function itself under the AIFMD and UCITSD V has been harmonized to a much larger extent than under IORPD II.[128]

The AIFMD 'transitional relief' regime'[129] suggests that the duties, delegation and depositary's liability regime are sufficiently harmonized on the European level for the introduction of a European passport. Under this regime, credit institutions appointed as an AIF depositary are allowed to be appointed under a 'mutual recognition regime' provided that the AIF home Member State in which the AIF is established for which the depositary is appointed has implemented this option in its AIFMD implementation laws.[130] Given the similarities under the UCITSD V depositary regime, similar considerations could be made regarding the introduction of a UCITSD V depositary passport.

This seems to suggest that the introduction of a 'cross-sectoral depositary passport' would require full harmonization of the depositary as a financial intermediary and also the harmonization of the IORP depositary duties, delegation and liability standards would be necessary for a consistent approach.

Similarly as for the 'management company passport' discussion, custodians already upon the introduction of ISD enjoyed an ('ancillary') European passport. As a compromise of introducing the European 'management passport' under UCITSD IV and the AIFMD, the depositary remained to be required to be established in the UCITS/AIF home Member State.

Modelled after this concept, indeed, a proportional 'cross-sectoral depositary passport' could be built upon the core activities of the safekeeping of assets and the performance of oversight duties. All depositaries and custodians perform at least the safekeep-

---

127 European Parliament, *Report of the Committee on Legal Affairs and Citizen's Rights on the 1993 UCITS Proposal*, A5-0268/1993, 1 October 1993, http://goo.gl/rRSdJO.
128 *See* for the AIFMD/UCITSD V depositary regime: Chapter 4; *See* for the IORPD II depositary regime: Chapter 5.
129 *See* Chapter 2, Section 2.1.2.2.2.
130 *Ibid.*

ing of assets at a minimum. Essentially, depositaries are custodians that perform, in addition to the safekeeping of assets, oversight duties.[131] For this reason, a 'cross-sectoral depositary passport' could be built on the basis of an harmonized authorization regime for custodians on the basis of the regulatory activity 'safekeeping of assets', whereas on the sectoral level a cross-sectoral consistent set of legislation applies additionally for custodians that act as depositaries.

---

131 *See* Chapter 7, Section 7.2.1.3.

9 CONCLUSION

This book intended to clarify whether a 'cross-sectoral'[1] depositary passport should be introduced which allows depositaries to perform cross-border services for not only IORPs and clients under MiFID II, but also AIFs and UCITS. The author takes the view in this book that not introducing an European passport for depositaries is a disregard of the fundamental freedom of services which characterizes the creation of an internal market for international financial services in the EEA that cannot be justified in terms of investor protection.

Consequently, this book explores the question whether depositaries in European investment law should be allowed to enjoy the right of a cross-sectoral European passport.

In supporting this thesis, this book addressed this question by answering the following sub-questions:

– What inconsistencies in attributing an European depositary passport are to be found in European investment law?
– To what extent do financial intermediaries have to be harmonized on the EEA level to obtain a European passport?
– Do the differences between depositaries and custodians justify the difference in treatment?
– What preconditions need to be fulfilled to introduce a European AIF/UCITS depositary passport and/or a cross-sectoral European depositary passport?

The questions needed were answered before a full European AIF and UCITS depositary passport and, eventually, a cross-sectoral depositary passport was considered.

9.1 THE EUROPEAN DEPOSITARY PASSPORT PARADOX

In practice, the same investment firms and credit institutions are acting as a custodian for discretionary mandates and 'execution only'[2] services under MiFID II/CRD IV, a depositary under the AIFMD/UCITSD V and a depositary/custodian under IORPD II. Part I showed that the European investment laws, i.e. MiFID II, CRD IV, the AIFMD, UCITSD V and IORPD II, are inconsistent in granting a depositary/custodian passport to these depositaries/custodians. They are inconsistent both throughout the directives and on a

---

1 European law had the tendency to first harmonize various sectors, such as the insurance and banking sector. Currently, European law not only harmonizes legislation within a certain sector but also harmonizes the legislative standards throughout various sectors as to ensure consistency.
2 *See* Annex I s. n. 1 and n. 2 MiFID II; Art. 25(4) MiFID II.

cross-sectoral basis. On a cross-sectoral basis, MiFID II and CRD IV have an 'ancillary' European passport for 'custodians' in place.[3] To the contrary, the AIFMD and UCITSD V require the depositary of UCITS and EEA-AIFs to be established in the UCITS/EEA-AIF home Member State,[4] whereas the same entities acting as a depositary/custodian under IORPD II have a 'de facto' European passport.[5] Not only are the European investment laws inconsistent throughout the directives, but also the directives itself are inconsistent. The AIFMD, for example, differentiates between a strict locational requirement for EEA-AIFs, whereas there is a 'quasi-depositary passport regime' in place for depositaries appointed for TC-AIFs.[6] The inconsistency in granting a European passport for depositaries under the European investment law directives lead to a 'European depositary passport paradox'.

For a better understanding of all legal issues related to the European depositary passport, it was of importance to examine the debate upon the European depositary passport in a historical context. For this purpose, the concerns raised upon introducing such a passport during the adoption of the various UCITS directives, the AIFMD, the ISD/MiFID I/II and IORPD I/II, have been studied in Part I. The 'ancillary European passport' for investment firms and credit institutions under MiFID II and CRD IV has never been updated to a full-fledged investment service as concerns have been raised related to the scope of 'safekeeping and administration' and, in practice, such a 'low margin service' is only being offered in connection with other investment services/activities. The non-harmonization in this area will, however, also in the future remain to raise a number of questions as to whether the European legal framework for custodians needs to be further harmonized and strengthened to ensure a level playing field in terms of investor protection measures across all Member States.[7] Part I showed that, notwithstanding the benefits of introducing a depositary/custodian passport, a European passport for UCITS and AIF depositaries has so far been multiple times considered, but not introduced. MEP Perreau de Pinninck after the introduction of the 'ancillary European passport' under the ISD and Second Banking Directive considered that a European depositary passport for UCITS should not be introduced for two reasons.[8] First, it was considered that the depositary function was going beyond mere performing the 'custodian' function under the ISD and Second Banking Directive. Second, the depositaries in the UCITS domain had not been harmonized to effectively perform the controlling function. This reasoning, however, did

---

3   Annex I n. 12 CRD IV; Annex I s. A MiFID II.

4   Art. 21(5) AIFMD and Art. 23(1) UCITSD V.

5   Art. 33(3) IORPD II.

6   *See also* C.P. Buttigieg, *The Case for A European Depositary Passport*, http://studylib.net/doc/13128849/the-case-for-a-european-depository-passport; *See also* S.N. Hooghiemstra, *Depositary Regulation* (D.A. Zetzsche ed, Kluwer 2015).

7   Question 3, Bank of New York Mellon response to the MiFID/MiFIR II questionnaire of MEP Markus Ferber – 12 January 2012.

8   European Parliament, *Report of the Committee on Legal Affairs and Citizen's Rights on the 1993 UCITS Proposal*, A5-0268/1993, 1 October 1993, http://goo.gl/rRSdJO.

not explain why currently a depositary passport has not been introduced under the substantially harmonized depositary function under the AIFMD and UCITSD V. Nor does this reasoning explain why depositaries and custodians under IORPD II enjoy a 'de facto European passport' under a minimum harmonized regime and why the AIFMD grants transitional relief for credit institutions and a quasi-depositary passport for TC-AIFs. For this reason, Part II set out under what conditions an European/TC passport could be granted to (AIF/UCITS) depositaries, whereas Part III addressed to what extent depositaries and custodians are different.

9.2 THE EEA'S APPROACH TOWARDS THE CROSS-BORDER PROVISION OF FINANCIAL SERVICES

Part II studied the EEA's approach towards the cross-border provision of financial services in more detail. In particular, the conditions under which European and TC passports are granted to EEA and TC financial intermediaries have been studied as to determine under what conditions a (cross-sectoral) European/TC passport could be granted to 'depositaries' and 'custodians'.

EEA law in regulating financial intermediaries has an 'internal dimension' and an 'external dimension'. The so-called 'internal dimension' is regulated by EEA secondary law that is based upon the four freedoms and regulates the cross-border provisions of financial services in the internal market by EEA financial intermediaries. The 'external dimension' regulates the cross-border provisions of financial services in the internal market by TC financial intermediaries and is based upon international law commitments and EEA secondary law.

EEA law in regulating both the 'internal dimension' and 'external dimension' has as its purpose to establish an internal market for financial services that enhances market efficiency and leads to economies of scale and scope. Authorization and notification requirements under European passport arrangements, for example, only need to be fulfilled in one Member State while having a large market to offer their financial products and services without worrying about multiple authorization applications and the establishment of subsidiaries that would have led to a duplication of legal costs. Prices in an EEA internal market for financial services decline as fixed costs are shared amongst a larger client base.[9] Firms may organize themselves anywhere in the EEA, in small and big Member States and, as a result, have the potential to maximize their efficiency and become more competitive. In addition to reducing transaction costs, financial institutions from either smaller or bigger EEA Member States may market products and services to all of the European Union's 500 million citizens, resulting in more revenue.

---

9   D.A. Zetzsche, *Drittstaaten im Europäischen Bank- und Finanzmarktrecht* 56 (G. Bachmann & B. Breig eds., Mohr Siebeck, Tübingen 2014).

The market access that an internal market facilitates may create negative externalities, such as the insolvency of financial intermediaries or fraud, that is particularly fuelled by 'risk asymmetry'.[10] Member States might be inclined by political and economic motivations to stimulate their financial services/products that are 'produced' in their Member States (production state) by subjecting their financial intermediaries and products to a minimum set of regulation and/or lax enforcement of the regulatory framework in place.[11] If those products and services are primarily marketed outside of that home Member State, the positive effects of lax regulation and supervision are being enjoyed by the home Member State as 'production state', whereas the negative effects of that are to be borne by 'distribution states', i.e. the host Member States. For this reason, prudential regulation is in place that intends to ward off any externalities resulting from 'risk asymmetry'. In the past, this has led to a large degree of legal fragmentation posing hurdles to the cross-border provision of financial intermediaries that could not be resolved by the 'four freedoms' due to the 'prudential carve-out' that justifies the infringements on the freedom movement of capital and establishment.

The 'prudential carve-out' under the 'four freedoms' impeded the establishment of an internal market for the cross-border provision of financial services in the internal market solely based on negative integration. Instead, positive integration by means of secondary legislation was established. The evolution since the 1980s was characterized by a gradual increase in detailed EEA financial law harmonization, more centralized rulemaking and implementation of the EEA legal framework for the cross-border provision of financial services. This ultimately resulted in 'joint principles', i.e. regulatory conditions, under which EEA financial intermediaries were granted a 'European passport'.

The so-called 'European passport' is at the heart of the EEA system for financial services. It is a general concept that lays down the conditions for the 'mutual recognition' principle. The general idea is that financial products or services that are 'produced' (and marketed) in a 'home Member State' may, under conditions set out in European legislative acts, be marketed throughout the internal market without incurring further conditions imposed by 'host Member States'. The concept of the European passport is now widespread and commonly used to enhance the development of the EEA internal market for financial intermediaries that are active in a wide range of sectors. The European passport and the overarching principle of 'mutual recognition' are based upon two cornerstones: the 'single rulebook', i.e. a thick set of harmonized rules, and a coordinated institutional framework for financial supervision comprising of 'home state control' and the ESFS that allows host Member States to defer supervision to home Member States and ESAs.[12] The European passport as regulatory tool is unique and not to be found in any other multilateral, regional or bilateral forms of

---

10 *See* D.A. Zetzsche, *Competitiveness of Financial Centers in Light of Financial and Tax Law Equivalence Requirements* 401-402 (R.P. Buckley, E. Avgouleas & D.W. Arner eds., Cambridge University Press 2016).

11 D.A. Zetzsche, *Drittstaaten im Europäischen Bank- und Finanzmarktrecht* 62-63 (G. Bachmann & B. Breig eds., Mohr Siebeck, Tübingen 2014).

12 N. Moloney, *Brexit, the EU and Its Investment Banker: Rethinking 'Equivalence' for the EU Capital Market*, LSE Legal Studies Working Paper No. 5/2017, 5, https://ssrn.com/abstract=2929229.

cooperation on the international level.[13] The reason for this is the degree of centralized rulemaking and supervision on the EEA level on which the regulatory tool is based.[14]

Along with the development of the European passport as primary regulatory concept for EEA financial intermediaries, the EEA developed its 'external dimension', i.e. the conditions under which TC financial intermediaries may provide financial services in the internal market. TC financial intermediaries are not subject to the same centralized rulemaking and supervision as EEA financial intermediaries. Moreover, the harmonization of financial regulation on the international level varies from sector to sector. Banking and insurance legislation are harmonized to a large degree, whereas other sectors, such as asset management, are hardly harmonized. For this reason, the EEA determines in EEA secondary legislation whether and to what extent TC financial intermediaries may provide certain services within the EEA.

The regulation of TC financial intermediaries that want to offer cross-border financial services in the internal market is based upon the same 'law and economics' considerations as the regulation of EEA financial intermediaries. The 'external dimension', on the one hand, offers benefits in terms of market efficiency and economies of scale and scope. On the other hand, however, the possible 'risk asymmetry' externalities resulting from granting market access are even bigger than for EEA financial intermediaries. In imposing regulation to these TC financial intermediaries in warding off externalities, international law obligations ensure that TC financial intermediaries are not treated on a discriminatory basis. The European Commission is representing the entire EU in a so-called common commercial policy to ensure a consistent approach. The obligations on the international law level that have to be taken into account when regulating TC financial intermediaries are laid down in the GATS, obligations arising from the EEA and EFTA treaty and bilateral trade agreements concluded between the European Commission and third countries.

The 'prudential carve-out' under both the 'four freedoms' and GATS prevents the establishment of an 'internal market with external dimension' for financial services.[15] Already upon the introduction of the First Banking Directive, it was recognized that only market access conditions in EEA secondary law could lead to the establishment of an 'internal market with an external dimension'.

The tendency of adopting a TC approach in secondary law has several advantages. First, a coordinated approach strengthens the position of the EU in international financial governance.[16] The centralized and coordinated approach at the EU level ensures an influential position in negotiating financial regulation on the international level. Second,

---

13 P.H. Verdier, *Mutual Recognition in International Finance*, 52 Harvard International Law Journal 56 (2011).
14 IOSCO, *IOSCO Task Force on Cross-Border Regulation – Final Report*, FR 23/2015, (2015), 31 et seq.
15 J. Marchetti, *The GATS Prudential Carve-Out* 280-286 (P. Delimatsis & N. Herger eds., Kluwer 2011).
16 N. Moloney, *The EU in International Financial Governance*, 1 Russell Sage Journal of the Social Sciences 138-152(2017).

the centralized foreign commercial policy towards third country market access leads to a level playing field for small and big Member States.[17] Big Member States have a stronger position not only in international financial governance, but could also negotiate market access in third countries on better terms. Finally, a coordinated approach of the internal market as huge 'distribution target' for offshore financial centres reduces the regulatory gap between 'production' and 'distribution states'. EEA financial regulation, whether third countries are bound to it or not on a bilateral basis, has an extraterritorial effect on third countries as being regarded as 'non-equivalent' on the EEA level forecloses market access.

The EEA's equivalency concept in overcoming 'risk asymmetry' has, however, to abide by the rules related to the external dimension of the four freedoms and the obligations arising out of GATS in regulating:

- EEA financial intermediaries with an external dimension;
- TC financial intermediaries within the EEA; and
- EEA financial intermediaries within third countries.

TC financial intermediaries, usually, enter the internal market by either establishing an EEA subsidiary or acquiring 'qualifying holdings'[18] and 'close links'[19] in EEA financial intermediaries.[20] EEA subsidiaries may then be authorized under the respective EEA sectoral legislative acts,[21] whereas EEA financial intermediaries in which a 'qualifying holding' or 'close link' is acquired may have already done so. EEA law preserves the internal market by demanding compliance with EEA 'qualifying holding' and delegation requirements. EEA law also requires groups and conglomerates to comply with the EEA requirements related to consolidated supervision and conglomerates.

Solely allowing EEA firms to be active within the internal market would be contrary to the GATS. For this reason, EEA law intends to offer a legal framework for TC firms that want to provide services within the EEA to avoid externalities that would put investor protection, the market integrity or the financial system in the EEA as a whole at risk. To this end, the EEA principle of 'mutual recognition' in the form of the equivalency of TC

---

17 D.A. Zetzsche, *Drittstaaten im Europäischen Bank- und Finanzmarktrecht* 80 et seq. (G. Bachmann & B. Breig eds., Mohr Siebeck, Tübingen 2014).

18 'Qualifying holding' under various sectoral EEA legislative acts means a direct or indirect holding in an investment firm which represents 10% or more of the capital or of the voting rights or a holding which makes it possible to exercise a significant influence over the management of the EEA financial intermediary in which that holding subsists; *See* for precise definitions: Art. 4(2) n. 12 MiFID II; Art. 4(1)(ah) AIFMD; *See* for a less detailed definition: Art. 2(1)(i) UCITSD V; Art. 13 n. 21 Solvency II; Art. 4 n. 36 CRR.

19 *See* for a definition of 'close links' under various sectoral EEA legislative acts means a situation in which two or more natural or legal persons are linked by participation in the form of ownership, direct or by way of control, of 20% or more of the voting rights or capital of an undertaking; *See* Art. 2(1)(i), (4) UCITSD V; Art. 4(1)(e) AIFMD; Art. 4 n. 38 Art. 4(2) n. 26 MiFID II.

20 D.A. Zetzsche, *Drittstaaten im Europäischen Bank- und Finanzmarktrecht* 81 et seq. (G. Bachmann & B. Breig eds., Mohr Siebeck, Tübingen 2014).

21 *See, e.g.* the AIFMD, UCITSD V, MiFID II, CRD II or Solvency II.

regulatory and supervisory frameworks is required by sectoral EEA secondary legislation to be in place in such a way that TC firms have access to the EEA. The TC regimes regulating this vary from sector to sector as some sectors, such as banking and insurance, are harmonized to a larger extent at the international level than other sectors (e.g. asset management). For this reason, some EEA secondary laws require TC firms to comply with 'stand-alone authorizations', whereas others grant access to the EEA on the basis of 'central negotiation' or even grant a European passport to TC financial intermediaries.

Originally, market access of EEA financial intermediaries in third countries was based upon bilateral and international treaties concluded by individual Member States or, to the extent there was an EEA legislative initiative with an 'external dimension', the European institutions.[22] A disadvantage of this was the fragmented landscape of market access for EEA financial intermediaries in third countries. Since an amendment of the Treaty of Nice, the EU common commercial policy became an exclusive competence of the EU.[23] To this end, various EEA secondary laws grant the European Commission a 'negotiation mandate' to ensure that EEA financial intermediaries are granted market access in third countries on a reciprocal basis.

The regulation of TC financial intermediaries that want to offer cross-border financial services in the internal market is based upon the 'internal dimension', i.e. the 'four freedoms', and the external dimension that includes international law commitments and EEA secondary law. The equivalency of TC regulatory and supervision regimes to which TC financial intermediaries are subjected to serves the basis of 'equivalency' that is required to be in place upon market access in the internal market. In addition, equivalency in EEA secondary law requires 'legal representation' in the EEA by means of subsidiaries, branches or 'legal representatives' to ensure compliance with EEA law. Both are complemented by cooperation and information exchange agreements that are required to be in place between the relevant Competent Authorities. Moreover, the European Commission and ESAs have a role in centralized rulemaking and supervision and, finally, TC financial intermediaries are subject to 'judicial control'.

9.3   DEPOSITARIES VERSUS CUSTODIANS

Part III clarified whether a difference in treatment of depositaries, on the one hand, and custodians, on the other hand, throughout European investment law is justified from an investor protection perspective. To this end, 'depositaries' in the AIFMD, UCITSD V and IORPD II, on the one hand, and 'custodians' under MiFID II, CRD IV and CSDR, on the other hand, were studied.

---

22 D.A. Zetzsche, *Drittstaaten im Europäischen Bank- und Finanzmarktrecht* 67 (G. Bachmann & B. Breig eds., Mohr Siebeck, Tübingen 2014).
23 Art. 3(1)(e) TFEU.

Depositaries under the AIFMD/UCITSD V perform a safekeeping and oversight role and custodians under CRD IV, MiFID II and the national level perform merely a safekeeping role. Despite this, the same entities that within individual Member States act as a depositary perform mainly safekeeping under MiFID II and safekeeping (and oversight duties) under IORPD II. At the same time, they are subjected to the same custody transfer laws that determine the legal scope of the safekeeping function. Part III clarified that this is the case because depositary law is a specialized area of custody law. The depositary is, thus, a 'specialized custodian'.

The authorization, conduct of business rules, prudential regulation, supervision and enforcement of credit institutions, investment firms and 'equivalent other entities' are considered under the various European directives to be appropriately addressing the investor and market protection risks related to the safekeeping function of custodians and depositaries.

The notion of 'depositary' under IORPD II, UCITSD V and the AIFMD is wider than the notion of pure 'custodian'.[24] Although the safekeeping task of depositaries and custodians prevents operational failures, the safekeeping task of the depositary/custodians alone does not mitigate the agency costs resulting from the actions of, in particular, (collective) asset managers related to those assets. To this end, depositaries under sectoral 'depositary laws' are required to perform oversight duties towards these (collective) asset managers. CRD IV, MiFID II and national equivalent regulations do not contain such an explicit obligation for custodians. This can be explained by the agency costs borne by AIF/UCITS investors and IORP members in relation to (collective) asset managers compared to individual investors related to investment firms. For this reason, IORPD II, UCITSD V and the AIFMD require additional conduct of business rules to be fulfilled for depositaries that in their capacity of acting as a custodian perform oversight duties. Depositary law is, thus, a separate area of law applying on top of the 'general law' targeting credit institutions, investment firms or 'other equivalent legal entities' authorized to act as a custodian.

9.4   TOWARDS A CROSS-SECTORAL DEPOSITARY PASSPORT

Part IV, on the basis of the outcome of the preceding parts, advocated in favour of introducing not only an AIF/UCITS depositary but a 'cross-sectoral European depositary passport' in European investment law. The introduction of a (cross-sectoral) depositary passport would enable depositaries to offer their services on the European level and to consolidate services on a cross-sectoral and cross-border basis.

Prior to introducing an AIF/UCITS or cross-sectoral depositary passport, Part IV answered whether the differences between depositaries and custodians justify the loca-

---

24 European Commission, *Impact Assessment – Commission Delegated Regulation Supplementing Directive 2009/65/EC of the European Parliament and of the Council with regard to obligations of depositaries* (C (2015) 9160 final), Annex 4.

tional restriction applicable to AIF/UCITS depositaries. Furthermore, Part IV clarified whether AIF, UCITS and IORP depositaries are sufficiently harmonized and, if not, what should be done to make the introduction of a cross-sectoral passport acceptable. A 'de facto European depositary passport' is granted to IORP depositaries, whereas this is not available for AIF/UCITS depositaries. This is highly remarkable as depositaries perform the same functions with the same underlying investor protection objective. This inconsistency can be rightfully called an 'European depositary passport paradox' as the eligible entities and, in particular, the depositary function itself under the AIFMD and UCITSD V have been harmonized to a much larger extent than under IORPD II.[25]

The AIFMD 'transitional relief regime'[26] suggests that the duties, delegation and depositary's liability regime are sufficiently harmonized on the European level for the introduction of a European passport. Under this regime, credit institutions appointed as an AIF depositary are allowed to be appointed under a 'mutual recognition regime' provided that the AIF home Member State in which the AIF is established, has implemented this option in their AIFMD implementation laws.[27] Giving the similarities under the UCITSD V depositary regime, similar considerations could be made regarding the introduction of a UCITSD V depositary passport.

This seems to suggest that the introduction of a 'cross-sectoral depositary passport' would require full harmonization of the depositary as a financial intermediary and also the harmonization of the IORP depositary duties, delegation and liability standards would be necessary for a consistent approach.

Similarly as for the 'management company passport' discussion, custodians already upon the introduction of ISD enjoyed an ('ancillary') European passport. As a compromise of introducing the European 'management passport' under UCITSD IV and the AIFMD, the depositary remained to be required to be established in the UCITS/AIF home Member State.

Modelled after this concept, indeed, a proportional 'cross-sectoral depositary passport' could be built upon the core activities of the safekeeping of assets and the performance of oversight duties. All depositaries and custodians perform at least the safekeeping of assets as a minimum. Essentially, depositaries are custodians that perform, in addition to the safekeeping of assets, oversight duties.[28] For this reason, a 'cross-sectoral depositary passport' could be built on the basis of an harmonized authorization regime for custodians performing the regulatory activity 'safekeeping of assets', whereas on the sectoral level a cross-sectoral consistent set of legislation applies additionally for custodians that act as depositaries.

---

25 *See* for the AIFMD/UCITSD V depositary regime: Chapter 4; *See* for the IORPD II depositary regime: Chapter 5.
26 *See* Chapter 2, Section 2.1.2.2.2.
27 *Ibid.*
28 *See* Chapter 7, Section 7.2.1.3.

Bibliography

A

Acharya, V., Philippon, T., Richardson, M. & Roubini N., *Prologue: A Bird's Eye View. The Financial Crisis of 2007-2009: Causes and Remedies* (V. Acharya & M. Richardson eds., Wiley 2009).

Amenc, N., Focardi, S., Goltz, F., Schröder, D. & Tang, L., *EDHEC-Risk European Private Wealth Management Survey*, EDHEC (2010).

Aragon, G.O. & Strahan, P.E., *Hedge Funds as Liquidity Providers: Evidence from the Lehman Bankruptcy* (August 2009), www.nber.org/papers/w15336 (accessed 30 September 2012).

Arnaboldi, F., *Deposit Guarantee Schemes – A European Perspective* (Springer 2014).

Arrow, K.J., *The Economics of Agency* 37-51 (J.W. Pratt & R.J. Zeckhauser eds., Harvard Business School Press 1985).

B

Bailey, R.E., *The Economics of Financial Markets* 22 (Cambridge University Press 2005).

Bande, A., *Banking Integration in the EU: A Process Marked by a Battle between Systems*, https://www.utwente.nl/en/bms/pa/staff/donnelly/Thesis%20-%20A%20%20Bande%2020%2008%2012.pdf.

Bergervoet, M., *De impact van de AIFM Richtlijn voor derde landen en in het bijzonder voor Curaçao*, 4 TvFR 120 (2014).

Boatright, J.R., *Ethics in Finance* 5 (Wiley-Blackwell 2014).

Bogdandy, A. von, *Founding Principles* (A. Von Bogdandy & J. Bast, eds., Hart Publishing 2010).

Broekhuizen, K.W.H. & W.A.K. Rank, *Grensoverschrijdende dienstverlening* 230-243 (A.J.C.C.M. Loonen et al., NIBE-SVV 2008).

Broekhuizen, K.W.H. & Rank, W.A.K., *Het Europees paspoort voor beleggingsonderne-mingen* 255-271 (D. Busch, D.R. Doorenbos, C.M. Grundmann-van de Krol, R.H. Maat-man, M.P. Nieuwe Weme & W.A.K. Rank, Kluwer 2007).

Bruni, L., Gilli, M. & Pelligra, V., *Reciprocity: Theory and Facts*, 55 International Review of Economics 1-11 (2008).

Bühler, T., *ELTIF – Eine neue Säule der Finanzierung der Europäischen Realwirtschaft*, 3 Recht der Finanzinstrumente 198 (2015).

Busch, D. & van der Velden, J.W., *Aansprakelijkheid en verhaal bij Fondsen voor Gemene Rekening*, Financieel Recht 161 (2009).

Busch, D., *Governance of the Single Resolution Mechanism* (D. Busch & G. Ferrarini, Oxford 2015).

Busch, D. & Ferrarini, G., *A Banking Union for a Divided Europe: An Introduction* (D. Busch & G. Ferrarini, Oxford 2015).

Busch, D. & Louisse, M., *MiFID II/MiFIR's Regime for Third-Country Firms* (D. Busch & G. Ferrarini eds., Oxford 2017).

Butter, F.A.G. den, *Managing Transaction Costs in the Era of Globalization* 58 (Edward Elgar Publishing 2012).

Buttigieg, C.P., *The 2009 UCITS IV Directive: A Critical Examination of the Framework for the Creation of a Broader and More Efficient Internal Market for UCITS*, https://ssrn.com/abstract=2137202.

Buttigieg, C.P., *The Alternative Investment Fund Managers Directive in Malta: Past, Present … What Next?*, https://ssrn.com/abstract=2602750.

Buttigieg, C.P., *The Case for A European Depositary Passport*, http://studylib.net/doc/13128849/the–case–for–a–european-depositary-passport

Buttigieg, C.P., *The Development of the EU Regulatory and Supervisory Framework applicable to UCITS: A Critical Examination of the Conditions and Limitations of Mutual Recognition*, March 2014, 66, http://sro.sussex.ac.uk/48285/1/Buttigieg%2C_Christopher_P..pdf.

C

Caruana, J., *Systemic Risk: How to Deal With It?* (BIS 2010).

Casey, J.P. & Lannoo, K., *The MiFID Revolution*, ECMI Policy Brief No. 3 (November 2006).

Casey, J.-P. & Lannoo, K., *The Mifid Revolution: A Policy View*, 7 Competition and Regulation Network Industries 515 (2006).

Casey, J.-P., *Shedding Light on the UCITS-MiFID Nexus and Potential Impact of MiFID on the Asset Management Sector*, ECMI Policy Brief No. 12, April 2008.

Casey, J.P. & Lannoo, K., *The MiFID revolution* (Cambridge University Press 2009).

Ciani, D., *European Investment Funds: The UCITS Directive of 1985 and the Objectives of the Proposal for a UCITS II Directive*, 4(2) Journal of Financial Regulation and Compliance 150-156 (1996).

Clerc, C., *The AIF Depositary's Liability for Lost Assets* (D.A. Zetzsche ed., Kluwer 2015).

Clouth, P., *Anlegerschutz. Grundlagen aus Sicht der Praxis*, 177 ZHR 112 (2013).

Coase, R.H., *The Problem of Social Cost*, 3 Journal of Law and Economics 1 (1960).

Conac, H.P., *Rights of the investor*, 105-134. (H.P. Conac, U. Segna & L. Thévenoz eds, Cambridge 2013).

Craig, P.P. & Búrca, G. de, *EU Law: Text, Cases, and Materials* 369 (6th edn., Oxford University Press 2015).

Crockett, A., Harris, T., Mishkin, F.S. & White, E.N., *Conflicts of Interest in the Financial Services Industry: What Should We Do About Them?*, 5 Geneva Reports on the World Economy (2003).

D

Davies, E., Dufour, A. & Scott-Quin, B., *The MiFID: Competition in a New European Equity Market* 163-197 (G. Ferrarini & E. Wymeersch, Oxford 2006).

Delmont, D.P., *Managing Hedge Fund Risk and Financing – Adapting to a New Era* 7 (Wiley 2011).

Dietrich, D., *Transaction Cost Economics and Beyond: Towards a New Economics of the Firm* (Routledge 1994).

Doelder, J. & Jansen, I.M., *Een nieuw Europees toezichtraamwerk*, 1/2 TvFR 17 (2010).

Dolan, T., *UCITS V Brings Convergence of the Depositary Role with AIFMD*, 1 JIBFL 64B (2015).

Dupont, P., *Rights of the Account Holder Relating to Securities Credited to its Securities Account*, 90-104. (H.P. Conac, U. Segna & L. Thévenoz eds., Cambridge 2013).

Dussart, S., F. Rodriguez, F. & Thouch, M., *La restitution des actifs par le dépositaire*, Joly Bourse 542 (2008).

E

Eichhorn, J. & Klebeck, U., *Drittstaatenregulierung der MiFID II und MiFIR*, 3 Recht der Finanzinstrumente 1 (2014).

Einsele, D., *Wertpapier als Schuldrecht: Funktionsverlust von Effektenurkunden, international Rechtsverkehr* (Tübingen: Mohr Siebeck 1995).

Eisenhardt, K.M. *Agency Theory: An Assessment and Review*, 14 Academy of Management Review 57-74 (1989).

F

Ferran, E. & Babis, V.S.G., *The European Single Supervisory Mechanism*, University of Cambridge Faculty of Law Research Paper No. 10 (2013).

Ferran, E. & Alexander, K., *Can Soft Law Bodies be Effective? Soft Systemic Risk Oversight Bodies and the Special Case of the European Systemic Risk Board*, https://ssrn.com/abstract=1676140.

Ferran, E., *Building an EU Securities Market* (Cambridge University Press 2004).

Ferran, E., *European Banking Union: Imperfect, But it Can Work* (D. Busch & G. Ferrarini, Oxford 2015).

Ferran, E., *Understanding the New Institutional Architecture of EU Financial Market Supervision*, Paper No. 29/2011 (2011).

Ferrarini, G. & Chiarella, L., *Common Banking Supervision in the Eurozone: Strengths and Weaknesses*, ECGI - Law Working Paper No. 223/2013 (2013).

Ferrarini, G. & Recine, F., *The Single Rulebook and the SSM: Should the ECB Have More Say in Prudential Rule-Making?* (D. Busch & G. Ferrarini, Oxford 2015).

Ferrarini, G., & E. Wymeersch, *Investor Protection in Europe: Corporate Law Making, the MiFID and Beyond* (Oxford University Press 2006).

Fischer-Appelt, D., *The European Securities and Market Authority: The Beginnings of a Powerful European Securities Authority?*, 1 Law and Financial Markets Review 21-32 (2011).

Fortado, L., *Lehman Segregated Accounts Appeal May Delay Hedge Fund Payouts*, www.bloomberg.com/apps/news?pid=newsarchive&sid=a2g8ad6oSj4Q.

Frase, D. *Overview* 4 (D. Frase ed., Sweet & Maxwell 2011).

Frase, D., *Custody*, in *Law and Regulation of Investment Management* (D. Frase ed., Sweet & Maxwell 2011).

Fridriksson, I., *The Banking Crisis in Iceland in 2008*, www.bis.org/review/r090226d.pdf.

G

Gaouaoui, S., *Conservation d'actifs, la Cour d'appel entérine la responsabilité des dépositaires*, 1025 Option finance 10 (2009).

Gasser, J. & Schwingshackl, M., *Asset Protection through Liechtenstein Annuities and Life Insurance*, (M. Gantenbein & M.A. Mata eds., John Wiley & Sons 2008).

Geiger, H., *Transnational Supervisory Recognition: A Macro-Jurisdictional Overview* (J. Burling, S.C. Chambers & K. Lazarus eds., Edward Elgar 2012).

Gelauf, G., *Subsidiarity and Economic Reform in Europe* (Springer 2008).

Gerner-Beuerle, C., *United in Diversity: Maximum versus Minimum Harmonization in EU Securities Regulation*, 3 Capital Markets Journal 317 (2012).

Gilson, R. & Kraakman, R., *Market Efficiency after the Financial Crisis: It's Still a Matter of Information Costs*, 100 Va. L. Rev. 313 (2014).

Goodhart, C., et al., *Financial Regulation: Why, How and Where Now?* 5 (Routledge 1998).

Goodhart, C., *The Central Bank and the Financial System* 434 (Palgrave Macmillan UK 1995).

Gortsos, Ch.V., *The Supervision of Financial Conglomerates under European Financial Law (Directive 2002/87/EC)*, 25 Banking & Financial Law Review 295-313 (2010).

Goutay, Ph., *Obligation de restitution des dépositaires: les arrêts du 8 avril 2009 de la Cour d'appel de Paris*, 2 RD Bancaire et Financier 166 (2009).

Greef, R.M.J.M de, *Herziening IORP richtlijn – Een verbetering?*, 50 TPV 27 (2016).

Greene, E.F., *Beyond Borders: Time to Tear Down the Barriers to Global Investing*, 48 Harv. Int'l L.J. 92 (2007).

Gregoriou, G. N. & Lhabitant, F.-S., *Madoff: A Riot of Red Flags* (EDHEC-Position Paper 2009).

Groffen, C.J., *UCITS V implementatie in Nederland*, 3 TvFR 114 (2016).

Gros, D., *The Economics of Brexit: It's not about the Internal Market*, https://www.ceps.-eu/publications/economics-brexit-it%E2%80%99s-not-about-internal-market (accessed 14 January 2017).

Grundmann-van de Krol, C.M. & Hijink, J.B.S., *Who is Afraid of a Single Rulebook?* 3-16 (F.G.B. Graaf, R.H. Maatman & L.J. Silverentand eds., Kluwer 2012).

Grundmann-van de Krol, C.M., *Regulering beleggingsinstellingen en icbe's in de Wft* (Boom Juridische Uitgevers 2013).

Grundmann-van de Krol, C.M., *Consultatiewetsvoorstel implementatie UCITS V in de Wft*, 49 Ondernemingsrecht 262 (2015).

Gruson, G., *Supervision of Financial Holding Companies in Europe: The EU Directive on Supplementary Supervision of Financial Conglomerates*, 36 The International Lawyer 1229-1260 (2002).

Gruson, M., *Foreign Banks and the Financial Holding Company* (M. Gruson & R. Reisner eds., Lexis Nexis Matthew Bender 4th ed. 2003).

Gruson, M., *Supervision of Financial Conglomerates in the European Union*, 198 Journal of International Banking Law and Regulation 363-381, 364 (2004).

Gruson, M., *Consolidated and Supplementary Supervision of Financial Groups in the European Union*, Institute for Law and Finance Johann Wolfgang Goethe-Universität Frankfurt, Working Paper Series No. 19 (2004).

Gruson, M., *Consolidated and Supplementary Supervision of Financial Groups in the European Union*, Der konzern, Teil 1, 65-93, Teil II, 249-265 (2004).

H

Haentjes, M., *Harmonisation of Securities Law: Custody and Transfer of Securities in European Private Law* 131-172 (Kluwer 2007).

Haentjes, M., *Clearing and Settlement – Ways Forward*, 5 Journal of International Banking Law and Regulation (2011).

Hamstra, I.M., *Gedragsregels voor Nederlandse beleggingsondernemingen handelend met cliënten buiten de Europese Economische Ruimte*, 6 V&O 122-125 (2010).

Hardin, R., *Collective Action* (Baltimore 1982).

Hoecke, M. van, *Do "Legal Systems" Exist? The Concept of Law and Comparative Law* 43-57 (S. Donlan & L. Heckendorn Urscheler eds., Ashgate 2014).

Hoecke, M. van, *Methodology of Comparative Legal Research*, http://rem.tijdschriften.-budh.nl/tijdschrift/lawandmethod/2015/12/RENM-D-14-00001#content_RENM-D-14-00001.5738700789.

Hohenwarter, D. & Plansky, P., *Die Kapitalverkehrsfreiheit mit Drittstaaten im Lichte der Rechtssache Holböck*, SWI 346 (2007).

Hollinger, P. & Chung, J., *Madoff Affair Sparks Demand for Revamp of Investment Fund Rules*, Financial Times, (13 January 2009), 15.

Holopainen, H., *Integration of financial supervision*, Bank of Finland Research Discussion Papers 12 (2007).

Hooghiemstra, S.N., *De AIFM-richtlijn en de aansprakelijkheid van de bewaarder*, 6 TvFR 178 (2013).

Hooghiemstra, S.N. *Wat is een beleggingsinstelling onder de AIFM-richtlijn?*, 3 Ondernemingsrecht 24 (2014).

Hooghiemstra, S.N., *Depositary Regulation* 480 (D.A. Zetzsche ed., Kluwer 2015).

Hooghiemstra, S.N., *The AIFM's Transposition in the Netherlands* (D.A. Zetzsche ed., Kluwer 2015).

Hövekamp, H. & Hugger, G., *Die Reichweite der Haftung der Depotbanken vor dem Hintergrund des Madoff-Skandals* 2015-2028 (S. Grundmann, B. Haar & H. Merkt eds., De Gruyter 2010).

J

Jans, J.H. & Squintani, L., Aragão, A., Macrory, R. & Wegener, B.W., *'Gold plating' of European Environmental Measures*, 6(4) Journal of European Environmental and Planning Law 417-435 (2009).

Jutzi, T., & Feuz, C., *MiFID II, AIFMD und UCITSD: Auswirkungen des EU-Vermögensverwaltungsrechts auf das grenzüberschreitende Geschäft Schweizer Finanzintermediäre*, Jusletter Next, 25. April 2016.

K

Kapstein, E.B., *Governing the Global Economy – International Finance and the State* 136 (Harvard University Press 1994).

Kaufmann, G. & Scott, K., *What Is Systemic Risk, and Do Bank Regulators Retard or Contribute to It?*, 7:3 The Independent Review 371 (2003).

Keijser T.R.M.P., *Financiële zekerheidsovereenkomsten*, 11 Ars Aequi 835-840 (2006).

Keijser, T.R.M.P., *A Custodian's Right of Use under Dutch Law?* 40-42 (T. Keijser ed., Report on A 'Right of use' for collateral takes and custodians), Presented to the UNIDROIT Secretariat (2003).

Kern, A. & Schmidt, A., *The Market in Financial Instruments Directive and Switzerland*, 1 GesKR 45 (2012).

Key, S.J., *Financial Integration in the European Community*, Board of Governors of the Federal Reserve System – International Finance Discussion Papers, No. 349 (April 1989).

King, M.R. & Maier, P., *Hedge Funds and Financial Stability: Regulating Prime Brokers Will Mitigate Systemic Risks*, 5 Journal of Financial Stability 283 (2009).

Klebeck, U. & Eichhorn, J., *Drittstaatenregulierung der MiFID II und MiFIR*, 3 RdF 1 (2014).

Klebeck, U. & Meyer, C., *Drittstaatenregulierung der AIFM-Richtlinie*, Recht der Finanzinstrumente 95 (2012).

Klebeck, U., *Interplay between AIFMD and the UCITSD* (D.A. Zetzsche ed., Kluwer 2015).

Klerk, J.E., & Slange, R., *UCITS V and beyond*, 1/2 TvFR 34-39 (2015).

Kobbach, J. & Anders, D., *Umsetzung der AIFM-Richtlinie aus Sicht der Verwahrstellen*, NZG 1170 (2012).

Kortleve, N. et al., *European Supervision of Pension Funds: Purpose, Scope and Design*, Netspar Design Papers No. 4 (Oct. 2011), 15-18.

Kost - de Sevres, N. & Sasso, L., *The New European Financial Markets Legal Framework: A Real Improvement? An Analysis of Financial Law and Governance in European Capital Markets from a Micro- and Macro-economic Perspective*, 7 Capital Markets Law Journal 30 (2011).

Kress, S., *Effizienzorientierte Kapitalmarktregulierung – eine Analyse aus institutionenökonomischer Perspektive* 59 (Wiesbaden 1996).

Kruithof, M., *Conflicts of Interest in Institutional Asset Management: Is the EU Regulatory Approach Adequate?*, 31, http://ssrn.com/abstract=871178.

L

Laaper, P., *Uitbesteding in de financiële sector - in het bijzonder van vermogensbeheer door pensioenfondsen* 57-60, 211 (Kluwer 2015).

Labeur, R.E. *Uniform derdelandenbeleid AIFMD: Nog een lange weg te gaan*, 10 TvFR 391-395 (2015).

Lachgar, K., *From the UCITS Directive to the Transposition of AIFMD: Exegesis of Evolution's Depositary Activity in Europe*, Joly Bourse (2014).

Lachgar, K., *Le rôle du dépositaire dans l'ère AIFM: 'business as usual' ou opportunité de différenciation?*, 749 Revue Banque (2012).

Lamandini, M., *When More is Needed: the European Financial Supervisory Reform and its Legal Basis*, 6 European Company Law 197-202 (2009).

Lannoo, K. & Levin, M., *Securities Market Regulation in the EU – Everything You Always Wanted to Know about the Lamfalussy Procedure*, CEPS Research Report in Finance and Banking, No. 33 (May 2004).

Lannoo, K., *EU Retail Financial market Integration: Mirage Or Reality?*, ECRI Policy Brief No. 3 (June 2008).

Lannoo, K, *The Great Financial Plumbing: From Northern Rock to Banking Union* 40 (Rowman and Littlefield International 2015).

Lannoo, K., *Brexit and the City*, https://www.ceps.eu/publications/brexit-and-city

Lannoo, K., *EU Financial Market Access after Brexit*, CEPS Policy Brief, September 2016, https://www.ceps.eu/system/files/Brexit%20and%20the%20financial%20sector_0.pdf

Larosière, J. de, *The High-Level Group on Financial Supervision in the EU*, 25 February 2009, http://ec.europa.eu/internal_market/finances/docs/de_larosiere_report_en.pdf

Lee, K., *Investor Protection in European Union: Post FSAP Directives and MiFID*, https://ssrn.com/abstract=1339305

Lehmann, M. & Manger-Nestler, C., *Die Vorschläge zur neuen Architektur der europäischen Finanzaufsicht*, 3 Europäische Zeitschrift für Wirtschaftsrecht 87 (2010).

Lehmann, M. & Zetzsche, D.A., *Brexit and the Consequences for Commercial and Financial Relations between the EU and the UK*, https://ssrn.com/abstract=2841333

Leland, H.E, *Quacks, Lemons, and Licensing: A Theory of Minimum Quality Standards*, 87 Journal of Political Economy 1328 (1978).

Lewis, A., Pretorius, R. & Radmore, E., *Outsourcing in the Financial Services Sector*, 106 C.O.B. 1 (2013).

Lieverse, C.W.M., *The Scope of MiFID II* (D. Busch & G. Ferrarini eds., Oxford 2017).

Llewellyn, D., *The Economic Rationale for Financial Regulation* (FSA 1999).

Löber, K.M., *The Developing EU Legal Framework for Clearing and Settlement of Financial Instruments*, European Central Bank – Legal Working Paper Series, No. 1 (February 2006).

Logue, K.D., & Slemrod, J.B., *Of Coase, Calabresi, and Optimal Tax Liability*, Law & Economics Working Papers Law & Economics Working Papers Archive: 2003-2009, University of Michigan Law School Year 2009, 3, http://repository.law.umich.edu/cgi/viewcontent.cgi?article=1097&context=law_econ_archive

Ludlow, P., *The Making of the European Monetary System: A Case Study of the Politics of the European Community* (Butterworth Scientific 1982).

Lumpkin, S.A., *Risks in Financial Group Structures*, 2 OECD Journal: Financial Market Trends 105-136 (2010).

M

Maffei, A., *Controverse autour des obligations du dépositaire*, 1 RD Bancaire et Financier étude 8 (2011).

Maggi, R., *MiFID II: Marktzugang, Umsetzung, Handlungsoptionen* (Zürich/Basel/Genf 2014).

Meerten, H. van & Ottow A.T., *The Proposals for the European Supervisory Authorities (ESAs): The Right (Legal) Way Forward?*, 1/2 TvFR 5 (2010).

Meerten, H. van, van den Brink, A. & de Vries, S.A., *Regulating Pensions: Why the European Union Matters* (Netspar Discussion Paper) 38, http://papers.ssrn.com/sol3/papers.cfm?abstract_id=1950765

Meester, B. de, *Liberalization of Trade in Banking Services – An International and European Perspective* 270 (Cambridge University Press 2014).

Micheler, E., *The Legal Nature of Securities: Inspirations from Comparative Law*, 131-149. (L. Gullifer & J. Payne eds, Hart Publishing 2010).

Micheler, E., *Intermediated Securities and Legal Certainty*, LSE Law, Society and Economy Working Papers No. 3 (2014).

Micheler, E., *Custody chains and Asset Values: why crypto securities are worth contemplating*, 3 Cambridge Law Journal 1-6 (2015).

Möllers, T., *Auf dem Weg zu einer neuen europäischen Finanzmarktaufsichtsstruktur – Ein systematischer Vergleich der Rating-VO (EG) Nr. 1060/2009 mit der geplanten ESMA-VO*, 8 Neue Zeitschrift für Gesellschaftsrecht 285 (2010).

Moloney, N., *Investor Protection and the Treaty: An Uneasy Relationship* 17-61 (G. Ferrarini, K.J. Hopt & E. Wymeersch eds., Kluwer 2002).

Moloney, N., *The European Securities and Markets Authority and institutional Design for the EU Financial Market. A Tale of Two Competences: Part (1) Rule Making*, 12 European Business Organization Law Review 41-86 (2011).

Moloney, N., *The European Securities and Markets Authority and Institutional Design for the EU Financial Market. A Tale of Two Competences: Part (2) Rules in Action*, 12 European Business Organization Law Review 177-225 (2011).

Moloney, N., *The Investor Model Underlying the EU's Investor Protection Regime: Consumers or Investors?*, 13 E.B.O.R. 169 (2012).

Moloney, N., *EC Securities Regulation* 216, 217 (3rd edn., Oxford University Press 2014).

Moloney, N., *Banking Union and the Implications for Financial Market Governance in the EU: Convergence or Divergence* (D. Busch & G. Ferrarini, Oxford 2015).

Moroni, T. & Wibbeke, L., *OGAW V: Die Sprunglatte für OGAW-Verwahrstellen liegt höher*, 3 Recht der Finanzinstrumente 187 (2015).

Motani, H., *The Proposed EU Legislation on Securities Holding*, 69. (H.P. Conac, U. Segna & L. Thévenoz eds., Cambridge 2013).

Mülbert, P. & Wilhelm, A., *CRD IV Framework for Banks' Corporate Governance* (D. Busch & G. Ferrarini, Oxford 2015).

Mülbert, P., *Anlegerschutz und Finanzmarktregulierung – Grundlagen*, 177 ZHR 160 (2013).

Müller, G., *Die Rechtsstellung der Depotbank im Investmentgeschäft nach deutschem und schweizerischem Recht* (Neckar-Druck- u. Verl. Ges. 1969).

Murphy, J.B., *The Philosophy of Positive Law: Foundations of Jurisprudence* (Yale University Press 2005).

N

Naveaux, V. & Graas, R., *Direct Action by Investors Against a UCITS Depositary – A Short-Lived Landmark Ruling?*, 7 Capital Markets Law Journal 455 (2012).

O

Ohl, K., *Die Rechtsbeziehungen innerhalb des Investment-Dreiecks* (Duncker & Humblot 1989).

Olsen, M., *The Logic of Collective Action: Public Goods and the Theory of Groups* (Harvard University Press 1971).

P

Paech, P., *Market Needs as Paradigm – Breaking up the Thinking on EU Securities Law*, 22-64. (H.P. Conac, U. Segna & L. Thévenoz eds., Cambridge 2013).

Paech, P., *Cross-Border Issues of Securities Law – European Efforts to Support the Securities Market with a Coherent Legal Framework, Study prepared for the European Parliament*, www.europarl.europa.eu/document/activities/cont/201106/20110606ATT20781/20110606ATT20781EN.pdf

Partsch, T., *Delegation* (D.A. Zetzsche ed., Kluwer 2015).

Peleckiene, V., Peleckis, K. & Duzeviciute, G., *New Challenges of Supervising Financial Conglomerates*, 5 Intellectual Economics 298-311 (2011).

Pierrat, M., *De la distinction entre obligations de moyens et obligations de resultat: pile ou face?* 15 Journal des Tribunaux 61 et seq (2011).

Pope, D. & Garzaniti, L., *Single Market-Making: EC Regulation of Securities Markets*, 14 (3) Company Lawyer 44 (1993).

Praag, E.J. van, *Het grensoverschrijdend financieel toezicht loopt tegen grenzen aan*, 9 TvFR 259 (2011).

R

Raas, R.P., *De AIFM Richtlijn en derde landen* 59-69 (N.B. Spoor, M. Tausk, J.B. Huizink & R.P. Raas eds., Kluwer 2012).

Rank, W.A.K., *Vermogensscheiding* (D. Busch & C.M. Grundmann-van de Krol eds., Kluwer 2009).

Raz, J., *The Concept of a Legal System* 141 (Clarendon Press 1980).

Rehm, H. & Nagler, J., *Verbietet die Kapitalverkehrsfreiheit nach 1993 eingeführteAuslanderungleichbehandlung?*, 15 Internationales Steuerrecht 861(2006).

Reiss, M., *Pflichten der Kapitalanlagegesellschaft und Depotbank gegenüber dem Anleger und die Rechte des Anlegers bei Pflichtverletzungen* (Duncker & Humblot 2006).

Riassetto, I. & Prüm, A., *La fonction de conservation du dépositaire, source de responsabilité civile, note sous Paris, 1ère Ch., Section H, 8 avril 2009, no. 2008/22218*, 3 Joly Bourse 191, §I-A-2 (2009).

Riassetto, I., *Obligation de restitution du dépositaire d'OPCVM*, 4 RD Bancaire et Financier Comm. 161, point 1-B (July 2010).

Riassetto, I. *L'obligation de restitution du dépositaire d'OPC en droit Luxembourgeois*, 30 Journal des Tribunaux Luxembourg 167 (2013).

Riassetto, I., *Moyens et procédures adéquats pour la mise en œuvre de l'obligation de contrôle des dépositaires d'OPC*, 10 Bulletin Joly Bourse (2013).

Riassetto, I., *Dépositaires – Quelles différences entre la directive OPCVM V et la directive AIFM?*, 4 RD Bancaire et Financier (2014).

Riassetto, I., *La clarification des obligations et de la responsabilité des dépositaires par la directive OPCVM V*, 98 Revue Lamy Droit des Affaires 31 (2014).

Riassetto, I., *Le nouveau régime applicable aux dépositaires issu de la directive OPCVM V*, 3 Bulletin Joly Bourse 113 (2015).

Riassetto, I., *Responsabilité de la société de gestion et du dépositaire d'un OPC envers les actionnaires d'une société cible, note sous Cass. com. fr. 27 mai 2015*, 4 RD Bancaire et Financier (2015).

Rooke, C.A., *MiFID en custodians: let op extra informatieverplichtingen!*, 1/2 TvFR 43-46 (2008).

S

Samuel, G., *An Introduction to Comparative Law Theory and Method* 81-82 (Hart Publishing 2014).

Sarna, D. E. Y., *History of Greed: Financial Fraud from Tulip Mania to Bernie Madoff* (Wiley 2010).

Schammo, P., *Equivalence-Based Regulation and EU/EEA Prospectus Law – The Shadow Regime* 493 (D. Prentice & A. Reisberg eds., Oxford University Press 2011).

Scharpf, F.W., *Negative and Positive Integration in the Political Economy of European Welfare States* (G. Marks ed, Sage Publisher 1996).

Schön, W., *Der kapitalverkehr mit Drittstaaten und das international Steuerrecht* 489-501 (R. Gocke, D. Gosch & M. Lang eds., C.H. Beck 2005).

Schröder, O. & Rahn, A., *Das KAGB und Private-Equity-Transaktionen – Pflichten für Manager von Private-Equity-Fonds und deren Verwahrstellen*, GWR 49 (2014).

Schwarcz, S.L., *Indirectly Held Securities and Intermediary Risk*, 2 Uniform Law Review 283 (2001).

Schwarcz, S.L., *Intermediary Risk in a Global Economy*, 6 Duke Law Journal 1541 (2001).

Schwarcz, S.L., *Systemic Risk*, 97 The Georgetown Law Journal 193 (2008).

Scott, H., *Reducing Systemic Risk Through the Reform of Capital Regulation*, 13 Journal of International Economic Law 763 (2010).

Seegebarth, N., *Stellung und Haftung der Depotbank im Investment-Dreieck* (Peter Lang Verlag 2004).

Seriere, V.P.G. de, *Recovery and Resolution Plans of Banks in the Context of the BRRD and the SRM: Some Fundamental Issues* (D. Busch & G. Ferrarini, Oxford 2015).

Sethe, R. *Das Drittstaatenregime von MiFIR und MiFID II*, 6 SZW/ RSDA 615 (2014).

Sharipo, J.C., *Investment, Moral Hazard, and Licensing*, 53 Review of Economic Studies 843 (1986).

Siekmann, H., *Das neue Europäische Finanzaufsichtssystem*, Working Paper Series 40 (Institute for Monetary and Financial Stability 2010).

Siekmann, H., *Die Europäisierung der Finanzmarktaufsicht*, Working Paper Series 47 (Institute for Monetary and Financial Stability 2011).

Siems, M., *Comparative Law* (Cambridge University Press, 2014).

Siena, J.R. & Eckner, D., *The AIFMD's Transposition in the United Kingdom* (D.A. Zetzsche ed., Kluwer 2015).

Siena, J.R., *Depositary Liability: A Fine Mess and How to Get Out of It* (D.A. Zetzsche ed., Kluwer 2015).

Singh, M. & Aitken, J., *The (Sizeable) Role of Rehypothecation in the Shadow Banking System* (IMF Working Paper 2010).

Sitkoff, R.H., *An Agency Costs Theory of Trust Law*, 89 Cornell Law Review 621 (2004).

Skouris, V., *the ECJ and the EFTA Court under the EEA Agreement: A Paradigm for International Cooperation between Judicial Institutions* 123-129 (C. Baudenbacher, P. Tressel & T. Örlygsson eds., Hart Publishing 2005).

Sloman, J., Wride, A., Garratt D., *Economics* 293 (Pearson 2012).

Smits, R.K.Th.J., *De AIFMD-bewaarder; praktische gevolgen voor Nederlandse belegging-sinstellingen*, 11 V&O 200-204 (2012).

Stefansson, A. & Saethorsson, T., *Cross-Border Issues in EU Deposit Guarantee Schemes: With a Focus on the Icelandic Case*, 63-82, http://pure.au.dk/portal-asb-student/files/12991/Thesis_without_Appendix.pdf

Stewart, F. & Yermo, J., *Pension Fund Governance: Challenges and Potential Solutions*, OECD Working Papers on Insurance and Private Pensions No. 18 (June 2008).

Steyer, R., *White-Label Funds on Rise for DC Plans*, Pensions & Investments, October 27, 2014, www.pionline.com/article/20141027/PRINT/310279972/white-label-funds-on-rise-for-dc-plans

Storck, M., *Particularisme de l'obligation de restitution incombant au dépositaire*, RTD com. 573, § I-B (2010).

T

Tausk, M., *De verplichting om een bewaarder te benoemen: alles gaat veranderen* 22-43 (N.B. Spoor, M. Tausk, J.B. Huizink & R.P. Raas, Kluwer 2012).

Tegelaar, J. & Haentjes, M., *Brexit: financieelrechtelijke gevolgen*, 74 Bedrijfsjuridische Berichten 257 (2016).

Thévenoz, L., *Intermediated Securities, Legal Risk, and the International Harmonization of Commercial Law*, 13 Stanford Journal of Law, Business & Finance 384-452 (2008).

Thévenoz, L., *Who holds (Intermediated) Securities? Shareholders, Account Holders, and Nominees?*, 3-4 Uniform Law Review 845-859 (2010).

Tison, M., *De bescherming van de beleggers in het kapitaalmarktrecht: de hobbelige weg naar een Europees ius commune*, https://papers.ssrn.com/sol3/papers.cfm?abstract_id=1142777

Trachtman, J.P., *Addressing Regulatory Divergence through International Standards: Financial Services* 27–41 (A. Mattoo & P. Sauvé eds., Oxford University Press, 2003).

Tuchschmid, N., Wallerstein, E. & Zanolin, A., *Hedge Funds and Prime Brokers: The Role of Funding Risk*, http://ssrn.com/abstract=1343673

U

Usher, J.A., *The Evolution of the Free Movement of Capital*, 31 Fordham International Law Journal 1533 (2007).

V

Vaplane, H. de, & Yon, J.P., *The Concept of Integrity in Securities Holding Systems*, 193-214. (H.P. Conac, U. Segna & L. Thévenoz eds, Cambridge 2013).

Velden, J.W.P.M. van der, *Babylonische bewaarders*, Tijdschrift voor Ondernemingsrecht 17 (2009).

Velden, J.W.P.M. van der, *Beleggingsfondsen naar Burgerlijk recht* (Kluwer 2008).

Velden, J.W.P.M. van der, *Hoofdstuk 25 Beleggingsinstelling en aansprakelijkheid in het zicht van de nieuwe regelgeving*, in *Aansprakelijkheid in de Financiële Sector* 976-977 (D. Busch, C.J.M. Klaassen & T.M.C. Arons eds., Kluwer Law 2013).

Vinuales, J., *The International Regulation of Financial Conglomerates: A Case-Study of Equivalence as an Approach to Financial Integration*, 37 California Western International Law Journal 1-61 (2006).

Voermans, W., *Gold-Plating and Double Banking: An Overrated Problem?* 79-88 (H. Snijders & S. Vogenauer eds. Sellier European Law Publishers 2009).

Vranken, J.B.M., *Methodology of Legal Doctrinal Research*, https://pure.uvt.nl/ws/files/1296852/Vranken_Methodology_of_legal_doctrinal_research_110118_publishers_embargo1y.pdf

Vuyst, V. de, *Internal Governance bij financiele conglomeraten* (Intersentia 2010).

W

Warner, E.W., *"Mutual Recognition" and Cross Border Financial Services in the European Community*, 55 *Law and Contemporary Problems* 7-28 (1992).

Weber, R.H. & Grünewald, S., *UCITS and the Madoff Scandal: Liability of Depositary Banks?*, www.zora.uzh.ch/20149/ (accessed 15 May 2017).

Wegman, H., *Investor Protection – Towards Additional EU Regulation of Investment Funds* (Kluwer 2016).

Wei, T.B., *The Equivalence Approach to Securities Regulation*, 225 Northwestern Journal of International Law & Business 1 (2007).

Wiggins, R.Z., Wedow, M. & Metrick, A., *European Banking Union B: The Single Resolution Mechanism*, Yale Program on Financial Stability Case Study 2014-5B-V1 (2014).

Worley, J.P.S., *UCITS III and the Freedom to Provide Fund Management Services*, www.avukati.org/common/fileprovider.ashx?id=633123978903617500 (accessed 8 July 2017).

Wymeersch, E., *Europe's Financial Regulatory Bodies* (H.S. Birkmose, M. Nevillie & K.E. Sørensen eds., Kluwer 2012).

Wymeersch, E., *Banking Union: Aspects of the Single Supervisory Mechanism and the Single Resolution Mechanism Compared*, ECGI – Law Working Paper No. 290 (2015).

Wymeersch, E., *The European Banking Union, a First Analysis*, Financial Law Institute Working Paper Series WP 2012-07 (2012).

Wymeersch, E., *The Single Supervisory Mechanism or 'sSM', Part One of the Banking Union*, European Corporate Governance Institute (ECGI) – Law Working Paper No. 240/2014 (2014).

Wymeersch, E., *The Single Supervisory Mechanism: Institutional Aspects* (D. Busch & G. Ferrarini, Oxford 2015).

Wymeersch, E., *The Institutional Reforms of the European Financial Supervisory System, an interim Report*, https://ssrn.com/abstract=1541968 (accessed 16 February 2017).

Wymeersch, E., *Europe's New Financial Regulatory Bodies*, 5, http://ssrn.com/abstract=1813811

Y

Yeoh, P., *The Challenges and Implications of Systemic Risks for Financial Regulation*, 31 Company Lawyer 389 (2010).

Yermo, J. & Marossy, A., *Pension Fund Governance*, Insurance and Private Pensions *Compendium for Emerging Economies Book 2 Part 1:4)b*, 7 www.oecd.org/finance/private-pensions/1815934.pdf

Z

Zaal, P.J. van, *Aanhouden van gelden door beleggingsondernemingen en betaaldienstverleners*, 9 TvFR 226-237 (2010).

Zebregs, B.J.A. *De CSD-verordening in het licht van de Capital Markets Union* (Ondernemingsrecht 2017/18).

Zetzsche, D.A., *Investment Law as Financial Law: From Fund Governance over Market Governance to Stakeholder Governance?*, in *The European Financial Market in Transition* (H.S. Birkmose, M. Nevillie & K.E. Sørensen eds., Kluwer 2012).

Zetzsche, D.A., *Drittstaaten im Europäischen Bank- und Finanzmarktrecht* 62-63 (G. Bachmann & B. Breig eds., Mohr Siebeck, Tübingen 2014).

Zetzsche, D.A., *Fondsregulierung im Umbruch - ein rechtsvergleichender Rundblick zur Umsetzung der AIFM-Richtlinie*, 1 ZBB 32 (2014).

Zetzsche, D.A. & Marte, T.F., *The AIFMD's Cross-Border Dimension, Third-Country Rules and the Equivalence Concept* 474 (D.A. Zetzsche ed., Kluwer 2015).

Zetzsche, D.A. & Marte, T.F., *AIFMD versus MiFID II/MIFIR: Similarities and Differences* (D.A. Zetzsche ed., Kluwer 2015).

Zetzsche, D.A. & Preiner, C.D., *Scope of the AIFMD* (D.A. Zetzsche ed., Kluwer 2015).

Zetzsche, D.A., *(Prime) Brokerage* (D.A. Zetzsche ed., Kluwer 2015).

Zetzsche, D.A., *The AIFMD and the Joint Principles of European Asset Management Law* (D.A. Zetzsche ed., Kluwer 2015).

Zetzsche, D.A., & Marte, T.F., *The AIFMD's Cross-Border Dimension, Third-Country Rules and the Equivalence Concept*, 474 (D.A. Zetzsche ed., Kluwer 2015).

Zetzsche, D.A., & Preiner, C.D., *ELTIFR versus AIFMD* (D.A. Zetzsche ed., Kluwer 2015).

Zetzsche, D.A., *Drittstaatenregelungen im EU-Finanzmarktrecht*, in *Finanzmarktregulierung zwischen Innovation und Kontinuität in Deutschland, Europa und Russland* (G. Bachmann ed., Mohr Siebeck 2014).

Zetzsche, D.A., *Prinzipien der kollektiven Vermögensanlage* (Mohr Siebeck 2015).

Zetzsche, D.A., *Verordnung über europäische langfristige Investmentfonds (ELTIF-VO) – Langfristigkeit im Sinne der Kleineranleger?*, 6 ZBB 362 (2015).

Zetzsche, D.A., *Competitiveness of Financial Centers in Light of Financial and Tax Law Equivalence Requirements* (R.P. Buckley, E. Avgouleas & D.W. Arner eds., Cambridge University Press 2016).

Zetzsche, D.A., *Aktivlegitimation gemäß § 78, 89 KAGB im Investment-Drei-und –Viereck* (M. Casper, L. Klöhn, W.H. Roth & C. Schmies eds, RWS Verlag 2016).

Zhao Li, *Securities Regulation in the International Environment*, 110-115, http://theses.-gla.ac.uk/691/1/2009zhaoliphd.pdf.

Zippelius, R., *Juristische Methodenlehre* (C.H.Beck 2012).

Zweigert, K. & Kötz, H., *Introduction to Comparative Law* 35 (Clarendon Press 1998).

INDEX

prime broker, 150, 151

prudential regulation, 33, 68-69, 116, 150-151, 154-155

R

rehypothecation, 140, 202, 209, 228, 303, 318, 353

reuse of assets, 160, 202, 209, 228, 348

right of use, 318, 353

risk asymmetry, 58-59, 62-64, 71, 84-89, 121-122, 132, 362-364

S

safeguarding of client assets, 268, 290-291, 295, 305, 324, 351

safekeeping, 259-261

securities settlement system, 196, 286

self-custody, 249, 267-269, 296, 316, 324

single rulebook, 69, 76-77, 133, 331, 342, 347

sub-custodian, 195-196

T

TC passport, 53, 58, 109, 132, 339, 361

trustees, 152, 271-273, 1-4, 6-11, 16-18

U

UCITS ManCo164-169